Visual Basic 4 Menu Items and Shortcuts

File

New Project	
Open Project	Ctrl+O
Save File	Ctrl+S
Save File As…	Ctrl+A
Save Project	
Save Project As…	
Add File	Ctrl+D
Remove File	
Make EXE File…	
Make OLE DLL File…	
Print Setup	
Print	Ctrl+P

Edit

Undo	Ctrl+Z
Redo	
Cut	Ctrl+X
Copy	Ctrl+C
Paste	Ctrl+V
Paste Link	
Delete	Del
Find	Ctrl+F
Replace	Ctrl+H
Indent	Tab
Outdent	Shift+Tab
Bring to Front	Ctrl+J
Send to Back	Ctrl+K
Align to Grid	
Lock Controls	

View

Code	F7
Form	Shift+F7
Procedure Definition	Shift+F2
Last Position	Ctrl+Shift+F2
Object Browser	F2
Debug Window	Ctrl+G
Project Window	Ctrl+R
Properties	F4
Toolbox	
Toolbar	
Color Palette	

Insert

Procedure	
Form	
MDI Form	
Module	
Class Module	
File	

Run

Start	F5
Start with Full Compile	Ctrl+F5
End	
Restart	Shift+F5
Step Into	F8
Step Over	Shift+F8
Step to Cursor	Ctrl+F8
Toggle Breakpoint	F9
Clear All Breakpoints	Ctrl+Shift+F9
Set Next Statement	Ctrl+F9
Show Next Statement	

Tools

Add Watch	
Edit Watch	Ctrl+W
Instant Watch	Shift+F9
Calls	Ctrl+L
Menu Editor	Ctrl+E
Custom Controls	Ctrl+T
References	
Set	
Check Out	
Check In	
Undo Check Out	
Options	

Add-Ins

Data Manager
Report Manager
Add-In Manager

Help

Contents	F1
Search for Help On…	
Obtaining Technical Support	
Visual Basic Books OnLine	
Learning Microsoft Visual Basic	
About Microsoft Visual Basic	

Keyboard Control Nudges

With the control selected:

Shift+*arrow key* = changes size of control one grid width

Ctrl+*arrow key* = moves control one grid width

Visual Basic 4 Data Types

Data Type Character	Declaration	Storage Size	Range
Byte		1 byte	0 to 255
Boolean		2 bytes	True or False
Currency	@	8 bytes	-922,337,203,685,477.5808 to 922,337,203,685, 477.5807
Date		8 bytes	January 1, 100 to December 31, 9999
Double	#	8 bytes	-1.79769313486232E308 to 4.94065645841247E-324 for negative values; 4.94065645841247E-324 to 1.79769313486232E308 for positive values
Integer	%	2 bytes	-32,768 to 32,767
Long	&	4 bytes	-2,147,483,648 to 2,147,483,647
Single	!	4 bytes	-3.402823E38 to-1.401298E-45 for negative values; 1.401298E-45 to 3.402823E38 for positive values
String (variable-length)	$	10 bytes (string length)	+0 to approximately 2 billion(approximately 65,400 for Microsoft Windows version 3.1 and earlier)
String (fixed-length)	$	Length of string	1 to approximately 65,400
User-defined (using Type)		Number required by elements	The range of each element is the same as the range of its data type
Variant (with numbers)		16 bytes	Any numeric value up to the range of a Double
Variant (with characters)		22 bytes + string length	Same range as for variable-length string

What's New in This Edition

 Use the quick reference list to look up all the individual new features that are conspicuously marked by the New to Visual Basic 4 icon.

- Coverage of the Standard, Professional, and Enterprise Editions of Visual Basic 4, as well as Visual Basic for Applications (VBA), which is now a subset of Visual Basic.

- 32-bit development for Windows 95 and Windows NT.

- Writing Visual Basic programs for Windows 95. Integrate Windows 95 components such as toolbars, status bars, tabbed notebooks, and progress bars.

- The new Visual Basic 4 Integrated Development Environment look and feel. (See Chapter 5.)

- Using the Visual Basic Object Browser. (See Chapters 5 and 14.)

- Improved debugging tools. (See Chapter 12.)

- The ability to add insertable objects, such as an Excel Worksheet or Word Document, to your Visual Basic toolbox. (See Chapter 14.)

- Using OLE Automation Objects and building objects that support OLE Automation and creating OLE objects with methods that can be programmed externally by other applications. (See Chapter 14.)

- Conditional compilation and the ability to use one code base to target multiple platforms. (See Chapters 5 and 15.)

- Version 3.0 of the Jet Database Engine. Data Access Objects (the DAO library) and the new data-bound controls. (See Chapter 16.)

- Extending the Visual Basic environment using add-ins. Use of OLE Custom Controls. (See Chapters 18 and 19.)

  - Including multimedia components in your programs. (See Chapter 20.)

    - Version 4.0 Help Files for Windows 95. (See Chapter 21.)

      - Using the improved Setup Toolkit. (See Chapter 22.)

Peter Norton's Guide to
Visual Basic™ 4
for Windows® 95

**Peter Norton,
and Harold and
Phyllis Davis**

SAMS
PUBLISHING
201 West 103rd Street
Indianapolis, Indiana 46290

We'd like to dedicate this book to our mothers: Virginia Palmer Davis and Barbara Owens Hopper.

Copyright © 1995 by Peter Norton

FOURTH EDITION

International Standard Book Number: 0-672-30615-8

Library of Congress Catalog Card Number: 94-67511

98 97 96 95   4 3 2 1

Interpretation of the printing code: the rightmost double-digit number is the year of the book's printing; the rightmost single-digit, the number of the book's printing. For example, a printing code of 95-1 shows that the first printing of the book occurred in 1995.

Composed in Goudy and MCPdigital by Macmillan Computer Publishing

Printed in the United States of America

Publisher and President	*Richard K. Swadley*
Acquisitions Manager	*Greg Weigand*
Development Manager	*Dean Miller*
Managing Editor	*Cindy Morrow*
Marketing Manager	*Gregg Bushyeager*

Acquisitions Editor
Sunthar Visuvalingam

Development Editor
Sunthar Visuvalingam

Production Editors
Mary Inderstrodt
Tonya Simpson

Copy Editors
Kim Hannel
Ryan Rader

Technical Reviewers
Robert Bogue
Sloan Thrasher

Editorial Coordinator
Bill Whitmer

Technical Edit Coordinator
Lynette Quinn

Formatter
Frank Sinclair

Editorial Assistant
Sharon Cox

Cover Designer
Tim Amrhein

Book Designer
Alyssa Yesh

Production Team Supervisor
Brad Chinn

Production
Angela D. Bannan, Carol Bowers, Charlotte Clapp Mike Dietsch, Louisa Klucznik Ayanna Lacey, Kevin Laseau Paula Lowell, Steph Mineart Brian-Kent Proffitt, Bobbi Satterfield, SA Springer Tina Trettin, Susan Van Ness Mark Walchle

Indexers
Charlotte Clapp
Jeanne Clark
Greg Eldred

Overview

Contents

Quick Reference to What's New in Visual Basic 4

You'll find some of these features nice to have and others to be significant advances or indicative of the future directions of Visual Basic.

Coding, Debugging, and Error-Trapping

Controls, Properties, Methods, and Events

Data-Centric and Database-Related Features

Integrated Development Environment (IDE)

Object Orientation/Object Linking and Embedding

Windows 95 Specific Features

Acknowledgments

The authors would like to thank Scott Clark of the Peter Norton Group, Clint Hicks, Sunthar Visuvalingam of Sams/Macmillan, and Matt Wagner of Waterside Productions, without all of whom *Peter Norton's Guide to Visual Basic 4 for Windows 95* would not have been written. We would also like to thank Robert L. Bogue for his conscientious technical review, and for his assistance in author review. His efforts have gone far beyond the normal call of duty.

Introduction

Peter Norton's Guide to Visual Basic 4 for Windows 95 is the fourth revised edition of the classic Peter Norton book on the Visual Basic programming language. It covers release 4 of Visual Basic, and emphasizes coverage of how the new release of Visual Basic interacts with the new version of Windows: Windows 95.

The concept of the Peter Norton series has always been to cover a topic in authoritative depth while providing enough information so that a beginner could learn the subject matter. In *Peter Norton's Guide to Visual Basic 4 for Windows 95*, I have tried to maintain this tradition. You'll find advanced discussions of topics including sophisticated component handling, creating OLE DLLs, database design, using the Windows API, and creating your own OLE controls. At the same time, enough background information is presented so that—even if you've never programmed before—you can be up and running with Visual Basic in a matter of minutes! In every case, not only do I show you *how* to do something, I also provide working code examples.

What Is in This Book?

Visual Basic is a tremendous toolbox of programming resources, and this book explores much of what is available. You will work your way up, from the most basic examples to the most polished. In the beginning of the book, you will get the essentials down, and then you will be able to progress beyond them, following the natural course of Windows programming development. You will start with a blank window, embellish it a little with color and graphics, and then start to add buttons and text boxes—which Visual Basic calls *controls*. When you become comfortable with the idea of controls, you will add dialog boxes, message boxes, and then menus. As you work your way through the book, you will get into the kinds of topics that real Windows applications deal with, such as the Clipboard, bitmaps and icons, and error handling. One chapter is devoted to debugging, and another to Dynamic Data Exchange (DDE), which is one of the techniques that enables you to communicate with other Windows applications such as Microsoft Excel or Word for Windows. You'll then move on to the greatly expanded role of Object Linking and Embedding (OLE) in Visual Basic.

Then you will press on to the realm of the expert: For starters, you will learn how to call outside functions including the Windows API from Visual Basic. This book is for whether you want to stick with pure Visual Basic and explore its many opportunities or if you want work with integrating Visual Basic with other applications and programming languages. All of this makes for quite an ambitious plan—learning how to design and put to work useful Windows applications with a minimum of trouble. But that is what Visual Basic does best.

As previously mentioned, your orientation will be about seeing your programs work and getting functioning results. To do that, however, you must understand what you are doing. Therefore, you will have to take the time to understand all the concepts involved with Visual Basic—concepts such as events, forms, methods, projects, and modules. You will see that Visual Basic is made of certain objects. For example, *forms*—which non-programmers tend to think of as *windows*—are objects that encapsulate appearance and functionality. This means you will have to take the time to understand those objects before you can work with them.

For that reason, the first and second chapters will get you started by exploring the concepts you will need. It is important to understand the relationship of Visual Basic 4 to Windows 95, as well.

Peter Norton's Guide to Visual Basic 4 for Windows 95 begins with an introduction to the background concepts of Visual Basic and Windows 95 programming. You'll quickly move on to explore fundamental Windows concepts and programming objects—such as windows, buttons, properties, and components—and then you'll work through some Windows programming concepts. You will also get an introduction to the essential Visual Basic programming concepts. Because these first chapters lay the foundation for the rest of the book, make sure you comprehend all of the basic ideas before continuing.

From then on, the book is as task-oriented as possible. Many of the chapters are purposely designed to cover one specific type of Visual Basic control—buttons, list boxes, combo boxes, dialog boxes, or menus, for example. In this way, you will build your expertise by building your windows—piece by piece—steadily adding more and more power to your Windows applications. This will enable you to handle any complexities you might encounter in a systematic, gradual way.

To add power to the programming part of your applications—rather than to the user-interaction part, which is handled by menus and buttons—you will investigate how to work with files and how to pass data in and out of the Windows Clipboard. Then you will continue with other, more advanced concepts, such as developing and using custom controls, using the Windows API, and linking to the C language, on your way to becoming a Visual Basic "wizard."

What Is New to Version 4?

The single most important aspect of this long-awaited and significant version of the Visual Basic programming environment is that it is now primarily intended to create 32-bit applications running under Windows 95 (or Windows NT).

Visual Basic 4 ships in three versions: the Standard, Professional, and Enterprise editions. Of these, the Professional and Enterprise editions ship with a separate application that enables you to still build 16-bit applications (as well as 32-bit). With the Standard Edition, you can only create 32-bit applications designed to run under 32-bit operating systems.

Note: This book deals exclusively in the development of 32-bit applications; however, there are no changes necessary to convert a standard 32-bit program into a 16-bit program. Even if your program uses items outside the standard features of Visual Basic, the conversion task is not that difficult.

As in previous releases of Visual Basic, the Professional Edition extends the capabilities of the Standard Edition with additional controls such as the Toolbar and Slider OLE Controls. In addition, the Professional Edition provides facilities for extending the Visual Basic environment and your Visual Basic applications in various ways.

The Enterprise Edition extends the capabilities of the Professional Edition by adding features to enable client/server development and tools to facilitate team development using Visual Basic.

The programming language used in Version 4 contains all of the commands included in Version 3. It is a superset of the Version 3 language, as well as being a superset of the Visual Basic for Applications 2.0 (VBA) language. However, in some cases Version 3 code will run under Version 4, but only because an intentional effort has been made to ensure backward compatibility. For example, in Visual Basic 3, 0 represented False and -1 represented True. You can still write code this way, but it is probably a better idea to use the new Boolean constants—for example: `CapFlag = True`.

The addition of Visual Basic for Applications to Visual Basic is an important step because it makes it easier to program OLE automation objects that are VBA-compliant and means that Visual Basic code can be easily transported between modules in applications that support it. Other new features include, in the Standard Edition:

- The introduction of OLE controls (OCXs) as a replacement for VBXs (which are limited to 16-bits).
- The ability to add insertable objects—such as an Excel Worksheet or a Word document—to your toolbox (and Visual Basic application).
- The option to conditionally compile.
- Extensive improvements to the functionality of—and your ability to customize—the Visual Basic development environment.
- The Object Browser facility.
- The ability to use OLE automation objects.
- The introduction of Data Access Objects (DAO) and new data-bound controls.
- The introduction of components that allow you to give applications a Windows 95 look and feel.

In addition, if you have the Professional and Enterprise Editions of Visual Basic, you will be able to

- Build applications that support OLE Automation; in other words, create OLE objects with methods that can be programmed externally by other applications.
- Develop add-ins that can extend the Visual Basic Integrated Development Environment (IDE).
- Create your own OLE Dynamic Link Libraries (DLLs).
- Use improved data access features of the new Jet engine Version 3.0.
- Use a number of new components optimized for Windows 95.

What You Will Need

If the question is what will you need to profitably read and enjoy this book, the answer is not much. However, at a minimum you will need to be running Windows 95—or NT—and at least the Standard Edition of Visual Basic 4. (Note that the Standard Edition of Visual Basic 4 will not run under 16-bit operating systems. End of story.) If you wish to work through the examples in Chapters 17 and 19, in which we talk about interfacing Visual Basic programs directly to Windows, to C programs, and to OLE controls, then you'll need a C++ compiler; preferably Microsoft's Visual C++. If you would like to create your own help files for your Visual Basic applications, a subject we consider in Chapter 21, then you'll need a word processor that can save files in .rtf format.

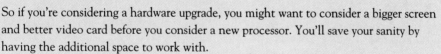

Tip: When programming in Visual Basic 4 or any visual programming tool, the more screen space you can get the better. By the time you open Windows for the project, the form you're working on, the form's code, the online help, the Books Online, and so on, you will find that you can never see everything that you want to see at the same time.

So if you're considering a hardware upgrade, you might want to consider a bigger screen and better video card before you consider a new processor. You'll save your sanity by having the additional space to work with.

Before you start learning about *programming* Windows 95 applications, you should familiarize yourself with the user interface concepts of Windows 95 such as windows, control boxes, minimize and maximize buttons, scrollbars, thumbs, and so on. Mostly, these concepts are not very different than the way they were under older versions of Windows. This means that if you are one of the more than 80 million current users of Windows, you already know what you need in this regard. If not, your best approach would be to spend a little time playing with Windows 95 so that you can get up to speed. Chapter 1, "Visual Basic and Windows Programming," covers the relationship of Visual Basic 4 to Windows 95 and explains where Windows 95 fits in with earlier versions of Windows.

To quickly get up to speed on fundamental Visual Basic concepts, the best bet is to have a look at Chapter 2, "The First Windows," and Chapter 3, "Buttons, Text Boxes, and an Alarm Clock Program." Chapter 4, "Programming in Visual Basic," provides a thorough introduction to the Visual Basic programming language. And Chapter 5, "The Visual Basic Integrated Development Environment (IDE)," is a guided tour of the enhanced Visual Basic development environment. You'll find in Chapter 5 an antidote to the "I don't know how to..." software blues.

As you can see, it is not necessary for you to bring a great deal of background knowledge to the Visual Basic 4 feast! *Peter Norton's Guide to Visual Basic 4 for Windows 95* will help you learn all you need to create polished, professional applications. If you're up for it, we'll take you to some of the most sophisticated and advanced corners of Visual Basic while we're at it. In any case, hang on! Visual Basic programming is fun! You can expect an informative and vastly entertaining journey.

1

Visual Basic and Windows Programming

Introduction

Release 4 of Visual Basic comes at an extremely exciting time, coinciding with the introduction of the Windows 95 operating system. Windows 95 is the first major upgrade to Windows, the world's most popular operating system, since Windows 3.0 was introduced in 1990. Not only does the substantial elapsed time between major versions create a situation in which Windows 95 incorporates major technical advances, it has also caused an unprecedented wave of popular interest in the new operating system.

As you'll see in *Peter Norton's Guide to Visual Basic 4 for Windows 95*, Visual Basic has also metamorphosed. Readers who have worked with earlier versions of Visual Basic (such as Visual Basic 3.0) will find much that is familiar in this important new release, although the cosmetics of the *Integrated Development Environment* (IDE) have changed quite a bit. (See Chapter 5 for a complete tour of the new IDE.)

However, the most significant changes to Visual Basic have to do with its tight integration with Windows 95. This involves a substantial refocusing of the role of Visual Basic. Conceptually, developers might now want to think of Visual Basic 4 as a glue that combines applications, objects, and tools within the Windows 95 environment to create custom solutions. (This is not to say that Visual Basic 4 can't be used in the same fashion as previous releases of Visual Basic, to write complete professional applications. It can. In fact, if you have programs or libraries of code written in earlier versions of Visual Basic, only minor modifications—if any—should be required to make them run under Visual Basic 4.)

The major changes that enable Visual Basic to function as a universal custom glue for Windows 95 include the following:

- The capability to create 32-bit code (although you can still create 16-bit applications using a separate 16-bit application shipped in the box with Visual Basic 4).
- The capability to implement components with a Windows 95 look and feel in your Visual Basic applications.
- The capability to create class modules and in-process OLE automation servers.
- The inclusion of *Visual Basic for Applications 2* (VBA2)—the macro language that is common to Excel, Access 7.0, Project 7.0, and other Microsoft applications—as a subset of Visual Basic 4.
- The inclusion with the Professional Edition of an editor designed to handle help files and hotspots within graphics.
- The inclusion with the Enterprise Edition of Visual Basic 4 of tools to make client/server and database development easier.

These are all significant topics and will be covered in detail in the appropriate places in this book. For now, in this first chapter, I'll take you on a quick tour that gives you the background information you need to get the most out of Visual Basic 4 and Windows 95.

The Evolution of the Windows Environment

Windows was first released in 1985. However, as noted previously, it did not really gain widespread acceptance until version 3.0 was released in May of 1990. These early versions of Windows were intended to build a *Graphical User Interface* (GUI) on top of the older, character-based DOS operating system. Users embraced Windows 3.0—and its upgrades, version 3.1 and Windows For Workgroups 3.11—with unprecedented enthusiasm.

Windows 95 has been designed to take advantage of advances in hardware and software technologies that have occurred in the years since the 3.x versions were released. Microsoft has attempted to do this without "breaking" older applications that were written to run under Windows 3.x. Almost every application written for Windows 3.x should run without modification in Windows 95.

Among the innovations important to programmers in Windows 95 are

- A 32-bit *Application Program Interface* (API) that is compatible with the API supported by Windows NT.

- A memory model without many of the limitations of earlier versions of Windows. This means that strings are no longer limited to 65,535 characters. They can be almost 2 billion characters in length.

- The capability to embed OLE objects within most Windows 95-compliant applications along with widespread adoption of drag-and-drop.

- The adoption of OLE custom controls (OCXs) in the place of VBX controls (VBXs) for use as components in programming applications.

Note: The terms OLE custom controls, OCXs, and OLE controls are used interchangeably. However, OCX controls seems to be Microsoft's latest version of their name. So that is what will be used here.

- Enhancement of the central registry facility as a way to store information about applications. This replaces the INI files that were used in Windows 3.x to maintain information about the system and application settings.

- Extensive improvement in the implementation of multimedia, including sounds, graphics, and animations.

- The introduction of a new look and feel in many components including taskbars, tabbed controls, and help files.

These topics by no means cover all of the new features introduced in Windows 95. (For example, Windows 95's adoption of the plug-and-play standard may turn out to be its most important innovation in the long run.) But they *are* important to programmers who would like to run their programs under 95—and take advantage of the exciting new capabilities of this operating system.

BASIC and Visual Basic: Some History

The BASIC (Beginner's All-Purpose Symbolic Instruction Code) programming language was invented in the early 1960s by two Dartmouth College professors, John G. Kemeny and Thomas Kurtz (for more details, see Chapter 4). Their intention was to create a language that was useful for teaching computer programming. At this, they were wildly successful.

From its earliest years, BASIC has been easy to understand, because it is close to English. It is also easy to learn to write because it is intuitive and *unstructured*, meaning that it isn't too fussy about how you organize programs and is flexible about how you use variables.

The trade-off for this ease of use was speed. Early versions of BASIC were slow because they were *interpreted*—that is, translated into code the computer could understand on-the-fly—rather than *compiled*—that is, run as a standalone executable program that has first been translated into machine code. (Visual Basic programs are, to this day, interpreted rather than compiled. When you compile a Visual Basic application, you are actually creating a file consisting of tokenized pseudo-code, termed *p-code*, which must be parsed by an interpreter on-the-fly before it is executed.)

Due to its lack of speed and ease of use—perhaps on the principle that "anything this easy can't really be good"—BASIC got the reputation in some circles as a "toy" programming language, not really suitable for serious work. Wouldn't those who thought of BASIC this way be surprised to find that Visual Basic is the world's most successful professional development tool? Over one million copies have been sold—more than any other programming language in history.

In the late 1980s, Alan Cooper—dubbed by some "the father of Visual Basic"—originated many of the concepts that have made Visual Basic so popular and successful as a Windows development tool. Cooper combined the easy-to-use BASIC as an underlying programming language with a visually intuitive way to create the appearance of applications and a straightforward mechanism for responding to events (for example, the user's click of the mouse).

Visual Basic and Windows Development

Prior to the release of Visual Basic, there was no easy way to program for Windows. The appearance and behavior of windows (with a small "w") on the screen (windows are called *forms* in developer parlance) had to be built in painstaking detail using the Windows API and by intercepting the internal Windows message stream. Old-time Windows developers might remember a time when a great deal of the effort in creating a Windows application went into coding and maintaining a giant `Case` statement that branched according to the intercepted Windows message.

> **Note:** Since the introduction of Visual Basic many other programming languages have "gotten visual." Microsoft and others now employ many of the same form layout concepts that Visual Basic made popular in Visual C++ and other visual programming tools.

Visual Basic ended most of this drudgery, making it fast, easy, and fun to create all kinds of programs that run under Windows.

Two concepts were crucial to this:

- A visual method of creating the application's appearance, including its forms, controls, and components on the form.
- The ability to attach code directly to each event of each element of the visual design.

If you know Visual Basic from previous versions you'll know—and, if you don't, as you'll see in a moment in Chapter 2, "The First Windows"—that Visual Basic does an excellent job of implementing these concepts. Indeed, VISUAL BASIC has become the visual development environment against which all others are judged.

Essentially, the first goal—creating the appearance of your application—is accomplished by working in much the same way as you would in a desktop publishing application: You draw your forms on the screen, set their properties, and add components from a toolbox.

Each object that has been created in this fashion has a list of appropriate events that can occur—or, as it is sometimes termed, *be fired*—either by the application's user or the system. Examples of events include clicking on a button, pressing a key, moving the mouse, and loading a form. It is an easy matter to associate the execution of your code with any of these events.

Strengths and Weaknesses of Visual Basic

One of the great strengths of Visual Basic is its capability to enable you to quickly and effortlessly turn out application interfaces that have functionality as prototypes—and beyond. VisualBasic's *Rapid Application Development* (RAD) environment is useful for rapidly refining interface design and development approaches. Additionally, in today's world, applications must be written that can be easily and quickly changed in response to external events. For example, an application might be based on regulations that are subject to change, such as the provisions of the Internal Revenue code. Visual Basic is perfect for this.

Note: Many other Rapid Application Development tools have come out since the advent of Visual Basic; however, none have been as successful, yet.

One effective way to use Visual Basic is to combine it with another programming tool such as C. Visual Basic can be used for creating the user interface and other parts of the application that might be subject to frequent change. *Dynamic Link Libraries* (DLLs) written in C can be used for computation-intensive routines that need to be optimized for speed. How to do this is discussed in detail in Chapter 17.

Note: Many of the speed problems that are generally associated with Visual Basic programs can be resolved by knowing how to use Visual Basic's data types correctly. This is covered in Chapter 4.

You could also create your own OLE controls in C (see Chapter 19) and use them in a Visual Basic program.

It should be noted that for several years Visual Basic has been used with considerable success as the sole development language for mission-critical applications at top development sites. There's almost nothing that can't be done in Visual Basic if you put your mind to it! Some special considerations do apply if you are using Visual Basic to create shrink-wrapped professional software, or for mission-critical applications that have little tolerance for error. (Of course, most of these considerations would also apply no matter what language you were using in these situations.)

The more complex and critical the application, the more important it is that you follow sound, modern coding practices. With large applications, you should try to create structured modules and avoid global variables. And resource consumption may need to be optimized (although this is less of an issue under Windows 95 than under Windows 3.x).

Techniques for bullet-proofing your applications will be covered in this book as we go along.

The Windows API and SDK

As you might know, the Windows *Application Programming Interface* (API) is a set of functions and procedures used to program Windows. Visual Basic is designed to work on many levels. Almost everything can be done with Visual Basic without using the Windows API. Generally speaking, you will need to use only the Windows API with your Visual Basic application if you need to send or receive configuration or status type information.

If you should get to the point that you want to do things that cannot be done in Visual Basic, the entire API is available to you. For example, using Visual Basic's native facilities, you cannot access areas of the screen that are not within a Visual Basic window. In Chapter 17, you will learn how to use the API to capture screen areas outside your Visual Basic application's normal control.

In general, using an API in Visual Basic is simply a matter of including the correct declaration for the API function or procedure in your Visual Basic program and then calling the API. An application that helps make it easy to do this—the API Text Viewer—ships with Visual Basic 4. Because Windows itself is largely written in C, the API declarations use C-type variables, and some adjustments are required to use them from within Visual Basic. These matters are discussed in detail in Chapter 17.

You should also know that the 32-bit APIs used by 32-bit applications to run under Windows 95 differ from the old 16-bit APIs. Of course, 16-bit applications will still run under Windows 95. (Indeed, this was one of Microsoft's primary goals in creating Windows 95.) Any applications you have written in older versions of Visual Basic should still run in the new environment.

The Professional and Enterprise editions of version 4 ship with separate 16-bit and 32-bit development applications. (But the Standard Edition only ships with the 32-bit version.) To create 32-bit applications that take advantage of the performance boost available under Windows 95, you will have to use the 32-bit version. This means using the 32-bit APIs rather than the older, 16-bit, versions, and using OLE controls rather than VBXs—which are 16-bit—in your applications.

As these are essentially the only differences between writing 16-bit and 32-bit Visual Basic applications that run under Windows 95, this book assumes you are writing 32-bit applications. (As you can see, it should not be terribly difficult to convert 16-bit applications to 32-bit provided that you have upgraded the 32-bit components as required.) I suggest you get started with 32-bit development as soon as possible. Microsoft has made no promises about how long it will continue to support 16-bit platforms.

The Windows API—in either 32-bit or 16-bit—is quite extensive. Literally hundreds of different function and procedure calls are involved. In addition, the API can be quite complex. To help with this, Microsoft ships the *Software Development Kit* (SDK). The SDK is not normally required for Visual Basic development, but if you're going to be using the API at all extensively in your projects, it would probably be a good idea to get a copy.

Tip: The Professional and Enterprise versions of Visual Basic include a help file for the 16-bit Windows API; however, more detailed documentation is available from Microsoft.

If you find that you need information on Windows APIs or other development issues that are not covered in the Visual Basic documentation, you might consider calling to join the Microsoft Developer Network. For a small yearly fee, they send you a CD containing a great deal of information on all of the Microsoft development tools. Microsoft Developer Network Customer service can be reached at (800) 759-5474.

In addition to online reference material explaining all APIs and their syntax, the SDK includes many tools that programmers will find useful including a font editor, a resource editor, and debugging and testing tools.

Using Visual Basic and C

From within Visual Basic you can also call any external library function or procedure that has been compiled in the Windows Dynamic Link Library (DLL) format. As with an API call, this simply involves placing the appropriate declaration in your VB program and then using the function or procedure in the library as you normally would.

Unfortunately, it is not easy to create your own DLLs—other than OLE DLLs, an important feature but special-case DLL that is new to version 4.0—from within Visual Basic. However, you can create—or license professionally created—DLLs in a language that does enable the creation of libraries of routines such as Delphi or C.

Chapter 17 includes a demonstration of the creation of a simple DLL in C and how you would call it from your Visual Basic program. In Chapter 17 you'll also find the minimum C source code required to create a DLL called from Visual Basic. You can use this as a template and add your own C routines to this DLL as you like.

Visual Basic for Applications

One of the most important new features in Visual Basic 4 is the inclusion of the *Visual Basic for Applications* (VBA) macro language as a supported subset of Visual Basic 4 in all versions—standard, professional, and enterprise.

Probably the most important implication of this is that you will be able to program embedded VBA-compliant applications (for example, Excel 7.0, Access 7.0, and Project) directly in Visual Basic. You'll learn more about how to do this using Object Linking and Embedding (OLE) automation in Chapter 14.

This also means that much of the macro code you write—for example, in Excel—is directly transportable to Visual Basic. It's as simple as copy and paste.

Of course, you could use *Dynamic Data Exchange* (DDE) to send VBA code to compliant applications for execution. DDE is explored in Chapter 13. Although DDE is still supported under Windows 95—and is very useful in certain situations, as will be explained in Chapter 13—OLE is a far more powerful interapplication communication technology. It will surely be worth your while to get to know OLE. OLE is covered in detail in Chapter 14.

Creating Reusable Objects in Visual Basic

Modern programming practice is overwhelmingly clear on the importance of coding in a way that creates reusable objects. Visual Basic has always been *object-based*—that is, built around objects. As you'll see in this book, release 4.0—in addition to introducing a number of important new ways to work with objects—also represents an incremental step toward true object orientation (known as *object-oriented programming*, or OOP).

Hard-core, object-oriented programming involves three concepts:

- **Inheritance:** Inheritance enables you to create a new object that is based on an existing object but with new or changed features. In Windows programming, this is sometimes called *sub-classing*.

- **Encapsulation:** Encapsulation means hiding the implementation details within an object. Only the methods necessary to get the object to do what it is supposed to are exposed to other parts of the application; how the methods are achieved is hidden. Encapsulation plays an important role in creating robust applications because it enables conceptual abstraction and isolation of problem areas.

- **Polymorphism:** Polymorphism enables you to implement the same method in different ways for different sub-classed objects. For instance, a display method displays an object, and the method name display is used with different objects. Each object does whatever is necessary to display the object.

Of these OOP concepts, encapsulation comes most naturally to Visual Basic. If you think about it, a form is an object encapsulating its appearance, components, and attached code. Release 4.0 provides new mechanisms for specifying the *scope*—that is, visibility—of routines and variables within Visual Basic modules. (See Chapter 4 for more on the new scoping rules.) This goes a long way toward enabling you to achieve true encapsulation. You'll see as we go along that there are various techniques that can be used—for example, avoiding the use of global variables, allowing access to modules only through specific access routines, and packaging reusable dialog boxes—to strengthen the object-orientation of your Visual Basic applications.

In addition, release 4.0 of Visual Basic is built upon a framework of object libraries, giving you the capability to browse and pick and choose among objects that you want to add to your applications. For more about this, see Chapter 5. An astonishingly powerful new feature is the capability to add any OLE object that is available in the Windows 95 Registry to your Visual Basic toolbox. Essentially, this gives you the capability to add any registered program or application into your Visual Basic projects using the OLE container control. (See Chapters 14 and 18 for more about this.)

Perhaps the single most important innovation—available in the Professional and Enterprise editions of version 4.0—is the capability to create OLE DLLs based on class modules. This feature will enable you—at least to some extent—to create a family of objects which can be used polymorphically, enabling you to write Object.display, regardless of what the underlying object is (providing it supports the display method). The most common use will probably be to create your own reusable code libraries. For further discussion, see Chapters 14 and 19.

Windows 95 and Windows NT

You will be pleased to know that applications written in 32-bit Visual Basic 4 under Windows 95 will, in general, run unchanged under Windows NT. (Of course, this can't be said of programs compiled under 16-bit Visual Basic that call the 16-bit APIs.) Releases of NT subsequent to 3.51 include common dialog boxes and components with a 95 look and feel; as you are probably aware, running under NT as well as 95 is a requirement for Microsoft's Windows 95 certification program. Because this would seem to indicate a long-term coming together of the platforms, it would be wise to test applications that you expect to maintain over time on both platforms.

What Direction has Visual Basic Taken with Release 4.0?

Release 4.0 of Visual Basic is catholic with a small *c*, meaning that all of the features of version 3.0 have been kept and many different kinds of new ones have been added. This means that Visual Basic is no longer a programming tool that anyone can expect to know all about without a great deal of study—although it is still possible to whip off quick applications with very little code in a matter of minutes.

Familiar features of the IDE have been enhanced considerably in ways that lead to greater productivity. For example, you no longer need to scroll to the top of the Property window to enter a value for a selected property; you can do it right at the entry for that property. Enhancements to the IDE are covered in Chapter 5.

As already hinted, probably the most notable change in direction in this long-awaited release of the world's most popular programming package are the many additions that address a software environment in which "we are all connected." These additions include tight integration with the Windows 95 operating system as well as heavy implementation of the use of OLE objects. Visual Basic can still be used by the hobby programmer creating applications for fun. Heavy-duty additions also make Visual Basic an excellent choice as an enterprise solution for welding together many different sorts of objects—perhaps including code modules, databases, and OLE servers—to efficiently and creatively solve industrial-strength, information-technology problems.

Obtaining Information about Visual Basic

As with previous versions of Visual Basic, Version 4's Help file (and hard copy documentation) is an excellent source of information about the product.

In addition, you should be aware that, with the Professional and Enterprise editions, all Visual Basic documentation is available online in one place by selecting Visual Basic Books OnLine from the Visual Basic Help menu. From Books OnLine, all topics available in the Visual Basic documentation can be accessed using a table of contents, an index, or by entering queries.

Do not underestimate the Object Browser (available from the View menu) as a source of information about available Windows 95 and Visual Basic objects and their properties and values. You can use this browser to find out everything you need to know about the contents of object libraries, available constants, and much more. See Chapter 5 for more details.

Summary

It's time to get down to brass tacks. This chapter has covered the fundamental concepts you need to get started. Changes in Visual Basic 4 to enable Visual Basic to better integrate with Windows 95 have also been discussed. In the next chapter, you'll take a first look at a Windows 95 window and learn how to use Visual Basic to write a simple program with the 95 look and feel. Veteran Visual Basic programmers may want to skim the material in Chapter 2, because, other than the Windows 95 aspects, this will probably seem fairly familiar. That isn't to say that there isn't plenty of material for the *power* programmer as well. Advanced OLE and DDE topics are covered. Also, tips and tricks on how to squeeze every bit of power and performance out of Visual Basic are sprinkled throughout the book.

2

The First Windows

Welcome to Visual Basic! In this chapter you will put together your first functioning Windows 95 programs, getting an introductory taste of event-driven programming. The chapter will cover the following topics:

- Windows 95 basics: terminology, look, and feel
- The parts of a Windows 95 window
- How to program in Windows 95
- Event-oriented programming
- Creating a window
- Adding text boxes to windows
- Adding buttons to windows
- Creating a Visual Basic project
- Running a Visual Basic program
- Saving work on disk

Here you will develop your first program, which places a welcoming message into a Windows text box in response to a button click. You also will find a discussion of some fundamental concepts of Windows and Visual Basic programming and programming design, which will be useful when you start creating your own programs.

Visual Basic is certainly one of the most exciting software packages in the PC marketplace and one of the revolutionary components in Windows programming. Visual Basic 4 is the latest version of one of the most popular and easiest-to-use visual-development environments ever. No longer does it take a great deal of patience, experience, and expensive software to produce valuable Windows applications. Under Visual Basic and similar programs, developing Windows programs is easier than ever. In this chapter you will put together your first two Visual Basic programs, which will run under Windows 95. Creating these programs will probably be easier than you think; Visual Basic will handle most of the details for you.

You can think of Visual Basic as an immense box of tools and resources, just waiting for you to use them. In other words, you have to know what is available—and all about the environment in which it is available—before you can take advantage of the many tools Visual Basic has to offer.

Accordingly, your tour of Visual Basic will begin with an examination of the environment in which you will work: Windows 95. Next, you will see how Visual Basic works in this environment and what tools it offers for you to manipulate that environment. Then, when you are ready, you will put Visual Basic to work and get quick, functional results. Now to begin by examining the host operating environment, Windows 95.

Windows 95 Terminology, Look, and Feel

Before you begin programming in Visual Basic, you should be very familiar with the way the user expects Windows programs to work, look, and feel. Even those of you familiar with Windows 3.*x* will find the new Windows 95 interface very different. Windows 95 adds to the familiar concepts from Windows 3.*x*. As a programmer you should understand how other programs in Windows react to clicks, double-clicks, drags, and so on, so that you can write your programs to respond similarly. This will make your user interface feel more Windows-like. When designing for Windows 95, particular attention should be paid to drag and drop, OLE, context menus, and interoperability. While these features have been in Windows programs in the past, they've never been implemented in the scale to which they have been implemented in Windows 95.

Before producing applications yourself, you should be familiar with the way a user expects a Windows application to work. In other words, there are many Windows conventions to be aware of and adhere to in your programs. (For example, in most Windows applications the File menu usually has an Exit item, and that item is always last. This is a standard part of the Windows interface in which you will be programming.) Although these conventions are discussed as you reach the appropriate topics, as well as in Appendix A of this book, there is no substitute for working with existing Windows applications to get a good feel for the Windows environment.

Pop-Up Menus

A new type of menu, the *pop-up menu*, is included with the Windows 95 interface. This menu can be accessed by clicking the right mouse button when selecting an object. The pop-up menu will appear next to the object as shown in Figure 2.1 and is *context sensitive*—it changes according to the current state of the object (for instance, if the printer is printing a document and the right mouse button is pressed while the cursor is positioned over the printer icon, a Pause Printing item will appear in the pop-up menu).

Figure 2.1.
A Windows 95 pop-up menu.

After a while, these conventions become quite automatic. For instance, in file list boxes, where the program shows which files are available to be opened, one click of the mouse should highlight a filename—this is called *selecting*. Two clicks should open the file—this is called *choosing*. On the other hand, Windows should be usable without a mouse at all—just with the keyboard—so you must provide keyboard support at the same time. In the case of file selection, the user would press the Tab key to move to the correct box, use the arrow keys to highlight a filename, and then press the Enter key to choose it.

You Should Use the Mouse for Program Design

For the purposes of program design, this book assumes that you have a mouse to go along with Visual Basic. Although it is possible to use Windows *applications* without a mouse, Windows *programmers* (or even experienced Windows users) are severely restricted without one, and their productivity is seriously hampered.

There are other conventions that Windows users expect. For instance, if there is an object that can be moved around the screen, users expect to be able to drag it with the mouse. They expect shortcut keys in menus; system menus that enable them to close a window; and windows that can be moved, resized, or minimized. As mentioned earlier, the best way to know what will be expected of your program is to work with existing Windows applications.

Tab Controls

Windows 95 makes use of a control that has become increasingly popular—the *tab control*. This control enables the user to navigate through different sheets of logically related information by pressing the various tabs. An example of a tab control is shown in Figure 2.2.

Figure 2.2.
A tab control.

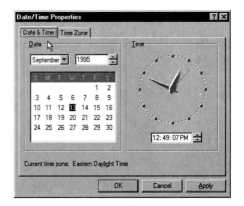

A typical Windows 95 window appears in Figure 2.3.

Figure 2.3.
A Windows 95 window.

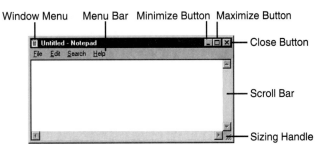

Window Menu   Menu Bar   Minimize Button   Maximize Button

Close Button

Scroll Bar

Sizing Handle

Before starting to program you should spend a little time reviewing Windows terminology; this will help you later in the book. At the upper left of the window in Figure 2.3 is the program icon, in this case a notepad. When clicked, this Notepad icon displays a *window menu* that typically enables the user to move the window, minimize it, or close it. To the right of the program icon is the title bar, or *caption bar* (Visual Basic refers to the text as the window's *caption*, not its title), which provides an easy way of identifying applications.

A New Look for the Control Box and New Name for the System Menu

In Windows 3.*x*, the system menu was accessed through the control box at the upper-left corner of the window. In Windows 95, the term *system menu* has been changed to *window menu* and the control box has been replaced with a miniature copy of the program's icon.

At the extreme right of the title bar are three buttons, two directly side-by-side and the third, separated from the other two, on the right side. Moving from left to right, the first two buttons are the Minimize and Maximize/Restore buttons. These buttons enable the user to reduce the window to an icon or expand it fully, to the whole screen. The third button—the one with the X on it—is the Close button. When pushed, this button closes the window.

Tip: In Windows 95, as in Windows 3.*x*, you can still close a window by double-clicking on the control box.

Under the title bar, a menu bar offering the currently available menu options for the application is normally present. Almost every stand-alone application will have a menu bar with at least one menu item in it: the File menu. This is the menu that conventionally offers the Exit item at the bottom, as in Figure 2.4.

Figure 2.4.
*A Windows 95 window with
the File menu displayed.*

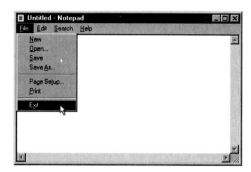

How Users Quit Windows Programs

The Exit item is the typical way for users to leave an application, so if your application supports file handling you should include the Exit item at the bottom of the File menu.

This is not to say that you should prevent the user from closing the program in other ways, such as an exit button.

Below the menu bar is the *client area*. Actually, the client area makes up the entire window under the menu bar except for the borders and scroll bars; in other words, it is the area that the window is designed to display. This is the drawing area—the area you will work with directly in Visual Basic. Here is where you will place buttons, list boxes, text boxes, and the other parts of your programs.

To the right of the client area is a vertical scroll bar, which is a common component of windows that display text. If there is too much text to fit in the window at once, scroll bars enable the user to move around within the document to look at some subsection of the whole.

At the bottom of the window is a horizontal scroll bar that scrolls the text in the client area horizontally. To the right of the horizontal scroll bar is the window's *sizing handle*. Everything in the window except the client area is called the *nonclient area*; even the border is part of the nonclient area. Visual Basic is responsible for maintaining the nonclient area of the window, and you are responsible for the client area.

A New Look and Functionality for Scroll Bars and Sizing Handles

With Windows 95 the shape of the *scroll box* has changed. (In previous versions of Windows, the scroll box was called the *thumb*.) The scroll bar retains its previous Windows functionality, providing the user with an indication of current document position. What's new is that the scroll box is now sized to show how much of the total document is displayed in the window. If the scroll box fills the entire length of the scrollbar, it means the entire document is being shown on the screen.

The window *sizing handle*, located at the lower-right corner of the window, is new to Windows 95. It encompasses an area of the window not previously used and makes it easier to resize a window. By the way, it also makes the Window more Mac-like in its appearance.

Windows Events

In a traditional or *procedural* application, program execution follows a defined path through the application, and it is the application itself, rather than an event, that controls the order in which code segments execute.

In *event-driven* programs, a system event or user action, such as pressing a button, executes an event procedure. Thus, the code executes in an order that depends on which events occur. This in turn depends on what the user does. That is the heart of graphical user interfaces and event-driven programming: *the user is in charge and your code responds to the user*.

Because the user's actions cannot be predicted, your code must make a few assumptions about what is going on when it executes. When assumptions are made—for example, that a text box has text in it before a command button is pushed—you should try to structure your application so those assumptions are always valid. An example of this kind of structuring is *disenabling*—set so they cannot be used—command buttons when you do not want the user to be able to click them.

An application under Windows 95 typically presents many possible options on the screen (in the form of visual objects) for the user to select. In this way, it represents event-driven and *object-oriented* programming. The programmer can no longer completely control the flow of the program. The user's choice determines the direction of the program as she selects among the options presented, and it is up to the program to respond correctly. For example, there might be three buttons on a window, as shown in Figure 2.5. Clearly, you cannot just write your program assuming that the user is going to push them in some particular sequence. Rather, you have to write separate code for each button.

That is the case in general, and it will have significant consequences for you in this book. Instead of the monolithic programs from the past that could be read from beginning to end, your code will necessarily be divided into smaller, modular sections, one section for one kind of event. For example, you might add to the window a text box in which you want the message "Welcome to Visual Basic!" to appear when the user clicks the button marked "Click Me." In that case, your program might appear as follows:

```
Private Sub ClickMe_Click()
      Message.Text = "Welcome to Visual Basic!"
End Sub
```

This code is specifically designed to handle one type of event—clicking the button marked Click Me.

Figure 2.5.
A window with three command buttons.

Visual Basic 4 adds a `Private` keyword. This keyword changes the scope of the procedure, or where it can be called from. This is explained more in Chapter 4. The code for a form with one click event in Visual Basic 4 appears as:

```
Option Explicit
Private Sub ClickMe_Click()
      Message.Text = "Welcome to Visual Basic!"
End Sub
```

(This assumes that the VB Environment Options item found under the Tools menu has been set to Require Variable Declaration. It also assumes that there are no other code or events in this form.)

Your programs will typically be collections of code sections such as that in the previous sidebar, one after the other. That is how event-driven programming works: you will largely be designing your code around the interface; that is, around the way you have set up the window—at least in the early part of this book. You will see how this works soon.

Besides being event-driven, Windows programming is also *object-oriented*. That is easy enough to see on the screen. Just pick up an object, such as an icon or paintbrush, and move it around. This bears some relationship to what is called *object-oriented programming*. This type of programming breaks up a program into discrete objects, each having its own code and data associated with it. In this way, each of the objects can be somewhat independent from the others.

Visual Basic 4 is the first version of VB to support true object-oriented methodologies, including the concepts of objects, object collections, classes, and inheritance. The object-oriented parts of Visual Basic 4 are covered in Chapter 14.

Using object-oriented programming is a natural for event-driven software, because it breaks the program up into distinct *objects*. An object can be anything: a button, a form, a control, and so on. You need to know only what you need them to do, not how they do it. That is the way you will be treating your windows and all the buttons, text boxes, and so on that you put in them. Each of these objects can have data and code associated with it. You might have heard of object-oriented programming, and you might suspect that it is difficult to do, but it turns out that Visual Basic automatically takes care of many details for you.

Now that you have your Windows background, you are ready to look at the programming tools you will be using in this book.

Visual Basic Programming: Forms, Methods, and Properties

Windows is designed for the user; and, prior to the release of Visual Basic, the programmer paid the price. In earlier programming environments, programming Windows was often an excruciating task. Today, the programmer is reaping the benefit of that same ease the user has enjoyed for so long. The computer itself is being enlisted as an aid for the programmer, not just for the user.

Note: Today there are several options to choose from if you want to design applications visually. Today almost all Windows programming tools enable you to design windows, or forms, visually. Currently, Visual Basic is the best-selling programming tool for Windows, but there have been many innovations making other tools viable options for Rapid Application Development (RAD) in Windows.

There are three major steps to writing an application in Visual Basic, and you will follow them throughout this book. They are

1. Draw the windows you want.
2. Customize the properties of buttons, text boxes, and other control objects used in the windows.
3. Write the code for events associated with the various controls.

The first step—drawing the window you want, complete with the buttons and menus—is where Visual Basic really shines. Before resource editors, like the integrated resource editor in Visual Basic, designing a window's appearance was a tedious process beset with difficulties; placement of buttons and controls was a tedious task. Adding additional features or removing them was also very difficult. Under Visual Basic, however, this whole process has become extraordinarily easy. Visual Basic enables you to simply draw—just like a paint program—your windows, as well as all the buttons, boxes, and labels you want. You see the actual appearance of your application at design-time, not just when the program is running.

Note: The visual design tools used in Visual Basic are available for other programming languages in Windows. The program that handles these tools is often called a resource editor. Visual C++ had a separate Resource Editor to manage its windows, menus, and so on, until version 2.0.

As you will see, adding or removing buttons or boxes works just as it would in a paint program. There is no difficult programming involved.

The next step in program design involves customizing the properties of the controls you have drawn. For example, you might give a window or button a certain caption, or change its color, or determine whether it is visible.

Note: Controls will remain visible at design-time whether or not their `Visible` property is set to `False`. This is so you can work with them. They will not appear when you run your program.

The final step is to write the code that responds to the events you consider significant—for instance, the click of a command button or the press of a key on the keyboard.

That is a basic outline of how Visual Basic programming works. Now to see it in practice.

In order to understand the way Visual Basic works, you are going to put together a one-window application that has one button and one text box. When the user clicks (or chooses) the button, the message Welcome to Visual Basic! should appear in the text box as shown in Figure 2.6.

Figure 2.6.
Your first program.

Start programming by starting Visual Basic under Windows 95. The VB display appears as in Figure 2.7. As with any new software, there are new terms and concepts to learn here.

Figure 2.7.
The Visual Basic program-
ming environment in
Windows 95.

Toolbar

Toolbox

Form

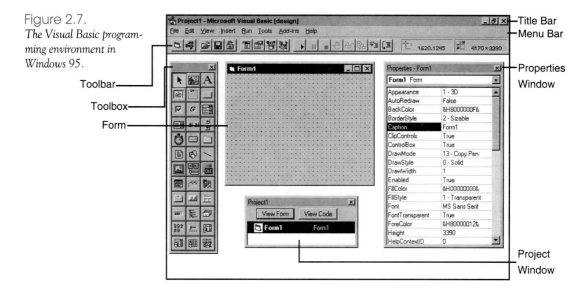

Title Bar
Menu Bar

Properties
Window

Project
Window

Forms

First, a window labeled Form1 appears in the center of the screen. This is the window you are designing; Visual Basic refers to windows that you customize as *forms*. As you can see, the form you
begin with has the appearance of a normal window. In fact, this is almost exactly the way your window will look when the application you are writing starts. Notice that Form1 already has a window
menu icon, a title bar, the Minimize and Maximize/Restore buttons, the Close button, a border, and
a client area.

The client area is filled with dots at regular intervals. These dots form a grid that helps you align
buttons and boxes when designing the window but disappears at run-time. In fact, your window is
already viable as it stands; as a program it will work, but it will not do much. If you tell Visual Basic
to run this program, a window labeled Form1 will appear on the screen. The parts of the window
that you already see, including the window menu and the Maximize, Minimize/Restore, and Close
buttons, will all be active. This is part of what Visual Basic provides for you. To try this out, move up
to the menu bar in the VB display at the top of the screen and select the Run menu as in Figure 2.8.

Choose the Start option from this menu. When you do, the screen changes, and Form1 appears just
like a normal window, as in Figure 2.9. (Instead of selecting Run from the menu bar, you could also
click the Start button on the toolbar or press F5 on the keyboard for the same result.)

Figure 2.8.
Visual Basic's Run menu.

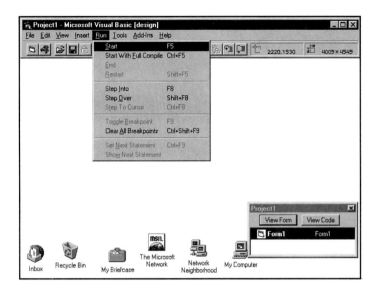

Figure 2.9.
Form1 running.

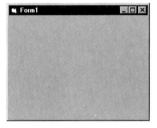

Your program is already running, although it is not very spectacular. You can move the window Form1 around the screen and resize it just like a normal window. The Minimize and Maximize buttons work as you would expect, minimizing Form1 down to an icon or expanding it so that it takes up the whole page. If you clicked the Close button, the window would close and the program would stop running. In addition, note that the dot grid that was present in the window when you started Visual Basic is gone now. These dots are present only at design-time to help you align objects in the window. (If you wanted to remove the grid altogether at design-time, you could uncheck the Show Grid item in the Environment Options box under the Tools menu.)

End the program now by opening the window menu in the window you have designed and selecting the Close option, or by selecting the End option from Visual Basic's Run menu, or by clicking the Close button on the window.

Setting Grid Width and Height

You can customize the grid cell width and height with Visual Basic 4 Found under the Environment Options tab in the Tools/Options dialog box, the grid default values are width = 120 and height = 120. These values are based in twips. 1440 twips equal one inch. The settings can range from 45 twips (the greatest concentration of dots) to 1485 twips (the least concentration of grid dots). The width and height values do not have to be set equally.

Properties

The window or, rather, the *form* you have been designing is pretty plain. So far, all you have is a single window named Form1; now you will start customizing it. Visual Basic treats forms under design, as well as boxes and buttons, as *objects*, and each different type of object can have certain *properties*. The object named Form1, for example, has properties associated with it that are normal for a window. These properties include the title or caption, color, visibility (whether it is visible on the screen at run-time), a certain screen position, and so on. A text box might have a different set of properties, including what text is currently displayed in it and what font is being used. In other words, an object's properties represent all of the data normally associated with that particular object.

To change the Caption property of Form1 so that the caption reads "My First Program" instead of "Form1," you have to use the Properties window on the screen as shown in Figure 2.10. The Properties window provides an easy way to set properties for all of the objects on a form. The Properties window is present only when you are designing your programs, not when you are running them.

Visual Basic 4 Makes Setting Properties Easier

In the Visual Basic 3.0 Properties window, changes were made by selecting the property to revise, selecting the settings box at the top of the Properties window, and then typing text or selecting options. This process was very tedious and distracted from the task at hand, designing windows. The Properties window in Visual Basic 4 has been redesigned. Now an object's properties can be changed by selecting the property and then typing or selecting the new property setting in the box to the right of the property name, as can be done in Visual C++. This box is appropriately named the Settings box.

Figure 2.10.
The Visual Basic 4
Properties window.

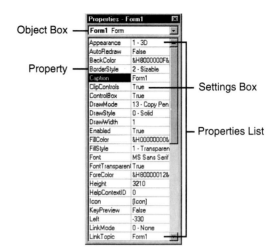

Object Box

Property

Settings Box

Properties List

Note: Be sure you know the terms used for each part of the Properties window because they are constantly referred to throughout the book.

As you work through the design process, you will place more and more objects on the screen, such as buttons, list boxes, check boxes, radio buttons, and labels. Each of these objects has a specific set of properties, such as color and size, that can be associated with each item. As you work on the different objects, the Properties window lets you change the properties of the object with which you are working. For example, you are working on Form1 now, so the Properties window holds the properties connected with this object. Notice that the title in the Properties window reads "Properties - Form1."

Properties That are not Available at Design-Time

It is possible that not all properties of a certain object will be available at design-time, that is when you are designing, and not running the program. For example, one of the properties associated with a filename list box is the name of the file currently selected. However, because no file is selected at design-time, that property will not appear in the Properties window. You will also run into rare occurrences where properties are available at design-time, but not run-time.

Look at the Form1 Properties window and use its scrollbar to view the entire list of properties associated with this window as shown in Figure 2.10. You will explore these options thoroughly later. Currently, the Caption property of the window is Form1.

Now, make sure that Caption is selected, as it is in Figure 2.10. (Do this by clicking the word Caption with the mouse.) The Settings box gives the current value of the selected property, which in this case is Form1. You can change the current value of the selected property simply by entering the new text so that it reads My First Program. Notice that as you type My First Program, the letters appear one-by-one in the title bar at the top of the form. Remember that Visual Basic calls a window's title bar a *caption bar*; thus, when you change the caption of a form, you are really changing its title.

That's all there is to it. You have renamed the window as My First Program. While you're at it, change the form's Name property from the default Form1 to frmFirst. The Name property is the property used to identify a form, or other design object, in the program's code. It is a good idea to specify meaningful names to your forms and design objects so your code will be more readable. For more information about what names are suggested for forms and controls, refer to Appendix A. If you ran the program now, that new caption would be present on the window's caption bar.

Now would be a good time for you to save your first program. Even though you've not done much to your program yet, it is a good idea to save frequently. So, select Save Project from the File menu, or press the Save Project button on the toolbar. You will see a dialog box asking you for the name of the form; enter my-first. Visual Basic will take care of the extension for you. Next you will see another dialog box asking for the name of the project; enter my-first again. When Visual Basic saves a project, it first saves all of the forms, modules, and classes, and then saves the project file.

Controls and the Toolbox

So far, you have seen how to work on the elementary properties of a form. There is another type of object in Visual Basic, however, besides the form: *controls*. Controls are all of the graphical objects that you can design and place on a form, such as list boxes, buttons, labels, and timers. In other words, a control is an object that is not itself a window and can be placed on a form. The window you are designing and creating is a form. A control is used for interaction with the user—she can manipulate check boxes, command buttons, and pushbuttons, for example. Together, forms and controls are called *objects* in Visual Basic because they are both treated like graphical objects.

If you are familiar with object-oriented programming, you already know that objects such as these not only have data associated with them, but also have built-in procedures that can be used, for instance, to move a button around the window. In C++ these object-connected procedures are called *member functions*; in Pascal and Visual Basic, they are called *methods*. You will learn about them soon.

Now you will find out how to add a text box to your first window by using the Visual Basic toolbox.

Because this is Visual Basic, you are going to draw the controls you want right on the form you are designing. This process works in much the same way as it does in a paint program, in which you would select a drawing tool and then draw with it. In this example, you select a control tool from the toolbox and then "paint" (draw) controls with it. You do that by selecting a tool from the Visual Basic toolbox, which is shown in Figure 2.11.

Figure 2.11.
The Visual Basic toolbox.

Balloon Help

Visual Basic 4 now comes equipped with *balloon help*. This means that whenever you move the mouse pointer over a button on the menu bar or a button in the toolbox while in VB design mode, a descriptive "balloon" will appear, providing the name of that button. This can be very helpful, especially with the many tools available in the toolbox—it can be difficult to remember exactly what each button does!

The toolbox will play a big part in this book, because it enables you to draw all of the controls you need. There are two ways to draw controls in Visual Basic. The first is to click the button in the toolbox corresponding to the control you want to add and then move the mouse pointer onto the form. Notice that the pointer becomes a crosshair, as shown in Figure 2.12. Place the crosshair where you want the upper-left corner of the control to appear. Now, hold the left mouse button down while dragging the crosshair until the text box is sized correctly. Release the mouse button and the box will appear.

Tip: You can also add a control to the form by double-clicking the control in the toolbox. A control with the standard size will be inserted on your current form.

Your goal now is to create a text box. Double-click on the text box tool; a default-sized text box appears in the middle of the form, as shown in Figure 2.13.

Figure 2.12.
Using the toolbox to draw a text box.

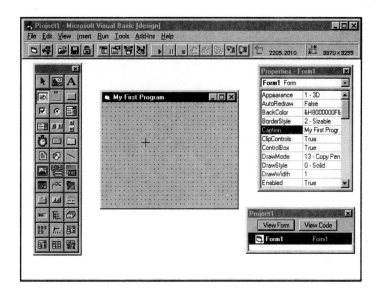

Figure 2.13.
A default text box.

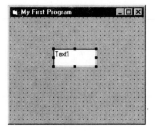

Note that the Properties window's caption now displays Properties - Text1. This is the name of the text box. The Name property holds the name of a control. This is how Visual Basic recognizes it; thus, when programming, you must refer to it in this way. In this case, the default name for your text box is Text1. As you can see, there are eight small, black squares on the edges of your new text box. These squares, called *sizing handles*, enable you to manipulate the size of the controls you are designing. By using them, you can stretch a control in any of the eight directions. To move the control itself, simply move the mouse pointer anywhere on the text box, then click and drag it. It is also possible to use keyboard and menu commands to move controls. You can find more information on moving controls without dragging in Chapter 5; however, unless you need precision positioning, using the mouse to drag the control is the best method to move a control.

Locking Control Positions

With Visual Basic 4 it is now possible to lock (and unlock) control positions so that they cannot be inadvertently moved after they are in the desired location. To lock all control positions on a specific form, select Lock Controls from the Edit menu or click the Lock Controls button on the toolbar. This locks all controls on the form in their present positions. Use this when you have completed designing the form so that you don't inadvertently move controls when you are writing code. This command toggles, so you can also use it to unlock the control positions. Notice that the little padlock on the Lock Controls button opens or closes as you lock or unlock the controls. Locking and unlocking controls affects only the selected form. Controls on other forms remain untouched.

Move the text box and resize the window until it corresponds roughly to Figure 2.14. Because the text box is selected, the Properties window is ready to display the properties you can set.

Now take a look at the properties—that is, the data items—in the Properties window as shown in Figure 2.14. This list presents every property of an object that you can set at design-time. You can scroll through the list to see what is available, such as BackColor (the background color behind the text), Font, Left and Top (the position of the top-left corner of the text box), and Width and Height.

Figure 2.14.
The properties list associated with the text box.

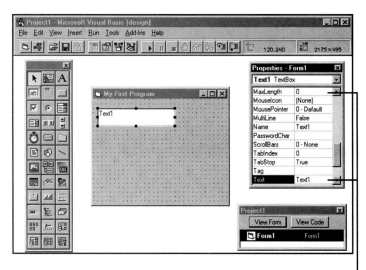

Properties List ⏋

That is how it works: You select a property of the object you are dealing with first, and manipulate that property using the Settings box to the right of the property name. When you select certain properties that have multiple fixed settings, a downward-pointing arrow appears to the right of the Settings box. When you click this arrow, the combo box opens to display a list of all of the options possible for that property, as shown in Figure 2.15.

Figure 2.15.
A property's multiple settings option.

Other controls that have multiple fixed settings use a Properties button to display the entire list of options for that property. This Properties button looks like a small square with an ellipsis inside it, as shown in Figure 2.16.

Figure 2.16.
A Properties button.

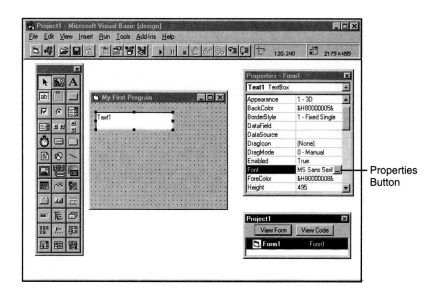

Properties Button

In this way, you do not have to remember long lists of numbers or codes—just select an object and use the settings options available. Select a property by clicking it with the mouse, and then click on the drop-down box's arrow or on the Properties button to display the entire list of options available. Scroll down to the Width property to see what its setting is. You may be surprised to find that your text box has a width of something like 2295.

The obvious next question is, 2295 what? Just what is the unit of measurement here? You might first assume that measurements on the screen would be in terms of pixels—the individual dots on the screen. Although measurements on the screen can be in pixels if you like (you will learn more about this topic later), the default measuring system for a Windows application should apply to all possible display devices, not just the screen. For example, a laser printer typically prints 300 dots per inch, so you would need some unit of measurement that is finer. Visual Basic uses *twips*, and there are 1440 of them per inch for the display on the corresponding device. You will see more about such measurements later. In the meantime, simply design your interface using the toolbox tools rather than concerning yourself with the actual location of the controls on your forms. However, you might notice that you can change the Width property, like all of the properties available at design-time, simply by editing the text in the Settings box of the Properties window. For example, if you changed the text box's Width property to 1440, you would see the text box grow or shrink to 1440 twips, or one inch, wide.

You can take advantage of this flexibility to change the text that appears in your text window. Right now it simply reads Text1, which is certainly not very interesting. Change it to Welcome to Visual Basic!—make sure that the text box is selected by clicking on it once, and then move to the Properties window. The property you want to change is called Text; find it and select it. Now just type the text in the Settings box to the right of Text (that is, the default Text1) by typing Welcome to Visual Basic!.

There! You have changed a property of the text box—that is, you have changed the text in the box from Text1 to Welcome to Visual Basic!. This new data becomes part of the object, and when you make this into a program the new text will appear in the text box. As you will see in a short while, you can also reach the properties of controls from the program code. In the meantime, resize the form by pulling the bottom border up until it is a few grid rows below the text box. Then select the Start option from the Run menu or click the Start button from the toolbar or press F5. At run-time, the window you have created and modified will look like the one in Figure 2.17.

Figure 2.17.
The modified window and text box.

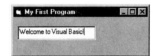

Note that when you run your program, the caption bar of Visual Basic itself, which has been displaying "Project1—Microsoft Visual Basic [design]," becomes "Project1—Microsoft Visual Basic [run]," indicating that the program is now running. As you can see, the new text appears in the text box: Welcome to Visual Basic!

So far, your program is an absolute success. You have displayed your own message, but the program as a whole is still not very interesting. The next step is to add a command button that the user can click to display the text in the text box, instead of having the text present immediately when the program runs.

Command Buttons

Stop the program either by choosing the Close option from the Window menu of the window you created, choosing the End option from Visual Basic's Run menu, pressing the End button on the VB toolbar, clicking the program's end button or double-clicking the control box. The Visual Basic design desktop reappears. Now choose the command button tool—the tool with a button shape in the toolbox, the second tool down on the right side. When you double-click this tool, a command button appears in the center of the form as shown in Figure 2.18.

Figure 2.18.
Creating a command button.

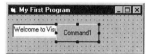

Move the command button to the right side of the form so that it does not obscure the text box. Because the command button is selected, the Properties Window contains all of its properties that you can work with at design-time. As you can see by scrolling through the properties list, this includes the default name of the control, Command1, at the top of the Properties window as well as in the Name property's Settings box; other properties such as Left, Top, Height, and Width as before; FontName and other properties having to do with fonts; and a number of other properties you have not seen before, such as TabStop.

In this case, you will change the caption of this button so that it says Click Me. Select the Caption property for the command button in the Properties window and change the text from Command1 to Click Me, as shown in Figure 2.19. As you do, Click Me appears letter-by-letter on the new command button. Next, change the default name, Command1, to something more easily distinguishable (thus, if you are looking at code, you will be able to discern which name goes with which control). In this case, call the command button cmdFirstButton. To do that, scroll down to the Name property and select it. Type in cmdFirstButton. That's all there is to it! (The cmd prefix is part of the generally accepted Visual Basic object-naming conventions—txt for a text box, cmd for a command button, and frm for a form. These conventions are discussed in the next chapter; a complete list appears in Appendix A.)

Figure 2.19.
The Properties window for the command button.

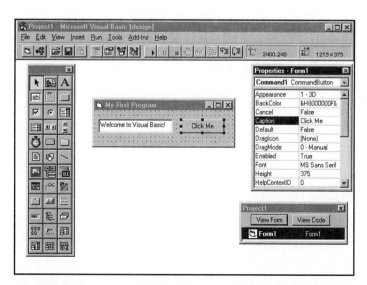

Somehow you have to connect the command button to the text box so that when you click the button, the text "Welcome to Visual Basic!" appears in the text box. This is where you will start writing your first lines of actual Visual Basic code. Your goal is to reach the Text property of the text box by using the program code. To do that, you have to know how VB refers to the properties of the different controls in the program.

The normal way to refer to a property in a Visual Basic program is *Object.Property*, where *Object* is the name of a form or control and *Property* is the name of the actual property itself. Thus, if you have a text box whose Name property is MyBox, you can simply refer to the text in its Text property as MyBox.Text. In another example, you can refer to the words (the caption) that appear on a command button named BigButton as BigButton.Caption.

A *method* is a procedure that is part of an object. Methods act only on the object to which they are attached. When you start dealing with the code routines that are built-in for many of the screen objects, you will find that they are accessed like this: *Object.Method*. It is very similar to accessing a property.

Note that it is important not to get a control's caption or some other text confused with the control's actual name. The Name property is the internal name of that control in Visual Basic, and the default name for your text box is Text1. A second text box would automatically be named Text2, a third Text3, and so on. You can see this default name by checking the Name property of the command button.

Change that default text box name now to txtFirstBox.

The txtFirstBox Text property in your program can be changed when the Click Me button is pressed by using the following Visual Basic statement:

```
txtFirstBox.Text = "Welcome to Visual Basic!"
```

If you delete the text in the text box at design-time, the text box will be empty when the program starts. When you execute the preceding code statement, the text "Welcome to Visual Basic!" will appear in the box.

As you know, your programs are going to be event-driven. They will be broken into sections specifically written to handle certain events, such as button pushes. This means that you have to connect your single line of code to the correct event. In this case, that event occurs when the user clicks the command button. To find the events associated with any object, just double-click on that object when designing your program. A new window, called the Code window, opens as in Figure 2.20.

Using the Code Window

The Code window contains a skeletal code outline for every event procedure (connected with a specific object) that you can write. This is exceptionally handy for two reasons. One is that it will save you some time setting up the outline for each procedure you want to write. The other reason is that the Code window indicates the kind of events that can have procedures attached. These might be `Click`, `DragDrop`, `DragOver`, `GotFocus`, and so on. In Figure 2.20, the following outline is already prepared for you:

```
Private Sub cmdFirstButton_Click()

End Sub
```

Figure 2.20.
The Code window.

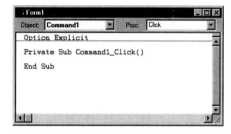

A New Way to View Code

Visual Basic 4 now offers you two ways to view your code:

One procedure at a time. This is the way code was presented in the Code window in previous versions of Visual Basic.

Full Module View. This method enables you to look at all of the procedures used in the module at one time. Here's how to set this up: Select Options… from the Tools menu to open the Options dialog box. Click the Editor tab and find the Full Module View check box to the right of the tab sheet. Select it by putting an X in the box; then click OK.

There are two types of procedures in Visual Basic: `Sub` procedures and `Function` procedures. The two differ in that *Function procedures* return values and *Sub procedures* do not.

`Sub` and `Function` procedures take arguments passed to them in Visual Basic as follows:

```
Sub MySub (A as Integer, B as Integer)
        :
        :
End Sub

Function MyFunc (C as Integer, D as Integer) as Boolean
        :
        :
MyFunc = True
End Function
```

Boolean Variables

Visual Basic 4 now has a Boolean data type that is used to store logical information. The possible values are `True` and `False`. In Visual Basic 4, zero will evaluate to `False` and any non-zero integer will evaluate to `True`. In prior versions of VB, zero was `False` and −1 was `True`. These values will still work as they are supposed to, thus maintaining backward code compatibility to previous versions of Visual Basic.

You will see how to set up your own `Sub` and `Function` procedures later, including what kind of data they can handle. For now, take a look at the `Sub` procedure that is already set up for you, in outline, in the Code window: `cmdFirstButton_Click()`. You can easily get to the Code window by double-clicking on the command button. The name of the `Sub` procedure `cmdFirstButton_Click()` indicates that this event procedure is connected with the command button cmdFirstButton, and that this is the `Sub` procedure that is executed when the user clicks that button.

Other events are associated with command buttons as well. Take another look at the Code window in Figure 2.20. The box on the right, below the caption bar, is called the Procedure box; it indicates what procedures are available for a particular object. If you click the down arrow to the right of the Procedure box, you will see a useful list of the available procedures, as in Figure 2.21.

Figure 2.21.
A Procedure box in the Code window.

In the left box just under the caption bar, the Code window also contains an Object box that lists all of the objects you have created so far. If you click the down arrow next to the Object box, a list of the object names appears as in Figure 2.22. You can attach event procedures to these objects.

You can see that txtFirstBox—your text box—is there, as well as your command button, cmdFirstButton. In addition, the form itself is listed because there are several events that can take place with forms. For example, when a form is first used by a program, it is considered an event, `Form_Load()`, as it is when the user clicks on the form during run-time, `Form_Click()`. In addition, there is another entry in the object list labeled (General). This is where the internal procedures will go when you write them; namely, the `Sub` and `Function` procedures you might write to do the real work of a program, whereas the rest is connected to events, such as the user clicking something, typing something, or just moving the mouse.

Figure 2.22.
An Object box in the Code window.

In this case, however, your code is entirely connected to a control that the user presses and consists of the following single line:

```
txtFirstBox.Text = "Welcome to Visual Basic!"
```

Put that line in the `cmdFirstButton_Click()` Sub procedure as follows:

```
Private Sub cmdFirstButton_Click()
      txtFirstBox.Text = "Welcome to Visual Basic!"
End Sub
```

To place it, position the insertion point (in Windows, the location where new text will go is called the *insertion point*, or *caret*; the term *cursor* is reserved for the mouse cursor) in the Code window between the two lines of the code template. Then enter the text as in Figure 2.23.

Figure 2.23.
Inserting Visual Basic code.

Making Your Programs Easier to Read

Note that you indented your single code line by pressing the Tab key first. Although not necessary, it is good programming practice to indent code lines in this manner. When your code gets more complex and includes multiple levels of `if`, `while`, and `for` statements, you will see that indenting helps make the code much easier to read and understand. There is more information about indenting and good programming practices in Chapter 4.

Indents and Outdents

Visual Basic 4 provides a new feature to help you make your code more readable: *indent* and *outdent*. They are located under Edit on the menu bar and can be accessed quickly by pressing Tab and Shift+Tab, respectively.

That's all the code necessary for `cmdFirstButton_Click()`. Close the Code window by choosing the Close option from the system menu. Now remove the text from your text box by clicking once on the text box. Scroll down the Properties list in the Properties window until you reach the `Text` property. Delete the text, Welcome to Visual Basic!, from that property's Settings box.

Quickly Identifying Events that Already Have Code

There is an easy way to keep track of the events that have code associated with them. If you look at the Procedure list in the Code Window—the drop-down list connected to the Procedure box—you will see that Visual Basic prints the names of all events with added code in bold, making them easier to pick out.

Now you are ready to run your program! To begin, choose the Start option from Visual Basic's Run menu or click the Start button on the toolbar. The window you have created appears on the screen along with the command button that states "Click Me" and the text box you emptied just a short while ago. When you click the button, the text Welcome to Visual Basic! will appear in the text box, as shown in Figure 2.24.

Figure 2.24.
Running your first program.

In fact, you do not have to run your program under Visual Basic. You can make it into a stand-alone Windows application. All you need to do is choose the Make EXE File… option from Visual Basic's File menu, as shown in Figure 2.25.

When you choose this option, a dialog box opens as in Figure 2.26. Notice that the default filename is automatically set to My-first. This is just fine. Click the OK button; Visual Basic creates a file called My-first.exe that can be run directly under Windows and will produce a fully functioning window.

Figure 2.25.
Visual Basic's File menu.

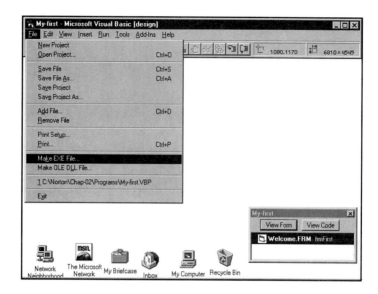

Figure 2.26.
The Make EXE File dialog box.

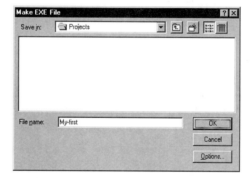

Congratulations! You have created your first complete Windows application.

What You Need to Run an .exe File

My-first.exe is not completely independent. Visual Basic .exe files require Visual Basic run-time libraries. In VB4 this means VB40016.dll is used for 16-bit applications and VB40032.dll for 32-bit applications. You also will need to include other files necessary for run-time execution. These files are listed in the Swdepend.ini, located in your Windows directory under the [VB Runtime] keyword. Typically, for 32-bit applications, vb40032.dll, vaen232.dll, vaen232.olb, mfcans32.dll, and msvcrt20.dll will be required.

The best way to determine what files are necessary for an application is to use the Application Setup Wizard. It will locate all of the files that you need to distribute and helps you build an application to install them on the users' computer. Chapter 22 contains more information on creating an installation program.

Visual Basic 4 Run-Time Libraries

The Visual Basic run-time library designation has changed with version 4. In Visual Basic versions one through three, the run-time libraries Vbrun*xxx*.dll, where *xxx* corresponds to the version number, were required. This means that Vbrun100.dll was required for Visual Basic 1 executables, Vbrun200.dll for Visual Basic 2 executables, and Vbrun300.dll for Visual Basic 3 executables. As you can see, this scheme has changed somewhat due to the two different executable application versions now available—16-bit and 32-bit (as mentioned above).

Forms, Modules, and Projects

You might wonder why Visual Basic gave the name My-first.exe to your application. The reason is that VB organizes tasks by *projects*, not by forms. An application can have a number of forms (that is, multiple windows) associated with it. Collecting everything together into a single project wraps it up into one easily managed package. Visual Basic allows only one project to be open at a time. Each project can have four different parts: form modules, class modules, standard modules, and resource files.

Visual Basic 4 includes two new kinds of program items: class modules and resource files. These are discussed in detail later in Chapter 4, "Programming in Visual Basic."

You already know that a form is a window you design in Visual Basic. (See Figure 2.27.) A form uses the .frm filename extension and contains descriptions of the image of the form itself and its controls, including its property settings. It can also contain subroutines that handle events and general procedures, as well as form-level declarations or constants, variables, and external procedures. Applications usually have at least one form; but, as you will see later, this is not technically necessary.

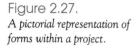

Figure 2.27.
A pictorial representation of forms within a project.

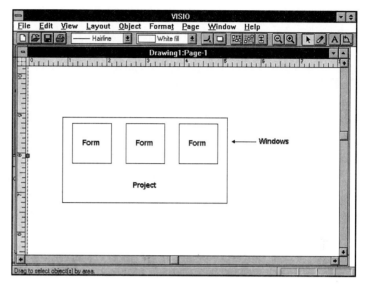

A Visual Basic *module* is made up of Visual Basic code, but code that is not directly related to a particular form. The procedures in a module can be reached from anywhere in the application. For example, you might want to define a Sub procedure that sorts data. This procedure is not directly concerned with input or output, but it can be vital to some applications. To avoid the necessity of having all code tied to one particular form, Visual Basic introduced the idea of a module that is designed to hold only code. To create a module, as you will do later, use the Module... item from Visual Basic's Insert menu. Normally, larger applications use modules to store procedures that are used throughout the application.

You can declare Sub and Function procedures in a module as Public or Private. Using the Public keyword enables them to be accessible to the rest of the application. Using the Private keyword permits access only from other routines within the module.

How Function and Sub Procedures Relate to the New Public and Private Keywords

The capability to control the scope of functions and subroutines using the Public and Private keywords is new to Visual Basic 4 In previous versions, all routines in modules were automatically available to be called (that is, they were Public). This is also the default in VB4.

Variables within a module can also be declared as Public (available to other modules) or Private (available only to the current module). (See Figure 2.28.) Declaring a module Public makes it accessible to the rest of the application. Private is the default and is equivalent to using the Dim statement. This means that the variables are not available outside the form or module. For more information about scope see Chapter 4. The Dim statement, however, is not as clear because it does not explicitly define the scope of the variable.

How Form and Module Level Variables Relate to the New Public and Private Keywords

In Visual Basic 4, module- and form-level variables can be declared as either Private or Public. In previous VB versions, variables were assumed to be Private unless the Global keyword was used.

Figure 2.28.
A pictorial representation of forms and modules within a project.

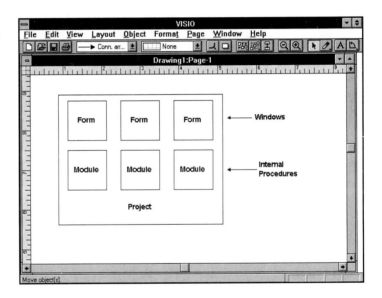

The New Class Modules, and Standard Modules

There are two new types of modules used in Visual Basic 4 (although one is an old friend with a new name): Class modules and Standard modules. *Class modules* use the filename extension .cls. They contain code, including subroutines, functions, methods, and procedures, and are used to create generic descriptions of objects. *Standard module* is the new name for the generic module type found in previous versions of Visual Basic. These modules contain subroutines and functions and use the .bas filename extension. Standard modules can contain `Public` or module-level declarations of types, constants, variables, external procedures, and `Public` procedures. Class modules are discussed in Chapter 14, and standard modules, because they are more frequently used, will be covered throughout the book.

Resource files use the .res filename extension and contain bitmaps, text strings, or other data that can be changed without having to re-edit a program's code. (See Figure 2.29.) For example, if an application needs to be changed to use a particular foreign language, all of the user-interface text strings and bitmaps for that language can be contained in one resource file. From there, changing the application to that language is easy. Only the resource file needs to be replaced, not the entire application. A project can contain only one resource file. You will learn more about resource files later in Chapter 15.

Figure 2.29.
A pictorial representation of forms, different types of modules, and a resource file within a project.

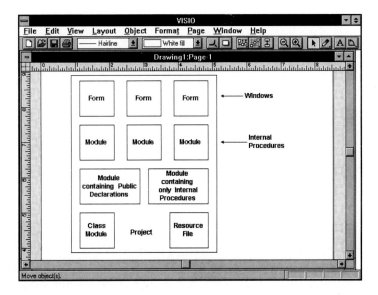

Using Visual Basic Projects

When you start Visual Basic, it automatically starts or creates Project1. To rename the project, select the Save Project or Save Project As... item from the File menu. (The first time Save Project is used it functions exactly the same as Save Project As, asking you for names for the new modules.) To work on a project that already exists, use the Open Project... item on the File menu, as shown in Figure 2.30.

To keep track of the current project, Visual Basic maintains a Project window. The contents of the Project window for your application are shown in Figure 2.31.

Figure 2.30.

The File menu with the Open Project item selected.

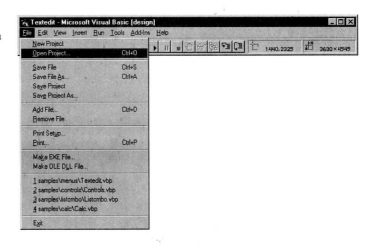

Figure 2.31.

Your Project window.

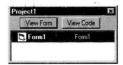

The Project window is useful when you have multiple forms or modules. Here, because you have only one form, you have not made too much use of it.

You might also notice in the Project window that the default name of your form is Form1.frm. The .frm file extension is normal for forms, just as the .bas extension is normal for Visual Basic code module files. Similarly, the .cls extension is the default for VB class modules. When Form1.frm is selected in the Project window, you can easily look back and forth between the form and the Code window, which holds all the code associated with the objects in the project, by clicking the buttons in the Project window: View Form or View Code. However, it is just as easy to double-click on an object to open up the Code window. (When you double-click on a form name in the Project window, the form is displayed in normal design mode.)

Projects themselves are saved as .vbp files with associated .frm, .bas, and .cls files stored separately. Initially, when you create a new project, including new forms and even modules, Visual Basic does not automatically create the corresponding files on disk. Instead, it is up to you to save the files you want (although Visual Basic will prompt you to save files when you leave, if you have not already done so). Now that you have created your own project, you need to make sure that you can save it to disk so that nothing is lost.

Saving Forms, Modules, and Projects

There are four Save items on the Visual Basic File menu: Save Project, Save Project As..., Save File, and Save File As.... The Save Project item saves all of the files associated with the current project on disk. When you save a project, you should give it a unique name. You could stick to using the default name, Project1, but that could lead to trouble later with another Project1. You would have to be very careful to make sure the project was not inadvertently overwritten later. Using the Save Project As... option, you can choose a name for the current project and save all of the associated files on disk. After the project is named, the Save Project item will save your work under that name as well. If you select Save Project and you have not ever saved the project before, it will be the same as selecting Save Project As.

You also can use the Save File item to save the currently selected form or module as opposed to the current project. Again, you should give it a unique name. This menu item opens a dialog box where you must specify the name of the file you want to save.

Saving Program Files in Text Format Only

Visual Basic 3.0 offered the option of saving .bas and .frm files as text as opposed to its proprietary binary format. The only purpose of the binary format was to retain backward compatibility with earlier versions of Visual Basic (that is, Visual Basic 1.0 and Visual Basic 2.0). As these older versions are no longer viable in today's programming world, that option has been removed from Visual Basic 4 When you save files now, Visual Basic automatically saves them as text; hence, they can be opened in a text editor such as Notepad as shown in Figure 2.32.

Figure 2.32.
A Visual Basic form opened in Notepad.

```
Welcome - Notepad
File  Edit  Search  Help
VERSION 4.00
Begin VB.Form frmFirst
   Caption         =   "My First Program"
   ClientHeight    =   1080
   ClientLeft      =   1755
   ClientTop       =   2385
   ClientWidth     =   4395
   Height          =   1485
   Left            =   1695
   LinkTopic       =   "Form1"
   ScaleHeight     =   1080
   ScaleWidth      =   4395
   Top             =   2040
   Width           =   4515
   Begin VB.CommandButton cmdFirstButton
      Caption      =   "ClickMe!"
      BeginProperty Font
         name      =   "MS Sans Serif"
         charset   =   0
```

That's it! The next time you start Visual Basic you can reload this project by using the Open Project… item from the File menu and by selecting My-first.vbp. To help you do this, Visual Basic 4 includes a Most Recently Used (MRU) file list. This list of most recently opened projects is added to the bottom of the File menu. Figure 2.30 shows four MRUs just above the Exit item. When you want to reopen a currently used project, just select the matching menu item.

The Save Before Run Option

It is good programming practice to set the Save Before Run option to "Yes, prompt." This option can be found under the Environment Options Dialog item in the Tools menu. When set to "Yes, prompt," Visual Basic will ask you if you want to save any changes you have made to your program before running it.

The No to All Button

In previous versions of Visual Basic, the program questioned the programmer several times whether she wanted to Save the Form, Save the Project, and so on upon exiting. If she did not, this meant pressing the No button several times in various interrogative (question) boxes.

For example, when trying to load a program in which there were many forms and some errors (perhaps one custom control was not loaded on the system), VB would put up a question box for every individual form, asking if the changes should be saved. What a tedious, lengthy process, answering No to every one!

In Visual Basic 4, a No to All button has been added, circumventing this process.

Adding More Power to Your Text Box

Before you finish your first application, you might notice that because the text "Welcome to Visual Basic!" appears in a text box, the user is free to edit it, even after the box has displayed your message. The text box is acting, for all intents and purposes, like a normal Windows text box. However, you can modify your program so that you are informed if any change is made to the text. In Visual Basic, changing the text in a text box is one of the events for which you can write code.

Read-Only Text Boxes

If you do not want the user to be able to change the text you display on a form, there are two methods that you can use. The first is to use a label instead of a text box. As you will see, you can write to a label at design-time, but the user cannot change the displayed text at run-time. In essence, this means that labels can act as read-only text boxes.

The other method is to use a new feature included with Visual Basic 4 A new property, `Locked`, can be set to either `False` or `True`. If set to `True`, the text in the text box cannot be changed by the user at run-time.

When the text in a text box is edited, a *text box change event* occurs. Because your text box is named txtFirstBox, this event would be called `txtFirstBox_Change()`. You can intercept that change by going back to the Visual Basic design screen and double-clicking on the text box. The Code window for the text box opens as in Figure 2.33. As you can see in the figure, the text `Change` event is already selected. This is where you will enter your new line of code.

Figure 2.33.
*The text box's Code window
displaying the Change
event's code template.*

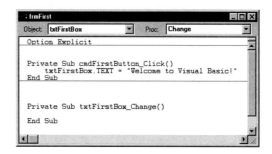

Suppose the text in the text box is edited and a text box change is generated. You may want to give the user the option of restoring the text to the original welcome message. You can do that by changing the caption of the command button from "Click Me" to something like "Restore Msg." This is easy to do because the caption of the command button is just a property of the command button that can be reached from the program. Because the command button's `Name` property is cmdFirstButton, you can simply make this Visual Basic assignment: cmdFirstButton.Caption = "Restore Msg" where you assign the string `"Restore Msg"` to the button's Caption property. You can do that by making this change to the `Sub` procedure `txtFirstBox_Change()`, as follows:

```
Private Sub txtFirstBox_Change()
      cmdFirstButton.Caption = "Restore Msg"
End Sub
```

Now, when you run the program, the usual window appears along with the Click Me button and the empty text box. However, as soon as the user changes the text in the text box, the button caption changes to Restore Msg as shown in Figure 2.34, indicating that the original message can be restored by pressing this button.

> **Tip:** In a professional application, the button would change its own caption back after it had been clicked to indicate, among other things, that it has completed its job. This can be done by assigning the caption property of the button within the `cmdFirstButton_click` procedure. This is something you might want to try to do on your own.

Figure 2.34.
The RestoreMsg button.

Throughout this book a complete listing of each program, including each control's properties settings and the complete code listings, will conclude each program section. Following is a table of object properties and a code listing for your first project.

Object	Property	Setting
Form	Caption	My First Program
	Name	frmFirst
Text Box	Name	txtFirstBox
	Text	(None)
Command Button	Caption	Click Me
	Name	cmdFirstButton

The code is as follows:

```
Private Sub cmdFirstButton_Click()
     txtFirstBox.Text = "Welcome to Visual Basic!"
End Sub

Private Sub txtFirstBox_Change()
     cmdFirstButton.Caption = "Restore Msg"
End Sub
```

That's almost it for this chapter. You now have the fundamentals of Visual Basic under your belt. In the next section of this chapter you will use what you know to work through a second mini-application. Then, in Chapter 3, you will start to look into Visual Basic in depth. Specifically, you will explore all there is to know about two of its most popular objects—the two that you are already familiar with—buttons and text boxes.

A Mini-Application

Turning on the light.

This program turns a light bulb on and off while the caption on the command button that the user presses toggles from ON to OFF.

To get going on this mini-application, start Visual Basic. A form named Form1 appears as the program opens. Using the Properties window, change this form's Name property from Form1 to frmBulb, and then change the Caption property from Form1 to Turning on the Light!. Next, change both the MaxButton and MinButton properties to False (this eliminates the Maximize and Minimize buttons from the form at run-time, not design-time). Now select the Icon property and press the Properties button (the square button with the ellipsis in it) that appears to the right of the Icon Settings box. The Icon dialog box opens. Scroll down to the directory where Visual Basic resides (usually VB), and then double-click on the Icons subdirectory. Scroll down in the Icons subdirectory until you reach Misc and double-click on it. Now, move your mouse pointer to the File Name menu until you find Lighton.ico. This property associates an icon with the form. Select it and then click OK. Visual Basic returns you to your form. Notice that after selecting the light bulb icon, it appears on the form at the upper-left corner.

You might have noticed that you could see not only the name of what you were selecting, but also a small image of the icon. This Windows 95 feature makes finding pictures and icons much easier than in previous versions of Visual Basic.

It is a good idea to save what you have done now—and to save periodically as you add to the application. To save the form and the entire project, select Save Project from the File menu. The Save File As dialog box opens first. This is where you will save the form on which you have been working. Select the directory where you want to place the project. In the File Name text box, change the filename to Bulb.frm and then click OK. Next, the Save Project As dialog box opens. In the File Name text box, change the default filename to LiteBulb.vbp and then click OK. Visual Basic returns you to the design desktop. Notice that the caption at the top of the screen now reads LITEBULB—Microsoft Visual Basic [design], and that the caption in the Project window says Litebulb. Also, the form that you just named Bulb.frm appears on the list in the Project window, as in Figure 2.35.

The New .vbp File Extension for Projects

In previous versions of Visual Basic, project files used a .mak file extension that was appended to the filename. With Visual Basic 4 that extension has been changed to .vbp, which stands, appropriately enough, for Visual Basic Program/Project.

Now resize the form window until it is approximately the same dimensions as Figure 2.35 (about 3 1/2-inches high and 3-inches wide). If you check the Height and Width properties, they should be set at 3600 and 3030, respectively.

Figure 2.35.
Designing the light bulb form.

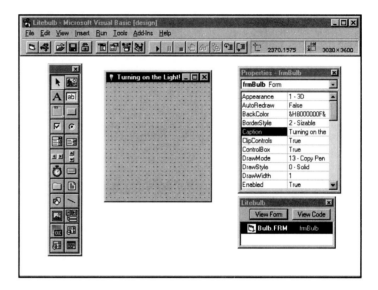

The caption bar that reads Turning on the Light! might have been cut off a bit as you resized the width of the form. Don't worry about that for now. When the program is running, the Maximize and Minimize buttons will disappear, making the rest of the caption visible.

Using the toolbox, double-click on the Command Button tool. A default-sized command button appears in the center of your form. Move it straight down until it is a few grid rows from the bottom of the form, as it is in Figure 2.36. As you move it, notice how the object aligns to the grid. In the Properties window, change the Name property from Command1 to cmdClose. Also, change the Caption property from Command1 to CLOSE. Click on the Font property and then press the Properties button that appears to the right of the Font Settings box. A Font dialog box opens displaying the font (in this case the default font is MS Sans Serif), font style, size, effects, and a sample. Change the Font Style from Regular to Bold and then click OK.

Now make another command button as you just did by double-clicking on the Command Button tool in the toolbox. A second default-sized command button appears in the center of your form. Change this command button's Name property to cmdOnOff, change its Caption property to read ON, then also change its Font property style to Bold as you did just a few minutes ago with the previous command button.

Figure 2.36.
The command buttons,
cmdClose and cmdOnOff,
placed on the light bulb form.

Double-click on the Picture Box tool on the toolbar (the top-center button). A default-sized picture box appears in the center of the screen, right on top of cmdOnOff. Move it up and slightly to the left above cmdOnOff. Make it smaller by resizing it as in Figure 2.37.

Figure 2.37.
The first picture box resized
and placed above
cmdOnOff.

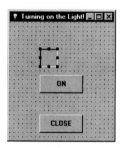

Double-click the Picture Box tool on the toolbar again to create a second picture box. Move this box up to the right of the first picture box and then resize it to match the first picture box.

Now, click on the first picture box you made—the one on the left. Change its Name property from Picture1 to picBulbOff. Change its BorderStyle property from 1-Fixed Style to 0-None; then click on the Picture property. Press the Properties button that appears to the right of the Settings box. The Load Picture dialog box opens. Scroll down to the directory where Visual Basic resides (usually VB), and then double-click on the Icons subdirectory. Scroll down the Icons subdirectory until you reach Misc and double-click on it. Now, move your mouse pointer to the File Name menu and scroll down the list until you find Lightoff.ico. Select it; then click OK. An unlit light bulb appears in the picture box on your form.

Move to the picture box on the right, named Picture2, and select it. Change its Name property to picBulbOn. Remove the border from the picture box using the BorderStyle property as you did before, and then select the Picture property and press the Property button again. The icon you want to appear in the picture box is C:\VB\ICONS\MISC\LIGHTON.ICO. When selected, the lit light bulb appears in the second picture box.

The last item you need to place on your form is a rectangle that surrounds cmdOnOff and the two picture boxes, as in Figure 2.38. Instead of double-clicking the Shape tool to create a default-sized rectangle, select (click once) the Shape tool and then move the mouse pointer to the form. The pointer arrow changes to a crosshair. Place the crosshair where you want the top-left corner of the rectangle to appear (above and to the left of picBulbOff). Depress the left mouse button and then drag the rectangle to where you want the lower-right corner (below and to the right of cmdOnOff). Now, change the Name property to shpRectangle, and change the BorderWidth property from 1 to 2. Look at Figure 2.38 and compare your form to it. If the rectangle seems a bit off or if the controls aren't lined up to your satisfaction, move or resize them until you are happy with them.

Figure 2.38.
The completed light bulb form.

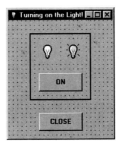

That's it for the objects on this form. Lock them in place by selecting Lock Controls from the Edit menu or by pressing the Lock Controls button on the toolbar. That way an object won't be moved inadvertently.

Now for the code that will make the program work.

First, when the program is running, the form should be centered on the screen. Double-click on the form itself. The Code window for the form opens with the cursor in the Sub Form_Load() code template. Move the mouse pointer to the Procedure list box and choose the arrow to the right of the box to display all of the procedures available for the form. Scroll up to Initialize and select it. Add a call to a subroutine called CenterForm as follows:

```
Private Sub Form_Initialize()
      'Center the form by calling CenterForm subroutine
      CenterForm Me
End Sub
```

Notice that after the call to the subroutine CenterForm is the word Me. Me is a Visual Basic keyword that is shorthand for "the current form" (in this case frmBulb). You could substitute frmBulb instead of using the keyword Me (that is, CenterForm frmBulb). The Me keyword is discussed in more depth in Chapter 15, "Advanced Control and Form Handling."

Also note in the code that there is a line prefaced with an apostrophe. In Visual Basic, an apostrophe marks a line of comments that the program does not see at run-time. It is good practice to add comments to your programs as you write them. If you need to return to a program at a later date and your descriptive comments are in place by each section of code, it will be easier for you to understand what the program is doing. If you write your comments well, every section of the application is spelled out for you.

> **Tip:** Use comments to describe each section of coding, and on lines where it is not apparent what is going on. The programs in this book do not include a lot of comments in the code because I had a whole book to describe the programs!

So, be a good programmer now! Add a comment that states what the line of code does that you just inserted.

Now it's time to add the subroutine that the Initialize event calls. Move your cursor to the very bottom of the Code window and select Procedure from the Insert menu. An Insert Procedure dialog box opens with the cursor in the Name text box. Type in CenterForm and make sure the Type radio button is set to "Sub" and the Scope is set to "Public"; then click OK. (The important concept of scope is discussed in Chapter 4, "Programming in Visual Basic.")

The template for the CenterForm subroutine appears on the screen with your cursor positioned above the End Sub. Add code so the subroutine appears as follows:

```
Public Sub CenterForm(F As Form)
      'Subroutine to center form
      F.Left = (Screen.Width - F.Width) / 2
      F.Top = (Screen.Height - F.Height) / 2
End Sub
```

Now move your mouse pointer to the Object list box and choose the arrow to the right of the box to display all of the objects available in your program. Scroll to cmdClose and select it. Then move your pointer to the Procedure list box and choose the arrow to the right of that box. Scroll to Click and select it. This moves you to the cmdClose Click event.

When the program is running and the user presses the Close command button, a Click event occurs. The function of this Close button is to close the light bulb window and also terminate the application. You must enter code at that Click event to make this happen. One way of doing this is the Unload command. It unloads the specified form. Because the close control is on the form you want to close you can enter the code Unload cmdClose.Parent as follows:

```
Private Sub cmdClose_Click()
      'End application when user presses Close button
      Unload cmdClose.Parent
End Sub
```

Using the Object and Procedure list boxes at the top of the Code window as you did a few minutes ago, move to the form's Initialize event. This is where you entered some code earlier.

At the moment, your two light bulb pictures are side-by-side on the form. When the application is running, the program will place them on top of each other, with one picture in front. When the user presses the cmdOnOff button, the picture that is hidden behind the first one will move to the front and become visible while the one that was in front moves behind and becomes invisible. That is how the light bulb turns on and off. One way to control the order in which objects appear back-to-front on the screen is by using the *ZOrder method*. ZOrder is the order in which forms appear on the screen. Think of multiple overlapping pages on your desk. Some of the pages are partially obscured (or completely obscured) by other pages that are on top of them. Windows works the same way. Objects can hide other objects because of their location in relationship to each other, or their ZOrder. For now, enter the code that positions the light bulb pictures within the `Initialize` subroutine, just above `End Sub`. When you are done the entire `Initialize` subroutine will appear as follows:

```
Private Sub Form_Initialize()
        'Center the form by calling CenterForm subroutine
        CenterForm Me

        'Position the light bulbs on top of each other
        picBulbOn.Left = 1200
        picBulbOn.Top = 600
        picBulbOff.Left = 1200
        picBulbOff.Top = 600

        'Make sure the program starts with picBulbOff on top
        picBulbOff.ZOrder 0
End Sub
```

Now, move to the cmdOnOff `Click` event using the Procedure and Object list boxes at the top of the Code window.

Before moving on to the final piece of code for this application (the `Click` event for cmdOnOff), save your work. Great!

Now you can add the code to the program that changes which picture of the lightbulb is shown, on or off, and changes the caption of the command button. The code to do this appears below:

```
Private Sub cmdOnOff_Click()
        'Change light bulb on or off
        If cmdOnOff.Caption = "ON" Then
                cmdOnOff.Caption = "OFF"
                'bring picBulbOn to front
                picBulbOn.ZOrder 0
        Else
                cmdOnOff.Caption = "ON"
                'bring picBulbOff to front
                picBulbOff.ZOrder 0
        End If
End Sub
```

Note: When you set the ZOrder method of an object to 0 the rest of the objects are pushed back, away from the top. You do not have worry about conflicting with the ZOrder of other objects.

When this program starts running, the light bulb will be off and the command button below the light bulb will state ON. When the user presses the ON button, the light bulb will light up. Simultaneously, the caption on the button the user just pressed will change to OFF. When the user presses the OFF button, the light bulb will turn off and the caption on the command button will once again state ON. Thus, there are two things happening at this `Click` event: the caption on the command button toggles and the light bulb turns on and off. Right now your cursor is centered in the cmdOnOff `Click` event. Following is the complete code for the program. In it you will, of course, find the cmdOnOff `Click` event and the final lines of code you need.

The properties of the objects used in this program should be set as follows:

Object	Property	Setting
Form	`Caption`	Turning on the Light!
	`Height`	3600
	`Icon`	Lighton.ico
	`MinButton`	False
	`MaxButton`	False
	`Name`	frmBulb
	`Width`	3030
Command Button	`Caption`	CLOSE
	`Font`	Style: Bold
	`Name`	cmdClose
Command Button	`Caption`	ON
	`Font`	Style: Bold
	`Name`	cmdOnOff
Picture Box	`BorderStyle`	0-None
	`Name`	picBulbOff
	`Picture`	Lightoff.ico
Picture Box	`BorderStyle`	0-None
	`Name`	picBulbOn
	`Picture`	Lighton.ico
Shape	`BorderWidth`	2
	`Name`	shpRectangle

The complete code listing is as follows:

```
Option Explicit

Public Sub CenterForm(F As Form)
        'Subroutine to center form
        F.Left = (Screen.Width - F.Width) / 2
        F.Top = (Screen.Height - F.Height) / 2
End Sub

Private Sub cmdClose_Click()
        'End application when user presses Close button
        Unload cmdClose.Parent
End Sub

Private Sub cmdOnOff_Click()
        'Change light bulb on or off
        If cmdOnOff.Caption = "ON" Then
                cmdOnOff.Caption = "OFF"
                'bring picBulbOn to front
                picBulbOn.ZOrder 0
        Else
                cmdOnOff.Caption = "ON"
                'bring picBulbOff to front
                picBulbOff.ZOrder 0
        End If
End Sub

Private Sub Form_Initialize()
        'Center the form by calling CenterForm subroutine
        CenterForm Me

        'Position the light bulbs on top of each other
        picBulbOn.Left = 1200
        picBulbOn.Top = 600
        picBulbOff.Left = 1200
        picBulbOff.Top = 600

        'Make sure the program starts with picBulbOff on top
        picBulbOff.ZOrder 0
End Sub
```

And that's it! It's time to run your program. Press F5 or the Start button on the toolbar, or select Start from the Run menu and watch your creation fly!

Figure 2.39.
*The light bulb application
running.*

If you would like to make your mini-application into a stand-alone program on the desktop, select Make EXE File from the File menu. A Make EXE File dialog box opens. The default name in the File Name text box is the name of the project. Place the file where you would like it to reside and then click OK. Run the program you just created, Litebulb.exe, from the Windows 95 desktop.

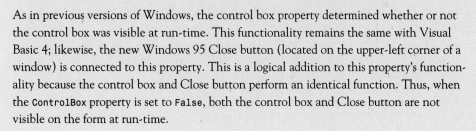

Enhanced Functionality of the Control Box Property

As in previous versions of Windows, the control box property determined whether or not the control box was visible at run-time. This functionality remains the same with Visual Basic 4; likewise, the new Windows 95 Close button (located on the upper-left corner of a window) is connected to this property. This is a logical addition to this property's functionality because the control box and Close button perform an identical function. Thus, when the `ControlBox` property is set to `False`, both the control box and Close button are not visible on the form at run-time.

Summary

In this chapter you learned about the parts of a Windows 95 window, window events, how to design and run a Visual Basic program, and how to save work on disk. You learned about the terms form, control, object, module, project, and others, as well as the elements of designing programs in Windows 95. You put together your first working Windows programs, using text boxes, command buttons, and pictures.

Congratulations, you've made a lot of progress! As a quick review, a summary of properties and events that you've worked with has been included next.

New Properties	Description
Caption	Holds the control's caption (title) on the screen.
Height	Holds the height of the object or form (the default measurement is in twips).
Left	When referring to controls, holds the control a certain distance from the left edge of its form. When referring to forms, holds the left edge of the form a certain distance from the left edge of the screen (the default measurement is in twips).
Locked	Available only for text boxes. This property locks the text in the text box; thus, the user cannot change the text at run-time.
Name	Holds the name you use for a form or control in code. For example, the `Text` property of a text box named Text1 is `Text1.Text`.

New Properties	Description
Text	Holds text associated with a text-oriented control such as a text box.
Top	When referring to controls, holds the top edge of a control a certain distance from the top edge of a form. When referring to forms, holds the top edge of a form a certain distance from the top edge of the screen (the default measurement is in twips).
Width	Holds the width of a control or form (default measurement is in twips).

New Events	Description
Change	Occurs when the contents (usually text) of a control change.
Click	Occurs when a form or control is clicked with the mouse.
Load	Occurs when a form is first loaded. Use it for initialization.

3

Buttons, Text Boxes, and an Alarm Clock Program

This chapter explores some very popular Windows controls: buttons, text boxes, labels, and option buttons. These controls provide the most fundamental methods of receiving input and displaying output in your programs. In particular, this chapter covers the following:

- Reading numbers into your programs
- Using labels
- Storing data in variables
- Scope and lifetime of variables
- Changing fonts
- Formatting text output
- How to cut and paste text
- Enabling and disabling buttons
- Quick-access keys
- Option (radio) buttons
- Reading individual keystrokes
- The Visual Basic Beep statement
- Using third-party controls

The programs you will develop here include a Windows calculator, a notepad that will enable you to select, cut, and paste text, an alarm clock, and an ASCII character-value finder. The alarm clock will show you how to work with fonts in Visual Basic, an asset to any program that uses text. The ASCII finder, a mini-application (how many times have you gone searching for an ASCII character chart?), will introduce you to more advanced programming concepts. You will also start to interpret and store the data you receive. This means that you will see how to use variables in Visual Basic. In other words, you are not only going to develop your user-interface skills in this chapter; you will also learn how to manipulate data in your programs.

Two of the most common Windows controls are text boxes and buttons. In fact, you used both of these controls in the previous chapter. Text boxes are an important user-interface text control in Visual Basic, and buttons are one of the chief command-interface controls (the other being menus, which you will see in Chapter 6, "Menus"). For those reasons, you will discover how to use both text boxes and buttons in depth in this chapter.

It is important to realize that text boxes are the primary means of character-string input in Visual Basic. This means that they can take the place of other Visual Basic instructions, such as the Print method or using the Printer object. (More about these items in Chapter 9, "Visual Basic Graphics.") Given the importance of both character input and output, text boxes are the first topic this chapter covers.

The whole idea of user-text interface—character-string input and output—brings you closer to the heart of programming in Visual Basic. To understand text handling and how to display data from your programs, you have to examine how to store it in the first place. That brings you to the topic of variables. In fact, your first application in this chapter will be a simple calculator that operates in its own window so that you can learn how to accept and display numeric values in text boxes.

In addition, you will learn about the difficulties of displaying graphic text characters in Windows. For example, the width of each character can be different, so it can be difficult to know exactly how far a group of characters has printed across the screen. Text boxes also have some pretty advanced capabilities. For instance, text boxes can be set up with more than one line, including word wrapping and scrollbars. You will handle all kinds of character-string input and output with text boxes and get commands from the user with command buttons. Also, you will retrieve specific text the user has marked. In Chapter 8, "File Handling in Visual Basic," you will put a small file-editing program together. You can get that started now by writing a notepad application that takes keystrokes and lets you store text. That is the plan for this chapter.

The Rich Text Box Control

Visual Basic 4 comes equipped with a rich text box control. This control can be found in the Custom Controls dialog box accessed from the Tools menu. To add the control to your toolbox, select Microsoft Rich Text Control from the Available Controls list, and then press OK. The rich text box control is a 32-bit control that will only run on 32-bit systems, such as Windows 95 and Windows NT 3.51 or higher.

Although the rich text box control works like its cousin, the regular text box control, letting users enter and edit text; it also provides several formatting features that are more advanced. These features include setting multiple font sizes, fonts, font styles, and colors; the capability to open and save files in both rich text format (.rtf) and ASCII format (.txt); and printing all or only part of the text contained in the rich text box.

For more information about the rich text box, see the "RichTextBox Control" topic in Visual Basic's on-line help.

Now to start with the calculator example.

A Calculator Program

The calculator is going to be remarkably simple, because it focuses only on text boxes and not a larger application. There will be just two text boxes, one for the first operand and one for the second, a button marked with an equal sign, and a text box to hold the sum of the two operands. When the user clicks on the equal button, the sum of the addition will appear in the result text box.

If you chose to install the samples that came with Visual Basic, you can find a more complex calculator in c:\vb32\samples\calc\calc.vbp. You will find that examining the code behind an application created by professional programmers such as those employed by Microsoft is a useful learning tool. The Visual Basic sample calculator is much more sophisticated than the one included here, but it employs the same principles that you will be using.

To get going, start Visual Basic and change the Caption property of the default window, which reads Form1, to Calculator by editing its Caption property in the Properties window. Now, save this form by selecting Save Project... from the File menu. The Save File As dialog box opens with the default form name Form1 in the filename text box. Change this to Calc; then, using the File menu, choose the directory where you would like the project to reside. Click OK. Next, the Save Project As dialog box opens, again with the cursor in the filename text box. Change the default Project1.vbp to Calc.vbp, and then click OK. Visual Basic returns you to the design window. These are the typical beginning steps of writing a new application, because the only way to name files in Visual Basic is with the Save option. Visual Basic does not even create files for the form and project until you save them. It is also a good idea to periodically save your work. You can do that now by selecting the Save Project item from the File menu.

Next, choose (double-click) the text box tool. A default-sized text box appears in the center of the form. Move it up to the top of the form and change its Name property to txtOperand1, as shown in Figure 3.1.

Figure 3.1.
Designing the calculator form.

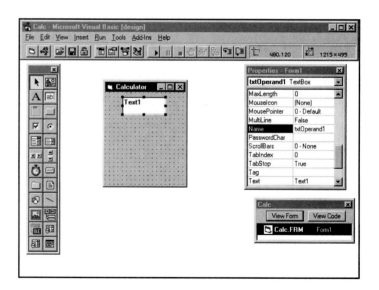

This text box, txtOperand1, is going to receive the first operand. The next text box will, of course, receive the second. Then there will be a button marked with an equal sign (=) and also a result text box. For simplicity's sake, this calculator will only perform addition, adding Operand1 + Operand2 to get a sum, but it would be a simple matter to add buttons for subtraction, multiplication, and division.

Double-click on the text box tool again and place the second text box one grid row below txtOperand1. Change this second text box's Name property to txtOperand2, as shown in Figure 3.2.

Figure 3.2.
*The calculator form with a
second text box.*

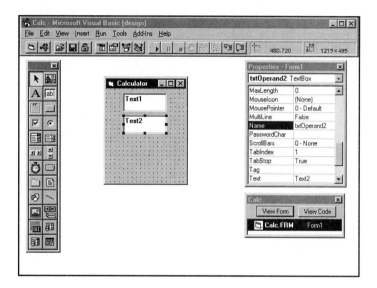

Now place a command button one grid row below the two boxes and change its Caption property to an equal sign (=). Rename the command button cmdEquals. Finally, place one last text box one grid row below the command button and change this last text box's Name property to txtResult. Figure 3.3 displays the calculator as it currently appears.

Figure 3.3.
The calculator template.

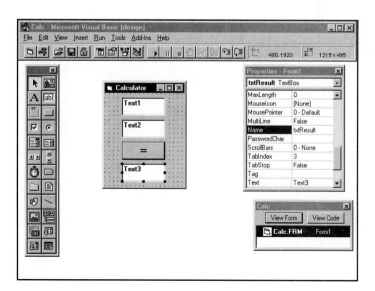

There are two more things to do and then you will have completely designed the calculator's appearance. First, remove the text from each text box—for example, `Text1`—by selecting each box's `Text` property and deleting what is there. Finally, add a plus sign (+) in front of txtOperand2 to indicate what operation you are performing. To do that, you will place a label on the form and set its `Caption` property to a plus sign.

Labels

As their name implies, *labels* are normally used to classify other controls on a form. Although your program can change the text in a label by referring to its `Caption` property, the user cannot. (This feature comes in handy when you want a read-only text box—a text box that the user cannot change. A label can act in this capacity.)

Making a Label Look Like a Text Box

Although labels often appear only as text, you can also put a box around them to make them look just like a text box. To do that, change the `BorderStyle` property from `0-None` to `1-Fixed Single`.

The label you want to add to your calculator form is a very simple plus sign. You can do that by choosing the label tool (second down on the left; it is marked with a large, uppercase A). A default-sized label appears in the middle of the form. Change its `Caption` property from `Label 1` to + in the Properties window, change its `Name` property to `lblPlus`, and then move it next to txtOperand2, as shown in Figure 3.4.

Figure 3.4.
The calculator form with
lblPlus added and positioned.

The plus sign on lblPlus seems small when compared with the other objects on the form. To make it bigger, click on the label's `Font` property. A Property box will appear to the right of the Settings box. Press the Property button (...), to the right of Font to open the Font dialog box. (More about this dialog box later in the chapter.) The default font size is 8 points; change it to 18 points. When you are finished, click OK. Your form should look similar to the one pictured in Figure 3.5.

Figure 3.5.
The completed calculator form.

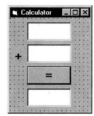

Another Way to Place Text Directly on a Form

Instead of placing text on a label by using its `Caption` property, you can place text directly on a form using the `Print` method. This will be discussed in Chapter 9.

You have to do one last thing before you move on to writing code. Click on the form to select it; then press the Lock Controls button on the toolbar. Notice that the padlock icon changes to a closed lock when you press the button. With the controls locked in place, none of them can be moved accidentally.

Now the calculator form is complete. All that remains is to write the code behind the form. The action here is simple. When the user clicks cmdEquals, you want to take txtOperand1, add it to txtOperand2, and place the sum in txtResult. However, to do this poses a problem. So far, you have only dealt with text in text boxes. How do you display numbers? And how do you store them in your program?

This is a very important concept. How can the input received from the user in text boxes be manipulated, especially if that input is supposed to represent numbers, not just text? In other words, your job now is to translate the text in txtOperand1 and txtOperand2 into numbers, add them in the program, and then display the result. All of this internal data handling brings up the next topic, *variables*, which you should explore before proceeding.

Variables in Visual Basic

In Visual Basic, variable names can be up to 40 characters long (including letters, numbers, and underscores), and they have only two naming rules.

- The first character must be a letter so Visual Basic does not assume that the name is a numeric value
- Reserved words such as `Sub` or `Function` cannot be used

The data types that are built into Visual Basic are shown in Table 3.1, along with their ranges of allowed values.

Table 3.1. Fundamental Visual Basic data types.

Type	Number of bytes	Character	Range
Integer	2 bytes	%	−32,768 to 32,767
Long	4 bytes	&	−2,147,483,648 to 2,147,483,647
Single	4 bytes	!	−3.402823E38 to −1.401298E−45 for negative values; 1.401298E−45 to 3.402823E38 for positive values.
Double	8 bytes	#	−1.79769313486232E308 to −4.94065645841247E−324 for negative values; 4.94065645841247E−324 to 1.79769313486232E308 for positive values
Currency	8 bytes	@	−922337203685477.5808 to 922337203685477.5807
String	1 byte per character	$	Strings can range in length from 0 to approximately 2 billion (approximately 65,535 for Microsoft Windows version 3.1 and earlier)
Byte	1 byte	(None)	0 to 255
Boolean	2 bytes	(None)	`True` or `False`
Date	8 bytes	(None)	January 1, 100 to December 31, 9999
Object	4 bytes	(None)	Any `Object` reference

Type	Number of bytes	Character	Range
Variant	16 bytes + 1 byte for each character	(None)	Null, Error, any numeric value up to the range of a Double or any character text, object, or array

Byte, Boolean, and Object: New Variable Data Types

There are three new data types used in Visual Basic 4: Byte, Boolean, and Object. The Byte data type is used to hold small, positive integer numbers ranging from 0 to 255. Using *Byte* variables to store binary data enables files to use less space and applications to run with less memory. It also prevents Visual Basic from performing any conversions on the data as it would if you tried to store a value such as this in a position of a string. A *Boolean variable* declaration should be used when a variable contains simple yes/no or on/off information. The default value of Boolean is False. *Object variables* are stored as 32-bit (4-byte) addresses that refer to objects within an application or within some other application. A variable declared as Object is one that can subsequently be assigned to refer to any actual object recognized by the application.

You Are Not Restricted to Built-In Data Types

Besides the built-in data types listed previously, you also can define your own aggregate data types with the Type statement, which defines data structures. The Type statement must be placed in the Declarations section of a standard module. User-defined types can be declared as Private or Public with the appropriate keyword. For example:

```
Private Type MyDataType
:
End Type
or
Public Type MyDataType
:
End Type
```

The user-defined data type is one of the most useful and most used concepts in programming. It will be discussed in depth in Chapter 4, "Programming in Visual Basic," and Chapter 11, "Advanced Data-Handling, Sorting, and Storing a Spreadsheet Program."

Type Conventions for Variables

The Currency type was originally designed to hold currency values, but it is useful for other reasons as well: For example, it stores numbers with 15-place accuracy to the left of the decimal place and 4-place precision to the right. These numbers are *fixed-point* numbers; that is, they always have four places to the left of the decimal point.

In calculations where you don't really need the range of a floating-point variable, but need a few decimal points for accuracy without the rounding errors, use the Currency type. Because Currency is stored as a fixed decimal point it does not have the range of floating-point numbers, but it is much more accurate because the floating-point number approximations don't need to be used.

> Floating-point numbers—Double and Single data types—pose the interesting problem that they are only numerical approximations. Consequently, they do not equate to precise numerical expressions. When working with currency and other applications where it is important to be exactly right, the Currency data type is the one to use.

There are certain characters in Visual Basic, for example ! and %, as indicated in Table 3.1, that can be used to indicate the type of variable intended when first used. For instance, if you want to use an integer value named `My_int`, you can indicate to Visual Basic that `My_int` is an integer by adding % to the end of it, like this: `My_int%`. Similarly, if you want to use a single, precision floating-point number called `My_float`, you can call it `My_float!`. Using these characters to type variables is called *implicit* typing.

The Variant Data Type

Visual Basic variables default to the Variant data type. In other words, if a variable is not declared as a particular data type, Visual Basic will assume that it is a Variant. The Variant data type can store arrays and objects, and numeric, date/time, or string data. You do not have to convert between these types of data when assigning them to a Variant variable. Variables will always store data of a particular type, but Visual Basic can handle that data more efficiently if you declare a variable of that type. Data types will be discussed in depth in Chapter 4.

How to Change the Default Data Types

You can change default data types with `Def[type]` statements. `Def[type]` statements are used at the module level to set the default data types for variables, arguments passed to procedures, and the return type for `Function` and `Property Get` procedures whose names start with the specified characters. A `Def[type]` statement works like this:

```
DefInt letterrange[, letterrange]
```

The argument `letterrange` uses the following syntax:

```
letter1[-letter2]
```

The `letter1` and `letter2` arguments specify the name range; you can set a default data type for this. Thus, `DefInt A-Z` indicates that you want all variables with the letters A–Z to be integers.

Other `Def[type]` options include `DefBool`, `DefByte`, `DefInt`, `DefLng`, `DefCur`, `DefSng`, `DefDbl`, `DefDate`, `DefVar`, `DefObj`, and `DefStr`. All `Def[type]` statements are defined in Visual Basic's help file.

In fact, there are two ways of indicating to Visual Basic that you want to use a certain name as a variable name. The first is to use the `Dim` statement to specifically declare a variable at the beginning of a procedure (you will see how to declare `Public` variables later), as in the following examples:

```
Dim My_int As Integer
Dim My_Double As Double
Dim My_VariableString As String
Dim My_FixedString As String * 20
```

This declaration type is referred to as an *explicit declaration* and is more proper from a programming point of view than the second type of declaration, *implicit declaration*. You do not have to declare a variable before using it; thus an implicit declaration simply uses the variable name where it is called, as follows:

```
My_int% = 5
```

Visual Basic automatically creates a variable with that name, so you could use it as if you had explicitly declared it. Although this is convenient, *it can lead to errors in your code if you misspell a variable name by mistake.*

Note in particular the last two explicit declarations in the code lines, `Dim My_VariableString As String` and `Dim My_FixedString As String * 20`. The first one is a string with variable length up to 65,525. The second one is explicitly declared a fixed length by adding `* 20` to the end of the declaration, which makes it a string of exactly 20 characters. You will take a closer look at strings later in this chapter when you deal with the built-in string statements and functions in Visual Basic.

There are several places to put such declarations and the placement of a variable's declaration affects the variable's scope.

> ### Variable Scope
>
> When you declare a variable within a procedure, only code within that procedure can access or change the value of that variable. In other words, it has a *scope* that is local to that procedure. Sometimes, however, you need to use a variable with a broader scope, such as one whose value is available to all of the procedures within the same module, or even to all of the procedures in your entire application. Visual Basic enables you to specify the scope of a variable when you declare it.

After examining the concept of scope, you will be ready to complete the calculator application.

Variable Scope in Visual Basic

As mentioned, a variable's scope refers to the regions in the application that can access it. There are several different levels of variable scoping, some of which are new to Visual Basic 4.

The first place to declare variables, either *explicitly* using a Dim or Static statement or *implicitly* by using the data type character, is at the procedure level. *Procedure-level variables* are recognized only in the procedure where they are declared. These are also known as *local* variables. For example, there are two definitions in the following code. Each is valid. The first one declares a standard variable whose value is lost after the procedure ends execution. The second declares a variable that maintains its values between calls. Figure 3.6 shows how variables are isolated from one another.

```
Dim intTemporary As Integer
```

or

```
Static intPermanent As Integer
```

Figure 3.6.
A pictorial representation of local variables.

Local variables declared with Static exist the entire time your application is running. Local variables declared with Dim exist only as long as the procedure is executing; in other words, every time you enter the procedure, the local variables are reinitialized. Therefore, you should not count on retaining the value in a local variable between procedure calls.

How to Make Local Variables Retain Their Data

You can, however, make local variables permanent by declaring them as `Static`. Visual Basic will not reinitialize a static variable at any time.

Declaring All Local Variables as `Static`

To make all local variables in a procedure static, place the `Static` keyword at the beginning of a procedure heading. For instance,

```
Static Function GrandTotal (Num)
```

This makes all the local variables in the procedure static regardless of whether they are declared with `Static` or `Dim` or are declared implicitly. You can place `Static` in front of any `Sub` or `Function` procedure heading, including event procedures and those that are also declared as `Private`.

The next two places where you declare variables are at the form and module levels (remember that a module can hold the general, non-user-interface code associated with an application). If you declare a form-level variable, that variable is accessible to all procedures in that form. The same goes for code modules: If you declare a module-level variable, that variable is accessible to all procedures in that module.

Depending on how it is declared, a variable is scoped as either a procedure-level (local) or module-level variable. Table 3.2 describes where a variable can be used given how it is defined. Figure 3.7 shows how the form- and module-level variables are separate and how the procedure variables are separate from one another.

Table 3.2. **Variable scope.**

Scope	Private	Public
Procedure-level	All identifiers are private to the procedure in which they appear.	Not applicable. You cannot declare public variables within a procedure.
Module-level	Identifiers are private to the module in which they appear.	Identifiers are available to all modules.

Figure 3.7.
A pictorial representation of procedure-level and module-level variables.

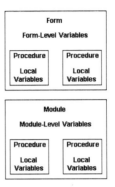

By default, a *module-level variable* is available to all of the procedures in that module, but not to code in other modules. You create module-level variables by declaring them with `Dim` or `Private` in the Declarations section at the top of the module. At the module level there is no difference between `Private` and `Dim`, but `Private` is preferred because it readily contrasts with `Public` and makes code easier to read.

The next level of variable is the `Public` level. Every procedure or line of code in an application has access to these variables. Thus, these variables are application-wide. To make a module-level variable available to other modules, use the `Public` keyword to declare the variable. The values in `Public` variables are available to all procedures in an application. Like all module-level variables, `Public` variables are declared in the Declarations section at the top of the module. One way to get to the Declarations section at the top of a module is to use the Object list box at the top of a module's Code window. Then using the down arrow to the right of the Objects list box, scroll until you find `(General)` and select it. In the Procedures list box, use the arrow to the right of that box to find `(declarations)`. Then you can enter the following declarations there:

```
Public My_Int As Integer
Public My_Double As Double
Public My_VariableString As String
Public My_FixedString As String * 20
```

Thus, at the procedure, form, and module or public levels, the structure would be as shown in Figure 3.8.

Using Multiple Variables with the Same Name

If `Public` variables in different modules share the same name, it is possible to differentiate between them in code. For example, if there is a `Public` integer variable `intX` declared in both Form1 and in Module1, you can refer to the public integers as `Module1.intX` and `Form1.intX` to get the correct values.

In the calculator application you will use procedure-level variables. Now it is time to get back to that application.

Figure 3.8.

A pictorial representation of variable scope.

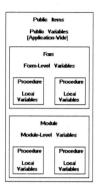

Using the Right Mouse Button to Show the Context Menu

When run under Windows 95, Visual Basic 4 makes use of the new pop-up menu feature you access with the right mouse button. If the right mouse button is clicked over any object on the Visual Basic design desktop—for instance, a form, a command button, a text box, or whatever—a pop-up menu appears next to that object, displaying various object-sensitive options, including View Code and Properties.

Storing the Calculator's Data

If you want to, you can store the calculator's data (the numbers typed by the user and the resulting sum) as single-precision numbers. You have designed things so that all action takes place when the user clicks cmdEquals, so let's take a look at that procedure. Double-click on cmdEquals to bring up the Code window that displays the Sub procedure for the Click event associated with it. It will appear as follows:

```
Private Sub cmdEquals_Click()

End Sub
```

So far, there is nothing in this procedure. Begin by reading the text in txtOperand1 and storing it in a single-precision variable named Op1, which you can declare as follows:

```
Private Sub cmdEquals_Click()
      Dim Op1 As Single

      :
End Sub
```

To convert txtOperand1.Text into a number, Visual Basic provides the Val() function, which works in the following way:

```
Private Sub cmdEquals_Click()
      Dim Op1 As Single
```

```
        'Convert text in Op1 to numbers
        Op1 = Val(txtOperand1.Text)


          :
End Sub
```

Val() will take a string and, moving from left to right, convert as much of it as it can into a numeric value. If it reaches illegal characters, it simply stops converting the text into a number.

Next, you do the same for txtOperand2, calling the resulting variable Op2, as follows:

```
Private Sub cmdEquals_Click()
        Dim Op1 As Single
        Dim Op2 As Single

        'Convert text in Op1 and Op2 to numbers
        Op1 = Val(txtOperand1.Text)
        Op2 = Val(txtOperand2.Text)


          :
End Sub
```

Besides the Val() function, Visual Basic also has the Str() function, which goes the other way, converting a number into a text string. Consequently, you can add the two numbers and display the results in txtResult.Text as follows:

```
Private Sub cmdEquals_Click()
        Dim Op1 As Single
        Dim Op2 As Single

        'Convert text in Op1 and Op2 to numbers
        Op1 = Val(txtOperand1.Text)
        Op2 = Val(txtOperand2.Text)

        'Two numbers added and reverted to text string
        txtResult.Text = Str(Op1 + Op2)

End Sub
```

That is all the code you need. Your calculator is ready. Just select the Start item from the Run menu, click the Start button on the toolbar, or press F5, and the calculator will function, as in Figure 3.9. You can type in floating-point numbers for the first two operands; when you click cmdEquals, the two will be added together. It might be a good idea to make txtResult into a label or change txtResult's Locked property to True so the user cannot modify it. The user can even modify the two operands after typing them—for example, to correct mistakes—because you used text boxes.

Figure 3.9.
The calculator application running.

Str and Str$ Both Return a String

In Visual Basic 3.0, `Str` returned a variant whereas `Str$` returned a string. In Visual Basic 4, `Str` and `Str$` both return a string.

Creating a Password Text Box Control

Another handy way of processing text box input is by using a password control. A character such as * or x can be specified for the text box property `PasswordChar`. This permits the text box to print out only a string of *s or xs, no matter what is typed. Even so, the actual text input by the user will be stored in the text box's `Text` property.

As is usual in Windows, the user can switch from text box to text box by pressing the Tab key (not Enter) as well as by using the mouse. However, this includes the result of the calculation, txtResult; thus the user can tab to txtResult. Because this is not convenient for data entry because the user should never want to directly enter the result, one change you might make to your program is to make sure that the Tab key will not move the *focus* to txtResult. When a control contains the insertion point in Windows, it is called *having the focus*. The way to make sure that txtResult no longer gets the focus while the user is tabbing around the text boxes is to set its `TabStop` property to `False`. (The default for text boxes and command buttons is `True`.)

You can do that by selecting the `TabStop` property for txtResult in the Properties window and setting it to `False` as in Figure 3.10. Note that the two options offered by the settings box are `True` or `False`, so the choice is easy.

Figure 3.10.
The TabStop property.

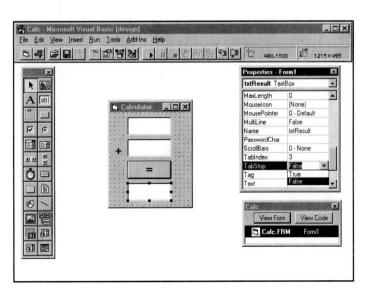

Setting the Tab Order

In the calculator application, the tab order should move from the text box at the top, txtOperand1, down successively through the controls, txtOperand2 and cmdEquals. You can establish this progression by setting the tab order. To do this, select (click once) txtOperand1 and then scroll down the Properties window until you reach TabIndex. Change, if necessary, the number in the TabIndex Settings box to 0. Now select txtOperand2. Change the value in the TabIndex Settings box associated with that object to 1. Finally, select cmdEquals and change its TabIndex setting to 2. That's all there is to setting the tab order on a form; just start at 0 and move consecutively through each object in the order you choose. Run the calculator program now and note that it opens with txtOperand1 in focus. Tab around the calculator to see the tab settings at work.

There is one more change you might want to make to your calculator application, one that will exercise yet another capability of command buttons. Because the Enter key is not specifically used for anything in the calculator program, it can be set to activate cmdEquals, making cmdEquals the *default button*. Thus, when the user presses the Enter key, it will be the same as clicking cmdEquals with the mouse. As is standard in Windows, the default button is surrounded by a thick black border so the user knows exactly which button is the default.

You can make cmdEquals into the default button simply by setting its Default property in the Properties window to True, as in Figure 3.11. (This will not affect the tab order, if you have set one.) Now when the user runs the program, she can select cmdEquals easily by pressing the Enter key.

Figure 3.11.
The calculator application with cmdEquals set as the default.

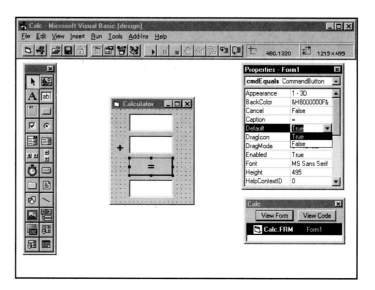

The full version of the calculator, complete with cmdEquals as the default button (notice the thick black border), appears in Figure 3.12.

You have made a good deal of progress as far as numeric user interaction is concerned, but there is more to come. So far, text boxes have shown themselves to be both handy and flexible, but this is only the tip of the iceberg, as it were. Because this is the chapter about text boxes and because they are so very important for both displaying and reading data, you will explore some of their more advanced capabilities next.

Figure 3.12.
The calculator application running.

Formatting Text

As you have seen, one way to display numbers as text in a text box is to use the str() function, as follows:

```
Private Sub cmdEquals_Click()
      Dim Op1 As Single
      Dim Op2 As Single

      'Convert text in Op1 and Op2 to numbers
      Op1 = Val(txtOperand1.Text)
      Op2 = Val(txtOperand2.Text)

      'Two numbers added and reverted to text string
      txtResult.Text = Str(Op1 + Op2)

End Sub
```

Here, you set the Text property of txtResult to str(Op1 + Op2). The str() does a good job of formatting numeric data in most cases. That is, it adds a space before and after the number it is to print out, and it even handles floating-point numbers. For example, if numbers get too big, it will print them out with an exponent, such as 1.2E+07. At this point, though, this is essentially unformatted output. You have no real control over the format of the text in txtResult.

To give you more control, Visual Basic includes the Format() function. With Format(), you can indicate the number of decimal places a number must have and the number of leading or trailing zeros, as well as formatting currency values. The following is the way to use Format(); the square brackets indicate that the format string is optional.

```
Format(expression[ ,format])
```

The *expression* argument specifies a number to convert. The *format* argument is a string made up of symbols that shows how to format the number. The most commonly used symbols are listed in Table 3.3. Take a look at the following examples to get used to the way the *Format* expression works.

Example	Value Returned
Format(1234.56, "#####.#")	1234.5
Format(1234.56, "00000.000")	01234.560
Format(1234.56, "###,###.0")	1,234.56
Format(1234.56, "$#,000.00")	$1234.56

As you can see, the # symbol is a placeholder telling Format() how many places you want to retain to the right of the decimal point. The 0 symbol acts the same way, except that if no actual digit is to be displayed at the corresponding location, a 0 is printed. In addition, you can specify other characters, such as $ or commas to separate thousands.

Table 3.3. Format symbols.

Symbol	Description
0	Digit placeholder; prints a trailing or leading zero in this position, if appropriate.
#	Digit placeholder; never prints trailing or leading zeros.
.	Decimal placeholder.
,	Thousands separator.
-, +, $, (,), (space)	Literal character. Characters are displayed exactly as typed into the format string.

To add thousands separators to your calculator, just change the Str() statement to a Format() statement, as follows:

```
Private Sub cmdEquals_Click()
      Dim Op1 As Single
      Dim Op2 As Single

      'Convert text in Op1 and Op2 to numbers
      Op1 = Val(txtOperand1.Text)
      Op2 = Val(txtOperand2.Text)

      'Two numbers added and reverted to text string
      txtResult.Text = Format(Op1 + Op2, "###,###,###.#######")

End Sub
```

The resulting change to the calculator is shown in Figure 3.13.

Figure 3.13.
*The calculator application
with a thousands separator in
txtResult.*

The Locked and Appearance Properties

There are two new exciting properties in Visual Basic 4. The first is found in the text box Property window. It is Locked. As the name implies, when set to True in the property's Settings box, the text box becomes locked. The cursor can be placed in the text box by the user, but the user cannot affect any changes to the text box's content. The second new property is located in the form's Properties window. It is Appearance. When the property value is set to 1-True (the default), the form automatically becomes three-dimensional, with beveled exterior edges. The window of an object such as a text box becomes cut out, surrounded by beveled edges.

Using the new properties mentioned previously, change the Locked property found in the txtResult Properties window to True. Then select the calculator form, frmCalc, and make sure that its Appearance property is set to True (also experiment with the other option, 0-Flat, to see what it looks like). Now run your calculator application. You'll be surprised at the quick results offered by these new properties.

The complete layout and code for the calculator application appears in Table 3.4 and Listing 3.1.

Table 3.4. Visual design of frmCalc in the calculator application. (Calc.vbp)

Object	Property	Setting
Form	Appearance	1-3D
	Caption	Calculator
	Name	frmCalc
Command Button	Caption	=
	Default	True
	Name	cmdEquals
Label	Caption	+
	Font	Size: 18
	Name	lblPlus

continues

Table 3.4. continued

Object	Property	Setting
Text Box	Caption	(None)
	Name	txtOperand1
	TabIndex	0
Text Box	Caption	(None)
	Name	txtOperand2
	TabIndex	1
Text Box	Caption	(None)
	Locked	True
	Name	txtResult
	TabStop	False

Listing 3.1. Code for the frmCalc form of the calculator application.

```
Option Explicit

Private Sub cmdEquals_Click()
    Dim Op1 As Single
    Dim Op2 As Single

    'Convert text in Op1 and Op2 to numbers
    Op1 = Val(txtOperand1.Text)
    Op2 = Val(txtOperand2.Text)

    'Two numbers added and reverted to text string
    txtResult.Text = Format(Op1 + Op2, "###,###,###.#######")

End Sub
```

Displaying Date and Time

Visual Basic also makes it easy to display the time and date with the Format() function. In fact, you can use the built-in Visual Basic function name Now to return the current time and date in numeric form, and use Format() to display that date and time. In this case, you can use special formatting characters: h, m, s and m, d, y. Format() is capable of producing text strings from Now in many different ways, depending on the way these characters are used and how many are used. Table 3.5 shows several examples of how the Format command can be used to format the current date and time.

Table 3.5. **Date and time formats.**

Format Syntax	Result
Format(Now, "m/d/yy")	3/20/95
Format(Now, "dddd, mmmm dd, yyyy")	Monday, March 20, 1995
Format(Now, "d-mmm")	20-Mar
Format(Now, "mmmm-yy")	March-95
Format(Now, "hh:mm AM/PM")	08:55 AM
Format(Now, "h:mm:ss a/p")	8:55:00 a
Format(Now, "d-mmmm h:mm")	20-March 8:55

As you can see, a variety of formats is available. In fact, by using the Now function with the format "ddddd ttt," t you can print the current date and time in an appropriate format for a computer in any country as set in the Regional Settings dialog box of the Windows 95 Control Panel. Some examples of how the date will be formatted with different country settings appears in Table 3.6.

Table 3.6. **International date and time formats.**

Country	Format syntax	Result
Canada (French)	Format(Now, "ddddd tttt")	95-03-20 20:55:00
Sweden	Format(Now, "ddddd tttt")	1995-03-20 20:55:00
United Kingdom	Format(Now, "ddddd tttt")	20/03/95 20:55:00
United States	Format(Now, "ddddd tttt")	03/20/95 8:55:00 PM

At this point, you have had a good introduction to the use of text boxes and command buttons with the calculator program, but now it is time to move on to a more powerful application. Your next project is to build a windowed notepad, complete with text boxes that include scrollbars.

A Notepad Application, Complete with Cut and Paste

Putting together a functioning notepad application might be easier than you think in Visual Basic. In fact, a notepad is really a multiline text box, and Visual Basic supports multiline text boxes automatically. To see how this works, start a Visual Basic project and change the Caption property of the form that appears to NOTEPAD. Then change its Name property to frmNotePad. Next, save the form and project, using the Save Project item from the File menu. Save the form as Notepad.frm and the project as Notepad.vbp.

To produce the multiline text box, simply double-click on the text box tool and stretch the resulting default-sized text box until it takes up most of the form, leaving room for a row of buttons at the bottom as in Figure 3.14.

Figure 3.14.
The notepad form being designed.

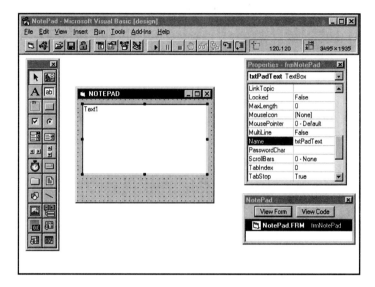

Now find the MultiLine property in the text box's Properties window. As indicated in the Settings list for that property, two settings, True and False, are allowed. The default is False, which means that text boxes can handle only a single line of text by default. Set this property to True to give your notepad multiline capability.

At this point, your pad is already functional. Just delete the default text, Text1, from the Text property using the Properties window, and change the Name property from the default, Text1, to txtPadText. Now run the program. The notepad appears, as in Figure 3.15, and you can write to it. In fact, the text box comes complete with word wrap. When you get to the end of a line, notice that the current word wraps in its entirety to the next line instead of being broken in the middle.

Figure 3.15.
The notepad at run-time with the text wrapping in the text box.

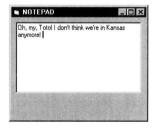

However, it is possible to do a great deal more here. For example, you can add a vertical scrollbar to the text box just by changing its `ScrollBars` property from `0-None` to `2-Vertical`. In fact, you can add horizontal scrollbars as well, but if you did so to a multiline text box, the word wrap would be automatically turned off. For that reason, you are not going to add a horizontal scrollbar. Unlike the scrollbars you will see later in this book, multiline text box scrollbars are managed entirely by Visual Basic. Adding them is easy. To add vertical scrollbars, just find the `ScrollBars` property in the Properties window. The Settings list indicates what is available: `0-None`, `1-Horizontal`, `2-Vertical`, or `3-Both`, as shown in Figure 3.16.

Figure 3.16.
The `ScrollBars` property options.

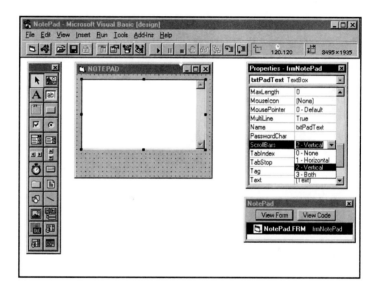

To add vertical scrollbars to the text box in your notepad, just select the Vertical option. A vertical scrollbar appears, as in Figure 3.17.

Figure 3.17.
The notepad application running, showing the vertical scrollbar in the text box.

Now you can scroll through a much larger document in your new notepad—up to 64 KB, in fact. This is the maximum string length in Visual Basic.

So far, everything you have done has been quite easy. Now it's time to press on and add more capabilities to your notepad. Specifically, you will add cut and paste so the user can select text, cut it, and paste it back in somewhere else.

Using Selected Text in Text Boxes

Normally, the user can mark or select text in a text box. For example, she can simply place the mouse cursor at some location, hold down the left button, drag the cursor to another location, and release it. In that case, the text between the two points is highlighted automatically. Windows has already given this capability to your text boxes. You already know that you can refer to the text in a text box as, for instance, `txtMyBox.Text`, where `txtMyBox` is the `Name` property you gave to the text box control and `.Text` is the text located in the `Text` property. But how can you only refer to a specific section of text?

> **Tip:** You can also select text by holding down the Shift key while using the arrow keys, Page Up, Page Down, Home, and End keys to maneuver. The text from where you started holding down the Shift key to where you end up will be selected. This works for most Windows applications as well as your text boxes.

In Visual Basic this is easy. Three properties associated with text boxes keep track of selected text: `SelStart`, `SelLength`, and `SelText`. These properties are not available at design-time and are called using code at run-time.

The first of these, `SelStart`, returns or sets the starting point of selected text and indicates the position of the insertion point if no text is selected. If `SelStart`'s index is set to `0`, the selected text starts just before the first character in the text box; if `SelStart` is equal to the length of text in the text box, it indicates a position just after the last character in the text box. Note that `SelStart` is a long integer because it has to be able to handle numbers up to 64KB. Setting `SelStart` greater than the text length sets the property to the existing text length. Changing `SelStart` changes the selection to an insertion point and sets `SelLength` to `0`.

The next property, `SelLength`, is also a long integer. It returns or sets the number of characters selected. Setting `SelLength` less than `0` causes a run-time error.

`SelText`, the final property, returns or sets the string containing the currently selected text. If no characters are selected, it consists of a zero-length string (`""`).

The proper syntax for these three properties is as follows:

```
object.SelStart [= index]
object.SelLength [= number]
object.SelText [= value]
```

If your program set these properties at run-time to SelStart = 0 : SelLength = 5, for instance, it would highlight the first five characters.

You will use these properties to add both the cut and paste features to the notepad by adding some command buttons. In particular, you will add three specific functions: Clear All—which deletes everything in the notepad's text box; Cut—which cuts the selected text; and Paste—which pastes the selected text at the insertion point.

The first button, Clear All, is easy. All you have to do is set the Text property of the text box to the empty string, "". To start, change the Name property of the notepad's text box to txtPadText in the Properties window. Now add a command button; then change its Caption property to CLEAR ALL and change its Name property to cmdClearAll. Position the button at the lower right corner of the form, as in Figure 3.18; then click on it twice to open the Code window. Your cursor is positioned within the Click event template for that button: cmdClearAll_Click(), which is exactly where you want it. Add the following code to the template, as follows:

```
Private Sub cmdClearAll_Click()
      'Clear text from txtNotePad
      txtPadText.Text = ""

End Sub
```

Figure 3.18.
The notepad with cmdClearAll positioned at the bottom of the form.

Object-Naming Conventions

When you first create an object—a form or control—Visual Basic sets its Name property to a default value. For example, all text buttons have their Name property initially set to Text*n*, where *n* is 1, 2, 3, and so on. Visual Basic names the first text box drawn on a form Text1, the second Text2, and so on. Visual Basic increments the number each time a new control is added to the form, making each name unique.

You may choose to keep the default name; however, when you have several controls of the same type, it makes sense to change their Name properties to something more descriptive. Because it may be difficult to distinguish controls and their type, especially while writing code, a naming convention can help. For example, txtMyBox is easily recognizable as a text box and cmdDoIt is readily understood to be a command button. This is especially true when an application consists of several forms and modules.

You can use a prefix to describe the class, followed by a descriptive name for the control. Using this naming convention makes the code more self-descriptive and groups similar objects alphabetically in the Code Window Object list box. Some of the conventions are listed in Table 3.7.

Table 3.7. Object-naming conventions.

Object	Prefix	Example
Command Box	cmd	cmdCancel
Form	frm	frmNew
Label	lbl	lblMessage
List Box	lst	lstEmployees
Option (Radio) Button	opt	optYes
Picture Box	pic	picBulbOn
Shape	shp	shpRectangle
Text Box	txt	txtResult
Timer	tmr	tmrAlarmClock

A complete list of the object-naming conventions is included in Appendix A, "Visual Basic Naming Requirements and Conventions."

Changing the Name of a Control at Design-Time

If you change the name of a control partway through the design process, you should know that Visual Basic *does not* go through the code and change the names of the procedures you have already written to match. That is *your* responsibility!

Now you can run your notepad application. When you do, the button becomes active and clicking on it deletes the text in txtPadText. However, after you have selected an object in Windows (by clicking on it, for example), the focus changes and the location of the insertion point is transferred to that object. This is the default action in Windows. If you click an object, that object gets the focus. In this example, the Clear All button retains the focus even after clearing the notepad. Note that it is surrounded by a thick, black border to indicate that it still has the focus. To get back to the pad, the user has to press the Tab key or click on the text window, which seems less than professional.

You can readily fix that problem, however, with the SetFocus method. Programmers familiar with object-oriented languages know that two types of programming constructions can be associated with an object: data and procedures. In Visual Basic an object's data items are referred to as *properties* and the procedures connected with it are called *methods*. You will see more about methods throughout this book. In the meantime, what concerns you here is the SetFocus method that is built into most controls. With it, you can move the focus back to the text box simply with the statement txtPadText.SetFocus.

You refer to methods the same way you refer to properties with the dot (.) operator. (Later on you will see that some methods take arguments.) When you transfer the focus back to the text box, the insertion point appears there again and starts blinking. cmdClearAll_Click() should appear as follows:

```
Private Sub cmdClearAll_Click()
      'Clear text from txtNotePad
      txtPadText.Text = ""

      'Set focus on txtPadText
      txtPadText.SetFocus
End Sub
```

That's all there is to it. Your notepad should look like the one in Figure 3.19.

Figure 3.19.
The notepad running with the Clear All button functioning.

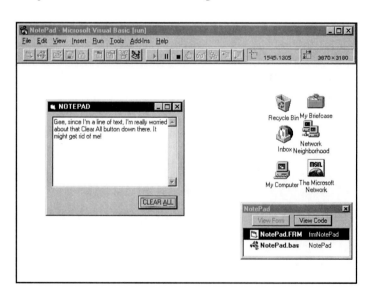

Now it is time to move on to cutting selected text in a text box.

How to Cut Selected Text

To start the process of cutting text, add another command button. Position it in the lower-left corner of the form; then change its Name property to cmdCut and change its Caption property to CUT. When the user presses this button, she wants the text selected in the text box to be cut. In reality, the program places the text in a temporary buffer so that it can be pasted later, if necessary. Begin by creating this temporary buffer. It should be a String type and should be named CutText. Because you want both the Cut and Paste procedures to have access to this buffer, CutText should be a Public variable, making it accessible from all parts of the notepad application.

Caution: In the Notepad application and the applications based on it, the Windows Clipboard has not been used to maintain simplicity. However, generally speaking, it is a bad idea to create a private clipboard that stores information. Windows users generally expect that when something is cut it will be copied to the Windows Clipboard.

To make a Public declaration, you have to open a module, which you can do by selecting the Module item from the Insert menu. A module Code window with the default name Module1 appears on your screen as in Figure 3.20.

Figure 3.20.
The CutText's Public
declaration.

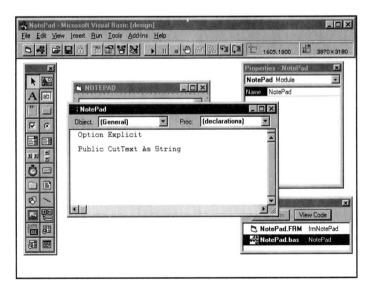

Change the module's Name property to NotePad using the Properties window. Then declare CutText as follows (and as is shown in Figure 3.21):

```
Public CutText As String
```

Now your buffer, CutText, is ready. You are prepared to cut the string itself in the notepad's text box. Before you do, however, you should save the selected text to the CutText buffer. To do that, close the NotePad module Code window and save it as Notepad.bas, using the Save Form item on the File menu. Next, using the regular Code window associated with frmNotePad, open the Click event for cmdCut, as follows:

```
Private Sub cmdCut_Click()

End Sub
```

Then save the cut text like this:

```
Private Sub cmdCut_Click()
        'Save cut text in buffer
        CutText = txtPadText.SelText


        :

End Sub
```

The next step is to cut the selected string itself. That turns out to be surprisingly easy. All you have to do is to replace txtPadText.SetText, the selected text, with an empty string, "". If no text was selected, no text is cut.

```
Private Sub cmdCut_Click()
        'Save cut text in buffer
        CutText = txtPadText.SelText
        txtPadText.SelText = ""


        :

End Sub
```

Finally, move the focus back to the text window, using the SetFocus method, as follows:

```
Private Sub cmdCut_Click()
        'Save cut text in buffer
        CutText = txtPadText.SelText
        txtPadText.SelText = ""

'Move focus to txtPadText
        txtPadText.SetFocus

End Sub
```

The Cut button is now functional. However, this is only half the story of a full notepad application. The next step is to enable the user to paste the text back into the text box.

How to Tell When an Object Has Got or Lost Focus

The `GotFocus` and `LostFocus` events occur when an object receives or loses focus. A `LostFocus` event is used mainly to verify and validate updates, or for reversing or changing conditions set up in the object's `GotFocus` procedure. An object can receive focus in three ways: selecting an object at run-time, using an access key to select a control at run-time (more about access keys later in the section "Using Access Keys"), and using the `SetFocus` method in code. You can see when some objects have the focus. For example, when a command button has the focus, it appears with a dotted, highlighted border around the caption.

Pasting text back in a text box can happen in two ways. First, the user can select some additional text in the text box, and then the program pastes over that text. Or the user might simply position the insertion point at a particular location and then the program is supposed to insert the text there. As it happens, Visual Basic takes care of these two cases almost automatically.

To get started, add another command button. Change its `Name` property to `cmdPaste` and change its `Caption` property to `PASTE`. Place this button between the other two, as in Figure 3.21, and then double-click on it to open the Code window. You can see that `cmdPaste_Click()` is already selected. All you have to do here is replace the selected text in the text window, `cmdPadText.SelText`, with `CutText`, the public string that holds the cut text. Visual Basic handles the details. If some text is selected, it is replaced with `CutText`. If no text is selected, `CutText` is added at the insertion point, exactly as it should be. The code for `cmdPaste_Click()` is as follows (note that you return the focus to the text box here, too):

```
Private Sub cmdPaste_Click()
        'Paste text back into text box
        txtPadText.SelText = CutText
        txtPadText.SetFocus
End Sub
```

You are almost done with the Paste button. The working notepad application, as it now stands, is shown in Figure 3.21.

Figure 3.21.
The notepad application running with all of the command buttons in place.

There are still a few problems, however. One occurs when the application starts. Although there is nothing to paste yet, the Paste button can still be pushed. Although it doesn't do anything, it would be better still if you could disable the button and gray the button caption when there is nothing to paste.

Don't despair! You can do this! One of the properties associated with a command button is the Enabled property. When this property is set to True, the button is enabled and can be clicked. When it is set to False, the button does not respond to the user and its caption is grayed. You can take advantage of this immediately. First, set the Enabled property of cmdPaste to False using the Properties window. You want to enable this button only when text has been placed in the CutText buffer. Because that is done only when the Cut button has been clicked, the code should be added to the Click event of cmdCut.

```
Private Sub cmdCut_Click()
        'Save cut text in buffer
        CutText = txtPadText.SelText
        txtPadText.SelText = ""

        'Enable paste button
        cmdPaste.Enabled = True

        'Move focus to txtPadText
        txtPadText.SetFocus

End Sub
```

(Remember that Visual Basic 4 handles Boolean variable types, so True and False can be used in place of -1 and 0, respectively, which would have been used in Visual Basic 3.0. The old values from previous versions of Visual Basic will be correctly translated.)

Now, when you start the application the notepad appears, as in Figure 3.22, with the Paste button grayed and disabled. As soon as you cut some text with the Cut button, the Paste button becomes active again.

Figure 3.22.
The notepad application running with the Paste button disabled.

In fact, having gone this far, you might as well enable the Cut and Clear All buttons only when it makes sense. In particular, you can enable these buttons after the user has started typing something into the notepad (that is, at the time there is text available to cut or clear). In this case, you can work with the text box's Change event. As you saw in the last chapter, this is one of the primary text box programming events. Whenever the contents of a text box change—for instance, when characters are typed in or if the program affects the text box's `Text` property—a corresponding `Change` event is generated. You can take advantage of that here to enable the Cut and Clear All buttons in your notepad after text has been typed for the first time.

To begin, set the `Enabled` property for both `cmdCut` and `cmdClearAll` to `False` at design-time using the Properties window. Now, when the notepad first appears at run-time, all three buttons—Cut, Paste, and Clear All—will be grayed. Next, click `txtPadText` twice to open the Code window. The following `Sub` procedure appears:

```
Private Sub txtPadText_Change()

End Sub
```

Just put the following code in as follows:

```
Private Sub txtPadText_Change()
        'Enable Cut and Clear All buttons
        cmdCut.Enabled = True
        cmdClearAll.Enabled = True
End Sub
```

That's it! The first time the user types in the text box, the two buttons, Cut and Clear All, will be enabled. Your notepad is becoming quite polished. Lock the controls on the form by selecting the form and then pressing the Lock Controls button on the toolbar.

While we're on the topic of command buttons, you should assign your buttons access keys.

Using Access Keys

An *access key* is used in a menu or command button to select an option with a single keystroke. By pressing the Alt key and a particular character, the user can quickly select an item without moving her hands from the keyboard. For example, if you made C the access key for your Cut button, the user could press Alt+C to select the button. Each access key should be unique among the currently available buttons or menu items.

Adding access keys is very simple. All you have to do is place an ampersand (`&`) in front of the character you want to use in the control's `Caption` property. For example, to make C the access key for the Cut button, change the button's `Caption` property to `&Cut`. To make P the access key for the Paste button, change that button's `Caption` property to `&Paste`. Finally, to change the Clear All button's access key to A (because you have already used C for the Cut button), change its `Caption` property to `Clear &All`. Visual Basic automatically changes the caption of each button, underlining the access key, as in Figure 3.23. It is that easy to set up access keys in Visual Basic.

Figure 3.23.
The notepad application running, showing access keys.

And that's it for the notepad for now. You will come back to it later in the book as part of a larger application. The code for the events appears in Table 3.8, Listing 3.2, and Listing 3.3.

Table 3.8. The event code for the notepad application. (Notepad.vbp)

Object	Property	Setting
Form	Appearance	1-3D
	Caption	Notepad
	Name	frmNotePad
Text Box	MultiLine	True
	Name	txtPadText
	ScrollBars	2 - Vertical
	Text	(None)
Command Button	Caption	CLEAR &ALL
	Enabled	False
	Name	cmdClearAll
Command Button	Caption	&CUT
	Enabled	False
	Name	cmdCut
Command Button	Caption	&PASTE
	Enabled	False
	Name	cmdPaste

Listing 3.2. Source code for Notepad.bas.

```
Public CutText As String
```

Listing 3.3. The complete code for Notepad.frm.

```
Option Explicit

Private Sub cmdClearAll_Click()
        'Clear text from txtNotePad
        txtPadText.Text = ""

        'Set focus on txtPadText
        txtPadText.SetFocus
End Sub

Private Sub cmdCut_Click()
        'Save cut text in buffer
        CutText = txtPadText.SelText
        txtPadText.SelText = ""

        'Enable paste button
        cmdPaste.Enabled = True

        'Move focus to txtPadText
        txtPadText.SetFocus

End Sub

Private Sub cmdPaste_Click()
        'Paste text back into text box
        txtPadText.SelText = CutText
        txtPadText.SetFocus
End Sub

Private Sub txtPadText_Change()
        'Enable Cut and Clear All buttons
        cmdCut.Enabled = True
        cmdClearAll.Enabled = True
End Sub
```

Now it is time to turn to another application: a windowed alarm clock.

An Alarm Clock Example

You still have a good deal to learn about text boxes and buttons. For instance, keystrokes can be read as they are typed in a text box, or display fonts can be changed. For that matter, an entirely different kind of button can be used: *option buttons*—the small, round buttons that are also referred to as *radio buttons*. You will take advantage of some of these capabilities with a new application: a digital alarm clock that lets you display the time and will notify you when a certain amount of time has passed. The application you are aiming for appears in Figure 3.24.

Figure 3.24.
The alarm clock application running.

To get going on this program, start a new Visual Basic project. A new form appears on the design desktop. Change the form's Caption property to ALARM CLOCK, and change its Name property to frmAlarmClock. Create a module by selecting the Module item from the Insert menu; then change its Name property to Alarm. Next, save the entire project by selecting Save Project from the File menu and save the form, module, and project as Alarm.frm, Alarm.bas, and Alarm.vbp, respectively.

Now you are ready to start. The first thing you can do is set up the text box that will accept the alarm setting. For example, the alarm setting in Figure 3.24 is 12:00:00. Draw a text box on the form, positioning it to correspond roughly to the one in Figure 3.24.

Change this text box's Name property to txtAlarmSetting and remove the default text, Text1, from the Text property so the text box is empty when the application starts. To keep this example relatively simple, you are only going to accept time in a restricted format: hh:mm:ss. Of course, in a professional application the time format would have to be more flexible. You have not restricted user input before, but Visual Basic enables you to do so by reading each keystroke as it is typed.

Interpreting Individual Keystrokes

Three events occur each time the user types a key in a control that has the focus: KeyDown, KeyUp, and KeyPress. The KeyPress event returns the standard type of character values you are used to dealing with in Visual Basic. The KeyDown and KeyUp events are generated when the user presses and releases a key, and each of these two event procedures receives two arguments: KeyCode and Shift. The KeyCode argument here is the *ANSI* code (not ASCII) for the key that was pressed or released. The Shift argument holds the state of the Shift, Alt, and Ctrl keys. It turns out that ANSI, not ASCII, is the standard Windows character set. Although the two character sets overlap considerably, they are not exactly the same.

KeyPress interprets the uppercase and lowercase of each character as separate key codes and, therefore, as two distinct characters. KeyDown and KeyUp interpret the uppercase and lowercase of each character using two arguments: KeyCode—which indicates the physical key, thus returning F and f as the same key; and Shift—which indicates the state of Shift + key and therefore returns either F or f. The Shift argument is a bit field with values that correspond to the bits, 1 for the Shift key, 2 for the Ctrl key, and 4 for the Alt key. Some, all, or none of these bits can be set, indicating that some, all, or none of the keys are pressed. For example, if both Ctrl and Alt are pressed, the Shift argument value is 6.

The reason KeyDown and KeyUp are useful is that they can read keys that have no standard ASCII value, such as the Delete key, arrow keys, or function keys. For instance, when the user presses the Delete key, KeyCode is equal to the constant vbKeyDelete. If the user presses the Insert key, KeyCode equals the constant vbKeyInsert. If you ever need to specify key codes, you should use the constants in the Visual Basic Object Library located in the Object Browser. This will be discussed in more detail in Chapter 11, "Advanced Data-Handling, Sorting, and Storing a Spreadsheet Program." For now, you will stick with the KeyPress event.

Your intention is to restrict the user's keystrokes to those allowed in txtAlarmSetting. Those characters are 0 through 9 and a colon (:). Your program will check to make sure that the typed key is in that range. To set up your procedure, double-click on the text box to open the Code window (if it is not already open); then select the KeyPress event from the Procedure list box. The following procedure template appears:

```
Private Sub txtAlarmSetting_KeyPress(KeyAscii As Integer)

End Sub
```

As you can see, Visual Basic passes one argument to a KeyPress event, KeyAscii, the typed key's ASCII value. Although KeyDown and KeyUp use ANSI key codes, KeyPress uses the ASCII set most programmers normally employ. In other words, this is just like a normal Sub procedure with one argument passed to it. You can make use of this immediately by checking the value of the key that was just typed, as follows:

```
Private Sub txtAlarmSetting_KeyPress(KeyAscii As Integer)
    Dim Key As String

    'Procedure checks for characters other than
    '0 through 9 and :
    Key = Chr(KeyAscii)
    If (Key < "0" Or Key > "9") Then
        If Key <> ":" Then

            :

        End If
    End If
End Sub
```

The code above first converts the ASCII code in KeyAscii to a character, for example, a string of length one, using the Visual Basic Chr() function like this: Key = Chr(KeyAscii). Then the program checks the value of that character against the allowed range. The < and > operators work for string comparisons as well as numeric comparisons in Visual Basic. They do this by comparing strings in alphabetical order, so 0 is less than 1 and c is greater than b.

Although you are restricting the user to the characters 0 through 9 and :, it would be good programming practice to permit text-editing characters such as the backspace and Delete keys. To keep things simple, though, you will not use text-editing characters in this application.

If the key that was typed is not within the allowed range, the program should delete it and beep to indicate an error. Deleting the key is easy, and `Beep` is a regular Visual Basic statement. You just have to set `KeyAscii` back to `0`, as follows:

```
Private Sub txtAlarmSetting_KeyPress(KeyAscii As Integer)
     Dim Key As String

     'Procedure checks for characters other than
     '0 through 9 and :
     Key = Chr(KeyAscii)
     If (Key < "0" Or Key > "9") Then
             If Key <> ":" Then
                     Beep
                     KeyAscii = 0
             End If
     End If
End Sub
```

That's it for checking the typed keys and for `txtAlarmSetting_KeyPress()`. Now you should add a label to the form. Double-click on the Label button in the toolbox. A default-sized label appears in the center of the form. Move it above txtAlarmSetting and stretch its width to match the text box as in Figure 3.24. Change the label's `Name` property to `lblAlarm` and change the `Caption` property to `Alarm Setting:`; then scroll up to the `Alignment` property and change it to `2-Center`. Now you are set as far as recording and storing the alarm setting goes. Your program will be able to read the alarm setting directly from the text box's `Text` property.

Easy Input Filtering

Visual Basic 4 includes a Masked Edit control that provides restricted data input as well as formatted data output. This control supplies visual cues about the type of data being entered or displayed. This will be discussed in depth in Chapter 15, "Advanced Control and Form Handling."

Displaying the Time

The next step in assembling the alarm clock is to set up the clock's display. Because you do not want the clock display to be edited from the keyboard (it will use system time), you can use a label here instead of a text box. Click on the label tool again and draw the label on the form, placing it near the top, and resize it until it looks roughly like the one in Figure 3.25. Delete the characters in the Settings box of the `Caption` property and change the `Name` property to `lblDisplay`. To display the time, the program will use the Visual Basic function `Time` like this: `lblDisplay.Caption = Time`.

Next, take a look at the label's `BorderStyle` property in the Properties window. Normally, labels do not have a border, but they can have the same type of border as a text box. If you click on the arrow to the right of the Settings box, you will see that the two options for `BorderStyle` are `0-None` and `1-Fixed Single`. Select `1-Fixed Single` to give the clock's display a border.

Figure 3.25.
The alarm clock form.

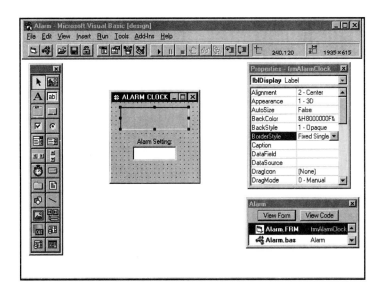

Two New Border Styles

Previous versions of Visual Basic included four settings for the BorderStyle property. These settings are still available with Visual Basic 4:

- 0-None. No borders or border-related elements are added to the form.

- 1-Fixed Single. This setting can include a control box, Close button, title bar, Maximize button, and Minimize button.

- 2-Sizable (default). This border makes a window resizable using any of the optional border elements: control box, title bar, Maximize button, and Minimize button.

- 3-Fixed Dialog. This setting can include a control box, Close button, and title bar. It does not include a Minimize or Maximize button and is not resizable.

There are two new settings for the BorderStyle property that apply only to a new Windows 95 window style, ToolWindow. A ToolWindow has a smaller title bar with no icon, no Maximize or Minimize buttons, and no entry on the Windows 95 taskbar. The new settings are as follows:

- 4-Fixed ToolWindow. This setting behaves like Fixed Double. It is not resizable and displays a Close button and title bar text in a reduced font size.

- 5-Sizable ToolWindow. This setting behaves like Sizable. It is resizable and displays a Close button and title bar text in a reduced font size.

So, the program now boils down to the following questions: How does the program keep the time updated, and what kind of event occurs often enough and regularly enough to make sure that the time in Display.Caption is current? Visual Basic has another type of control for exactly this kind of use: timers.

Visual Basic Timers

A *timer* is just that: it can produce a specific event, called a Timer event, at a predetermined interval. Its control symbol is a small clock, both in the toolbox and on the form. The control is visible at run-time, but not at design-time. Double-click on the Timer tool. A Timer object appears in the center of the form. Move it to an unobtrusive place, where it will not get in the way of the other objects, as in Figure 3.26. Change the default Name property from Timer1 to tmrAlarmClock.

Figure 3.26.
The alarm clock form with a timer placed to the right.

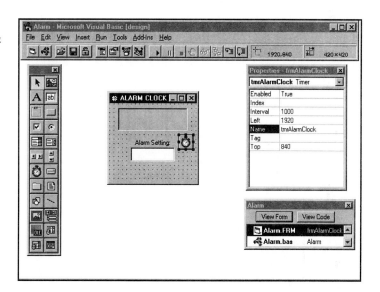

The next step is to set the timer's Interval property. This property tells how often the Timer event occurs. Make sure that the timer is selected; then highlight the Interval property in the Properties window. The Interval property is measured in milliseconds—that is, in thousandths of a second. Because you do not want to put a significant burden on the rest of the system while the application is running, you will update the clock only once a second. For that reason, enter 1000 in the Interval property's Settings box for this timer.

Now you are ready to write the actual procedure that will be run every time the timer ticks. Because you set it to 1000, this will be every second. Double-click on the timer to open the Code window. The procedure where your cursor is positioned is the one you want.

```
Private Sub tmrAlarmClock_Timer()

End Sub
```

You can start by checking whether the time is up—that is, whether the string returned by the Visual Basic function `Time` is the same as the time for which the alarm is set. This amounts to the function `Time` equaling `txtAlarmSetting.Text`. If the time is up, an alarm will sound. Even though this train of thought is entirely logical, it might not work. If Windows is performing some action, or if the clock's window is being moved, the timer might not be called for a while. For that reason, the program should actually check whether `Time` is greater than or equal to `txtAlarmSetting.Text`, as follows:

```
Private Sub tmrAlarmClock_Timer()
      'Timer checking whether >= txtAlarmSetting.Text
      If (Time >= txtAlarmSetting.Text) Then
            :
      End If

      :
End Sub
```

If the condition is `True`, the `Beep` statement can be used like this:

```
Private Sub tmrAlarmClock_Timer()
      'Timer checking whether >= txtAlarmSetting.Text
      If (Time >= txtAlarmSetting.Text) Then
            Beep
      End If

      :
End Sub
```

Well, that's it! When the time has elapsed, this procedure will make the clock beep; and because it is called once a second, the alarm clock will keep beeping when it has finished, once a second. (How's that for annoying?) However, this is incomplete as it stands. Alarm clocks usually have two settings: Alarm On and Alarm Off. For instance, now that your alarm is on, you need to shut it off.

> **Note:** You might notice that there is no way to set the alarm for a time earlier than the current time. This would prevent you from using this alarm clock to wake you up in the morning. If you wanted to add this feature, you would need to add code to determine whether or not the alarm has been silenced, in addition to the code that turns it on and off.

For that reason, you need to add two option (radio) buttons to your form. Double-click on the Option Button tool in the toolbox. A default-sized option button appears in the center of the form. Move it down below txtAlarmSetting and to the left. Change its `Name` property to `optAlarmOn`, then change its `Caption` property to `Alarm On`. Make a second option button and place it to the right of the first one. Change its `Name` property to `optAlarmOff` and change its `Caption` property to `Alarm Off`. Look at Figure 3.24 for the placement of these option buttons. Make sure that the `Value` property of `AlarmOn`—the Alarm Off button—is set to `True`.

The procedure connected with the two option buttons can communicate with the current procedure, tmrAlarmClock_Timer(), through a Public variable that will be called AlarmOn. Thus, if AlarmOn is True *and* the function Time >= txtAlarmSetting.Text, the program should beep. This can be added in the following way:

```
Private Sub tmrAlarmClock_Timer()
      'Timer checking whether >= txtAlarmSetting.Text
      If (Time >= txtAlarmSetting.Text And AlarmOn) Then
            Beep
      End If

        :
End Sub
```

The last thing to do here is to update the display, because this procedure is called when the time changes. You can do that as follows:

```
Private Sub tmrAlarmClock_Timer()
      'Timer checking whether >= txtAlarmSetting.Text
      If (Time >= txtAlarmSetting.Text And AlarmOn) Then
            Beep
      End If

      lblDisplay.Caption = Time
End Sub
```

As mentioned, because this procedure is called once a second the beeping will continue until the Alarm Off radio button is clicked, which will make the Public variable AlarmOn False. Now it's time to set up AlarmOn itself. You can make it Public by double-clicking on the AlarmOn.bas module in the Project window. The (General) section of the Alarm.bas declarations procedure opens. Declare AlarmOn as follows:

```
Public AlarmOn As Boolean
```

At this point, the timer and clock are ready to function, although the clock display will appear in a smaller font than the one in Figure 3.24. Changing the font size comes later. For now, compare the alarm setting to the current time and update the display on the screen. Make sure that the controls are locked on the form.

Everything is ready except the AlarmOn variable and the rest of the code behind the option buttons that make AlarmOn active. Without them, the alarm part of the clock cannot work.

Using Option (Radio) Buttons

Option buttons—often called radio buttons—work in a group. Only one of the option buttons that appear on a form can be selected at a time. You use option buttons to select one option from among several mutually exclusive choices—for example, choices when it is either one or the other, such as yes or no, male or female, and on or off.

More on Grouping Option Buttons Together

Another way to make option buttons work as a group is to enclose them in a *frame* by using the frame tool in the Visual Basic toolbox. Note that you must draw the frame on the form and then draw the option buttons onto the frame. Otherwise, the option buttons will not be grouped within the frame. (This also means that you cannot use the double-click method to add option buttons to a frame.) The option buttons in such a frame are separate from the rest of the option buttons on the form.

Visual Basic takes care of the details of turning option buttons on and off; if one of a group of option buttons is clicked, the one that was "on," with the dot in the center, is automatically turned "off." So far, your alarm clock form should appear as the form in Figure 3.27.

Figure 3.27.
The alarm clock form at design-time with the option buttons placed toward the bottom.

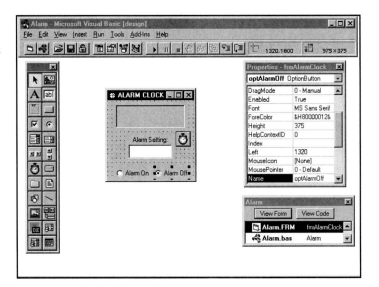

Together, the two option buttons on your form make up an *option button group*. Because they are part of the same form (and not enclosed by separate frames), Visual Basic will turn them on and off so that only one is selected at a time. When the clock starts, the AlarmOff option button should be selected. A Value property is associated with each option button, indicating whether the button is selected. If True, the button is selected with the black dot showing in the center of the button. If the Value property is False, the opposite is, of course, true. You can set the Value property at both de-sign-time and run-time. So, right now, set the Value property for optAlarmOff to True. Notice that if the optAlarmOn Value property was set to True when you changed the Value property for optAlarmOff to True, the Value property for optAlarmOn automatically changed to False.

Earlier in this chapter, you named the option buttons `optAlarmOff` and `optAlarmOn`. The variable `optAlarmOn` could be set to `True` or `False` by using the values of `optAlarmOn.Value` or `optAlarmOff.Value`. However, groups of buttons—in fact, groups of controls—like this are usually handled in a different way in Visual Basic. Normally, the group of buttons is made into a *control array*.

Control Arrays

Control arrays are the preferred way to handle groups of controls in Visual Basic. For example, imagine that you have a number of buttons as in Figure 3.28.

Figure 3.28.
A pictorial representation of a group of buttons.

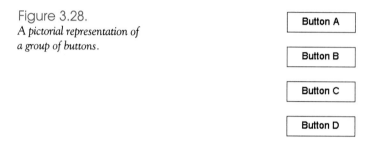

In this case, you would have to write a separate event handler for each button. For instance, if you were interested in the `Click` event, you would have `ButtonA_Click()`, `ButtonB_Click()`, `ButtonC_Click()`, and `ButtonD_Click()`. This could be awkward (and tedious for the programmer) if the buttons performed essentially the same action with a few variations, just as a group of controls usually does. The easier way to handle such button groups is to give them all the same name. If you do so, Visual Basic automatically gives them separate *index numbers* (you might have noticed the `Index` property associated with most controls in the Properties window). Thus, if you changed the button names in Figure 3.28 to MyButton, Visual Basic would give the first one an index of 0, the next an index of 1, and so on. (See Figure 3.29.)

Figure 3.29.
A pictorial representation of a control array.

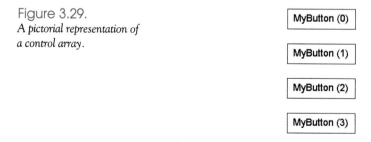

Consequently, instead of four separate event procedures such as `ButtonA_Click()` to `ButtonD_Click()`, there would be only one procedure for each event instead of four, and Visual Basic would automatically pass the index number corresponding to the button that was clicked. Therefore, the `Click` event would consist of the following:

```
Private Sub MyButton_Click(Index As Integer).
```

To see this in action, change the `Name` property of the right option button on your Alarm Clock form from `optAlarmOff` to `optAlarmOnOff`. Next, do the same for the option button on the left: Change its `Name` property from `AlarmOn` to `AlarmOnOff`. When you change the second `Name` property, a question box appears on the screen, as shown in Figure 3.30, with the message: Do you want to create a control array? Click Yes. Visual Basic automatically adds the correct index value for that option button.

Figure 3.30.
The control array question box.

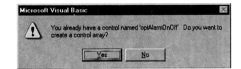

Another Way to Create a Control Array

After placing one control of a proposed control group on a form, select the control and then copy it, using Ctrl+C on the keyboard, or the Copy item from the Edit menu, or by clicking the right mouse button to open the pop-up menu for that object. Next, paste the copied control onto the form, using either Ctrl+V or the Paste item from the Edit menu, or the pop-up menu. When you do, the Visual Basic question box pictured in Figure 3.30 will appear. Click Yes and a new control will appear on the form, named appropriately as part of a control array. You can continue to paste in as many copies of the same control as you want.

Now, double-click on either option button to open the Code window. Your cursor will be positioned within the following procedure template:

```
Private Sub optAlarmOnOff_Click(Index As Integer)

End Sub
```

Notice the first line. Because you have set up `optAlarmOnOff` as a control array, Visual Basic automatically passes the index of the button pushed. When you check the value of `index`, it is easy to determine which button was pushed. Thus, you can write one procedure for both buttons. This is exactly the idea behind creating groups of controls. It makes for less work for the programmer (and is less confusing because it is more organized!) So, all the alarm clock application has to do in the current procedure is to determine which button has been clicked by checking the `index` parameter. In this case, 0 indicates the Alarm Off button and 1 indicates the Alarm On button. Then, using the index value from `optAlarmOnOff`, the program correctly sets the public variable `AlarmOn`. That is the ultimate job of these option buttons: to set the public variable `AlarmOn`. Do that as follows:

```
Private Sub optAlarmOnOff_Click(Index As Integer)
        'Checking radio button Index value and
        'setting AlarmOn
        If (Index = 1) Then
                AlarmOn = True
        Else
                AlarmOn = False
        End If
End Sub
```

That's all there is to it. The alarm clock is almost finished. The last change to make will be to the clock display itself. As it stands, the time is displayed in standard system-font characters, but you can improve that significantly.

There is one more point worth mentioning here—if you had designed the alarm clock in a slightly different order than you have by putting the alarm setting text box on the form after the option buttons, it would cause a small problem. The option button, rather than the alarm Settings box, would have the focus first when the application started running. To give the alarm Settings box the default focus, set it first in the tab order. TabIndex is a control property that sets that order. The control with a TabIndex value of 0 gets the default focus; then you can tab around the form to the other controls at will. (The other controls have tab indices of 1, 2, 3, and so on.) In fact, by using TabIndex you can rearrange the way the user tabs from control to control on the form.

Selecting Fonts

Some of the properties associated with labels and text boxes have to do with fonts. If you click on Font in the Properties window and then select the Properties button that appears to the right of the Settings box, a Font dialog box appears, as in Figure 3.31.

Figure 3.31.
The Visual Basic Font dialog box.

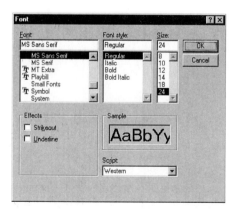

As you can see in Figure 3.31, there are several different items associated with this property. Font refers, of course, to the font selected. Font Style refers to the font's appearance: Regular, Italic, Bold, and Bold-Italic. The next item to the left is Size, referring to the font size in points. There are 72 points to the inch. Visual Basic permits selections from between 8 and 30 points. Effects also refers to a font's appearance. There are two possibilities: Strikeout and Underline. Finally, there is a large window to the bottom right that shows a sample of the font—and other options—you have selected.

You can select the type of font used in the alarm clock by using the Font property at design-time. For this example, you will just use the standard font, MS Sans Serif, and expand it from 8 to 24 points. To do that, select lblDisplay and using the Properties window, select the Font property. Press the Properties button that appears and then scroll down the Size list box until you reach 24. Select it; then press OK. And that's it! The running application appears in Figure 3.24, shown earlier in the chapter, and the code, event by event, appears in Table 3.9, Listing 3.4, and Listing 3.5.

Table 3.9. The frmAlarm for the alarm clock application. (Alarm.vbp)

Object	Property	Setting
Form	Appearance	1-3D
	Caption	Alarm Clock
	Name	frmAlarmClock
Label	Alignment	2 - Center
	Caption	Alarm Setting:
	Name	lblAlarm
Label	Caption	(None)
	Font	Size: 24
	Name	lblDisplay
Option (Radio) Button	Caption	Alarm Off
	Index	0
	Name	optAlarmOnOff(0)
Option (Radio) Button	Caption	Alarm On
	Index	1
	Name	optAlarmOnOff(1)
Timer	Name	tmrAlarmClock

Listing 3.4. Code for Alarm.bas.

```
Public AlarmOn As Boolean
```

Listing 3.5. Code for alarm.frm.

```
Option Explicit

Private Sub optAlarmOnOff_Click(Index As Integer)
        'Checking radio button Index value and
        'setting AlarmOn
        If (Index = 1) Then
                AlarmOn = True
        Else
                AlarmOn = False
        End If
End Sub

Private Sub tmrAlarmClock_Timer()
        'Timer checking whether >= txtAlarmSetting.Text
        If (Time >= txtAlarmSetting.Text And AlarmOn) Then
                Beep
        End If

        lblDisplay.Caption = Time
End Sub

Private Sub txtAlarmSetting_KeyPress(KeyAscii As Integer)
        Dim Key As String

        'Procedure checks for characters other than
        '0 through 9 and :
        Key = Chr(KeyAscii)
        If (Key < "0" Or Key > "9") Then
                If Key <> ":" Then
                        Beep
                        KeyAscii = 0
                End If
        End If
End Sub
```

You will now continue to explore the user interface, using Microsoft's Common Control OLE Custom Control Module to enhance the look and feel of your applications. Then you will design a rather handy mini-application titled "Easy ASCII."

Third-Party Custom Controls

Third-party custom controls are easy to add to any project. These controls extend the available tools of Visual Basic in useful, creative ways. Many custom controls are included with Visual Basic 4 and can be added to the Visual Basic toolbar at any time.

Third-party controls are installed on your system like any other program, by selecting Run from the Start menu and typing `a:\setup`. In the case of those controls included with Visual Basic 4, no installation is required because the controls were installed along with Visual Basic.

Controls can be added to a project using the Custom Controls… item on the Tools menu (or you can press Ctrl+T). Just select the control that you would like to add to the toolbar by checking the box next to that control as in Figure 3.32 and then clicking OK. Visual Basic will add the new control to the toolbar.

Figure 3.32.
Adding a new control to a project.

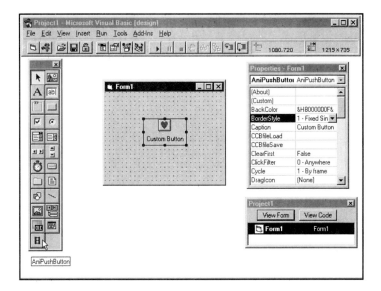

Open the Custom Controls dialog box and have a look around. On the right is a list of available controls and insertable objects. Below that list is a frame that shows the name of the selected control and its path.

To the right of the Available Control list is a set of three check boxes: Insertable Objects, Controls, and Selected Items Only. When the Insertable Objects box is checked (an *insertable object* is an object of an application that is a type of custom control), the Available Control list will show insertable objects, such as a Microsoft Excel chart. If the Controls box is checked, controls with .ocx and .vbx filename extensions will be shown. If the Selected Items Only box is checked, the Available Controls list will show only those items that you have selected to include in that particular project.

The Evolution of Controls: VBX to OCX

When Visual Basic first came out it was apparent that there would need to be a way to extend Visual Basic's capabilities. For this reason Microsoft came out with the VBX architecture, which enabled programmers to extend the capabilities of Visual Basic.

Since that time, Microsoft has developed OLE technology and has decided to start moving Visual Basic to the new OLE standard. As a result, a new format was developed for add-in controls. This is the OCX format. Hence, controls are now called OLE controls, or OLE custom controls.

OCXs have several advantages over their VBX predecessors, not the least of which is speed. Because OCXs can be written for the 32-bit architecture of Windows 95 and Windows NT, they will run faster than the old 16-bit VBX controls.

There is a Browse button that will display a Browse dialog box. Using this dialog box, you can add an .ocx or .vbx to the Available Controls list. You should note that a control or insertable object that is used in a project cannot be removed from that project.

Microsoft's Common Control OLE Custom Control Module

One of the control sets available with Visual Basic 4 is a Microsoft module, listed in the Available Controls list as Comctl OLE Custom Control Module (comctl32.ocx). If you add this .ocx to your project, eight custom controls are added to the Visual Basic toolbox:

- TabStrip control
- Toolbar control
- ImageList control
- StatusBar control
- Progress Indicator control
- TreeView control
- ListView control
- Slider control

The new Windows 95 interface incorporates each of these controls. Therefore, using these tools it is easy for you to design a form that looks and functions exactly like one available from Microsoft.

The controls in this section are all 32-bit controls and will only run on 32-bit operating systems, such as Windows 95 or Windows NT 3.51 or higher.

The TabStrip Control

The TabStrip control is a device that enables the user to navigate among logical *sheets* of information—you can think of them as dividers in a notebook. This control is meant to suggest an equal standing among the different sheets. By using a Tab control, you can include a large amount of related information and possible user choices on one form.

The control contains one or more Tab objects grouped in a Tabs collection. Table 3.10 contains brief descriptions of how various properties affect the tabstrip's appearance and performance:

Table 3.10. TabStrip properties.

Property	Description
MultiRow	Sets whether the control can have more than one row of tabs.
Style	This property has two settings: `0-Tabs` or `1-Buttons`. If set to Buttons, the TabStrip looks like push buttons; if set to Tabs, it appears, of course, as tabs.
TabFixedHeight	This property is only activated when the `TabWidthStyle` property is set to `2-Fixed`. `TabFixedHeight` sets the height of the tabs in a TabStrip control.
TabFixedWidth	Just like the `TabFixedHeight` property, this property is only activated when the `TabWidthStyle` property is set to `2-Fixed`. `TabFixedWidth` sets the width of the tabs in a TabStrip control.
TabWidthStyle	This property's settings are as follows: `0-Justified`. This setting only works if the `MultiRow` property is set to `True`. If this is the case, then each tab is wide enough to accommodate its caption and each tab spreads to span the width of the control. `1-Non-Justified`. This setting makes each tab wide enough to accommodate its caption, but it does not spread each tab to the width of the control, making for jagged rows. `2-Fixed`. Fixed sets all tabs to the width set in the `TabFixedWidth` property.

For more information on this new control, check with Visual Basic's on-line help under "TabStrip Control." An example of a TabStrip control on a form is shown in Figure 3.33.

Figure 3.33.
The TabStrip control added to a form.

The Toolbar and ImageList Controls

These two controls are companion controls that work together. The *toolbar* is a popular device that was originally created for Windows 3.1 applications. With Windows 95, the toolbar has been graphically redesigned, although its functionality remains the same. The Toolbar control enables you to add, delete, move, raise, and lower buttons within a toolbar. It also supports a customization feature, enabling the user to add her favorite buttons to the toolbar.

The ImageList control defines the button images and captions that appear on the toolbar. But this control is not only a warehouse for pictures; it can perform some nifty graphics—for instance, using the Overlay method, you can create a composite image from two different (yet same-sized) images.

ImageList controls are designed to be used in conjunction with other controls such as ListView, TabStrip, and TreeView. ImageList can give these controls the images they need for their lists, tabs, or trees.

The ImageList's custom properties box appears in Figure 3.34. Figure 3.35 shows a toolbar's custom Properties box, and Figure 3.36 shows a sample program that uses both a toolbar and an ImageList control. For more information about these two controls, see Visual Basic's on-line help under "ImageList Control" and "Toolbar Control."

Figure 3.34.
The ImageList Control Properties dialog box.

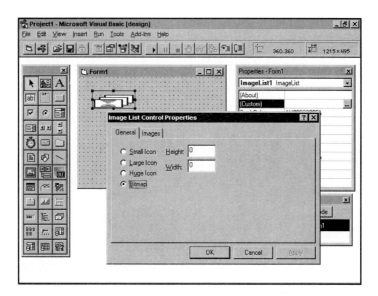

Figure 3.35.
The Toolbar control linked
to the ImageList control.

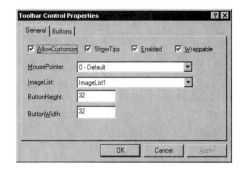

Figure 3.36.
A sample program running,
showing an active Toolbar
control.

StatusBar Control

The status bar was incorporated into early versions of Microsoft Word for Windows. It became a popular feature and has appeared increasingly in other applications. It has been completely incorporated into the Windows 95 interface—one very visible instance of it is its presence on the Windows 95 desktop. Usually a status bar appears at the bottom of a window, although the control allows for placement also at the top, right, or left. A status bar can consist of one window, displaying a single line of text, or it can be divided into multiple windows, with a text or information display in each pane.

A StatusBar control is made up of *panel objects*—objects that can contain text and/or a bitmap. Several properties control the appearance of the individual panels, including `Alignment`, `Bevel`, and `Width`.

In the Visual Basic design desktop, you can use the StatusBar's `Custom` property to easily design a status bar.

You can see an example of how the StatusBar control appears in Figure 3.37. To learn more about this control, check out "StatusBar Control" in Visual Basic's on-line help.

Figure 3.37.
A StatusBar control
positioned at the bottom of a
form, showing a message, the
time, and date.

ProgressBar Control

Also called a *Progress Indicator Control*, the ProgressBar control gives an indication of how far a lengthy process is from completion. A progress bar works much like a gauge but without the same accuracy; a gauge measures values continuously, whereas a progress bar uses chunky rectangles that approximate an operation's relative progress. You can set the range of the control—minimum and maximum values—and how quickly the control advances from the minimum value to the maximum value.

Figure 3.38 shows an example of how the ProgressBar control looks. Look at the "ProgressBar Control" topic in Visual Basic's on-line help for more information.

Figure 3.38.
A running program, showing a ProgressBar control being used.

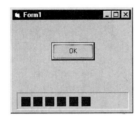

The TreeView and ListView Controls

These controls provide the capability to display a collection of items to the user. The Windows 95 interface uses these controls when it displays folders. The TreeView control provides hierarchical information about items and enables the expansion or collapse of parts of the tree. An example of this can be found in the left pane of the Windows 95 Explorer. The ListView control supports a single-level list that can be displayed as large and small icons or a details view. This is the view that you see when you open a directory.

As stated earlier, the TreeView control works with the ImageList control. To connect an ImageList to a TreeView control set the TreeView's `ImageList` property to the name of that ImageList. An example of a TreeView control is shown in Figure 3.39 and an example of a ListView control is shown in Figure 3.40.

Figure 3.39.
*The TreeView control in
action.*

Figure 3.40.
*The ListView control in
action.*

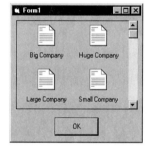

Slider Control

The Slider control is used for setting values within a continuous range as opposed to a series of discrete values. Many applications used scrollbars in the past for this purpose, but it was difficult to make accurate settings because there was no information through which to scroll. You can set the minimum and maximum positions, tick marks, the position of the slider, and the selection range. An example of a slider control is shown in Figure 3.41. For more information on this control, check out Visual Basic's on-line help.

Figure 3.41.
*A Slider control in use on a
form.*

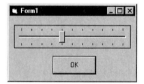

Now it is time to move on to the last application in this chapter. It includes skills that you have already learned and a few new programming techniques that will come in handy in the future.

An ASCII Application

Easy ASCII. A mini-application that helps find ASCII key value equivalents.

Because you have already completed several applications and are becoming familiar with the Visual Basic programming environment, this project will start out a touch differently. The many skills you have learned and demonstrated by completing your own applications will be put to use here without too much in the way of step-by-step instructions. You know how to draw controls onto a form and then change their properties. You know how to change from one object and procedure to another in the Code window. You've come quite far in only a few chapters; you should be proud of yourself! By this time, you can do a great deal by yourself.

First, you will read a brief description of the events behind the project and what controls you will need to use. A picture of the finished form will give you an idea of where to place these controls and a table of their property settings will help you prepare them. Finally, you will read a description of the various parts of the application, covering programming concepts and structures that will help fill in the rest.

Easy ASCII is an application that will display the ASCII equivalent of a pressed key. The questions to ask are: What should the user interface look like and what events are activated by the controls on that user interface?

To answer the first question, the user will need some object that shows her keyboard entry when she presses a key. As you have discovered in this chapter, a text box is perfect for that job. Also, there needs to be some kind of object that will display the ASCII value of the key pressed. You don't want the user to be able to manipulate the contents of this object, so a label would be a good choice. So far, you will need one text box and one label for the application. The only other considerations are practical ones. The user should be able to clear the text box and label of their contents. A command button with the caption Clear All—like the one in the notepad application—would be ideal. And finally, the text box that shows the user's input and the label that shows the equivalent ASCII value should be labeled so the user knows what she is seeing. As you have discovered, two labels would work well for that purpose. When counting the controls necessary for the project, the total comes to one text box, one command button, and three labels.

Now for the second question: What events are activated by the controls on that user interface? When the user presses a key, that key character shows up in the text box. Thus, the text box's KeyPress event must play a role here. As discussed earlier in the chapter, the KeyPress event does not recognize all keys on the keyboard—it does not include keys such as Delete, Insert, or End. For those, the application must turn to the KeyDown event associated with the text box. The label showing the ASCII value will change each time a new key is pressed; therefore, use the label's Caption property. But where is this change affected? Again, the event is linked to the text box. The last object, the command button, is clicked to clear the contents of both the text box and label showing ASCII values. This falls into the realm of the command button's Click event.

To get going on your own Easy ASCII application, start Visual Basic. Using Figure 3.42 and Table 3.11, draw the controls on the form; then change their corresponding properties. (The controls in the table work from the top of the form down.) When you are finished placing controls on the form, use the Lock Controls button on the toolbar to lock the controls. Remember to save your work as you go along!

Figure 3.42.
The Easy ASCII form with controls in place.

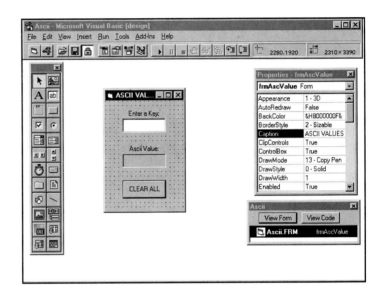

Table 3.11. The object properties for the Easy ASCII form.

Object	Property	Setting
Form	Caption	ASCII VALUES
	MaxButton	False
	MinButton	False
	Name	frmAscValue
Label	Alignment	2-Center
	Caption	Enter a Key:
	Font	Style: Bold
	Name	lblEnterKey
Text Box	Font	Style: Bold
	Name	txtEnterKey
	Tab Index	0
	Text	(None)

Object	Property	Setting
Label	Alignment	2-Center
	Caption	Ascii Value:
	Font	Style: Bold
	Name	lblValue
Label	Alignment	2-Center
	BorderStyle	1-Fixed Single
	Caption	(None)
	Font	Style: Bold
	Name	lblAscResult
Command Button	Caption	CLEAR ALL
	Default	True
	Font	Style: Bold
	Name	cmdClear

The controls are named in a way that is descriptive of the function they perform. To start writing the code behind the controls, start with the object that has the least number of functions—the command button. As in the notepad application, the command button's Click event clears controls of their contents. Thus, the code for the button uses the empty string ("") expression. Also, because the application revolves around the text box, it is a good idea to make sure the focus is there.

```
Private Sub cmdClear_Click()
    txtEnterKey.Text = ""
    lblAscResult.Caption = ""
    txtEnterKey.SetFocus
End Sub
```

Now move to the center of operations, the text box. The main event is KeyPress. First, it is a good idea to clear the text box of the previous character (if there is one); otherwise the box would eventually fill up.

The KeyAscii argument of the KeyPress event is the integer that is the numeric ASCII equivalent of the key pressed. Thus, the Caption property of the label, lblAscResult (the object on the form that shows the user the ASCII value), should be equated to KeyAscii.

The next part of the KeyPress event concerns keys that KeyPress recognizes and returns a value for, but that are not expressed on the screen as a character. These include the Backspace, Tab, and Enter keys. Thus, the application will return a numeric value if the Backspace key is pressed, but nothing would appear in the text box indicating which key was pressed. So, the answer is to fill the text box's Text property with a string that is the name of the key pressed. If…Then loops could be used (that is, If KeyAscii = 8 Then) but multiple If…Then loops in a row can get confusing. An easier statement to use is Select Case. The Select Case syntax looks like this:

```
Select Case TextExpression
[Case ExpressionList n
       [Statements n]]
[Case Else
       [ElseStatments]]
End Select
```

ExpressionList n represents a delimited list of `Case` possibilities where *n* equals one particular selection.

Thus, the `Select Case` statement works like a very large `If…Then` loop, but it contains all of the selections that multiple `If…Then` loops would hold, using much simpler syntax. (The `Select Case` statement will be discussed in greater detail in the next chapter, "Programming in Visual Basic.") To put the `Case` statement into use, the entire code for the text box's `KeyPress` event is as follows (notice how the `Select Case` statement works):

```
Private Sub txtEnterKey_KeyPress(KeyAscii As Integer)
       If txtEnterKey.Text <> "" Then
              txtEnterKey.Text = ""
       End If

       Select Case KeyAscii
              Case 8
                     txtEnterKey.Text = "[Backspace]"
              Case 9
                     txtEnterKey.Text = "[Tab]"
              Case 13
                     txtEnterKey.Text = "[Enter]"

              Case Else
       End Select

       lblAscResult.Caption = KeyAscii
End Sub
```

The final part of the code for this application involves keys that the `KeyPress` event does not recognize. Clearly, these keys exist on the keyboard, but there is no ASCII equivalent for keys such as Delete, Insert, and End. This is where the text box's `KeyDown` event comes into play. The `KeyDown` event uses the argument `KeyCode`. `KeyCode` is just what it says it is, a key code, such as the constant `vbKeyDelete` (the Delete key), whose value is 46 or the constant `vbKeyInsert` (the Insert key), whose value is 45. Constants will be discussed in Chapter 4. (If you ever need to specify key codes, you should use the constants in the Visual Basic Object Library located in the Object Browser.) In this program, the constants, such as `vbKeyDelete` and `vbKeyInsert`, are declared for each `Case` and the result is placed in the text box individually as a string. Of course, there are many more keys on the keyboard that have not been used in this instance, such as the function keys and other editing keys. If you wanted to add them to Easy ASCII, you could look up their constants in the Visual Basic Object Library.

Before displaying the complete code for the project, including the KeyDown event, there is one more Sub procedure that should be discussed. It is Sub Form_Activate(), or the Activate event for the form. Activate is a very straightforward event. It occurs when a form becomes the active window. Using the Activate event, the focus can be set immediately on the text box, before the user even makes a move. For that reason, you will use the Activate event to set focus on txtEnterKey.

A sample of running Easy ASCII application appears in Figure 3.43. The code, event by event, appears in Listing 3.6.

Figure 3.43.
The Easy ASCII application running.

Listing 3.6. **The Easy Ascii application. (Ascii.vbp)**

```
Option Explicit

Private Sub cmdClear_Click()
      txtEnterKey.Text = ""
      lblAscResult.Caption = ""
      txtEnterKey.SetFocus
End Sub

Private Sub Form_Activate()
      txtEnterKey.SetFocus
End Sub

Private Sub txtEnterKey_KeyDown(KeyCode As Integer, Shift As Integer)
      Const vbKeyDelete = 46
      Const vbKeyInsert = 45
      Const vbKeyEnd = 35

      Select Case KeyCode
            Case vbKeyDelete
                  lblAscResult.Caption = "Delete Pressed!"
                  txtEnterKey = "[[Delete]"
                  'Note that delete gets two brackets!
                  'This is because Delete, deletes the first one
            Case vbKeyInsert
                  lblAscResult.Caption = "Insert Pressed!"
                  txtEnterKey = "[Insert]"
            Case vbKeyEnd
                  lblAscResult.Caption = "End Pressed!"
                  txtEnterKey = "[End]"
```

continues

Listing 3.6. continued

```
            Case Else

        End Select
End Sub

Private Sub txtEnterKey_KeyPress(KeyAscii As Integer)
        If txtEnterKey.Text <> "" Then
                txtEnterKey.Text = ""
        End If

        Select Case KeyAscii
                Case 8
                        txtEnterKey.Text = "[Backspace]"
                Case 9
                        txtEnterKey.Text = "[Tab]"
                Case 13
                        txtEnterKey.Text = "[Enter]"

                Case Else
        End Select

        lblAscResult.Caption = KeyAscii
End Sub
```

Take your new program for a test run. If you wanted to, you could turn it into an executable application and keep it on your desktop for easy reference. No more searching for that ASCII numbering chart!

That's it for this chapter. In Chapter 4 you will examine Visual Basic programming in depth, including syntax, data types, flow-control statements, and static and dynamic arrays.

Summary

In this chapter you put not only text boxes and buttons to work, but also a wide variety of Visual Basic techniques and methods. You have seen how to read in numbers and store them, what variable scope means and how to take advantage of it, how to make buttons into default buttons, how to enable and disable buttons, and how to let the user tab from one control to the next in a program. Another major topic covered here was the use of alternate fonts and changing a font's appearance and size. You have seen some more advanced techniques such as adding access keys to buttons, interpreting individual keystrokes, and setting up entire control arrays. You discovered that control arrays are useful when there are several similar controls performing similar functions. You also learned how a control's Index property identifies the selected control, thus saving you from writing separate procedures for each radio button in the alarm clock application.

The following tables identify the new properties and events you've learned in this chapter.

New Property	Description
BorderStyle	Sets type of border for control or form from the available options.
Default	If True, this property makes its control the default (gets focus when the form opens).
Enabled	If True, the control is enabled. If False, disabled (grayed).
Font	Sets font type used in certain objects, such as text boxes and labels. Various options included in this property are Font, Font Style, Size, and Effects.
Index	Sets a control's index value. Used in control arrays. When a control in a control array is clicked or chosen, the value in its Index property is passed to the event procedure.
MultiLine	If available and set to True, this property enables a text control to support multiple lines of text.
ScrollBars	Determines whether a text-oriented control will have vertical and/or horizontal scrollbars.
SelStart	The starting location of text selected in a text-oriented control. This property is not available at design-time and must be inserted using code.
SelLength	The length of the selected text in a text-oriented control. This property is not available at design-time and must be inserted using code.
SelText	A string holding the selected text from a text-oriented control. This property is not available at design-time and must be inserted using code.
TabIndex	Sets the control's place in the tab order (for example, the control with TabIndex 3 follows the control with TabIndex 2).
TabStop	Determines whether the user can tab to a control. Settings: True or False.

New Event	Description
KeyDown	Occurs when the user presses a key while an object has the focus. It uses the Shift argument to determine whether the Alt, Ctrl, or Shift keys have been pressed.
KeyPress	Occurs when the user presses and releases an ANSI key. Unlike KeyDown and KeyUp, KeyPress does not indicate the physical state of the keyboard; instead, it passes a character.
KeyUp	Occurs when the user releases a key while an object has the focus. It uses the Shift argument to determine whether the Alt, Ctrl, or Shift keys have been pressed.

4

Programming in Visual Basic

Introduction

The BASIC programming language was invented in 1963 by John Kemeny and Thomas Kurtz at Dartmouth College. BASIC was originally designed as a teaching language and emphasized clarity as opposed to speed or efficiency. In other words, BASIC statements were intended to be as close as possible to English language statements. Early BASIC was intended to let the user concentrate on methods and tasks needed to solve programming tasks, not technical issues involving compiling and linking with computer hardware.

One cost of this ease of use was run speed—because early BASIC was interpreted rather than compiled. In addition, BASIC programs were not structured. The logic and flow control was accomplished through the use of GOTO or GOSUB statements with line numbers as their arguments. This resulted in what is termed *spaghetti code*—code that branches back and forth in such a confusing way that it is difficult to understand a program's logic and flow control.

> **Note:** Many programming languages today still have GOTO statements but their use has been limited by most professional programmers to very unique circumstances when GOTO statements are the only way to do something and make it make sense.
>
> Many professional programming shops have banned the use of the GOTO keyword in whatever language they are using. Although GOTO can make things work if you end up lost in a program's flow, it is almost never the best answer.

However, over the years BASIC improved quite a bit. For example, Microsoft's QuickBasic, first introduced in 1982, added modern programming capabilities. Users could produce compiled programs. (Qbasic, an interpreter-only version of QuickBasic, shipped with MS-DOS versions 6.x and earlier.) With all the advances, BASIC has remained first and foremost a language that is easy to understand. BASIC syntax and keywords are used in ways that are intuitively close to their English counterparts.

This chapter presents all you need to know about the workings of the Visual Basic variant of the BASIC programming language. While the material it covers is important—how constants are used, type and scope of variables, logical program flow control, and string manipulation—it is also straightforward. Of all programming languages, Visual Basic is one of the easiest to understand.

In the first three chapters of this book you saw how easy and intuitive it is to write Visual Basic programs. The material in this chapter may seem, by comparison, rather technical. But bear in mind that you don't need to absorb it all at once. This chapter is designed to be useful as a one-stop reference tool. When questions about the Visual Basic programming language come up as you create applications, you can use it as a quick, easy way to find what you need to know.

By the time you have finished this chapter you will know how to write and structure Visual Basic programs. You will have also learned how to tap into the power and flexibility available in the Visual Basic programming environment.

What's Still BASIC in Visual Basic?

The story goes that a great seer who was supposed to know the answers to all questions about the future of computer software was asked, "Will BASIC still be around in the year 2500?"

Lo and behold, the answer came back, "Yes, there will be a BASIC, but it won't be anything like BASIC today."

In actuality, those used to the syntax of older BASICs will find much of the programming language unchanged in Visual Basic. For instance, the following QuickBasic code sample prints *123* on three separate lines followed on another line by, *Blast Off!*, at the top of the screen. (See Figure 4.1.)

```
QuickBasic Demonstration program

CLS

FOR I = 1 TO 3
      PRINT I
NEXT I

PRINT "...Blast Off!"
PRINT
END
```

Figure 4.1.
The sample QuickBasic Blast Off! program.

As you can see, the essentially identical code in Visual Basic produces the same output, except this time at the top of a window. (See Figure 4.2.)

```
Private Sub Form_Click()

'Visual Basic for Windows Demo Program

For I = 1 To 3
   Print I
```

```
Next I

Print "...Blast Off!"

End Sub
```

If you require variable declarations by placing an `Option Explicit` statement in the general declarations of the form or if you have the Require Variable Declaration checked in the Tools | Options dialog box you will get an error message that the variable `I` is not defined. You can either define `I` as an integer with the statement `Dim I As Integer` or you can remove the variable declaration requirement. The importance of requiring variable typing as a sound programming practice is discussed later in this chapter.

Figure 4.2.
*The sample Visual Basic
Blast Off! program.*

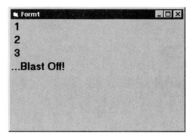

Both sets of code are the same. The only difference is that the code in the Visual Basic program is enclosed within the form's *click event*. To view the output, therefore, the user must click the form. This code could have been placed in another form event just as easily.

You might recall from the first three chapters of this book that VB programs are largely made up of code placed in Windows events. This is the primary difference between Visual Basic and older versions of Basic. In addition, Visual Basic provides a rich and varied language with many options and possibilities. But the core programming language retains much of the syntax and flavor of older Basics. This chapter presents the essential elements of this basic core.

Visual Basic Data Types

Table 4.1 shows data types that are recognized in Visual Basic.

Table 4.1. Visual Basic data types.

Data type	Character	Conventional Variable Prefix
Boolean	(None)	bln
Byte	(None)	byt
Integer	%	int

Data type	Character	Conventional Variable Prefix
Long	&	lng
Single	!	sng
Double	#	dbl
Date	(None)	dte
Currency	@	cur
String	$	str
Object	(None)	obj
Variant	(None)	vnt

The default data type is Variant. In other words, if a variable is not declared as something else—in one of the two ways you will see in a minute—Visual Basic assumes it is a variant.

Legal Variable Names

In order for a variable name to be recognized by Visual Basic, the name

- Must begin with an alphabetic character.
- Can't contain an embedded period or type-declaration character.
- Must be unique within its same scope.
- Must be no longer than 255 characters. Only the first 40 characters are significant in the sense that they must be unique.

A variable is declared to be a particular type either by appending the data type character listed in Table 4.1 to the variable name or by using the Dim statement.

Using the first method, often called *implicit typing*, the following are statements that tell VB that a variable is of a specific type:

```
strFirstName$ = "Dennis" 'strFirstName is a string
intNumEmployees% = 1200  'intNumEmployees is an integer
curPay@ = 999.99 'curPay is a Currency Variable.
```

Tip: Use explicit typing rather than implicit typing to improve a program's readability and easily avoid certain kinds of program bugs. Implicit typing is not very acceptable in many programming shops.

The second method of declaring a variable's type is known as *explicit typing*. The Dim (short for dimension) statement is used. Here is the syntax of the Dim statement:

```
Dim varname[([subscripts])][As [New] type][, varname[([subscripts])][As [New] type]] . . .
```

The Dim statement has these parts:

- *varname*—The name of the variable; must be a legal variable name as described above.
- *subscripts*—The dimensions of an array variable; up to 60 multiple dimensions can be declared. The subscripts argument uses the following syntax:

  ```
  [lower To] upper [,[lower To] upper] . . .
  ```

  When not explicitly stated in lower, the lower bound of an array is controlled by the Option Base statement. The lower bound is zero if no Option Base statement is present.

- New—A keyword used to indicate that a declared object variable is a new instance of a Visual Basic object or an externally createable OLE Automation object. The New keyword can't be used to declare variables of any intrinsic data type and can't be used to declare instances of dependent OLE Automation objects. OLE and OLE objects are covered in depth in Chapter 14.

- *type*—The data type of the variable; it can be Byte, Boolean, Integer, Long, Currency, Single, Double, Date, String (for variable-length strings), String * length (for fixed-length strings), Object, Variant, a user-defined type, or an object type. Use a separate As type clause for each variable you declare (this means that multiple variables can be declared with one Dim statement).

The following are examples of explicit variable declarations using the Dim statement:

```
Dim strFirstName As String
Dim intNumEmployees As Integer
Dim curPay As Currency
Dim intBlock As Integer, strStrong As String.
```

To explicitly declare a variable as a variant, the As Variant keyword should be used in the declaration, or the As block can be left off the Dim statement completely.

```
Dim vntBooks
Dim vntBooks  As Variant
```

Both examples above are explicit declarations of the variable vntBooks as type variant.

Why use variant variables? The good news about variants is that since they can be any type, your conversions will be taken care of for you. You don't have to worry about what kind of information is stored in the variable. Also, there are occasions where you might want to store multiple types of information in one variable. For example, you might want NumEmployees to be an integer for internal calculation purposes and a string for display. If you have declared an integer version—intNumEmployees—and a string version—strNumEmployees—you will have to convert back and forth using the `Str$()` and `Val()` functions. In this example, `strNumEmployees` might equal `Str$(intNumEmployees)` and `intNumEmployees` might equal `Val(strNumEmployees)`.

The bad news about variants is that if you know what type of data you will be using—string, integer, boolean, and so on—using a variant data type will consume more memory and will be expensive in terms of run-time speeds. Variants are notoriously slow, particularly when used as a loop counter. Also, if the type of your information is changing, you might want to force a change of variable type. Otherwise, it can be easy to make coding errors by not fully realizing the effects of automatic conversion. However, one good use for variants is storing object information. This will be discussed in Chapter 11, "Advanced Data Handling, Sorting, and Storing a Spreadsheet Program."

On the whole, it is probably wisest not to use variants when you have a pretty good idea of what kind of information is going to be stored in a variable.

The recommendation is even stronger to use the explicit variable typing style (using the `Dim` statement) rather than the implicit style (using data type characters). This is a matter of *style*. Many fine programmers prefer to implicitly type their variables rather than explicitly declare them. You will recognize code written in the implicit style because of all the percent signs (`%`), dollar signs (`$`), and exclamation points (`!`) hanging around after variable names.

But it has become generally recognized that it is usually a better practice to explicitly declare variables. In order to require the explicit declaration of variables in your code, add the keywords

```
Option Explicit
```

at the beginning of each module. The Visual Basic environment can be set to automatically add the `Option Explicit` keywords to the beginning of any form or module. Go into the Environment tab of the Options setting on the Tools menu and make sure that Require Variable Declaration is checked.

What the `Option Explicit` statement does is generate a syntax error if it finds any undeclared variables. The primary advantage of this is that it avoids potentially difficult-to-debug problems arising from typographic errors in keyboard entry of variable names. For example, in the following sample code only one string variable named `strNumSkull` is intended. But by mistake, one of the `strNumSkull` calls was typed in with one letter "l" instead of two.

```
Option Explicit

Dim strNumSkull As String

Private Sub Form_Load ()

strNumSkull = strNumSkul + 1

End Sub
```

Without the `Option Explicit` settings, this could be a surprisingly hard kind of error to trace. But when it's on, an instant `Undeclared Variable` message from Visual Basic appears on the screen. (See Figure 4.3.)

Figure 4.3.
The error message generated
by Visual Basic.

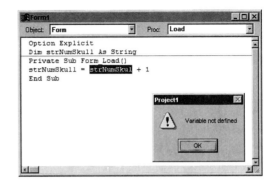

It is important to carefully choose your variable names. The variable naming conventions suggested in the third column of Table 4.1 are recommended by Microsoft in the Office Development Kit (ODK). But the two most important things in naming variables—whether or not you follow the MS ODK conventions—are to make the contents of the variable clear, and to be consistent.

Good Names for Variables

- Variable names should fully and accurately describe the values represented by the variable.
- Cryptic abbreviations should be avoided.
- Ambiguous names should be avoided.
- Good variable names express what the variable is, not how it is calculated or obtained.
- Good variable names avoid computer terminology.
- Good variable names make sense when read in English.
- Boolean variables should be given names that imply True or False. Positive Boolean names should be used. For example, naming a variable `NotFound` could lead to confusion in the statement `if not NotFound`.
- Avoid two or more variable names with similar meanings in one program.
- Avoid misspelled words and words that are commonly misspelled in variable names.

One other variable naming technique in Visual Basic that you should know about is the `Def` statement. When used at the module level, this statement sets the default data type for variables starting with the letters in the specified range. Table 4.2 lists the variants of the `Def [type]` statements. Here are some examples:

```
DefBool T    'all variables starting with T default to Boolean
DefInt A-Z   'all variables default to integer
DefStr A-Q   'variables starting A-Q default to string.
```

Table 4.2. Visual Basic **Def** statements.

Statement	Data Type
DefBool	Boolean
DefByte	Byte
DefInt	Integer
DefLng	Long
DefCur	Currency
DefSng	Single
DefDbl	Double
DefDate	Date
DefStr	String
DefObj	Object
DefVar	Variant

Note: As mentioned earlier, it is generally not accepted to use implicit definitions. However, if you do use them, the Def[*Type*] statements will be helpful in keeping all variables starting with a letter the same type.

Modules, Subroutines, and Functions

The building blocks that make up Visual Basic projects are called *modules*. VB modules come in three general flavors. The first flavor is the *form*. Simple applications can consist of a single form with all the code for that application residing in the single module. You have seen forms used in the Alarm, Calculator, and NotePad applications created in the last chapter. Form modules when they are saved have the file suffix .frm.

As you write applications that are larger and more complicated, you will add additional form modules. Soon your projects will have quite a few form modules. At some point you will find that there is common code being executed in a number of different forms. Since you don't want to duplicate the same code in two—or more—places, you can create a separate *module* containing the procedures that implement the common code. The separate module—which is shared by the various forms—has no component visible at run-time. It is called a *standard module*. Standard module files are saved with the .bas extension. They are generally used as libraries for the other parts of an application.

Class Modules for Creating Objects with Custom Properties and Methods

Class modules are saved with a .cls extension. They are used to define classes, or *blueprints* of objects, and are new to Visual Basic 4. New objects created using class modules can have their own customized properties and methods.

Class modules are very similar to forms, except that class modules are not visible at run-time, whereas forms can be visible. Each class module defines one class. The Sub and Function procedures in a class module are the methods of the class; the module-level variables and property procedures in a class module are the properties of the class. Class modules bring some object-oriented programming capabilities to Visual Basic, and as such, represent an important advance. They will be discussed in more detail in Chapter 15, "Advanced Control and Form Handling." Table 4.3 is a comparison of the three different types of Visual Basic modules.

Table 4.3. Types of modules.

	Form	*Standard*	*Class*
File Suffix	.frm	.bas	.cls
Different Types	Standard form, MDI form		
Invocation on	Form, MDI Form		
Insert Menu	Form, MDI Form	Module	Class Module
Can Contain	Graphical descriptions of form, its controls, and property settings; form level type; constant and variable declarations; procedures that handle events; general procedures	Global or module level type; constant and variable declarations; external procedures; global procedures	Form level type, constant and variable declarations constant and variable delcarations; procedures that handle events; general procedures
Visible at run-time?	Usually	Never	Never
Related Files	Binary information required by a .frm file is stored in a companion .frx file		

	Form	*Standard*	*Class*
Comments	Forms are the foundation for most VB applications.	Often used as a library of routines for forms in an application.	Can be used as the basis for an entire class of objects using the `As New` keywords.

How does Visual Basic put all these different kinds of modules together? When you add a module to a project, the project file gets updated with the name of the new module file, for example, MyForm.frm, MyLib.bas, or MyObj.cls. There is one Visual Basic project file for each project. It is an ASCII text file with a .vbp extension. This is the kind of file Visual Basic looks for when you tell it to open a project.

Note: In addition to pointing to a project's modules, the .vbp file also contains other information such as the name of the executable file created by the project, its icon, version information, and add-on controls required by the project. Many of these are set in the Executables Options screen shown in Figure 4.4.

Figure 4.4.
The Executables Options screen.

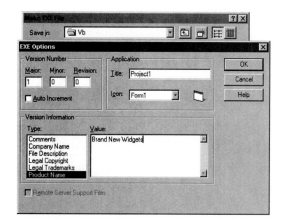

Figure 4.5 shows a portion of a simple .vbp file from the TString project you'll create later in this chapter.

Just as modules are the building blocks upon which Visual Basic projects are made, *procedures* are the substance out of which modules are made. As you can see from Table 4.4, modules can also include other kinds of information such as declarations. With form modules, graphic information that is placed by drawing on the screen is also included.

Figure 4.5.
TString.vbp opened in Notepad.

Table 4.4. Types of procedures.

	Sub	*Function*	*Property*
Returns a Value?	Never explicitly returns value (see discussion).	Always returns a value (but value can only indicate success or failure of operation (see discussion).	May return the value of a property.
Default type	N/A	Variant.	Variant.
Default scope	`Public`; except that event `Sub` procedures are `Private` by default.	`Public`.	N/A— applies to the module containing the property procedure.
Can be placed in…	Form modules, standard modules, class modules.	Form modules, standard modules, class modules.	Form modules, class modules.
Types of…	General `Sub` procedures; event `Sub` procedures.	N/A	`Property Let` (sets the value of a property; `Property Get` (returns the value of a property); `Property Set` (sets a reference to an object).

Procedures are also generally known as *subroutines*.

There are two kinds of Sub procedures: *general procedures* and *event procedures*. You have already seen a number of examples of event procedures in applications created in the first three chapters of this book. An event procedure is invoked whenever an object in Visual Basic recognizes that an event has occurred. Examples are the form's Load event and a command button's Click event, Private Sub Form_Load(), and Private cmdOK_Click().

An event procedure for a control combines the control's name, as set in the .Name property, with an underscore (_) and the event name—for example, cmdOK_Click.

An event procedure for a form combines the word Form with an underscore (_) and the event name—for example, Form_Load or Form_Click. (The form .Name property is not used in the syntax of form events.) For MDI (Multiple Document Interface) forms, the event combines the word MDIForm with an underscore (_) and the event name—for example, MDIForm_Unload. (MDI forms are discussed in Chapters 7 and 15.

A Programming Tip

If you are going to change the names of your controls, for example, it might be a good idea to change the Name property of your first command button from Command1 (the default) to cmdOK—make the change *before* you start putting code in the event procedure. If you change the name of a control after writing code in a procedure attached to it, you must also change the name of the procedure to match the new name. Otherwise, Visual Basic won't match the procedure to the control. When a procedure name does not match a control name, Visual Basic considers it a general procedure.

General procedures tell your program how to perform a specific task. They will only be executed if specifically invoked in an application. This is also termed *calling* a procedure.

One reason for using general procedures is because different event procedures need the same actions performed. A good programming strategy is to put the common statements in a general procedure and have each event procedure call the general procedure. This eliminates code duplication, makes the logic in the application easier to follow, and makes maintaining the program easier.

Earlier, you created a procedure to center a form. That was a general-purpose procedure. This is a common "utility" type function that many people keep in a standard module so they can include it in all of their applications.

Incidentally, a general `Sub` procedure (as opposed to a function) does not normally return a value to the procedure that invoked it. However, it is often a good idea to use one of the `Sub` procedure's arguments to return information. Here is the syntax of the general `Sub` procedure:

```
[Private ¦ Public] [Static] Sub name [(arglist)]
       [statements]
       [Exit Sub]
       [statements]
End Sub
```

The syntax of the general `Sub` procedure is as follows:

- `Public`—Indicates that the `Sub` procedure is accessible to all other procedures in all modules. If used in a private module (one that contains an `Option Private` statement), the procedure is not available outside the project. The scope of routines and variables is covered in more detail later in this chapter.

- `Private`—Indicates that the `Sub` procedure is accessible only to other procedures in the module where it is declared. Routines and variables are discussed in more detail later in this chapter.

- `Static`—Indicates that the `Sub` procedure's local variable values are retained between calls. The `Static` attribute doesn't affect variables that are declared outside the `Sub`, even if they are used in the procedure.

- *name*—The name of the `Sub`; follows standard variable naming conventions.

- *arglist*—A list of variables representing arguments that are passed to the `Sub` procedure when it is called. Multiple variables are separated by commas. Following is a further explanation of `arglist`.

- *statements*—Any group of statements to be executed within the body of the `Sub` procedure.

The *arglist* portion of the `Sub` statement has the following syntax and parts:

```
[[Optional][ByVal ¦ ByRef][ParamArray] varname[( )] As type]
```

The *arglist*—argument list—portion of general `Sub` statement arguments work like this:

- `Optional`—Indicates that an argument is not required. If used, all subsequent arguments in *arglist* must also be optional and declared using the `Optional` keyword. All `Optional` arguments must be `Variant`. `Optional` can't be used for any argument if `ParamArray` is used.

- `ByVal`—Indicates that the argument is passed by value.

- `ByRef`—Indicates that the argument is passed by reference. See the following discussion.

- `ParamArray`—Used only as the last argument in *arglist* to indicate that the final argument is an `Optional` array of `Variant` elements. The `ParamArray` keyword lets you provide an arbitrary number of arguments. It cannot be used with `ByVal`, `ByRef`, or `Optional`.

- *varname*—The name of the variable representing the argument; follows standard variable naming conventions.

- *type*—The data type of the argument passed to the procedure; may be Byte, Boolean, Integer, Long, Currency, Single, Double, Date, String (variable length only), Object, Variant, a user-defined type, or an object type.

In the default mode, arguments are passed to Sub procedures by reference. Passing arguments by reference, either as the default or by using the ByRef keyword, gives the procedure access to the actual value of the variable, not just a copy of it. This means that the procedure has the power to permanently change the value of the variable.

On the other hand, if you pass a value by using the ByVal keyword, only a copy of the variable is passed to the procedure. If the procedure then changes the value of the variable, the change affects *only* the copy of the variable and not the original. Use of the ByVal keyword is an effective way to isolate subroutines from the rest of a program. In addition, it is often required when calling functions external to Visual Basic.

The syntax of the Function statement works like this:

```
[Public ¦ Private] [Static] Function name [(arglist)] [As type]
        [statements]
        [name = expression]
        [Exit Function]
        [statements]
        [name = expression]
End Function
```

This is very similar to the Sub statement, except that the Function, Exit Function, and End Function statements are used instead of the corresponding Sub statement. And, significantly, functions are typed and return a value. In fact, the syntax of the subparts of this statement are the same as those listed for Subs.

Function procedures differ from Sub procedures in three ways:

1. Usually, functions are called by including the function name and arguments on the right side of a larger statement or expression.

2. Function procedures themselves have a type, just like variables. The function type determines the type of the return value of the function. The type is set using the As clause in the Function statement. If no type is set, the function defaults to variant.

3. Functions return a value. This value is returned by assigning it to the function name within the function procedure. When the function is called as part of a larger expression, the return value of the function becomes part of the larger expression.

The Return Value of a Function

Sometimes the return value of a function serves only a nominal purpose or checks that no errors have occurred. For example, a function might return `True` if no errors have taken place during its operations, and `False` if otherwise. The real work of the function might not involve returning values, or the value could be returned as an argument rather than the function value. For an example of this, see the `GetPrivateProfileString` function in the sample INI application in Chapter 8, "File Handling in Visual Basic."

The following is an example of a function and how to call the function that compares two integers. If the first one is bigger than the second one, it returns `True`; otherwise, it returns `False`.

```
Public Function IsBiggerThan (A As Integer, B As Integer) As Integer
If A > B then
        IsBiggerThan = True
Else
        IsBiggerThan = False 'A<= B
End if

End Function

If IsBiggerThan(I,J) Then
        MsgBox "I is bigger than J!"
End If
```

Property procedures are used to create and manipulate custom properties. When you create a property procedure, the new property belongs to the module containing the procedure. Visual Basic provides three kinds of property procedures:

1. `Property Let` sets the value of a property.

2. `Property Get` returns the value of a property.

3. `Property Set` sets a reference to an object.

The syntax of these statements is almost identical to the `Sub` and `Function` statement syntax that has already been explored in some detail. Custom properties and the use of the Property Procedure are discussed in detail in Chapter 15.

Scope and Lifetime of Variables and Procedures

The term *scope* is about who can see whom. What parts of a program can see—or talk to—other parts? What subroutines or variables are visible, and where are they visible? Procedures can be visible (meaning they can be called) or invisible (meaning they cannot be called) to other procedures outside their module. Similarly, variables can be visible or invisible at procedure, module, and project levels. Variables declared in a procedure are visible only within the procedure. They lose their values between calls to their procedures unless they have been declared with the `Static` keyword. This sounds rather confusing, but really is rather straightforward. Take a look at variable scoping in Table 4.5 first.

Table 4.5. The scope of variables in Visual Basic.

Declared In	Private Keywords	Used to Declare	Scope	Public Keywords	Scope
Procedure	`Dim`	Variables	Local to the procedure in which they appear	Not applicable —you cannot declare public variables from within a procedure	N/A
	`Const`	Constants	Local to the procedure in which they appear	N/A	N/A
	`Static`	Variables (see discussion)	Local to the procedure in which they appear	N/A	N/A
Declarations section of Module	`Private`	Variables	Private to the module (available to all procedures within the module)	`Public`; used for variables and constants. `Global`; maintained for backwards compatibility (use `Public` in preference)	Available to all modules in a project.
	`Private` `Const`	Constants	Private to the module (available to all procedures within the module)	`Public`; used for variables and constants. `Global`; maintained for backward	Available to all modules in a project

continues

Table 4.5. continued

Declared In	Private Keywords	Used to Declare	Scope	Public Keywords	Scope
				compatibility (use `Public` in preference)	
	`Dim` (defaults to Private)	Variables (maintained for backward compatibility; use `Private` in preference)	Private to the module (available to all procedures within the module)	`Public`; used for variables and constants. `Global`; maintained for backward compatibility (use `Public` in preference)	Available to all modules in a project
	`Const` (defaults to Private)	Constants	Private to the module (available to all procedures within the module)	`Public`; used for variables and constants. `Global`; maintained for backward compatibility (use `Public` in preference)	Available to all modules in a project

What this really boils down to is that there are three variable scopes that are important in Visual Basic. Think about it this way: A variable can be known in all modules and procedures in a program, in which case it is a global variable and should be declared as `Public` in the declarations section of a standard module. It can be visible to all procedures within a module, in which case it is a module-level variable and should be declared in the declarations section of the module using `Private`. Or the variable is local to a procedure—and only visible within that procedure—in which case it should be declared within the procedure using a `Dim` or `Static` keyword.

Variables can be declared at the procedure level with the `Static` keyword. Variables declared this way retain their values as long as the code is running. You can declare all the local variables within a procedure as static by using the `Static` keyword in front of the procedure heading. For example:

```
Static Function MyFunc (Num As Integer) As Integer
    :
End Function
```

This causes all local variables in the procedure MyFunc—regardless of whether they are declared with Static, Dim, or implicitly—to be static.

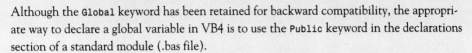

Using the Public Instead of the Global Keyword

Although the Global keyword has been retained for backward compatibility, the appropriate way to declare a global variable in VB4 is to use the Public keyword in the declarations section of a standard module (.bas file).

The statement line of a procedure contains either the Public or Private keyword. Here are some examples:

```
Private Sub cmdOK_Click()

Public Static Sub MySub(MyNum As Integer)
Private Function MyFunc(MyNum As Integer) As Boolean

End Sub
```

By default, procedures are public (except event procedures, which are private by default). A private procedure is one that can only be seen by other procedures in its module. A public procedure can be called or seen by any procedure in any module in the project. Table 4.6 is a summary of the availability of procedures.

Table 4.6. **Scope of procedures in Visual Basic.**

Scope	Procedures with Public Keyword	Procedures with Private Keyword
Accessible within Module?	Yes	Yes
Accessible to procedures in other Modules within project?	Yes	No

There is only one more thing you need to know about scoping: Modules also have scope. The default scope of a module is public, meaning that public variables, constants, and procedures in the module are potentially visible to other projects. But you can use the Option Private statement to make these items invisible outside the project. The syntax of this statement is

```
Option Private Module
```

This phrase must appear in a module before any statements or declarations. (Even when the Option Private statement is used, all public variables, constants, and procedures are available throughout the project.) The concepts involved in using objects from outside a project are discussed further in Chapter 15.

Constants

Constants are used in programs for two reasons. First, they serve to replace a string or numeric value that is constant and reappears within the program a number of times. Second, they serve to make code easier to read by replacing numbers that in and of themselves have no meaning. A constant is a meaningful name that takes the place of a number or string that does not change. For example, the constant PointsPerInch might take the place of the number 72. A constant is somewhat like a variable, but a constant cannot be modified or assigned a new value to it, as is possible with a variable.

There are two kinds of constants in Visual Basic:

1. *Intrinsic*, also called *system-defined*, constants are provided by Visual Basic or some other application that provides an object library. For a list of the constants available, select Object Browser from the View menu (or F2). On the top drop-down list, select VB—VB Objects and Procedures. Scroll down the list in the left box until you reach Constants. Double-click the word Constants. A list of the available constants appears in the right box. When you select a constant, it tells you the value for the constant and what the constant represents. You may use any of these constants in your programs in contexts where they make sense (or use the numeric equivalents—but using the constant makes things clearer and less prone to typographic errors). Here are some examples of intrinsic VB constants:

   ```
   vbBringToFront = 0
   vbBlue = 16711680
   vbXorPen = 7
   ```

Naming Conventions for Intrinsic Constants and Their Uses

Intrinsic constants in Visual Basic 4 are treated differently than in previous versions of Visual Basic. In earlier versions of Visual Basic, constant names were capitalized with underscores. For example:

```
TILE_VERTICAL
```

In Visual Basic 4, constant names are in a mixed-case format. The first two letters indicate the originating object library. Constants in the Visual Basic library start with vb. An example of this is

```
vbTileVertical
```

In previous versions of Visual Basic, built-in constants had to be loaded into a project by adding a provided text file. In Visual Basic 4, if a constant is listed in the Object Browser, you can just use it with no further ado.

2. *Symbolic* or *user-defined* constants are created by the programmer who declares them using the `Const` statement. User-defined constants follow the scoping rules outlined in the previous section of this chapter. That is, if they are declared within a procedure they are local to that procedure, and if they are declared in the declarations section of a module, they can either be private to that module or global in scope if the `Public` keyword is used. For example:

```
Public Const ProgramName = "My Sample Program"
```

It is a good idea to set user-defined constants apart from variables and intrinsic constants by prefixing them in a standard way, possibly with **con**. Here are some more examples of user-defined constant declarations following this convention:

```
Const conPi = 3.14159265358979
Public Const conMaxPlanets = 9
Const conReleaseDate = #6/1/95#
Public Const conVersion = "04.10.A"
Const conShipName = "Starship Enterprise"
```

Arrays

The purpose of an array is to allow you to refer to a series of variables by the same name and to use an index to tell them apart. This can often help you simplify your code. You can set up loops that deal efficiently with any situation based on the index number. Arrays have a first element—called the *lower bound*—and a last element—called the *upper bound*. All the elements of the array are contiguous between the lower and the upper bound.

A Visual Basic Programming Tip

Because Visual Basic allocates space for each indexed array element, try not to declare arrays any larger than necessary.

There are two kinds of arrays: *fixed-size* and *dynamic*. Fixed-size arrays have a set number of elements; the size of dynamic arrays can change at run-time. First, a look at fixed-size arrays. In terms of scope, there are three ways to declare a fixed-size array:

1. To create a public array, use the `Public` statement in the declarations section of a module. For example:

```
Public DonutTypes(100) As String
```

2. To create a module-level array, use the `Dim` statement in the declarations section of a module. For example:

```
Dim CreamContentPerFlav(100) As Integer
```

3. To create a local array, use the `Static` statement within a procedure to declare the array. (Note that local fixed-size arrays must be static.) For example:

```
Public Sub GetID()
Static EmploySS(150) As Long
:
End Sub
```

By default, the index on the array starts at 0—the lower bound. This means that the declaration

```
Dim CreamContentPerFlav(100) As Integer
```

has set up an array of integers with the index going from 0 to 100—the upper bound. By now, this is pretty much established as a reasonable way of setting up arrays, but you don't have to do it this way. You can change the default lower bound for arrays to 1 by placing an `Option Base` statement in the declarations section of a module like this:

```
Option Base 1
```

Now, `Dim CreamContentPerFlav(100) As Integer` would set up an array going from 1 to 100. You can also change the lower and upper bounds of an array explicitly to any number you'd like, using the `To` keyword. For example:

```
Dim CreamContentPerFlav (1 to 100) As Integer    'Sets up an array with lower
                                                 'bound of 1 and upper bound
                                                 'of 100

Public DonutTypes (50 To 75) As String           'Sets up an array with lower
                                                 'bound of 50 and upper bound
                                                 'of 75
```

Visual Basic arrays can have more than one dimension. If you haven't run into multidimensional arrays before, perhaps the easiest way to think of them is as tables. In fact, VB arrays can have has many dimensions has you like. Each dimension can be declared with or without the `To` keyword. For example

```
Dim MultiDim (5, 1 To 75, 9, 0 To 9)
```

sets up a variant array in which the first dimension has 6 elements, the second has 75, and the third and fourth both have 10 (6 by 75 by 10 by 10). The total number of elements in the array is the product of the four dimensions, or 45,000.

A Bit About `LBound()` and `UBound()`

The `LBound()` and `UBound()` functions, which are built into Visual Basic, return the lower and upper bounds, respectively, of an array. For one-dimensional arrays, they can be used simply by placing the name of the array in the function call:

```
intflavors = UBound(DonutTypes)
```

For multidimensional arrays, you signal which dimension you want returned by the argument placed after the comma in the function call. For example:

```
LBound(MultiDim, 3)
```

If the dimension is omitted, 1 is assumed.

A Programming Tip

The storage needs of arrays increase dramatically as you add dimensions. Be particularly careful not to make arrays any larger than they need to be with multidimensional variant arrays.

Sometimes you might not know exactly how big to make an array. The answer to this problem is to set up a *dynamic array* rather than a fixed-size array. Dynamic arrays can be resized when a program is running by the program itself through the use of the ReDim statement. The ability to conveniently and easily resize arrays is a great feature of VB. It helps you to manage memory consumption efficiently and means that you can make an array large only when you need it to be large.

Here's how it works. Declare an array using one of the three methods for declaring a fixed-size array, but don't put any number of elements in the declaration (leave the inside of the parentheses blank):

```
Dim DonutTypes () As String
```

Allocate the actual number of elements, using the ReDim statement:

```
Public Sub DoStuff()
Const conDuncan = 125
ReDim DonutTypes(conDuncan) As String
End Sub
```

Because ReDim is an executable statement, it must appear within a procedure and cannot be placed in declaration sections of your code. The ReDim statement can be used the same way an array declaration statement is used to set up as many dimensions. ReDim is used at the procedure level to declare dynamic-array variables and allocate or reallocate storage space. Its syntax works like this:

```
ReDim [Preserve] varname(subscripts) [As type][, varname(subscripts) [As type]] . . .
```

The ReDim statement syntax has these parts:

- **Preserve**—Preserves the data in an existing array when you change the size of the last dimension.
- **Varname**—The name of the variable; follows standard variable naming conventions.

- Subscripts—The dimensions of an array variable; up to 60 multiple dimensions may be declared. The subscripts argument uses the following syntax:

  `[lower To] upper [,[lower To] upper]...`

  When not explicitly stated in `lower`, the lower bound of an array is controlled by the `Option Base` statement. The lower bound is zero if no `Option Base` statement is present.

- Type—A data type of the variable; may be `Byte`, `Boolean`, `Integer`, `Long`, `Currency`, `Single`, `Double`, `Date`, `String` (for variable-length strings), `String * length` (for fixed-length strings), `Object`, `Variant`, a user-defined type, or an object type. Use a separate `As type` clause for each variable being defined. For a Variant containing an array, type describes the type of each element of the array, but does not change the Variant to some other type.

One problem with the `ReDim` statement is that each time it is executed, all current values in the array are lost. This is fine if you just want to use the dynamic aspect of the array to save on memory usage or if you are preparing the array for assignment of new values. But if you want to change the size of the array without losing its contents, you must use the `Preserve` keyword. Here's an example of how it works:

```
ReDim Preserve DonutTypes (Ubound (DonutTypes)+1)
```

This statement adds an additional element to the array without losing the values of the existing elements. But note some limitations of the `Preserve` keyword: only the upper bound of the last dimension in a multidimensional array can be changed. If you try to change any dimension other than the last, or the lower bound of the last dimension, a run-time error will be generated. Thus,

```
ReDim Preserve MyMatrix (25, UBound(MyMatrix,2) + 1)
```

adds one element to the second dimension of the array `MyMatrix`. But

```
ReDim Preserve MyMatrix(Ubound(MyMatrix, 1) + 1, 25)
```

generates an error.

User-Defined Data Types

It is possible to combine variables of several different types to create user-defined types—known as *structs* in the C programming language. User-defined types are useful when you want to create a single variable that records several related pieces of information. This can be a very powerful way to organize information in programs. A user-defined type is created using the `Type` statement, which must be placed in the `Declarations` section of a standard module. User-defined types can be declared as private or public with the appropriate keyword. For example:

```
Private Type YourDataType
```

or

```
Public Type YourDataType
```

For instance, a user-defined type could be created that records information about a computer system:

```
' Declarations (of a standard module)
Private Type SystemInfo
        CPU As Variant
        Memory As Long
        VideoDriver As String
        HardDrive As String
End Type
```

Or, a user-defined type could be created for all employees at a company:

```
Public Type Employee
        JobTitle As String
        SS As Long
        Wage As Currency
End Type
```

After a user-defined type is set up, local, private module-level, or public module-level variables of the same user-defined type can be declared:

```
Dim MySystem As SystemInfo, HackersSystem As SystemInfo
Dim Fairweather As Employee, Hacker As Employee
```

Table 4.7 shows the scoping rules for user-defined types and variables you can create based on those types.

Table 4.7. User-defined types and variable scoping rules.

Procedure/Module	You can create a user-defined type as	Variables of a user-defined type can be
Procedures	Not applicable	Local only
Standard modules	Private or public	Private or public
Form modules	Private only	Private only
Class modules	Private only	Private only

Assigning and retrieving values from user-defined types works with the . operator the same way that properties work with controls. For example, values would be assigned as follows:

```
HackersSystem.CPU = "Pentium"
Hacker.JobTitle = "Consultant"
```

To retrieve values, switch the equation around:

```
Text1.Text = Hacker.JobTitle
```

or

```
If HackersSystem.CPU = "Pentium" Then
```

Note that user-defined types can contain fixed-size or dynamic arrays as one (or more) of their elements. Here are some examples:

```
Private Type SystemInfo
     CPU As Variant
     Memory As Long
     VideoDriver As String
     HardDrives (15) As String 'fixed-size array
End Type

Private Type SystemInfo
     CPU As Variant
     Memory As Long
     VideoDriver As String
     HardDrives ()  As String 'dynamic array
End Type
```

Values within the arrays in a user-defined type are accessed as follows:

```
Dim HackersSystem As SystemInfo
HackerSystem.HardDrives(0) = "2.4 Gig SCSI"
```

You can also declare arrays of user-defined types:

```
Dim OurComputers (50) As SystemInfo
```

And access these as you would any array:

```
OurComputers (10).CPU = "SPARC"
OurComputers(I).HardDrives(2) = "420M IDE"
```

String Manipulation

The term *string* is short for *text string*. A text string refers to plain text using the 256-character ANSI (American National Standards Institute) character set used by Windows to represent keyboard input. Text string data is sometimes referred to as ASCII text.

Strings are represented by one of the major Visual Basic data types. The codes for the characters in the string data type range from 0 to 255. Characters 0 through 127 correspond to the letters and symbols on a standard American keyboard. Characters 128 through 255 represent special characters, such as letters in international alphabets, typographic symbols, accents, and fractions.

String manipulation is an extremely important topic because, in the end, almost all manipulation of source code comes down to manipulating strings. In other words, the code in your program itself can be thought of as string data.

Also, most user keyboard input consists of string input. To interpret what the user has typed, and to do anything useful with it, your programs must make plentiful use of string manipulation techniques.

Fortunately, Visual Basic is an extremely capable language when it comes to string manipulation. Many powerful built-in functions that can help you to interpret, translate, and manipulate strings are available for your use. Table 4.8 shows some of the more commonly used Visual Basic string manipulation functions.

Table 4.8. Common Visual Basic string manipulation functions.

Function: ASC

Syntax	Asc(*String*)
Returns	Character code corresponding to the first letter in a string.

Function: CHR

Syntax	Chr(*Char_Code*)
Returns	The character corresponding to the ANSI Char_Code (from 0 – 255, inclusive) entered.
Comments	Char_Codes 0–31 are the standard, nonprintable ASCII codes. Values 8, 9, 10, and 13 convert to backspace, tab, linefeed, and carriage return characters, respectively. They have no graphical representation, but depending on the application may significantly affect the visual display of text.

Function: FORMAT

Syntax	Format(Expression [,format[,firstdayofweek [,firstweekofyear]]])
Returns	Formats an expression using the instructions in the format expression.
Comments	Commonly used to format dates and times, but can be used to generally format strings. See the Format function in Visual Basic Help.

Function: INSTR

Syntax	InStr([*Start*,] *String1*, *String2*[,Compare])
Returns	First occurrence of *String2* within *String1*
Comments	*Start* is a numeric expression that sets the starting point of the search. If it is left off, searching is started at the first character of *String1*. Compare indicates

continues

Table 4.8. continued

the type of string comparison being made. If it is set to 0, the default, a binary comparison is made. By setting `Compare` to 1, you will cause `InStr` to do a textual comparison ignoring upper- and lowercases.

Function: LCASE

Syntax	LCase(*String*)
Returns	A string converted to lowercase.

Function: LEFT

Syntax	Left(*String*, *Length*)
Returns	The specified number of characters from the left side of a string.

Function: LEN

Syntax	Len(*String*)
Returns	The number of characters in a string.
Comments	If `Len` is used on a variable that is typed as neither string nor variant, it returns the number of bytes required to store the variable (not its character count).

Function: LTRIM

Syntax	LTrim(*String*)
Returns	A copy of the string without leading spaces.

Function: MID

Syntax	Mid(*String*, Start[,*Length*])
Returns	The specified number of characters from a string.
Comments	If *Length* is left out or there are fewer *Length* characters, all characters from the start to the end of the string are returned.

Function: RIGHT

Syntax	Right(*String*,*Length*)
Returns	The specified number of characters from the right side of a string.

Function: RTRIM

Syntax	RTrim(*String*)
Returns:	A copy of the string without trailing spaces.

Function: STR

Syntax	Str(*Number*)
Returns	A string representation of a number.

Function: STRCOMP

Syntax	StrComp(*String1, String2* [,*compare*])
Returns	-1 if *String1* is less than *String2*, 0 if *String1* equals *String2* and 1 if *String1* is greater than *String2*. If either *String1* or *String2* is null, it returns null.
Comments	*Compare* indicates the type of string comparison being made. If it is set to 0, the default, a binary comparison is made. By setting compare to 1, you will cause StrComp to do a textual comparison, ignoring upper- and lowercases.

Function: STRCONV

Syntax	StrConv(*string, conversion*)
Returns	If conversion = 1, puts String in uppercase; if conversion = 2, lowercases the string; if conversion = 3, uppercases the first letter of every word in a string. Constants for the conversion value are as follows: vbUpperCase = 1 vbLowerCase = 2 vbProperCase = 3

Function: TRIM

Syntax	Trim(*String*)
Returns	A copy of the string without leading or trailing blanks.

Function: UCASE

Syntax	UCase(*String*)
Returns	A string converted to uppercase.

Function: VAL

Syntax	Val(*String*)
Returns	The numeric value of a string.
Comments	Val stops reading the string argument at the first character it can't recognize as part of a number.

There are only a few more things to cover about strings, and then you will be ready to put what you have learned to use.

You should know that there are two ways to make string comparisons: binary or text. A *binary text* comparison is based on the internal binary representation of the characters involved. A<B<a<b is an example of a typical binary search order. *Text* search order is based on case-insensitivity. In a text sort, A=a<B=b.

Which method of comparing strings is used is set by using the Option Compare statement. The syntax of this statement is:

```
Option Compare {Text | Binary}
```

It must appear before any declarations or statements in a module. If you do not use the `Option Com-pare` statement, Visual Basic will default to binary comparison.

You should also be aware that quite a few string manipulation functions come in two flavors. When you place a `$` at the end of the function name, it returns a string value. When you leave the `$` off, the function returns a variant value. It is generally a better idea to use the form that returns a string and add any conversions, both for clarity and to improve performance.

Although variants handle type conversions automatically and are possibly more convenient, there are some reasons for using string variables instead. For instance, if the information you are dealing with consists primarily of strings, you will save on resources by using string rather than variable typing. Also, if you use explicitly typed string variables, you will know if an intentional or unintentional conversion to another type is taking place. Finally, as you will see in Chapter 8, if you use string variables, you can write directly to random-access files.

Table 4.9 lists functions that return a string variable when `$` is appended to the function name. These functions have the same usage and syntax as their variant equivalents.

Table 4.9. Functions that return strings with $ appended to the function's name.

Chr$	CurDir$	Date$	Dir$
Error$	Format$	Hex$	Input$
InputB$	LCase$	Left$	LeftB$
Mid$	MidB$	Oct$	Right$
RightB$	RTrim$	Space$	Str$
String$	Time$	Trim$	UCase$

That's all there is to it! Now put what you have learned to good use and manipulate a few strings.

String Manipulation Code Example

This sample string manipulation program will tell how many times a character occurs in a string. Start a new Visual Basic project. Select the default form, `Form1`, and scroll down the Properties window until you reach `Name`. Change that property to `frmStringMa`. Next, scroll up the Properties window until you find Caption, and change that property to String Manipulation. Then save the form and project by selecting the Save Project... item from the File menu. Save the form as String.frm and the project as String.vbp.

Using the text box tool on the toolbar, add two text boxes and two labels to the form. Then add two labels and two command buttons. Using the Properties window, change their properties to reflect the following table. Position the controls using Figure 4.6 as a guide.

Object	Property	Setting
Form	Appearance	1-3D
	BorderStyle	3-Fixed Dialog
	Caption	String Manipulation
	Name	frmStringMa
Label	Caption	Enter a Character to
		Search for:
	Name	lblChar
Text Box	Caption	T
	Name	txtSearchChar
Label	Caption	Enter a String to Search:
	Name	lblString
Text Box	Caption	MY COUNTRY 'TIS OF THEE
	Name	txtSS
Command Button	Caption	DO IT!
	Default	True
	Name	cmdDoIt
Command Button	Caption	CANCEL
	Name	cmdCancel

Before you enter the following code, notice two things. First, the character text entry box has been limited to one character by setting the Maximum property to 1. The user can only enter one character in this box. Second, this program is case-sensitive. This means that if you tell it to search for a lowercase y, it will not find it if only an uppercase Y is present in the search string.

The complete code for the application appears in Listing 4.1.

Figure 4.6.
The Character Search
application template.

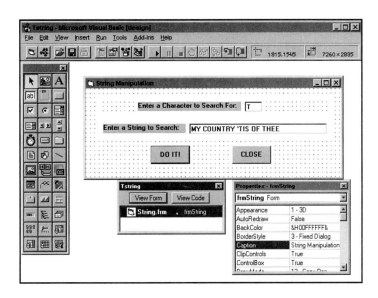

Listing 4.1. The String Manipulation application (String.vbp).

```
Option Explicit

Private Sub cmdClose_Click()
Unload cmdClose.Parent
End Sub

Private Sub cmdDoit_Click()
Dim C As String, SS As String, L As Integer, I As Integer
Dim CharCount As Integer, TS As String

CharCount = 0

If txtSearchChar.Text = "" Or txtSS.Text = "" Then
      MsgBox "You Must Enter a Character and a String to Search!"
      Exit Sub
Else
      C = txtSearchChar.Text
      SS = Trim$(txtSS.Text)
      L = Len(SS)

      For I = 1 To L
            If InStr(I, SS, C) <> 0 Then
                  CharCount = CharCount + 1
                  I = InStr(I, SS, C)
            End If
      Next I

      If CharCount = 1 Then
            TS = "time"
      Else
            TS = "times"
      End If
```

```
        MsgBox C & " occurs " & Str$(CharCount) & " " & TS & " in " & SS

End If

End Sub

Private Sub txtSearchChar_Click()
txtSearchChar.Text = ""
End Sub

Private Sub txtSS_Click()
txtSS.Text = ""
End Sub
```

The logic for the program occurs in the cmdDoIt_click routine. Each time the InStr function finds a match, CharCount is increased by one and the starting search character in the next InStr call is moved to one after the match. Finally, CharCount is checked to see whether the singular or plural of *time* should be used in the message box. That's all there is to it. When you run the program, enter a character to search for and a string to search, then press the DO IT! button. The application window should look like Figure 4.7.

Figure 4.7.
The String Manipulation application running.

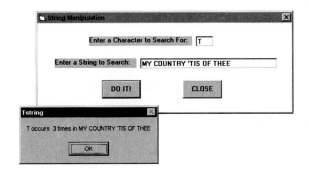

Flow Control Statements

Flow control statements—also called *control structures*—are the logical statements that cause programs to execute loops. These commands also tell programs under what conditions they should stop execution. In many ways, logical program control is the nuts and bolts of program creation. Control structures let you control the flow of your program's execution. If left unchecked by control-flow statements, a program's logic will flow through statements from left to right, top to bottom. Although some very simple programs can be written with this one-way flow, most of the power and utility of any programming language comes from its capability to change statement order with structures and loops. As such, it is a very important topic. Fortunately, Visual Basic includes a few very powerful flow control statements that are intuitive and easy to learn. There are two kinds of flow control statements: those that are primarily used to make decisions—If, Select Case—and those which are used to repeat operations—Do, For…Next and While…Wend. Each kind of statement has a number of variations. All are presented in Table 4.10.

Table 4.10. **Flow control statements.**

Statement: `If...Then...Else`

Purpose	Conditional execution; branching.
Syntax	`If condition then statements [Else elsestatements]`. Or, you can use the following, more versatile syntax:
	`If condition then [statements]`
	`[ElseIf condition-n Then[elseifstatements]]…`
	`[Else[elsestatements]]`
	`End If`

Subparts of the `If...Then...Else` Statement

Part	*Description*
`Condition`	One or more of the following two types of expressions: a numeric or string expression that evaluates to `True` or `False`. If condition is `Null`, the condition is treated as `False`. An expression of the form `TypeOf objectname Is objecttype`.
	The `objectname` is any object reference, and `objecttype` is any valid object type. The expression is `True` if `objectname` is of the object type specified by `objecttype`; otherwise, it is `False`.
`Statements`	One or more statements separated by line breaks; executed if condition is `True`.
`Condition-n`	Same as `condition`.
`Elseifstatements`	One or more statements executed if associated `condition`-n is `True`.
`Elsestatements`	One or more statements executed if no previous condition or `condition`-n expression is `True`.
Comments	You can use the single-line form (first syntax) for short, simple tests. However, the block form (second syntax) provides more structure and flexibility than the single-line form and is usually easier to read, maintain, and debug.

Statement: `Select Case`

Purpose	Execution depending on condition; branching.

Syntax	

```
Select Case testexpression
[Case expressionlist-n[statements-n]]...
[Case Else
[elsestatements]]
End Select
```

Subparts of the Select Case Statement

Part	Description
Testexpression	Any numeric or string expression.
Expressionlist-n	Delimited list of one or more of the following forms: expression, expression To expression, and Is comparisonoperator expression. The To keyword specifies a range of values. If you use the To keyword, the smaller value must appear before To. Use the Is keyword with comparison operators (except Is and Like) to specify a range of values. If not supplied, the Is keyword is automatically inserted.
Statements-n	One or more statements executed if testexpression matches any part of expressionlist-n.
Elsestatements	One or more statements executed if testexpression doesn't match any of the Case clause.
Comments	Use a single Select Case statement to replace a number of If...Then...Else statements. This provides greater clarity and more easily maintainable code.

Statement: Do...Loop

Purpose	Repeats a block of statements while a condition is True or until a condition becomes True.
Syntax	

```
Do [{While | Until} condition]
[statements]
[Exit Do]
[statements]
Loop
```

Or, you can use this equally valid syntax:

```
Do
[statements]
```

continues

Table 4.10. continued

	`[Exit Do]`
	`[statements]`
	`Loop [{While ¦ Until} condition]`
Statement: For...Next	
Purpose	Executes a block of code the number of times specified by a counter variable.
Syntax	`For counter = start To end [Step step]`
	`[statements]`
	`[Exit For]`
	`[statements]`
	`Next [counter]`

Subparts of the For...Next Statement:

Part	Description
`Counter`	Numeric variable used as a loop counter. The variable can't be an array element or an element of a user-defined type.
`Start`	Initial value of counter.
`End`	Final value of counter.
`Step`	Amount counter is changed each time through the loop. If not specified, step defaults to one. The step argument can be either positive or negative. The value of the step argument determines loop processing as follows:

Value	Loop executes if
Positive	Counter <= End
Negative	Counter >= End

After the loop starts and all statements in the loop have executed, `step` is added to `counter`. At this point, either the statements in the loop execute again (based on the same test that caused the loop to execute initially), or the loop is exited and execution continues with the statement following the `Next` statement.

Statements	One or more statements between `For` and `Next` that are executed the specified number of times.
Comments	`Do` loops work well when you don't know how many times the statements in your loop should be executed. When you know the code must be executed a specified number of times, a `For...Next` loop is more efficient.

Statement: `While...Wend`

Purpose	Executes a block of statements as long as a condition is true.
Syntax	`While condition`
	`[statements]`
	`Wend`

Generally the `Do` loop provides a more structured and powerful method of execution control.

Summary

Wow! This chapter offered a lot of information. But most of it is pretty straightforward and logical. And you don't have to remember it all. Just use the chapter as a reference guide.

In this chapter, you have learned about

- Visual Basic data types
- Modules, subroutines, and functions
- Scope and lifetime of variables and procedures
- Constants
- Fixed-size and dynamic arrays
- User-defined types
- String manipulation functions
- Flow-control statements

Also, you wrote a program that uses concepts of string manipulation to determine the number of times a given letter occurs in a string.

Just remember: In a language as rich as Visual Basic, no one remembers all the details about everything. What is important is to get a sense of the general concepts and the way they are implemented. You can always look up syntax. By reading this chapter, you've come a long way toward understanding key concepts that will help you master Visual Basic.

5

The Visual Basic Integrated Development Environment (IDE)

Whether Visual Basic is an old friend or a new one, this chapter will have something for you. Visual Basic 4 is the latest updated version of the world's most popular programming software. But, besides that, Visual Basic comes to the world in a brand new operating system—Windows 95—as well. It's as if Visual Basic has acquired a new wardrobe (its updated Integrated Development Environment, or IDE) and moved into a new, larger, more modern house (Windows 95) all at the same time. So, although Visual Basic will appear familiar to you—the toolbox, Properties window, Project window, and so on are still there—there are many new features just waiting for discovery.

This chapter will cover the following topics:

- The Visual Basic 4 tool and menu bars
- The toolbox and Properties window
- The Project and Code windows
- Design desktop options
- Setting compiler options
- Navigating within projects
- Visual Basic forms are ASCII text
- The Project (.vbp) file

First, the chapter will take a look at the big picture and describe what you initially see when you start Visual Basic 4 right after installing it. Then the focus will move to close-up looks at the various parts of the Visual Basic design desktop, comparing it to its predecessor Visual Basic 3.0. The chapter will continue with a discussion of the new Visual Basic 4 options that you can use to set the work environment to suit your tastes and work needs. The chapter will show you how to align and size controls using some new Visual Basic 4 tools. All of this, of course, is part of the Visual Basic Integrated Development Environment (IDE)—your programming workplace.

It's time for a tour of the Visual Basic desktop, starting from the top and the menu bar, and then working around to the toolbar, Properties window, and Project window.

Visual Basic Right Out of the Box

So, you've installed Visual Basic 4 (and Windows 95) and want to get going on building new applications right away. After you discover what is new in Windows 95, it's time to move on to Visual Basic 4 and become acquainted with its new looks and many new features and options. Figure 5.1 displays the Professional/Enterprise Edition of Visual Basic 4. (If you are using the Standard Edition, the IDE might appear slightly different.)

Figure 5.1.
The Visual Basic 4 Professional/Enterprise Edition right out of the box.

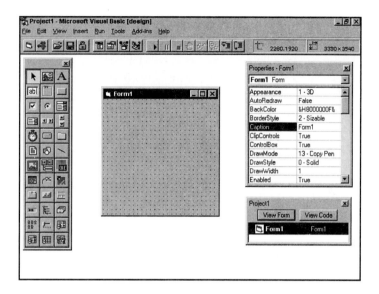

The first thing you might have noticed is that the toolbar buttons and toolbox tools are now in color! It's like moving from a black-and-white television to a color model. As you look around the Visual Basic 4 design desktop, you see that the titles on the menu bar have changed, several new buttons on the toolbar have been added (and some deleted), the toolbox contains many new controls, and the Properties window looks rather different.

Just for the sake of comparison, take a look at Figure 5.2. This figure displays Visual Basic 3 running under Windows 95.

Figure 5.2.
Visual Basic 3 running under Windows 95.

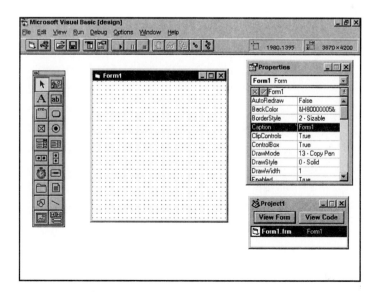

Now compare Figures 5.1 to 5.2. Of course, running Visual Basic 3.0 under Windows 95 makes it take on some of the looks of the new operating environment: The Control box is changed to a project icon, for instance. But the differences between the two Visual Basic versions are apparent when such IDE elements as the toolbar and toolbox are compared.

It's time to zoom in on the different parts of the IDE and see what has changed.

The New Menu Bar

The Visual Basic 4 menu bar contains some new menu titles and has left off some old ones. Many of the menu items have been redistributed to other menus, had their shortcuts changed, or have been removed from the IDE altogether.

The File Menu

As you probably know, the file menu is used to start a new project, open a project that already exists, or save a project. Using the file menu, you can also add files such as standard modules, class modules, and forms to a project, as well as print an application's code or forms as text or images. This is also where you can make an executable file (.exe) of your project.

The following table is a comparison of the menu items found on the File menu in Visual Basic 3 and Visual Basic 4. (This table is set up as the menus appear in the IDE with separator bars.)

Visual Basic 4 File Menu		Visual Basic 3.0 File Menu	
New Project		New Project	
Open Project	Ctrl+O	Open Project	
Save File	Ctrl+S	Save Project	
Save File As	Ctrl+A	Save Project As	
Save Project		New Form	
Save Project As		New MDI Form	
Add File	Ctrl+D	New Module	
Remove File		Add File	Ctrl+D
Print Setup		Remove File	
Print	Ctrl+P	Save File	Ctrl+S
Make EXE File		Save File As	Ctrl+A
Make OLE DLL File		Load Text	
Exit		Save Text	
		Print	Ctrl+P
		Make Exe File	
		Exit	

As you can see, some menu items have been moved to new positions on the menu and others are not there at all. The three Visual Basic 3 form creation items—New Form, New MDI Form, and New Module—have been moved from this menu to a new Visual Basic 4 menu: Insert. The Open Project item now has a shortcut key (Ctrl+O), and the Load Text and Save Text Visual Basic 3 menu items have been eliminated.

Note: The Load and Save text options have been deleted because Visual Basic 4 always saves in text format.

If you are running the Professional or Enterprise Editions of Visual Basic 4, there is a completely new item on the Visual Basic 4 menu: Make OLE DLL File. This item uses an OLE Automation Server with your custom properties and methods to create a Dynamic Linked Library (.dll). However, the only way to access the DLL's functionality is by using OLE Automation. All of this is discussed in Chapters 14 and 15.

The Edit Menu

The Edit menu is where you can perform cut, copy, and paste operations on controls and code; undo a change you have made (Undo, or Ctrl+Z, can be *very* useful!); and use the search engine to find or replace a specific word or phrase.

The Visual Basic 4 Edit menu is pretty similar to its Visual Basic 3 parent, but there are a few additions that you should note:

- In the previous version of Visual Basic, there were three Find menu items: Find (Ctrl+F), Find Next (F3), and Find Previous (Shift+F3). These three items have been replaced with a single Find item (Ctrl+F) on the Visual Basic 4 Edit menu. When you access the new Find dialog box, you will discover that a sophisticated search engine has been added to Visual Basic 4, incorporating the old functionality of the three menu items into one dialog box.

- The Replace item's shortcut has been changed from Ctrl+R to Ctrl+H.

- Below the Find and Replace section are two new menu items: Indent (Tab) and Outdent (Shift+Tab). These items can be used to indent or outdent entire sections (or a single line) of code. Just select the section of code you want to indent or outdent and select either menu item.

- The bottom section of the menu still contains some old friends, but with new shortcuts: Bring to Front (Ctrl+J), Send to Back (Ctrl+K), and Align to Grid. The new addition to this section—Lock Controls—is very handy. This item locks all the controls on a form so that they can't be inadvertently moved.

Tip: When you've completed the visual design of a form, either temporarily or permanently, lock down the controls. This will prevent you from accidentally moving them when you go to access the code menus for the controls by double-clicking.

What You See is What You Get: The View Menu

The Visual Basic 4 View menu is very similar to a page layout application's View menu. Using it, you can toggle between a form and the Code window, and open desktop windows such as the toolbox, toolbar, Color Palette, and Project and Properties windows.

With Visual Basic 4 the View menu has changed radically. There are several new additions that are really handy and one that deserves special mention—the *Object Browser*.

Here's a comparison of the old and new View menus:

Visual Basic 4 View Menu		*Visual Basic 3 View Menu*	
Code	F7	Code	F7
Form	Shift+F7	New Procedure	
Procedure Definition	Shift+F2	Next Procedure	Ctrl+Down
Last Position	Ctrl+Shift+F2	Previous Procedure	Ctrl+Up
Object Browser	F2	Procedure Definition	Shift+F2
Debug Window	Ctrl+G	Toolbar	
Project	Ctrl+R		
Properties	F4		
Toolbox			
Toolbar			
Color Palette			

The new View menu includes a new item, Form, that is a companion to the old menu item Code. These items let you quickly toggle between a form and its Code window.

The New Procedure item found on the old Visual Basic 3 menu has been moved to a new Visual Basic 4 menu, Insert, and is discussed in the next section.

The Visual Basic 4 View menu groups all of the desktop elements—the Debug window, Project window, Properties window, toolbox, toolbar, and Color Palette—all on one menu. In the previous version of Visual Basic, these items were split between the View menu and the window menu. (The Window menu does not exist in the new Visual Basic IDE. Its contents have been redistributed onto the View, Tools, and Add-Ins menus.)

The Object Browser

The Object Browser, a completely new tool found in Visual Basic 4, is accessed using the View menu. The Object Browser is a dialog box that lets you examine the contents of an object library for information about the objects contained in that library. If you have Visual Basic 4 open right now, open up the Object Browser and take a look at it. If you don't have Visual Basic 4 open, refer to Figure 5.3.

Figure 5.3.
The Visual Basic 4 Object
Browser.

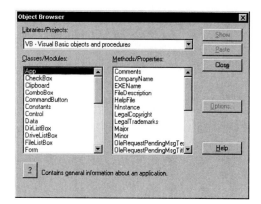

The Object Browser displays information in three levels. To use the browser, start at the top of the window and select from the available libraries—including your own open Visual Basic project—in the Libraries/Properties list box. Next, depending upon what you selected in the Libraries/Properties list box, use the Classes/Modules list box to select the module or class that you are interested in. Finally, select the object's procedure, method, or property from the Methods/Procedure list box.

The Object Browser is a very flexible tool that you can use to do the following:

- Quickly move from one spot to another in a large Visual Basic project. To move to a specific procedure in a certain module, select your project in the Libraries/Projects list box. Next, find the module's name and the procedure you want to view in the Classes/Modules and Methods/Properties list boxes, and then press the Show button. The procedure you selected appears in the Code window.

- Paste code skeletons or complicated lines of code into your projects. To do this, find the place in the Code window where you want to paste the code and place the cursor's insertion point there. Open the Object Browser using the View menu, or press F2. Select the library, the object, and then the property or method you want to use. Press the Paste button. The code is automatically transferred to the place where you left the cursor in the Code window.

- Display available classes from object libraries and procedures contained within a project, or explore libraries of other applications. If there are OLE servers installed on your system, the browser will also display OLE Automation objects from the servers. Anything you find in the browser you can use in a project.

For more information on this wonderful new tool, look in Visual Basic online help for the Object Browser (Visual Basic Help) topic.

The New Visual Basic 4 Insert Menu

Insert, a new menu on the toolbar, is the menu you use to add new forms or modules to a project. On this menu you find the old Visual Basic 3.0 File and View menu items New Form, New MDI Form, New Module, and New Procedure (without the *New* designation). These four items have been moved to a menu of their own and are accompanied by a completely new critter: the Class Module.

Here's what you'll find on the Insert menu:

Procedure
Form
MDI Form
Module
Class Module
File

The first item on the menu, Procedure, creates (of course) a new procedure; however, Visual Basic 4 has changed the way procedures are scoped. The next two figures show a comparison of the Visual Basic 3 New Procedure dialog box (shown in Figure 5.4) and the Visual Basic 4 Insert Procedure dialog box (shown in Figure 5.5) with its new options.

Figure 5.4.
The Visual Basic 3 New Procedure dialog box.

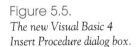

Figure 5.5.
The new Visual Basic 4 Insert Procedure dialog box.

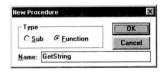

As you can see, there are now three possible procedure types—Sub, Function, and Property—and a choice of whether the procedure is Public or Private. Plus, by checking one box, you can easily make all local variables static. Scope is discussed in detail in Chapter 4, and creating your own properties and methods using procedures and class modules is discussed in Chapter 14.

The mention of class modules brings the discussion to this new Visual Basic 4 module type. As you probably already know, the standard .bas module is a container for procedures and declarations used by other parts of an application. A class module uses a .cls filename extension and is the foundation of object-oriented programming in Visual Basic. Using class modules, you can create new objects that include custom properties and methods, which can be used by other objects in an application. A complete discussion of creating objects using class modules can be found in Chapter 14, "Connecting to Other Windows Applications: OLE 2."

Ready, Set, Start: The Run Menu

The Visual Basic Run menu is used to run (start)—either straight through, line-by-line, or procedure-by-procedure—an application that you want to test. It also ends the application after it has been stopped by bugs and adds debugging tools such as breakpoints.

In version 4 of Visual Basic, the many items from the old Visual Basic 3 Run and Debug menus have been combined into one complete Run menu. Several new program start and debugging menu items have been added, and some have been renamed. Here's a comparison of the new Visual Basic 4 Run menu and the old Run and Debug menus.

Visual Basic 4 Run Menu		*Visual Basic 3 Run Menu*	
Start	F5	Start	F5
Start with Full Compile	Ctrl+F5	End	
End		Restart	Shift+F5
Restart	Shift+F5		
Step Into	F8	**Visual Basic 3 Debug Menu**	
Step Over	Shift+F8	Add Watch	
Step to Cursor	Ctrl+F8	Instant Watch	Shift+F9
Toggle Breakpoint	F9	Edit Watch	Ctrl+W
Clear All Breakpoints	Ctrl+Shift+F9	Calls	Ctrl+L
Set Next Statement	Ctrl+F9	Single Step	F8
Show Next Statement		Procedure Step	Shift+F8
		Toggle Breakpoint	
		Clear All Breakpoints	
		Set Next Statement	
		Show Next Statement	

Debugging and debugging tools are explained in-depth in Chapter 12; the new compile options, including the new Start with Full Compile menu item are discussed later in "The Options Dialog Box" section.

The New Tools Menu

The Tools menu is used to add debugging features such as a watch to a variable, check what procedure calls are uncompleted after an application has been run, add third-party controls to a project, and set the IDE's options.

This new menu is a combination of parts of the old Visual Basic 3.0 Debug, Options, and Window menus, with some excellent new additions.

The Visual Basic 4 Tools Menu

Add Watch	
Edit Watch	Ctrl+W
Instant Watch	Shift+F9
Calls	Ctrl+C
Menu Editor	Ctrl+E
Custom Controls	Ctrl+T
References	
Get	
Check Out	
Check In	
Undo Check Out	
Options	

If you are familiar with previous versions of Visual Basic, the first section of the menu that contains the Watch and Calls items is familiar to you. The next item, Menu Editor (Ctrl+E) is the old Visual Basic 3 Menu Designer (from the now defunct Windows menu) with a new shortcut designation.

Custom Controls, the next item down on the menu, is new to Visual Basic 4. This is where you go to add third-party .ocx controls and insertable application objects such as Excel or CorelDraw to a project's toolbox. Adding custom controls to projects is discussed in Chapter 3 and Chapter 18.

Another new Visual Basic 4 menu item, References, is used to make another application's objects available to your code by setting a reference to that application's object library. This menu item is used extensively when creating custom OLE Automation Servers. An in-depth look at the References dialog box is available in Chapter 14.

The final item on the menu, Options, is a combination of the two items found on the old Visual Basic 3 Options menu with some new features. If you select the Option menu item, an Options dialog box with several tabs—Environment, Project, Editor, and Advanced—opens on the screen.

The Options Dialog Box

As you can see in Figure 5.6, there are four tab pages that present groups of options. The following list shows what each tab page lets you do.

Figure 5.6.
The Visual Basic 4 Options dialog box.

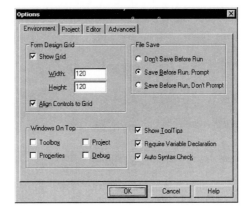

Environment:

- Set grid dot spacing, whether the grid will show, and whether controls drawn on forms will snap to the grid.
- Set File Save options: whether the project is saved before it runs and whether the IDE prompts you to save the project.
- Select windows that will always be on top.
- Show tooltips (balloon help) and set required variable declaration (using the Option Explicit statement) and syntax checking.

Project:

- Set the Start-Up form and project name.
- Connect a help file to a project.
- Set the Start Mode. (This is used when creating OLE Servers and is discussed in Chapter 14.)
- Set the name of the .exe file for the current project.
- Create a brief description of the application. (This is used when the project's object library is displayed in the References and Object Browser windows and is discussed in Chapter 14.)

Editor:

- Set the Code window environment, including special fonts and colors for specific text types such as Comment Text, Keyword Text, Syntax Error Text, and so on.

- Set the number of spaces for a tab's width.

- Determine how code is viewed: The Full Module view check box lets you see every procedure in the Code window at once, instead of viewing the code one procedure at a time.

Advanced:

- Set project loading options, including upgrading custom controls from .vbx to .ocx and background loading. (This only applies if there is an .ocx control upgrade available on your system.)

- Select error trapping options: Break on all errors, unhandled errors, or in a Class Module.

- Set OLE DLL restrictions (available only with the Professional and Enterprise Editions of Visual Basic 4). This is used for testing a DLL within a project and makes the DLL behave as it would when used in-process with another application. (Check out Chapter 14 for a discussion of this topic.)

- Set compile options (see the following sidebar).

- Add command line and conditional compilation arguments.

Setting the New Compile Options

Visual Basic 4 comes with several new compile options located on various menus.

- Found under the Run menu, Start with Full Compile makes sure a program is fully compiled before it starts. This option should be used if you are testing an OLE server project.

- Two check boxes found on the Advanced tab page of the Options dialog box, Compile on Demand and Background Compile, work together. Compile on Demand sets whether an application is fully compiled before it starts or whether it is compiled as the code is needed (which lets the program start faster). Background Compile only works if the Compile on Demand item is selected. If this option is checked, a project is compiled in the background during run-time when the computer is idle.

- At the bottom of the Advanced tab page of the Options dialog box is a text box that accepts Conditional Compilation Arguments. These arguments let you selectively compile specific parts of an application.

The Visual Basic 4 *Operating Environment* manual deals extensively with these compilation options.

The New Add-In Menu

There are three available items on the new Visual Basic 4 Add-In menu: Data Manager, Report Manager, and Add-In Manager. The first two items were available on the (now extinct) Visual Basic 3 Window menu. The third item, Add-In Manager, is brand new to Visual Basic 4. With this option, you can select and manage add-ins (OLE Servers), which are extensions that can add special capabilities to the Visual Basic development environment. For instance, if you are using the Professional or Enterprise Editions of Visual Basic 4, you can create custom OLE servers. These OLE servers are add-ins that you can use in your applications. Two sample applications that ship with Visual Basic 4, Spy.vbp and Align.vbp, found in the Visual Basic Samples directory, demonstrate and use add-in techniques. (Align.vbp, an OLE DLL, is used in the "Aligning Controls on a Form" section later in this chapter.) If you assign a new add-in, Visual Basic saves that information in the [Add-Ins16] or [Add-Ins32] sections of Vb.ini.

Note: Microsoft has recommended that programmers use the Registry to store their information, but Microsoft programs such as Visual Basic still use INI files. INI files are an acceptable way to store information about the configuration of a program for a while.

What's New on the Help Menu

The Visual Basic 4 Help menu contains the same items that it did in release 3.0: Contents, Search for Help On…, Obtaining Technical Support, Learning Microsoft Visual Basic, and About Microsoft Visual Basic. The Learning Microsoft Visual Basic item is especially useful. It consists of nine online lessons that cover topics ranging from "How Visual Basic Works" to "Working with Forms and Controls" to "Introduction to OLE Automation Objects."

If you are running the Professional or Enterprise Editions of Visual Basic 4, Visual Basic Books Online is a really handy addition. This menu item gives you access to all Visual Basic 4 documentation in one place. Using Visual Basic Books Online, you can find all the available information from the various Help libraries with one search. There are three ways to use Visual Basic Books Online.

Note: The interface used for Visual Basic 4's Books Online is very similar to the interface used by Microsoft on both its Technet and Developer Network browsers. If you've used either one of these products, you will be right at home with Visual Basic Books Online.

1. Use the table of contents that appears at the left of the window (see Figure 5.7) and navigate through each library just as you would with the Windows 95 Explorer.

Figure 5.7.
Visual Basic Books Online. Using the Contents to search for a topic.

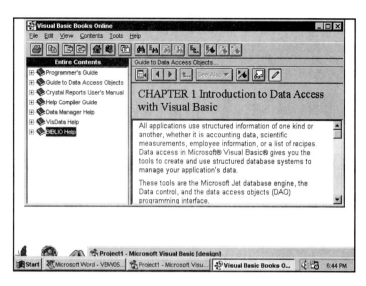

2. Select Query from the Tools menu (or press Ctrl+F) to search all or selected libraries for a specific word or phrase, as shown in Figure 5.8.

Figure 5.8.
The Query dialog box.

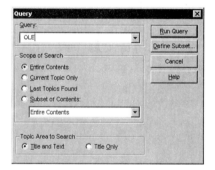

3. Use the alphabetical keyword index to search for specific keywords in all or selected libraries.

Context-Sensitive Help

Release 4 of Visual Basic comes with context-sensitive help. This means a help topic for a specific part of the Visual Basic IDE can be accessed without going through the help menu. For instance, to open the help topic for any control in the toolbox, select the control in question using the mouse, and then press F1 on the keyboard. The help topic for that control will appear on the screen. For another example, to quickly reach the help topic for any keyword in the Code window, place the cursor within that keyword and press F1.

Here's a list of what parts of the Visual Basic IDE are context-sensitive:

- All Visual Basic windows: the Code window, the Properties window, and so on
- Toolbox controls
- Objects (controls) on a form
- The individual properties found within the Properties window
- Event procedures in the Code window
- Keywords including statements, events, properties, methods, functions, and so on
- Error messages

Shortcuts

Keyboard shortcuts can make any task easier and faster, be it one performed in a word processing application or a page layout program. Visual Basic makes good use of mnemonic shortcuts that speed you on your way while designing an application.

For use as a handy reference guide, here is a list of Visual Basic 4's menu shortcuts. Many of them are new or changed from the previous version. They are listed alphabetically by their functionality.

Function	Shortcut
Add File	Ctrl+D
Bring to Front	Ctrl+J
Calls	Ctrl+L
Clear All Breakpoints	Ctrl+Shift+F9
Code Window	F7
Copy	Ctrl+C
Custom Controls	Ctrl+T
Cut	Ctrl+X
Delete	Del
Debug Window	Ctrl+G
Edit Watch	Ctrl+W
Find	Ctrl+F
Form	Shift+F7
Help Contents	F1
Indent	Tab

continues

Function	Shortcut
Instant Watch	Shift+F9
Last Position	Ctrl+Shift+F2
Menu Editor	Ctrl+E
Object Browser	F2
Open Project	Ctrl+O
Outdent	Shift+Tab
Paste	Ctrl+V
Print	Ctrl+P
Procedure Definition	Shift+F2
Project Window	Ctrl+R
Properties Window	F4
Replace	Ctrl+H
Restart	Shift+F5
Save File	Ctrl+S
Save File As	Ctrl+A
Send to Back	Ctrl+K
Set Next Statement	Ctrl+F9
Start	F5
Start with Full Compile	Ctrl+F5
Step Into	F8
Step to Cursor	Ctrl+F8
Step Over	Shift+F8
Stop Running a Project	Ctrl+Break
Toggle Breakpoint	F9
Undo	Ctrl+Z

There are other shortcuts that are functional, depending upon the window—Code window, Form window, Menu Editor window, and so on—that you are using. All of these shortcuts are listed in Visual Basic's online Help under the "Shortcut keys, design environment" topic.

The New Pop-Up Menus

Visual Basic 4 comes with a handy new feature: *pop-up menus* (also called *context menus*). These menus provide easy access to actions that are frequently performed when developing an application. To access a pop-up menu, position the mouse pointer over the object you are working with and click the right mouse button. The pop-up menu appears on the screen right next to the object.

The Toolbar

Moving down the screen from the menu bar is the new Visual Basic 4 toolbar. It is used to quickly access commonly used commands such as adding a form or module to a project, opening the Menu Editor window, running an application, and so on.

The Visual Basic 4 toolbar has some new additions, as shown in Figure 5.9.

Figure 5.9.
The Visual Basic 4 toolbar.

Finding Out what All Those Buttons Do Using Balloon Help

Visual Basic 4 comes complete with Tool Tips (also known as balloon help). When you place the mouse pointer over a button on the toolbar or the toolbox, a small window appears that describes what the button does. Figure 5.10 shows the tooltip for the save project button.

Figure 5.10.
A Visual Basic 4 tooltip.

The Visual Basic 4 Toolbox

As you can see in Figure 5.12, the Visual Basic Professional/Enterprise Edition toolbox is loaded with a multitude of tools—36 to be exact. This collection is made up of 21 standard controls and 15 custom controls.

The standard controls are contained within the Visual Basic .exe file and are always included in the toolbox. Figure 5.11 shows the standard controls that are contained in the toolbox.

Custom controls, on the other hand, are insertable objects (.ocx controls or application objects such as Excel) that can be added to or removed from the toolbox as you wish. The custom controls that are standard with the Visual Basic 4 Professional/Enterprise editions are shown in Figure 5.12.

Figure 5.11.
Visual Basic's standard controls. (These controls cannot be removed from the toolbox.)

Figure 5.12.
The Custom Controls in the Visual Basic 4 Professional/ Enterprise Edition.

You can change which custom controls are automatically loaded into a new 32-bit project by editing the Auto32ld.vbp file (use the Autoload.vbp file for 16-bit setup). To edit this file, select Open Project from the Visual Basic File menu. In the Open Project dialog box select Auto32ld.vbp, and then click the Open button. To remove a custom control, select Custom Controls from the Tools menu and uncheck the boxes of the control you want to remove. Click OK to close the Custom Control dialog box. Then save the Auto32ld project and close it. When you open a new project, the control that you removed will not be loaded. For more information about the Auto32ld.vbp file and what you can add for automatic project loading, see Chapter 4, "Managing Projects," of the *Programmer's Guide* that ships with Visual Basic 4.

The New Data-Bound Custom Controls

There are three new data-bound controls that will help you with building database applications. They include the data-bound list box, data-bound combo box, and data-bound grid.

In order to use these controls, you need to add them to your project using the Custom Controls dialog box found under the Tools menu. Also, you must register the Data Access Object (DAO) library using the References dialog box found under the Tools menu. A data access object is an object that is defined by the Microsoft Jet database engine. For more information about the Jet database engine and DAO, look in Visual Basic online help under Data Access Overview.

Aligning Controls on a Form

A few nifty new items have been added to Visual Basic 4 that will assist in aligning and sizing controls.

The first one, available in all editions of Visual Basic, is a keyboard operated nudge. Select the control whose width or height you want to change, and hold down the Shift key while pressing the arrow buttons. For example, Shift+Right Arrow stretches a control one grid width to the right; Shift+Down Arrow stretches a control one grid width larger vertically.

This next alignment/sizing tool is only available with the Professional and Enterprise Editions of Visual Basic 4. The tool is actually a project, Align.vbp, that is included in the Samples directory. Align.vbp is actually an OLE DLL with specially coded methods that align and size controls, using their Height, Width, Top, and Left properties. (It's actually very educational to look at Align.vbp's code to see how it works.) Here's how you use this Alignment tool in your projects:

1. Start Visual Basic and open the Align.vbp project.
2. Run the application. When you do, no forms appear on the screen (which is the way it's supposed to be). Minimize the instance of Visual Basic that is running the application.
3. Start another instance of Visual Basic and open the project in which you want to use the alignment/sizing tools, or start a new project.
4. Using the Add-Ins menu, select the Add-In Manager item to open that dialog box. In the Add-In Manager dialog box, put an X in the Align Sample Add-In check box, and then click OK.

That's it! Take a look at your Add-Ins menu now. Align and Size, two new items with fly-out menus, have been added to the menu. To align or size controls, select the controls you want to move or size, and click on the appropriate menu item such as Align | Bottom Align or Size | Width. These two add-in menu items are shown in Figure 5.13.

The About item found under the Align menu item gives a brief description of how the add-in works.

Figure 5.13.
The Align and Size add-in
menu items.

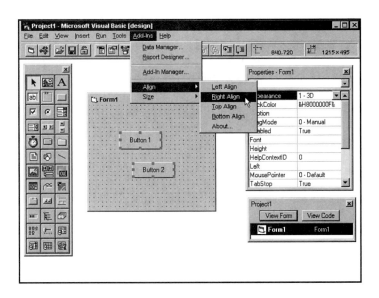

Controls and Their Properties

It's time to move past the Visual Basic 4 IDE to the much improved Properties window, shown in Figure 5.14. As you probably know, this window is used to set a control's design-time properties. To select the module, form, or control whose properties you want to set, either click on the object or select it from the Object box at the top of the Properties window.

Figure 5.14.
The Visual Basic 4
Properties window.

A few new features are incorporated into the Properties window:

* To set a property, select the property's name from the list on the left side of the window. In the Settings box to the right of the property, type or select the new property setting. (Those who are familiar with Visual Basic 3 will realize what a great change this is. In the previous version of Visual Basic, the programmer had to select the property's name, and then move to the top of the Properties window to change the property setting.)

- To set a property that has predefined settings, click on the property's Settings box and then click the Properties button that appears to the right of the Settings box. (A Settings box with a down arrow is shown in Figure 5.14.) There are two types of Settings boxes: those with a down arrow that display a list of possible settings (such as the Cancel property), and those with an ellipsis (…) that display a dialog box (such as the Font property).

The Project Window

The next window, the Project window (shown in Figure 5.15), is much as it was in Visual Basic 3.0. You can use it to view forms and modules or view the Code window associated with a particular object.

Figure 5.15.
The Visual Basic 4 Project window for the sample Align project.

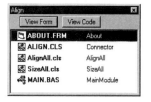

The New Project File Extension: .vbp

Visual Basic 4 uses a new file extension when a project is saved. In previous versions, the project extension was .mak (as in MyProg.mak). Now, the project file extension is .vbp (as in MyProg.vbp), which stands for Visual Basic Project.

Each time you save a project, Visual Basic updates the .vbp project file, which contains the same file list that appears in the Project window. But the project file contains much more than just the information shown in the Project window. It contains everything the computer needs to know about a project, from the project's name to what help file is associated with the project. The .frm and .vbp files are actually ASCII text files that you can view in any ASCII editor such as Notepad. Figure 5.16 shows the Align sample application's project file.

For in-depth information on the various lines that can appear in a .vbp project file, look in Appendix A of the Visual Basic *Programmer's Guide*, which ships with Visual Basic 4.

Figure 5.16.
Part of a .vbp project file displayed in Notepad.

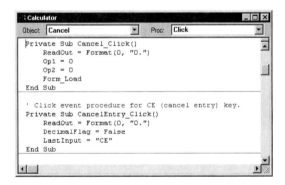

```
Class=Connector; ALIGN.CLS
Module=MainModule; MAIN.BAS
Class=AlignAll; AlignAll.cls
Class=SizeAll; SizeAll.cls
Form=ABOUT.FRM
ProjWinSize=87,734,250,343
ProjWinShow=2
HelpFile=""
ExeName32="Align32.DLL"
ExeName="Align16.EXE"
Command=""
Name="Align"
HelpContextID="0"
StartMode=1
Description="Align Addin Sample"
VersionCompatible32="0"
VersionCompatible=""
MajorVer=1
MinorVer=0
RevisionVer=0
AutoIncrementVer=0
ServerSupportFiles=0
VersionCompanyName=" "
```

The Code Window

The last IDE window to be explored in this chapter is the Code window. This is where you, the programmer, add the behind-the-scenes wiring that makes the visual part of the application—the forms—do what it's supposed to do. An example of what a Visual Basic code window looks like appears in Figure 5.17.

Figure 15.17.
The Visual Basic 4 Code window.

```
Object: Cancel          Proc: Click
Private Sub Cancel_Click()
    ReadOut = Format(0, "0.")
    Op1 = 0
    Op2 = 0
    Form_Load
End Sub

' Click event procedure for CE (cancel entry) key.
Private Sub CancelEntry_Click()
    ReadOut = Format(0, "0.")
    DecimalFlag = False
    LastInput = "CE"
End Sub
```

For those of you who are familiar with prior releases of Visual Basic, you have probably noticed that the Visual Basic 4 Code window looks pretty much the same, but there is a fundamental change as to how code is viewed.

Using the Options dialog box described earlier in "The New Tools Menu" section of this chapter, you can change many aspects of the code's appearance in the window, including the fonts used, font size, text color, and how the code is actually viewed. There are two ways to view the code in Visual

Basic 4. The first, the default for Visual Basic, is procedure-by-procedure view. This lets you see only one procedure at a time (for example, only the Click event for a command button). The other way to view code is by checking Full Module View on the Editor Page of the Options dialog box. This lets you see every procedure contained in a module at one time. To move to another event, just scroll down the Code window.

Unfortunately, the code that makes an application work usually has to be debugged, too. The Code window contains some sophisticated tools to help with the debugging process. For a discussion about using the debugging tools built into the Code window, see Chapter 12.

Summary

This chapter took you for a tour of the Visual Basic 4 IDE. On the first IDE tour stop, you discovered what was new about the Visual Basic 4 menu bar: the new menus on the menu bar, the locations where some old menu items had been redistributed, and the functionality of new menu items. After that, the tour moved to the toolbar, where you discovered which old buttons have been removed and which new ones have been added, as well as what each button does. Next, you took a look at the toolbox, what each tool does, and which controls can be removed from the toolbox.

From there, the Visual Basic 4 IDE tour moved on to three important windows: the Properties, Project, and Code windows. In the discussion of the Properties window, you discovered the new way that properties' values are set in Visual Basic 4. While looking at the Code window, you saw that there are now two ways to view a project's code.

With the release of Visual Basic 4, this flexible and powerful programming tool has been given an IDE worthy of its development capabilities. Those unfamiliar with previous versions of Visual Basic will find using the new and updated tools that the Visual Basic programming environment supplies easy and efficient. For those who are experienced Visual Basic programmers, this IDE is an old friend whose strong points have been improved and expanded.

6

Menus

This chapter examines a very important feature of Windows: menus. You will see how easy it is to add custom menus to your programs. This chapter covers the following topics:

- Designing menus and adding them to programs
- Enabling and disabling menu items and menus
- Menu access keys
- Menu shortcut keys
- Separator bars
- How to end a Visual Basic program
- Adding check marks to menu items
- Pop-up menus
- Adding menu items at runtime
- Creating a font menu that lets the user select fonts
- Giving programs their own icons in Windows 95

In addition, you will write a demonstration Tic-Tac-Toe Game. The idea behind this exercise is to see control arrays at work. It does not include the code to play tic-tac-toe, although the buttons can be clicked, making them display X or O. Also, you will write a phone book application in which you will add people's names to a menu. Finally, you will start to work on building the Editor application. When it is finished, the Editor will let you read in files up to 64 KB, edit them, and write them back out. Menus are a big part of any Windows application, and creating them is a good skill to have.

The next step in creating useful Windows applications is to add menus. In fact, you have already used many menus in Visual Basic. For example, Visual Basic's File menu appears in Figure 6.1 with the various parts labeled.

Figure 6.1.
The Visual Basic File menu.

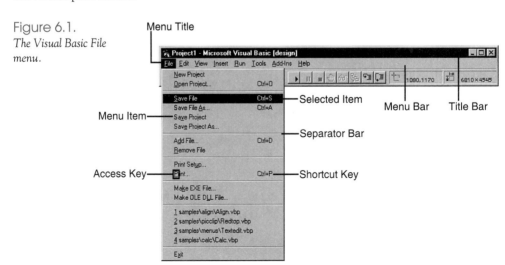

There are a number of elements in a menu that you should be familiar with before you read about building them. The first of these elements, of course, is the *menu bar*, which indicates all the menus that are currently available in an application. The menu bar appears immediately below the *title bar* (the caption bar that reads "Project1 - Microsoft Visual Basic [design]") on the form and contains one or more *menu titles*. When a menu title such as File is clicked, a menu containing a list of *menu items* drops down. Menu items can include commands such as Open and Save As…, separator bars, and submenu items. Each menu item that the user sees corresponds to a menu control defined in the Menu Editor.

Releasing the mouse button while an item is selected chooses that item. If the item is followed by an ellipsis (…), it opens a dialog box that can read more information from the user. In addition, items can be *grayed* or *disabled*. They can also be *checked* with a check mark (✓) by them, indicating that a certain option has been turned on. Finally, menu items can be grouped together with a *separator bar*, as shown in Figure 6.1. As you can see in Figure 6.1, all the save options are grouped together. Similarly, both print items are also grouped together. You will explore most of these menu parts— menu bars, menu items, disabled items, checked items, and separator bars—in this chapter.

Designing and implementing menus in Visual Basic is not difficult. In this chapter, you will see a number of examples. In particular, you will start a small file editing program that will be finished later, after you learn the mechanics of loading and saving files. You will also update the alarm clock application into a menu-driven program. However, the first example will be a Tic-Tac-Toe Game. There is not enough space here to develop the code necessary to let the computer play; games can be long programs to write. Therefore, this will be a game for two human players.

A Menu-Driven Tic-Tac-Toe Game

Start the Tic-Tac-Toe Game by beginning a new Visual Basic project. For this project, you will need a form and nine command buttons.

There is an easy and quick way to create the command buttons and place them in an array at the same time. Place the first one on the form, and then resize and reposition it in the upper-left corner. Next, change its Name property to cmdTTT and remove the text from the Caption property. Finally, scroll to the Font property and select it. Click the Property button that appears to the right of the Settings box, and then change the font style to Bold and the font size to 18. Click OK. Now copy the command button by using the Copy item from the Edit menu, by pressing Ctrl+C, or by using the pop-up menu activated by the right mouse button. Select the form and paste the new buttons on by using the Paste item from the Edit menu, by pressing Ctrl+V, or by using the right mouse button pop-up menu. When you create the second button by pasting it in, a Visual Basic window opens, asking whether you want to create a control array. Answer yes. Writing one click procedure will be much easier than writing nine!

Place the buttons as shown in Figure 6.2. Then, using Table 6.1, change the objects' properties. Save the form and project by selecting the Save Project item from the File menu. Save the form as Tictac.frm and the project as Tictac.vbp.

Figure 6.2.
The Tic-Tac-Toe template.

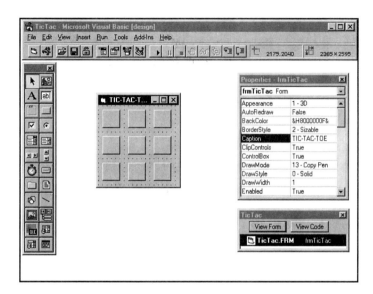

Table 6.1. Property settings for the Tic-Tac-Toe form.

Object	Property	Setting
Form	Appearance	1-3D
	Caption	TIC-TAC-TOE
	MinButton	False
	MaxButton	False
	Name	frmTicTac
Command Button	Caption	(None)
	Font	Style: Bold Size: 18
	Index	0
	Name	cmdTTT
Command Button	Caption	(None)
	Font	Style: Bold Size: 18
	Index	1
	Name	cmdTTT

Object	Property	Setting
Command Button	Caption	(None)
	Font	Style: Bold Size: 18
	Index	2
	Name	cmdTTT
Command Button	Caption	(None)
	Font	Style: Bold Size: 18
	Index	3
	Name	cmdTTT
Command Button	Caption	(None)
	Font	Style: Bold Size: 18
	Index	4
	Name	cmdTTT
Command Button	Caption	(None)
	Font	Style: Bold Size: 18
	Index	5
	Name	cmdTTT
Command Button	Caption	(None)
	Font	Style: Bold Size: 18
	Index	6
	Name	cmdTTT
Command Button	Caption	(None)
	Font	Style: Bold Size: 18
	Index	7
	Name	cmdTTT

continues

Table 6.1. **continued**

Object	Property	Setting
Command Button	`Caption`	(None)
	`Font`	Style: Bold
		Size: 18
	`Index`	8
	`Name`	cmdTTT

Now, you can immediately write the procedure that operates the control array. Double-click on a command button to open the Code window.

Because the command buttons are grouped in an array, Visual Basic automatically passes an *Index argument* to the Click event subroutine. If you arranged the buttons in random order on the form, don't worry. In this case, it doesn't matter which index belongs to which button because the button's caption is set up like this: `cmdTTT(Index).Caption`.

However, the program has to know when to put an X or an O on a particular button. That's easy to do by declaring a public variable called `XTurn`. When `XTurn` is `True`, it is X's turn; when it is `False`, it is O's turn. You can declare that variable by adding a module (select Module from the Insert menu) and making the following declaration:

```
Public XTurn As Boolean
```

After entering the variable declaration, change the module's `Name` property to `TicTac`, and save the module using the Save Form item from the File menu. Name it Tictac.bas. (You should know that this public variable, `XTurn`, could have been placed in the form's `(General) (declarations)` section instead, because this application only contains one form.)

Setting the button's `Caption` property to X or O is easy now. You can do it as follows:

```
Private Sub cmdTTT_Click(Index As Integer)
    If (XTurn) Then
            cmdTTT(Index).Caption = "X"
            XTurn = False
    Else
            cmdTTT(Index).Caption = "0"
            XTurn = True
    End If
End Sub
```

You need to do one other thing before you are ready to use this application: You must set `XTurn` to True. This is because x goes first in the game of tic-tac-toe. Therefore, enter the following code in the `form_load` procedure:

```
XTurn = True
```

This alternates the characters that appear when the user clicks the different command buttons. Notice that in this simple program you did not check whether the button had been clicked already or whether someone had won the game. These are two things you should do if you intend to develop this into a realistic Tic-Tac-Toe Game.

Note: In Chapter 7 you will revisit the Tic-Tac-Toe Game and prevent someone from clicking on a square that has already been clicked on.

The user should also be given some way to start over. A good way to do this is to add a New Game option, which involves initializing the xTurn variable and clearing all the command buttons that make up the squares on the tic-tac-toe board. This is where menus come into play, because New Game is exactly the kind of item found in a menu. In addition, an Exit item should be added to the menu because all applications that have menus should have an Exit item.

Adding a Menu to the Tic-Tac-Toe Game

Designing menus in Visual Basic is not as hard as you might expect. Actually, it's rather easy. Each menu item is a control itself, and the primary event associated with it is the Click event. To get these new types of controls onto the form, however, you have to design them first, using the Menu Editor. They cannot simply be painted on the form using the toolbox tools.

To open the Menu Editor onto the screen, select Menu Editor from the Tools menu, press Ctrl+E, or use the right mouse button pop-up menu. The Menu Editor appears on your screen as pictured in Figure 6.3.

Figure 6.3.
The Visual Basic Menu Editor.

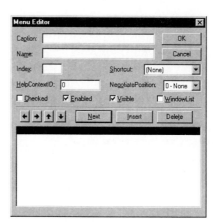

You can get started on your menu by specifying the menu's caption. Call it File because applications often have a File menu, and that is where the user expects to find the Exit item. (After you learn about file handling in Chapter 8, "File Handling in Visual Basic," you can modify the Tic-Tac-Toe Game to save the current game to a file.) To create a File menu so that File will appear on the menu bar, type File in the Caption text box at the top of the Menu Editor as shown in Figure 6.4. In addition, each menu item has to be given a name so that the program can refer to it. (This enables you to switch menus around in the menu bar or change them altogether, as you will see later.) For this menu title, type the name mnuFile in the Name text box.

Figure 6.4.
The Menu Editor with a File caption and name.

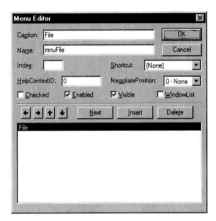

Menu-Naming Conventions

When naming menu items, you should try to follow these guidelines:

- Item names should be unique within a menu, but they can be repeated in different menus to represent similar or different actions.

- Item names can be single, compound, or multiple words.

- Each item name should have a unique mnemonic access character for users who choose commands with keyboards. The access character should be the first letter of the menu title, unless another letter offers a stronger mnemonic link; no two menu titles should use the same access character. (Assigning access and shortcut keys will be discussed later in this chapter.)

- An ellipsis, (...), should follow names of commands that require more information before they can be completed.

- Keep the item names short. This makes finding the correct menu Click event easier. Also, if your application is localized into another language, the length of words tends to increase by approximately 30 percent, and you might not have enough space to adequately list all menu items.

Although you can create your own naming conventions, the following syntax has been generally adopted:

Menu Element	Syntax	Example
Menu Title	mnu*MenuTitle*	mnuFile
Menu Item	mnu*MenuTitle*Item	mnuFileExit
Menu Array Items	mnu*MenuTitle*Array	mnuFileMRU
Submenu Item	mnu*SubmenuTitle*Item	mnuFontSize

You might have noted that as you typed the word File in the Caption box, the same word appeared in the main list box below it. As you can see in Figure 6.4, File is highlighted in the main list box. This is where the menus you are designing will appear. So far, you only have the caption of one menu: File. The next step is to add the New Game and Exit items.

The insertion point should be right after the last name you typed in the Name text box (mnuFile). Press Enter on the keyboard (notice that the Next button has the focus, so when you press the Enter key, the Next button gets pushed), or click on the Next button with the mouse pointer. This ends the item and moves the highlight bar in the main list box down one line. The Caption and Name boxes are automatically cleared in preparation for receiving the next menu item. Type New Game in the Caption text box, and in the Name text box type mnuFileNewGame (meaning the New Game item in the File menu). Again, the text New Game appears in the main list box. This item should be the first menu item in the File menu. For that reason, click the right-pointing arrow in the bar that is above and to the left of the main list box. When you do this, the New Game entry is indented with four dots in the list box, as in Figure 6.5.

Figure 6.5.
The Menu Editor showing
New Game indented.

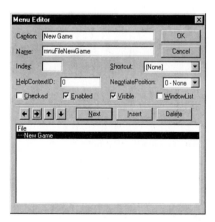

The indent means that New Game is an item in the File menu, not a menu itself. In fact, New Game is the first item. Now, use the keyboard to press Enter or the mouse to click the Next button again; as a result, the main list box highlight bar moves down one more line. Once again, the Caption and Name text boxes are cleared.

What About Menus Within Menus?

Visual Basic enables you to have menus within menus. You do this by using successive levels of indentation. Each menu you create can include up to four levels of *submenus*. A submenu branches off another menu to display its own menu items.

The next item in the File menu is Exit. Type Exit in the Caption text box and then type mnuFileExit in the Name text box. Notice that you did not have to click the right pointing arrow again to indent Exit in the list box. It was indented automatically for you as you continued to add items to the File menu. If you wanted to remove the automatic indentation, you would click on the arrow pointing left above the main list box. Your menu design is now complete and is shown in Figure 6.6.

Figure 6.6.

The completed menu in the Menu Editor.

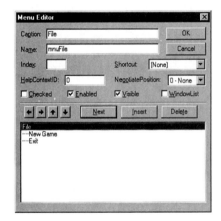

Close the Menu Editor by clicking OK. When you do, you will see that a File menu has been added to the Tic-Tac-Toe Game template, as shown in Figure 6.7.

As mentioned earlier, the design process primarily adds controls to the template. Now that you have added the controls, you can treat them like any other controls. Consequently, you can attach code to them just as easily. To see how this works, click on the File menu in the tic-tac-toe menu bar. The menu opens showing the two items you put in, New Game and Exit, as in Figure 6.8.

Figure 6.7.
The Tic-Tac-Toe template
with a File menu.

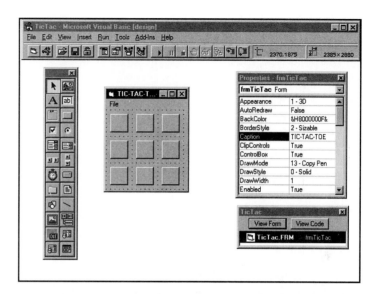

Figure 6.8.
The File menu open on the
Tic-Tac-Toe template.

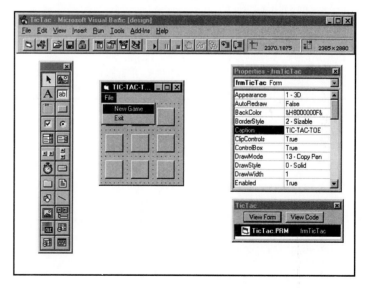

These two menu items are simply controls, like buttons or text boxes. To open the Code Window, for example, just click on the New Game item. The Code Window opens, holding a Sub procedure code skeleton like this (recall that you gave the New Game item a name of mnuFileNewGame):

```
Private Sub mnuFileNewGame_Click()

End Sub
```

When the user chooses this item, this Sub procedure is executed. In other words, you will be using the Click event for menu items, just as you did for command buttons. In this case, the user wants to start a new Tic-Tac-Toe Game, so you will have to reset the variable called XTurn like this:

```
Private Sub mnuFileNewGame_Click()

    :

    XTurn = True

    :

End Sub
```

Coding Menu Items

It is a good idea not to add too much code to a menu's Click event. A better programming practice would be to call a subroutine from the menu's event rather than put extensive code there. The reason for this is that another control, such as a command button, might have the same functionality as the menu. In that situation, placing code in one routine that is called from both the menu item and the command button would save time, as well as simplify logic and debugging.

Next, you need to set the Caption property of each command button to "". As an added touch, you can set the focus (the thick black outline that appears around a command button) to the top left button, cmdTTT(0), although this is not necessary.

```
Private Sub mnuFileNewGame_Click()
    Dim ButtonCount As Integer

    XTurn = True

    For ButtonCount = 0 To 8
        cmdTTT(ButtonCount).Caption = ""
    Next ButtonCount

    cmdTTT(0).SetFocus
End Sub
```

Here, you are using a For...Next loop to move from one command button to the next. The variable ButtonCount is used as the counter. (You might recall that this programming syntax was discussed in Chapter 4, "Programming in Visual Basic.")

Now the New Game item in the File menu is active. Making the Exit option active is even easier. Open the File menu on frmTicTac and click on the Exit item. A new Sub procedure template appears: mnuFileExit_Click(). All you want to do here is close the form. To do that use the Unload statement.

```
Private Sub mnuFileExit_Click()
      Unload frmTicTac
End Sub
```

Finally, you want to terminate the program, so you should use the new Visual Basic 4 Sub procedure Terminate. Using the Object list box in the Code window, scroll to and select Form. Then, using the Procedure list box, scroll to and select Terminate. The new Sub procedure appears in the Code window. Here you want to use the End statement, which terminates the program.

```
Private Sub Form_Terminate()
      End
End Sub
```

Terminate and Initialize: Two New Form Events

Terminate and Initialize are new Form events in Visual Basic 4. They occur, respectively, after the form has been unloaded from memory (such as after the Form Unload event) and before a form is loaded into memory (such as before the Form Load event).

Using the Unload and End statements is not strictly necessary. Thus, it is not essential that the End statement be placed in the tic-tac-toe's Form event. Unloading all forms will end an application in and of itself automatically in most cases. However, employing the Unload and End statements as described earlier is a good programming practice.

And that's it for the Tic-Tac-Toe Game. Everything is ready to go, and it was that quick! The completed, operating version appears in Figure 6.9. The complete code for the project is in Listing 6.1 (Tictac.vbp). Every time a user clicks on a command button, an X or O (in alternating sequence) appears. To start over, select the New Game item from the File menu. To quit the application, select Exit. Note that this is a demonstration program only. As mentioned earlier, the program allows you to click a command button that has already been clicked and does not stop even when someone wins. The idea here is to demonstrate the menus. Listing 6.1 shows the code for the Tictac.bas module, and Listing 6.2 shows the complete code for Tictac.frm.

Figure 6.9.
*The Tic-Tac-Toe application
running.*

Listing 6.1. The Tic-Tac-Toe Game (Tictac.vbp).

```
Public XTurn As Boolean
```

continues

Listing 6.1. **continued**

```
Option Explicit

Private Sub cmdTTT_Click(Index As Integer)
        If (XTurn) Then
                cmdTTT(Index).Caption = "X"
                XTurn = False
        Else
                cmdTTT(Index).Caption = "0"
                XTurn = True
        End If
End Sub

Private Sub Form_Terminate()
        End
End Sub

Private Sub mnuFileExit_Click()
        Unload frmTicTac
End Sub

Private Sub mnuFileNewGame_Click()
        Dim ButtonCount As Integer

        XTurn = True

        For ButtonCount = 0 To 8
                cmdTTT(ButtonCount).Caption = ""
        Next ButtonCount

        cmdTTT(0).SetFocus
End Sub

Private Sub Form_Load()
        XTurn = True
End Sub
```

At certain times, command buttons should be used for options. At other times, menus should be used instead. Generally, command buttons are used when the options they represent are so frequently used that it is acceptable to have them continually presented on the form. On the other hand, commands such as the ones you used in the Notepad in Chapter 3—Cut, Paste, and Clear All—are usually part of a menu and not displayed as command buttons. In fact, why not modify the Notepad so that it uses menus instead of command buttons? The example will point out how close command buttons and menus are from a Visual Basic programming point of view. Of course, many applications use both buttons and menus to achieve the same functionality. You can do this, too! And the Notepad project will get you started on an application that will be completed when you learn more about files: a File Editor.

Beginning the Editor Example

There is absolutely nothing wrong with the Notepad you developed in Chapter 3, but its use is very limited. In particular, the contents of the Notepad disappear when the application is closed. It would be much better if the Notepad contents could be saved on disk. Then, when the user reopened the application, the preexisting files could be read in and modified.

Toward that end, you are going to modify the Notepad application, incorporating menu selections. Later, in Chapter 8, you will be able to add the actual mechanics of Visual Basic file handling. To get going, open Notepad.vbp using the Open Project item from the File menu. Then save the project as Editor.vbp, using the Save Project As… item from the File menu. Finally, save both Notepad.frm and Notepad.bas as Editor.frm and Editor.bas, respectively, using the Save File As… option from the File menu. Next, change the Form's Caption property from NOTEPAD, to EDITOR. Now you are ready to design the Editor's menu system.

With Editor.frm displayed on the design desktop, open the Menu Editor by selecting Menu Editor from the Tools menu, by pressing Ctrl+E, or by using the right mouse button pop-up menu. Because the leftmost menu on Windows applications is normally the File menu, type File first, as the caption of that menu title. Give this menu a name of mnuFile. After you have entered the caption and name, press Enter or click the Next button to move down to the first entry that will go on this menu. To make the first item Load File…, type Load File… in the Caption text box. Indent it by clicking the arrow above the main list box that points right. In addition, give this item the name mnuFileLoad, and then press Enter. You can also make a provision to save files with a Save File… item. Add that next, giving it the name mnuFileSave. After that, you need a final menu item, Exit, which is expected on a File menu.

Because Exit does not fit in with Load File… and Save File…, you can set it off as its own group by placing a *menu separator* on the menu drop-down box. A separator on a menu is a horizontal line that divides menu items into groups. (Some separators appear on the File menu shown in Figure 6.1.) Note that Exit is set off from the rest of the menu items with a separator on Visual Basic's File menu as well. To specify a menu separator, simply type a hyphen, -. Do that now, by typing a hyphen as the Caption, and then enter mnuSep1 as the name and press Enter or click the Next button. Finally, enter Exit as the last item on the File menu, entering mnuFileExit in the Name text box. At this point, the Menu Editor should look like Figure 6.10.

Close the Menu Editor by clicking OK. Editor.frm should now look like Figure 6.11.

Figure 6.10.
The Menu Editor window
for Editor.frm.

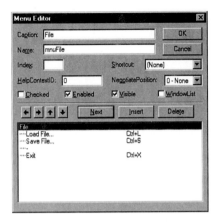

Figure 6.11.
The Editor template with the
File menu selected.

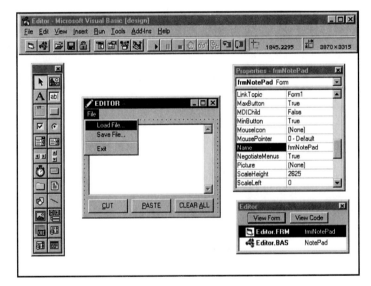

As you can see, the separator was inserted, setting the Exit item off from the others. Grouping menu items in this way is often a good idea because it is easier to find commands related to one another.

Unfortunately, the only File menu item you can make active at this time is the Exit item. (You will have to wait until you have expertise with files before you can set up Load File... and Save File....) Click on the Exit item to make that template appear. Just add the Unload statement here to close the form. Then using the Code window, find the Terminate procedure for the Form and type End in that template to terminate the application.

```
Private Sub mnuFileExit_Click()
        Unload frmNotePad
End Sub

Private Sub Form_Terminate()
        End
End Sub
```

The Edit menu usually follows the File menu in word processors and editors, so add that menu now. Open the Menu Editor again and click on the blank line below the last entry (....Exit) in the main list box. Now move up to the Caption box and type Edit and then mnuEdit in the Name box. Note that because you left the Menu Editor and came back, the automatic indentation was turned off. Thus, Edit is made into a menu bar item without the four dots before it, as in Figure 6.12.

Figure 6.12.
The Menu Editor, showing
the added Edit menu.

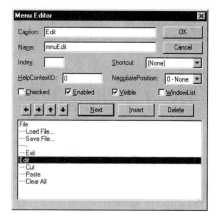

Because the Notepad's command buttons will be supplanted with menu items, the three items in the Edit menu should be Cut, Paste, and Clear All. Enter them one at a time, making sure that they are indented and give them the names mnuEditCut, mnuEditPaste, and mnuEditClear, respectively. At this point, the Menu Editor should look like Figure 6.12 and frmNotePad should look like Figure 6.13.

The only work remaining is to transfer the procedures from cmdCut, cmdPaste, and cmdClearAll to the menu items. Because each menu item is a Click event, they can be transferred whole. This is also easy to do in Visual Basic. Just double-click on the first button, cmdCut, to open the Code window as in Figure 6.14.

Remember that in the Notepad application you implemented your own clipboard, which is not a recommended approach, but rather was used here for illustration.

Figure 6.13.
The Editor template with the Edit menu added.

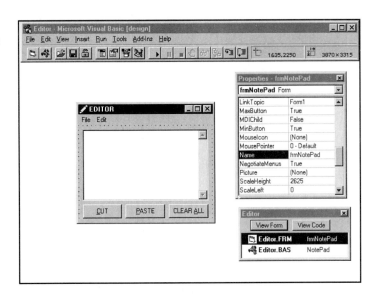

Figure 6.14.
The Click *event associated with* cmdCut.

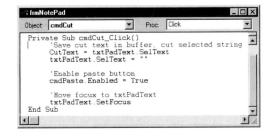

Because this button is named cmdCut, the Sub procedure appears as follows:

```
Private Sub cmdCut_Click()
        'Save cut text in buffer
        CutText = txtPadText.SelText
        txtPadText.SelText = ""

        'Enable paste button
        cmdPaste.Enabled = True

        'Move focus to txtPadText
        txtPadText.SetFocus

End Sub
```

Much of this will be the same under the menu system. Just change the name to mnuEditCut_Click(), which is the name of the Cut item on the Edit menu, as follows:

```
Private Sub mnuEditCut_Click()
        'Save cut text in buffer
```

```
        CutText = txtPadText.SelText
        txtPadText.SelText = ""

        'Enable paste button
        cmdPaste.Enabled = True

        'Move focus to txtPadText
        txtPadText.SetFocus

End Sub
```

> **Note:** The quickest way to accomplish the following changes is to change the name of the existing click procedures for each of the buttons to the names of the menu items.

As soon as you make this change and move the cursor to another line, Visual Basic checks the Object list to see whether this new name corresponds to an object that already exists. In this case it does, so Visual Basic assigns this procedure to the mnuEditCut menu control. Note that this is indicated by the Object list box at the top of the Code window, which now reads mnuEditCut, as in Figure 6.15.

Figure 6.15.
The mnuEditCut_Click event in the Code window.

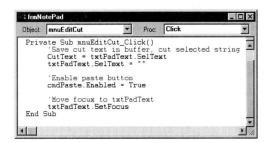

How Visual Basic Treats Unfamiliar Procedures

If Visual Basic does not recognize the new name of a procedure, it puts it in the form object named (General), assuming that it is not directly connected with an already existing object.

Next, you can do the same thing for the other buttons. The Paste procedure, cmdPaste_Click(), looks like this at present:

```
Private Sub cmdPaste_Click()
        'Paste text back into text box
        txtPadText.SelText = CutText
        txtPadText.SetFocus
End Sub
```

You might recall that the cut text is saved in a public variable named `CutText`. Here you are just pasting it back into the text box on the Notepad. You can change this to `mnuEditPaste_Click()` easily enough by editing the name of the `Sub` procedure until it appears as follows:

```
Private Sub mnuEditPaste_Click()
     'Paste text back into text box
     txtPadText.SelText = CutText
     txtPadText.SetFocus
End Sub
```

That's it for Paste. Now handle the Clear All button the same way. Using the Object and Procedure list boxes, move to the `cmdClearAll_Click()` event. Simply change that `Click` event from

```
Private Sub cmdClearAll_Click()
     'Clear text from txtNotePad
     txtPadText.Text = ""

     'Set focus on txtPadText
     txtPadText.SetFocus
End Sub
```

to the following, using `mnuEditClear_Click()`:

```
Private Sub mnuEditClear_Click()
     'Clear text from txtNotePad
     txtPadText.Text = ""

     'Set focus on txtPadText
     txtPadText.SetFocus
End Sub
```

Now that you have made the menu items active, you can start making the changes to the code itself. First, you no longer need to set the focus to other objects because, in the absence of buttons, the text box will always have the focus. For that reason, remove the `txtPadText.SetFocus` line from all the procedures so that they appear as follows:

```
Private Sub mnuEditClear_Click()
     'Clear text from txtNotePad
     txtPadText.Text = ""
End Sub

Private Sub mnuEditCut_Click()
     'Save cut text in buffer
     CutText = txtPadText.SelText
     txtPadText.SelText = ""

     'Enable paste button
     cmdPaste.Enabled = True
End Sub

Private Sub mnuEditPaste_Click()
     'Paste text back into text box
     txtPadText.SelText = CutText
End Sub
```

Next, you might recall that you started the Notepad with all three buttons grayed, and you enabled the Cut and Clear All buttons only after the user typed something into the text box. In other words, after there was a change in `txtPadText`, these controls were enabled in the following way:

```
Private Sub txtPadText_Change()
     'Enable Cut and Clear All buttons
     cmdCut.Enabled = True
     cmdClearAll.Enabled = True
End Sub
```

Menu items have an `Enabled` property just as command buttons do. You are probably more accustomed to seeing grayed menu items than grayed button captions. All you have to do to gray the menu items on your menu is to change the references from button `Enabled` properties to menu item `Enabled` properties. In other words, what was `cmdCut.Enabled` becomes `mnuEditCut.Enabled`, and what was `cmdClearAll.Enabled` becomes `mnuEditClear.Enabled`.

```
Private Sub txtPadText_Change()
     'Enable Cut and Clear All menu items
     mnuEditCut.Enabled = True
     mnuEditClear.Enabled = True
End Sub
```

In addition, you might remember that the Paste button was enabled only after some text was cut. This code was placed in the procedure `cmdCut_Click()` (which is now labeled `mnuEditCut_Click()`). That reference can change also from `cmdPaste.Enabled` to `mnuEditPaste.Enabled`.

```
Private Sub mnuEditCut_Click()
     'Save cut text in buffer
     CutText = txtPadText.SelText
     txtPadText.SelText = ""

     'Enable paste menu item
     mnuEditPaste.Enabled = True
End Sub
```

Now all the references to buttons in the code have been replaced by references to menu items. Delete the buttons from the form. To do that, unlock the controls using the Lock Controls button on the Toolbar or by using the pop-up menu. Then click on the buttons while depressing the Shift key to select all three. Next, select the Clear item from the Edit menu or press the Delete key. When the buttons are gone, readjust the size of the text box to absorb the space left by the button's absence.

Well, you're almost finished! The final step is to make sure that all the Edit menu items—Cut, Paste, and Clear All—are grayed when the application starts, before the user starts typing. As you might expect, you can change that at design-time, using the Menu Editor. Open the Menu Editor, and then click on the Cut item in the main list box to highlight it. Click on the Enabled check box to deselect it or turn it off. The Enabled check box is above the Next button. When deselected, the ✓ (check mark) disappears, as is shown in Figure 6.16.

Figure 6.16.
The Menu Editor with the
Cut item's Enabled option
deselected.

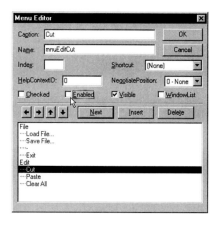

Next, do the same for the other two menu items in the Edit menu—Paste and Clear All. When you are finished, click OK. Now, when the Editor application is run, the Edit menu items originally appear grayed as in Figure 6.17. When the user starts typing, the Cut and Clear All items become active. When something is actually cut, the Paste item becomes enabled as well.

Figure 6.17.
The Editor application
running with the Edit menu
disabled.

Menu items are enabled and disabled with the Enabled property. Setting it to True enables the menu items, whereas setting it to False disables them. This capability is extremely valuable. It ensures that the user cannot choose an option before it is possible, such as attempting to cut text before there is any text to cut.

You must keep track of the items that have been disabled, however. And you should realize that users find large menus with virtually all items grayed to be unattractive and frustrating. If you have many grayed items, a better option would be to remove those items from the menu altogether and replace them when they become enabled again. You will see how to do this later in this chapter.

For now, all the code in the Editor so far appears, event by event, in Listing 6.2.

Listing 6.2. The Editor Application, Version 1 (Editor.vbp).

The code for the Editor.bas module is as follows:

```
Public CutText As String
```

Finally, here is the rest of the code for the Editor application as it stands:

```
Option Explicit

Private Sub Form_Terminate()
        End
End Sub

Private Sub mnuEditClear_Click()
        'Clear text from txtNotePad
        txtPadText.Text = ""
End Sub

Private Sub mnuEditCut_Click()
        'Save cut text in buffer
        CutText = txtPadText.SelText
        txtPadText.SelText = ""

        'Enable paste menu item
        mnuEditPaste.Enabled = True
End Sub

Private Sub mnuEditPaste_Click()
        'Paste text back into text box
        txtPadText.SelText = CutText
End Sub

Private Sub mnuFileExit_Click()
        Unload frmNotePad
End Sub

Private Sub txtPadText_Change()
        'Enable Cut and Clear All menu items
        mnuEditCut.Enabled = True
        mnuEditClear.Enabled = True
End Sub
```

There are still some ways to improve the Editor application. One is to add another menu to it so that the user can select the actual font used in the text. Because this operation will expose you to more of what menus are all about from a programmer's point of view, that is what to look into next.

Selecting Fonts from Menus

If you have worked with word processors that allow you to switch fonts, you know that such alternative fonts are exactly the kind of option that should be put in a menu. Most users do not normally change fonts often enough to make it worthwhile to have all the font options visible all the time. Some of the fonts that come with Windows 95 are displayed in Figure 6.18.

Figure 6.18.
Some of the fonts that come
with Windows 95.

Another Way to Change Fonts in an Application

Instead of adding a font menu to an application, the code for your program could call a Font dialog box. Using this type of dialog box and other common dialog box types are discussed in the next chapter.

The text in the Editor text box can be changed to any one of these fonts simply by changing the FontName property of the text box. However, there is a drawback. When the font is changed in a text box, all the text is automatically changed to that font. For that reason, only one font can be used in a text box at a time. With that restriction in mind, it's time to add a font menu to the Editor application.

Using Different Fonts in One Document

If you want to use different fonts in a single document, use the Print method, which applies to forms and picture boxes. In fact, Print is the general way to display text in Visual Basic. It can be used, for example, if it is necessary to write to an editor that can handle multiple fonts, formatting options, and more than 32 KB of text (the Text Box limit). In that case, however, the programmer would be responsible for such operations as scrolling and selecting text. You will see how to use Print later in Chapter 9, "Graphics."

To add a Font menu, open the Menu Editor and add a new menu caption, Font, after the Clear All edit item. Name the menu mnuFont. Then give the Font menu five items—Arial, Courier, MS Sans Serif, MS Serif, and Times New Roman—as shown in Figure 6.19. You could write a separate Click event procedure for each menu item, but now that you have five of them, setting up a control array is simpler. It is much easier (and less time consuming!) to let Visual Basic pass an Index to an event procedure, as it did earlier for the tic-tac-toe buttons, than to write separate procedures yourself.

In fact, it is just as easy to have Visual Basic pass an Index to a menu event procedure as it is to pass an Index to a button event procedure. To do this, give each menu item (Arial, Courier, MS Sans Serif, MS Serif, and Times New Roman) the same control name, `mnuFontNameArray`, in the Name text box. As far as Visual Basic is concerned, each menu item has the same name. To differentiate between them, Visual Basic needs an Index. Unfortunately, Visual Basic does not automatically assign indices to menu items as it did to the buttons earlier. You have to use the Index text box (refer to Figure 6.19) to set an Index for each menu item. In this case, you can simply give the Indexes 0 through 4 to the five fonts, as shown in Table 6.2. To do that, just select each menu item in turn and fill in the Index box as shown in Table 6.1.

Table 6.2. Font menu items for the Editor application.

Menu Item	Name	Index
Arial	`mnuFontNameArray`	0
Courier	`mnuFontNameArray`	1
MS Sans Serif	`mnuFontNameArray`	2
MS Serif	`mnuFontNameArray`	3
Times New Roman	`mnuFontNameArray`	4

Figure 6.19.
The open Menu Editor showing the completed Font menu.

Close the Menu Editor by clicking OK. Now you are ready to write some code. As you can see in Figure 6.20, a new menu (Font) has been added to the Editor form.

When you click on any of the menu items in this menu, the Code window opens with a template for `mnuFontNameArray_Click()`, as follows:

```
Private Sub mnuFontNameArray_Click(Index As Integer)

End Sub
```

Figure 6.20.
*The Editor form with the
new Font menu.*

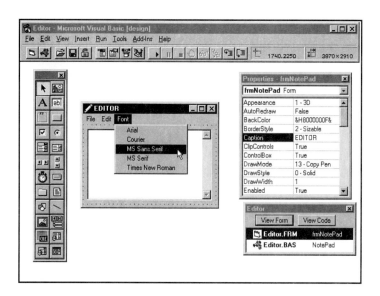

Your goal here is to select the appropriate font, depending on which selection is made. Because the menu item's index is passed, you can use it to set the font. The name of the text window in the Editor is `txtPadText`, so the property you want to set is `txtPadText.Font = "FontName"`. You can do that with a `Select Case` statement. (`Select Case` statements were discussed in Chapter 4.) In `mnuFontNameArray_Click()`, the code would appear like this:

```
Private Sub mnuFontNameArray_Click(Index As Integer)

    Select Case Index
            Case 0
                    txtPadText.Font = "Arial"
            Case 1
                    txtPadText.Font = "Courier"
            Case 2
                    txtPadText.Font = "MS Sans Serif"
            Case 3
                    txtPadText.Font = "MS Serif"
            Case 4
                    txtPadText.Font = "Times New Roman"
    Case Else

    End Select
End Sub
```

That's all there is to selecting a font, so now the Font menu is active. When the Editor application is running, the font can be selected from this menu and all the text will change at once. However, there is no easy way to tell from the font menu which font is currently selected. This is normally indicated in Windows applications with a check mark; applications often indicate which option is currently active by putting a check mark next to the appropriate menu item. As you might expect, you can do this, too. In the next section, you will add this capability to the Editor program.

Marking Menu Items with Check Marks

Open the Menu Editor again. To make sure that a default font appears checked when the Editor first starts, select MS Sans Serif, and then click on the Checked box above the arrow buttons, as in Figure 6.21. The Checked property will be used to add check marks to the menu items. When True, the item appears with a check mark, ✓; when False, it appears without a check mark. After checking the Checked box, click OK to close the Menu Editor.

Figure 6.21.
The Menu Editor with MS Sans Serif and the Checked property selected.

When the user selects a new font, the check mark should be removed first from the Font menu. You can do this by looping over each menu item and setting the Checked property, mnuFontNameArray(0-4).Checked, to False. Finally, you should add a check mark to the new font, which is simply an element of mnuFontNameArray, as follows:

```
Private Sub mnuFontNameArray_Click(Index As Integer)
    Dim UnCheck As Integer

    Select Case Index
        Case 0
            txtPadText.Font = "Arial"
        Case 1
            txtPadText.Font = "Courier"
        Case 2
            txtPadText.Font = "MS Sans Serif"
        Case 3
            txtPadText.Font = "MS Serif"
        Case 4
            txtPadText.Font = "Times New Roman"
    Case Else

    End Select
```

```
    For UnCheck = 0 To 4
          'Remove check mark from font
          mnuFontNameArray(UnCheck).Checked = False
    Next UnCheck

    'Add check mark to new font
    mnuFontNameArray(Index).Checked = True
End Sub
```

Now the Font menu is fully functional. When the user clicks on a new font, not MS Sans Serif, the check mark is removed from MS Sans Serif and placed in front of the new font, as in Figure 6.22. In this way, the user can keep track of the font currently selected. The code for the Editor application so far appears in Listing 6.3.

Figure 6.22.
Check marks in the Editor application's Font menu.

Listing 6.3. The Editor Application, Version 2 (Editor.vbp).

The code for the Editor.bas module is as follows:

```
Public CutText As String
```

Here is the rest of the code for the Editor application as it stands:

```
Option Explicit

Private Sub Form_Terminate()
      End
End Sub

Private Sub mnuEditClear_Click()
      'Clear text from txtNotePad
      txtPadText.Text = ""
End Sub

Private Sub mnuEditCut_Click()
      'Save cut text in buffer
      CutText = txtPadText.SelText
      txtPadText.SelText = ""

      'Enable paste menu item
      mnuEditPaste.Enabled = True
End Sub

Private Sub mnuEditPaste_Click()
      'Paste text back into text box
      txtPadText.SelText = CutText
```

```
End Sub

Private Sub mnuFileExit_Click()
        Unload frmNotePad
End Sub

Private Sub mnuFontNameArray_Click(Index As Integer)
        Dim UnCheck As Integer

        Select Case Index
               Case 0
                       txtPadText.Font = "Arial"
               Case 1
                       txtPadText.Font = "Courier"
               Case 2
                       txtPadText.Font = "MS Sans Serif"
               Case 3
                       txtPadText.Font = "MS Serif"
               Case 4
                       txtPadText.Font = "Times New Roman"
        Case Else

        End Select

        For UnCheck = 0 To 4
               'Remove check mark from font
               mnuFontNameArray(UnCheck).Checked = False
        Next UnCheck

        'Add check mark to new font
        mnuFontNameArray(Index).Checked = True
End Sub

Private Sub txtPadText_Change()
        'Enable Cut and Clear All menu items
        mnuEditCut.Enabled = True
        mnuEditClear.Enabled = True
End Sub
```

The Editor application is looking better and better! However, a number of features are still missing (besides its inability to work with files, yet). *Access keys* are used in most complete Windows applications that use menus. For instance, one letter of a menu name or item is underlined, indicating the letter plus Alt key that will select that option. Also, *shortcut keys*, such as Ctrl+A, are similarly used. Naturally, you can add those options to your Visual Basic programs as well.

Adding Access Keys to Menus

Access keys enable the user to open a menu by pressing the Alt key and typing a designated letter. Adding an access key to a menu is as easy as adding command buttons to a form. Just place an ampersand, &, in front of the letter to be designated. For example, if Cut was changed to &Cut in the

Menu Editor, C would become the access key for the Cut item on the Edit menu. Access keys should be unique to their level; no two menu titles on the menu bar should have the same access key, nor should two menu items in the same menu have the same access key.

In the Editor application, you will use the first letter of each item's name as its access key, with a few exceptions. Because two menu names begin with F (File and Font), you could use F for the File menu access key and O for the Font menu. In addition, because both Cut and Clear All appear on the Edit menu, you could use C for the Cut item's access key and A for Clear All, as you did when you originally designed the Notepad's command buttons. You will not give access keys to the fonts because you do not expect the user to switch fonts often enough to need them. Finally, even though the Exit option begins with E, make X the access key. The Windows convention is to give Exit X as an access key. Many users are accustomed to using it that way, and very few menu items are likely to begin with X. All the access keys used in the Editor application are marked with an ampersand in Figure 6.23.

Figure 6.23.
The Menu Editor window
with access keys assigned.

Now when you run the Editor application, the access keys will be underlined, as in Figure 6.24.

Figure 6.24.
The Editor application
running, showing the new
access keys.

The Editor program looks much more professional. But, there is one last addition that will really jazz it up—shortcut keys.

Adding Shortcut Keys to Menus

You have probably seen shortcut keys in menus already. For example, the Visual Basic File menu in Figure 6.1 has four shortcut keys for handling file operations. Ctrl+D is a shortcut for adding a file. Ctrl+S is a shortcut for saving a file. The shortcut for Save File As... is Ctrl+A, and Ctrl+P is the shortcut for the Print item. A shortcut key immediately runs a menu item's code, no matter where the user is in the application. You can add shortcuts like this to the Editor application as well.

To do that, open the Menu Editor again. Select shortcut keys with the Shortcut list box that appears to the right side of the window. As in most cases, Visual Basic is capable of presenting you with all the options available. Instead of having to look them up, the options are displayed on the screen when you click on the arrow next to the Shortcut box, as in Figure 6.25.

Figure 6.25.
Shortcut keys in the Menu Editor.

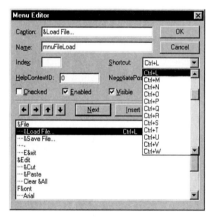

The first menu item you might give a shortcut key to is the Load File item on the File menu. Because you will have no other use for the Ctrl+*key* combinations such as Ctrl+A or Ctrl+M in your application, you can use them as shortcut keys. Ctrl+*letter* key combinations are often easier to remember than function key combinations, although function key combinations are also available in the Shortcut drop-down list. To connect Ctrl+L with the Load File item, just highlight that item in the main list box (as in Figure 6.25), and select Ctrl+L from the Shortcut list box. When you do, Ctrl+L appears in the main list box on the same line as the Load File... item.

In this way, you can keep going by choosing shortcut keys for most of the items, as shown in Figure 6.26. To make these keys active when you are finished selecting shortcut keys in the Menu Editor, click OK and then run the Editor application. As you can see in Figure 6.27, the shortcut keys are now displayed in the menus themselves, next to the items they represent—and they work!

Figure 6.26.
The completed shortcut keys in the Menu Editor.

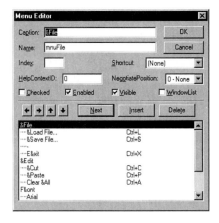

Figure 6.27.
The Editor application running, showing the new shortcut keys.

About the Scope of Access and Shortcut Keys

Keep in mind that a menu has to be open for an access key to be available from that menu. Shortcut keys such as Ctrl+X and Shift+F3 are available even when the menu is closed. For that reason, shortcut keys should be unique throughout all menus, not just where they are located.

For the time being, that's it for developing the Editor application. It has shown you a great deal about menu design, including how to gray items in a menu when they are inactive, how to mark menu items with a check mark, how to use access keys and separator bars, and now how to use shortcut keys. In fact, the Editor is becoming a well-polished application. Consequently, you should give the application its own icon. As it turns out, that is easy enough to do. Visual Basic comes with a library of some 400 icons, ready for use. But first, a little about a feature used extensively in Windows 95: *pop-up menus*.

Pop-Up Menus

As you already know, pop-up menus, or *context menus*, are a new feature of the Windows 95 interface and are also available in many commercial applications. Virtually anywhere you click with the right mouse button on the Windows 95 desktop will display a pop-up menu. This is also true for the Visual Basic 4 design desktop, as shown in Figure 6.28.

Figure 6.28.
A pop-up menu on the VB4 design desktop.

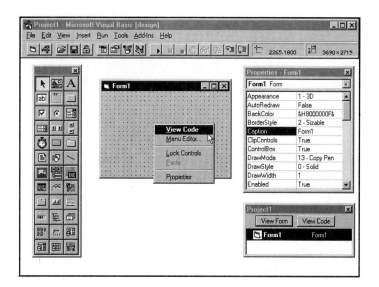

These pop-up menus are easy to add to any application. To display a pop-up menu at run-time, use the PopupMenu method. For example, to display a menu named mnuFile when the user clicks a form with the right mouse button, add the following code to the Form's MouseUp event:

```
Private Sub Form_MouseUp(Button As Integer, Shift As Integer, X As Single, Y As Single)
      If Button = 2 Then
      'Right mouse button clicked
             PopupMenu mnuFile
      End If
End Sub
```

Next, open the Menu Editor. Create a menu with caption &File and the name mnuFile. Under the File menu, create a menu item named mnuFileSurprise with the caption &Surprise!. Using the arrow pointing right, indent this menu item, as in Figure 6.29. (Pop-up menus must have at least one menu item to work.) Then click OK to close the Menu Editor.

Now, run the test project. Click the right mouse button anywhere on the form. Surprise! As you can see in Figure 6.30, a small menu, with only the surprise item in it, appears.

Figure 6.29.
The test form's Menu Editor is open, displaying the menu settings.

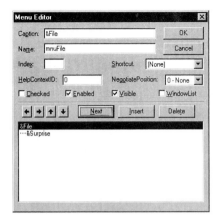

Figure 6.30.
The test form running with a pop-up menu displayed.

There are a couple of wrinkles to this. Only one pop-up menu can be open at a time. A pop-up menu cannot be displayed while a menu control is active. And any code following the display of the pop-up menu will not run until the user selects an item from the pop-up menu or cancels it (in this example, by clicking somewhere else on the form).

It's time to refine the pop-up menu a bit. In this example so far, the Surprise menu item is visible on the normal menu below File. Often, when using pop-up menus, the pop-ups activate items not normally visible on the menu bar. The way to do this is to return to the Menu Editor and uncheck the File menu's Visible property (so there is no ✓ in the check box). Also, while you are at it, why not add two more items to the File menu: &Birthday Presents and &Christmas Presents. Give them the captions mnuFileBirthday and mnuFileChristmas, respectively. The menu editor should look like it does in Figure 6.31. When you are done, click OK.

Now, run the project again. You might notice that the form appears to have no menus. Click anywhere in the form's Client Area with the right mouse button and the pop-up menu will appear, as in Figure 6.32, showing the three menu items.

Figure 6.31.
The test form's Menu Editor, showing the completed File menu.

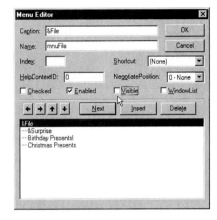

Figure 6.32.
The test application running, with the pop-up menu open.

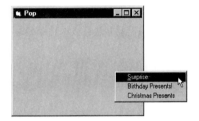

The Negotiate Position Setting in the Menu Editor

New in Visual Basic 4 is the Negotiate Position setting in the Menu Editor. Negotiate Position determines the location of menus belonging to an embedded OLE object placed in a Visual Basic MDI (Multiple Document Interface) application. These topics will be discussed further in Chapters 14, "Connecting to Other Windows Applications," and 15, "Advanced Control and Form Handling."

Listing 6.4 shows all the code necessary to make the pop-up application work. Of course, you still have to create the menu, but as you can see actually displaying the pop-up menu is easy.

Listing 6.4. The Popup program (popup.frm).

```
Option Explicit

Private Sub Form_MouseUp(Button As Integer, Shift As Integer, X As Single, Y As Single)
    'Right mouse button clicked
```

continues

Listing 6.4. continued

```
    If Button = 2 Then
        PopupMenu mnuFile
    End If
End Sub
```

Now return to the Editor application. It's time to give it an icon.

Giving the Editor Application an Icon

Icons are stored in the Icons directory and are broken into 12 groups, each with its own subdirectory: Arrows, Comm (for communication), Computer, Dragdrop, Elements, Flags, Industry, Mail, Misc (for miscellaneous), Office, Traffic, and Writing. The Writing category sounds appropriate for an Editor application, so that category should be explored for an appropriate icon. A complete copy of the icon library is included in the Visual Basic documentation. Figure 6.33 shows some icons available in the Writing library.

Figure 6.33.
The Visual Basic icons from the Writing subdirectory.

The Pencil01 icon looks about right for the Editor application. To use it, you must associate the icon with the Editor program's form.

Reopen the Editor project. Select the form itself, and scroll to the Icon property in the Properties window. When that property is selected, a Property Button appears to the right of the Settings box. Click on it to open the Load Icon dialog box as shown in Figure 6.34.

Use the Directories box in this dialog box to switch to Visual Basic's Icons/Writing directory. Load the Pencil01 icon by highlighting Pencil01 and then clicking Open. Notice that the pencil icon appears at the upper left corner of the form. At this point, the icon is associated with the Editor application's form, which still bears the Name `frmNotePad`. This is where Visual Basic takes the icon from that will be associated with an .Exe file. Select the Make EXE File... item from the Visual Basic File menu. The Make EXE File dialog box opens, as shown in Figure 6.35.

Figure 6.34.
The Load Icon dialog box.

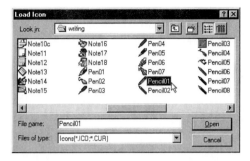

Figure 6.35.
The Make EXE File dialog box.

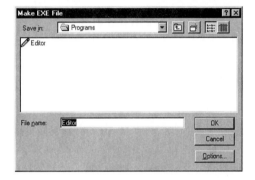

Next, click on the Options button. The EXE Options dialog box opens, as in Figure 6.36.

Figure 6.36.
The EXE Options dialog box.

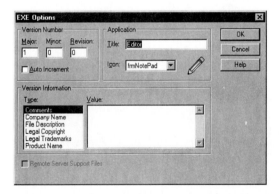

As you can see in the EXE Options dialog box, Pencil01 has become the icon for the Editor application. Click OK to close the EXE Options dialog box, and then click OK on the Make EXE File dialog box. Visual Basic then creates Editor.exe. To run your application from the Windows 95 desktop, just open the folder where Editor.exe is located. Click on it to select it. Next, use the File menu or the pop-up menu to create a shortcut to Editor.exe. Pull this shortcut icon out of the folder window onto the Windows 95 desktop. Close the file folders to get them out of the way, and then double-click on the Shortcut to Editor icon to run the program. The Shortcut and Running Editor application are shown in Figure 6.37.

Figure 6.37.
The Editor application running with the Shortcut to Editor icon to the right on the Windows 95 desktop.

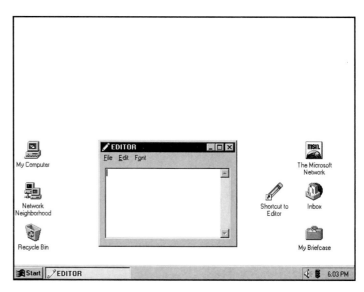

That's it for the Editor for now. You will return to it later when you are able to add file support. In the meantime, there is more to learn about menus. For instance, menu items can be changed at runtime. To see how to do this, you are going to adapt one of your old programs—the alarm clock from Chapter 3.

Changing Menu Items at Runtime

As you might recall, the alarm clock program has two option buttons—Alarm On and Alarm Off. You can convert this application to use a menu, just as you did for the Editor application. In particular, your goal here is to have one menu, Alarm, with one item on it. At first, that item will be Alarm Off. When selected at runtime, it will change to Alarm On, and so on, toggling back and forth as necessary.

To start this conversion, open the Alarm project and view frmAlarm. Save the project as Alarm2.vbp, using the Save Project As... item on the File menu. Save the form and module as Alarm2.frm and Alarm2.bas, respectively, using the Save File As... item from the File menu. Then open the Menu Editor. All you need to do here is create a single menu named &Alarm, with the Name of mnuAlarm. Then add one item to the Alarm menu, Alarm Off. Name that item mnuAlarmOnOff. Be sure to indent the menu item, and then click OK.

Now, double-click on one of the option buttons to open the Code window and display that control's code.

```
Private Sub optAlarmOnOff_Click(Index As Integer)
     'Checking radio button Index value and
```

```
        'setting AlarmOn
        If (Index = 1) Then
                AlarmOn = True
        Else
                AlarmOn = False
        End If
End Sub
```

As you might recall, AlarmOn was a public variable that determined whether the program would beep when the allotted time elapsed. You can change this Sub procedure code, rewriting it in the following way:

```
Private Sub mnuAlarmOnOff_Click()
        If (AlarmOn) Then
                AlarmOn = False
                'Toggle alarm
                mnuAlarmOnOff.Caption = "Alarm On"
        Else
                AlarmOn = True
                'Toggle alarm
                mnuAlarmOnOff.Caption = "Alarm Off"
        End If
End Sub
```

And that's it! You can delete the option buttons now, using the Visual Basic Edit menu, because all code reference to them has been removed. Resize the form to adjust for the missing option buttons. By changing the Caption property of the single menu item, it is possible to change that menu item at runtime. When the alarm clock application is run now, the menu name Alarm appears in the menu bar. Opening it reveals the Alarm On item. When the user clicks on Alarm On, the menu closes, the item changes to Alarm On, and the Alarm clock starts, as in Figure 6.38. In this way, the user can toggle between the Alarm On and Alarm Off items.

Figure 6.38.
The Alarm Clock program running, showing the Alarm menu.

The other way to do this is to use the menu item's Visible property instead. If you had two menu items—mnuAlarmOn (Alarm On) and mnuAlarmOff (Alarm Off), for example—setting mnuAlarmOn.Visible to True would display the Alarm On menu item and setting mnuAlarmOff.Visible to False would hide it, as follows:

```
Private Sub mnuAlarmOnOff_Click()
        If (AlarmOn) Then
                AlarmOn = False
                'Toggle alarm
                mnuAlarmOn.Visible = True
                mnuAlarmOff.Visible = False
        Else
```

```
            AlarmOn = True
            'Toggle alarm
            mnuAlarmOn.Visible = False
            mnuAlarmOff.Visible = True
      End If
End Sub
```

This is a way to hide options in menus when necessary, especially to avoid presenting too many grayed options. Setting the `Visible` property this way can be an important part of menu design.

The alarm clock program can also function with check marks. For instance, check marks are designed for cases in which the user toggles between two options, such as on and off. To put check marks into the alarm clock's Alarm menu, open the Menu Editor again and set up a new menu with the Caption text `&Alarm` and the Name text `mnuAlarm`. Then put an Alarm On item onto this menu and name it `mnuAlarmOn`, as in Figure 6.39.

Figure 6.39.
The new Alarm menu for
the Alarm Clock application.

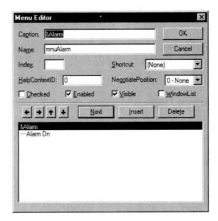

Close the Menu Editor, and then click on the Alarm On menu item to open the Code window, showing that item's `Click` event.

```
Private Sub mnuAlarmOn_Click()

End Sub
```

You can check the Alarm On item and set the public variable `AlarmOn` appropriately, as follows:

```
Private Sub mnuAlarmOn_Click()
      If (AlarmOn) Then
            AlarmOn = False
            mnuAlarmOn.Checked = False
      Else
            AlarmOn = True
            mnuAlarmOn.Checked = True
      End If
End Sub
```

This way, the Alarm On item toggles between being checked and unchecked, corresponding to the state of the alarm, as in Figure 6.40. (Make sure to eliminate the old `mnuAlarmOnOff_Click()` Sub procedure entirely. Otherwise, it will be automatically placed by Visual Basic in the general declarations section of the code because it will not recognize it.) Another variation of the previous menu designs is to have two items, Alarm On and Alarm Off, and place a check mark in front of the appropriate one.

Figure 6.40.
The Alarm Clock application with the Alarm On item checked.

That's it for the alarm clock application for now. The entire code for the program so far is shown in Listing 6.5.

Listing 6.5. **The Alarm2 Clock Application (Alarm2.vbp).**

```
Public AlarmOn As Boolean
```

Here is the rest of the code for the alarm clock application:

```
Option Explicit

Private Sub mnuAlarmOn_Click()
      If (AlarmOn) Then
              AlarmOn = False
              mnuAlarmOn.Checked = False
      Else
              AlarmOn = True
              mnuAlarmOn.Checked = True
      End If
End Sub

Private Sub tmrAlarmClock_Timer()
      'Timer checking whether >= txtAlarmSetting.Text
      If (Time >= txtAlarmSetting.Text And AlarmOn) Then
              Beep
      End If

      lblDisplay.Caption = Time
End Sub

Private Sub txtAlarmSetting_KeyPress(KeyAscii As Integer)
      Dim Key As String
```

continues

Listing 6.5. **continued**

```
        'Procedure checks for characters other than
        '0 through 9 and :
        Key = Chr(KeyAscii)
        If (Key < "0" Or Key > "9") Then
                If Key <> ":" Then
                        Beep
                        KeyAscii = 0
                End If
        End If
End Sub
```

As you have seen, it is possible to change a menu item's caption at runtime, as well as make it visible or invisible. However, this does not cover all the possibilities. What if you wanted to add or delete completely new menus at run-time? That is the next option that will be explored.

Adding and Deleting Menu Items

Suppose that you wanted to write a menu-driven phone book application, a program you can use to keep track of the phone numbers of friends. Such an application might have two text boxes in it. One text box for holding a name and the other for holding the corresponding phone number. If all the stored names appear in a menu, selecting one is easy. When a name is chosen from the menu, it appears in the name text box, and the corresponding phone number appears in the phone number text box. However, it must be taken into account that such a menu list of names could grow or shrink.

In Visual Basic, menu items can be added with the `Load` statement and removed with the `Unload` statement. (As you will see, `Load` and `Unload` can be used for many Visual Basic controls.) To do this, however, the menu items must be part of a control array and must use the same click procedure, although their indices will be different. The reason for this is that entirely new code for a new click procedure cannot be added at runtime. Rather, Visual Basic must already have the code framework necessary to handle the new menu item.

Using `Load` and `Unload` is not difficult. For instance, if you had a menu item named `mnuGeekArray` whose index was 0, you could add another item named `mnuGeekArray(1)` in the following way:

```
Load mnuGeekArray(1)
```

This adds another item right below the last item. To add a new item to the menu itself, you could load a string into `mnuGeekArray(1)`'s `Caption` property like this:

```
Load mnuGeekArray(1)
mnuGeekArray(1).Caption = "Load File..."
```

Similarly, you could remove items using `Unload`. Suppose, for example, that you had added these file handling items to a menu in the following way:

```
Load mnuGeekArray(1)
        mnuGeekArray(1).Caption = "Load File..."
    Load mnuGeekArray(2)
        mnuGeekArray(2).Caption = "Check Spelling"
    Load mnuGeekArray(3)
        mnuGeekArray(3).Caption = "Format Text"
    Load mnuGeekArray(4)
        mnuGeekArray(4).Caption = "Save File As..."
```

Now, suppose you wanted to remove the Load File... item. In a control array, Visual Basic allows only the last item to be removed with `Unload`. So the operation would have to be performed by moving all the other items up and then deleting the last item, as follows:

```
Dim Shuffle As Integer


    For Shuffle = 1 to 3
        mnuGeekArray(Shuffle).Caption = mnuGeekArray(Shuffle + 1).Caption
    Next Shuffle

    Unload mnuGeekArray(4)
End Sub
```

Note, in this case, that the indices of each surviving item are decremented by one. You would have to account for that in code. Note also that you did nothing with the first item in the array, `mnuGeekArray(0)`. This is a defect of using `Load` and `Unload` for menu items. A control array cannot be set up unless there is at least one element in place at design-time, and items created at design-time cannot be unloaded at runtime. No matter what you do, you must always have one element of the control array in the menu. But, because you do not know before runtime which items should be placed in the menu (for example, the names of which friends), what Caption should it be given at design-time?

External Resource Files and Menu Captions

In Visual Basic 4, external Resource Files can now be used to load the strings that make up Visual Basic menu captions. This is useful when combined with the new conditional compilation feature in Visual Basic 4, because it allows the programmer to prepare one version of a program that can easily be customized for different languages and locations. A further discussion of this topic will be held in Chapter 15, "Advanced Control and Form Handling."

When designing a menu, the usual solution to this problem is to give the 0 item (the one that starts the control array) an invisible menu item as a caption. That way, all subsequent menu items that are added will come after this invisible 0 item. Now you will see how this works in practice.

Start a new project and create a module. Change the module's Name property to `Phone`. Then change the form's Name property to `frmPhone` and change its Caption property to PHONE BOOK. Save the project, using the Save Project item from the File menu. Save the form, module, and project as Phone.frm, Phone.bas, and Phone.vbp, respectively. Using Figure 6.41 and Table 6.3 as guides, create the form. (The table works down from the top of the form.)

Table 6.3. Visual implementation of the Phone Book application.

Object	Property	Setting
Form	Appearance	1-3D
	Caption	PHONE BOOK
	MaxButton	False
	MinButton	False
	Name	frmPhone
Label	Caption	Name:
	Font	Style: Bold
	Name	lblName
Text Box	Caption	(None)
	Name	txtName
Label	Caption	Number:
	Font	Style: Bold
	Name	lblNumber
Text Box	Caption	(None)
	Name	txtNumber

Now, open the Menu Editor. The menu in the phone book application can conceivably expand to save phone directories on disk, so in the Caption box call it &File. Name it, of course, mnuFile. Next, add the first menu item, giving it the Caption &Add Current Name and using the Name mnuFileCurrent. (Don't forget to indent it!) Add a separator bar by typing a hyphen (-) in the Caption box and giving it the Name mnuSep1. After that, add another item using a Caption such as NArray and give it the Name mnuFileNArray. In addition, give mnuFileNArray an Index of 0 by putting a 0 in the Index text box below the Name text box. Now, make it invisible by clicking on the Visible box so the ✓ in that check box disappears. To quickly recap, the control array will be named mnuFileNArray(), and you will be able to refer to specific items in the array using mnuFileNArray(1), mnuFileNArray(2), and so forth. (Note that because mnuFileNArray(0) will always remain invisible, you could give it any caption you wanted.) Finally, add the last two items. Add another separator bar with the Caption being a hyphen and the Name mnuSep2. Then add what is at the bottom of any File menu, E&xit, with a Name of mnuFileExit.

Figure 6.41.
The Phone Book project form with text boxes and labels in place.

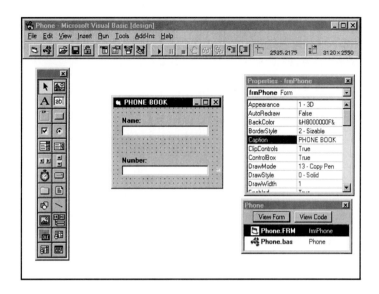

If you run the program, you will see the menu, as displayed in Figure 6.42. You might have noticed that there is nothing between the two separator bars. This is because NArray is invisible. When the code is in place, the names entered into the phone book will be placed between the two separators.

Figure 6.42.
The Phone Book application running, showing the File menu.

This is how the program will work: The user will be able to type a name into txtName and then type a phone number into txtNumber. Then, when the user selects the Add Current Name option from the File menu, the program will add that name to the menu, simultaneously adding the name to the File menu right below the separator bar. After the user finishes entering names in this manner, she should select a name from the menu. That name, along with the corresponding phone number, will appear in the text boxes.

You can start adding code to the program by clicking on the Add Current Name item on the File menu. This opens the Code window, positioning the cursor within the Sub procedure template for mnuFileCurrent_Click().

```
Private Sub mnuFileCurrent_Click()

End Sub
```

The first thing you want to keep track of is the number of menu items available at one time. Declare a variable called Quantity as Static. Static means that the variable's value will not change between successive calls.

```
Private Sub mnuFileCurrent_Click()
     Static Quantity As Integer

         :

End Sub
```

Because you are adding a person's name in this procedure, the first action should be to increment Quantity by one (static variables are initialized to 0) and load a new menu item, like this:

```
Private Sub mnuFileCurrent_Click()
     Static Quantity As Integer

         Quantity = Quantity + 1
         Load mnuFileNArray(Quantity)

         :

End Sub
```

Next, load the name now in the name text box, txtName, into the new menu item's Caption property this way:

```
Private Sub mnuFileCurrent_Click()
     Static Quantity As Integer

         Quantity = Quantity + 1
         Load mnuFileNArray(Quantity)
         mnuFileNArray(Quantity).Caption = txtName

         :

End Sub
```

Now, to store the people's names and their telephone numbers, set up two string arrays named People() and Telephone(). These arrays have to be broader in scope than just the current procedure, because when the user clicks on a person's name in the menu to retrieve data, the corresponding Click procedure will have to read from these arrays to fill txtName and txtNumber. For that reason, declare People() and Telephone() as form-level arrays. To do that, select the (General) item from the Code window Object list box, and make sure the Procedure list box says (declarations). Then add the following declarations, as shown in Figure 6.43.

```
Dim People(0 To 10) As String
Dim Telephone(0 To 10) As String
```

Figure 6.43.

The frmPhone *Code window, showing the general declarations section.*

Placing these arrays in the general declarations section makes them form-level arrays, accessible to all procedures in the form. Now you can go back to mnuFileCurrent() and enter the rest of the code that will store the current name and number.

```
Private Sub mnuFileCurrent_Click()
        Static Quantity As Integer

        Quantity = Quantity + 1
        Load mnuFileNArray(Quantity)
        mnuFileNArray(Quantity).Caption = txtName

        'Make list of people's names visible
        mnuFileNArray(Quantity).Visible = True

        'Data from name text box
        People(Quantity) = txtName

        'Data from number text box
        Telephone(Quantity) = txtNumber
End Sub
```

With mnuFileCurrent_Click() now complete, the user can add friends' names to the File menu at runtime.

The next step after adding names is to retrieve them on demand. When that happens, a mnuFileNArray_Click() event occurs. Note that the first item, mnuFileNArray(0), is simply the placeholding invisible item. The next item, mnuFileNArray(1), corresponds to the first name in the menu under the separator bar. MnuFileNArray(2) corresponds to the second name under the separator bar, and so on. To write the mnuFileNArray Click subroutine, find and click on mnuFileNArray in the Code window's Object box. This Sub procedure appears as follows:

```
Private Sub mnuFileNArray_Click(Index As Integer)

End Sub
```

When the user clicks on a name in the menu, this procedure is called with an index number that corresponds to the item chosen. Because the program stores the names and numbers with the same index as the menu items themselves, the application can display the requested name and number on the screen in the following way:

```
Private Sub mnuFileNArray_Click(Index As Integer)
        txtName = People(Index)
        txtNumber = Telephone(Index)
End Sub
```

That's all there is to it.

Finally, add the code that activates the Exit item. Change to the `mnuFileExit_Click` event, using the Code window or by clicking on the Exit item in the form's file menu. Close the form by using the `Unload` statement: `Unload frmPhone`. Then change to the Form's `Terminate` event, using the Object and Procedure list boxes. Enter the `End` statement there to terminate the application. The code placement is as follows:

```
Private mnuFileExit_Click()
      Unload frmPhone
End Sub

Private Form_Terminate()
      End
End Sub
```

And that's it for the phone book application for now. The entire code for the application so far, including the string array coding that stores people's names and telephone numbers, is displayed in Listing 6.6.

Listing 6.6. The Phone Book Application (Phone.vbp.).

The properties in this application should be set as follows:

Object	Property	Setting
Form	Appearance	1-3D
	Caption	PHONE BOOK
	MaxButton	False
	MinButton	False
	Name	frmPhone
Label	Caption	Name:
	Font	Style: Bold
	Name	lblName
Text Box	Caption	(None)
	Name	txtName
Label	Caption	Number:
	Font	Style: Bold
	Name	lblNumber
Text Box	Caption	(None)
	Name	txtNumber

The menu settings for Phone.frm are as follows:

Caption	Name	Indentation	Other Information
File	mnuFile	0	(None)
Add Current Name	mnuFileCurrent	1	(None)
- (Separator)	mnuSep1	1	(None)
NArray	mnuFileNArray	1	Index = 0
			Visible = False
- (Separator)	mnuSep2	1	(None)
Exit	mnuFileExit	1	(None)

Finally, here is the rest of the code for the application:

```
Option Explicit

Dim People(0 To 10) As String
Dim Telephone(0 To 10) As String

Private Sub Form_Terminate()
      End
End Sub

Private Sub mnuFileCurrent_Click()
      Static Quantity As Integer

      Quantity = Quantity + 1
      Load mnuFileNArray(Quantity)
      mnuFileNArray(Quantity).Caption = txtName

      'Make list of people's names visible
      mnuFileNArray(Quantity).Visible = True

      'Data from name text box
      People(Quantity) = txtName

      'Data from number text box
      Telephone(Quantity) = txtNumber
End Sub

Private Sub mnuFileExit_Click()
      Unload frmPhone
End Sub

Private Sub mnuFileNArray_Click(Index As Integer)
      txtName = People(Index)
      txtNumber = Telephone(Index)
End Sub
```

Run the phone book application. It now stores names and numbers when they are typed into the text boxes and the Add Current Name item from the File menu is selected. Each time a new name and number is added, that name is added to the menu, as in Figure 6.44. To retrieve a telephone number for any name, just select the menu item.

Figure 6.44.
The functioning Phone Book application, showing names added to the File menu.

You have come a long way in your work with menus in this chapter, but there is one thing you did not do: make items such as Load File… and Save File… active. Usually, selecting a menu item with an ellipsis like this opens a dialog box. Because of this, you will learn about dialog boxes in the next chapter.

Summary

You learned how to work with menus in this chapter. In fact, you saw much of what is possible with menus. In particular, you learned how to design menus using the Menu Editor, how to incorporate them into programs, and how to add code to specific menu items. Also, you discovered how to enable and disable menu items, how to add and use menu access and shortcut keys, as well as how to add separator bars, menus within menus, and check marks. You learned about pop-up menus and creating a font menu that enables the user to switch fonts. And you developed a phone book application that lets the user add menu items at runtime, using control arrays. Two other practical topics you covered in this chapter were how to end a program using the `Unload` statement, and using the `End` statement in the form's `Terminate` event. Also, you learned how to assign an icon to a program and set up an .exe file. Congratulations!

New Properties	Description
`Checked`	Indicates whether a menu item appears with a check mark in front of it (if `True`) or not (if `False`).
`Icon`	Holds the path and filename of the icon that Visual Basic will associate with an application's .exe file.
`Visible`	Indicates whether a control or form is visible (`True`) or not (`False`).

New Statements	*Description*
`End`	Ends a Visual Basic application.
`Load`	Adds a form or control into memory.
`Unload`	Removes a form or control from memory.

New Method	*Description*
`PopupMenu`	Displays a pop-up menu on an `MDIForm` or `Form` object at the current mouse location or at specified coordinates.

7

Dialog Boxes and a Database Program

In this chapter you will discover how to work with multiple windows—specifically, dialog boxes. You will add dialog boxes to your programs, making the dialog boxes appear on the screen when required. You will also learn the basics of the Multiple Document Interface (MDI). In fact, this chapter covers all these topics:

- Visual Basic programs without windows
- Parsing a program command line
- Message boxes
- Input boxes
- Creating and using dialog boxes
- Connecting dialog boxes to menu items
- An introduction to the workings of the Multiple Document Interface (MDI)
- Toolbars and status bars
- How scroll bars work
- Combo boxes
- List boxes
- An introduction to the Common Dialog control

You will develop some good programs in this chapter—a command-line parser, a Windows shell program that will start Windows applications, and a Control Panel application window. Also, you will start working on the database application. Like the Editor application, the database program will extend over a few chapters, and you will pick up skills, such as file handling, as they are covered. You will also update the Tic-Tac-Toe program to use message boxes. And you will learn some other skills: how to run a Visual Basic program without any windows at all, how to set colors in Visual Basic, and how to use the Multiple Document Interface (MDI), which can maintain a number of windows inside a larger one—just like the Windows Program Manager. You will also discover all permutations of the `InputBox()` and `MsgBox()` functions. Dialog boxes are an important part of almost any Windows program, and the knowledge you pick up here will be handy when you set one up on your own.

So far, all of your programs have involved a single window—one form. However, it is very common for applications to use many windows: dialog boxes, message boxes, warning boxes, help windows, and all sorts of other windows. Perhaps the most common type of window is a dialog box. You will learn quite a bit about different types of multiple form applications in this chapter.

Visual Basic provides some built-in windows that you can use for just this purpose: `MsgBox()` and `InputBox()`. These two Visual Basic statements display a message and the second one, InputBox, also receives string input from the user.

First, you will create a windowless application: the command-line parser. Then you will learn about the MsgBox() and InputBox() functions. Next, you will see how to work with multiple forms in general—how to create a second form when designing your application, how to display it, how to address the properties of other forms, and how to hide them again.

After that, you will see how to create and use dialog boxes. If you have used Windows, you know that dialog boxes play an integral part in getting information from the user. So far, you have handled tasks such as numeric input, string input, and option selection by using buttons and menus. In commercial applications, these same tasks are often handled with dialog boxes. You will also spend a good deal of time in this chapter with some of the controls that are often associated with dialog boxes—combo boxes and list boxes. And you will see how the Multiple Document Interface (MDI) works. With all that in mind, it is time to start by discovering that some applications need no windows. Then the chapter will move on to MsgBox() and InputBox(), the two simplest types of dialog boxes available.

No Windows Needed

It may surprise you to learn that you do not need any windows in a Visual Basic program. To see how this works, start Visual Basic and remove the default form, Form1, using the Remove File item from Visual Basic's File menu. Add a module, using the Module item from the Insert menu. This module will have the default name Module1. As you may recall, you store code that is not associated with any form in Visual Basic modules. If you add a Sub named Main() to the module's (General) object, Visual Basic will execute it. No forms are needed. For example, put the following code in the (General) section of Module1 (when you do, Visual Basic will automatically add Main to the Procedure list box):

```
Public Sub Main()
      Beep
End Sub
```

When you run the program, it will simply execute the Visual Basic Beep statement and then exit. It's that simple to write a windowless program in Visual Basic!

More Uses for a Windowless Program in Windows

Note that you can do much more with Windows programs that do not display windows—especially with those that can communicate with other Windows programs using Dynamic Data Exchange (DDE is discussed in Chapter 13, "Connecting to Other Windows Applications: DDE.") You will discover later in this chapter that Load() and Show() can be used to load and display windows, even from a program that does not have any windows originally.

Creating a Command-Line Parsing Program

Sometimes it is useful to pass arguments to a program that you have written. For example, you might want to pass a file's name to a program for the program's use. Or, you might want to send different flags to a program, telling it what to do depending upon the value of the flag.

It's time to write an application that illustrates the concept of the windowless program. You will do this by simply parsing the command line and sending up a message box saying which flag has been passed. Of course, the message box itself is literally a window, but this program can be considered an example of a windowless program, because instead of passing out a message, it could go on and do something else.

How to Set Execution-Line Arguments in Windows 95

Using the Taskbar at the bottom of the screen, click Start, and then select Run. Enter the name of the program you want to run in the File list box. At the end of the program line, skip a space and enter the flag.

In this example, `C:\vb\parse.exe /a`, /a is the *command-line argument*. This is also called a *command-line flag*.

To set a command-line argument for an application you are creating in the Visual Basic development environment, select the Options item from the Tools menu and click the Advanced tab. On the Advanced tab sheet, enter your command-line argument in the appropriate text box.

In the program that you are about to write you will use a special variable, which is referred to as a function in the Microsoft documentation. The special variable `Command` is used to return the command-line arguments.

To begin, open Visual Basic and remove Form1 from the program by selecting the Remove File option from the File menu. Next, insert a module using the Insert menu on the menu bar. Change this module's Name property to Parse, and save the module and project by selecting the Save Project item from the File menu. Save the module as Parse.bas and the project as Parse.vbp.

Select the module in the Program Window and click the View Code button (or double-click the module Listing in the Program Window). Add the following code to the (General) section of the module, as in Figure 7.1:

```
Public Sub Main()
     Dim Msg As String ' Declare variable.

     If Command = "" Then     ' If no command line.
          Msg = "There is currently no command-line string."
```

```
    Else                 ' Put command line into message.
        Msg = "The command-line string is: '" & Command & "'"

    End If

    MsgBox Msg            ' Display message.

End Sub
```

Figure 7.1.
Adding code to the Parse module.

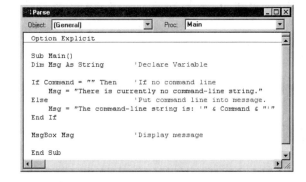

When you run the project, the message "There is currently no command-line string" appears on the screen, as in Figure 7.2. Once you click OK in the message box, the program stops running.

Figure 7.2.
The Parse application running, with the message box displayed.

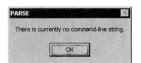

Using the Tools menu, select the Options item. Click the Advanced tab. Move the cursor down to the Command Line Argument text box. In that box, enter the command-line argument, /Cuddly Teddy Bear, as shown in Figure 7.3.

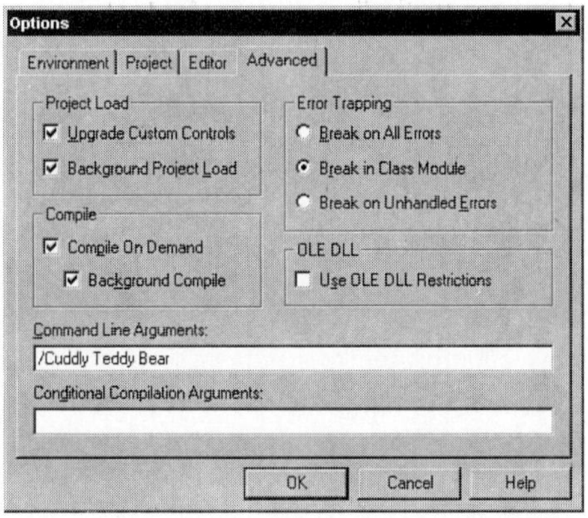

Figure 7.3.
The Project Options dialog box with a command-line argument entered into the Command Line Argument text box.

After you are finished entering the command-line argument, click OK and run the project. The message box will appear as it did before, but this time the message is "The command-line is: '/Cuddly Teddy Bear' as displayed in Figure 7.4.

Figure 7.4.
The Parse application running with a command-line argument shown in the message box.

The next thing to do is to create an executable program from the Parse application. Select the Make Exe File... option from the File menu. The Make EXE dialog box opens. In the File Name text box, enter the program's name: Parse.exe. Select the directory where you would like the exe file to reside. Then click OK. Close Visual Basic and, using the Windows 95 Taskbar, select Run. In the dialog box, enter the path where the program resides on your hard drive and Parse.exe, followed by "This is a test." This is shown in Figure 7.5.

Figure 7.5.
The Windows 95 Run dialog box with Parse.exe and the command line "This is a Test" entered in the Command Line text box.

After you have entered the path, file name, and command line, click OK. A message box opens displaying, "The command-line is 'This is a Test'" as shown in Figure 7.6.

Figure 7.6.
The Parse application running, showing the command-line message box.

Congratulations! You have created your first windowless program *and* you have learned how to use a genuinely useful programming function: parsing a program's command line.

Displaying a Message Box with MsgBox

The first function covered here, MsgBox, enables only a restricted dialog. You place a message on the screen in a window, and the user is restricted to communicating back through buttons. In other words, MsgBox displays a message in a dialog box, waits for the user to choose a button (such as, Yes, No, or

Cancel), and returns a value to the program, indicating which button was chosen. The way MsgBox syntax works is as follows:

```
MsgBox(prompt[, buttons][, title][, helpfile, context])
```

The MsgBox function syntax uses these arguments:

- prompt—A string expression, which is displayed as the message in the dialog box.
- buttons—A numeric expression that is the sum of values, specifying the number and type of buttons to display, the icon style to use, the identity of the default button, and the modality of the message box. Visual Basic constants (prefixed with vb—for example, vbYesNoCancel) can be used in place of a sum of numbers.
- title—A string expression that is displayed in the title bar of the message box. If the Title argument is omitted, Visual Basic automatically puts the application's name in the title bar.
- helpfile—A string expression that identifies the Help file to use to provide a help link to that message box.
- context—A numeric expression that is the Help context number for the appropriate topic, assigned by the Help file's author.

The buttons argument lets you select from a number of options, such as displaying OK buttons, Abort, Retry, or Ignore buttons, Cancel buttons, or even icons such as a Stop sign, an information symbol—a lowercase i in a balloon, and others, as indicated in Table 7.1. The values in that table can be added together. For example, to display Yes, No, and OK buttons along with a Stop sign, you would use a button value of 4 + 16 = 20. In another example, a message box displaying the Retry and Cancel buttons with the default focus set on the second button, and an Exclamation mark, would have a value of 5 + 256 + 48 = 309. Note that even if you do not specify a value for the button argument, Visual Basic still places an OK button in the message box for the user to select. The return values for the MsgBox function are in Table 7.1. These values enable the program to determine which button was pushed.

Table 7.1. Button argument settings for the MsgBox function.

Constant	Value	Description
vbOKOnly	0	Displays OK button only.
vbOKCancel	1	Displays OK and Cancel buttons.
vbAbortRetryIgnore	2	Displays Abort, Retry, and Ignore buttons.
vbYesNoCancel	3	Displays Yes, No, and Cancel buttons.
vbYesNo	4	Displays Yes and No buttons.
vbRetryCancel	5	Displays Retry and Cancel buttons.

continues

Table 7.1. continued

Constant	Value	Description
vbCritical	16	Displays stop sign icon.
vbQuestion	32	Displays question mark icon.
vbExlamation	48	Displays exclamation mark icon.
vbInformation	64	Displays information sign icon.
vbDefaultButton1	0	First button has the default focus.
vbDefaultButton2	256	Second button has the default focus.
vbDefaultButton3	512	Third button has the default focus.
vbApplicationModal	0	The application is modal; the user must respond to the message box before continuing work in the current application.
vbSystemModal	4096	The system is modal; all applications are suspended until the user responds to the message box.

The first group of values—0 through 5—describes the number and type of buttons displayed in the dialog box. The second group—16, 32, 48, and 64—describes the icon style. The third group—0, 256, and 512—determines which button is the default. The final group—0 and 4096—determines the modality of the message box. (When the numbers are added together to create a final value for the button argument, only one number from each group should be chosen.)

The constants in the preceding table are specified by Visual Basic. Because of this, the constants can be used anywhere in place of the actual value in code. For example, a message box containing a Stop sign—whose value = 16—and Yes and No buttons—whose value = 4—could be written like this:

```
MsgBox "Stop!", 20, "Sample Stop Box"
```

If you were to use the Visual Basic constants, however, the same line of code would be written like this instead:

```
MsgBox "Stop!", vbYesNo + vbCritical, "Sample Stop Box"
```

Tip: Use Visual Basic's constants to make your code more readable. It's much easier to understand what vbYesNo + vbCritical is than 20.

Table 7.2. **MsgBox** return values.

Constant	Value	Button Chosen
vbOK	1	OK
vbCancel	2	Cancel
vbAbort	3	Abort
vbRetry	4	Retry
vbIgnore	5	Ignore
vbYes	6	Yes
vbNo	7	No

Some common uses for message boxes include information messages, About boxes—which describe the application and its authors—and error messages.

> **Tip:** Use message boxes whenever you can. In a single line of code you can get valuable feedback from the user, or inform them of an error message, without taking the time to design a special dialog box.

To start making an information box, open Visual Basic and put a command button in the middle of the default form, Form1. Change the button's `Caption` property to `Info` and double-click the command button. The following `Sub` procedure code skeleton appears:

```
Private Sub Command1_Click()

End Sub
```

You can use the `MsgBox` function to display a simple information message: "That button opens an Information box!" Along with this message will be an information symbol—an i inside a circle whose value = 64—as well as an OK button and a Cancel button—whose value = 1.

```
Private Sub Command1_Click()
MsgBox "That button displays an Information box!",
➥vbOKCancel + vbInformation, "Information"
End Sub
```

Notice that you can also use `MsgBox` as a statement, not a function, which is what you are doing here, because you are not interested in a return value. When the Info button is clicked, your message appears on the screen like in Figure 7.7. And that's it! You're already using elementary dialog boxes.

Figure 7.7.

A trial Information message box.

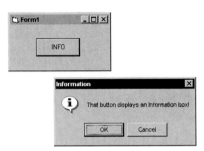

You can see an example of an error message box if you modify the Tic-Tac-Toe game from Chapter 6. Open Tictac.vbp and using the Save File As... and Save Project As... items from the File menu, save the project and its associated files as Tictac2.frm, Tictac2.bas, and Tictac2.vbp.

You might recall that the user could click any button, changing it to an X or an O, whether it had been selected before or not. That can be fixed by checking the clicked button's caption. If the button has already been selected, an error message should appear on the screen.

In the original program there was a call to a control array that handles the button clicks. This was the corresponding event procedure:

```
Private Sub cmdTTT_Click(Index As Integer)
    If (XTurn) Then
        cmdTTT(Index).Caption = "X"
        XTurn = False
    Else
        cmdTTT(Index).Caption = "0"
        XTurn = True
    End If
End Sub
```

An error message with an exclamation point inside a bright yellow triangle—whose constant is `vbExclamation` —can be added easily, as shown in Figure 7.8. If a previously selected button is chosen again, the program will leave the `Sub` procedure after displaying the Error message, and the doubly selected button will not be changed. Add the following to the top of the `cmdTTT_Click` procedure:

```
    If (cmdTTT(Index).Caption <> "") Then
    'Send up error message if button selected twice
        MsgBox "That button was already clicked!", 48, "Error!"
        Exit Sub
    End If
```

That's all for the Tic-Tac-Toe game. It's time to turn to another interesting application that displays every type of message box available with the `MsgBox` function. In essence, this program is a message box displayer. The radio buttons are in arrays and grouped within *frames*. A frame is an object that provides a visual and functional container for controls. It is an object that has a solid border around it and a caption at the top. In Figure 7.9, there are four frames. The one on the left has the caption Buttons, the one next to it says Icons, the one to the right of the form says Defaults, and the fourth frame below Icons and Defaults says Modality. When radio buttons are placed in frames they automatically group together so that no more than one option button can be selected.

Figure 7.8.

An error message box added to the Tic-Tac-Toe game.

Caution: You cannot just drag an option button over a frame to add it to the frame. Instead, you must actually draw the option button on the frame. This means you can't draw an option button in a frame using the shortcut of double-clicking the control in the toolbox.

Tip: To determine whether an option control is bound to a frame, simply drag the frame. If the option button moves with the frame, it is bound to the frame; if it doesn't move with the frame then it is not bound to the frame and will need to be redrawn on it. (Another way to "redraw" an existing control in a frame is to use Cut and Paste. Select the control—an option button, perhaps—then either press Ctrl+X on the keyboard or select Cut from the Edit menu. Next, use the mouse pointer to select the frame on which you want to draw the cut control, then press either Ctrl+P on the keyboard or select Paste from the Edit menu. The cut control will appear on the frame.)

To start the application and create the form shown in Figure 7.9, open a new project in Visual Basic. Change Form1's Name property to frmMsg and change its Caption property to Message Box Options. Save the form and project by selecting the Save Project item from the File menu. Save the form and project as Msgbox.frm and Msgbox.vbp, respectively.

Next, draw four frames on the form in roughly the same positions as shown in Figure 7.9. Change their Caption properties to correspond to Figure 7.9. Then draw a radio button inside one of the frames—the frame captioned "Buttons," for example. Change that button's `Name` property to `optButton`. Next, change its `Caption` property from Option1 to OK Button Only. Now, click the radio button to make sure that it is selected. Go into the Edit menu and select Copy, press Ctrl+C, or use the pop-up menu to copy the button. When you copy the option button, it will become deselected. Return to the form and select the frame captioned Button (so you can see the eight black handles around the frame's edge). Then, select Paste from the Edit menu, press Ctrl+V, or use the pop-up menu. Visual Basic will ask you whether you want to create a control array. Answer Yes. Move that new option button to where it belongs under the first button. Change its Caption property to OK and Cancel Buttons. If you scroll down the Property Window, you will see that the radio button has also been named optButton. If you look at its Index property, you will see that its Index is now 1. (The first option button's Index is 0.)

Continue in this manner until all the option buttons for that frame are created. Move on to the next frame, Icons, and repeat the process by first creating a new option button, changing its Name property to optIcons, and copying and pasting in the remaining buttons for that frame. Then move on to the final two frames, using Figure 7.9 as a guide and Table 7.3 to set the properties.

Figure 7.9.
The MsgBox form completed.

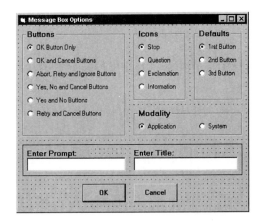

Table 7.3. Object properties for frmMsg.

Object	Property	Setting
Form	Appearance	1-3D
	Caption	Message Box Options
	Name	frmMsg
Frame	Caption	Buttons
	Name	Frame1
Option Button	Caption	OK Button Only
	Index	0
	Name	optButton
	Value	True

Object	Property	Setting
Option Button	Caption	OK and Cancel Buttons
	Index	1
	Name	optButton
	TabStop	False
Option Button	Caption	Abort, Retry, and Cancel Buttons
	Index	2
	Name	optButton
	TabStop	False
Option Button	Caption	Yes, No, and Cancel Buttons
	Index	3
	Name	optButton
	TabStop	False
Option Button	Caption	Yes and No Buttons
	Index	4
	Name	optButton
	TabStop	False
Option Button	Caption	Retry and Cancel Buttons
	Index	5
	Name	optButton
	TabStop	False
Frame	Caption	Icons
	Name	Frame2
Option Button	Caption	Stop
	Index	0
	Name	optIcons
	Value	True
Option Button	Caption	Question
	Index	1
	Name	optIcons
	TabStop	False

continues

Table 7.3. continued

Object	Property	Setting
Option Button	Caption	Exclamation
	Index	2
	Name	optIcons
	TabStop	False
Option Button	Caption	Information
	Index	3
	Name	optIcons
	TabStop	False
Frame	Caption	Defaults
	Name	Frame3
Option Button	Caption	1st Button
	Index	0
	Name	optDef
	Value	True
Option Button	Caption	2nd Button
	Index	1
	Name	optDef
	TabStop	False
Option Button	Caption	3rd Button
	Index	2
	Name	optDef
	TabStop	False
Frame	Caption	Modality
	Name	Frame4
Option Button	Caption	Application
	Index	0
	Name	optMod
	Value	True
Option Button	Caption	System
	Index	1
	Name	optMod
	TabStop	False

Object	Property	Setting
Shape	BorderColor	White
	Name	Shape1
Label	Caption	Enter Prompt:
	Name	Label1
Text Box	Name	txtPrompt
	Text	(None)
Label	Caption	Enter Title:
	Name	Label2
Text Box	Name	txtTitle
	Text	(None)
Command Button	Caption	OK
	Default	True
	Name	cmdOK
Command Button	Caption	Cancel
	Name	cmdCancel

Tip: Although it might seem pointless to name shapes, labels, and frames because you rarely reference them in code, it is important to remember that things that are obvious now may not be so obvious when you return to the program in a few years. *Remember to always name controls and forms.*

When you have finished placing the frames and option buttons on the form, it is time to turn to the two labels, two text boxes, and rectangle surrounding them. Place the labels and text boxes on the screen in approximately the same position as in Figure 7.9. Change their Name and Caption properties to reflect the properties listed in Table 7.3. Then, using the shape tool on the toolbar, draw a rectangle around the list and text boxes. Size and reshape it until you are happy with it. Finally, add the two command buttons at the bottom of the form, cmdOK and cmdCancel.

When the application is running, the user chooses the message box options that she or he wants. These selected options return specific Index values to the program. The program then uses these values to form the desired message box. These values are placed in a public variable named, appropriately enough, WhichMessage. The user actions that the program centers around are the click events for the option button arrays. The final click event that triggers all the others is the OK button's click event. That is where WhichMessage is placed. (See Figures 7.10 and 7.11.)

`WhichMessage` is an integer that is the sum of its parts, the publicly declared variables `Button`, `IconTp`, `Default`, and `Modality`. Each of these variables corresponds to one particular option button array. For example, the variable `Button` coincides with the `optButton` array; `IconTp` corresponds to the `optIcons` array, and so on. The value of the variable equals the value of the selected option. Each of these values are displayed in Table 7.1. When added together, they equate to `WhichMessage`, which corresponds to the `Button` argument of the `MsgBox` function.

The complete code, event by event, appears in Listing 7.1.

Figure 7.10.
The MsgBox application running after the user has selected certain message box options, but before she clicks OK.

Figure 7.11.
The resulting message box after the user has clicked OK.

Listing 7.1. The MsgBox application (Msgbox.vbp).

```
Option Explicit

Dim Button As Integer
Dim IconTp As Integer
Dim Default As Integer
Dim Modality As Integer
Dim WhichMessage As Integer
Dim Title As String
Dim Prompt As String

Private Sub cmdCancel_Click()
      Unload cmdCancel.Parent
End Sub

Private Sub cmdOK_Click()
      WhichMessage = Button + IconTp + Default + Modality
      MessageBox WhichMessage
End Sub
```

```
Public Sub MessageBox(W As Integer)

Dim RetVal As Long
Dim ReturnString As String

        RetVal = MsgBox(Prompt, W, Title)

        Select Case RetVal
                Case 1
                        ReturnString = "You pressed OK!"
                Case 2
                        ReturnString = "You pressed Cancel."
                Case 3
                        ReturnString = "You pressed Abort."
                Case 4
                        ReturnString = "You pressed Retry."
                Case 5
                        ReturnString = "You pressed Ignore."
                Case 6
                        ReturnString = "You pressed Yes!"
                Case 7
                        ReturnString = "You pressed No."

        Case Else
                ReturnString = "Internal Error!"

        End Select

        frmMsg.Caption = ReturnString

End Sub

Private Sub Form_Initialize()
        Prompt = "This is the Prompt."
        Title = "This is the Title."
        Button = 0
        IconTp = 16
        Default = 0
        Modality = 0
        optDef(1).Enabled = False
        optDef(2).Enabled = False
End Sub

Private Sub optButton_Click(Index As Integer)
Button = Index

        Select Case Index
                Case 0
                        optDef(1).Enabled = False
                        optDef(2).Enabled = False
                Case 2, 3
                'enable second and third button default
                        optDef(1).Enabled = True
                        optDef(2).Enabled = True
                Case 1, 4, 5
                'enable second  buttons
                        optDef(1).Enabled = True
                        optDef(2).Enabled = False
        End Select
```

continues

Listing 7.1. continued

```
End Sub

Private Sub optDef_Click(Index As Integer)
     Default = Index * 256
End Sub

Private Sub optIcons_Click(Index As Integer)
     IconTp = (Index + 1) * 16
End Sub

Private Sub optMod_Click(Index As Integer)
     Modality = Index * 4096
End Sub

Private Sub txtPrompt_LostFocus()
     Prompt = txtPrompt.Text
End Sub

Private Sub txtTitle_Change()
     Title = txtTitle.Text
End Sub
```

Context-Sensitive Help for Message and Input Boxes

In Visual Basic 4.0, message boxes (and input boxes) can now be set to trigger context-sensitive help files. This can be set by adding `Helpfile` and `Context` arguments to the `MsgBox()` or `InputBox()` function call. When these two arguments are supplied, a Help button appears on the message or input box. Help files are discussed in detail in Chapter 21, "Creating a Windows 95 Help File."

Since the icons and general appearance of message boxes like these look like standard message boxes in commercial Windows 95 applications, using `MsgBox()` in your programs can make them appear more professional. And, as indicated, you can receive a limited amount of information back from `MsgBox`—which button the user clicked. However, that limits the user's input options to Yes, No, Cancel, Abort, Retry, Ignore, and OK. On the other hand, the next function you will explore, `InputBox()`, has no such restriction. The `InputBox` function displays a prompt in a dialog box and waits for the user to input text or choose a button. After the user is finished, `InputBox` returns the contents of the text box.

An *InputBox()* Application— A Windows Shell

To see how `InputBox()` functions, you are going to create an application that uses it. In this case, you will use Visual Basic's `Shell()` function, which can start Windows applications. The way Shell syntax works is as follows:

```
Shell (pathname[, windowstyle])
```

The Shell function syntax uses these arguments:

- *Pathname*—the name of a program to execute any required arguments or command-line switches.

- *Windowstyle*—a number corresponding to the style of the window in which the program will run. If Windowstyle is omitted, the program will start minimized.

The Windowstyle argument uses the values shown in Table 7.4.

Table 7.4. The Shell function's **Windowstyle** types and values.

Constant	Value	Description
vbNormalFocus	1	The program window has the focus and is located at its default size and position.
vbMinimizedFocus	2	The program window is displayed as an icon with focus.
vbMaximizedFocus	3	The program window has the focus and is maximized.
vbNormalNoFocus	4	The program window is next located to its default size and position, though the calling Visual Basic program retains focus.
vbMinimizedNoFocus	6	The program window is displayed as an icon, and the calling Visual Basic program retains focus.

If the Shell function is able to execute the program, it returns the program's *task ID*. A task ID is a unique number identifying the program. The task ID will not be used in this program.

You can create your own application called Windows Shell, which will start applications on request. To get the name and path of the application to start, use the InputBox() function. InputBox syntax appears as follows:

```
InputBox(prompt [,title][, default][, xpos][, ypos][, helpfile, context])
```

The InputBox function syntax uses these arguments:

- *prompt*—a string expression displayed as the message in the dialog box.

- *title*—a string expression in the title bar of the dialog box. If the title argument is left out, the application name is placed in the title bar.

- *default*—a string expression displayed in the text box as the default response if no other input is provided by the user. If the default argument is left out, the text box is displayed empty.

- *xpos*—a numeric expression that specifies, in twips (there are 1440 twips per inch), the horizontal distance of the dialog box's left edge from the left edge of the screen. If xpos is omitted, the dialog box is centered horizontally.

- *ypos*—a numeric expression that specifies, in twips, the vertical distance of the dialog box's upper edge from the top of the screen. If the *ypos* argument is left out, the dialog box is vertically positioned one-third of the way down the screen.

- *helpfile*—a string expression that identifies the Help file to use to provide corresponding Help for the dialog box. If `helpfile` is a provided argument, `context` must also be included.

- *context*—a numeric expression that represents the Help context number assigned to the appropriate Help topic by the author. When `helpfile` and `context` are supplied, a Help button automatically appears in the dialog box.

Unlike message boxes, input boxes do not display icons. Also, they only come in the OK and Cancel button flavor. Input boxes will, however, enable you to accept any string input by the user. To use an input box, you specify the prompt—or message in the box—and, if you wish, the title of the input box, a default string input, and positioning coordinates. If you do not specify the input box's position, it will automatically appear in the center of the screen.

To see all of this in action, start a new Visual Basic project. Change Form1's `Caption` property to Windows Shell and change its Name property to frmShell. Save the project, using the Save Project item from the File menu. Save the form and project as Shell.frm and Shell.vbp, respectively.

Now, select the form and open the Menu Editor. Create one menu captioned &File and named mnuFile. Add two items to the file menu: &Run... and E&xit. Give them the names mnuFileRun and mnuFileExit. Assign access and shortcut keys to the menu items as shown in Figure 7.12. When you are finished designing the menu, click OK.

Figure 7.12.
The new File menu for the Windows Shell application.

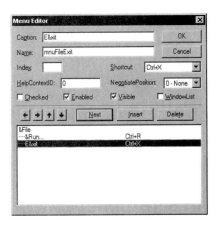

Next, click on the File menu, and then click the Run menu item to open the Code Window. Your cursor will be displayed in the mnuFileRun Click event template:

```
Private Sub mnuFileRun_Click()

End Sub
```

In this Sub procedure, you want to get specific string input. So, an input box would work admirably in this situation. Actually, because the menu item, Run…, has an ellipsis after it, the user expects a dialog box to appear. When the string is returned from the InputBox function, it can be passed on to the Shell function, as follows:

```
Private Sub mnuFileRun_Click()
     Dim RetVal As Long

     RetVal = Shell(InputBox("Application to run:", "Run…"), vbNormalFocus)

End Sub
```

In this case, the code asks for an input box that has the prompt, Application to run: and the caption Run… in the title bar. It then passes the string that was entered by the user back to the Shell function, along with a Window-style argument of vbNormalFocus, requesting a normal window with focus.

In addition, you should make the File menu's Exit item active as well, by placing the End statement in the mnuFileExit_Click() Sub procedure as follows:

```
Private Sub mnuFileExit_Click()
     Unload Me
End Sub
```

In the preceding code, Me is equivalent to the present form; thus, frmShell could be put in place of the Me keyword (for example, Unload frmShell).

At this point, you are all set. When the Windows Shell application runs, a simple window appears on the screen with a File menu. When the user opens the File menu, two items are available: Run… and Exit. When the user clicks Run…, a dialog box opens as shown in Figure 7.13. Then, the user can type the name of a Windows application to run, perhaps Calc.exe, to start the calculator that comes with Windows. (Remember that you must enter the path where Calc.exe resides if it is not in your path, for example: C:\Windows\Calc.exe.) When OK is clicked, the application starts and functions normally.

Figure 7.13.
The Windows Shell application running.

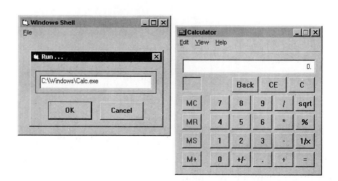

Unfortunately, there is a problem with this application. As it stands, the user has to remember the name and correct path of the application she wishes to run. At the end of this chapter you will solve this problem by adding a Browse button that calls the Common Dialog control. This will let users specify the desired application easily, without having to remember the file's name or location.

For now, it is time to consider the look of the input box. At present, it is less than optimal. This can be a hang-up unless you can design your windows explicitly for your programs. As you can see, the prompt appears at the top of the dialog box and the text box is some distance away at the bottom. A better option is to design the dialog box you want to use yourself. That is the topic for the next section.

Creating Applications with Multiple Windows

As you might expect, it is not difficult to create multiple form programs in Visual Basic. It is time to revise the Windows Shell program to use a dialog box designed by you. To do that, you need a new form. This is easily done by selecting the Form item from the Insert menu. The new form, called Form1, appears on the screen as in Figure 7.14.

Figure 7.14.
The new form added to the Windows Shell program.

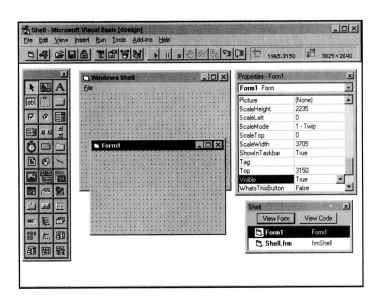

All along through this book, you have been giving forms names, though it might have seemed unnecessary. This is where form names come into play—with multiple forms. If both forms have distinct names, it is easy to recognize them in the Project Window. And using the Project Window, it is easy to switch between them, just by clicking on the name of the form you want to see.

The First Form

When multiple forms are involved, a question arises. Which one does Visual Basic start first when the application opens? It would be awkward if Visual Basic decided to place the dialog box on the screen by itself. The default in Visual Basic is that the first form created in an application is the first form that opens when the application runs.

The `Form_Initialize` Event

In Visual Basic 4, starting a form now triggers a `Form_Initialize` event. This event is activated *before* the form is loaded. It is a great place for initialization code.

When the first form is started, a `Form_Initialize` event is generated and a `Form_Load` event is generated for that form. As you have seen, `Form_Load` is a special event that occurs just as a form is about to appear. If your application depends on a number of windows being on the screen at the same time, `Form_Load` can be used on the first window—the one Visual Basic displays first—to display the other windows. You will learn a great deal about the `Form_Initialize` and `Form_Load` events later.

The question now is, how are other windows displayed? After you have designed the dialog box, how will you be able to place it on the screen when you want it to appear? Visual Basic has several ways of handling this task. For example, the two statements `Load` and `Unload` add and remove forms into and out of memory. In this way, `Load` and `Unload` work in much the same way they did with menu items in the previous chapter. Here, however, the forms can be added and removed by using their Name properties like this:

```
Load Form1
```

```
Unload Form1
```

Note, though, that simply loading a form does not display it. Display is handled by the `Show` method. As you have seen before, as with the `SetFocus` method, a *method* is similar to a procedure, but it is tied to an object (a control or form) just like a property. In other words, a property is made up of data attached to the object, and a method is a procedure attached to the object.

The `Show` method automatically makes a `Load` event occur if the form has not already been loaded; thus, `Show` will load the form and then display it. If the form has already been loaded, `Show` makes only the form appear on the screen and there is no need for the `Load` event to occur again. In fact, if code is executed that uses a property or method that has not been already loaded into memory, Visual Basic automatically loads it before executing that statement.

The opposite of `Show` is `Hide`. `Hide` has the same two-tiered nature as `Show`. If a form is visible on the screen, `Hide` makes it invisible, though the form is still loaded into memory. It takes an `Unload` statement to remove the form from memory. Together, `Show` and `Hide` are the two methods that handle dialog box appearances and disappearances. For example, if you changed the Name property of the second form you created in the Windows Shell program to frmRunDialog, the following statement would be needed to load and display the form:

```
frmRunDialog.Show 1
```

The number 1 is an argument that makes the dialog box modal. (If you recall, this is the same value you saw in Table 7.4.) There is another way to write this code statement, though. Instead of using the number 1, which can be a bit cryptic when reading through code, you could use one of the new constants supplied with Visual Basic, like this:

```
frmRunDialog.Show vbFocusNormal
```

When a number of forms are on the screen, you may wonder how to refer to the controls and properties of a particular form. The solution is to simply use the form as part of that control's or property's name, like this:

```
Form1.mnuFileExit
```

or

```
frmAnalyze.txtBigBox
```

Until now, when there was only one form, there was no need to specify the form name when referring to a control. Visual Basic simply assumed that the current form was the one desired. With multiple forms, however, all you need to do is specify the form's Name property along with the property or method you want to access.

In other words, you used to refer to a control's property set as follows: Control.Property. Now, there might be a number of forms to choose from, so you can specify the same thing like this:

```
Form.Control.Property.
```

In addition, now that you know a little bit about methods, you can refer to them by form as well:

```
Form.Method.
```

But, put the Windows Shell application away for a while. When you close the project, make sure that you have changed the new form's Name property to frmRunDialog and save the form as Run.frm.

Right now it's time to discover another type of multiple form applications—MDIs.

Introduction to MDI Applications

Another important concept regarding multiple windows applications is the *Multiple Documents Interface* (or MDI). The idea is a familiar one to most Windows 95 users, even if they don't realize that they have been using MDI applications. Because part of this chapter deals with multiple form programs, it seems appropriate to introduce them here. It is time for you to become acquainted with

MDIs. That way, you will be able to move ahead when MDI applications are discussed in detail in Chapter 15, "Advanced Control and Form Handling."

In MDI applications many child windows can be opened. These child windows are all the same. An MDI application can have many child windows, but there can be only one parent window per application. Most Windows word processing programs, such as Microsoft Word and WordPerfect, are good examples of familiar MDI applications.

To create a simple MDI application, start a new Visual Basic project. As usual, the default form, Form1, appears on the design desktop. As soon as the MDI form is added, this default form will become the child form. Add that MDI form now by selecting the MDI item from the Insert Menu. A new form, MDIForm1, appears on the screen. That new form is the parent form.

Notice that the icons in the Project Window and the upper-left corner of each form are different for MDI child and parent forms. Also, the default gray background of the MDI form is darker. This difference is shown in Figure 7.15.

Figure 7.15.
The VB desktop, displaying the different types of form icons on the forms and in the Project Window.

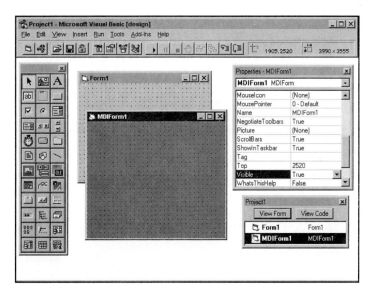

Now select Form1 and turn your attention to its Properties window. Change both its Name and Caption properties to frmChild. Also, change the MDIChild property to True. (Notice that when you set this property to True, the icon next to frmChild in the Properties window changes to an MDI icon.) Next, click on MDIForm1 to select it. Open the Menu Editor by selecting the Menu Editor item from the Tools menu. Create a &File menu and Name it mnuFile. Add two menu items to the File menu: &New and E&xit, naming them mnuFileNew and mnuFileExit, respectively. (Don't forget to use the right pointing arrow to indent the two menu items.) Next, create another menu title, &Window, and name it mnuWindow. Make sure to click the left pointing arrow to remove the indenting. Also, be sure to check the `WindowList` box property for the Window menu, as shown in Figure 7.16. Give each menu item shortcut keys as well. (These are also shown in Figure 7.16.) When you are finished designing the menu, click OK.

Figure 7.16.
The completed menu entries
for the MDI test application.

Next, add the following code to the `mnuFileNew` click event:

```
Private Sub mnuFileNew_Click()
        Dim X As New frmChild

        X.Show

End Sub
```

That's all there is to it! You now have a simple, fully functioning MDI application, as in Figure 7.17.

Figure 7.17.
The test MDI application.

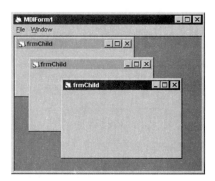

It's time to go to town and make this MDI application a little more interesting. Why not add a counter that keeps track of the number of open child forms. To do this, create a module by choosing Module from the Insert menu. Change that module's `Name` property to MDI; then in that module's Code Window, declare `ChildCounter` as a public integer variable, like this:

```
Public ChildCounter As Integer
```

Next, close the module's Code Window and save the entire project, using the Save Project item from the File menu. Save the Parent form, MDIForm1, as `Parent.frm`; the Child form, frmChild, as `Child.frm`; the module as `MDI.bas`; and the project as `MDI.vbp`.

Now add the code that will keep track of the number of open forms, and simultaneously change the child forms' captions. Open the Code Window associated MDIForm1. There, in the form's Load event and in the menu items `mnuFileExit` and `mnuFileNew` click events, you will use the publicly declared variable `ChildCounter` to keep track of the open child forms. Enter the code as follows:

```
'MDIForm1 code

Private Sub MDIForm_Load()
        ChildCounter = 1
End Sub



Private Sub mnuFileExit_Click()
        End
End Sub

Private Sub mnuFileNew_Click()
        Dim X As New frmChild

        ChildCounter = ChildCounter + 1
        X.Show

End Sub
```

Now add the code to `frmChild` that changes the captions of the new child forms and also subtracts one from the `ChildCounter` every time a child form is unloaded.

```
'frmChild code

Private Sub Form_Initialize()
        Me.Caption = Me.Caption & " #" & Str(ChildCounter)
End Sub

Private Sub Form_Unload(Cancel As Integer)
        ChildCounter = ChildCounter - 1
End Sub
```

And that's it! You now have a crude counting method that tracks Child forms, as in Figure 7.18.

You might have noticed, however, that this counter does not always work in the way you might like. Use this example: With the application running, open four child forms. Now, using the Close button on the second child form, close that form. Next, open another new Child form. Compare the captions. Unfortunately, there are now two `frmChild #4` forms on the screen, as in Figure 7.19.

Figure 7.18.
The MDI application running, showing added child forms.

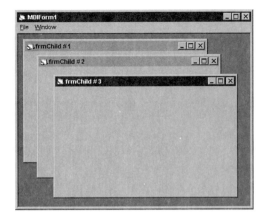

Figure 7.19.
The MDI application, with misnamed child forms.

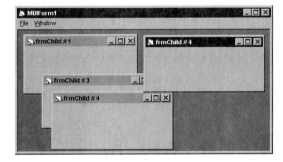

Techniques for tracking child forms more accurately are discussed in Chapter 15, "Advanced Control and Form Handling."

It is time to add a status panel to the bottom of the application that displays the value of the variable ChildCounter.

First, add the 3D panel custom control to your toolbox. To do that select the Custom Controls... item from the Tools menu. A Custom Controls dialog box opens with an Available Controls list box on the left side. Scroll down this list box until you find Sheridan 3D Controls (Threed32.ocx). Select it and make sure that an X appears in the box to the right of Sheridan 3D Controls. (If you ever want to remove a custom control from the toolbox, use the Available Controls list box. Just deselect, or uncheck, the custom control.) Now click OK. When Visual Basic returns you to the design desktop, new control tools are added to the toolbox. Notice how the toolbox changes shape to accommodate the new buttons, as in Figure 7.20.

Now, using one of the new controls you just added to the toolbox, select an SS Panel (the one on the bottom row on the left). Draw a 3D panel on MDIForm1. Select the panel's Align property and change it to 2-Align Bottom. As soon as you do that, the panel snaps to the bottom of the form, as shown in Figure 7.21. Stretch the panel horizontally, making it wider, to each side edge of the form. Using the Properties Window, remove the text from the panel's Caption property.

Figure 7.20.
The toolbar expanded to accommodate the new object tools.

Now you can have a little fun with the label's three-dimensional capabilities. All of these capabilities are, of course, properties of the object. Scroll to the BevelInner property and change it from 0-No Bevel to 1-Inset Bevel. Notice that the property below it, BevelOuter, is already set to 2-Raised Bevel. This is its default. Next, move down to the BevelWidth property and change it to 2, and do the same for the BorderWidth property. You can experiment with these four settings, seeing which one affects what look, and find the panel look that you like.

Figure 7.21.
The 3D label aligned to the bottom of MDIForm1.

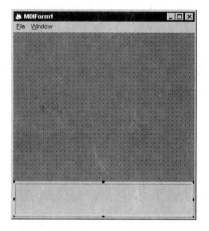

Now add two labels to the panel by selecting the label tool on the toolbar and drawing the labels one above the other as in Figure 7.22. Change the Name property of the top label to lblCaption and then change its Caption property to Child Counter is:. Change its Alignment property to 2-Center. Set the lower label's Name property to lblCounter and delete any text from its Caption property. Scroll to the Align property and change it, also, to 2-Center.

Figure 7.22.
The MDIForm1 3D panel and labels positioned correctly.

Next, open the MDIForm1 Code Window and add the following code to the Initialize event:

```
Private Sub MDIForm_Initialize()
      ChildCounter = 0
      lblCounter.Caption = Str(ChildCounter)
End Sub
```

Finally, add the following code to the Initialize and Unload events of frmChild:

```
Private Sub Form_Initialize()
      Me.Caption = Me.Caption & " #" & Str(ChildCounter)
      MDIForm1.lblCounter.Caption = Str(ChildCounter)
End Sub

Private Sub Form_Unload(Cancel As Integer)
      ChildCounter = ChildCounter - 1
      MDIForm1.lblCounter.Caption = Str(ChildCounter)
End Sub
```

Now run the application. The new label, lblCaption, keeps track of the value of the public variable ChildCounter, as in Figure 7.23.

Figure 7.23.
The MDI application running, showing the number of open child forms.

The properties of the objects used in the MDI application should be set as shown in Table 7.5.

Table 7.5. The MDI application (MDI.vbp).

Object	Property	Setting
Form (child)	Caption	frmChild
	MDIChild	True
	Name	frmChild
MDIForm (parent)	Caption	
	Name	MDIForm1
3D Panel	Align	2-Align Bottom
	BevelInner	1-Inset Bevel
	BevelOuter	2-Raised Bevel
	BevelWidth	3
	BorderWidth	1
	Caption	(None)
	Name	Panel3D1
Label	Alignment	2-Center
	Caption	Child Counter is:
	Name	lblCaption
Label	Alignment	2-Center
	Caption	(None)
	Name	lblCounter

The menu settings for frmChild are shown in Table 7.6.

Table 7.6. The frmChild menu.

Caption	Name	Indentation	Other Information
&File	mnuFile	0	(None)
&New	mnuFileNew	1	Shortcut: Ctrl+N
E&xit	mnuFileExit	1	Shortcut: Ctrl+X
&Window	mnuWindow	0	WindowList = True (Checked)

The variable `declaration` in MDI.bas is as follows:

```
Option Explicit

Public ChildCounter As Integer
```

Listing 7.2. The complete code for **MDIForm1**, the parent form.

```
Option Explicit

Private Sub MDIForm_Initialize()
      ChildCounter = 0
      lblCounter.Caption = Str(ChildCounter)
End Sub

Private Sub mnuFileExit_Click()
    End
End Sub

Private Sub mnuFileNew_Click()
      Dim X As New frmChild

      ChildCounter = ChildCounter + 1
      X.Show

End Sub
```

Listing 7.3. The complete code for the child form, **frmChild**.

```
Option Explicit

Private Sub Form_Initialize()
      Me.Caption = Me.Caption & " #" & Str(ChildCounter)
      MDIForm1.lblCounter.Caption = Str(ChildCounter)
End Sub

Private Sub Form_Unload(Cancel As Integer)
      ChildCounter = ChildCounter - 1
      MDIForm1.lblCounter.Caption = Str(ChildCounter)
End Sub
```

That's it for the mini-MDI application for now. It's good that you have become acquainted with MDIs. In Chapter 15, MDI applications are discussed in depth. For now, it is time to return attention to the Windows Shell program and add a custom dialog box to the application.

Creating Custom Dialog Boxes

You may recall that the dialog box generated by Visual Basic was not very interesting graphically: The text was at the top of the dialog box and the file input box at the very bottom. It's easy to add a custom dialog box to your Windows Shell application. To do that, open the project and view the second form you added earlier, frmRunDialog. This form is going to become your custom dialog box. First, change its Caption property to Run..., just as the Visual Basic input box was labeled earlier.

The job of this dialog box is to accept a string—the name of the Windows application to run. So you will need a text box in it. Place a text box in the upper half of the form, as in Figure 7.24, and remove the default text from the Text property. That way it appears blank. Then change the text box's Name property to txtFile. Also, this form will not need either a maximize or minimize button, because this is a modal dialog box. The user cannot do anything else in the application until dealing with this box. So, find the MinButton and MaxButton properties and set both of them to False. The buttons will still be visible at design-time, but will disappear at run-time.

Figure 7.24.
The text box positioned in the Run... dialog box.

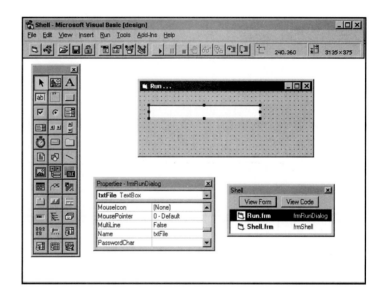

In addition, as with most dialog boxes, this custom dialog box does not need to be resized. So, change the frmRunDialog property BorderStyle to 1-Fixed Single. Fixed single is a fixed-size, single-width border. When a fixed border type is selected, Visual Basic also removes the Size option from that form's system menu. The custom dialog box will also need two buttons: OK and Cancel. In particular, note that most dialog boxes should have a Cancel option, especially if the dialog box is modal. This option gives the user a way out if the choices she has made up to that point were in error or unintentional. For that reason, double-click the command button tool twice, once for each new button, and position the buttons below the text box, as in Figure 7.25. Change the left one's Caption property to OK and its Name property to cmdOK. Then change the right command button's Caption and Name properties to Cancel and cmdCancel, respectively. Also, scroll up to the Cancel button's Cancel property. The default setting for this property is False; set it to True.

The Cancel Property for Command Buttons

Command buttons now come with a Cancel property available in the Properties Window. (This property was available in previous versions of Visual Basic, but only in code, not in the Properties Window.) When this property is set to True and the application is running, the user can quickly cancel the form by pressing the Esc key on the keyboard.

Figure 7.25.
The custom dialog box form.

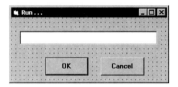

Now that you have designed the dialog box's appearance, it is time to move behind the scenes and start working on the code that will make this box active. The event that makes the dialog box appear is the mnuFileRun click event on frmShell. Open the File menu on that form and click the Run… item.

This procedure should be changed to simply display your new custom dialog box. The Shell function and its accompanying code, currently in this procedure, will be moved to another event. Change the mnuFileRun click event to read:

```
Private Sub mnuFileRun_Click()
      frmRunDialog.Show vbNormalFocus
End Sub
```

Recall that even if frmRunDialog is not in memory when the Show method is executed, Visual Basic will automatically load it. In fact, you can run the program right now. When the Run… item in the File menu is clicked, your custom dialog box will appear. On the other hand, there is no way to get rid of it now, because it is application modal. If you try to switch to the Windows Shell form, you will get a beep—although it is possible to switch to other Windows applications.

After you are finished running the application, end it by selecting the End item from the Run menu, by pressing the End button on the toolbar, or by pressing the Close button on the application's windows.

The real action in the application takes place in the click procedures associated with the buttons on frmRunDialog. When the user clicks the OK button, the program is supposed to execute the Windows application whose path and name were typed in the text box. So bring up the OK button's code skeleton by double-clicking it. The following template appears in the code window:

```
Private Sub cmdOK_Click()

End Sub
```

Because this is the procedure connected to the OK button, this is where the application will execute. This is where you put the orphaned shell function and private function Exists code. (Insert a private function into the code by selecting Procedure… from the Visual Basic Insert menu.)

```
Private Sub cmdOK_Click()
        Dim RetVal As Long
        Dim FileName As String

        FileName = txtFile.Text

        If Exists(FileName) Then
                RetVal = Shell(FileName, vbNormalFocus)

        Else
                MsgBox "Please try again with a file that actually exists!",
                ➥vbExclamation    , "Shell Program"

        End If

        frmRunDialog.Hide


End Sub


Private Function Exists(F As String) As Boolean
        'Tests for the existence of a file

        Dim X As Long

        On Error Resume Next
        X = FileLen(F)

        If X Then
                Exists = True

        Else
                Exists = False

        End If

End Function
```

Before the end of the cmdOK_Click Sub procedure and before the execution of the Windows application, the dialog box should be hidden. Thus, when the Windows application finishes, the program will return to the original Windows Shell form, not the dialog box. That is why the hide method was used just above the End Sub.

Consequently, after the user clicks the OK button, the dialog box disappears and the selected application starts. In addition, while you are here, you should make the OK button the default. To do that, set the cmdOK button's Default property to True.

Determining Whether a Window is Visible

The code can determine whether a form is hidden or visible at run-time by using the Visible property. If Form.Visible is True, the form is shown; if False, the form is hidden.

The other button in the dialog box is the Cancel button. If the Cancel button is clicked, the dialog box should be hidden and the application should return to the original window. A line of code should be added to the Click event for that button, as follows. Figure 7.26 shows the completed Windows Shell application.

```
Private Sub cmdCancel_Click()
     frmRunDialog.Hide
End Sub
```

This returns the user to the original form and restores the focus to it. Nothing else is required. That's all there is to it. The properties of the objects used in the Windows Shell application should be set as shown in Table 7.7.

Figure 7.26.
The Windows Shell application running, showing the custom dialog box.

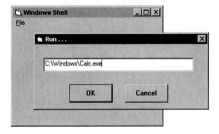

Table 7.7. The Windows Shell Application (Shell.vbp).

Object	Property	Setting
Form	Caption	Windows Shell
	Name	frmShell
Form	BorderStyle	1-Fixed Single
	Caption	Run…
	MaxButton	False
	MinButton	False
	Name	frmRunDialog
Text Box	Name	txtFile
	Text	(None)

Object	Property	Setting
Command Button	Caption	OK
	Default	True
	Name	cmdOK
Command Button	Cancel	True
	Caption	Cancel
	Name	cmdCancel

Table 7.8 shows the menu settings for `frmRunDialog`.

Table 7.8. The menu settings for `frmRunDialog`.

Caption	Name	Indentation	Other Information
&File	mnuFile	0	(None)
&Run…	mnuFileRun	1	(None)
E&xit	mnuFileExit	1	(None)

Listing 7.4. The code for `frmShell`.

```
Option Explicit

Private Sub mnuFileExit_Click()
     Unload Me
End Sub

Private Sub mnuFileRun_Click()
     frmRunDialog.Show vbNormalFocus
End Sub
```

Listing 7.5 shows the code for `frmRunDialog`.

Listing 7.5. The code for `frmRunDialog`.

```
Option Explicit

Private Sub cmdCancel_Click()
     frmRunDialog.Hide
End Sub

Private Sub cmdOK_Click()
     Dim RetVal As Long
     Dim FileName As String
```

continues

Listing 7.5. continued

```
        FileName = txtFile.Text

        If Exists(FileName) Then
                RetVal = Shell(FileName, vbNormalFocus)

        Else
                MsgBox "Please try again with a file that actually exists!",
                ➥vbExclamation     , "Shell Program"

        End If

        frmRunDialog.Hide

End Sub

Private Function Exists(F As String) As Boolean
        'Tests for the existence of a file

        Dim X As Long

        On Error Resume Next
        X = FileLen(F)

        If X Then
                Exists = True

        Else
                Exists = False

        End If

End Function
```

As you can see, there really is very little code for such a powerful application, and each line of code is tied to its own event. In this way, event-driven programming can save you a good deal of work when it comes to user-interface handling. So far, you have been dealing mostly with the user-interface. But in the next chapter, when you start working with files, you will start to add more code for internal data processing behind the scenes. Earlier in this chapter, you saw how to use InputBox as a dialog box of sorts, but now you have seen that it is almost as easy to create your own dialog boxes. The result is usually worth the trouble in Visual Basic. Just compare your custom dialog box in Figure 7.26 with the default InputBox in Figure 7.13.

In fact, there are many types of controls you can find in dialog boxes. Buttons and text boxes are only two of them. For instance, your next application will include a control panel that will let you set different aspects of the main window with various controls, including scroll bars. Generally, control panels are very popular in large-scale Windows applications. You will investigate that next.

Adding a Control Panel to Your Applications

You can start a new application to demonstrate how control panels work in Windows applications. As you probably know, a control panel is used to customize certain aspects of an application. In this example, you will use it to set some properties of the main window: the background color, the height and width of the window, and the main window's caption. Also, this program will give you experience with changing the properties of another window from the current one. And you will use a new type of control: *scroll bars*.

As is normal when starting a new application, change the default form's Name and Caption properties. In this case, change them to frmTestWindow and Test Window, respectively. Then save the project using the Save Project item from the File menu. Save the form as Test.frm and the project as Panel.vbp. Now you are ready to start.

Add a second form by selecting the Form item from the Insert menu. Change its Name and Caption properties to frmControlPanel and Control Panel, respectively. Using the Save File item from the File menu, save this form as Panel.frm. Put a text box, which should be Named txtNewCaption, onto frmControlPanel. Add a label with the Caption property 'Application Caption' and an Alignment property of 2-Center, as in Figure 7.27.

Figure 7.27.
Starting the Control Panel application with the text box and label placed near the top of frmControlPanel.

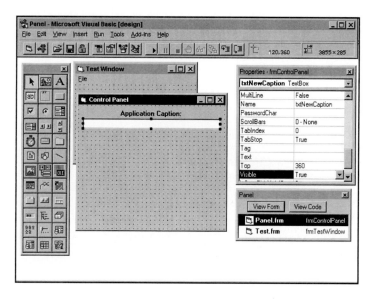

Delete the text from txtNewCaption so the text box appears blank. This box will be used to change the name of the test window, if the user desires. This kind of change will go into effect when the user clicks an OK button. Put that control on the form toward the bottom as in Figure 7.29. Name it cmdOK and change its Caption property to OK. Also add a Cancel button, giving it the name of cmdCancel. As an added touch, make the OK button the default by changing that property to True and changing the Cancel button's Cancel property to True.

As you may have suspected, the Cancel button does nothing more than hide frmControlPanel. Add that code like this:

```
Private Sub cmdCancel_Click()
      frmControlPanel.Hide
End Sub
```

On the other hand, you will be doing more work in this procedure because of the way the control panel application will work. Rather than keeping track of the changes made, you can just set the relevant properties of the test window, after the OK button has been clicked. For example, the way to set the test window's new caption in this procedure is as follows:

```
Private Sub cmdCancel_Click()
      frmTestWindow.Caption = txtNewCaption.Text
      frmControlPanel.Hide
End Sub
```

Notice the first line in the code above:

```
frmTestWindow.Caption = txtNewCaption.Text
```

In general, the way to refer to the properties of another form is to use the form's Name property first. If you wanted to change the properties of one of frmTestWindow's controls, you could refer to it as `frmTestWindow.Control.Property`.

Note that you should also load the current settings of the test window's properties into the control panel's controls when the application opens. For instance, when the control panel is opened for the first time, the text box should read Test Window, because that is the current caption of the test window. Next, you will manipulate the size of the main window.

Using Scroll Bars

The default unit of measurement in Visual Basic is a twip, or 1/1440th of an inch. This means that the two properties the control panel will be changing, the test window's height and width, are measured in twips. You could just use a text box in the control panel to set new sizes in terms of twips.

This would involve the `Val()` function and setting the two appropriate test window properties, `frmTestWindow.Height` and `frmTestWindow.Width`. However, it is not so easy to get a feel for 1/1440th of an inch. Instead, you could use a popular Windows control for easily converting a numerical value into a smooth range that is graphically manipulated—scroll bars.

You have seen scroll bars many times in Windows applications. (See Figure 7.28.) In fact, you used them yourself when you developed the multiline text box for the Notepad application in Chapter 3, although Visual Basic took care of all the scroll bar details there. Now it is up to you. There are five scroll bar properties that concern you here: `Min`, `Max`, `Value`, `LargeChange`, and `SmallChange`.

Figure 7.28.

The parts of a scroll bar.

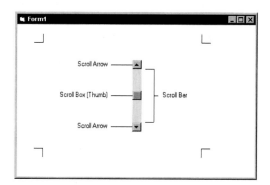

`Min` is the numerical value that indicates the minimum value assigned to the scroll bar. `Max` is the numerical value that indicates the maximum values assigned to the scroll bar. Both of the properties are set by the programmer, and their values can be set anywhere from 0 to 32,767. The `Value` property, whose default is 0, is an integer value corresponding to the position of the *scroll box* in the scroll bar. (The scroll box is the small square within the scroll bar that slides up and down in a vertical scroll bar or left and right in a horizontal scroll bar.) When the scroll box position is at the minimum value (`Min`), it moves to the left-most position in a horizontal scroll bar or to the top position in a vertical scroll bar. When the scroll box is at the maximum value (`Max`), the scroll box moves to the right-most or bottom position. Similarly, a value halfway between the bottom and top of the range places the scroll box in the middle of the scroll bar.

The `LargeChange` property indicates the amount that `Value` should change each time the user clicks the bar above or below the scroll box. The `SmallChange` property indicates the amount that `Value` should change when the user clicks one of the arrows at the top or bottom of a scroll bar. With the exception of `Value`, all these properties can be set at design-time.

There are two main scroll bar events: `Change` and `Scroll`. Change occurs *after* the scroll box is moved. Scroll occurs *as* the scroll box is moved, but does not occur if the scroll arrows or scroll bar is clicked. In your Control Panel application, the value of the scroll bars should not be read until the OK button is clicked.

Now you will see how this works in practice. Select frmControlPanel and double-click the vertical scroll bar tool in the Visual Basic toolbox. A default-sized scroll bar appears in the control panel window. Change its `Name` property to vsbNewHeight. You will be using a total of five scroll bars in the application. They will correspond to the height and width of the test window, and to three test colors—red, green, and blue—for its background color. Place this first scroll bar over to the left of the control panel, as in Figure 7.29.

Figure 7.29.
The Control Panel with its first scroll bar.

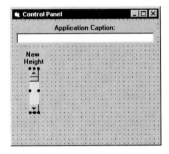

Next, you have to decide the `Min` and `Max` values for this scroll bar. Because there are 1,440 twips to an inch, you can design your window size in inches. For example, to have a minimum window size of 1×2 (height $\times$ width) and a maximum of 5×7, this translates into a twip range of 1440×2880 and 7200×10080. This scroll bar, appropriately named vsbNewHeight, sets the test window's height. This means that the properties you should set at design-time are `vsbNewHeight.Min = 1440` and `vsbNewHeight.Max = 7200`. Similarly, when you design a scroll bar to change the test window's width, you can call it vsbNewWidth. VsbNewWidth.Min will equal 2880, and VsbNewWidth.Max will equal 10800.

To set those properties, click the scroll bar vsbNewHeight on your developing control panel. Using the Properties window, scroll to the `Min` property. Its default value is 0; change this to `1440`. Next, click the `Max` property. Its default value is 32767. Set it to `7200`. In addition, you have to specify values for `LargeChange`—when the user clicks the scroll bar above or below the scroll box—and `SmallChange`—when the user clicks the scroll arrows at either end of the scroll bar. For the purposes of this demonstration, you can use `vsbNewHeight.LargeChange = 1000`, and `vsbNewHeight.SmallChange = 500`. Change those properties accordingly in the Properties window. Now the scroll bar will be active when the program runs. For instance, you will be able to read the scroll bar's setting simply by reading `vsbNewHeight.Value`. So there should be a label above the scroll bar to indicate what it does. Put a label there now, as in Figure 7.32, whose `Caption` property is New Height. Change the label's `Alignment` property to 2-Center.

Next, create another vertical scroll bar. Change its `Name` property to vsbNewWidth and position it to the right of the first one. Put a label above it whose caption reads New Width. Then, change the new scroll bar's `Min` and `Max` properties to 2880 and 10080, respectively. For the `LargeChange` and `SmallChange` properties, you can use 1000 and 500 as you did with the previous scroll bar.

Now add the necessary code to the OK button. When the user clicks the OK button, she wants the test window properties `frmTestWindow.Height` and `frmTestWindow.Width` to equal `vsbNewHeight.Value` and `vsbNewWidth.Value`, respectively. So, you can add these lines to the OK button's click event:

```
Private Sub cmdOK_Click()
        frmTestWindow.Caption = txtNewCaption.Text
        frmTestWindow.Height = vsbNewHeight.Value
        frmTestWindow.Width = vsbNewWidth.Value
        frmControlPanel.Hide
End Sub
```

To see this code in action, you have to add code to the test window to open the control panel in the first place. Go back to the test window, frmTestWindow, select it, and then open the Menu Editor by selecting the Menu Editor item from the Tools menu. For this window, you can create a single menu, whose caption is File and whose name is `mnuFile`. This menu should have two items, Control Panel... and Exit. Name them `mnuFileControlPanel` and `mnuFileExit`, respectively.

In fact, while you are in the Menu Editor, why not add access keys and shortcut keys to the menu? Put an ampersand (&) in front of the first letters of each Name (except for Exit). For example, change File to &File, change Control Panel to &Control Panel, and then change Exit to E&xit. Next, associate shortcut keys with both menu items—perhaps Ctrl+C for Control Panel and Ctrl+X for Exit. The completed menu is displayed in Figure 7.30.

Figure 7.30.
The Menu Editor open, showing the completed File menu for frmTestWindow.

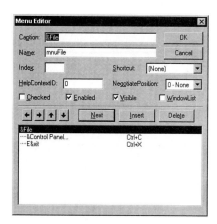

After finishing the menu, click OK to return to the design desktop. Open the Code Window for the Control Panel item on the new File menu by clicking it. A code template for that item opens, as follows:

```
Private Sub mnuFileControlPanel_Click()

End Sub
```

When the user selects this item, the Control Panel's controls should be loaded with the current settings for the test window. Then the control panel should appear on the screen. In other words, the following should happen:

1. Load `frmControlPanel.txtNewCaption.Text` with `frmTestWindow.Caption`.

2. Load `frmControlPanel.vsbNewHeight.Value` with `frmTestWindow.Height`.

3. Load `frmControlPanel.vsbNewWidth.Value` with `frmTestWindow.Width`.

The scroll box in the scroll bars will move to match the number placed in the `Value` property. After you load the defaults, the Control Panel should appear on the screen. To see the values of the scroll bars and to display the form, use the following code:

```
Private Sub mnuFileControlPanel_Click()
        frmControlPanel.txtNewCaption.Text = frmTestWindow.Caption
        frmControlPanel.vsbNewHeight.Value = frmTestWindow.Height
        frmControlPanel.vsbNewWidth.Value = frmTestWindow.Width

        frmControlPanel.Show

End Sub
```

The way to refer to the properties of another form is by referring to the properties' full name, including the form on which they are placed. In addition, before starting the application, you should make the Exit item on the File menu active, using the following `Sub` procedures:

```
Private Sub mnuFileExit_Click()
        Unload Me
End Sub

Private Sub Form_Terminate()
        End
End Sub
```

Now start the application and click on the Control Panel... item on the File menu. When you do, the Control Panel opens and displays the current defaults for the test window's caption and size. Try testing the various controls on the control panel to see if the program is working. If you change the text in the text box and click the OK button, the control panel disappears and the caption in the test window will change to match the new caption. If you use the scroll bars, you can reset the test window's size. This is really no great savings, because the test window can be easily resized just by dragging its edges, but it is still impressive to see as an example.

In fact, you should really give some indication of the new size of the main window as the scroll bars are manipulated. It is always good to give as much visual feedback as possible in a Windows application. If the user changes the window size by mistake, she could still click the Cancel button. It would be a good idea here to draw a rectangle in the control panel to represent the screen and another to represent the test window to show their relative sizes. Rectangles and other simple graphic figures will be discussed in depth later in Chapter 9, "Visual Basic Graphics."

It's time to start work on changing the color of the test window. The background color—the color behind the text—is kept in the BackColor property and is the color you want to manipulate. The foreground color—the color of the text itself—is kept in the ForeColor property.

Note that colors in Windows are determined by three independent settings: a red setting, a green setting, and a blue setting. To take care of all three, you need three vertical scroll bars. You can create them by clicking the vertical scroll bar tool. Position them next to the two you already have made. Place a label above the first new one, captioned Red; a label above the second one, captioned Green; and a third label above the final scroll bar, captioned Blue. Call the scroll bars Name properties vsbNewRed, vsbNewGreen, and vsbNewBlue.

In addition, you can actually provide some direct visual feedback and indicate what color you are selecting. Doing so will introduce you to the scroll bar Change event at the same time. Create a label named lblNewColor and place it in the space between the OK and Cancel buttons at the bottom of the control panel as in Figure 7.31. Delete any text from its Caption property, then give it a fixed, single border by changing its BorderStyle property (you may recall that labels do not have a border by default) to 1-Fixed Single. This is where the color will be displayed that is selected with the scroll bars.

Figure 7.31.
The completed control panel template.

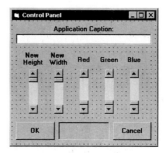

Now that the design of the control panel is finished, lock the controls on the form using the Lock Controls button on the toolbar or the pop-up menu.

Setting Colors in Visual Basic

As mentioned, there are three color settings in a color value under Visual Basic. Each can range from 0 to 255, and they can be put together to form a long integer. This long integer is what you can place in properties such as frmTestWindow.BackColor or lblNewColor.BackColor. LblNewColor is the name of the label you have added to show the color combination represented by the scroll bar values. In fact, Visual Basic provides a special function, the RGB() function, to combine these values. For example, the background color of lblNewColor can be set like this (where vsbNewRed.Value, for example, is the name of the Value property of the red scroll bar):

```
lblNewColor.BackColor = RGB(vsbNewRed.Value, vsbNewGreen.Value, vsbNewBlue.Value)
```

In other words, you need to pass the three color values red, green, and blue, in order, to the `RGB()` function. The function will return a setting that can be used in the `BackColor` and `ForeColor` properties. For that reason, you should give each color value scroll bar a `Min` property of `0` and a `Max` property of `255`. You can also use `SmallChange` and `LargeChange` values of `10` and `20`. After setting these properties in the scroll bars, click vsbNewRed to open the associated `Sub` procedure:

```
Private Sub vsbNewRed_Change()

End Sub
```

This is the event procedure called whenever `vsbNewRed.Value` is changed. Although you could simply read this value when the OK button is clicked and change `frmTestWindow.BackColor` accordingly, you can use this event to keep track of the currently selected color and display it in `lblNewColor`, as follows:

```
Private Sub vsbNewRed_Change()
      lblNewColor.BackColor = RGB(vsbNewRed.Value, vsbNewGreen.Value, vsbNewBlue.Value)
End Sub
```

Now whenever the user changes the setting of the Red scroll bar, the color of `lblNewColor` changes to match. In fact, you can do the same thing in the `Change` event procedures of all three scroll bars, like this:

```
Private Sub vsbNewRed_Change()
      lblNewColor.BackColor = RGB(vsbNewRed.Value, vsbNewGreen.Value, vsbNewBlue.Value)
End Sub

Private Sub vsbNewGreen_Change()
      lblNewColor.BackColor = RGB(vsbNewRed.Value, vsbNewGreen.Value, vsbNewBlue.Value)
End Sub

Private Sub vsbNewBlue_Change()
      lblNewColor.BackColor = RGB(vsbNewRed.Value, vsbNewGreen.Value, vsbNewBlue.Value)
End Sub
```

Make these changes and run the program. When you do, you can change the color in `lblNewColor` by moving the scroll bars around and adjusting the color components in it. In addition, the color that the user creates using the scroll bars needs to be transferred to the test form when the user clicks OK. That code can be added to the OK button's click event:

```
frmTestWindow.BackColor = RGB(vsbNewRed.Value, vsbNewGreen.Value, vsbNewBlue.Value)
```

Now the user can select the color of the test window and see what color she has selected at the same time. When the OK button is clicked, the `BackColor` property of txtTestWindow changes instantly, turning the window to the selected color. That's almost it for your Control Panel application. At this point, it is mostly functional. The last step is to load the original background color from the test window into the control panel when it first starts. To do that, you can load the original color, `frmTestWindow.BackColor`, into `frmControlPanel.lblNewColor.BackColor`. Since this is a demonstration program, you are not going to dissect this color onto separate settings for each scroll bar.

Object	Property	Setting
Command Button	Caption	OK
	Default	True
	Name	cmdOK
Command Button	Cancel	True
	Caption	Cancel
	Name	cmdCancel
Label	BorderStyle	1-Fixed Single
	Caption	(None)
	Name	lblNewColor

The menu settings for `frmTestWindow` are shown in Table 7.10.

Table 7.10. The menu settings for `frmTestWindow`.

Caption	Name	Indentation	Other Information
&File	mnuFile	0	None
&Control Panel...	mnuFileControl Panel	1	Shortcut: Ctrl+C
E&xit	mnuFileExit	1	Shortcut: Ctrl+X

Listing 7.6. The code associated with `frmTestWindow`.

```
Option Explicit

Private Sub Form_Terminate()
      End
End Sub

Private Sub mnuFileControlPanel_Click()
      frmControlPanel.txtNewCaption.Text = frmTestWindow.Caption
      frmControlPanel.vsbNewHeight.Value = frmTestWindow.Height
      frmControlPanel.vsbNewWidth.Value = frmTestWindow.Width
      frmControlPanel.lblNewColor.BackColor = frmTestWindow.BackColor
      frmControlPanel.Show
End Sub

Private Sub mnuFileExit_Click()
      Unload Me
End Sub
```

Listing 7.7. The rest of the code for `frmControlPanel`.

```
Option Explicit

Private Sub cmdCancel_Click()
    frmTestWindow.Caption = txtNewCaption.Text
    frmControlPanel.Hide
End Sub

Private Sub cmdOK_Click()
    frmTestWindow.Caption = txtNewCaption.Text
    frmTestWindow.Height = vsbNewHeight.Value
    frmTestWindow.Width = vsbNewWidth.Value
    frmTestWindow.BackColor = RGB(vsbNewRed.Value, vsbNewGreen.Value,
    ➥vsbNewBlue.Value)

    frmControlPanel.Hide
End Sub

Private Sub vsbNewBlue_Change()
    lblNewColor.BackColor = RGB(vsbNewRed.Value, vsbNewGreen.Value,
    ➥vsbNewBlue.Value)
End Sub

Private Sub vsbNewGreen_Change()
    lblNewColor.BackColor = RGB(vsbNewRed.Value, vsbNewGreen.Value,
    ➥vsbNewBlue.Value)
End Sub

Private Sub vsbNewRed_Change()
    lblNewColor.BackColor = RGB(vsbNewRed.Value, vsbNewGreen.Value,
    ➥vsbNewBlue.Value)
End Sub
```

Creating List Boxes

List boxes are used when there are a number of limited choices present. The user cannot type into the list box to create a new choice; she can only select what is there. On the other hand, a combo box is used for suggested choices. That is, the user can enter her own choice in the combo box's text box or select one of the options from the drop-down list. Say, for example, that you have a list of customized Windows applications that your Windows Shell application is capable of starting. You could present the choices using a list box. Or, you might want to present the different file attribute options—plain file, read-only, hidden, and so on—when writing to a file. In general, list boxes can be useful when there are a number of choices from which to pick. Because list boxes can have a scroll bar, a greater number of selections can be shown in them than in a menu. This makes list boxes a popular item in a dialog box.

Note: Sometimes programmers use combo boxes like list boxes; that way, the user cannot enter values in the combo box that do not exist in its list. This is a useful technique to use when presenting a large quantity of information on a small or crowded form.

As an example, you will put together a mini-database program. Databases usually sort their data records according to some key. You can do that here with a list box. Suppose that this database program is used to keep track of a pharmacy's inventory or even the contents of your own medicine cabinet. You might want to keep track of the following things:

- Name of product
- Quantity of product in stock
- Comments about product

For instance, if you had seven bottles of aspirin, each containing 100 tablets, the data might appear as follows:

- Name of product: Aspirin
- Quantity of product in stock: 7
- Comments about product: Bottles of 100 each

Each of these data items—Aspirin, 7, and Bottles of 100 each—is called a *field* in a database. Together, these three fields make up one *record*. To set up your application, you could add a menu to the main window with an item named Find Record.… When selected, a dialog box would open with a list box that cataloged the names associated with each record: Aspirin, Bandages, Cold Cream, Lipstick, Perfume, and so on. (See Figure 7.33.)

Figure 7.33.
A pictorial representation of a Find Record... menu.

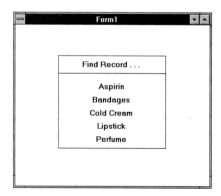

By double-clicking one of those names, the user could bring up the corresponding record. The dialog box would disappear, and the record's data would be placed into text boxes in the application's main window.

One of the list box properties that can help immensely is Sorted. If Sorted is set to True, Visual Basic will keep all the list box items sorted alphabetically. In other words, Visual Basic will automatically sort all the products.

To design this application, start a new Visual Basic project. Using the Properties window, change the Name and Caption properties of the default form to frmDatabase and Database, respectively. Then save the project using the Save Project item from the File menu. Save the form as Database.frm and the project as Database.vbp.

You will need three text boxes on this form. Give the text boxes the names txtNameField, txtNumberField, and txtCommentField. Delete the text in the three text boxes' Text property settings boxes. In fact, you can make the comment box, txtCommentField, a multiline text box so that a considerable amount of text can be stored there. To do that, change txtCommentField's Multiline property to True. Then add a vertical scroll bar by changing the ScrollBar property to 2-Vertical. Next, add three labels to the form. Place one to the left of each text box and give them the corresponding captions Name:, Number:, and Comment:. (Change the labels' Alignment properties to 1-Right Justify.) The completed form is shown in Figure 7.36.

Next, add a menu captioned &File (and named mnuFile) with the following items in it: &Add Item, &Find Item…, &Save File…, &Load File…, and E&xit. The Names of those menu items should be mnuFileAdd, mnuFileFind, mnuFileSave, mnuFileLoad, and mnuFileExit, respectively. Put separator bars between &Find Item… and &Save File…, and between &Load File… and E&xit. Also, add the appropriate access and shortcut keys. (The complete settings for the menu are listed at the end of this chapter in Table 7.10.) The completed menu appears in Figure 7.34.

Figure 7.34.
The frmDatabase completed menu.

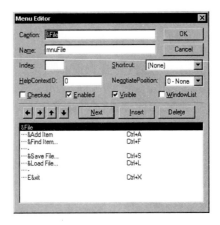

At this point, the application's main window should look like the one in Figure 7.35.

Figure 7.35.
The completed database template window.

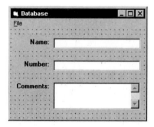

The first menu choice, Add Item, is available so the user can fill the database with information. After editing the three text boxes, the user can select Add Item to add the new information to a new record in the database. The next item, Find Item…, will open the dialog box holding the product name of each record. When the user double-clicks a product name in the list, the dialog box will disappear and the correct record will appear in the main window. You will learn how to add the code for the next two menu items, Save File… and Load File in Chapter 8, "File-Handling in Visual Basic." You already know how to handle the last item on the menu, Exit.

First, you will write the `mnuFileAdd_Click()` procedure. Click the Add Item menu choice, opening the following subroutine template:

```
Private Sub mnuFileAdd_Click()

End Sub
```

When the user clicks Add Item, she wants the current contents of the text boxes to be stored in the database. You can do that by setting up some public variables. Note that they should be public, not form-level variables, because the dialog box—an entirely separate form—will need to reach them as well. Open a module by selecting the Module item from the Insert menu. Change the module's Name property to `Database`, then save the file as Database.bas. Now, add the following declarations to the module:

```
Public Names(100) As String
Public Quantity(100) As String
Public Comments(100) As String
Public TotalRecords As Integer
```

> **Tip:** Normally, Visual Basic starts arrays with a 0 element. If this element is not needed, you can set *Option Base 1*. Using this setting, Visual Basic will not allocate a 0 element, saving memory.

In this way, you are setting aside enough space to hold records for 100 products. Also note that you are keeping track of the total number of records in a public integer named TotalRecords. Now you are free to fill those arrays with data, using the text boxes in the main window before clicking on Add Item. Thus, the data can be stored in the database arrays using the `mnuFileAdd_Click()` event. Note that you increment TotalRecords first, because you are adding a new record.

```
Private Sub mnuFileAdd_Click()
      TotalRecords = TotalRecords + 1
      Names(TotalRecords) = txtNameField.Text
      Quantity(TotalRecords) = txtNumberField.Text
      Comments(TotalRecords) = txtCommentField.Text

      :

End Sub
```

Suppose, for example, that the user is about to create the first record and the text boxes hold the following data:

> Name of product: Aspirin
>
> Quantity of product in stock: 7
>
> Comments about product: Bottles of 100 each

The program would set Names(1) to Aspirin, Quantity(1) to 7, and Comments(1) to Bottles of 100 each. Having stored the data, the application would have to add the name of the product, Aspirin, to the automatically alphabetized list box, so the user could easily select the records. You can do that with the AddItem method. Note that this is a *method*. This means that you will have to attach it to the name of the list box you want to change. For example, you can call the list box that holds all the products' names' lstName. Thus, you would include this line at the end of mnuFileAdd_Click(), as follows:

```
frmRecord.lstName.AddItem txtNameField.Text
```

The final thing you should add to the Add Item click event is a way to clear the text boxes after the new item has been entered and set the focus on the txtNameField text box. To do that, add the following code right before the End Sub in the mnuFileAdd click event:

```
txtNameField.Text = ""
txtNumberField.Text = ""
txtCommentField.Text = ""
txtNameField.SetFocus
```

FrmRecord is the name of the second form, which appears when the user wants to select a record. (You will design this form shortly.) In general, you use the method AddItem in Visual Basic in the following way:

```
object.AddItem item, index
```

The AddItem method syntax has these arguments:

- Object—a required object expression, such as frmRecord.lstName.
- Item—a required string expression specifying the item to add to the object. An example of an Item is txtNameField.Text.
- Index—an optional integer specifying the position within the object where the new item is placed. If a valid value is supplied for Index, the item is placed in that position within the object. If Index is omitted, the item is added at the proper sorted position, if the Sorted property is set to True—or at the end of the list, if Sorted is set to False.

In this example, the list box `Sorted` property will be set to `True`, accordingly sorting the items automatically. Thus, you will not have to specify an `Index` for your entries.

Conversely, to remove an item, you can use the `RemoveItem` method:

```
object.RemoveItem Index
```

The `RemoveItem` method syntax uses these two arguments:

- `Object`—a required object expression, such as `frmRecord.lstName`.
- `Index`—a required integer representing the item's position within the object. For the first item in a ListBox or ComboBox, the index = 0.

Here, the `Index` is not optional. You must use it to specify which item to remove from the list.

That's it for adding an item. The next step is to find items on demand.

The actual work of finding a record is done by the second form, `frmRecord`. Add that to the `mnuFileFind_Click` subroutine like this:

```
Private Sub mnuFileFind_Click()
      frmRecord.Show
End Sub
```

That's it for `mnuFileFind_Click()`. Now you can design the dialog box named frmRecord. Create a second form by selecting the Form item from the Insert menu. Change the new form's `Caption` property to Find Record… and change its `Name` property to frmRecord. Remove the Min and Max buttons by setting those properties to `False`. Also, give it a fixed border by selecting the BorderStyle property and changing the setting from 2-Sizable to 1-Fixed Single. Save the form as `Record.frm`.

Next, add a list box to the form by double-clicking the list box tool in the VB toolbox (fifth one down on the right). Give this list box the `Name` property you have already used, lstName. Set its `Sorted` property to `True`. That way, the entries in the list box will appear in alphabetical order. Note that the `Name`, lstName, appears in the list box. It will be gone at runtime. There are no scroll bars on this list box, but they will appear automatically if the list becomes too long for the list box.

Figure 7.36.
The Find Record… dialog box template.

Now add the two normal control buttons for a dialog box—OK and Cancel. See Figure 7.36 for their placement. Give them the Names cmdOK and cmdCancel, respectively. It is a good idea to make the OK button the default, so set the cmdOK Default property to True as well. As before, it is easy to write the Cancel button procedure. All you have to do is hide frmRecord, like this:

```
Private Sub cmdCancel_Click()
      frmRecord.Hide
End Sub
```

Now you can work on the dialog box's OK button procedure. When the user clicks the OK button or double-clicks the desired item in the list box, she has made her choice and the program should display the corresponding record. Suppose, for example, that your dialog box looks like that depicted in Figure 7.33.

Clicking Aspirin should fill the text boxes in the main window with the data already stored by using the Add item, as follows:

> Name of product: Aspirin
>
> Quantity of product in stock: 7
>
> Comments about product: Bottles of 100 each

In general, you can determine which item is selected in a list box—one item is always selected in list boxes—by using the following list box properties:

Text	The currently selected item.
List	A String array containing all the items.
ListIndex	The index of the selected item. 0 corresponds to the first item.
ListCount	The total number of items in the list.

One of the most commonly used properties in this application is Text—the string that holds the currently selected item. However, the other properties are very useful, too. In this case you have to find the record corresponding to the selection and display it. You can find the correct record with a loop in frmRecord's cmdOK_Click(), like this:

```
Private Sub cmdOK_Click()
      Dim WhichRecord As Integer

      For WhichRecord = 1 To 100
            If Names(WhichRecord) = lstName.Text Then
                  Exit For
            End If
      Next WhichRecord
      :
End Sub
```

Tip: In a production application you would not use numbers to define the range of the `For` command. You would have constants defined that would specify how many records the array could hold.

Numbers that don't have any specific meaning are sometimes called "magic numbers" by programmers. Generally, they should be avoided. These numbers can cause serious headaches when used in a large project. In this simple example, there are two places in the code that you would have to find to change the maximum number of records the program can handle. Imagine what trouble you would have in a 10,000-line program with 20 forms!

It is a much better idea to define a descriptively named constant that holds the value required. For example:

```
Const MaxRecords = 100
    :
For WhichRecord = 1 To MaxRecords
```

Here, the code is just comparing the selected product name with the product name of each record. When it does find the selected name, the program leaves the loop. At this point, you can fill in the fields on the main form correctly and hide `frmRecord`, as follows:

```
frmDatabase.txtNameField.Text = Names(WhichRecord)
frmDatabase.txtNumberField.Text = Quantity(WhichRecord)
frmDatabase.txtCommentField.Text = Comments(WhichRecord)

frmRecord.Hide
```

Note that the important events for list boxes are `Click`—when the user makes a *selection*—and `DblClick`—when the user makes a *choice*. Double-clicking an item is the same as clicking the OK button, so you can call the `cmdOK_Click` procedure in the `DblClick` procedure as follows:

```
Private Sub lstName_DblClick()
      cmdOK_click    'Double clicking is the same as pressing OK.
End Sub
```

The only remaining thing to do is to make the Exit item active in the frmDatabase menu. You can do this in the usual way, using the click event for the Exit item and the form's `Terminate` event:

```
Private Sub mnuFileExit_Click()
      Unload Me
End Sub

Private Sub Form_Terminate()
      End
End Sub
```

The completed application appears in Figure 7.37. The application receives the record data through the text boxes on frmRecord. The user types the pertinent information into each box, then when done, selects the Add Item option from the File menu. That record is then put in memory and the item name appears in the list box. When the user wants to retrieve a record, she selects the product name from the list box and clicks OK. The program sorts through the stored data until it finds the correct entry and displays it in the text boxes on frmRecord. Why not try it out for yourself, now? Most likely, you will find that your database is a success!

Figure 7.37.
*The Database application
running.*

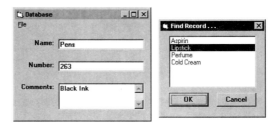

Note, however, that the code was duplicated in both the lstName_DblClick() and cmdOK_Click() events. One way to avoid this is to place this code into a module and call it from these two procedures. So, if you create a public subroutine called GetItem that contains the code in both events, both lstName_DblClick() and cmdOK_Click() can be revised to the following:

```
Private Sub lstName_DblClick()
     GetItem
End Sub

Private Sub cmdOK_Click()
     GetItem
End Sub
```

Using the Project Window, open the Database.bas module. This is where you declared the public variables Names, Quantity, Comments, and TotalRecords earlier. These declarations as well as the code you will put in this module can be reached from every section of the entire application. You can place GetItem in this module very simply. After the public declarations, skip a line and type the code into the Code Window. Visual Basic automatically uses the name of this new procedure, GetItem, from the declaration in the first line: Public Sub GetItem(). When writing code in the new module, you will have to refer to a form's control by including the form's name. That way, the module knows which control on which form to use. It is like an address. When sending a letter, you need the person's name and a street address, plus the city and state to make sure that the letter arrives. In programming, the person's name is equivalent to the property or event (of a control), the street address is equivalent to the control itself, and the city and state are equivalent to the form. To take this one step further, here's an example:

Martha Jones
12 Baskerville Street
Hometown AZ

If you were to call a control's event using the previous address form, it would look like this:

```
Text (property)
txtNameField
frmDatabase
```

Conversely, if Martha's address were placed into proper Visual Basic syntax, her address would look like this:

```
Hometown AZ.12 Baskerville Street.Martha Jones
```

Using the same form, the control event would appear as follows:

```
frmDatabase.txtNameField.Text
```

This is how an application knows where to look for controls and their events. So, the code in the module should be entered as follows:

```
Public Sub GetItem()
      Dim WhichRecord As Integer

      For WhichRecord = 1 To 100
              If (Names(WhichRecord) = frmRecord.lstName.Text) Then
                      Exit For
              End If
      Next WhichRecord

      frmDatabase.txtNameField.Text = Names(WhichRecord)
      frmDatabase.txtNumberField.Text = Quantity(WhichRecord)
      frmDatabase.txtCommentField.Text = Comments(WhichRecord)

      frmRecord.Hide

End Sub
```

The public arrays `Names()`, `Quantity()`, and `Comments()` are not attached to any form, of course. This module is just like any other file associated with the current project. Thus, it is saved and loaded along with the others. The code for the entire database program, as it stands, appears in Listing 7.8. (Remember that you have not yet added any code for the Save File… and Load File… items. That will come later in Chapter 8.)

Connecting to External Database Systems

If you are an advanced Visual Basic programmer interested in databases, the Visual Basic Open Database Connectivity (ODBC) dynamic link libraries enable you to connect to many external database systems, such as Microsoft SQL.

The properties for the controls in this application should be set as in Table 7.11.

Table 7.11. The Database application (Database.vbp).

Object	Property	Setting
Form	Appearance	1-3D
	BorderStyle	1-Fixed Single
	Caption	Find Record...
	MaxButton	False
	MinButton	False
	Name	frmRecord
List Box	Name	lstName
	Sorted	True
Command Button	Caption	OK
	Default	True
	Name	cmdOK
Command Button	Cancel	True
	Caption	Cancel
	Name	cmdCancel
Form	Appearance	1-3D
	Caption	Database
	Name	frmDatabase
Label	Alignment	1-Right Justify
	Caption	Name:
	Name	Label1
Text Box	Name	txtNameField
	Text	(None)
Label	Alignment	1-Right Justify
	Caption	Number:
	Name	Label2
Text Box	Name	txtNumberField
	Text	(None)
Label	Alignment	1-Right Justify
	Caption	Comment:
	Name	Label3

Object	Property	Setting
Text Box	Multiline	True
	Name	txtCommentField
	Scroll Bars	2-Vertical
	Text	(None)

The menu settings for frmDatabase are in Table 7.12.

Table 7.12. The menu settings for frmDatabase.

Caption	Name	Indentation	Other Information
&File	mnuFile	0	(None)
&Add Item	mnuFileAdd	1	Shortcut: Ctrl+A
&Find Item	mnuFileFind	1	Shortcut: Ctrl+F
-	mnuSep1	1	(None)
&Save File	mnuFileSave	1	Shortcut: Ctrl+S
&Load File	mnuFileLoad	1	Shortcut: Ctrl+L
-	mnuSep2	1	(None)
E&xit	mnuFileExit	1	Shortcut: Ctrl+X

The code included in the module Database.bas should be

```
Option Explicit

Public Names(100) As String
Public Quantity(100) As String
Public Comments(100) As String
Public TotalRecords As Integer

Public Sub GetItem()
     Dim WhichRecord As Integer

     For WhichRecord = 1 To 100
            If (Names(WhichRecord) = frmRecord.lstName.Text) Then
                  Exit For
          End If
     Next WhichRecord

     frmDatabase.txtNameField.Text = Names(WhichRecord)
     frmDatabase.txtNumberField.Text = Quantity(WhichRecord)
     frmDatabase.txtCommentField.Text = Comments(WhichRecord)

     frmRecord.Hide

End Sub
```

Listing 7.8. The complete code for `frmRecord`.

```
Option Explicit

Private Sub cmdCancel_Click()
frmRecord.Hide
End Sub

Private Sub cmdOK_Click()
        GetItem
End Sub

Private Sub lstName_DblClick()
        GetItem
End Sub
```

Listing 7.9. The code for `frmDatabase`.

```
Option Explicit

Private Sub Form_Terminate()
        End
End Sub

Private Sub mnuFileAdd_Click()
        TotalRecords = TotalRecords + 1
        Names(TotalRecords) = txtNameField.Text
        Quantity(TotalRecords) = txtNumberField.Text
        Comments(TotalRecords) = txtCommentField.Text

        frmRecord.lstName.AddItem txtNameField.Text

        txtNameField.Text = ""
        txtNumberField.Text = ""
        txtCommentField.Text = ""
        txtNameField.SetFocus

End Sub

Private Sub mnuFileExit_Click()
        Unload Me
End Sub

Private Sub mnuFileFind_Click()
        frmRecord.Show
End Sub
```

Creating Your Own Data Types

As the database program stands, you are maintaining three arrays of data:

```
Pubic Names(100) As String
Public Quantity(100) As String
Public Comments(100) As String
```

In fact, fields like this are usually gathered into their own type as discussed in Chapter 4, "Programming in Visual Basic." In general, such a type declaration appears as follows:

```
Type TypeName
      ElementName As VariableType
      [ElementName As VariableType]
      [ElementName As VariableType]
      :
End Type
```

Thus, you could make a `Record` type for your database, adding it under the public variable `TotalRecords`, like this:

```
Public TotalRecords As Integer

Type Record
      Name As String * 50
      Quantity As String * 20
      Comments As String * 200
End Type
```

This code defines a new data type, `Record`, which contains the fields shown previously. Note that you are giving each string a definite size. The `* 50`, `* 20`, and `* 200` indicate that number of characters in a string (for example, 50 characters in the `Name` string and 20 characters in the `Quantity` string). These are *fixed-length strings*. That means that even if the name of a product such as Aspirin is only 7 characters long, Visual Basic will pad the string to the right of the last letter, n, making it 20 characters long. You can declare an array of this data type and call it `TheData`, as follows:

```
Public TotalRecords As Integer
Public TheData(100) As Record

Type Record
      Name As String * 50
      Quantity As String * 20
      Comments As String * 200
End Type
```

When to Use Fixed-Length Strings

Strings do not need to have a fixed length in a type declaration as above, except when they are used to set up records for random-access files. This is discussed in Chapter 8.

You can use this new array to combine the three separate arrays—`Names`, `Quantity`, and `Comments`—in the Database program into one array—`TheData`. There are only two subroutines that need to change in the application, `mnuFileAdd_Click()` and `GetItem()`. In `frmDatabase`, the procedure for adding an item should be changed to the following:

```
Private Sub mnuFileAdd_Click()
      TotalRecords = TotalRecords + 1
```

```
        TheData(TotalRecords).Name = txtNameField.Text
        TheData(TotalRecords).Quantity = txtNumberField.Text
        TheData(TotalRecords).Comments = txtCommentField.Text

        frmRecord.lstName.AddItem txtNameField.Text

        txtNameField.Text = ""
        txtNumberField.Text = ""
        txtCommentField.Text = ""
        txtNameField.SetFocus

End Sub
```

Then the `GetItem()` subroutine in the module Database.bas changes in a similar manner as shown in the following code. Also, a line of code should be added to change the procedure for looking up an item.

```
Public Sub GetItem()
        Dim WhichRecord As Integer

        For WhichRecord = 1 To 100
                If (RTrim(TheData(WhichRecord).Name)) =
                ➥RTrim(frmRecord.lstName.Text) Then
                        Exit For
                End If
        Next WhichRecord

        frmDatabase.txtNameField.Text = TheData(WhichRecord).Name
        frmDatabase.txtNumberField.Text = TheData(WhichRecord).Quantity
        frmDatabase.txtCommentField.Text = TheData(WhichRecord).Comments

        frmRecord.Hide

End Sub
```

Recall that you are using a fixed-length string for all fields. Because Visual Basic pads such spaces to the right, the above line of code using the `RTrim` function removes those extra spaces. The `RTrim` function simply trims any spaces off the right side of strings before comparing them to the item in the list box.

Note: The `RTrim` function is part of a family of functions that trim spaces, or whitespace, from a string. `RTrim` removes spaces from the end of the string. `LTrim` removes spaces from the beginning of the string. `Trim` removes spaces from both the beginning and the end of the string. These functions are useful in removing unintentional spacing, as well as dealing with fixed length strings.

The revised database program, complete with its own data type, Record, appears in Listing 7.10.

The code included in the module Database.bas is shown in Listing 7.11.

Listing 7.10. The revised database application (Database.vbp).

```
Option Explicit

Public TheData(100) As Record
Public TotalRecords As Integer

Type Record
        Name As String * 50
        Quantity As String * 20
        Comments As String * 200
End Type

Public Sub GetItem()
        Dim WhichRecord As Integer

        For WhichRecord = 1 To 100
                If (RTrim(TheData(WhichRecord).Name)) =
                ➡RTrim(frmRecord.lstName.Text) Then
                        Exit For
                End If
        Next WhichRecord

        frmDatabase.txtNameField.Text = TheData(WhichRecord).Name
        frmDatabase.txtNumberField.Text = TheData(WhichRecord).Quantity
        frmDatabase.txtCommentField.Text = TheData(WhichRecord).Comments

        frmRecord.Hide

End Sub
```

Listing 7.11. The complete code for `frmRecord`.

```
Option Explicit

Private Sub cmdCancel_Click()
        frmRecord.Hide
End Sub

Private Sub cmdOK_Click()
        GetItem
End Sub

Private Sub lstName_DblClick()
        GetItem
End Sub
```

Listing 7.12. The code for `frmDatabase`.

```
Option Explicit

Private Sub Form_Terminate()
        End
End Sub

Private Sub mnuFileAdd_Click()
        TotalRecords = TotalRecords + 1

        TheData(TotalRecords).Name = txtNameField.Text
        TheData(TotalRecords).Quantity = txtNumberField.Text
        TheData(TotalRecords).Comments = txtCommentField.Text

        frmRecord.lstName.AddItem txtNameField.Text

        txtNameField.Text = ""
        txtNumberField.Text = ""
        txtCommentField.Text = ""
        txtNameField.SetFocus

End Sub

Private Sub mnuFileExit_Click()
        Unload Me
End Sub

Private Sub mnuFileFind_Click()
        frmRecord.Show
End Sub
```

And, now, on to the next type of list box. Or is it a text box? Wait! It's both—it's a *combo box*.

Creating Combo Boxes

The difference between combo boxes and list boxes is that combo boxes combine a list box with a text box. This way users can type in their own text, if they do not want to select one of the offered choices. There are three types of combo boxes. The first style, *drop-down combo,* is the default setting (`Style Property = 0`). It is a standard combo box with the arrow detached from the text box. When the user clicks the arrow, the list of items to choose from drops down. The second style, a *simple combo* (`Style Property = 1`), displays the entire list all the time. During design, the box must be drawn large enough to display all the entries on the list. The final type, a *drop-down list box* (`Style Property = 2`), displays a list of items from which the user must choose. It is very similar to a list box; but unlike a list box, the list is not displayed until the arrow to the right of the box is clicked. The key difference between this and a drop-down combo box is that the user cannot type just anything into the box. The user can only select an item from the list.

Because the drop-down list box, style 2, is most similar to a regular list box, it will be covered first, before you start working with the default drop-down combo box.

It is easy to adapt the database application to use a drop-down list box instead of a normal list box. All you have to do is delete the list box, lstName, from frmRecord and replace it with a combo list box. To do that, select the original list box then press the Delete key or select Clear from the Edit menu. Then click the combo box tool in the toolbox (fifth down on the left) and draw it on the form where the list box used to be. (The combo box can only be stretched horizontally. If you try to stretch it vertically, it automatically snaps back to one line width.) Change the new combo box's Style property to 2-Dropdown List, and change its Name property to cboName. There are only a few minor changes to the code in the module, Database.bas, and frmRecord—and the new combo list box is complete. Open the Code window for frmRecord and find the old lstName_DblClick event.

Change the code to reflect the new control's name and change the event from DblClick to Click. A drop-down list box does not support the double-click event; it does support the single one. So the new event would look like this:

```
Private Sub cboName_Click()
        GetItem
End Sub
```

In the module Database.bas, the if/then loop that includes the call to the old list box lstName should be changed. The old line of code reads:

```
If (RTrim(TheData(WhichRecord).Name) = RTrim(frmRecord.lstName.Text) Then
        Exit For
End If
```

Only the new combo list box name is substituted for the old list box name, as follows:

```
        If (RTrim(TheData(WhichRecord).Name) = RTrim(frmRecord.cboName.Text) Then
                Exit For
        End If
```

Also, the mnuAddItem_Click event on frmDatabase calls the old list box like this:

```
frmRecord.lstName.AddItem txtNameField.Text
```

Change that call to reflect the new combo box:

```
frmRecord.cboName.AddItem txtNameField.Text
```

As you can see from Figure 7.38, using a drop-down list box enables the Find Record… dialog box to be considerably more compact. Using a drop-down list box is that easy.

Figure 7.38.

The Database application with a drop-down list box.

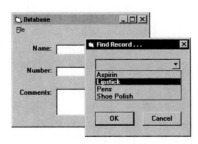

Text can change or be edited in the text box forming part of the simple combo and drop-down combo boxes. Therefore, two very important events connected to these two types of combo boxes are `Click` and `Change`. You already know about the `Click` event. The `Change` event occurs when the text in the text box is changed. In addition, a simple combo box, Style 1, supports the double-click event. (The drop-down combo does not.) The following are some of the properties associated with these two types of combo boxes:

- Text—the currently selected item in the text box.
- List—the string array containing all the items
- ListIndex—the index of the selected item. The first item's index is 0, the second 1, and so on. If the user enters text rather than making a selection, this property is set to -1.
- ListCount—the total number of items in the list.

In fact, the properties of a combo box are similar to the properties of a list box.

To see how this works, get ready to alter the database program again. This time `frmRecord` will display a combo box instead of a drop-down list box. The advantage of this is that the user can simply type the product's name instead of searching through what might be a long list. Unfortunately, this introduces the possibility that the selected entry might not correspond to a record at all. The user might incorrectly type the entry or type something that simply does not exist.

That is something the program will have to check for when the user clicks OK. In the meantime, open the database application in Visual Basic. Select the drop-down list box you just added. Because the drop-down list box is a Style 2 combo box, you can simply change the Style property to select a different type. For this exercise, use combo box Style property 1-Simple Combo. A simple combo box is virtually the same as a Style 0, drop-down combo box, except that the list of selected choices is always visible. The name of the changed combo box remains the same; delete any text found in the Text Property Settings box. Stretch the combo box vertically to take up the empty space in the middle of the form. Because the simple combo supports a double-click event, the code should be changed back from click to double-click, as follows:

```
Private Sub cboName_DblClick()
      GetItem
End Sub
```

Then the selection in the simple combo box must correspond to one of the records. To do that, add this code to the Database.bas module in the `GetItem` subroutine:

```
Public Sub GetItem()

Dim WhichRecord As Integer
Dim Matched As Boolean

Matched = False

For WhichRecord = 1 To 100
      If (RTrim(TheData(WhichRecord).Name)) =
      ➥RTrim(frmRecord.cboName.Text) Then
            Matched = True
```

```
        Exit For
    End If
Next WhichRecord

If (Matched) Then
    frmDatabase.txtNameField.Text = TheData(WhichRecord).Name
    frmDatabase.txtNumberField.Text = TheData(WhichRecord).Quantity
    frmDatabase.txtCommentField.Text = TheData(WhichRecord).Comments
    frmRecord.Hide
Else
    MsgBox "Sorry! I can't find that record! Try again, please…",
    ➥vbExclamation, "Database"
End If

End Sub
```

Thus, if the program cannot find the record that was entered into the combo box's text box, an error message pops up and lets the user start over. After this change, the program functions as before.

However, if the user enters the name of a record that does not match one of the existing records, an error box opens, as in Figure 7.39.

Figure 7.39.
The Database application running with the error box on the screen.

Adding a Browse Button and Common Dialog Control to the Shell Application

A short while ago, the Windows Shell application was put away until needed again. Well, that time has come. You may recall that a Browse button was going to be added to the application. When the Browse button is pushed a common dialog box opens, letting the user easily select a file after looking around the directory tree. For that reason, a common dialog box control needs to be added to frmRunDialog, as well as a command button captioned Browse.

To get going, open the Windows Shell program and view frmRunDialog. Next, find the Common Dialog tool on the toolbar (bottom tool on the right). Double-click the tool to add a Common Dialog control to `frmRunDialog`. Next, using the Properties Window, select the (Custom) property. When you click the property, a Property button appears to the right of the Settings box. Press the Property button to open the Common Dialogs Control Properties dialog box. (Why not call it the CDCP dialog box for brevity's sake!) At the top of the CDCP dialog box is a set of tabs. Make sure the Open/Save As tab is at the front of the tab group. If it is not, click it, and that tab will come to the front. Find the `DialogTitle` text box and enter Select File for Running; then move down the CDCP dialog box until you find the DefaultExt (Default Extension) text box. In that box enter `Exe`. Finally, in the Filter text box, enter `Execution Files (*.exe)¦*.exe¦All Files (*.*)¦*.*`. The completed CDCP dialog box appears in Figure 7.40.

Figure 7.40.
The completed Common
Dialogs Control Properties
dialog box.

When you are finished entering the settings in the CDCP dialog box, click OK. Most of the properties for your custom common dialog box are now set. To finish, add a command button to the right of txtFile. Change its `Caption` property to Browse and its `Name` property to cmdBrowse. To complete the changes to the Windows Shell program, add the following code to the new command button's Click event:

```
Private Sub cmdBrowse_Click()

        frmRunDialog.CommonDialog1.flags = &h1000& Or &h800& Or &h4&
        frmRunDialog.CommonDialog1.Action = 1

        If frmRunDialog.CommonDialog1.filename <> "" Then
                txtFile = frmRunDialog.CommonDialog1.FileName
        End If

End Sub
```

And that's all there is to it! Run your project and try it out. When you click the Browse button, the familiar common dialog file selection box comes up as in Figure 7.41. When you select a file and click OK, it will appear in the txtFile text box!

Figure 7.41.
The Windows Shell program
with the added Browse
command button.

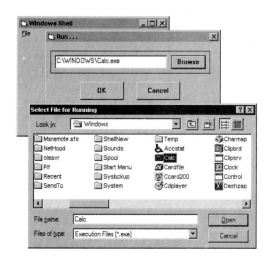

A Word About Common Dialog Boxes and Flags— Something Old and Something New!

First something old: By setting the `action` = property of the common dialog control, you tell the common dialog control which dialog box to display.

Each kind of dialog box uses different flags that set the options used in that dialog box. These flags are easily found by using the Help file that comes with Visual Basic. In the example you just created, the `&h1000&` flag means that the user can only place a valid file name in the text box. The `&h800&` flag means that the user can only enter valid paths. The `&h4&` flag hides a read-only check box. The use of the Or connector means that these three flags are all on. Another way to write these same flags would be to add them together. Thus, the original line of code:

```
frmRunDialog.CommonDialog1.flags = &h1000& Or &h800& Or &h4&
```

could also be expressed as:

```
frmRunDialog.CommonDialog1.flags = &h1804&
```

Here's one of the new parts about common dialogs: With Visual Basic 4.0 these flags can be set as properties at design-time. There is no need to put them into code. The way to do this is to press the Settings Box to the right of (Custom) on the common dialog control's Properties Window. This opens the Common Dialogs Control Properties dialog box (CDCP, for short). Choose a tab for the type of common dialog box desired—Open/Save As, Font, Color, etc. Flags can be set in the text box provided, but they must be an integer value (not the hexadecimal values listed above). Use the Object Browser to find these values. (On the Object Browser dialog box—found under the VB View menu—select Microsoft Common Dialog Control from the Libraries/Projects list box, and then select the constant type desired from the Classes/Modules list box). For instance, using the above example, `&h1000&` = 4096, `&h800&` = 2048, and `&h4&` = 4. Add these integers together and put that sum, 6148, into the Flag text box on the CDCP. It's that simple!

Common dialog boxes will be discussed further in Chapter 18, "Using Custom Controls."

Common Dialog Action Properties

The common dialog `Action` properties are now accessed with greater functionality, using the following methods: `ShowOpen`, `ShowSave`, `ShowFont`, `ShowColor`, `ShowPrinter`, `ShowHelp`. The `Action` method that was used previously in Visual Basic 3.0 and earlier versions still works. The example in this chapter uses it.

Summary

In this chapter you learned about message boxes and input boxes. Then you moved on to multiple forms and designing your own custom dialog boxes. You also covered the typical kinds of controls found in dialog boxes: scroll bars, list boxes, and combo boxes. Then you saw how to connect dialog boxes to menu items, and how the Multiple Document Interface (MDI) works. For that reason, you are no longer restricted to a single form application. The sky is, definitely, the limit! You have seen how to create and use multiple-window programs in Windows. That is useful for almost anything you will write. For example, many programs include dialog boxes—word processors, database programs, file-handling programs, applications with control panels, even graphics paint programs. And then, you took a first look at Common Dialog boxes. Using dialog boxes is a necessary skill for the Windows programmer and now this skill is yours, too!

New Property	Description
ForeColor	The foreground color of forms and controls. It is set with the RGB() function.
LargeChange	Holds the amount that a scroll bar has changed when a user clicks on the area between the scroll box and scroll arrow.
List	A string array containing all the items in a list-oriented control.
ListCount	The total number of items in the list of a list-oriented control.
ListIndex	The index of the selected item in a list-oriented control. This index starts at 0, thus the first item in the list has a ListIndex value of 0. The second item has a ListIndex value of 1. And so on.
Max	Holds the maximum value that a scroll bar's Value property can be.
MDIChild	This property indicates whether the form is a Child form of and MDI Parent form. If set to True, the form is displayed inside the MDI Parent form.
Min	Holds the minimum value that a scroll bar's Value property can be.
SmallChange	Holds the amount that a scroll bar has changed when a user clicks on a scroll arrow.
Sorted	If set to True, a list-oriented control will keep its list sorted alphabetically.
Value	The current value of a scroll bar control.

New Event	Description
DblClick	Occurs when a form or control is double-clicked.

New Method	Description
Hide	Removes a form or control from the screen.
Show	Displays a form or control on the screen.

8

File Handling in Visual Basic

The most common way to keep data around after a program ends is to store it in files. In this chapter, you will learn how to work with files in Visual Basic 4. The topics covered here include the following:

- Creating, opening, and closing files
- Reading and writing files
- The End of File (EOF()) and Length of File (LOF()) functions
- Sequential files
- Random-access files
- Directory list boxes
- File list boxes
- Drive list boxes
- The Seek statement
- The Get and Put statements
- How to handle file errors
- Reading and storing initialization data using private and public profile strings
- Common dialog controls

You will add file-handling capabilities to some of the programs you have already developed, specifically the Editor and Database programs. Most Windows programs use files of some sort, so the skills you pick up here will be important for all types of programs: graphics programs, word processors, database programs, and so on.

You might recall that your Editor program had two menu choices that were never implemented: Load File... and Save File.... Until now, all the data that the programs handled has been rather temporary. When an application closes, the data is gone—unless it is stored in a file.

The file-manipulation statements system in Visual Basic is, of course, Windows-based, so if you are familiar with Open, Close, and Save, you already have a head start. As you might expect, however, things are very different when it comes to interacting with the user. For example, users normally pick filenames for the files they are saving, using dialog boxes in Windows applications. Incidentally, this is why dialog boxes were covered (in Chapter 7) before files. You will see how to deal with user-interface issues as you set up your own file dialog boxes.

Two of the boxes that you will use for the Editor application are Save File... and Load File.... In addition, you will see how to work with structured files in which the data is broken into specific records as it was in the Database application in the last chapter. In fact, you will modify that application in this chapter, giving it file-saving capabilities. With this and the other topics coming up, why not get started right away!

Saving Data in a File

If you want to add file support to the Editor application, you should start with the Save File... item. After all, the user creates and saves files before opening them again.

When the user selects the Save File... item from the File menu, a dialog box should appear on the screen. The dialog box could contain a list box and two command buttons, OK and Cancel. That way the user could type the name of the file that she wanted to save, and the program would create a file with that name and then store the data there. To put this into practice, start Visual Basic and open the Editor project. Using the Save File As... and Save Project As... items from the File menu, save the form, module, and project as Editor2.frm, Editor2.bas, and Editor2.vbp, respectively.

Double-click on Editor2.frm in the Project window to view the form. If you look at the File menu, you will see that the Save File... item already exists but it is disabled. You need to enable this option before you work on it. Enter the Menu Editor and click the Enable check box and close the Menu Editor. Then click the Save File option to open the Code window. The cursor will appear centered in the following code template:

```
Private Sub mnuFileSave_Click()

End Sub
```

To save the user's current document, a Save File... dialog box needs to appear on the screen. Why not name that dialog box `frmSave`? That name gives a clear indication of what the form does. So, to display the frmSave dialog box, which you will design in just a minute, the following lines of code should be added to the `mnuFileSave Click` event:

```
Private Sub mnuFileSave_Click()
      frmSave.Show
End Sub
```

Now you can create the dialog box. Add a new form to the project by selecting the Form item from the Insert menu. Change the Name and Caption properties of the form to `frmSave` and `Save File...`, respectively. Then save the form as Save.frm, using the Save Form item from the File menu. There should be four objects on the form: a text box, a label that gives some hint of what the text box is for, and two command buttons (OK and Cancel). Add these controls to your form by placing them as shown in Figure 8.1. Change the objects' properties to those listed in Table 8.1.

Table 8.1. The visual design of the Save form.

Object	Property	Setting
Form	Appearance	1-3D
	BorderStyle	3-Fixed Dialog
	Caption	Save File...

continues

Table 8.1. continued

Object	Property	Setting
	MaxButton	False
	MinButton	False
	Name	frmSave
Label	Alignment	2-Center7
	Caption	Save File As:
	Font	Style: Bold
	Name	lblSave
Text Box	Name	txtFileName
	Text	(None)
Command Button	Caption	OK
	Default	True
	Font	Style: Bold
	Name	cmdOK
Command Button	Cancel	True
	Caption	Cancel
	Font	Style: Bold
	Name	cmdCancel

Figure 8.1.
The Save File... dialog box.

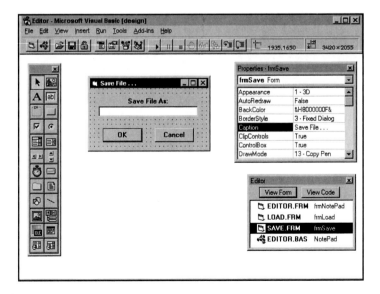

When you are finished adding and positioning the controls on the form, lock them using either the Lock Controls button on the Toolbar or the pop-up menu.

Now you move on to the code that makes the dialog box work. The Cancel button procedure is easy, so do that first. If the user presses the Cancel button, the form should disappear from the screen. Put the code that makes that happen into the Cancel button's `Click` event, like this:

```
Private Sub cmdCancel_Click()
      Unload cmdCancel.Parent
End Sub
```

The real work of this dialog box is done when the user clicks the OK button. Double-click that button now to open the `Click` event's template.

```
Private Sub cmdOK_Click()

End Sub
```

When the program reaches this point, there should be a filename in `txtFileName`. Then the application is supposed to save that document, which consists of `frmNotepad.txtPadText.Text`, using that filename. Three steps are involved in this process: first, creating or opening the specified file; second, writing the data to the file; and third, closing the file. You can look at each of these steps in order as you build `cmdOK_Click()`. Each step tells you something about the Visual Basic file system.

Opening Files in Visual Basic

To open or create a file in Visual Basic, simply use the `Open` statement. However, some consideration must be given to the way a file is opened or created. In particular, there are five ways to open files in Visual Basic. Each technique corresponds to how the files are used (form defines function, *and* function defines form). The available file modes are as follows:

- Sequential Input/Output
- Sequential Append
- Random Input/Output
- Binary Input/Output

The Types of Visual Basic Files

The first two file modes are associated with sequential files. Sequential files are usually used for text files; the file is written from beginning to end and read in the same way. There is no jumping around. Working with sequential files is like using cassette tapes. If the user wants to hear something at the end of the tape, she has to pass by everything in front of it first. In the same way, if some text were wanted at the end of a file opened for sequential access, all of the text that preceded the specific text would have to be read.

If sequential files are like cassette tapes, random files are like compact discs. Unlike a cassette, the user can simply move around at will on a CD without going through all the intervening magnetic tape. A program can move around in a random-access file in the same way, taking data from whatever location wanted. The price you pay as the programmer for using random-access files is that the data must be carefully sectioned into records, so that the program knows exactly where specific data resides. For example, if the records created in the database application were all the same size, they would work perfectly in a random-access file. When the twentieth record was needed, the application could simply skip over the first 19 records and access it. Because text—such as the text stored in the Editor application—is not neatly sectioned into records of the same size, that text should be saved using a sequential file.

The last entry in the previous list deals with binary files. Visual Basic does not interpret the contents of a binary file at all. Executable (.exe) files are binary files, and they are treated on a byte-by-byte basis in Visual Basic. To copy such a file to a new location, every byte of the original file would have to be read in, and then sent to the new file. The amount of data read by a sequential or random-access file can be set; binary files are always dealt with fully on a byte-to-byte basis.

Each of these three file access types—sequential, random, and binary—has its own set of Visual Basic statements. Because this can get confusing, a collection of the most common Visual Basic file-handling statements, organized by file type, is available in Table 8.2.

Table 8.2. Some common Visual Basic file statements, organized by access file type.

Access File Type	Some Visual Basic Statements
Sequential	`Close, Line Input #, Open, Print #, Write #; Input [function]`
Random	`Close, Get, Len, Open, Put, Type…End Type`
Binary	`Close, Get, Open, Put, Seek; Input [function]`

Your job here is to save the Editor application's current document. That can be accomplished by opening a sequential file. There are three ways to open sequential files:

1. For input
2. For output
3. For append

A file is opened for input if it is to be read by the application, for output if data will be written to it, and for append if data will be added to the end of it. These three modes are consistent with the concept of opening a file and then working with the data from beginning to end. For example, if a file was opened for sequential output and a first string was written to it to be followed by a second string, that second string would go directly after the first. This would continue for any subsequent strings, one after the other. To read them in again, the application would have to close the file and then open it for input. Then the data could be read back from beginning to end.

Random files, in which the application can move around at will, do not have any such restrictions. When a file is opened for random access, it is open for *both* input and output. However, the data has to be sectioned into records.

In this case, the Editor application is writing the document to disk, so the file will be opened for sequential output. Visual Basic's `Open` statement syntax works like this:

```
Open pathname [For mode] [Access access] [lock] As [#]filenumber
➥[Len = reclength]
```

The `Open` statement syntax uses these arguments:

- *pathname*—a string expression that specifies a filename. It can include a directory and drive.
- *mode*—a keyword specifying the file mode: `Append`, `Binary`, `Input`, `Output`, or `Random`.
- *access*—a keyword specifying the operations permitted on the open file: `Read`, `Write`, or `Read Write`.
- *lock*—a keyword specifying the operations permitted on the open file by other processes: `Shared`, `Lock Read`, `Lock Write`, and `Lock Read Write`.
- *filenumber*—a valid file number in the range 1 to 511, inclusive.
- *reclength*—a number less than or equal to 32,767 bytes. For files opened for random access, this value is the record length. For sequential files, this value is the number of characters buffered.

In this case, the user wants to write to the filename in `txtFileName.Text`, so you can use the following `Open` statement to open that file:

```
Open frmFileName.Text For Output As # 1
```

Actually, this file might not even exist. The user might want the application to create it. That is handled automatically by the `Open` statement. If the file does not exist and the user tries to open it for anything but input, Visual Basic will create the file. Note that when an existing file is opened for output and is then written to, the original contents of the file are destroyed. (If you want an application to add to the end of a sequential file while retaining what was there before, open the file for append.) Now you can start the Editor application's Save File... dialog box with this line in the `cmdOK_Click()` event:

```
Private Sub cmdOK_Click()

        Open txtFileName.Text For Output As #1   'Open file

    :

End Sub
```

This file will be referred to as file #1 when the application wants to write to it or close it. Note, however, that there is the possibility of error when a file is opened this way. The user might have specified an invalid path or misspelled the filename. To handle such errors, you can include an `On Error GoTo` statement, like this:

```
Private Sub cmdOK_Click()

     On Error GoTo FileError

     Open txtFileName.Text For Output As #1  'Open file

     :

End Sub
```

Now, if an error occurs, the program will jump automatically to the label `FileError`. Following the instructions in `FileError`, the application will place a message box on the screen and execute a `Resume` statement to bring the user back to the erroneous line so that she can try again.

```
Private Sub cmdOK_Click()

     On Error GoTo FileError

     Open txtFileName.Text For Output As #1        'Open file

     :

     Exit Sub

FileError:
     MsgBox "File Error", 48, "Editor"    'MsgBox for file error
     Resume Next

End Sub
```

How Errors that are Not Trapped are Handled

If the previous statement was not placed in code, there would have been no way for the application to *trap* a filename error. Visual Basic notifies the user of trapped errors directly with a message box. This is undesirable (and unprofessional) in most applications!

Therefore, if the filename is legal and the corresponding file can be opened, the application will do so. If there is a problem, the application indicates that fact and lets the user change the file specification for another attempt.

More About Errors

Chapter 12, "Error Handling and Debugging," goes into more detail about specific kinds of errors that can occur in this and other situations. That chapter discusses the `On Error GoTo` and `Resume` statements in depth. It also shows you how to trap most possible disk and file errors.

At this point, now that you have inserted the Open statement into code, the file is open. The next step is to get the application to write the user's document to the open file.

Writing to Files in Visual Basic

The usual way to write to a sequential file is by using either the Print # or Write # statements. Visual Basic's Print # statement syntax works as follows:

```
Print #Filenumber, [outputlist]
```

The Print # statement syntax uses this argument:

- *outputlist*—an expression or list of expressions to print.

The *outputlist* argument uses these possible settings:

```
[{Spc(n) ¦ Tab[(n)]} [expression] [charpos]
```

The settings definitions are as follows:

- Spc(*n*)—used to insert space characters in the output; *n* is the number of space characters to insert.
- Tab(*n*)—used to position the insertion point to an absolute column number; *n* is the column number. Use Tab with no argument to position the insertion point at the beginning of the next print zone.
- *expression*—a numeric or string expression to print.
- *charpos*—specifies the insertion point for the next character. A semicolon is used to specify the insertion point immediately after the last character is displayed. If charpos is omitted, the next character is printed on the next line.

The Write # statement uses the following syntax:

```
Write #filenumber, [outputlist]
```

The Write # statement uses these arguments:

- *filenumber*—any valid file number.
- *outputlist*—one or more comma-delimited number or string expressions to write to a file.

The two statements Print # and Write # are different. Write # inserts commas between the separate items in the outputlist as it writes them to the file, places quotation marks around strings, and inserts a new (blank) line at the end of the file. This is more useful if you are storing data, because it is easier to retrieve in this format. Because you do not want any of these added characters, you will use Print # instead. Actually, because you only want to send a single string (frmNotepad.txtPadText.Text) to the file, your Print # statement should appear as follows:

```
Private Sub cmdOK_Click()

        On Error GoTo FileError

        Open txtFileName.Text For Output As #1'Open file
        Print #1, frmNotePad.txtPadText.Text'Write document

        :

        Exit Sub

FileError:
        MsgBox "File Error", 48, "Editor"    'MsgBox for file error
        Resume Next
End Sub
```

That's all there is to writing the text to the file. Closing the file is not much harder. Use the Close statement like this:

```
Private Sub cmdOK_Click()

        On Error GoTo FileError

        Open txtFileName.Text For Output As #1    'Open file
        Print #1, frmNotePad.txtPadText.Text              'Write document
        Close #1                                  'Close file

        :

        Exit Sub

FileError:
        MsgBox "File Error", 48, "Editor"    'MsgBox for file error
        Resume Next

End Sub
```

Close #1 closes file number 1, the file you are working on. After closing the file, the Sub procedure ends, using the Exit Sub statement placed in the code earlier. At this point, the file has been successfully written to disk. (If it has not—such as when an invalid filename was entered—the user has been alerted to that fact.)

Closing All the Files at Once

If the Close statement is used without a file number, Visual Basic will close all open files in an application.

If the file handling has gone smoothly, the final step is to hide the Save File... dialog box, frmSave, in the following way:

```
Private Sub cmdOK_Click()

        On Error GoTo FileError
```

```
        Open txtFileName.Text For Output As #1    'Open file
        Print #1, frmNotePad.txtPadText.Text              'Write document
        Close #1                                  'Close file

        Unload cmdOK.Parent

        Exit Sub

FileError:
        MsgBox "File Error", 48, "Editor"    'MsgBox for file error
        Resume Next

End Sub
```

To see this in action, make the preceding changes and then try typing some lines of text into the Editor and saving them, as shown in Figure 8.2. When you do, you will find that the text is indeed saved to disk in the file you choose.

Figure 8.2.
Saving a file in the Editor application.

Note that the text in the file is stored as one long string without hard returns (unless they are present in the original document). That's it for the Save File... item on the File menu. Your Editor application is a bit more polished now that it writes a sequential text file to disk. The next step is to read files back into the Editor's Load File... item. It's time to look into that process.

Using the Visual Basic File Controls

The first step in reading the contents of a file is to get the name of that file. However, that is not just a simple matter of asking the user to type the filename in a text box. The application has to be able to search the disk, just as any other similar Windows application would, and let the user select from what is already there. Visual Basic provides three special controls for doing exactly that: *disk list boxes*, *directory list boxes*, and *file list boxes*.

The tools for creating these file controls are near the middle of the Visual Basic toolbox. These controls will do much of the work for you. They will search the disks and directories automatically. There are various properties that you can work with that are associated with each control.

Start this process by designing a dialog box for the Load File… option. Add a new form to the project by selecting the Form item from the Insert menu. Change the form's Caption to Load File… and change its Name property to frmLoad. Save the form, using the Save Form item from the File menu, as Load.frm.

First, connect it to the Load File… menu item by clicking on that item in frmNotepad's File menu. The following code skeleton appears in the Code window:

```
Private Sub mnuFileLoad_Click()

End Sub
```

To display the Load File… dialog box that you are about to design, simply show it in the following way:

```
Private Sub mnuFileLoad_Click()
     frmLoad.Show
End Sub
```

To design frmLoad, use Figure 8.3 for object placement and use Table 8.3 to set the objects' properties.

Table 8.3. The object properties for frmLoad.

Object	Property	Setting
Form	Appearance	1-3D
	BorderStyle	3-Fixed Dialog
	Caption	Load File…
	MaxButton	False
	MinButton	False
	Name	frmLoad
Drive List Box	Font	Style: Bold
	Name	drvChange
Directory List Box	Font	Style: Bold
	Name	dirLook
File List Box	Font	Style: Bold
	Name	filFind
Command Button	Caption	OK
	Default	True
	Font	Style: Bold
	Name	cmdOK

Object	Property	Setting
Command Button	Cancel	True
	Caption	Cancel
	Font	Style: Bold
	Name	cmdCancel

Figure 8.3.
The completed Load File...
dialog box template.

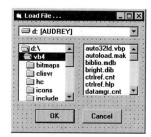

When you are finished adding and positioning the controls on the form, lock them using either the Lock Controls button on the Toolbar or the pop-up menu.

The form includes the three new controls: a directory list box, a drive list box, and a file list box. Note that the drive list box is a drop-down list box. Also, notice that all three list boxes are already active, showing the drive, directory, and file list that was current when you placed the controls on the form.

The user will be able to load any existing file, using the combination of drive, directory, and file list boxes. She can use the drive list box to specify the drive, the directory list box to specify the directory in that drive, and the file list box to indicate the actual file to open. That file can be opened in two ways: by double-clicking on the filename in the file list box, or by selecting the name in the file list box and then clicking OK.

As usual, making the Cancel button active is easy. Just unload the dialog box when that button is clicked.

```
Public Sub cmdCancel_Click()
      Unload cmdCancel.Parent
End Sub
```

Now to turn to the file controls. At this point, the three list boxes (drive, directory, and file) are not communicating with one another. They are only showing independent information for the current directory on the disk. If you were to run the program at this point and change the disk in the disk box list, the other two boxes would not respond to the change. To get them to communicate, you have to know a little more about what the important events are for each of them. That is covered next.

Drive List Boxes

The drive list box is a drop-down list box. The current drive is indicated in the box. When the user clicks on the attached arrow, the list box drops down, showing other available drives. When the user picks one, a `Change` event occurs in the list box. Because you have set the name of the drive list box to `drvChange`, the event procedure is `drvChange_Change()`. The property that holds the selected drive is `drvChange.Drive`.

Your next task is to pass on this new drive, `drvChange.Drive`, to the directory list box, `dirLook`. To do that, you just need to pass the `drvChange.Drive` information on to the `dirLook.Path` property. A picture of the information pass would look something like Figure 8.4.

Figure 8.4.
A pictorial representation of the information pass from the Drive list box to the Directory list box.

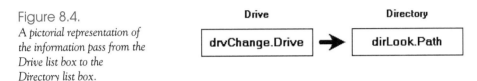

To put that into code, double-click on the Drive list box to bring up the `Change` event for that control.

```
Private Sub drvChange_Change()

End Sub
```

Pass the `Drive` property of `drvChange` to `dirLook`'s `Path` property in the following way:

```
Private Sub drvChange_Change()
     dirLook.Path = drvChange.Drive
End Sub
```

That's all it takes to connect the drive and directory boxes together. In fact, you can run the program right now. When you do, click on the Load File... item of the Editor's File menu. The dialog box that you have been designing, `frmLoad`, appears and displays the current drive, the directory, and the files in that directory. If you click on the drive box, the drop-down list of all the drives in your system appears. Clicking on one of those drives changes you to that drive, causing a ripple effect through to the directory list box, which also changes to list the directories on that new drive.

The next step in your program is to connect the directory list box with the file list box. Thus, when the directory is changed, the files displayed will be the files in that directory.

Directory List Boxes

The directory list box displays the directories available on a certain drive. It is a simple list box that is always displayed (unlike a drop-down list box such as the drive list box). The working drive is displayed on the top line, with that drive's directories below it. If there are more directories than space allowed (this spaced allotment is set by you, the programmer, at design-time), a vertical scrollbar appears automatically on the right side of the box. The current directory appears as a shaded folder. Its subdirectories appear as nonshaded closed folders just below it. At this point, here's what happens:

1. When the user changes the directory by clicking on a new directory, a dirLook_Change() event occurs and the new path is placed in dirLook.Path.

2. When the user changes drives, drvChange.Drive is passed to dirLook.Path.

This passing of data from drvChange.Drive to dirLook.Path also generates a dirLook_Change() event. Thus, the only event you need to be concerned about here is dirLook_Change(), which is handling both the drive and directory changes.

When a dirLook_Change() event occurs, the application needs to communicate the news to the file list box. This can be accomplished by passing the dirLook.Path data on to the Path property of filFind. Figure 8.5 is a drawing of the information being passed from control to control.

Figure 8.5.

A pictorial representation of data being passed from the drive list box to the directory list box, and then passed on to the file list box.

To do this in code, click on the directory list box to bring up its procedure template in the Code window:

```
Private Sub dirLook_Change()

End Sub
```

The goal here is to pass any changes in the dirLook.Path property down to filFind.Path. That will happen if you enter the following code:

```
Private Sub dirLook_Change()
      filFind.Path = dirLook.Path
End Sub
```

So, every time a change occurs in the working directory (or the working drive) the file list box will know about it. After you make this change, run the program again. You will find that the list boxes are all connected. For example, when you click on the drive list box to change the drive, the change is automatically communicated to the directory list box, which changes to display the new set of available directories. This change in turn communicates to the file list box, which displays the files available in the new working directory.

On the other hand, if you change the working directory in the directory list box, that change is also communicated to the file list box, which shows the available files in the new directory. To recap briefly, the important events here are drvChange_Change and dirLook_Change, and the important properties to be transferred are `dirLook.Drive`, `dirLook.Path`, and `filFind.Path`. The way that the selected filename is actually read by the program is by using the `FileName` property attached to `filFind`—hence, `filFind.FileName`. If this were drawn, it would look something like Figure 8.6.

Figure 8.6.
A pictorial representation of the filename selection.

You might note, also, that although you can select a new drive with a single click, it takes two clicks to select a new directory in the directory list box. This difference has to do with the difference between drop-down and normal list boxes. Two clicks are necessary in a directory list box so that users can move up and down through the list using the arrow keys, without changing the working directory to each highlighted entry along the way. Thus, the change is postponed until the user reaches the desired directory.

Your next task is to integrate the file list box into the program. When the user double-clicks on the file's name, the application should open that file and load it into the Editor. Therefore, the next step on this journey through file-handling is a look at file list boxes.

File List Boxes

The file list box shows the files in the current working directory. Like the directory list box, the file list box is a simple list box; its list is always displayed. If the list is too long for the box, a vertical scrollbar automatically appears. The files shown in the list box correspond to two properties: `Path` and `Pattern`. The `Path` property holds the displayed directory's path name. The `Pattern` property holds the file specification, such as .exe. The default pattern is *.*.

Although you are not going to do it in this demonstration program, you could include a text box to get a file specification from the user, transferring the appropriate text from the text box to a file list box's `Pattern` property. It would look something like this:

```
filBigList.Pattern = txtBigBox.Text
```

Note that you might have to separate the pattern string from a longer string if the user happened to specify both path and pattern in the same text box—for example, `C:\Data\Thesis.Phd`. A line of code like this could be put into the text box's `Change` event procedure.

Back to business now. File list boxes can respond to click or double-click events. Because it is normal to let the user select a file from a file list box and then close that dialog box by double-clicking on a file's name, code should be added to the `filFind_DblClick()` procedure. Note that this is the same as selecting a file and then clicking on the OK button, so one procedure should be written to be used by both events. You did that before by placing a public subroutine in a code module and then calling that general procedure from two event procedures. It's time to do that again. However, there is another way to do the same thing, which you might want to try here.

First, double-click on the file list box to open the Code window, and then select the `filFind_DblClick()` procedure using the Procedure list box at the top of the Code window. That template appears as follows:

```
Private Sub filFind_DblClick()

End Sub
```

This subroutine should be the same as the `cmdOK_Click` subroutine, but because `cmdOK_Click` is also a `Sub` procedure (just like `filFind_DblClick()`), you can call it like this:

```
Private Sub filFind_DblClick()
      cmdOK_Click
End Sub
```

You should know that if `cmdOK` were part of a control array, you would have had to pass an index, like this: `cmdOK(3)_Click()`.

That's all there is to it. Now you need to add the code for `cmdOK_Click()`, the action hot spot. Double-click on the OK button (or use the Object and Procedure list boxes to find `cmdOK` and its `Click` event) to bring up that `Sub` procedure:

```
Private Sub cmdOK_Click()

End Sub
```

At this point, the user is trying to open a file. The correct drive is in `drvChange.Drive` and the correct path is in `dirLook.Path`. Now you need the name of the actual file selected by the user. As mentioned earlier, the current selected filename is kept in the file list box's `FileName` property, so you do have the file's complete specification. You are ready to write the code that will open the file.

Drive, Directory, and File Controls are Still Lists

Remember that because the drive, directory, and file controls are still list boxes, you can use their `List`, `ListCount`, and `ListIndex` properties as well.

One way of opening the required file is to actually change to the new drive (`dirChange.Drive`) with the Visual Basic `ChDrive` statement, change to the new path (`dirLook.Path`) using the `ChDir` statement, and then open the file itself (`filFind.FileName`). There is no need to change the default drive and directory at the operating system level. You can assemble the complete file specifications yourself.

Setting Drive, Directory, and File at the Same Time

The Editor application can change the `FileName` property of a file list box to set the drive, path, and pattern of the files displayed in the file list box all at once.

What If a Program Requires Support Files?

Changing the drive and directory like this is useful if the user is about to run a program in that directory—using the `Shell` statement, for example. The program itself will search for the supporting files it might need, such as .dll or .dat files.

The `Path` property of the directory list box, `dirLook.Path`, usually represents a complete path, including the drive letter (for instance, `c:\vb32\icons\misc`). You can add that to the `filFind.FileName` if a backslash is added after the path, like this:

```
Dim TheFile As String

TheFile = dirLook.Path + "\" + filFind.FileName
```

Here, `TheFile` is a local variable that can be used in the `cmdOK_Click()` procedure. However, this is not quite good enough. If the user happens to be in the root directory of a drive, such as d:, the contents of `dirLook.Path` would be `d:\`. If the current file is Thesis.Phd, the variable `FileName`, which is equal to `dirLock.Path + "\" + filFind.FileName`, would be `d:\\Thesis.Phd`. There would be one backslash too many. To avoid this, the code should check the last character of `dirLook.Path`. If the last character is a backslash, the program should not add another one.

```
Dim TheFile As String

If (Right(dirLook.Path, 1) = "\") Then
    TheFile = dirLook.Path + filFind.FileName
Else
    TheFile = dirLook.Path + "\" + filFind.FileName
End If
```

`Right` is a function that returns a specified number of characters from the right side of the string. In this case, one character from the right side of `dirLook.Path`.

Another Way to Handle the Missing Backslash

A slightly more sophisticated method of handling the issue of the missing backslash is to write a function that adds one if necessary. Here's an example of a public function that does just that:

```
Public Function FixPath(InPath As String) As String
'sticks a backslash on the end of InPath if there is not one there already

Dim T As String

T = InPath
If Right$(T, 1) <> "\" Then T = T + "\"
```

```
FixPath = T

End Function
```

The advantage to writing a function is that it can be called from any routine. That way, the backslash code only needs to be written once, and not repeated in several Sub procedures.

Now the variable TheFile holds the complete file specification of the file that the application is supposed to open. You can open it using an Open statement. Because you are using sequential file access and you want to read the file, you can open it for Input in the following way:

```
Dim TheFile As String

If (Right(dirLook.Path, 1) = "\") Then
    TheFile = dirLook.Path + filFind.FileName
Else
    TheFile = dirLook.Path + "\" + filFind.FileName
End If

Open TheFile For Input As #1
```

Once again, there is the possibility of errors here. For example, the disk with the file might have been inadvertently removed. So you should put in some error-handling code. That might appear as follows in the cmdOK_Click() event:

```
Private Sub cmdOK_Click()

        On Error GoTo FileError

        :

        Exit Sub

FileError:
        MsgBox "File Error", 48, "Editor"    'MsgBox for file error
        Resume Next

End Sub
```

If there were any file errors, the application would simply display a message box, allowing the user to try again after the problem was fixed. Now you can put this all together—the routine for opening the file and the error-handling:

```
Private Sub cmdOK_Click()
        Dim TheFile As String

        On Error GoTo FileError

        If (Right(dirLook.Path, 1) = "\") Then
                TheFile = dirLook.Path + filFind.FileName
```

```
            Else
                    TheFile = dirLook.Path + "\" + filFind.FileName

            End If

            Open TheFile For Input As #1

            :

            Exit Sub

    FileError:
            MsgBox "File Error", 48, "Editor"    'MsgBox for file error
            Resume Next

    End Sub
```

At this point, you no longer need to use the file controls. The file has been selected and opened. The next step is to read in the data.

Reading from Files in Visual Basic

The standard ways to read a sequential file in Visual Basic are `Input #`, and `Line Input #`, `Input`.

`Input #` is a statement that reads data from an open sequential file and assigns the data to *variables*. The `Input #` syntax looks like this:

`Input #filenumber, varlist`

Its arguments are as follows:

- *filenumber*—any valid file number.
- *varlist*—a comma-delimited list of variables that are assigned values read from a file.

`Line Input #` is a statement that reads a line from an open sequential file and assigns it to a *string variable*. The `Line Input #` syntax works like this:

`Line Input #filenumber, varname`

Its arguments are as follows:

- *filenumber*—any valid file number.
- *varname*—a valid string variable name.

Finally, `Input` is a function that returns characters from an open sequential or binary file. Its syntax appears as follows:

`Input(number, [#]filenumber)`

The arguments that accompany this function are as follows:

- *number*—any valid numeric expression specifying the number of characters to return.
- *filenumber*—any valid file number.

If you use `Input #` to fill `frmNotePad.txtPadText.Text`, it might look like this:

```
Input # 1 frmNotePad.txtPadText.Text
```

The problem with `Input #`, however, is that it expects the items in the file to be separated by commas, spaces, or carriage returns. For numbers, this means that when `Input #` encounters the first comma, space, or carriage return, it assumes that the current number is finished. For strings, `Input #` terminates the string when it reaches a comma or carriage return. This is certainly unacceptable here, because the text of the document read in by the Editor application might contain commas. Also, the user might have deliberately put in carriage returns, or she might be trying to read in another application's document that has carriage returns in it.

Similarly, the `Line Input #` statement reads strings from files until it encounters a carriage return. Then it quits. That means that the Editor application would have to read in each line of the file—if it is divided into lines separated by carriage returns—separately. One way to do that would be as follows:

```
Dim Dummy As String

Do Until EOF(1)
        Line Input # 1, Dummy
        frmNotePad.txtPadText.Text = txtNotePad.txtPadText.Text +
        ➥Dummy + Chr(13) + Chr(10)
Loop
```

Here, the `EOF()` function is used to make up the condition for the loop. This function takes a file number as its argument—the `(1)`—and returns a value of `True` when the end of the file is reached. So the application continues to read lines from the file until it reaches the end of that file. In addition, each time a line is read, carriage returns and line feed characters are added to the end of the line. These characters need to be added at the end of each line because `Line Input #` treats those two characters purely as delimiters between strings and then deletes them.

A better option than either `Input #` or `Line Input #` is the `Input()` function. This function is specially made to read strings, and it does not suppress carriage returns or line feeds. Unlike the `Input #` statement, the `Input()` function returns all of the characters it reads, including commas, carriage returns, linefeeds, quotation marks, and leading spaces. To use this function, however, you will have to indicate the exact number of bytes you want read by the program. When you do that, the `Input()` function returns a string that can be assigned to `frmNotePad.txtPadText.Text`. The number of bytes you want to specify is simply the length of the file in bytes. You can use another file function, `LOF()`, to get that information for you. Like `EOF()`, `LOF()` takes a file number as an argument. `LOF()` returns the length of the indicated file in bytes, although the file must be open for `LOF()` to work. Thus, the entire file, `txtPadText.Text`, can be read by the program using this code:

```
frmNotePad.txtPadText.Text = Input(LOF(1), #1)
```

Limitations of the `Input()` Function

The `Input()` function is limited to reading files of 32,767 bytes if the file has been opened for sequential or binary access. However, if longer files need to be read, the file length can be checked using `LOF()`, and then the file can be read several times in succession until all necessary data is obtained.

You can add your `Input` statement to the `cmdOK_Click()` event this way:

```
Private Sub cmdOK_Click()
      Dim TheFile As String

      On Error GoTo FileError

      If (Right(dirLook.Path, 1) = "\") Then
            TheFile = dirLook.Path + filFind.FileName

      Else
            TheFile = dirLook.Path + "\" + filFind.FileName

      End If

      Open TheFile For Input As #1
      frmNotePad.txtPadText.Text = Input(LOF(1), #1)        'Read File

      Exit Sub

FileError:
      MsgBox "File Error", 48, "Editor"    'MsgBox for file error
      Resume Next

End Sub
```

The line of added code places the string that is read directly into the Editor's text box, `txtPadText`.

All that remains now is to close the file and hide the dialog box, `frmLoad`, at the same time. That can be accomplished like this:

```
Private Sub cmdOK_Click()
      Dim TheFile As String

      On Error GoTo FileError

      If (Right(dirLook.Path, 1) = "\") Then
            TheFile = dirLook.Path + filFind.FileName

      Else
            TheFile = dirLook.Path + "\" + filFind.FileName

      End If

      Open TheFile For Input As #1
      frmNotePad.txtPadText.Text = Input(LOF(1), #1)  'Read File
      Close #1                                        'Close File
```

```
        Unload cmdOK.Parent

        Exit Sub

FileError:
        MsgBox "File Error", 48, "Editor"    'MsgBox for file error
        Resume Next

End Sub
```

The Load File… dialog box is complete. To use it, simply start the program and select the Load File… item from the File menu. The Load File… dialog box opens, as shown in Figure 8.7. As you can see, the file list box presents the filenames in alphabetical order. To open a file, just double-click on it, or select it and click OK. When you do, the OK button Click procedure fires, opening the specified file and reading it into the Editor. At that point, you can edit it and save it to the disk again, using the Save File… option.

Figure 8.7.

The Editor application running, showing the fully functional Load File… dialog box.

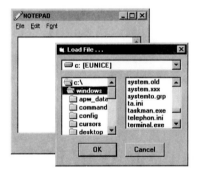

That's the end of the entire Editor application. You have made every part of the program operational. All the code, form-by-form, appears in Listings 8.1, 8.2, 8.3, and 8.4. The properties in this application should be set as shown in Table 8.4.

Table 8.4. The Editor Application. (Editor2.vbp)

Object	Property	Setting
Form	Appearance	1-3D
	Caption	EDITOR
	Icon	c:\vb\icons\writing\pencil01.ico
	Name	frmNotePad
Text Box	MultiLine	True
	Name	txtPadText
	ScrollBars	2-Vertical
	Text	(None)

continues

Table 8.4. continued

Object	Property	Setting
Form	Appearance	1-3D
	BorderStyle	3-Fixed Dialog
	Caption	Save File…
	MaxButton	False
	MinButton	False
	Name	frmSave
Label	Alignment	2-Center
	Caption	Save File As:
	Font	Style: Bold
	Name	lblSave
Text Box	Name	txtFileName
	Text	(None)
Command Button	Caption	OK
	Default	True
	Font	Style: Bold
	Name	cmdOK
Command Button	Cancel	True
	Caption	Cancel
	Font	Style: Bold
	Name	cmdCancel
Form	Appearance	1-3D
	BorderStyle	3-Fixed Dialog
	Caption	Load File…
	MaxButton	False
	MinButton	False
	Name	frmLoad
Drive List Box	Font	Style: Bold
	Name	drvChange
Directory List Box	Font	Style: Bold
	Name	dirLook

Object	Property	Setting
File List Box	Font	Style: Bold
	Name	filFind
Command Button	Caption	OK
	Default	True
	Font	Style: Bold
	Name	cmdOK
Command Button	Cancel	True
	Caption	Cancel
	Font	Style: Bold
	Name	cmdCancel

The menu settings for `frmNotePad` are shown in Table 8.5.

Table 8.5. The menu settings for `frmNotePad`.

Caption	Name	Indentation	Other Information
&File	mnuFile	0	(None)
&Load File…	mnuFileLoad	1	Shortcut: Ctrl+L
&Save File…	mnuFileSave	1	Shortcut: Ctrl+S
-	mnuSep1	1	(None)
E&xit	mnuFileExit	1	Shortcut: Ctrl+X
&Edit	mnuEdit	0	(None)
&Cut	mnuEditCut	1	Shortcut: Ctrl+C
&Paste	mnuEditPaste	1	Shortcut: Ctrl+P
Clear &All	mnuEditClear	1	Shortcut: Ctrl+A
&Font	mnuFont	0	(None)
Arial	mnuFontFArray	1	Index = 0
Courier	mnuFontFArray	1	Index = 1
MS Sans Serif	mnuFontFArray	1	Index = 2
MS Serif	mnuFontFArray	1	Index = 3
Times New Roman	mnuFontFArray	1	Index = 4

Listing 8.1. The code in the module, Editor2.bas.

```
Option Explicit

Public CutText As String
```

Listing 8.2. The code for `frmLoad` (the Load File... dialog box).

```
Option Explicit

Private Sub cmdCancel_Click()
      Unload cmdCancel.Parent
End Sub

Private Sub cmdOK_Click()
      Dim TheFile As String

      On Error GoTo FileError

      If (Right(dirLook.Path, 1) = "\") Then
            TheFile = dirLook.Path + filFind.FileName

      Else
            TheFile = dirLook.Path + "\" + filFind.FileName

      End If

      Open TheFile For Input As #1
      frmNotePad.txtPadText.Text = Input(LOF(1), #1)'Read File
      Close #1'Close File
      Unload cmdOK.Parent
      Exit Sub


FileError:
      MsgBox "File Error", 48, "Editor"    'MsgBox for file error
      Resume Next

End Sub

Private Sub dirLook_Change()
      filFind.Path = dirLook.Path
End Sub

Private Sub drvChange_Change()
      dirLook.Path = drvChange.Drive
End Sub

Private Sub filFind_DblClick()
      cmdOK_Click
End Sub
```

Listing 8.3. The code for `frmSave` (the Save File... dialog box).

```
Option Explicit

Private Sub cmdCancel_Click()
        Unload cmdCancel.Parent
End Sub

Private Sub cmdOK_Click()

        On Error GoTo FileError

        Open txtFileName.Text For Output As #1'Open file
        Print #1, frmNotePad.txtPadText.Text'Write document
        Close #1'Close file

        Unload cmdOK.Parent

        Exit Sub

FileError:
        MsgBox "File Error", 48, "Editor"    'MsgBox for file errror
        Resume Next

End Sub
```

Listing 8.4. The rest of the code for `frmNotePad`.

```
Option Explicit

Private Sub mnuEditClear_Click()
        'Clear text from txtNotePad
        txtPadText.Text = ""
End Sub

Private Sub mnuEditCut_Click()
        'Save cut text in buffer
        CutText = txtPadText.SelText
        txtPadText.SelText = ""

        'Enable paste menu item
        mnuEditPaste.Enabled = True
End Sub

Private Sub mnuEditPaste_Click()
        'Paste text back into text box
        txtPadText.SelText = CutText
End Sub

Private Sub Form_Terminate()
        End
End Sub

Private Sub mnuFileExit_Click()
        Unload frmNotePad
End Sub
```

continues

Listing 8.4. **continued**

```
Private Sub mnuFileLoad_Click()
      frmLoad.Show
End Sub

Private Sub mnuFileSave_Click()
      frmSave.Show
End Sub

Private Sub mnuFontNameArray_Click(Index As Integer)
      Dim UnCheck As Integer

      Select Case Index
            Case 0
                  txtPadText.Font = "Arial"
            Case 1
                  txtPadText.Font = "Courier"
            Case 2
                  txtPadText.Font = "MS Sans Serif"
            Case 3
                  txtPadText.Font = "MS Serif"
            Case 4
                  txtPadText.Font = "Times New Roman"
            Case Else

      End Select

      For UnCheck = 0 To 4
            'Remove check mark from font
            mnuFontNameArray(UnCheck).Checked = False
      Next UnCheck

      'Add check mark to new font
      mnuFontNameArray(Index).Checked = True
End Sub

Private Sub txtPadText_Change()
      'Enable Cut and Clear All menu items
      mnuEditCut.Enabled = True
      mnuEditClear.Enabled = True
End Sub
```

By this point, you have opened sequential files for input and output. And, as mentioned earlier, if you wanted to add to the end of a sequential file, you could open it in the Append mode. In that case, everything written to the file would be added to the end of the contents already in the file.

Well, that's it for sequential files. Now you move along to the next type: *random-access files.*

Using Random-Access Files in Visual Basic

It is time to move past sequential files to random-access files. These kind of files break up their data into records, all having the same format but usually different data. As you might remember, in the last chapter you set up the Database program's data, using exactly those kinds of records.

```
Type Record
Name As String * 50
Quantity As String * 20
Comment As String * 200
End Sub

Public TheData(100) As Record
```

To show it visually, each record of `TheData(n)` (in which *n* is the index number of the record) could appear as shown in Figure 8.8.

Figure 8.8.
A pictorial representation of the Database application's record array.

Well-organized files could be made from such records, as shown in Figure 8.9.

Figure 8.9.
A pictorial representation of records organized into files.

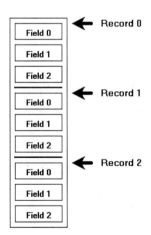

As you might recall, the database application has five items on its File menu, as shown in Figure 8.10. They are Add Item, which adds the current record to the database; Find Item…, which locates a specified record; Save File…; Load File…; and Exit. Everything works in the menu except the two file items. It is time to make them do something now. And to implement those changes, you will use random-access files.

Figure 8.10.
The Database application at design-time with the File menu open.

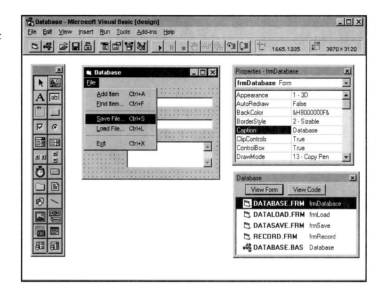

Writing Random-Access Files

Open the Database project to get going. If you do not want to overwrite the application as it currently stands, use the Save File As... and Save Project As... items on the Visual Basic File menu. Save the forms, module, and project as Database2.frm, Record2.frm, Database2.bas, and Database2.vbp.

Note: You might have noticed that Database2 is longer than the eight characters that filenames have been limited to since the advent of DOS. With the introduction of Windows 95, files can have "long" names that can contain spaces and some punctuation. Look forward to being able to actually figure out what your files are without opening them.

Start by adding the code that will save a selected file. This file is chosen after the user selects the Save File... item, `mnuFileSave`, from the File menu on Database2.frm. Open the `Click` event associated with the Save File... item by double-clicking on that item with the mouse. The following template appears in the Code window:

```
Private Sub mnuFileSave_Click()

End Sub
```

When the user clicks on this item, she wants to save the database in a particular file. So a dialog box very similar to the one you just designed for the Editor application needs to appear on the screen. In fact, you can use that very same dialog box here. To add that form to the Database program, select the Add File... option from the File menu. Find the form Save.frm and then click Open. Now, you need to save the form in your Database project. Make sure Save.frm is highlighted in the Project window, and then select the Save File As... item from the File menu. The Save File As... dialog box appears. Move through the file directory until you find the place where Database.vbp and its associated forms reside. Change the filename of the form to DataSave.frm, using the FileName list box. Press Save. It's that easy to add a form, such as a premade dialog box, to a project. Imagine how easy it would be to build a Visual Basic application, using your own custom-designed forms. Plus, using the same custom-designed forms makes your applications more uniform.

You can now add the code to the frmDatabase Code window that makes Datasave.frm appear on the screen:

```
Private Sub mnuFileSave_Click()
      frmSave.Show
End Sub
```

Next, you have to make some changes to the frmSave code. At the moment, it is set up to store sequential files. That needs to be changed so that it stores random-access files. Switch to the frmSave Code window using the Project window, or double-click anywhere on that form. Using the Object and Procedure list boxes at the top of frmSave's Code window, change to the Click event for cmdOK. When you do, the following procedure will appear in the Code window:

```
Private Sub cmdOK_Click()

      On Error GoTo FileError

      Open txtFileName.Text For Output As #1'Open file
      Print #1, frmNotePad.txtPadText.Text'Write document
      Close #1'Close file

      Unload cmdOK.Parent

      Exit Sub

FileError:
      MsgBox "File Error", 48, "Editor"    'MsgBox for file error
      Resume Next

End Sub
```

Because you want to use random file access this time, the file must be opened in the Random mode.

```
Private Sub cmdOK_Click()

      On Error GoTo FileError

      Open txtFileName.Text For Random As #1 Len = Len(TheData(1)) 'Open file
      Print #1, frmNotePad.txtPadText.Text'Write document
      Close #1'Close file

      Unload cmdOK.Parent

      Exit Sub
```

```
FileError:
        MsgBox "File Error", 48, "Editor"    'MsgBox for file error
        Resume Next

End Sub
```

In the changed line of code, the record length that will be used is indicated by Len(TheData(1)). This returns the length in bytes of the record size. Next, the application should write the entry array of records, TheData(), out to that file. So it is time to look into the options for writing random-access files.

The most common user-interface statements for both binary and random-access files are Get # and Put #. Put # will be used here for writing the files and Get # will be used later when reading the files.

The Put # statement writes from a variable to a disk file. Its syntax appears as follows:

```
Put [#]filenumber, [recnumber ], varname
```

The arguments that Put # uses are as follows:

- *filenumber*—any valid file number.
- *recnumber*—a record number (when reading from Random mode files) or a byte number (when reading from Binary mode files) where the reading begins.
- *varname*—a valid variable name into which data is read.

If a record number is not specified when the Put # statement is used, Visual Basic simply places the record after the last one in the file. The total number of records is stored in the public integer TotalRecords, so the records can be written out as follows (note that if TotalRecords = 0, no records will be written):

```
Private Sub cmdOK_Click()
        Dim AllRecords As Integer

        On Error GoTo FileError
        Open txtFileName.Text For Random As #1 Len = Len(TheData(1))    'Open file

        For AllRecords = 1 To TotalRecords
                Put #1, , TheData(AllRecords)
        Next AllRecords

        Close #1'Close file

        Unload cmdOK.Parent

        Exit Sub

FileError:
        MsgBox "File Error", 48, "Database"    'MsgBox for file error
        Resume Next

End Sub
```

Also, as shown in the preceding code, make sure to change the error message box title from Editor to Database.

And that's it! Now you can use the Database's Save File... option. When you do, the Save File... dialog box appears on your screen as in Figure 8.11.

Figure 8.11.
The Database application running with the Save File... menu item completely functional.

At this point, the file is written to disk. If you want to write a specific record instead of all of them at once, you could specify the record number in the following way:

```
Put # 1, 5, TheData(23)
```

This writes record 5 in the file, filling it with the twenty-third record of the TheData array. In this way, random access is completely random. The application has access to all records in the file, so it can move around at will, writing records in the order that the user specifies. This works in a similar way in Get #, as you will see next. Now you can read the records back into the file.

Reading Random-Access Files

You copied the Save File... dialog box from the Editor application to your database. Now it is time to do the same with the Load File... dialog box. Once again, select the Add File... option from the File menu. Find the form Load.frm, and then click Open. Now you need to save the form in the Database project. Select the Save File As... item from the File menu. The Save File As... dialog box appears. Move through the file directory until you find the place where Database.vbp and its associated forms reside. Then change the filename of the form to DataLoad.frm, using the File Name list box. Press Save.

Next, open the Code window for frmDatabase and find the Click event associated with mnuFileLoad. When you do, the following template will appear in the Code window:

```
Private Sub mnuFileLoad_Click()

End Sub
```

Now add the line of code that will show the Load File dialog box:

```
Private Sub mnuFileLoad_Click()
     frmLoad.Show
End Sub
```

Close that Code window and then double-click on the OK button on the Load File... form. This brings up the important procedure for that form, cmdOK_Click(), which already contains the following code:

```
Private Sub cmdOK_Click()
      Dim TheFile As String

      On Error GoTo FileError

      If (Right(dirLook.Path, 1) = "\") Then
            TheFile = dirLook.Path + filFind.FileName

      Else
            TheFile = dirLook.Path + "\" + filFind.FileName

      End If

      Open TheFile For Input As #1
      frmNotePad.txtPadText.Text = Input(LOF(1), #1) 'Read File
      Close #1'Close File
      Unload cmdOK.Parent

      Exit Sub

FileError:
      MsgBox "File Error", 48, "Editor"    'MsgBox for file error
      Resume Next

End Sub
```

Once again, you can change the code so that the file is opened for random access, like this:

```
Private Sub cmdOK_Click()
      Dim TheFile As String

      On Error GoTo FileError

      If (Right(dirLook.Path, 1) = "\") Then
            TheFile = dirLook.Path + filFind.FileName

      Else
            TheFile = dirLook.Path + "\" + filFind.FileName

      End If

      Open TheFile For Random As #1 Len = Len(TheData(1)) 'Open File
      frmNotePad.txtPadText.Text = Input(LOF(1), #1) 'Read File
      Close #1
      'Close File
      Unload cmdOK.Parent

      Exit Sub

FileError:
      MsgBox "File Error", 48, "Editor"    'MsgBox for file error
      Resume Next

End Sub
```

The `Put #` statement used in the last section *writes* from a variable to a disk file. Conversely, the `Get #` statement *reads* from an open disk file into a variable (for example, `Get #` can take records from a file). The `Get #` syntax works like this:

```
Get [#]filenumber, [recnumber ], varname
```

`Get #` uses the following arguments:

- `filenumber`—any valid file number.
- `recnumber`—a record number (when reading from Random mode files) or a byte number (when reading from Binary mode files) where the reading begins.
- `varname`—a valid variable name into which data is read.

As with the `Put #` statement, if a record number is not specified when using the `Get #` statement, Visual Basic simply gets the next record from the current position in the file.

Your first job here is to find out how many records are in the file. That can be achieved simply by dividing the length of the file by the size of each record. Then the program can read the data in like this, record-by-record:

```
Private Sub cmdOK_Click()
Dim TheFile As String
Dim NumLines As Integer
Dim FindThemAll As Integer

     On Error GoTo FileError

     If (Right(dirLook.Path, 1) = "\") Then
           TheFile = dirLook.Path + filFind.FileName

     Else
           TheFile = dirLook.Path + "\" + filFind.FileName

     End If

     Open TheFile For Random As #1 Len = Len(TheData(1)) 'Open File

     NumLines = LOF(1) / Len(TheData(1))
     For FindThemAll = 1 To NumLines
           Get #1, , TheData(FindThemAll)
     Next FindThemAll

     Close #1'Close File
     Unload cmdOK.Parent

     Exit Sub

FileError:
     MsgBox "File Error", 48, "Database"    'MsgBox for file error
     Resume Next

End Sub
```

Notice that, again, the name of the error title box was changed from Editor to Database.

Simply loading a file does not make the database active, however. The application also has to load the record names read by the `Get #` statement into the sorted combo box `cboName`, which is located on the Find Item... dialog box (`frmRecord`). There, a record can be selected by the user. To load the record names into that list box, the program must first erase all current entries, using the `RemoveItem` method. Then the new entries can be loaded from `TheData()` into `frmRecord.cboName`.

```
Private Sub cmdOK_Click()
Dim TheFile As String
Dim NumLines As Integer
Dim FindThemAll As Integer
Dim TotalRecords As Integer

    On Error GoTo FileError

    If (Right(dirLook.Path, 1) = "\") Then
        TheFile = dirLook.Path + filFind.FileName

    Else
        TheFile = dirLook.Path + "\" + filFind.FileName

    End If

    Open TheFile For Random As #1 Len = Len(TheData(1))    'Open File

    NumLines = LOF(1) / Len(TheData(1))
    For FindThemAll = 1 To NumLines
        Get #1, , TheData(FindThemAll)
    Next FindThemAll

    Close #1                    'Close File

    For FindThemAll = 1 To TotalRecords
        frmRecord.cboName.RemoveItem 0
    Next FindThemAll

    TotalRecords = NumLines

    For FindThemAll = 1 To TotalRecords
        frmRecord.cboName.AddItem TheData(FindThemAll).Name
    Next FindThemAll

    frmDatabase.txtNameField.Text = TheData(1).Name
    frmDatabase.txtNumberField.Text = TheData(1).Quantity
    frmDatabase.txtCommentField.Text = TheData(1).Comments

    Unload cmdOK.Parent

Exit Sub

FileError:
    MsgBox "File Error", 48, "Database"    'MsgBox for file error
    Resume Next

End Sub
```

And that's it! The application now reads in the file and fills the program variables correctly. The Database application's Load File... dialog box is now fully functional. When the application is running, it will appear on the screen as in Figure 8.12.

Figure 8.12.
The Database program running, showing the fully functional Load File... dialog box.

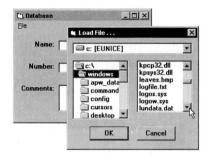

That's the end of the Database application for now. All the code, form-by-form, appears in Listings 8.5, 8.6, 8.7, 8.8, and 8.9. Listing 8.5 shows the code for the module Database2.bas.

Listing 8.5. The code for the module Database2.bas.

```
Option Explicit

Public TheData(100) As Record
Public TotalRecords As Integer

Type Record
  Name As String * 50
  Quantity As String * 20
  Comments As String * 200
End Type

Public Sub GetItem()
Dim WhichRecord As Integer
Dim Matched As Boolean

  Matched = False

  For WhichRecord = 1 To 100
    If (RTrim(TheData(WhichRecord).Name)) = RTrim(frmRecord.cboName.Text) Then
      Matched = True
      Exit For
    End If
  Next WhichRecord

  If (Matched) Then
    frmDatabase.txtNameField.Text = TheData(WhichRecord).Name
    frmDatabase.txtNumberField.Text = TheData(WhichRecord).Quantity
    frmDatabase.txtCommentField.Text = TheData(WhichRecord).Comments
    frmRecord.Hide

  Else
    MsgBox "Sorry! I can't find that record! Try again, please...",
    ➥48, "Database"

  End If

End Sub
```

Listing 8.6. The code for `frmDatabase`.

```
Option Explicit

Private Sub Form_Terminate()
End
End Sub

Private Sub mnuFileAdd_Click()
TotalRecords = TotalRecords + 1

TheData(TotalRecords).Name = txtNameField.Text
TheData(TotalRecords).Quantity = txtNumberField.Text
TheData(TotalRecords).Comments = txtCommentField.Text

frmRecord.cboName.AddItem txtNameField.Text

txtNameField.Text = ""
txtNumberField.Text = ""
txtCommentField.Text = ""
txtNameField.SetFocus

End Sub

Private Sub mnuFileExit_Click()
  End
End Sub

Private Sub mnuFileFind_Click()
    frmRecord.Show
End Sub

Private Sub mnuFileLoad_Click()
    frmLoad.Show
End Sub

Private Sub mnuFileSave_Click()
    frmSave.Show
End Sub
```

Listing 8.7. The code for DataLoad.frm.

```
Option Explicit

Private Sub cmdCancel_Click()
    Unload cmdCancel.Parent
End Sub

Private Sub cmdOK_Click()
    Dim TheFile As String
    Dim NumLines As Integer
    Dim FindThemAll As Integer
    Dim TotalRecords As Integer

    On Error GoTo FileError
```

```vb
    If (Right(dirLook.Path, 1) = "\") Then
        TheFile = dirLook.Path + filFind.FileName

    Else
        TheFile = dirLook.Path + "\" + filFind.FileName

    End If

    Open TheFile For Random As #1 Len = Len(TheData(1))     'Open File

    NumLines = LOF(1) / Len(TheData(1))
    For FindThemAll = 1 To NumLines
        Get #1, , TheData(FindThemAll)
    Next FindThemAll

    Close #1                     'Close File

    For FindThemAll = 1 To TotalRecords
        frmRecord.cboName.RemoveItem 0
    Next FindThemAll

    TotalRecords = NumLines

    For FindThemAll = 1 To TotalRecords
        frmRecord.cboName.AddItem TheData(FindThemAll).Name
    Next FindThemAll

    frmDatabase.txtNameField.Text = TheData(1).Name
    frmDatabase.txtNumberField.Text = TheData(1).Quantity
    frmDatabase.txtCommentField.Text = TheData(1).Comments

    Unload cmdOK.Parent

    Exit Sub

FileError:
    MsgBox "File Error", 48, "Database"    'MsgBox for file error
    Exit Sub

End Sub

Private Sub dirLook_Change()
    filFind.Path = dirLook.Path
End Sub

Private Sub drvChange_Change()
    dirLook.Path = drvChange.Drive
End Sub

Private Sub filFind_DblClick()
    cmdOK_Click
End Sub
```

Listing 8.8. **The code for DataSave.frm.**

```
Option Explicit

Private Sub cmdCancel_Click()
    Unload cmdCancel.Parent
End Sub

Private Sub cmdOK_Click()
    Dim AllRecords As Integer

    On Error GoTo FileError
    Open txtFileName.Text For Random As #1 Len = Len(TheData(1))    'Open file

    For AllRecords = 1 To TotalRecords
        Put #1, , TheData(AllRecords)
    Next AllRecords

    Close #1'Close file

    Unload cmdOK.Parent

Exit Sub

FileError:
    MsgBox "File Error", 48, "Database"    'MsgBox for file error
    Resume Next

End Sub
```

Listing 8.9. **The code for frmRecord.**

```
Option Explicit

Private Sub cboName_DblClick()
    GetItem
End Sub

Private Sub cmdCancel_Click()
    frmRecord.Hide
End Sub

Private Sub cmdOK_Click()
    GetItem
End Sub
```

Again, note that the entire record array does not need to be read in at one time. In fact, the application could read in only one record at a time if that was what you, the programmer, wanted to do. This would save a significant amount of memory in the process. For example, if the data was saved in a file named Db.dat, the subroutine that looks up records, GetItem(), could be changed to read them one at a time. The GetItem() routine at present looks like this:

```
Public Sub GetItem()
    Dim WhichRecord As Integer
    Dim Matched As Boolean

    Matched = False

    For WhichRecord = 1 To 100
        If (RTrim(TheData(WhichRecord).Name)) = RTrim(frmRecord.cboName.Text) Then
            Matched = True
            Exit For
        End If
    Next WhichRecord

    If (Matched) Then
        frmDatabase.txtNameField.Text = TheData(WhichRecord).Name
        frmDatabase.txtNumberField.Text = TheData(WhichRecord).Quantity
        frmDatabase.txtCommentField.Text = TheData(WhichRecord).Comments
        frmRecord.Hide

    Else
        MsgBox "Sorry! I can't find that record! Try again, please...",
        ➡48, "Database"

    End If

End Sub
```

If you were to make this change to the Database application, it would appear like this:

```
Public Sub GetItem()
    Dim WhichRecord As Integer
    Dim Matched As Boolean

    Matched = False

    For WhichRecord = 1 To 100
        If (RTrim(TheData(WhichRecord).Name)) = RTrim(frmRecord.cboName.Text)Then
            Matched = True
            Exit For
            End If
    Next WhichRecord

    Open "Db.Dat" For Random As # 1 Len = Len(TheData(1))
    Get # 1, WhichRecord, TheData(WhichRecord)
    Close # 1

    If (Matched) Then
        frmDatabase.txtNameField.Text = TheData(WhichRecord).Name
        frmDatabase.txtNumberField.Text = TheData(WhichRecord).Quantity
        frmDatabase.txtCommentField.Text = TheData(WhichRecord).Comments
        frmRecord.Hide

    Else
        MsgBox "Sorry! I can't find that record! Try again, please...",
        ➡48, "Database"

    End If

End Sub
```

In this way, the program could move around in the file, retrieving the specific records desired by the user.

At this point, your file expertise is almost complete. Note, however, that you do not have to specify the record number in the previous `Get #` statement if you don't want to specify one. Instead, you could use the `Seek #` statement.

Using the *Seek* # Statement

The `Seek #` statement can be extremely useful because it sets the position for the next read or write within a file opened using the `Open` statement. Its syntax works like this:

```
Seek [#]filename, position
```

The arguments for this statement are defined as follows:

- *filename*—any valid filename.
- *position*—a number in the range 1 to 2,147,483,647, inclusive, which indicates where the next read or write should occur.

Thus, the line from the `GetItem` subroutine

```
Get # 1, WhichRecord, TheData(WhichRecord)
```

could be changed to include the `Seek #` statement, like this:

```
Seek # 1, WhichRecord
Get # 1, , TheData(WhichRecord)
```

Using the `Get #`, `Put #`, and `Seek #` statements together gives you a great deal of control over files. In particular, with the statements, a program could work byte-by-byte in binary files.

A Visual Basic Trick

If you simply want to copy files, you could use the Visual Basic `FileCopy` command.

Handling Application Initialization Information Using Profile Strings (.ini Files)

Many times when writing a program, you would like it to remember settings and values from the last time the application ran. This type of memory, which is a user preference, is a good example of what a sophisticated Windows program should be able to do.

Fortunately, Windows provides an easy ASCII-based way to read and write this kind of information using *profile strings*. These profile strings are aptly named because they are normally used to profile user preferences and application settings. There are two kinds of profile strings: *public* and *private*. Public strings are stored in the Win.ini file, which is probably familiar to most Windows users. A section of a Win.ini file appears in Figure 8.13. Private strings are placed in files named by the programmer, although the convention is to store private profile string information in files with a .ini designation in the Windows directory.

Using the Registry to Save Program Settings

Initialization files have been included in Visual Basic 4 to facilitate backwards compatibility. A new method of initialization has been devised that uses the Registry to save program settings. This will be discussed in Chapter 14, "Connecting to Other Windows Applications: Object Linking and Embedding 2."

Figure 8.13.
A portion of a Win.ini file.

You probably know that it is not a terrific idea to clutter up Win.ini files; you should use private profile strings for your applications. Here's an example: If you wrote a program called Mysamp.exe, you could use a private profile file named C:\Windows\Mysamp.ini. (If the user leaves off the C:\Windows, the private profile functions know to look in the local Windows directory for it by default.)

In order to save to and read a value from Private .ini files, you need to know three things:

1. The name of the file.

2. The name of the section it appears in (you will see this in brackets).

3. The keyword for the value (this appears before the = sign). For example, the .ini file Mysamp.ini might look like this:

```
[Name of User]    *this is the section
LastName=Smith  *Lastname is the Keyword.
```

In addition, because the profile string functions are Windows Applications Programming Interface (API) functions, there are a few tricks that you must master when calling them. When you have learned these tricks, however, you will have no problem giving your applications an excellent memory, much like that of the proverbial elephant.

Using the API Viewer to Browse Through Declares, Constants, and Types

A new feature of Visual Basic 4 is an API Viewer that allows you to browse through declares, constants, and types included in the provided text file that contains API information. The Viewer can copy the declarations for these items onto the Clipboard, and then the paste facility can be used to deliver the calls to Visual Basic code. To open the Viewer located in the VB\WinApi group, double-click on the ApiLod32 object. (This is the 32-bit version of the API Viewer; if you are writing 16-bit code, you need to open ApiLod16.)

There are three Private Profile functions you can use:

- `GetPrivateProfileString`
- `GetPrivateProfileInt`
- `WritePrivateProfileString`

These functions are part of the Windows API. They are external to Visual Basic, so they must be declared in a Visual Basic project. The declarations should be placed in the `(General)` `(declaration)` section of a form. Alternatively, they should be placed in the `(General)` `(declaration)` section of a .bas Module and declared `Public`. This second option would be used if the functions were to be called from more than one form. It is very important to get the declarations exactly right. The following are the three declarations (each of these `Declare` statements is one long line and should be entered as one line in Visual Basic):

```
Public [Private] Declare Function WritePrivateProfileString Lib "kernel32" _
        Alias "WritePrivateProfileStringA" _
        (ByVal lpApplicationName As String, ByVal lpKeyName As Any, _
        ByVal lpString As Any, ByVal lplFileName As String) As Long

Public [Private] Declare Function GetPrivateProfileInt Lib "kernel32" _
        Alias "GetPrivateProfileIntA" (ByVal lpApplicationName As String, _
        ByVal lpKeyName As String, ByVal nDefault As Long, _
        ByVal lpFileName As String) As Long

Public [Private] Declare Function GetPrivateProfileString Lib "kernel32" _
        Alias "GetPrivateProfileStringA" (ByVal lpApplicationName As String, _
        ByVal lpKeyName As Any, ByVal lpDefault As String, _
        ByVal lpReturnedString As String, ByVal nSize As Long, _
        ByVal lpFileName As String) As Long
```

Tip: Visual Basic 4 enables you to split lines of code that are too long. Before Version 4 all of the preceding lines would have had to be on one line, making it difficult to see all of the arguments. Visual Basic 4 added the line continuation character support from Visual Basic for Applications. This character is an underscore (_). It is placed at the end of the line with at least one preceding space. This tells Visual Basic that you really want the next time to be included with the current line.

You should note that the preceding declarations are for 32-bit code. If you are writing for 16-bit code, you should use the 16-bit API Viewer (ApiLod16.exe) to copy the declarations from Win31Api.txt.

The following is a sample of what the calls to these functions might look like. For the sake of clarity, implicit variable declarations are used in this example so that you can see what type of variables need to be used. The names of the variables in these examples describe the intended contents of the variables:

```
x% = GetPrivateProfileString (SectionName$, KeyWord$, DefaultValue$, _
ReturnValue$, LengthofReturnValue%,FileName$)

ReturnValue% = GetPrivateProfileInt(SectionName$,KeyWord$,Default%,FileName$)

x% = WritePrivateProfileString(SectionName$, KeyWord$,Value$,FileName$)
```

Soon you will see how easy it is to use these functions in an actual application. But, before you put together a demonstration program that uses them, a few things need to be pointed out.

First, there is no way to save a numeric value directly using these functions. `WritePrivateProfileString` is the only function available for saving information, and it saves a string. Therefore, if you want to save an integer, you must first convert it to a string using the `Str()` function.

Next, both `GetPrivateProfileString` and `WritePrivateProfileString` return integer values that indicate whether they could successfully perform their tasks. `0` (or `False`) means failure; anything else indicates success. It is a good idea to test for successful completion in your applications before continuing.

Finally, the `ReturnValue$` string in `GetPrivateProfileString` must be declared as a fixed-length string. For instance, consider the declaration: `Dim ReturnValue As String * 50`. If you forget to use the `* 50` to define a fixed-length string and declare it normally (`Dim ReturnValue As String`) the `GetPrivateProfileString` will generate an error message (and probably crash your system). The argument following `ReturnValue$` in `GetPrivateProfileString` is the length of `ReturnValue$`. This should be set using the `Len()` function. An example of this is `Len(ReturnValue$)`.

That's all there is to it. Now it's time to put this into practice.

The Sample INI Program, Stage 1

To get going with the demo program, start a new project in Visual Basic. Change the default form's `Name` and `Caption` properties to `frmIni` and `Sample INI Program`, respectively. Then save the project using the Save Project item on the File menu. Save the form as Ini.frm and the project as Ini.vbp.

Design the test form referring to Figure 8.14 as a model for the various objects' placement. Use the following table to set the objects' properties.

Object	Property	Setting
Form	Appearance	1-3D
	Border	1-Fixed Single
	Caption	Sample INI Program
	Name	frmIni
Label	Alignment	2-Center
	Caption	Enter Value:
	Name	lblValue
Text Box	Name	txtValue
	Text	(None)
Shape	BorderColor	White
	Name	Shape 1
Label	BorderStyle	1-Fixed Single
	Caption	(None)
	Name	lblDemo
Text Box	MultiLine	True
	Name	txtDisplay
	ScrollBars	3-Both
	Text	(None)
Command Button	Caption	STORE: WritePrivateProfileString
	Default	True
	Name	cmdStore
Command Button	Caption	RECALL: GetPrivateProfileString
	Name	cmdGet
Command Button	Caption	Close
	Name	cmdClose

Figure 8.14.
The Sample INI template.

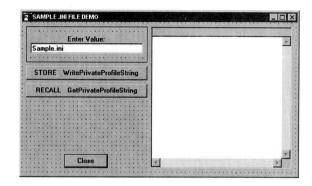

Start a new module by selecting the Module option from the Insert menu. A default module Code window, Module1, appears on the screen. Change the module's `Name` property to `SampleINI`, and then save the module using the Save File item on the File menu. Save the module as Ini.bas. Add the following declarations for the profile functions to the module (remember that each declare is a very long line):

```
Declare Function WritePrivateProfileString Lib "kernel32" Alias _
    "WritePrivateProfileStringA" (ByVal lpApplicationName As String, _
    ByVal lpKeyName As Any, ByVal lpString As Any, _
    ByVal lplFileName As String) As Long

Declare Function GetPrivateProfileInt Lib "kernel32" Alias _
    "GetPrivateProfileIntA" (ByVal lpApplicationName As String, _
    ByVal lpKeyName As String, ByVal nDefault As Long, _
    ByVal lpFileName As String) As Long

Declare Function GetPrivateProfileString Lib "kernel32" Alias _
    "GetPrivateProfileStringA" (ByVal lpApplicationName As String, _
    ByVal lpKeyName As Any, ByVal lpDefault As String, _
    ByVal lpReturnedString As String, ByVal nSize As Long, _
    ByVal lpFileName As String) As Long
```

Next, add the following code to `frmIni`, using the Object and Procedure list boxes to find each object's event:

```
Option Explicit

Dim IniFileName As String

Private Sub Form_Initialize()
  IniFileName = "c:\windows\sampini.ini"
End Sub

Private Sub cmdClose_Click()
  Unload cmdClose.Parent
End Sub

Private Sub cmdGet_Click()
  Dim x As Long
  Dim Temp As String * 50
  Dim lpAppName As String, lpKeyName As String, lpDefault As String,
  ➥lpFileName As String
```

```
    lpAppName = "Things to Remember"
    lpKeyName = "Value"
    lpDefault = "Sampini.ini"
    lpFileName = "Sampini.ini"

    x = GetPrivateProfileString(lpAppName, lpKeyName, lpDefault, Temp,
    ➥Len(Temp), lpFileName)

    If x = 0 Then
      Beep
    Else
      txtValue.Text = Trim(Temp)
      frmIni.Caption = "I remember: " & Temp
      RefreshDisplay txtValue.Text
    End If

    End Sub

Private Sub cmdStore_Click()
    Dim lpAppName As String, lpFileName As String, lpKeyName As String,
    ➥lpString As String
    Dim U As Long

    lpAppName = "Things to Remember"
    lpKeyName = "Value"
    lpString = txtValue.Text
    lpFileName = "Sampini.ini"

    U = WritePrivateProfileString(lpAppName, lpKeyName, lpString, lpFileName)

    If U = 0 Then
      Beep
    End If

    RefreshDisplay lpString
End Sub

Private Sub RefreshDisplay(Value As String)
    Dim ExpectedOutput As String
    Dim Crlf As String

    Crlf = Chr$(13) + Chr$(10) 'Crlf stands for Carriage return/line feed

    ExpectedOutput = ExpectedOutput + "[Things to Remember]"
    ExpectedOutput = ExpectedOutput + Crlf + "Value="
    ExpectedOutput = ExpectedOutput + Value
    txtDisplay.Text = ExpectedOutput
    lblDemo.Caption = "Contents of " & UCase$(IniFileName)

End Sub
```

There! Your application now writes a keyword (whatever is entered in the Value text box) and places it in the Sampini.ini file beneath a [Things to Remember] Section heading. This puts some of the file access tools introduced in this chapter to good use. The contents of Sampini.ini are displayed in the text box. Try entering different values in the Value box. The Sample API program is shown in Figure 8.15 as it should now appear.

Figure 8.15.
The Sample INI application running.

The Sample INI Program, Stage 2

At this point, you've successfully used the private profile functions to write to and read from an .ini file. Now you can take this one step further as a real application. Place a check box on the lower left of the form, as shown in Figure 8.16. Change the Name and Caption properties of the check box to chkStart and RECALL on Start-Up, respectively. The idea here is that if the user selects chkStart when exiting, Sampini.ini will remember the value set when the application closes. Also, add a View command button to the form to allow the user to update the display. Place this new command button below the Store and Recall command buttons, as in Figure 8.16. Change the new command button's Name property to cmdView and its Caption property to VIEW: C:\Windows\Sampini.ini.

Now add the following code to the new controls' event procedures (the form Load and Unload events), and add a few more lines to the RefreshDisplay subroutine as follows:

```
Private Sub cmdView_Click()
  RefreshDisplay txtValue.Text
End Sub

Private Sub Form_Load()
  Dim Y As Long, lpAppName As String, lpKeyName As String
  Dim lpDefault As Long, lpFileName As String, nDefault As String
  Dim Temp As String * 50
  Dim x As Long

  lpAppName = "Start Up"
  lpKeyName = "Checked"
  lpDefault = 0
  lpFileName = "Sampini.ini"

  x = GetPrivateProfileString(lpAppName, lpKeyName, lpDefault, Temp, _
                              Len(Temp), lpFileName)
  Y = Val(Trim(Temp))

  If Y = 1 Then
    chkStart.Value = 1
    x = GetPrivateProfileString("Things to Remember", "Value", "Sampini.ini", _
                                Temp, Len(Temp), lpFileName)
```

```
      If x = 0 Then
        Beep
      Else
        txtValue.Text = Trim(Temp)
        frmIni.Caption = "I remember: " & Temp
        RefreshDisplay txtValue.Text
      End If

   Else
     chkStart.Value = 0

   End If
End Sub

Private Sub Form_Unload(Cancel As Integer)
   Dim x As Integer, lpAppName As String, lpKeyName As String
   Dim U As Integer, lpstring As String, lpFileName As String

   lpAppName = "Start Up"
   lpKeyName = "Checked"
   lpFileName = "Sampini.ini"

   x = chkStart.Value
   lpstring = Str(x)
   U = WritePrivateProfileString(lpAppName, lpKeyName, lpstring, lpFileName)

   If U = 0 Then
     Beep
   End If

End Sub

Private Sub RefreshDisplay(Value As String)
   Dim ExpectedOutput As String
   Dim Crlf As String
   Dim chkval As Integer

   Crlf = Chr$(13) + Chr$(10) 'Crlf stands for Carriage return/line feed
   ExpectedOutput = "[Start Up]"
   ExpectedOutput = ExpectedOutput + Crlf + "Checked= "
   chkval = Abs(chkStart.Value)

   ExpectedOutput = ExpectedOutput + Str$(chkval) + Crlf + Crlf
   ExpectedOutput = ExpectedOutput + "[Things to Remember]"
   ExpectedOutput = ExpectedOutput + Crlf + "Value="
   ExpectedOutput = ExpectedOutput + Value

   txtDisplay.Text = ExpectedOutput
   lblDemo.Caption = "Contents of " & UCase$(IniFileName)

End Sub
```

That's all it takes. By checking the RECALL on Start-Up check box, the contents of Sampini.ini will appear in txtDisplay the next time the application is started. Run the application now and see what happens.

The complete code for the application is given in Listings 8.10 and 8.11. Table 8.6 shows how to set the properties for the controls in the Sample INI program.

Figure 8.16.
*The Sample INI application
completed and running.*

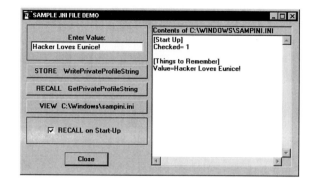

Table 8.6. The Sample INI property settings.

Object	Property	Setting
Form	Appearance	1-3D
	BorderStyle	1-Fixed Single
	Caption	Sample INI Program
	Name	frmIni
Label	Alignment	2-Center
	Caption	Enter Value:
	Name	lblValue
Text Box	Name	txtValue
	Text	(None)
Shape	BorderColor	White
	Name	Shape 1
Label	BorderStyle	1-Fixed Single
	Caption	(None)
	Name	lblDemo
Text Box	MultiLine	True
	Name	txtDisplay
	Text	(None)
Command Button	Caption	Close
	Name	cmdClose
Command Button	Caption	STORE: WritePrivateProfileString
	Name	cmdStore

continues

Table 8.6. continued

Object	Property	Setting
Command Button	Caption	RECALL: GetPrivateProfileString
	Name	cmdGet
Command Button	Caption	VIEW: C:\Windows\Sampini.ini
	Name	cmdView
Check Box	Caption	RECALL on Start-Up
	Name	chkStart
Shape	BorderColor	White
	Name	Shape 2

Listing 8.10. The code for Ini.bas.

```
Declare Function WritePrivateProfileString Lib "kernel32" Alias _
    "WritePrivateProfileStringA" (ByVal lpApplicationName As String, _
    ByVal lpKeyName As Any, ByVal lpstring As Any, _
    ByVal lplFileName As String) As Long

Declare Function GetPrivateProfileInt Lib "kernel32" Alias _
    "GetPrivateProfileIntA" (ByVal lpApplicationName As String, _
    ByVal lpKeyName As Any, ByVal nDefault As Long, _
    ByVal lpFileName As String) As Long

Declare Function GetPrivateProfileString Lib "kernel32" Alias _
    "GetPrivateProfileStringA" (ByVal lpApplicationName As String, _
    ByVal lpKeyName As Any, ByVal lpDefault As String, _
    ByVal lpReturnedString As String, ByVal nSize As Long, _
    ByVal lpFileName As String) As Long
```

Listing 8.11. The complete code for `frmIni`.

```
Option Explicit

Dim IniFileName As String

Private Sub cmdView_Click()
    RefreshDisplay txtValue.Text
End Sub

Private Sub Form_Load()
    Dim Y As Long, lpAppName As String, lpKeyName As String
    Dim lpDefault As Long, lpFileName As String, nDefault As String
    Dim Temp As String * 50
    Dim x As Long

    lpAppName = "Start Up"
    lpKeyName = "Checked"
```

```
        lpDefault = 0
        lpFileName = "Sampini.ini"

        x = GetPrivateProfileString(lpAppName, lpKeyName, lpDefault, _
        Temp, Len(Temp), lpFileName)
        Y = Val(Trim(Temp))

        If Y = 1 Then
            chkStart.Value = 1
            x = GetPrivateProfileString("Things to Remember", "Value", "Sampini.ini", _
            Temp, Len(Temp), lpFileName) 'this line is connected _
            to the one above

            If x = 0 Then
                Beep

            Else
                txtValue.Text = Trim(Temp)
                frmIni.Caption = "I remember: " & Temp
                RefreshDisplay txtValue.Text

            End If

        Else
            chkStart.Value = 0

        End If
End Sub

Private Sub Form_Unload(Cancel As Integer)
    Dim x As Integer, lpAppName As String, lpKeyName As String
    Dim U As Integer, lpstring As String, lpFileName As String

    lpAppName = "Start Up"
    lpKeyName = "Checked"
    lpFileName = "Sampini.ini"

    x = chkStart.Value
    lpstring = Str(x)
    U = WritePrivateProfileString(lpAppName, lpKeyName, lpstring, lpFileName)

    If U = 0 Then
        Beep
    End If

End Sub

Private Sub cmdClose_Click()
    Unload cmdClose.Parent
End Sub

Private Sub cmdGet_Click()
    Dim x As Long
    Dim Temp As String * 50
    Dim lpAppName As String, lpKeyName As String, lpDefault As String,
    ➥lpFileName As String
```

continues

Listing 8.11. continued

```
    lpAppName = "Things to Remember"
    lpKeyName = "Value"
    lpDefault = "Sampini.ini"
    lpFileName = "Sampini.ini"

    x = GetPrivateProfileString(lpAppName, lpKeyName, lpDefault, _
    Temp, Len(Temp), lpFileName)

    If x = 0 Then
        Beep

    Else
        txtValue.Text = Trim(Temp)
        frmIni.Caption = "I remember: " & Temp
        RefreshDisplay txtValue.Text

    End If

End Sub

Private Sub cmdStore_Click()
    Dim lpAppName As String, lpFileName As String, lpKeyName As String, _
    lpstring As String
    Dim U As Long

    lpAppName = "Things to Remember"
    lpKeyName = "Value"
    lpstring = txtValue.Text
    lpFileName = "Sampini.ini"

    U = WritePrivateProfileString(lpAppName, lpKeyName, lpstring, lpFileName)

    If U = 0 Then
        Beep
    End If

    RefreshDisplay lpstring
End Sub

Private Sub RefreshDisplay(Value As String)
    Dim ExpectedOutput As String
    Dim Crlf As String
    Dim chkval As Integer

    Crlf = Chr$(13) + Chr$(10) 'Crlf stands for Carriage return/line feed
    ExpectedOutput = "[Start Up]"
    ExpectedOutput = ExpectedOutput + Crlf + "Checked= "
    chkval = Abs(chkStart.Value)

    ExpectedOutput = ExpectedOutput + Str$(chkval) + Crlf + Crlf
    ExpectedOutput = ExpectedOutput + "[Things to Remember]"
    ExpectedOutput = ExpectedOutput + Crlf + "Value="
    ExpectedOutput = ExpectedOutput + Value

    txtDisplay.Text = ExpectedOutput
    lblDemo.Caption = "Contents of " & UCase$(IniFileName)

End Sub
```

The Common Dialog Control

As you discovered in the last chapter, it is easy to add the standard File Open common dialog box to a program. You might recall that you used this control to add a Browse button to the Windows Shell program.

Actually, in addition to the File Open dialog, the common dialog control can be used to display the standard File Save dialog, Color dialog, Font dialog, Print dialog, or Printer Setup dialog, or start the Windows Help engine. Table 8.7 lists the methods you can use to invoke these different dialogs. In addition, it shows the Action property that will start the common dialog. Setting the Action property was the way these dialogs were started in Visual Basic 3, and the older method still works.

Table 8.7. Methods used to invoke different dialog boxes.

Method	Action Property	Common Dialog Type	Description
	0	No Action	
ShowOpen	1	File Open	
ShowSave	2	File Save As	
ShowColor	3	Color Controls	
ShowFont	4	Font Selection	Flags property must be set to vbCFScreenFonts, vbCFPrinterFonts, or vbCFBoth before showing the box. (If you don't set the flag, you will get an error message saying no fonts exist.)
ShowPrinter	5	Print Setup	Set Flags to vbPDPrintSetup prior to using the method.
ShowHelp	6	Runs WinHelp.exe	

The options for these dialogs can be set using the Flags property. Object.Flags = is set before the common dialog is displayed. You can use either the Visual Basic constant or its value in the Flags setting. To apply more than one flag to a given common dialog, join them with an Or conjunction, as in this example:

```
CommonDialog1.Flags = vbOFNOverwritePrompt Or vbOFNHideReadOnly
```

`CommonDialog1.ShowSave` will display the File Save As dialog box with the Read-Only check box hidden. If the user tries to select a file that already exists, a message will inform her that the file already exists and ask if she wants to overwrite it.

Tables 8.8, 8.9, and 8.10 show all of the possible constant `Flags` and their values. As you can see, there isn't much to using common dialog boxes. (Of course, this control just displays the dialog boxes. It doesn't do the actual work of saving files, setting colors, or printing. You, as the programmer, must use the return values that the controls send back in order to do that!)

Table 8.8. `Flags` property settings for the Color dialog box.

Constant	Value	Description
CCFullOpen	&H2&	Causes the entire dialog box, including the portion that enables the user to create custom colors, to be displayed when the dialog box appears on the screen. Without this flag, the user must choose the Define Custom Colors command button to display this portion of the dialog box.
CCPreventFullOpen	&H4&	Disables the Define Custom Colors command button and prevents the user from defining custom colors.
CCRGBInit	&H1&	Sets the initial color value for the dialog box.
CCShowHelp	&H8&	Causes the dialog box to display a Help button.

Table 8.9. `Flags` property settings for the File dialog box.

Constant	Value	Description
OFNAllowMultiSelect	&H200&	Specifies that the File Name list box allows multiple selections. (The user can select more than one file at run-time by pressing the Shift key and using the up- and down-arrow keys to select the desired files.)
OFNCreatePrompt	&H2000&	Specifies that the dialog box prompts the user to create a file that does not currently exist. This `Flag` automatically sets the `vbOFNPathMustExist` and `vbOFNFileMustExist` `Flags`.
OFNExtensionDiffernt	&H400&	Indicates that the extension of the returned filename is different from the extension specified by the `DefaultExt` property.

Constant	Value	Description
OFNFileMustExit	&H1000&	Specifies that the user can enter only names of existing files in the File Name text box. If this Flag is set and the user enters an invalid filename, a warning is displayed.
OFNHideReadOnly	&H4&	Hides the Read Only check box.
OFNNoChangeDir	&H8&	Forces the dialog box to set the current directory to what it was when the dialog box was opened.
OFNNoReadOnlyReturn	&H8000&	Specifies that the returned file will not have the Read Only attribute set and will not be in a write-protected directory.
OFNOverwritePrompt	&H2&	Causes the Save As dialog box to generate a message box if the selected file already exists. The user must confirm whether to overwrite the file.
OFNPathMustExist	&H800&	Specifies that the user can enter only valid paths. If this Flag is set and the user enters an invalid path, a warning message is displayed.
OFNReadOnly	&H1&	Causes the Read Only check box to be initially checked when the dialog box is created. This Flag also indicates the state of the Read Only check box when the dialog box is closed.
OFNShareAware	&H4000&	Specifies that sharing violation errors will be ignored.
OFNShowHelp	&H10&	Causes the dialog box to display the Help button.

Table 8.10. Flag property settings for the Font dialog box.

Constant	Value	Description
CFApply	&H200&	Specifies that the dialog box enables the Apply button.
CFANSIOnly	&H400&	Specifies that the dialog box allows only a selection of the fonts that use the Windows character set. If this Flag is set, the user will not be able to select a font that contains only symbols.

continues

Table 8.10. continued

Constant	Value	Description
CFBoth	&H3&	Causes the dialog box to list the available printer and screen fonts. The hDC property identifies the device context associated with the printer.
CFEffects	&H100&	Specifies that the dialog box enables strikethrough, underline, and color effects.
CFFixedPitchOnly	&H4000&	Specifies that the dialog box selects only fixed-pitch fonts.
CFForceFontExist	&H10000&	Specifies that an error message box is displayed if the user attempts to select a font or style that does not exist.
CFLimitSize	&H2000&	Specifies that the dialog box selects only font sizes within the range specified by the Min and Max properties.
CFNoSimulations	&H1000&	Specifies that the dialog box does not allow graphic device interface (GDI) font simulations.
CFNoVectorFonts	&H800&	Specifies that the dialog box does not allow vector-font selections.
CFPrinterFonts	&H2&	Causes the dialog box to list only the fonts supported by the printer, specified by the hDC property.
CFScalableOnly	&H20000&	Specifies that the dialog box allows only the selection of fonts that can be scaled.
CFScreenFonts	&H1&	Causes the dialog box to list only the screen fonts supported by the system.
CFShowHelp	&H4&	Causes the dialog box to display a Help button.
CFTTOnly	&H40000&	Specifies that the dialog box allows only the selection of TrueType fonts.
CFWYSIWYG	&H8000&	Specifies that the dialog box allows only the selection of fonts that are available on both the printer and on the screen. If this Flag is set, the vbCFBoth and vbCFScalableOnly flags should also be set.

To show you how some of these Flags property constants work, here is a demonstration program that displays all possible versions of the control.

A Common Dialog Demo Application

This application uses one form and a list box to display various types of dialog boxes from which to choose. Start Visual Basic and change the `Name` and `Caption` of the default form to `frmCDdemo` and `Common Dialog Demo`, respectively. Then save the project using the Save Project option on the File menu. Save the form as CdDemo.frm and the project as CdDemo.vbp.

Next, design the form using Figure 8.17 as a guide. Table 8.11 lists the various objects' properties settings that should be applied.

Table 8.11. The visual design of the Common Dialog Demo.

Object	Property	Setting
Form	Appearance	1-3D
	Caption	Common Dialog Demo
	Name	frmCDdemo
Label	Caption	Choose a type of Common Dialog:
	Name	Label1
List Box	Font	Font: Courier
	Name	lstDiags
Command Button	Caption	OK
	Default	True
	Name	cmdOK
Command Button	Cancel	True
	Caption	Cancel
	Name	cmdCancel
Common Dialog	Name	CommonDialog1

Figure 8.17.
The Common Dialog Demo application template.

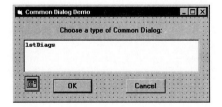

When the user runs the application, she selects a dialog box that she would like to see by either clicking on the item name in the list box and then clicking on the OK button, or by double-clicking on the item in the list box. Hence, two events are the key players in this application: cmdOK_Click() and lstDiags_DblClick(). Both of these events perform the same action of opening the selected dialog box, so a public subroutine should be written that can be called from both events. Keep that in mind while one other point is discussed that ties into these click events and the public subroutine.

When the user selects a dialog box to view, the application has to know in some way exactly which dialog box has been selected. This can be accomplished during the Form_Load event. In that event, the AddItem property of the list box, lstDiags, can be used to form an array of dialog boxes. Each time a new dialog box type is added to the array, that box is given a ListIndex property value, just as an array of option buttons uses an Index property value. This ListIndex property can then be used in the public subroutine to call the correct box, using the box's constant. (The constants are listed in Tables 8.8 through 8.10.)

First, you add the code to the Form_Load event to create the dialog box array. Open the Code window and select the Form Load event using the Object and Procedure list boxes at the top of the Code window. When you do, the event template appears in the window as follows:

```
Private Sub Form_Load()

End Sub
```

Now add the code that forms the array:

```
Private Sub Form_Load()
    lstDiags.AddItem "No Common Dialog - Action = 0"
    lstDiags.AddItem "Open Dialog     - Action = 1"
    lstDiags.AddItem "Save As Dialog  - Action = 2"
    lstDiags.AddItem "Color Dialog    - Action = 3"
    lstDiags.AddItem "Font Dialog     - Action = 4"
    lstDiags.AddItem "Printer Setup   - Action = 5"
    lstDiags.AddItem "Runs WinHelp    - Action = 6"
End Sub
```

Next, enter the two calls to the public subroutine that you are going to write. One call goes in the cmdOK_Click() event and the other in the lstDiags_DblClick() event. Use ShowBox as the name for the subroutine, like this:

```
Private Sub cmdOK_Click()
    ShowBox
End Sub

Private Sub lstDiags_DblClick()
    ShowBox
End Sub
```

One sideline task is to make the Cancel button functional. When the user clicks this button, she expects the window to close. Enter that code like this:

```
Private Sub cmdCancel_Click()
    Unload cmdCancel.Parent
End Sub
```

Now you go to the heart of the program, the public subroutine ShowBox(). Because the dialog boxes are set up in an array in lstDiags, each dialog box has a different ListIndex value. This value can be used to identify the type of dialog box the user has chosen. This would be a great place for a Select Case statement, using the ListIndex property to select the correct case. Add a public subroutine named ShowBox by selecting Procedure from the Visual Basic Insert menu. The complete code for the program, including the ShowBox routine, is in Listing 8.12.

Listing 8.12. The Control Dialog Demo application. (CdDemo.vbp)

```
Option Explicit

Private Sub cmdCancel_Click()
  Unload cmdCancel.Parent
End Sub

Private Sub cmdOK_Click()
  ShowBox
End Sub

Private Sub Form_Load()
  lstDiags.AddItem "No Common Dialog - Action = 0"
  lstDiags.AddItem "Open Dialog      - Action = 1"
  lstDiags.AddItem "Save As Dialog   - Action = 2"
  lstDiags.AddItem "Color Dialog     - Action = 3"
  lstDiags.AddItem "Font Dialog      - Action = 4"
  lstDiags.AddItem "Printer Dialog   - Action = 5"
  lstDiags.AddItem "Runs WinHelp     - Action = 6"
End Sub

Private Sub lstDiags_DblClick()
  ShowBox
End Sub

Public Sub ShowBox()
  Dim Which As Integer

  Const OFNFileMustExist = 4096       'Constant values found in Object Browser
  Const OFNAllowMultiselect = 512
  Const OFNShowHelp = 16
  Const OFNOverwritePrompt = 2
  Const CCFullOpen = 2
  Const CFBoth = 3
  Const PDPrintSetup = 64
  Const HelpContents = 3
```

continues

Listing 8.12. continued

```
If lstDiags.ListIndex = 0 Or lstDiags.ListIndex = -1 Then
  MsgBox "Sorry, no Dialog selected!"
Else
  Which = lstDiags.ListIndex

  Select Case Which
    Case 1
      'Open File
      'Action = 1

      CommonDialog1.Flags = OFNFileMustExist Or OFNAllowMultiselect
      'Demonstration flags set so that use can only enter existing files,
      ' and can multi-select files

      CommonDialog1.ShowOpen

    Case 2
      'Save As File
      'Action = 2

      CommonDialog1.Flags = OFNShowHelp Or OFNOverwritePrompt
      'flag shows the Help button and prompts before allowing a
      'a file to be over written

      CommonDialog1.ShowSave

    Case 3
      'Color
      'Action = 3

      CommonDialog1.Flags = CCFullOpen
      'flag starts the box with custom color dialog

      CommonDialog1.ShowColor

    Case 4
      'Font
      'Action = 4

      CommonDialog1.Flags = CFBoth
      'Flags property must be set to vbCFScreenFonts, vbCFPrinterFonts
      'or vbCFBoth or font dialog won't display

      CommonDialog1.ShowFont

    Case 5
      'Printer Setup
      'Action = 5

      CommonDialog1.Flags = PDPrintSetup
      'setting this flag shows the print setup box

      CommonDialog1.ShowPrinter

    Case 6
      'Help
      'Action = 6
```

```
        CommonDialog1.HelpFile = "VB.HLP"
        'show VB.hlp

        CommonDialog1.HelpCommand = HelpContents
        'show contents

        CommonDialog1.ShowHelp

    End Select

  End If

End Sub
```

You have now written the entire Common Dialog demo application. Run the program and try it out. Select the different types of dialog boxes available in the list box and check them out. The Common Dialog demo application is shown running in Figure 8.18. It's that easy to create a powerful application in Visual Basic.

Figure 8.18.
The Control Dialog demo application completed and running.

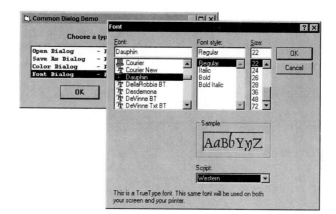

Summary

In this chapter, you have seen Visual Basic's file-handling statements, you have seen how they work in practice, and now you have added file-handling capabilities to two of your major applications: the Database, which uses random file access; and the Editor, which uses sequential file access.

You discovered how to use the powerful file controls provided by Visual Basic: directory list boxes, drive list boxes, and file list boxes. And you saw how these controls make it much easier for you to present file selection choices in a graphic and user-friendly fashion.

Moreover, you studied and used the six dialog boxes included in the Common Dialog control. You also learned to create and read private profile strings (.ini files).

In general, you discovered how to create, open, work with, and close files in Visual Basic. Also, you learned a number of sophisticated techniques for dealing with information contained in files. As mentioned at the beginning of this chapter, file-handling is an important part of any program, so your newfound skills can be put to use over and over again!

New Property	Description
Action	Used with common dialogs, this property returns or sets the type of dialog box to be displayed. (This property is not available at design-time.)
Drive	Determines the selected drive in a drive list box control.
FileName	This property holds the name of the file currently selected in a File list box.
Flags	Sets the options for different types of dialog boxes.
ListIndex	In a list box, this property returns or sets the index of the currently selected item in the control. (It is not available at design-time.)

New Function	Description
EOF()	Returns a value that indicates whether the end of a file has been reached.
GetPrivateProfileInt	Returns an integer stored in a private profile file.
GetPrivateProfileString	Allows you to retrieve a string stored in a private profile file.
Input	Returns characters from an open sequential or binary file.
LOF()	Returns the size, in bytes, of a file opened using the Open command.
Right	Returns a specified number of characters from the right side of a string.
WritePrivateProfileString	Allows you to store a string in a private profile file.

New Statement	Description
Close	Concludes input/output to a file opened using the Open statement.
Get #	Reads from an open disk file into a variable.
Input #	Reads data from an open sequential file and assigns the data to variables.

`Open`	Enables input/output to a file.
`Print #`	Writes display-formatted data to a sequential file.
`Put #`	Writes from a variable to a disk file.
`Seek #`	Sets the position for the next read or write within a file opened using the `Open` statement.
`Write #`	Writes raw data to a sequential file.

9

Visual Basic Graphics

This chapter is dedicated to a very exciting feature of Visual Basic: *graphics*. There is more to Visual Basic design than just putting text in text boxes or using flat gray backgrounds. The material covered in this chapter includes the following:

- Animation
- Drawing individual points in different colors
- Drawing lines in different styles
- Drawing circles
- Drawing rectangles
- Loading graphics images on disk into graphics controls
- Filling figures with patterns and colors
- Using the printer in Visual Basic
- Desaware's Animated Button Control (Anibtn32.ocx)
- Changing graphics coordinate systems to plot data easily
- How to draw text outside of text boxes

The programs developed in this chapter include an animation example, which sends a small rocket ship flying smoothly up the window, and an example showing how to plot data in a graph that will be tailored to the size of your window. The main graphics program is in the next chapter, where you design and write a fully functional Windows paint program. The skills you learn in this chapter are applicable every time you want to draw in a window, and that's not only in paint programs. You could have drawn a small rectangle in the earlier control panel application, for example, to give users some visual feedback about the new size setting of the test window. You will draw a rectangle on the screen—and outside your window—later in this book when you write a screen-capture program. Plenty of examples of graphics are used in Visual Basic applications from game boards to puzzles to screen savers, and you will learn how to draw these types of figures in this chapter. You will see that you can display text outside a text box. For example, you can place text on the form itself as a word processing program would. To do that, you must "draw" the text by using graphics techniques.

You might not have been expecting to see the subject of handling text in a chapter on graphics. In an environment such as Windows, which is a graphical user interface (GUI), everything is presented as graphics, including text. If you have read standard books about programming, you are probably used to seeing text treated differently than graphics. In this chapter, however, you will see that Visual Basic treats it in the same way. If text is not in a specifically text-oriented control such as a text box, label, or list box, it is treated just like any other graphic.

In addition to text, of course, this chapter explores the rest of Visual Basic's extensive graphics capabilities. You will draw points, lines, rectangles, circles, ellipses, and other graphical objects. You will even discover how to change their color, width, and fill pattern. You will see how to protect drawings in case they are covered temporarily by other windows, and how to load pictures from files. In addition, you will learn how to send your graphics to the printer, which is much easier than you might imagine. With all this in store, it's time to get going!

Drawing with Visual Basic

There are two main types of objects you can draw on in Visual Basic: forms and picture boxes. You are already familiar with forms, and you have had a bit of an introduction to picture boxes. Just to recap, picture boxes are simply boxes like any other, such as text boxes, which can be placed on forms. Their primary function is as a container for custom drawn graphics. To start, you will draw a single point in a picture box.

Drawing Points

The first Visual Basic graphics function to take a look at is the PSet() method, which sets a pixel on the screen.

To use PSet(), start Visual Basic. Change the Name and Caption of the default form to frmGraphics and Graphics, respectively. Then save the form and project as Graphics.frm and Graphics.vbp.

Next, find the AutoRedraw property in the Properties window and set it to True. This property indicates that Visual Basic should redraw the graphics on the form if part or all of it is covered temporarily by another window. This is especially important if you place graphics code in the Form_Load() event. If you do, and the AutoRedraw property is set to False, no graphics will appear on the form when the application is running.

The coordinate system in Visual Basic uses *twips* (1/1440th of an inch) by default. You might wonder why the twip is the default measurement instead of the screen pixel. The answer is that Visual Basic is intended to operate in a device-independent manner. Thus, you can draw on the printer just as easily as on the screen. But because printers have a resolution that is considerably higher than a monitor screen—a typical laser printer has a resolution of 300 to 600 dots per inch (dpi)—a more precise measurement system was needed. Hence, the twip. As a programmer, you might be used to other units such as pixels, centimeters, or points. (A point is often used to measure the dimensions of a font. 72 points equal one inch. One twip is 1/20th of a point.) Later, you will see that the basic unit of measurement can be switched to pixels, centimeters, or other systems. For this example, twips will be used.

The coordinate system starts at (0,0) in a form or picture box. X and Y increase to the right and down, respectively. A drawing of this would appear as shown in Figure 9.1.

Figure 9.1.
A pictorial representation of the coordinate system.

This coordinate system should be used when drawing a pixel, which can be placed in the center of frmGraphics. To do that, you can get the size of the form from the Properties window. For example, your form might be about three inches high by five inches wide. In twips, that would be 4320×7200. In that case, the PSet() method would appear as follows:

```
PSet (4320 / 2, 7200 / 2)
```

This statement sets the pixel in the center of the form. The syntax of PSet works like this:

```
object.PSet Step (x, y), color
```

The arguments for this method are as follows:

- object—An object expression that evaluates to an object. This is an optional argument. If object is omitted, the form with the focus is assumed to be the object.
- step—A keyword specifying that the coordinates are relative to the current graphics position given by the CurrentX and CurrentY properties. This argument is optional.
- (x, y)—This argument is required. It is a set of single-precision values that indicates the horizontal (X-axis) and vertical (Y-axis) coordinates of the point to set.
- color—A long integer value indicating the RGB color specified for a point. This argument is optional. If omitted, the current ForeColor property setting is used. The RGB function or the QBColor function can be used to specify the color.

There is another way, however, to center the pixel without knowing the size of the form beforehand: by using the ScaleWidth and ScaleHeight properties.

Four built-in properties can be used to determine the dimensions of a form or picture box: Height, Width, ScaleHeight, and ScaleWidth. It might appear that the appropriate properties to use to determine the form's center would be Width and Height. However, these properties correspond to the outer width and height of the window and include the title bar, menu bar, and so on. The dimensions of the client area within the window are determined by using ScaleWidth and ScaleHeight, as shown in Figure 9.2. (The default measurement for these two properties is twips.)

Figure 9.2.
The different height and width properties of a form.

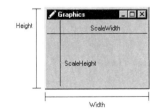

ScaleWidth and ScaleHeight can be used to find the center of a form and place a pixel there as follows:

```
PSet (ScaleWidth / 2, ScaleHeight / 2)
```

This code line should be executed as soon as the form appears on the screen; thus it should appear in the Form_Activate() event, which runs when the form first appears. Open the Code window and find that event, and then place the PSet() code line in the Code window as follows:

```
Private Sub Form_Activate()
     PSet (ScaleWidth / 2, ScaleHeight / 2)
End Sub
```

Check to make sure that the form's color properties are set correctly for this example. First, look at the BackColor property. If it is not set to white, select the white square in the color palette that appears when the Property button is pressed. Next, look at the ForeColor. Make sure that black is selected. Finally, change the tiny pixel to a large dot. That way it won't be missed when the application runs (one pixel is very small and rather easily overlooked). Scroll up to the DrawWidth property. The DrawWidth property default is 1, meaning 1 pixel. Change that to 50 (as in 50 pixels wide). Now run the program. When you do, a large dot 50 pixels in diameter appears at the center of the form as in Figure 9.3. Note that you could have used other events also to display this pixel, such as the Form_Click() event. If this event was used, the black dot would appear when any location on the client area was clicked.

Figure 9.3.
The Graphics application with a large dot, 50 pixels in diameter, centered on frmGraphics.

Now do the same thing in a picture box. Add a picture box to the form and size it to take up most of the window. Set the picture box's AutoRedraw property to True and change its Name property to picTest. The following code can be added to the Form_Activate() event:

```
Private Sub Form_Activate()
    PSet (ScaleWidth / 2, ScaleHeight / 2)
    picTest.PSet (picTest.ScaleWidth / 2, picTest.ScaleHeight / 2)
End Sub
```

The PSet() method is connected to the object on which you want to draw (recall Object.Method). When it is used without an Object argument, Visual Basic assumes that the object is the form. If an object's name is used (such as picTest.PSet, earlier), that object is PSet's target. Again, be sure that the DrawWidth property of the Picture Box is set to 50, and then run the program. The picture box is there, where you placed it, and a large dot is positioned at its center as in Figure 9.4. Note that the picture box obscures the dot on the form. This will be true in general. Any controls placed on a form are positioned on top of the form's graphics, thereby covering them.

So far, nothing too exciting has happened; you have drawn a large dot in black. It's time to make the black spot more colorful.

Figure 9.4.
The picture box on
`frmGraphics` *with a black*
dot positioned at the box's
center.

Selecting Colors

There are several ways to set colors in Visual Basic. The predefined color values are found in two places: in the Visual Basic Help File under Color | Color Constants, or in the Object Browser. Every color value in Visual Basic is a long integer, and many such values are ready to use, such as the constants named `vbRed` and `vbBlue` (as shown in Table 9.1). In addition, you can assign system colors using the system color constants, as defined in Table 9.2. A form's `BackColor` property—its background color—can be set to the current system-wide standard by setting it equal to `vbWindowBackground`. These Visual Basic constants are built into Visual Basic 4, so they do not need to be declared in a module as they were in Visual Basic 3.

Table 9.1. Visual Basic predefined colors.

Constant	Value	Description
vbBlack	0x0	Black
vbRed	0xFF	Red
vbGreen	0xFF00	Green
vbYellow	0xFFFF	Yellow
vbBlue	0xFF0000	Blue
vbMagenta	0xFF00FF	Magenta
vbCyan	0xFFFF00	Cyan
vbWhite	0xFFFFFF	White

Table 9.2. Visual Basic system colors.

Constant	Value	Description
vbScrollBars	0x80000000	Scrollbar color.
vbDesktop	0x80000001	Desktop color.
vbActiveTitleBar	0x80000002	Color of the title bar for the active window.

Constant	Value	Description
vbInactiveTitleBar	0x80000003	Color of the title bar for the inactive window.
vbMenuBar	0x80000004	Menu background color.
vbWindowBackground	0x80000005	Window background color.
vbWindowFrame	0x80000006	Window frame color.
vbMenuText	0x80000007	Color of text on menus.
vbWindowText	0x80000008	Color of text in windows.
vbTitleBarText	0x80000009	Color of text in caption, size box, and scroll arrow.
vbActiveBorder	0x8000000A	Border color of active window.
vbInactiveBorder	0x8000000B	Border color of inactive window.
vbApplicationWorkspace	0x8000000C	Background color of multiple-document interface (MDI) applications.
vbHighlight	0x8000000D	Background color of items selected in a control.
vbHighlightText	0x8000000E	Text color of items selected in a control.
vbButtonFace	0x8000000F	Color of shading on the face of command buttons.
vbButtonShadow	0x80000010	Color of shading on the edge of command buttons.
vbGrayText	0x80000011	Grayed (disabled) text.
vbButtonText	0x80000012	Text color on pushbuttons.
vbInactiveCaptionText	0x80000013	Color of text in an inactive caption.
vb3DHilight	0x80000014	Highlight color for 3D display elements.
vb3DDKShadow	0x80000015	Darkest shadow color for 3D display elements.
vb3DLite	0x80000016	Second lightest of the 3D colors after vb3DHilight.
vbClrInfoText	0x80000017	Color of text in ToolTips and the What's This help panel.
vbClrInfoBack	0x80000018	Background color of ToolTips and the What's This help panel.

Let's set the dot's color in the graphics application to magenta. This is very easy to do. All you have to do is add the Visual Basic color constant, `vbMagenta`, to the `PSet()` method in the `Color` argument position, like this:

```
Private Sub Form_Activate()
    PSet (ScaleWidth / 2, ScaleHeight / 2)
    picTest.PSet (picTest.ScaleWidth / 2, picTest.ScaleHeight / 2), vbMagenta
End Sub
```

Run your test application now and check out the groovy dot.

There are other ways to set color in Visual Basic. One is the `RGB()` function. `RGB()` returns a whole number representing an RGB color value. Its syntax works like this:

```
RGB (red, green, blue)
```

The `RGB()` function syntax has these arguments:

- `red`—A number in the range 0 to 255, inclusive, that represents the red component of the color.

- `green`—A number in the range 0 to 255, inclusive, that represents the green component of the color.

- `blue`—A number in the range 0 to 255, inclusive, that represents the blue component of the color.

As described earlier, each color value can range from 0 (when the color is excluded entirely) to 255 (when the color is at its strongest). For a pure red dot, you could make the red argument equal to 255 and the two other arguments equal to 0. Try that now in place of the call for magenta:

```
Private Sub Form_Activate()
    PSet (ScaleWidth / 2, ScaleHeight / 2)
    picTest.PSet (picTest.ScaleWidth / 2, picTest.ScaleHeight / 2),
    ➥RGB(255, 0, 0)
End Sub
```

If you run the application now, you will see that the dot is indeed red.

Another way to set the color is to use the constant value for a particular color. These values can be found using the Object Browser on the View menu. Make sure the Library/Project list box says VB. Then scroll down the Classes/Modules list box until you find Constants and select it. Next, scroll down to the name of the Visual Basic color constant you are looking for—`vbBlue`, for instance. When it is selected, the constant's value appears at the bottom of the Object Browser. In this case, `vbBlue` is equal to `16711680`. Take that number and put it onto the end of the `PSet()` code in place of the `RGB()` function like this:

```
Private Sub Form_Activate()
    PSet (ScaleWidth / 2, ScaleHeight / 2)
    picTest.PSet (picTest.ScaleWidth / 2, picTest.ScaleHeight / 2), 16711680
End Sub
```

When the program runs now, the dot will be blue.

Yet another way to set the color is to use the value found in Table 9.1 and convert it to a hexadecimal. For instance, in Table 9.1 the value for green is `0xFF00`. If you omit the `0x` and use the `FF00` within a hexadecimal setting (`&HFF00&`), the dot will be green. Change the `PSet` code to reflect that, and then see whether the dot is green.

```
Private Sub Form_Activate()
    PSet (ScaleWidth / 2, ScaleHeight / 2)
    picTest.PSet (picTest.ScaleWidth / 2, picTest.ScaleHeight / 2), &HFF00&
End Sub
```

The final way to specify colors is using the `QBColor()` function. `QBColor()` returns the RGB color code corresponding to a color number. Its syntax works as follows:

```
QBColor (color)
```

The argument for `QBColor` is as follows:

- `color`—A whole number in the range 0 to 15, as described in Table 9.3.

Table 9.3. Settings for the `QBColor` `Color` argument.

Number	Color
0	Black
1	Blue
2	Green
3	Cyan
4	Red
5	Magenta
6	Yellow
7	White
8	Gray
9	Light Blue
10	Light Green
11	Light Cyan
12	Light Red
13	Light Magenta
14	Light Yellow
15	Bright White

Let's change the dot's color one more time. This time, change it to light cyan, whose number is 11 in Table 9.3, using the QBColor() function. Change the PSet code to the following:

```
Private Sub Form_Activate()
    PSet (ScaleWidth / 2, ScaleHeight / 2)
    picText.PSet (picText.ScaleWidth / 2, picTest.ScaleHeight / 2),
    ➥QBColor(11)
End Sub
```

That's it for the chameleon spot. But, of course, this is only the beginning of Visual Basic's graphics capabilities. Next, you will draw lines.

Finding the Color at a Particular Screen Location

If you ever want to determine the color of a particular position on the screen, you can use the Point method, Object.Point (x,y), which returns the corresponding long integer color value.

Drawing Lines

The Line tool in the Visual Basic toolbox enables you to draw lines at design time. Using it is easy. Lines can be drawn in two ways using the tool. When the tool is double-clicked, a small line appears with two sizing handles on the form. The line can then be resized and positioned using the handles. The other way to draw a line is to select (click once) the tool and then move the mouse to the form. The mouse pointer changes to a crosshair. Position the crosshair where you would like the line to begin and depress the left mouse button and keep it down. Drag the line to where you would like it to end, and release the mouse button.

Lines can be added in code also. To draw lines that appear at run-time, use the Line() method, which draws lines and rectangles on an object. Its syntax works like this:

```
object.Line Step (x1, y1) - Step (x2, y2), color, B F
```

The Line() method syntax has the following arguments:

- object—An expression that evaluates to an object. This argument is optional. If object is omitted, the form with the focus is assumed to be object.

- Step—A keyword specifying that the starting point coordinates are relative to the current graphics position given by the CurrentX and CurrentY properties. This argument is optional.

- (x1, y1)—Single-precision values indicating the coordinates of the starting point for the line or rectangle. The ScaleMode property determines the unit of measure used. This argument is optional. If this is omitted, the line begins at the position indicated by CurrentX and CurrentY.

- `Step`—An optional keyword specifying that the end point coordinates are relative to the line starting point.

- `(x2, y2)`—Single-precision values indicating the coordinates of the end point for the line being drawn. This argument is required.

- `color`—An optional long integer value indicating the RGB color used to draw the line. If omitted, the `ForeColor` property setting is used. The `RGB` function or `QBColor` function can be used to specify the color.

- `B`—Causes a box to be drawn using the coordinates to specify opposite corners of the box. This argument is optional.

- `F`—If the `B` option is used, the `F` option specifies that the box is filled with the same color used to draw the box. You can't use `F` without `B`. If `B` is used without `F`, the box is filled with the current `FillColor` and `FillStyle`. The default value for `FillStyle` is transparent. This argument is optional.

Again, notice that this is a method; consequently, you can specify the object where the lines will be drawn. Like the `PSet()` method, if no object is specified, Visual Basic will assume that the object is the current form.

To draw a line, two points are usually involved: the beginning and end of the line, `(x1, y1)` and `(x2, y2)` respectively. When the `Step` argument is used in front of either of them, the point is placed relative to the current graphics position as specified by (`CurrentX`, `CurrentY`). In addition, a line's color can be set using any of the methods described for the dot example. The next section discusses the last two arguments, `B` and `F`, which are used to draw rectangles.

If you want to draw a single line diagonally across a form, the `Line()` method can be used as follows:

```
Line (0,0)-(ScaleWidth, ScaleHeight)
```

That's all that's required—just the two endpoints of the line. Visual Basic draws the line so that the first endpoint, not the second, is included. Remove the picture box from your graphics application by selecting it and pressing the Delete key. Next, change the `Load_Activate()` event to look like this:

```
Private Sub Form_Activate()
    Line (0,0)-(ScaleWidth, ScaleHeight)
End Sub
```

Running the program now results in a window like the one shown in Figure 9.5. Remember that the `DrawWidth` property of the form is set at `50`. That is why the line is so wide.

Figure 9.5.
The test Graphics application with a wide diagonal line across frmGraphics.

You could make the line blue by adding a color argument, like this:

```
Private Sub Form_Activate()
    Line (0,0)-(ScaleWidth, ScaleHeight), vbBlue
End Sub
```

Another way to specify that this line should be blue without passing a color value to the `Line()` method is to set the object's `ForeColor` property. All forms and picture boxes have this property, which changes the color of the foreground. All controls that can display text also have this property, which determines the color of the text (except for command buttons, which only have a `BackColor` property). When text or other graphics figures are drawn and a color is not specified, `ForeColor` is used as the default. That color can be specified for a particular object, as in the following example. (Recall that if an object is not specified for a graphical method, the current form is used.)

```
Private Sub Form_Activate()
    ForeColor = vbBlue
    Line (0,0)-(ScaleWidth, ScaleHeight)
End Sub
```

Until this object's `ForeColor` is changed again, it will be blue. You should note that changing the `ForeColor`, however, does not change the color of text or other graphics already on objects. By specifying the `ForeColor` property, therefore, a number of forms or picture boxes can be in an application, all with a different `ForeColor`. There are other drawing properties associated with these types of objects, and some of them are explored next.

What Properties Are Available for an Object?

A good way to get an idea of which properties are available for a specific object is to look at the list in the Properties window. Keep in mind that the Properties window only lists those properties available at design-time, not at run-time. To find a complete list of a control's design-time and run-time properties, search for that object type in Visual Basic's online Help index. For each type of object, all the properties are explicitly listed.

To draw lines and figures, an artist needs a pencil, pen, or charcoal, perhaps. When you use Visual Basic to create lines, dots, and graphics, you are the artist. But where is the drawing tool? Each object that displays graphics contains a "graphics pen." One of the properties associated with this graphics pen is the `DrawWidth` property, which you have already used in this chapter. To recap, the `DrawWidth` property is set at a default value of 1 pixel. The greater the value of the property, the wider the line. To see some different line widths, you could set up the following loop. For a change of pace, put this code in the form's `Click` event. That way, the loop will be activated when the user clicks anywhere on the client area of the form. Remove the code from the `Form_Activate()` event and add the following code to the `Form_Click()` event:

```
Private Sub Form_Click()
    Dim I As Integer

    For I = 1 To 9
        DrawWidth = I
        Line (0, I * ScaleHeight / 10)-(ScaleWidth, I * ScaleHeight / 10)
    Next I

    DrawWidth = 1      'Reset DrawWidth to 1
End Sub
```

This example displays a window with lines that grow steadily thicker as they proceed down the form as in Figure 9.6. Run the application and click on the form. The lines will draw in succession down the window.

Figure 9.6.
The test Graphics window with thickening lines.

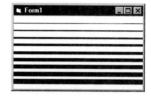

In addition to the line's width, the line's style can also be specified using the LineStyle property. The default is a solid line, but a line could also be broken up into dots or dashes. There are seven different line styles from solid to dotted to transparent, and all are represented in Table 9.4.

Table 9.4. The **DrawStyle** property's values.

Setting	Description
0	Solid (Default)
1	Dash
2	Dot
3	Dash-Dot
4	Dash-Dot-Dot
5	Transparent
6	Inside Solid

The LineStyle property returns or sets a value that determines the line style for output from graphics methods. Its syntax works like this:

```
object.DrawStyle [= number]
```

The DrawStyle property syntax has these parts:

- object—An expression that evaluates to an object in the Applies To list.
- number—An integer specifying line style, as described in Table 9.4.

The *inside solid* line (DrawStyle = 6) deserves some special mention. When a box is drawn with a thick line, the line is usually centered on the edge of the box. Thus the box ends up slightly larger than intended because the thick line is half in and half out of the box. The inside solid line, on the other hand, is drawn so that it is entirely inside the box, even when a line is thick.

So, to return to the test graphics application, open up the Code window again and find the Form_Click() event. The loop that you put in to draw the progressively thicker lines is still there:

```
Private Sub Form_Click()
Dim I As Integer

For I = 1 To 9
DrawWidth = I
Line (0, I * ScaleHeight / 10)-(ScaleWidth, I * ScaleHeight / 10)
Next I
DrawWidth = 1      'Reset DrawWidth to 1

End Sub
```

Move that to the Form_Activate() event by cutting and pasting the code into that event. Then add the following loop that will draw the seven types of lines. The code will appear as follows:

```
Private Sub Form_Activate()
    Dim I As Integer

    For I = 1 To 9
        DrawWidth = I
        Line (0, I * ScaleHeight / 10)-(ScaleWidth, I * ScaleHeight / 10)
    Next I

    DrawWidth = 1      'Reset DrawWidth to 1

End Sub


Private Sub Form_Click()
    Dim I As Integer

    Cls

    For I = 1 To 7
        DrawStyle = I - 1
        Line (0, I * ScaleHeight / 8)-(ScaleWidth, I * ScaleHeight / 8)
    Next I

End Sub
```

Check the form's Property window to be sure that the DrawWidth property is set back to 1. When the program is running, it first draws the thickening lines in the window, and then waits for the user to click the form. When that happens, seven different types of lines are drawn progressively down the form, as in Figure 9.7.

Figure 9.7.
The test Graphics application showing the different line styles.

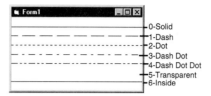

Using a `DrawWidth` Greater than 1 Alters Line Styles

It should be noted that using a `DrawWidth` property value greater than 1 makes line styles 1 through 4 produce solid lines rather than a series of dots or dashes.

So far, you have changed the thickness of lines and their style. You can even go further, in fact, and specify how a newly drawn line affects the drawings already there. The `DrawMode` property affects which type of graphics pen is used for drawing.

As mentioned, you can think of each graphics object as having a pen. This pen can draw in different styles. If the `DrawWidth` property is set to 6, for example, the pen draws lines or circles that are six pixels wide, or it draws dots that are six pixels in diameter. If you change `DrawMode` to 4, the pen changes into a "Not Pen," which draws the inverse of the color set in the `ForeColor` property. So, if `ForeColor` is set to black for instance, a Not Pen draws in white. `DrawMode` values range from 1 to 16, as shown in Table 9.5.

The `DrawMode` property returns or sets a value that determines the appearance of output from a graphics method or the appearance of a Shape or Line control. Its syntax works like any project associated with an object (*Object.Property*) as follows:

```
object.DrawMode [= number]
```

The `DrawMode` property syntax has these parts:

- `object`—An object expression that evaluates to an object.
- `number`—An integer specifying appearance, as described in Table 9.5.

Table 9.5. The settings for the **DrawMode** property.

Number	Pen Type	Description
1	Blackness	
2	Not Merge Pen	Inverse of setting 15 (Merge Pen).
3	Mask Not Pen	Combination of the colors common to the background color and the inverse of the pen.

continues

Table 9.5. continued

Number	Pen Type	Description
4	Not Copy Pen	Inverse of setting 13 (Copy Pen).
5	Mask Pen Not	Combination of the colors common to both the pen and the inverse of the display.
6	Invert	Inverse of the display color.
7	Xor Pen	Combination of the colors in the pen and in the display color, but not in both.
8	Not Mask Pen	Inverse of setting 9 (Mask Pen).
9	Mask Pen	Combination of the colors common to both the pen and the display.
10	Not Xor Pen	Inverse of setting 7 (Xor Pen).
11	Nop	No operation. Output remains unchanged. In effect, this setting turns drawing off.
12	Merge Not Pen	Combination of the display color and the inverse of the pen color.
13	Copy Pen (Default)	Color specified by the ForeColor property.
14	Merge Pen Not	Combination of the pen color and the inverse of the display color.
15	Merge Pen	Combination of the pen color and the display color.
16	Whiteness	

Some of these pen types deserve special mention. The Invert Pen, DrawMode = 6, inverts the color of what is on the screen when it draws. For instance, if you draw over a black area with an Invert Pen, white will appear. Conversely, if you draw over a white area, black will appear. Or, if you draw over a green area, red (the inverse of green) will appear. This capability can create striking visual effects. Use this on the test graphics application in the Form_Click() event. The following code will draw two broad diagonal bands on the form and invert what is underneath them when the form is clicked.

```
Private Sub Form_Click()
    DrawMode = 6
    DrawWidth = 9

    Line (0, 0)-(ScaleWidth, ScaleHeight)
    Line (0,ScaleHeight)-(ScaleWidth,0)
End Sub
```

Now when you run the application, the window first appears as in Figure 9.6. When you click on the window, however, two diagonal bands appear and invert whatever they draw over, as in Figure 9.8.

Figure 9.8.
The test Graphics application, showing diagonal lines drawn with an Invert Pen.

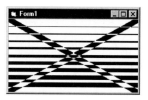

Another pen type, the Xor Pen (DrawMode = 7), is commonly used in animation. Xor (Exclusive Or) is a bit-wise operator much like And and Or. These operators compare the individual bits of two operands and produce a result based on a bit-by-bit comparison. For example, when Or is used on two bits that have a value of 1, the result is 1. If two bits both have a 0 value and Or is applied, the result is 0. The general action of these operators is shown in the following chart:

If bit 1 is:	AND bit 2 is:	The result is:
0	0	0
0	1	1
1	0	1
1	1	0

When the Xor Pen is used for drawing, the drawing color and the colors being drawn over on the window are interpreted by the Xor operator. So, if a graphic is being drawn on a white window with an Xor Pen, for example, the graphic's drawing color will be inverted (if the graphic is being drawn in white, its color will be inverted to black). The reason for this is that the color value of the drawing is compared by the Xor operator to the white background. Because white's color value is 1, using the previous chart, the white background would be bit 1 (with a value of 1), and the white pen doing the drawing would be bit 2 (with a value of 1). Thus, the result would be 0 or the inverse, black.

Anything can be drawn on a screen with an Xor Pen to make it appear. Then when that same object is drawn with an Xor Pen again, the object disappears because the original display is restored. Animation often works this way. For example, a white screen is drawn on using an Xor Pen whose color is white. The result is a black graphical figure. When the same figure is drawn again using the white Xor Pen, the graphical figure is erased and the white screen is restored.

Using Xor to Encrypt Data

As described earlier, anytime the Xor operator is applied to a value twice, the original value is restored. The logical Xor operator can also be used to encrypt data. To do so, just apply the Xor operator to the data, byte-by-byte, with some value or values such as the characters in a password. The result is encrypted data. To reverse the process, use the Xor operator again with the same value or values to reproduce the original exactly. This process is called *Xor encryption*.

It's time to move on to another Line() method capability: drawing rectangles.

Drawing Rectangles

You have seen that the Line() method enables you to draw lines at design-time. Another graphics control found in the Visual Basic toolbox, the *Shape* control, can produce a number of shapes including rectangles, ovals, squares, circles, rounded rectangles, and rounded squares. The shape of the object drawn is selected at design-time by setting the Shape property in the Properties window. Because these shapes are controls, their Top, Bottom, Left, Right, Height, and Width properties can, of course, be set in an application.

Suppose that you draw a rectangle on a form using the Shape tool and you name it shpRectangle. Then with the appropriate code added to the application, when the application runs, the width of that rectangle will double when the user clicks on the form. The rectangle-doubling code would look like this:

```
Private Sub Form_Click()
    shpRectangle.Width = 2 * shpRectangle.Width
End Sub
```

The Shape control is not usually used for producing program output, however. Instead, it is used to enhance the design and visual appeal of an application's windows. You might recall that in previous chapters, you have used rectangles on different forms to group controls. To produce normal graphics rectangles in code, the Line method is used again. It might seem a bit odd to use the Line method to draw a box, but that's exactly what the B argument of the Line() method is for. Recall that the method's syntax looks like this:

```
object.Line Step (x1, y1) - Step (x2, y2), color, B F
```

When a line is drawn in Visual Basic, the endpoints are specified. Similarly, when a rectangle is drawn, only two points are required—the upper-left and lower-right corners—as shown in Figure 9.9.

Figure 9.9.

A pictorial representation showing the upper-left and lower-right coordinates for a rectangle.

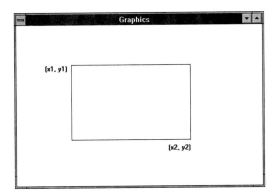

Because both the line and the rectangle patterns are uniquely specified by two points, Visual Basic will draw rectangles and lines with the Line() method. You can see how this works by modifying the test Graphics application to draw a few rectangles. At the moment, the Form_Activate() event contains the following code:

```
Private Sub Form_Activate()
    Dim I As Integer

    For I = 1 To 9
        DrawWidth = I
        Line (0, I * ScaleHeight / 10)-(ScaleWidth, I * ScaleHeight / 10)
    Next I

    DrawWidth = 1

End Sub
```

Rewrite the code as follows:

```
Private Sub Form_Activate()

    DrawWidth = 8
    Line (0, 0)-(ScaleWidth / 2, ScaleHeight / 2), , B
    Line (ScaleWidth / 4, ScaleHeight / 4)-(3 * ScaleWidth / 4, 3 *
    ➡ScaleHeight / 4), , B
    Line (ScaleWidth / 2, ScaleHeight / 2)-(ScaleWidth, ScaleHeight), , B

End Sub
```

This example generates the window shown in Figure 9.10.

Figure 9.10.
The test Graphics application with three rectangles drawn on frmGraphics.

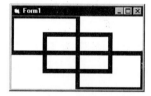

The thick lines at the edges of Figure 9.10 are half inside and half outside the edge of the client area. This can be fixed by using the Inside Line DrawStyle like this:

```
Private Sub Form_Activate()

    DrawWidth = 8
    DrawStyle = 6
    Line (0, 0)-(ScaleWidth / 2, ScaleHeight / 2), , B
    Line (ScaleWidth / 4, ScaleHeight / 4)-(3 * ScaleWidth / 4, 3 *
    ➡ScaleHeight / 4), , B
    Line (ScaleWidth / 2, ScaleHeight / 2)-(ScaleWidth, ScaleHeight), , B

End Sub
```

Now the rectangles are drawn so that the thick border is inside the boundaries as in Figure 9.11. That's the way inside lines work. They do not overlap the figure's boundaries. You can also change the DrawMode to use a different pen setting. Why not try the Invert Pen, DrawMode = 6, for example. Add that to the Form_Activate() event like this:

```
Private Sub Form_Activate()

        DrawWidth = 8
        DrawStyle = 6
        DrawMode = 6
        Line (0, 0)-(ScaleWidth / 2, ScaleHeight / 2), , B
        Line (ScaleWidth / 4, ScaleHeight / 4)-(3 * ScaleWidth / 4, 3 *
        ➥ScaleHeight / 4), , B
        Line (ScaleWidth / 2, ScaleHeight / 2)-(ScaleWidth, ScaleHeight), , B

End Sub
```

Figure 9.11.

The test Graphics application with all the rectangles drawn within the client area.

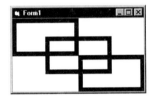

The addition of the DrawMode line creates rectangles like those in Figure 9.12. Generally, rectangles can be made as easily as lines.

Figure 9.12.

Rectangles drawn in the test Graphics application, using the Invert Pen.

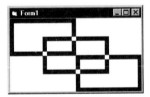

The rectangles shown in Figure 9.12 could also be filled with different colors and patterns. That is discussed next.

Filling Figures with Patterns

You now have drawn enclosed graphics figures for the first time, but Visual Basic goes much further. Fill patterns can be specified so that boxes are automatically filled. Actually, the rectangles that you have already drawn were filled with the default pattern, which is transparent. That's only one of eight fill patterns available, however. The others include horizontal or vertical lines, diagonal lines, and solid color. The property that controls fill patterns is FillStyle. The FillStyle property returns or sets the pattern used to fill Shape controls as well as circles and boxes created with the Circle and Line graphics methods. Its syntax works like this:

```
object.FillStyle [= number]
```

The FillStyle property syntax has these parts:

- object—An object expression that evaluates to an object.
- number—An integer specifying the fill style, as described in Table 9.6.

Table 9.6. Settings for the FillStyle property.

Number	Description
0	Solid
1	(Default) Transparent
2	Horizontal Line
3	Vertical Line
4	Upward Diagonal
5	Downward Diagonal
6	Cross
7	Diagonal Cross

Let's put this into action in the test Graphics application. You can draw eight rectangles on frmGraphics and then fill them, one-by-one, with the different patterns corresponding to each FillStyle property setting. Again, use the Form_Activate() event to see this work. Change the code that is presently in that procedure to the following:

```
Private Sub Form_Activate()

    Dim X As Long
    Dim Y As Long
    Dim I As Integer

    X = ScaleWidth
    Y = ScaleHeight

    For I = 0 To 3
        FillStyle = I
        Line ((2 * I + 1) * X / 9, Y / 5)-((2 * I + 2) * X / 9, 2 * Y / 5)
        ➥, , B
        FillStyle = I + 4
        Line ((2 * I + 1) * X / 9, 3 * Y / 5)-((2 * I + 2) * X / 9, 4 * Y / 5)
        ➥, , B
    Next I

End Sub
```

Make sure the form's DrawWidth property is set to 1.

As you can see, all eight fill patterns appear in Figure 9.13. These built-in patterns can be used to create visual effects in Visual Basic programs.

Figure 9.13.
The test Graphics application, showing different fill styles.

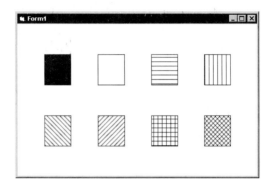

Just to recap, the B argument was used to draw rectangles. The F argument is only used to specify that the fill pattern will be drawn with the same color as the rectangle. If F is not specified—and F can only be used with B, not alone—the current FillColor is used. FillColor is just like BackColor and ForeColor, except that it is used exclusively as the fill pattern color. Like ForeColor and BackColor, it is a property associated with graphical objects such as picture boxes and forms, and like other properties, it remains set until it is changed again. You will learn more about FillColor later in this chapter when you draw circles.

Before ending the rectangle discussion, though, it is worth noting something important. Drawing solid white rectangles (with white borders) is a standard way to delete text on forms and picture boxes. (Of course, the solidly filled rectangle could also match the form if it were red, for instance.) Because text is treated as graphics in both forms and picture boxes, it can't be erased by being selected and then deleted. Instead, it has to be removed from the screen as with any graphic. But more about that later. Now you can draw some circles.

Drawing Circles in Visual Basic

Visual Basic makes circle drawing easy. All you have to do is use the Circle() method. This method draws a circle, ellipse, or arc on an object. Its syntax works like any other method (*Object.Method*):

```
object.Circle Step (x, y), radius, color, start, end, aspect
```

The Circle() method syntax uses the following arguments:

- object—An optional object expression that evaluates to an object. If object is omitted, the form with the focus is assumed to be object.

- **Step**—An optional keyword specifying that the center of the circle, ellipse, or arc is relative to the current coordinates given by the `CurrentX` and `CurrentY` properties of `object`.

- **(x, y)**—A required single-precision value indicating the coordinates for the center point of the circle, ellipse, or arc. The `ScaleMode` property of `object` determines the units of measure used.

- **radius**—A required single-precision value indicating the radius of the circle, ellipse, or arc. The `ScaleMode` property of `object` determines the unit of measure used.

- **color**—An optional long integer value indicating the RGB color of the circle's outline. If this is omitted, the value of the `ForeColor` property is used. You can use the RGB function or `QBColor` function to specify the color.

- **start, end**—Optional single-precision values. When an arc or a partial circle or ellipse is drawn, `start` and `end` specify (in radians) the beginning and end positions of the arc. The range for both is `-2` pi radians to `2` pi radians. The default value for start is `0` radians; the default for end is `2 * pi` radians.

- **aspect**—An optional single-precision value indicating the aspect ratio of the circle . The default value is `1.0`, which yields a perfect (nonelliptical) circle on any screen.

You can see the `Circle()` method at work by drawing a few circles. Start with a fill style that includes downward diagonals and a simple red circle, as in the following example:

```
Private Sub Form_Activate()

    FillStyle = 5           'Downward Diagonals
    ForeColor = RGB(255, 0, 0)  'Red
    Circle (ScaleWidth / 4, ScaleHeight / 4), ScaleHeight / 5

End Sub
```

This code produces a red circle filled with downward diagonals and a black fill pattern, not a red one. If you were drawing boxes, you could fix that by using the F argument, but there is no F option for the `Circle()` method. In this case, you should set the `FillColor` property to equal the current `ForeColor`, as follows:

```
Private Sub Form_Activate()

    FillStyle = 5           'Downward Diagonals
    ForeColor = RGB(255, 0, 0)  'Red
    FillColor = ForeColor
    Circle (ScaleWidth / 4, ScaleHeight / 4), ScaleHeight / 5

End Sub
```

Now both the circle and fill pattern are red. The `Circle()` method can do more, though. With it, you can also draw ellipses and arcs. To draw an ellipse, the `Aspect` argument must be used. The *aspect ratio* indicates the vertical to horizontal ratio for ellipses. When a circle is drawn, the `Aspect` argument is set to the default value of 1.0. It's just as easy to draw an ellipse. To draw a circle and then an ellipse that is twice as high as it is wide, for example, you can use an aspect ratio of 2, as follows:

```
Private Sub Form_Activate()

    Circle (ScaleWidth / 4, ScaleHeight / 4), ScaleHeight / 5
    FillStyle = 2

    Circle (ScaleWidth / 2, ScaleHeight / 2), ScaleHeight / 3, , , , 5
    ➥      'Ellipse

End Sub
```

The resulting graphics display appears in Figure 9.14.

Figure 9.14.

A circle and ellipse drawn on the test Graphics form.

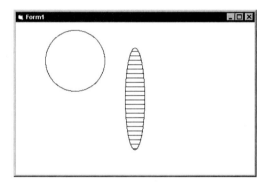

You can also draw arcs, which are partial circles, by specifying the Start and End arguments. These arguments are measured in radians. The range for both is -2 to 2 pi. Add an arc to the sample Graphics form, from 0 (the 3 o'clock position) to pi (moving counterclockwise to the 9 o'clock position) as follows:

```
Private Sub Form_Activate()

    Circle (ScaleWidth / 4, ScaleHeight / 4), ScaleHeight / 5
    FillStyle = 2
    Circle (ScaleWidth / 2, ScaleHeight / 2), ScaleHeight / 3, , , , 5
    ➥      'Ellipse

    Circle (3 * ScaleWidth / 4, 3 * ScaleHeight / 4), ScaleHeight / 5,
    ➥ , 0, 3.1415 'Arc

End Sub
```

The resultant arc appears in Figure 9.15 along with a companion circle and ellipse. You might have noticed that even though a FillStyle is specified for the arc, it is not filled. This is because the arc is not a closed figure.

Figure 9.15.
*The test Graphics application
with a circle, ellipse, and arc
drawn on* `frmGraphics`.

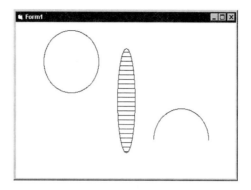

The Blanker Demo Sample Graphics Application

Visual Basic 4 comes with many sample applications. One of them, the Blanker Demo, demonstrates many of the drawing techniques discussed here. To check this out, start Visual Basic, and then open the Blanker project located under Samples\Graphics. When the program is loaded, run it and try the many available options.

That's it for the primary, built-in drawing methods `PSet()`, `Line()`, and `Circle()`. You have produced some interesting effects with them. Visual Basic also enables you to do many more things with graphics. For instance, predrawn pictures can be loaded into either forms or picture boxes. And that is the next topic of discussion.

Loading Pictures

Pictures can be loaded into picture boxes, image controls, or forms by using the `LoadPicture()` function or by assigning them to the object's `Picture` or `Icon` property. In particular, `LoadPicture()` can be used with four types of files: .ico (icons), .bmp (bitmap files), .rle (run-length encoded files), and .wmf (Windows metafiles). These types of files can also be loaded into picture boxes, image controls, or forms at design-time by setting their `Picture` properties to the correct filename.

The image control functions much like a picture box when loading and displaying images. The image control uses fewer system resources and repaints faster than a picture box control, but it supports only a small portion of the properties, events, and methods associated with picture boxes. Although an image control can be placed within a container, an image control can't act as a container. It differs from a picture box in that it automatically changes its size to fit the picture loaded into it. Also, by setting its `Stretch` property to `True`, the size of the image control can be adjusted after a picture is loaded into it, consequently stretching the picture to match the new size.

Saving Pictures on Disk

Just as pictures can be loaded using the `LoadPicture()` function, pictures can be saved using the `SavePicture()` function. This is discussed in Chapter 10, "The Mouse and a Mouse-Driven Paint Program."

Now to put this into practice by loading an icon into a picture box. You might recall that Visual Basic comes with many icons. The one you want here is a stoplight stored in Icons\Traffic\Trffc10a.ico. To load that icon into a picture box, start by placing a picture box control on the Graphics application's form. Name the new picture box `picTest`. Then enter the following line of code in `frmGraphic`'s `Click` event (remove any previous code from that event and any code in the `Form_Activate()` event, also):

```
Private Sub Form_Click()
    picTest.Picture = LoadPicture("c:\vb\icons\traffic\trffc10a.ico")
End Sub
```

When you use the preceding code line, make sure the path of the trffc10a.ico icon is correct for your system.

The traffic light icon is now assigned to the picture box. When the application is running, it will appear in the control when the form is clicked, as in Figure 9.16.

Figure 9.16.
The stoplight icon loaded into a picture box in the test Graphics application.

Note that the icon is placed in the upper-left corner of the picture box. If this were an image control, it would have automatically resized itself, shrinking around the icon. But, you can also do that with a picture box by changing its `AutoSize` property in the Properties window to `True`. When you do, the picture box automatically snaps to the correct size, as in Figure 9.17. (If the icon had been larger than the picture box, the box would have grown to accommodate the icon.)

Figure 9.17.
The stoplight icon loaded into the picture box with the `AutoSize` property set to `True`.

Files with the .bmp extension can also be loaded this way. This capability can be valuable for customizing the appearance of a window. To create such a .bmp file, draw the figure you want in an application such as Windows Paint or CorelDRAW, and then save it in .bmp (bitmap) format. Next, read it in with a line like the following one:

```
Private Sub Form_Activate()
    picMyProject = LoadPicture ("c:\windows\image.bmp")
End Sub
```

The window in Figure 9.18 was produced by loading a .bmp file directly with the `LoadPicture()` function.

Figure 9.18.
A .bmp file loaded into a picture box using the `LoadPicture()` *function.*

At this point, you know how to use graphics in Visual Basic relatively well, as well as how to load graphics files directly into your own projects. Next, you will explore methods for displaying text.

Before ending this discussion of nontext graphics, however, a point deserves to be made. In your test Graphics application, you have set the `frmGraphic`'s `AutoRedraw` property to `True`. This means that Visual Basic automatically restores the graphics to a form that has been temporarily obscured by other windows. To do this, however, Visual Basic needs to store the entire graphics image, which uses a huge amount of memory.

There is another way to do the same thing—by restoring the graphics images using code. The image must be redrawn every time a `Form_Paint()` event occurs. This event is generated when an obscured part of the client area is uncovered. That's when the application is supposed to repaint the image. The easiest way to do this is to simply redraw everything in the client area by putting the correct code in the `Form_Paint()` event. You will do this in a few pages. If you are going to use `Paint` events, however, you should know two more things:

1. `Paint` events do not occur if `AutoRedraw` is set to `True`.
2. If `AutoRedraw` is set to `False`, graphics cannot be drawn in the `Form_Load()` `Sub` procedure.

Now you move on to displaying text.

Displaying Text in Visual Basic

In Visual Basic, graphical text (text that does not appear in text-oriented controls) can be printed in three places: on forms, in picture boxes, and on the printer. This section takes a look at the use of all three.

Before beginning, though, it is important to understand that text is indeed treated as graphics. That means the ANSI code of each character is not stored. When you print a character on a form, a picture of that character appears, and that is all. The text itself is not somewhere in memory, as it would be in a text or list box. To write an Editor application that doesn't use a text box as a base—and, therefore, can go beyond the 64KB limit—you, the programmer, would have to handle all the screen details yourself.

You have already seen the Visual Basic fonts that were available when you designed the Notepad application. Now it's important to concentrate on how to print when it comes to graphical text. Printing text can be more involved than you might think, because most fonts in Windows do not have characters of the same width. Fonts whose characters are all the same width are called *monospace* or *nonproportional* fonts. An example of a monospaced font is Courier. Fonts with different character widths—*variable-width* or *proportional* fonts—are much more common. Some variable-width fonts are Arial, Helvetica, and Times New Roman. Because Windows normally uses the latter, you will have to be careful about printing. To add more text to the end of a printed string, for example, you would have to figure out just where that string ends.

To print graphical text, simply use the `Print` method. Note that the `Print` method only applies to objects that can display text, such as forms, picture boxes, and the printer. Its syntax looks like this:

```
object.Print outputlist
```

The `Print` method syntax uses the following arguments:

- `object`—An optional object expression that evaluates to an object.
- `outputlist`—An optional expression or list of expressions to print. If omitted, a blank line is printed.

The `outputlist` argument has the following syntax and parts:

```
{Spc(n) | Tab(n)} expression charpos
```

- `Spc(n)`—Used to insert space characters in the output; *n* is the number of space characters to insert. This argument is optional.
- `Tab(n)`—An optional argument used to position the insertion point at an absolute column number; *n* is the column number. Use `Tab` with no argument to position the insertion point at the beginning of the next print zone.
- `expression`—Optional numeric or string expressions to print.

- charpos—Specifies the insertion point for the next character. This argument is optional. Use a semicolon to position the insertion point immediately following the last character displayed. Use `Tab(n)` to position the insertion point at an absolute column number. Use `Tab` with no argument to position the insertion point at the beginning of the next print zone. If `charpos` is omitted, the next character is printed on the next line.

Because `Print` is a method, it can be used together with the name of an object (*Object*.*Method*). If an object name is omitted, Visual Basic assumes that the method refers to the current form. For example, a string of text could be printed using the following code example:

```
frmMyApp.Print "Way to go!"
```

To see the result of this line, you can put it in the `Form_Load` `Sub` procedure of the test Graphics application, and then run the application (be sure to set the form's `AutoRedraw` property to `True` or the graphics won't print).

```
Private Sub Form_Load()
    frmGraphics.Print "Way to go!"
End Sub
```

The result appears in Figure 9.19.

Figure 9.19.
The test Graphics application with a text string positioned in the upper-left corner of frmGraphics.

The text appears in the upper-left corner of the form. Why? Because the text appears at the coordinates (0,0). Text is printed at the current graphics output position, as set by the properties (`CurrentX`, `CurrentY`), with both quantities measured in twips. To begin the text exactly in the middle of the form, add the following code:

```
Private Sub Form_Load()

    CurrentX = ScaleWidth / 2
    CurrentY = ScaleHeight / 2

    frmGraphics.Print "Way to go!"
End Sub
```

The result of that code addition appears in Figure 9.20.

Figure 9.20.
The text string started at
frmGraphic's center.

Notice in the previous definition for the Print method's syntax that a comma or semicolon can be added to the charpos argument. These characters determine where the text cursor will be left when printing finishes. If a semicolon is used, the text cursor is placed immediately after the printed text; thus, the next printed line of text would immediately follow it. For example, the following lines of code produce the same result as the one you just used:

```
Private Sub Form_Load()
    CurrentX = ScaleWidth / 2
    CurrentY = ScaleHeight / 2

    frmGraphics.Print "Way ";
    frmGraphics.Print "to go!"

End Sub
```

On the other hand, if a comma is used in place of the semicolon, a tab is inserted into the text. This means that the text cursor is placed in the next print zone. The default length for a tab is the width of 14 average characters of the current font. The following code, for example, creates the output in Figure 9.21:

```
Private Sub Form_Load()
    frmGraphics.Print "Way ", "to go! "
End Sub
```

Figure 9.21.
The test Graphics application
with tabbed text output on
frmGraphics.

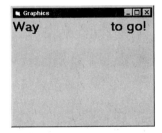

This might look a bit odd when using a sentence, but it could be used to print data tables in neat columns. For instance, Tab(20) tabs over to a print zone that starts at 20 average character widths rather than 14.

Suppose that you wanted to print the following table:

Region	Product
East	Plums
West	Strawberries
North	Apples
South	Grapefruit

It could be printed using the Print method. To begin, move down a few lines to make some room at the top of frmGraphics. Every time Print is used without an argument, it moves the text cursor to the next line. So add three Prints to skip three lines, like this:

```
Private Sub Form_Load()
    Print
    Print
    Print

    :

End Sub
```

Next, add customized tabs into the table in the following way:

```
Private Sub Form_Load()
    Print
    Print
    Print

    Print Tab(13); "Region"; Tab(30); "Product"
    Print
    Print Tab(13); "East"; Tab(30); "Plums"
    Print Tab(13); "West"; Tab(30); "Strawberries"
    Print Tab(13); "North"; Tab(30); "Apples"
    Print Tab(13); "South"; Tab(30); "Grapefruit"

    :

End Sub
```

To distinguish the table, draw a rectangle around it like this:

```
Private Sub Form_Load()
    Print
    Print
    Print

    Print Tab(13); "Region"; Tab(30); "Product"
    Print
    Print Tab(13); "East"; Tab(30); "Plums"
    Print Tab(13); "West"; Tab(30); "Strawberries"
    Print Tab(13); "North"; Tab(30); "Apples"
    Print Tab(13); "South"; Tab(30); "Grapefruit"

    DrawWidth = 2
    Line (650, 400)-(3600, 2000), , B
    Line (650, 930)-(3600, 930)

End Sub
```

The final table appears in Figure 9.22, printed (as with all text) in the object's `ForeColor`.

Figure 9.22.
A tabbed table printed on
frmGraphics.

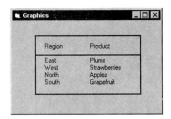

Of course, you could also print to a picture box. Double-click on the picture box tool to add one to `frmGraphics`. Change its `Name` property to `picText`. Now change the code in `Form_Load()` to the following:

```
Private Sub Form_Load()
    picText.Print "This is most certainly a very long string for such a small
picture box!"
End Sub
```

Set the picture box's `AutoRedraw` property to `True` (if you don't, you can't print graphics into the box from the `Form_Load()` event), and run the application.

As you can see in Figure 9.23, the string is much too long for the picture box, so the text is cut off on the right. To fix this problem, you would have to know when to skip to the next line. To know that, you would have to know the length of the text string as it will appear on the screen. The length can be determined using the `TextWidth` method.

Figure 9.23.
Text truncated in a picture
box on frmGraphics.

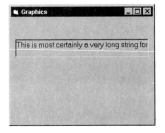

Determining String Length on the Screen

Two methods can be used to determine text string dimensions on the screen. In an environment that uses variable-width fonts, these methods can be invaluable. The two methods are `TextHeight` and `TextWidth`.

Determining the Height of a Text String

`TextHeight` can be used to determine the height of text, like this:

```
Dim HowHigh As Integer
HowHigh = TextHeight ("I am a tall sentence!")
```

Then, to position the text cursor down five lines, `5 * HowHigh` should be added to `CurrentY`.

Here's an example. Suppose that you want to determine the length of the string `Frodo is a hobbit`. That code would look like this:

```
Dim StringLength As Integer
StringLength = picText.TextWidth ("Frodo is a hobbit.")
```

You might recall from the discussion of string manipulation in Chapter 4, "Programming in Visual Basic," that the `Len` function can also be used to determine the length of a string. `Len` will be used shortly.

But what if your picture box, `picText`, is not big enough to print the string on one line? Then the string must be broken in two. To check where the line should be broken, use the `TextWidth` method.

Start this example by setting up a string array, as follows:

```
Private Sub Form_Load()
    Static MyText(4) As String

    :

End Sub
```

Next, load each word into the array like this:

```
Private Sub Form_Load()
    Static MyText(4) As String

    MyText(1) = "Frodo "
    MyText(2) = "is "
    MyText(3) = "a "
    MyText(4) = "hobbit."

    :

End Sub
```

Then the code should loop over each word, adding it to a string that will be printed while simultaneously checking to see whether the string is too long for `picText`.

```
Private Sub Form_Load()
    Static MyText(4) As String
    Dim FirstLine As String
    Dim LineCheck As String
    Dim Word As Integer
```

```
        MyText(1) = "Frodo "
        MyText(2) = "is "
        MyText(3) = "a "
        MyText(4) = "hobbit. "

        LineCheck = ""
        FirstLine = ""

        For Word = 1 To 4
            LineCheck = LineCheck + MyText(Word)

            If picText.TextWidth(LineCheck) > picText.ScaleWidth Then
                Exit For

            Else
                FirstLine = LineCheck

            End If
        Next Word

        :

End Sub
```

If the string is too long, a second line must be created in the following way:

```
Private Sub Form_Load()
        Static MyText(4) As String
        Dim FirstLine As String
        Dim SecondLine As String
        Dim LineCheck As String
        Dim Word As Integer
        Dim Line2Word2 As Integer

        MyText(1) = "Frodo "
        MyText(2) = "is "
        MyText(3) = "a "
        MyText(4) = "hobbit. "

        LineCheck = ""
        FirstLine = ""
        SecondLine = ""

        For Word = 1 To 4
            LineCheck = LineCheck + MyText(Word)

            If picText.TextWidth(LineCheck) > picText.ScaleWidth Then
                Exit For

            Else
                FirstLine = LineCheck

            End If
        Next Word

        Line2Word2 = Word
```

```
    For Word = Line2Word2 to 4
        SecondLine = SecondLine + MyText(Word)
    Next Word

    :

End Sub
```

Finally, the text can be printed using the following additional code:

```
Private Sub Form_Load()
    Static MyText(4) As String
    Dim FirstLine As String
    Dim SecondLine As String
    Dim LineCheck As String
    Dim Word As Integer
    Dim Line2Word2 As Integer

    MyText(1) = "Frodo "
    MyText(2) = "is "
    MyText(3) = "a "
    MyText(4) = "hobbit. "

    LineCheck = ""
    FirstLine = ""
    SecondLine = ""

    For Word = 1 To 4
        LineCheck = LineCheck + MyText(Word)

        If picText.TextWidth(LineCheck) > picText.ScaleWidth Then
            Exit For

        Else
            FirstLine = LineCheck

        End If
    Next Word

    Line2Word2 = Word

    For Word = Line2Word2 to 4
        SecondLine = SecondLine + MyText(Word)
    Next Word

    picText.Print FirstLine
    picText.Print SecondLine

End Sub
```

The result of all this work appears in Figure 9.24. Word wrapping is a common problem when printing with variable-width fonts. Unlike text boxes, which must remain in one font, printing text in this way can use multiple fonts. Fonts could be varied to include such formatting as bold, underline, and italics. However, this can make string widths even more unpredictable.

Figure 9.24.
*The word-wrapping example
in the test Graphics
application.*

To recap, Table 9.7 shows font properties found in the Visual Basic Font dialog box and their descriptions.

Table 9.7. Visual Basic Font properties.

Property		Description
Font Name		Name of font such as Courier or Times New Roman.
Font Size		Size of font in points (there are 72 points to the inch).
Font Style:	Regular	Changes the appearance of the font
	Bold	
	Italic	
	Bold Italic	
Effects:	Strikeout	Changes the appearance of the font.
	Underline	

More Uses for `TextHeight` and `TextWidth`

`TextHeight` and `TextWidth` have many other uses. For example, text can be centered on a form by using them together with the `ScaleWidth` and `ScaleHeight` properties. Or they can be used to find the average width of a character by finding the width of a long string and then dividing that width by the number of characters in the string.

Because formatting text for output in a restricted space is a common problem, some code should be developed that will help. To start, use the `Form_Load()` event and the picture box you added recently, `picText`. If you were to print a long string in that picture box, you would want to break the print string (call it `TheString`) into several lines to fit. A function named `GetWord()`, which you will write shortly, could be used to return the next word in `TheString`. Also, the code could loop until it returned an empty string, `""`, signifying that the print string is exhausted. The code for that might appear as follows:

```
Private Sub Form_Load()
    Dim TheString As String
    Dim NextWord As String
    Dim Graphic As String
    Dim TempString As String

    TheString = "I wish we had a daffodil garden."

    Graphic = ""
    NextWord = GetWord()

    Do While NextWord <> ""

        :

    Loop

End Sub
```

Using the `Do While` loop set up in the preceding code, the line is assembled to print—which is held in the variable `Graphic`—until it gets too long. Then the line is printed and the loop starts over on the next line. The line length can be checked using a temporary string, `TempString`, in the following way: `TempString = Graphic + NextWord`. If `TempString` becomes too long for the picture box, it is time to print the line.

```
Private Sub Form_Load()
    Dim TheString As String
    Dim NextWord As String
    Dim Graphic As String
    Dim TempString As String

    TheString = "I wish we had a daffodil garden."

    Graphic = ""
    NextWord = GetWord()

    Do While NextWord <> ""

        TempString = Graphic + NextWord
            If picText.TextWidth(TempString) > picText.ScaleWidth Then
                picText.Print Graphic
                Graphic = NextWord

        Else

            :

        End If

    Loop

End Sub
```

If you are printing `"I wish we had a daffodil garden."`, the first time through the variable `Graphic` equals `""`, and `TempString` (whose value is `Graphic + NextWord`) equals `"I "`. The next time through the loop, `TempString` equals `"I wish "`, and so on, until `TempString` is too long to fit horizontally in the picture box. If the line is not too long, on the other hand, the current word is added to `Graphic`. Then the next word of the string is retrieved by the variable `NextWord` and the loop starts again.

```
Private Sub Form_Load()
    Dim TheString As String
    Dim NextWord As String
    Dim Graphic As String
    Dim TempString As String

    TheString = "I wish we had a daffodil garden."

    Graphic = ""
    NextWord = GetWord()

    Do While NextWord <> ""

        TempString = Graphic + NextWord
            If picText.TextWidth(TempString) > picText.ScaleWidth Then
                picText.Print Graphic
                Graphic = NextWord

        Else
                Graphic = TempString

        End If

    NextWord = GetWord()
    Loop

        :

End Sub
```

That's it, except for one last detail. The lines have been printed when they get too long, but the final words that make up the last line still need to be printed. After that, `remainder` is printed using the following additional line of code, and then the `Form_Load()` event code is complete.

```
Private Sub Form_Load()
    Dim TheString As String
    Dim NextWord As String
    Dim Graphic As String
    Dim TempString As String

    TheString = "I wish we had a daffodil garden."

    Graphic = ""
    NextWord = GetWord()

    Do While NextWord <> ""

        TempString = Graphic + NextWord
            If picText.TextWidth(TempString) > picText.ScaleWidth Then
                picText.Print Graphic
                Graphic = NextWord

        Else
```

```
                    Graphic = TempString

                End If

        NextWord = GetWord()
    Loop

    picText.Print Graphic      'print remainder of text

End Sub
```

The final step is to write the function `GetWord()`. This is the function that returns the next word in `TheString`. This function needs a copy of `TheString` so that it can retrieve each successive word, but a copy of `TheString` can't be passed every time because the code would chop off and return the first word over and over. Instead, a public string, perhaps called `Original`, should be declared in a module. That way, it will be accessible to all parts of the application. The public declaration in the module would look like this:

```
Public Original As String
```

Or it could be made into a form-wide variable by declaring it in the `(General)` declarations section of the Code window, like this:

```
Dim Original As String
```

The new public variable `Original` can be filled immediately in `Form_Load()`, like this:

```
Private Sub Form_Load()
    Dim TheString As String
    Dim NextWord As String
    Dim Graphic As String
    Dim TempString As String

    TheString = "I wish we had a daffodil garden."
    Original = TheString

    Graphic = ""
    NextWord = GetWord()

    Do While NextWord <> ""

        TempString = Graphic + NextWord
            If picText.TextWidth(TempString) > picText.ScaleWidth Then
                picText.Print Graphic
                Graphic = NextWord

        Else
                Graphic = TempString

        End If

        NextWord = GetWord()
    Loop

    picText.Print Graphic      'print remainder of text

End Sub
```

Now write the function GetWord(). The task here is to chop off the first word of the string Original. In other words, the code should find the first space in that string and return everything up to and including the space. If this were the beginning of the loop, Original would be filled with "I wish we had a daffodil garden.". The GetWord() function should return "I " and then truncate Original, leaving it as "wish we had a daffodil garden.". There are a few cases that need to be handled in this function.

First, begin with the easy one in which Original has no spaces in it, meaning that it is either an empty string, "", or a single word. In that case, that word or empty string should be returned. And, because words are being chopped off of the variable named Original, the variable named TheString should become an empty string, indicating that there is nothing left. That code would appear as follows:

```
Private Function GetWord() As String

    If InStr(Original, "") = 0 Then      'No words left
        GetWord = Original
        Original = ""

    Else

    :

    End If

End Function
```

In this example, the Visual Basic function InStr() is used. This function determines the position of the first occurrence of one string within another. In other words, InStr() searches through the string contents of the variable named Original to determine whether there is a space in that string. In this case, if InStr(Original, "") = 0, there is no space in Original. Notice that you must return a value from the GetWord function. That return value is assigned to the function name using this code:

```
Private Function GetWord() As String

    If InStr(Original, "") = 0 Then      'No words left
        GetWord = Original
        Original = ""

    Else

    :

    End If

End Function
```

On the other hand, if there is a space in Original, that string has at least two words in it. The first word should be returned and then cut out of the string to prepare for the next time GetWord is called. That can be accomplished as shown in the following example, using the Visual Basic functions Left(String, n) and Right(String, n). These functions return the leftmost and rightmost n characters (in which n is the number of characters).

```
Private Function GetWord() As String

    If InStr(Original, "") = 0 Then      'No words left
        GetWord = Original
        Original = ""

    Else

        GetWord = Left(Original, InStr(Original, ""))
        Original = Right(Original, Len(Original) - InStr(Original, ""))

    End If

End Function
```

That's it for the GetWord function. And that also completes the string-printing routine. Now it can be used to print to picture boxes with a result like that in Figure 9.25. In this case, the application prints "I wish we had a daffodil garden." correctly in the small picture box, picText. The code for this routine appears in Table 9.8 and Listing 9.1.

Figure 9.25.
The text squeezed into
picText.

Using the String-Printing Routine with a Form

As it stands, this routine is limited to printing in picture boxes. That can be changed, however, to work on forms. The code must be generalized, or placed in a module in its own subroutine. That subroutine could appear as follows:

```
Sub PrintString(Frm As Form)

    :    '[All code from Form_Load() event here

End Sub
```

Then all references in the code to picText should be changed to Frm. From then on, any form could be passed to the Sub procedure PrintString().

Table 9.8. The visual implementation of the **frmString** form.

Object	Property	Setting
Form	Caption	Print String Example
	Name	frmString
Picture Box	AutoRedraw	True
	Name	picText

Listing 9.1. The Code for the **frmString** form.

```
Option Explicit

Dim Original As String

Private Sub Form_Load()
    Dim TheString As String
    Dim NextWord As String
    Dim Graphic As String
    Dim TempString As String

    TheString = "I wish we had a daffodil garden."
    Original = TheString

    Graphic = ""
    NextWord = GetWord()

    Do While NextWord <> ""

        TempString = Graphic + NextWord
            If picText.TextWidth(TempString) > picText.ScaleWidth Then
                picText.Print Graphic
                Graphic = NextWord

        Else
            Graphic = TempString

        End If

    NextWord = GetWord()
    Loop

    picText.Print Graphic     'print remainder of text


End Sub

Private Function GetWord() As String

    If InStr(Original, "") = 0 Then    'No words left
        GetWord = Original
        Original = ""

    Else
```

```
        GetWord = Left(Original, InStr(Original, ""))
        Original = Right(Original, Len(Original) - InStr(Original, ""))

    End If

End Function
```

Now turn to the topics of animation and custom-designed icons.

Creating Your Own Animation

It would be best if Visual Basic supported two-dimensional arrays of screen or printer bits, because then bitmaps could be moved around in any direction. But it doesn't, although you could interface to the underlying Windows system calls for bitmap support. However, there are ways around this.

Picture box controls are the best bet for animation. They can be moved easily around the screen. Visual Basic moves the associated bitmap around almost instantaneously, and can even switch rapidly between picture boxes to create animation effects.

The rocket ship is referred to in graphics as a *sprite*, which means that it is a simple bitmap that doesn't change but is moved around on the screen. To move it around, the rocket ship must first be loaded into a picture box or image control. That can be accomplished using the LoadPicture function. However, the picture must be drawn in an application such as Windows 95 Paint, and then saved in .bmp format. It can be read in with a line like the following:

```
Private Sub Form_Click()
    Image1.Picture = LoadPicture("c:\windows\image.bmp")
End Sub
```

The window in Figure 9.18, for instance, was produced in this way, by loading a .bmp file directly with LoadPicture. Any size of image can be created up to full-screen size, or part of a larger one could be used if a section was cut from the larger bitmap.

You could easily create the rocket as a small .bmp file, using Windows 95 Paint or some other application. Then you could load it into a picture box or image control and move it around the screen using the Move method, which moves Visual Basic objects.

Copying the Screen to the Clipboard and Windows Paint

You can load copies of what has appeared on the screen into forms or picture boxes. If you press Print Screen while in Windows, Windows pastes a copy of the complete screen to the Clipboard. Pressing Ctrl+Print Screen copies only the active window. From there, the screen capture can be pasted into Windows Paint. Then you could work on it and save it as a .bmp file that could be loaded into a Visual Basic graphics object.

Setting the Mouse Cursor to an Icon

The mouse cursor can be changed to an icon as it moves around the window by using the `MousePointer` property of controls and forms. As the mouse cursor passes over that form or control, it changes into the corresponding icon, which can also be changed at run-time. If you design your own icons, you can produce some interesting results.

Visual Basic provides an extensive icon library in the subdirectories of the Icons directory. You might recall that you have already used a few of these icons for several projects. A rocket icon, perfect for this example, can be found in the Icon subdirectory under Industry\Rocket.

Creating Your Own Icons

Visual Basic 3.0 included a program called Icon Works that allowed programmers to create their own icons. Unfortunately, Visual Basic 4 does not include this application. To make your own icons, use any icon program (such as the one included with the Windows 95 Software Development Kit (SDK) or Norton's Icon Editor application) that comes bundled with many programming tools. Creating icons is easy and fun, and adds a distinctive, professional touch to one's applications.

Start a new project in Visual Basic and set the form's `Caption` property to `Sprite` and its `Name` property to `frmSprite`. Save the form and project as Sprite.frm and Sprite.vbp, respectively. Next, add a command button and picture box as shown in Figure 9.26.

Figure 9.26.
The rocket ship application template just before the form's `BackColor` *property is set to black.*

Change the properties of the objects as follows:

Object	Property	Setting
Form	BackColor	Black
	Caption	Sprite
	Iconc:	\vb\icons\industry\rocket.ico
	Name	frmSprite
Command Button	Caption	Click Me!
	Name	cmdBlastOff
Picture Box	Appearance	0-Flat
	AutoSize	True
	BackColor	Black
	BorderStyle	0-None
	Name	picRocket

When you change the BackColor property for both the form and picture box to black, the picture box will effectively disappear. Don't worry about this! If you need to move the picture box to a new position, temporarily change its BackColor so that it is visible. When the program runs, the rocket icon will fill the black picture box.

If you would like to add some stars or planets, you could use the shape tool to create small circles, and then change the BackColor properties of these circles to red, yellow, blue, and so on.

Open the Code window and bring up the Form_Activate() event, as follows:

```
Private Sub Form_Activate()

End Sub
```

Then add this line:

```
Private Sub Form_Activate()
    picRocket.Picture = LoadPicture("c:\vb\icons\industry\rocket.ico")
End Sub
```

(Make sure that the path call in the preceding line of code is correct for your system.)

All that remains is the animation. This can be accomplished using the Move method. The Move method moves an MDI form, form, or control, and it does not support named arguments. Its syntax works like this:

```
object.Move left, top, width, height
```

The Move method syntax uses these arguments:

- object—An optional object expression that evaluates to an object. If the object argument is omitted, the form with the focus is assumed to be object.
- left—A required single-precision value indicating the horizontal coordinate (x-axis) for the left edge of object.
- top—An optional single-precision value indicating the vertical coordinate (y-axis) for the top edge of object.
- width—An optional single-precision value indicating the new width of object.
- height—An optional single-precision value indicating the new height of object.

The location of the top left of the picture box is (picRocket.Left, picRocket.Top). You can move the rocket ship picture box up the screen by changing the Top argument value successively using a loop, as follows:

```
Private Sub cmdBlastOff_Click()
    Dim GoingUp As Integer

    For GoingUp = picRocket.Top to 0 Step -50
        picRocket.Move picRocket.Left, GoingUp
    Next GoingUp
End Sub
```

That's it. The rocket ship now blasts off and moves smoothly up the window when the Click Me! button is pressed. Because the bit manipulations are handled by internal functions, the picture box moves up the screen quickly.

Now add some code to move the rocket from the top of the form back down to the bottom. Put the code in the picture box's double-click event, like this:

```
Private Sub picRocket_DblClick()
    Dim GoingDown As Integer
    Dim bottom As Integer

    bottom = frmSprite.ScaleHeight - picRocket.Height

    For GoingDown = picRocket.Top To bottom Step 50
        picRocket.Move picRocket.Left, GoingDown
    Next GoingDown
End Sub
```

When you run the program, press the Click Me! button to make the rocket fly to the top of the screen. Then double-click on the rocket itself to make it fly backward to the bottom of the screen. Figure 9.27 shows the rocket application running. The entire program appears in Listing 9.2.

Figure 9.27.
The Sprite Rocket applica-
tion running.

Listing 9.2. **The code for sprite.frm in the Sprite Rocket application (Sprite.vbp.).**

```
Option Explicit

Private Sub cmdBlastOff_Click()
    Dim GoingUp As Integer

    For GoingUp = picRocket.Top To 0 Step -50
        picRocket.Move picRocket.Left, GoingUp
    Next GoingUp
End Sub

Private Sub Form_Activate()
    picRocket.Picture = LoadPicture("c:\vb32\icons\industry\rocket.ico")
End Sub

Private Sub picRocket_DblClick()
    Dim GoingDown As Integer
    Dim bottom As Integer

    bottom = frmSprite.ScaleHeight - picRocket.Height

    For GoingDown = picRocket.Top To bottom Step 50
        picRocket.Move picRocket.Left, GoingDown
    Next GoingDown
End Sub
```

Because you have already assigned Rocket.ico to the Icon property of the form, the rocket icon will automatically be used if you create an .exe file for the application. To create an executable file, use the Make EXE File... item on the Visual Basic File menu.

Make sure to type in the .exe extension after the name you assign the executable (Sprite.exe), as shown in Figure 9.28. Otherwise, Windows 95 will not recognize the file as an executable. After the .exe file is created, Rocket.exe can be put on the Windows 95 desktop as a shortcut, as shown in Figure 9.29.

Figure 9.28.
Creating the .exe file with an
associated icon.

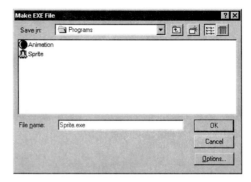

Figure 9.29.
Rocket.exe on the Windows
95 desktop.

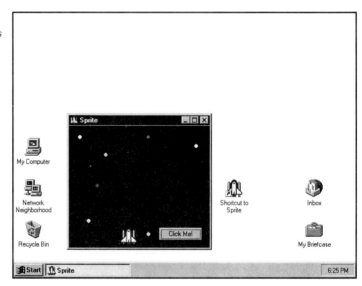

Now for another interesting animation using a third-party tool included with Visual Basic: *Desaware Animated Button Control.*

The Desaware Animated Button Control

This third-party control comes bundled with Visual Basic 4. Start a new project and add the tool to the toolbox by selecting Custom Controls… from the Tools menu or by pressing Ctrl+T on the keyboard. Find Desaware Animated Button Control in the Available Controls list box. (If you don't see it there, use the Browse button to find Anibtn32.ocx.) Select it, making sure that the check box has an X in it, and then click OK. The control is added to the bottom of the Visual Basic toolbox, as shown in Figure 9.30.

Now save the form and project as Animation.frm and Animation.vbp, respectively.

Figure 9.30.
The Desaware AniButton Control added to the toolbox.

Double-click on the AniButton control to add it to the form. Resize and position it on the form as shown in Figure 9.31.

Figure 9.31.
The AniButton control positioned on the form.

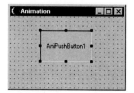

Now add the other controls to the form, setting their properties as follows:

Object	Property	Setting
Form	BorderStyle	3-Fixed Dialog
	Caption	Animation
	Icon	c:\vb\icons\elements\moon08.ico
	MaxButton	False
	MinButton	False
AniPushButton	BackColor	Purple
	BorderStyle1-	Fixed Single
	Caption	(None)
	Cycle	1-By Frame
	Name	AniPushButton1
Command	Caption	&Start
Button	Name	cmdStart

continues

Object	Property	Setting
Command	Cancel	True
Button	Caption	Sto&p
	Enabled	False
	Name	cmdStop
Timer	Interval	150
	Name	Timer1

The animated button control is a flexible pushbutton control that allows you to use any icon, bitmap, or metafile to define your own button controls. Control types include animated buttons, multistate buttons, and animated check boxes. Each animated button can contain zero or more images and an optional text caption. An animated button can be thought of as a series of frames that are displayed in sequence. The Picture property can be used to load images into the animated button control. The Frame property indicates which picture is currently accessible through the Picture property. In other words, the Frame property is an index of the array of images in the control.

Normally, this control would be used to show different pictures each time the button is clicked by the user. In this case, it will be used a little differently. Instead of making the user press the button to see the different pictures, code will simulate the user's button click, and a timer will set the rate of each "click." Thus, the AniButton will actually create an animation, for this example, of the revolving phases of the moon.

An easy way to set each "Frame" is to use the Custom property found in the Properties window. When it is selected, a Properties button appears to the right of the Settings box. When this button is pressed, the AniButton Control Properties dialog box appears on the screen. This dialog box uses the Tabbed Notebook metaphor to display many of the available properties. Have a look around each tab sheet to get an idea of what is available.

For this project, you should select the Frame Settings tab. This tab sheet makes it easy to load the various desired pictures for the AniButton. To get started, notice that a small list box to the upper left of the tab sheet indicates which frame is presently displayed. At the moment, 1 is listed, as shown in Figure 9.32.

When a picture is loaded into a frame, it will appear in the display box beneath the small horizontal scrollbar. Each time a picture is loaded, the frame count will increment by one.

To load the first icon, press the Load... command button. This opens a dialog box with Open - Frame 1 on the title bar. Change the file type listed from Bitmaps to Icons, as shown in Figure 9.33.

Move to the Visual Basic Icons subdirectory, and select Elements. Click on the icon Moon02.ico, and then click the Insert button. The Open dialog box disappears and the icon is loaded into Frame 1.

Figure 9.32.
*The Anibutton Control
Properties dialog box with the
Frame Settings tab sheet to
the fore.*

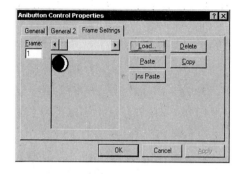

Figure 9.33.
*Loading an icon into a
frame.*

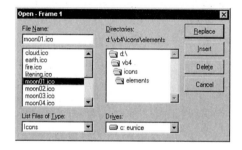

Press the right arrow on the scrollbar to move to Frame 2. The moon icon in the display box disappears, and the display box then shows an empty Frame 2. Again press the Load… button. This time, select Moon3.ico and press Insert. The Open dialog box again disappears and the second icon is loaded into Frame 2. Follow this list to continue loading icons until you have reached Frame 8.

Frame	Icon
1	c:\vb\icons\elements\moon02.ico
2	c:\vb\icons\elements\moon03.ico
3	c:\vb\icons\elements\moon04.ico
4	c:\vb\icons\elements\moon05.ico
5	c:\vb\icons\elements\moon06.ico
6	c:\vb\icons\elements\moon07.ico
7	c:\vb\icons\elements\moon08.ico
8	c:\vb\icons\elements\moon01.ico

When you are finished, scroll through the frames one by one to make sure they are all there, and then press OK. The AniButton control is now loaded.

Add the code that simulates the user's click. If the focus is set on the AniButton, a SendKeys call for a space (ASCII character 32) can be used to do just that. Because the Timer control will be used to count the interval between simulated clicks, the SendKeys call should go there.

```
Private Sub Timer1_Timer()
    Dim i As Integer

    AniPushButton1.SetFocus
    SendKeys (Chr(32))

    For i = 1 To 1000
        Timer1.Enabled = False
    Next i

    Timer1.Enabled = True

End Sub
```

Now add the code that activates the Start and Stop command buttons:

```
Private Sub cmdStop_Click()
    Timer1.Enabled = False
    cmdStop.Enabled = False
    cmdStart.Enabled = True
End Sub

Private Sub cmdStart_Click()
    Timer1.Enabled = True
    cmdStart.Enabled = False
    cmdStop.Enabled = True
End Sub
```

This code enables and disables the timer, thereby starting or stopping the moon animation. Also, when the program starts, the Stop button is disabled until the Start button is pushed. When the Start button is pressed, that button becomes disabled until the user presses the Stop button. Notice that you added access keys to the command buttons, too. Instead of clicking on the buttons, Alt+S can be pressed for start and Alt+P can be pressed for stop.

And that's all there is to it! Run the program and watch the moon phases rotate. You might notice that the animation does not stop sometimes when the Stop button is pressed. This is because the Stop button is being pressed while the AniButton is cycling through its paces. To be sure the animation does stop, press Alt+P. Figure 9.34 shows the Moon Phase program in action.

Figure 9.34.
The Moon Phase program running.

The entire program appears in Listing 9.3.

Listing 9.3. The code for the frmAnimation form of the Moon Phase Animation Program (Animation.vbp).

```
Option Explicit

Private Sub cmdStop_Click()
    Timer1.Enabled = False
    cmdStop.Enabled = False
    cmdStart.Enabled = True
End Sub

Private Sub cmdStart_Click()
    Timer1.Enabled = True
    cmdStart.Enabled = False
    cmdStop.Enabled = True
End Sub

Private Sub Timer1_Timer()
    Dim i As Integer

    AniPushButton1.SetFocus
    SendKeys (Chr(32))

    For i = 1 To 1000
        Timer1.Enabled = False
    Next i

    Timer1.Enabled = True

End Sub
```

That's it for animation and for the exploration of screen graphics for this chapter. Now you'll learn about printer graphics.

Using a Printer in Visual Basic

When it comes to graphics, the printer is used just as much as a picture box or form. In particular, the Print method can be used as it was before, except that it is now used with a Printer object that corresponds to the default printer loaded by the Windows Control Panel. To print "I wish we had a daffodil garden." on the printer in underlined, 18 point, Courier text, the following code should be used:

```
Private Sub Form_Activate()
    Printer.FontName = "Courier"
    Printer.FontSize = "18"
    Printer.FontUnderline = True
    Printer.Print "I wish we had a daffodil garden."
End Sub
```

Similarly, CurrentX and CurrentY can be used to position printer output on the page, as measured in twips.

```
Private Sub Form_Activate()
    Printer.FontName = "Courier"
    Printer.CurrentX = 1440
    Printer.CurrentY = 2880

    Printer.Print "I wish we had a daffodil garden."
End Sub
```

This code indicates where the graphics should go on the page. You could skip to the next page, in fact, using the NewPage method like this:

```
Private Sub Form_Activate()
    Printer.FontName = "Courier"
    Printer.NewPage
    Printer.CurrentX = 1440
    Printer.CurrentY = 2880
    Printer.Print "I wish we had a daffodil garden."
End Sub
```

In fact, because Visual Basic is designed to be device-independent, there is little more to learn here. As you might recall, the Printer object supports the other graphics methods seen earlier in the chapter (PSet, Line, and Circle), and it includes normal graphical properties, such as ScaleHeight and ScaleWidth. So a circle could be drawn using the following additional line of code:

```
Private Sub Form_Activate()
    Printer.FontName = "Courier"
    Printer.CurrentX = 1440
    Printer.CurrentY = 2880
    Printer.Print "I wish we had a daffodil garden."
    Printer.NewPage
    Printer.Circle (ScaleWidth / 4, ScaleHeight / 4), ScaleHeight / 5
End Sub
```

One method you have not seen before, however, is PrintForm. This method will print an entire form, as shown in the following example:

```
Private Sub Form_Activate()
    Form1.PrintForm
End Sub
```

Note, however, that this code prints with only pixel resolution—as though it were a direct transcription from the screen. If higher-resolution graphics are desired, use the Print method.

That's it for printing. Now you turn to manipulating the Visual Basic coordinate system.

Changing Coordinate Systems

Sometimes the default coordinate system, which looks like Figure 9.35, is not optimal for what you want to present.

Figure 9.35.

A pictorial representation of the default coordinate system.

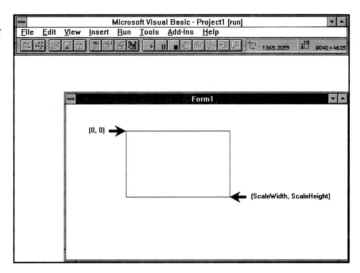

Suppose that you want to display the following data for your telephone bills month by month, as follows:

Month	Phone Bill ($)
January = 1	200
February = 2	95
April = 4	350
May = 5	105

If you use these data values, it would be much better if the window were set up as shown in Figure 9.36.

Figure 9.36.

A pictorial representation of the coordinate position for charting telephone bills month by month.

You can set up a window in exactly this way, using the Scale method. Scale defines the coordinate system for a Form, Picture Box, or Printer, and it does not support named arguments. Its syntax works like this:

```
object.Scale (x1, y1) - (x2, y2)
```

The Scale method syntax has these parts:

- object—An optional object expression that evaluates to an object in the Applies To list. If object is omitted, the Form object with the focus is assumed to be object.

- x1, y1—Optional single-precision values indicating the horizontal (x-axis) and vertical (y-axis) coordinates that define the upper-left corner of the object. Parentheses must enclose the values. If these are omitted, the second set of coordinates must also be omitted.

- x2, y2—Optional single-precision values indicating the horizontal and vertical coordinates that define the lower-right corner of the object. Parentheses must enclose the values. If these are omitted, the first set of coordinates must also be omitted.

This method sets the new coordinates for the beginning point at the left of the client area and the ending point to the right. To do this in your program, you need only one statement:

```
Scale (0, BigY)-(BigX, 0)      'Assuming a (0,0) origin
```

The variables BigY and BigX are the greatest Y and X values, respectively, that have to be plotted. To find those values, the following code should be put into the Form_Paint() procedure. This procedure is called every time Windows has to redraw the form.

Start a new project and change the Name and Caption properties of the default form to frmPlotter and Phone Bills. Save the form and project as Plotter.frm and Plotter.vbp. Now place the following code in the Form_Paint() event:

```
Option Explicit

Dim X(4) As Single   'Form-level variables placed in (General) declarations
Dim Y(4) As Single
Dim BigX As Single
Dim BigY As Single
Dim FindBig As Integer

Private Sub Form_Paint()
      'plotting program, assumes origin is (0,0)

    Cls

    X(1) = 1
    Y(1) = 200
    X(2) = 2
    Y(2) = 95
    X(3) = 4
    Y(3) = 350
    X(4) = 5
    Y(4) = 105

    BigX = 0

    For FindBig = 1 To UBound(X)
        If X(FindBig) > BigX Then
            BigX = X(FindBig)
        End If
    Next FindBig
```

```
        BigY = 0

        For FindBig = 1 To UBound(Y)
            If Y(FindBig) > BigY Then
                BigY = Y(FindBig)
            End If
        Next FindBig

        Scale (0, BigY)-(BigX, 0)     'Assuming (0,0) origin

        :

End Sub
```

The window needs to be set up to correctly plot the telephone bill values month by month as shown in Figure 9.37.

Figure 9.37.
A pictorial representation of the coordinate positions.

These values should be plotted directly. That can be accomplished using the following code in the form's `Paint` event:

```
Private Sub Form_Paint()
    'plotting program, assumes origin is (0,0)

    Cls

    X(1) = 1
    Y(1) = 200
    X(2) = 2
    Y(2) = 95
    X(3) = 4
    Y(3) = 350
    X(4) = 5
    Y(4) = 105

    BigX = 0

    For FindBig = 1 To UBound(X)
        If X(FindBig) > BigX Then
            BigX = X(FindBig)
        End If
    Next FindBig

    BigY = 0

    For FindBig = 1 To UBound(Y)
        If Y(FindBig) > BigY Then
            BigY = Y(FindBig)
        End If
    Next FindBig
```

```
    Scale (0, BigY)-(BigX, 0)      'Assuming (0,0) origin

    CurrentX = X(1)
    CurrentY = Y(1)

    For FindBig = 1 To UBound(X)
        Line -(X(FindBig), Y(FindBig))
    Next FindBig

End Sub
```

A `Form_Resize()` event should also be added. This event is fired when the form is resized. The call to replot the data should be put there.

```
Private Sub Form_Resize()
    Form_Paint
End Sub
```

This code calls the `Form_Paint()` event, which will replot the data if the form is resized. The result of all this appears in Figure 9.38. If you run the application, you will find that your plotter is a success!

Figure 9.38.
*The running Plotter
application.*

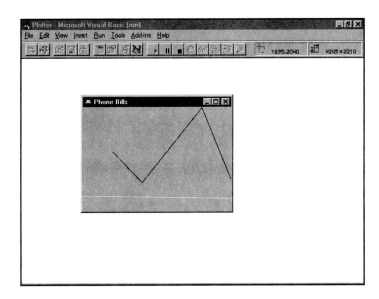

The complete code for the application appears in Table 9.9 and Listing 9.4.

Table 9.9. The visual design of the **frmPlotter** form.

Object	Property	Setting
Form	Caption	Phone Bills
	Name	frmPlotter

The complete code for frmPlotter is in Listing 9.4.

Listing 9.4. The code for the frmPlotter form of the Plotter application (Plotter.vbp).

```
Option Explicit

Dim X(4) As Single    'Form-level variables placed in (General) declarations
Dim Y(4) As Single
Dim BigX As Single
Dim BigY As Single
Dim FindBig As Integer

Private Sub Form_Paint()
     'plotting program, assumes origin is (0,0)

    Cls

    X(1) = 1
    Y(1) = 200
    X(2) = 2
    Y(2) = 95
    X(3) = 4
    Y(3) = 350
    X(4) = 5
    Y(4) = 105

    BigX = 0

    For FindBig = 1 To UBound(X)
         If X(FindBig) > BigX Then
             BigX = X(FindBig)
         End If
    Next FindBig

    BigY = 0

    For FindBig = 1 To UBound(Y)
         If Y(FindBig) > BigY Then
             BigY = Y(FindBig)
         End If
    Next FindBig

    Scale (0, BigY)-(BigX, 0)    'Assuming (0,0) origin

    CurrentX = X(1)
    CurrentY = Y(1)

    For FindBig = 1 To UBound(X)
         Line -(X(FindBig), Y(FindBig))
    Next FindBig

End Sub

Private Sub Form_Resize()
    Form_Paint
End Sub
```

That is all of the coverage of graphics in this chapter. It's time to move now to Chapter 10, where you will write a mouse-driven Paint program, incorporating the mouse with your newfound graphics abilities.

Summary

In this chapter, you learned a great deal about graphics handling in Visual Basic. The chapter described how to draw points, lines, rectangles, circles, and ellipses, and how to draw them in different colors using various methods. Also, you learned how to fill closed shapes with a variety of patterns. The chapter explored picture loading from files directly into picture boxes, image controls, and forms. It also presented easy and quick custom graphics animation using the Move method. You learned about the AutoRedraw property and its capability to preserve graphics on a form and to redraw the graphics when necessary. You discovered how to print text in a picture box or form, as well as on the printer. Finally, you looked into the graphics coordinate system available in Visual Basic and learned how to alter it to better fit your graphics needs. Graphics methods such as these can add visual appeal to your applications, bringing with them both color and pizzazz. Imagine how inviting such visual variations would be to the users of your programs!

New Property	Description
AutoRedraw	When set to True for a form, it stores a copy of the form and redraws it automatically when necessary (for instance, if the form is covered by another window and then uncovered, or if the form is resized).
AutoSize	If set to True, this property makes a picture box snap to the size of the picture in the box.
CurrentX	Holds the current graphics X coordinate position. This can be defined for lines, boxes, circles, and printed text.
CurrentY	Holds the current graphics Y coordinate position. This can be defined for lines, boxes, circles, and printed text.
DrawMode	Sets the way the graphics pen affects the original window data when a figure is drawn (see Table 9.5).
DrawStyle	Sets the style of the graphics pen used (see Table 9.4).
DrawWidth	Sets the width in pixels of the graphics pen.
FillColor	Sets the color used when filling graphics figures.
ScaleHeight	The height of a form's client area.
ScaleWidth	The width of a form's client area.

New Methods	Description
Circle	Draws a circle, ellipse, or arc.
Line	Draws a line or rectangle.
Move	Moves a control in a form.
Point	Returns the color of a point in a form.
Print	Prints in picture boxes, forms, or on the printer.
PSet	Sets a pixel's position.
Scale	Sets the graphics coordinate scale.
TextHeight	Returns the height of a text string.
TextWidth	Returns the width of a text string.

10

The Mouse and a Mouse-Driven Paint Program

In this chapter, you will discover how to use mouse and read mouse events, including location and mouse button information. You will also use graphics skills learned in Chapter 9 to write a fully functional Windows paint program. In addition, the following topics will be covered:

- Drawing with the mouse
- The MouseDown and MouseUp events
- The MouseMove event
- Stretching graphics images
- Saving graphics images in disk files
- Using the Windows Clipboard to copy and paste
- Changing the graphics scale from twips to pixels

The major program in this chapter is the Paint program, which will draw points, lines, boxes, circles, and graphical text. The application will print the graphics images the user creates and store them on disk. Also, it will open files and save them whenever the user desires. This program is pretty large, and it teaches you a few things about program design, such as the need for creating modular program code. The skills learned in this chapter can be applied to larger applications of your own or to setting up a user-interface. If you want to include a painting capability in your own programs, the information discussed here will be useful. In addition, you will pick up the skills to handle the mouse in code. This is invaluable for all kinds of applications, particularly word processors, spreadsheets, business form-design programs, and many others.

In this chapter, you will study the mouse and learn how to put what you have learned in the previous chapter—graphics—together with the mouse by creating a mouse-driven paint program. Certainly, you have already used the mouse, one of the two most important user interface tools in Windows (the other being the keyboard) throughout this book by responding to the Click event for various controls. There is much more to mouse manipulation, however. For instance, it is possible to get the precise location of the mouse pointer when the user clicks or releases a button. It's time to delve into all of this by investigating one of the basic mouse events: MouseDown.

MouseDown Events

A MouseDown event is generated when the user positions the mouse cursor on a form and presses a mouse button. This event is not the same as a Click event. In a Click event, the user must press and release the mouse button. A MouseDown event occurs when the user simply presses a mouse button down. These kinds of events are recognized by forms, picture boxes, labels, and any control that includes a list. Note that controls such as buttons respond only to Click events, not to MouseDown events.

In a MouseDown event, a program receives considerably more information than with a Click event. To see this, begin by putting together the Paint program. Start Visual Basic and change the default form's `Caption` and `Name` properties to `Paint` and `frmPaint`, respectively. Also, change its `AutoRedraw` property to `True`. Then save the form and project as Paint.frm and Paint.vbp.

Now click on the form to bring up the Code window and find the `Form_MouseDown()` event. When you do, the following code skeleton will appear in the Code window:

```
Private Sub Form_MouseDown(Button As Integer, Shift As Integer, X As Single, Y As Single)

End Sub
```

A few of the `MouseDown` arguments that are passed to this procedure will probably be new to you: `Button`, `Shift`, `X`, and `Y`. The `Button` and `Shift` arguments pass the mouse button and keyboard shift state information, and the `X` and `Y` arguments report the position of the mouse cursor. The application can make use of that information by reporting the cursor's position when the user presses a mouse button. To do that, create two new text boxes, `txtTest1` and `txtTest2`. Put `txtTest1` to the left of the form and `txtTest2` to the right. The mouse position can be transferred to the text boxes using the `X` and `Y` arguments in the `MouseDown` event:

```
Private Sub Form_MouseDown(Button As Integer, Shift As Integer, X As Single, Y As Single)
    txtTest1.Text = Str(X)
    txtTest2.Text = Str(Y)
End Sub
```

Run the program and press a mouse button. The `MouseDown` event will occur when any mouse button is pressed. When you do click the mouse button, the cursor's position is reported in twips in the two text boxes. This is how an application directly reads information about the mouse cursor's position.

Now look at the other two arguments passed to `MouseDown`: `Button` and `Shift`. Both of these arguments are integers. The `Button` argument describes which mouse button is pressed by encoding that information in its lowest three bits. If a picture were drawn of the bits, it would look something like Figure 10.1 (recall that an integer is two bytes, or 16 bits long).

Figure 10.1.
A pictorial representation of the `Button` *argument integer.*

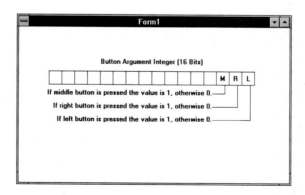

The `MouseMove` event procedure can be used to respond to an event caused by moving the mouse. The button argument for `MouseDown` and `MouseUp` differs from the button argument used for `MouseMove` (which will be discussed in the next section). For `MouseDown` and `MouseUp`, the button argument indicates exactly one button per event—left, middle, or right. For `MouseMove`, it indicates the current state of all buttons.

The `Button` argument can only take one of three values, shown in Table 10.1.

Table 10.1. Values for the **Button** argument (**MouseDown** and **MouseUp** events).

Constant	Button Value	Bit Field Value	Description
vbLeftButton	1	0000000000000001	Left button is pressed.
vbRightButton	2	0000000000000010	Right button is pressed.
vbMiddleButton	4	0000000000000100	Middle button is pressed.

Note in particular that the `Button` argument cannot be **0** because at least one button must be pushed to fire the `MouseDown` event. Put this information to use in your program. Add another text box, `txtTest3`, below the other two and toward the middle. This box will report which button causes the `MouseDown` event by using a `Select Case` statement.

```
Private Sub Form_MouseDown(Button As Integer, Shift As Integer, X As Single, Y As Single)
      txtTest1.Text = Str(X)
      txtTest2.Text = Str(Y)

      Select Case Button
      Case 1
      txtTest3.Text = "Left Button"
      Case 2
      txtTest3.Text = "Right Button"
      Case 4
      txtTest3.Text = "Middle Button"
End Select
```

Now when you run the program, it reports not only the position of the mouse cursor when the `MouseDown` event occurs, but also which button causes it. For example, if you press the left mouse button, you might see something like the window in Figure 10.2.

Figure 10.2.
The mouse information window.

Besides X, Y, and `Button`, the `Shift` argument also returns some very useful information. This integer indicates whether the Alt, Ctrl, or Shift keys have been pressed when the mouse button was clicked. This information is encoded in the last three bits of `Shift`, as shown in Figure 10.3.

Figure 10.3.
A pictorial representation of the Shift bit field.

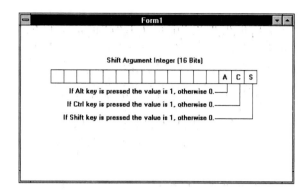

The Shift argument can take on three values, as shown in Table 10.2.

Table 10.2. Values for the **Shift** argument.

Constant	Shift Value	Bit Field Value	Description
vbShiftMask	1	0000000000000001	Shift key is pressed.
vbCtrlMask	2	0000000000000010	Ctrl key is pressed.
vbAltMask	4	0000000000000100	Alt key is pressed.

So far, you have seen that the MouseDown event reports four things: the X position of the mouse cursor, the Y position of the mouse cursor, which mouse button is pushed, and which key (Alt, Ctrl, or Shift) is pushed. MouseDown also has an important use in paint programs. It is usually used to start a drawing operation.

If the user wants to draw a line in a paint program, for example, she might press the left mouse button once to indicate where the line will begin, drag the mouse to the other end of the line, and then release the button. She expects the program to draw a line between the two locations. In Visual Basic terms, those steps can be translated like this: save the point where the MouseDown event occurs, which can be called the Anchor point (AnchorX, AnchorY); set the current graphics position to that same point; and then perform the drawing operation when the mouse button is released. In other words, when the user presses a mouse button, the program records that position. When the user releases it, the application draws a line, a box, or whatever figure is required.

To get going on this, remove the three text boxes—txtTest1, txtTest2, and txtTest3—from the form. Change the Form_MouseDown() event to the following:

```
Private Sub Form_MouseDown(Button As Integer, Shift As Integer, X As Single,
➥Y As Single)
     If Button = 1 Then   'Left button pressed
     AnchorX = X
     AnchorY = Y
     CurrentX = X
     CurrentY = Y
     End If
End Sub
```

The variables AnchorX and AnchorY should be made into public variables, so that any routine in the application can tell where the MouseDown event occurs. This process is useful if the program is supposed to draw a line from the anchor point to the current location when the mouse button is released. Insert a module into the Paint project and change its Name property to Paint. Then save the module as Paint.bas. Declare AnchorX and AnchorY there, as follows:

```
Public AnchorX As Integer
Public AnchorY As Integer
```

Now the anchor point can be accessed from any part of the application.

You might wonder why these variables have been declared as integers instead of Single, like the Button arguments X and Y. Because AnchorX and AnchorY are equated to X and Y in the MouseDown event, it would seem logical to declare them as Single. There are a few reasons for this. First, an integer takes up less space. Also, there is no need to worry about using the different variable types—integer and single. They will automatically translate when one encounters another.

It's time to put this to work and start drawing!

MouseMove Events

One capability of a paint program should be to draw continuously when the user moves the mouse cursor. The user should be able to press the mouse button and drag the mouse to create a freehand drawing by leaving a trail of pixels. To do that, the application needs to know where the mouse cursor is at any particular time. That can be accomplished using the MouseMove event. Every time the mouse is moved across a form or selected controls (file list boxes, labels, list boxes, or picture boxes), a MouseMove event is generated. MouseMove events are not usually generated for each pixel the mouse moves over. Instead, Windows generates only a certain number of these events per second. Still, that will be good enough for the paint application.

The Code window template for the MouseMove event looks like this:

```
Private Sub Form_MouseMove(Button As Integer, Shift As Integer, X As Single,
➥Y As Single)

End Sub
```

Just like the MouseDown event, the MouseMove event uses Button, Shift, X, and Y arguments. The Button argument in a MouseMove event reports the complete state of the mouse buttons. It can report whether more than one button is being pressed. The values that the Button argument can report are shown in Table 10.3.

Table 10.3. Values for the MouseMove Button argument.

Constant	Shift Value	Bit Field Value	Description
vbLeftButton	1	0000000000000001	Left button is pressed.
vbRightButton	2	0000000000000010	Right button is pressed.
vbLeftButton + vbRightButton	3	0000000000000011	Left and Right buttons pressed.
vbMiddleButton	4	0000000000000100	Middle button is pressed.
vbLeftButton + vbMiddleButton	5	0000000000000101	Left and middle buttons pressed.
vbMiddleButton + vbRightButton	6	0000000000000110	Middle and right buttons pressed.
vbLeftButton + vbMiddleButton + vbRightButton	7	0000000000000111	All three buttons pressed.

When the user presses the left mouse button, the anchor point (AnchorX, AnchorY) is set and that same location is set as the current graphics location (CurrentX, CurrentY). Next, the user keeps the mouse button depressed and drags the mouse to a new location. As the user drags the mouse, the application should draw on the screen, following the mouse cursor's movements. To put that into code, bring the Form_MouseMove() event up in the Code window. Then enter the following code:

```
Private Sub Form_MouseMove(Button As Integer, Shift As Integer, X As Single,
➥Y As Single)
      If Button = 1 Then       'Left Button Is pressed
      :
      End If
End Sub
```

Now add the code that will draw on the form as the mouse cursor moves. When this procedure is entered, the user has already moved from the original MouseDown location. Because the graphics position is set to that original location, you only need to draw from the graphics position to the current position. Do that using the Line method:

```
Private Sub Form_MouseMove(Button As Integer, Shift As Integer, X As Single,
➥Y As Single)
      If Button = 1 Then       'Left Button Is pressed
      Line -(X, Y)
      End If
End Sub
```

The entire code for the project so far should look like the following. (Remember that `AnchorX` and `AnchorY` are publicly declared in Paint.bas.)

```
Option Explicit

Private Sub Form_MouseDown(Button As Integer, Shift As Integer, X As Single,
➥Y As Single)
     If Button = 1 Then  'Left button pressed
     AnchorX = X
     AnchorY = Y
     CurrentX = X
     CurrentY = Y
     End If
End Sub

Private Sub Form_MouseMove(Button As Integer, Shift As Integer, X As Single,
➥Y As Single)
     If Button = 1 Then       'Left Button Is pressed
     Line -(X, Y)
     End If
End Sub
```

Paint programs are expected to draw all sorts of objects such as lines and rectangles. For these items, the position where the mouse button is released needs to be determined.

MouseUp Events

To draw a line, the user moves the mouse cursor to where she wants to start the line (the anchor point), presses the left mouse button, drags the mouse to another end point, and then releases the button to complete the line. The anchor point, (`AnchorX,AnchorY`), is already set, so when the user presses the left mouse button down, that information is stored. Now the code needs to be written that will report where the mouse button is released. That can be accomplished using the `MouseUp` event. The `MouseUp` code template looks like this:

```
Private Sub Form_MouseUp(Button As Integer, Shift As Integer, X As Single,
➥Y As Single)

End Sub
```

In the procedure, the application should check whether the mouse button was released and, if so, draw the line from (`AnchorX,AnchorY`) to the current position (`X,Y`). That code would look like this:

```
Private Sub Form_MouseUp(Button As Integer, Shift As Integer, X As Single,
➥Y As Single)
     If Button = 1 Then       'Checking to see if button released
                              'is the left button
     Line (AnchorX, AnchorY)-(X, Y)
     End If
End Sub
```

This creates a problem, however. Although the line is drawn, the code is still drawing over all the intermediate positions with the `MouseMove` procedure:

```
Private Sub Form_MouseMove(Button As Integer, Shift As Integer, X As Single,
➥Y As Single)
    If Button = 1 Then      'Left Button Is pressed
    Line -(X, Y)
    End If
End Sub
```

In other words, the application is drawing freehand and drawing lines at the same time. Usually, paint applications solve this problem by letting the user select only one drawing tool at a time. You can do the same thing by setting up a toolbox of command buttons as shown in Figure 10.4. These buttons correspond to the painting operations supported by the application: Draw, Line, Box, Circle, Text, and Clear All.

Figure 10.4.
The Paint application template with buttons.

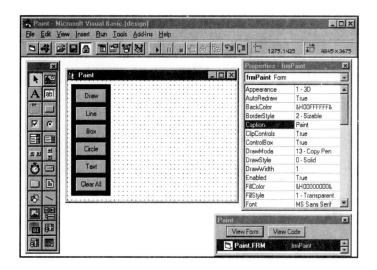

Use Figure 10.4 to position the command buttons on your template. Also, draw a rectangle around the buttons, using the Shape tool to group them and separate them from the drawing area. Use the following table to set the buttons' properties.

Object	Property	Setting
Form	AutoRedraw	True
	BackColor	White
	BorderStyle	2-Sizable
	Caption	Paint
	Name	frmPaint

continues

Object	Property	Setting
Command Button	Caption	Draw
	Name	cmdDraw
Command Button	Caption	Line
	Name	cmdLine
Command Button	Caption	Box
	Name	cmdBox
Command Button	Caption	Circle
	Name	cmdCircle
Command Button	Caption	Text
	Name	cmdText
Command Button	Caption	Clear
	Name	cmdClear
Shape	BackColor	Dark Blue
	BackStyle	1-Opaque
	BorderWidth	2
	BorderColor	Dark Blue
	Name	shpRectangle

When you are finished adding and placing controls, lock them on the form by using either the Lock Controls button on the toolbar or the pop-up menu.

Paint applications often have a different mouse cursor (typically a crosshair) in the drawing area than the one used to select the tools from the toolbox (an arrow). You can do that here, too. Forms and most controls have a `MousePointer` property that enables the programmer to specify the mouse cursor style as it passes over that form or control. You can change the cursor to any of those shown in Table 10.4 by using the Properties window.

Table 10.4. The cursor styles available for the **MousePointer** property.

Setting	Description
0	Shape determined by the object (default)
1	Arrow
2	Cross (crosshair pointer)
3	I-Beam
4	Icon (small square within a square)

Setting	Description
5	Size (four-pointed arrow pointing north, south, east, and west)
6	Size NE SW (double arrow pointing northeast and southwest)
7	Size N S (double arrow pointing north and south)
8	Size NW SE (double arrow pointing northwest and southeast)
9	Size W E (double arrow pointing west and east)
10	Up Arrow
11	Hourglass (wait)
12	No Drop
13	Custom icon specified by the MouseIcon property

Change the form's mouse cursor to a cross, for example, by using the Properties window. Select frmPaint, and then scroll down the Properties window until you find MousePointer. Select that property, and then press the Property button that appears to the right of the Settings box. Move down the list of cursor styles until you find 2-Cross and select it.

The buttons in the toolbox will use the same cursor: an arrow. Change each command button's MousePointer property to 1-Arrow. Now you are set. When the application is running, the cursor will switch between the arrow and cross depending upon its position on the Paint window.

You can make one of the command buttons, cmdClear, active immediately. This button simply clears the drawing area. Because that's done with the Cls statement, just add this line to the cmdClear_Click() event:

```
Private Sub cmdClear_Click()
      Cls
End Sub
```

In addition, you can have each button set a flag to indicate to the rest of the application which drawing tool is in use. A MouseUp event means something different if the user is drawing lines or circles. Because these flags should be public, they should be added to the module, Paint.bas, below the AnchorX and AnchorY variable declarations.

```
Option Explicit

Public AnchorX As Integer
Public AnchorY As Integer
Public DrawFlag As Boolean
Public LineFlag As Boolean
Public BoxFlag As Boolean
Public CircleFlag As Boolean
Public TextFlag As Boolean
```

There are now two kinds of data available to any part of the program: the anchor point (AnchorX, AnchorY), and a set of flags that tell which drawing tool is active. To set the flags, you can make each button in the toolbox set the corresponding flag while the rest are reset. That way, the drawing operation in use is available to the entire application. This lets you divide the code into smaller event procedures rather than handling everything in one giant procedure. Doing so makes your program modular, which is very important for larger applications. To set these flags, add the following call to a new procedure (FindTheFlag) to each command button's Click event. (You will write FindTheFlag shortly.)

```
Private Sub cmdDraw_Click()
        FindTheFlag "DRAW"
End Sub

Private Sub cmdLine_Click()
        FindTheFlag "LINE"
End Sub

Private Sub cmdBox_Click()
        FindTheFlag "BOX"
End Sub

Private Sub cmdCircle_Click()
        FindTheFlag "CIRCLE"
End Sub

Private Sub cmdText_Click()
        FindTheFlag "TEXT"
End Sub
```

Now move to the module Paint.bas, and add the following procedure in that Code window below the publicly declared variables (add the public subroutine FindTheFlag by selecting Procedure from the Visual Basic Insert menu):

```
Option Explicit

Public AnchorX As Integer
Public AnchorY As Integer
Public DrawFlag As Boolean
Public LineFlag As Boolean
Public BoxFlag As Boolean
Public CircleFlag As Boolean
Public TextFlag As Boolean

Public Sub FindTheFlag(Which As String)

        Which = UCase$(Which)

        DrawFlag = False
        LineFlag = False
        BoxFlag = False
        CircleFlag = False
        TextFlag = False

        Select Case Which
        Case "DRAW"
        DrawFlag = True
```

```
         Case "LINE"
         LineFlag = True

         Case "BOX"
         BoxFlag = True

         Case "CIRCLE"
         CircleFlag = True

         Case "TEXT"
         TextFlag = True

         Case Else
         MsgBox "We goofed here, Frodo!"

         End Select

End Sub
```

You could have added the code that sets the flags in each command button's Click event instead of calling a public procedure, but that would defeat the idea of modularity. If you were to return to the code at some later date and make changes, the flag-changing code is contained in one procedure, not five Click events.

The buttons are done now and the toolbox is finished. The only thing that remains is to use the flags with the new mouse events. From now on, the application can just check the public variables DrawFlag, LineFlag, BoxFlag, CircleFlag, and TextFlag to find out which tool is active. To check whether DrawFlag is True in the MouseMove event, add the following:

```
Private Sub Form_MouseMove(Button As Integer, Shift As Integer, X As Single,
➥Y As Single)
         If Button = 1 Then         'Left Button Is pressed

         If DrawFlag Then
         Line -(X, Y)
         End If

         :

         End If
End Sub
```

If the DrawFlag is active, the cursor will draw a freehand line.

This code solves the problem of drawing lines and drawing freehand at the same time. Now, if the user selects the Line tool, she can tack down one end of the line by pressing the mouse button, and then move to the other end and release it to create the line.

Paint programs usually do more than this, though. Normally, they display the line after one end has been tacked down at the anchor point, giving the impression of stretching the line into shape. That line becomes permanent when the mouse button is released. You can do that here, too, by checking whether the LineFlag is True in the MouseMove event like this:

```
Private Sub Form_MouseMove(Button As Integer, Shift As Integer, X As Single,
➥Y As Single)
        If Button = 1 Then          'Left Button Is pressed

        If DrawFlag Then
        Line -(X, Y)
        End If

        If LineFlag Then
        :
        End If

        End If
End Sub
```

The way to create the illusion of stretching or dragging a graphic object is to use the Xor Pen. To use that pen, the ForeColor and DrawMode properties have to change. The ForeColor property is set equal to the BackColor. The DrawMode property is changed to 7 (the setting for the Xor Pen) as follows:

```
Private Sub Form_MouseMove(Button As Integer, Shift As Integer, X As Single,
➥Y As Single)
        Dim TempColor As Long
        Dim TempMode As Integer

        If Button = 1 Then          'Left Button Is pressed

        If DrawFlag Then
        Line -(X, Y)
        End If

        If LineFlag Then
        TempColor = ForeColor
        TempMode = DrawMode
        ForeColor = BackColor
        DrawMode = 7              'Xor mode

        :

        End If

        End If
End Sub
```

When the Xor Pen is used, the ForeColor is compared by the Xor operator to what is already on the screen. Because you want the line to show up as the user stretches it, you will want it to be a different color from the background. If the foreground color is made the same as the background color temporarily, using the Xor Pen displays black. Thus, you end up with a black line on the standard white foreground. To erase that line and restore the background, you only need to draw it on the screen again in the same place with the Xor Pen. In MouseMove, the plan is to erase the last line drawn by the Xor Pen from the anchor point to the mouse cursor and draw a new line from the anchor point to the new mouse cursor's position. Do that in the following way:

```
Private Sub Form_MouseMove(Button As Integer, Shift As Integer, X As Single,
➥Y As Single)
        Dim TempColor As Long
        Dim TempMode As Integer
```

```
        If Button = 1 Then        'Left Button Is pressed

        If DrawFlag Then
        Line -(X, Y)
        End If

        If LineFlag Then
        TempColor = ForeColor
        TempMode = DrawMode
        ForeColor = BackColor
        DrawMode = 7        'Xor mode
        Line (AnchorX, AnchorY)-(CurrentX, CurrentY)
        Line (AnchorX, AnchorY)-(X, Y)

        :

        End If

        End If
End Sub
```

To finish the MouseMove event, replace the original values in the ForeColor and DrawMode properties like this:

```
Private Sub Form_MouseMove(Button As Integer, Shift As Integer, X As Single,
➡Y As Single)
        Dim TempColor As Long
        Dim TempMode As Integer

        If Button = 1 Then        'Left Button Is pressed

        If DrawFlag Then
        Line -(X, Y)
        End If

        If LineFlag Then
        TempColor = ForeColor
        TempMode = DrawMode
        ForeColor = BackColor
        DrawMode = 7          'Xor mode
        Line (AnchorX, AnchorY)-(CurrentX, CurrentY)
        Line (AnchorX, AnchorY)-(X, Y)
        ForeColor = TempColor
        DrawMode = TempMode
        End If

        End If
End Sub
```

That's it! Now the user can tack down one end of a line by pressing the left mouse button, move the mouse around while stretching a line from that point, and then release the mouse button to make the line permanent. Note that you also have to update the other event procedures to take the new flags into account. The MouseDown event is not going to change because it only sets the anchor point and the current graphics location. The MouseUp event needs to be updated, though, so that it draws lines only if LineFlag is True. That can be accomplished using the following code:

```
Private Sub Form_MouseUp(Button As Integer, Shift As Integer, X As Single,
➥Y As Single)
        If Button = 1 Then        'Checking to see if button released
                                  'is the left button

        If LineFlag Then
        Line (AnchorX, AnchorY)-(X, Y)
        End If
        End If
End Sub
```

The lines and freehand drawing components of the Paint application are now complete. All the code so far appears in Table 10.5, Listing 10.1, and Listing 10.2. You have made a good deal of progress. You set up a Paint program that lets the user draw freehand or create lines. With this version of the Paint program you should be able to make artwork similar to Figure 10.5. As you know, however, it is as easy to draw rectangles or boxes as it is to draw lines, so that's the next part to add to the Paint application.

Figure 10.5.
The Paint application with the Draw and Line command buttons working.

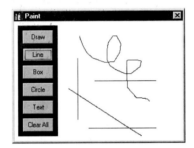

Table 10.5. Visual design of the **frmPaint** form.

Object	Property	Setting
Form	AutoRedraw	True
	BackColor	White
	BorderStyle	2-Sizable
	Caption	Paint
	MousePointer	2-Cross
	Name	frmPaint
Command Button	Caption	Draw
	MousePointer	1-Arrow
	Name	cmdDraw
Command Button	Caption	Line
	MousePointer	1-Arrow
	Name	cmdLine

Object	Property	Setting	
Command Button	Caption	Box	
	MousePointer	1-Arrow	
	Name	cmdBox	
Command Button	Caption	Circle	
	MousePointer	1-Arrow	
	Name	cmdCircle	
Command Button	Caption	Text	
	MousePointer	1-Arrow	
	Name	cmdText	
Command Button	Caption	Clear	
	MousePointer	1-Arrow	
	Name	cmdClear	
Shape	BackColor	Dark Blue	
	BackStyle	1-Opaque	
	BorderWidth	2	
	BorderColor	Dark Blue	
	Name	shpRectangle	

Listing 10.1. The code of the Paint.bas module.

```
Option Explicit

Public AnchorX As Integer
Public AnchorY As Integer
Public DrawFlag As Boolean
Public LineFlag As Boolean
Public BoxFlag As Boolean
Public CircleFlag As Boolean
Public TextFlag As Boolean

Public Sub FindTheFlag(Which As String)

     Which = UCase$(Which)

     DrawFlag = False
     LineFlag = False
     BoxFlag = False
     CircleFlag = False
     TextFlag = False
```

continues

Listing 10.1. continued

```
        Select Case Which
                Case "DRAW"
                        DrawFlag = True

                Case "LINE"
                        LineFlag = True

                Case "BOX"
                        BoxFlag = True

                Case "CIRCLE"
                        CircleFlag = True

                Case "TEXT"
                        TextFlag = True

                Case Else
                        MsgBox "We goofed here, Frodo!"

        End Select

End Sub
```

Listing 10.2. The code of the `frmPaint` form.

```
Option Explicit

Private Sub cmdBox_Click()
        FindTheFlag "BOX"
End Sub

Private Sub cmdCircle_Click()
        FindTheFlag "CIRCLE"
End Sub

Private Sub cmdClear_Click()
        Cls
End Sub

Private Sub cmdDraw_Click()
        FindTheFlag "DRAW"
End Sub

Private Sub cmdLine_Click()
        FindTheFlag "LINE"
End Sub

Private Sub cmdText_Click()
        FindTheFlag "TEXT"
End Sub
```

```
Private Sub Form_MouseDown(Button As Integer, Shift As Integer, X As Single,
➥Y As Single)
      If Button = 1 Then   'Left button pressed
              AnchorX = X
              AnchorY = Y
              CurrentX = X
              CurrentY = Y
      End If
End Sub

Private Sub Form_MouseMove(Button As Integer, Shift As Integer, X As Single,
➥Y As Single)
      Dim TempColor As Long
      Dim TempMode As Integer

      If Button = 1 Then       'Left Button Is pressed

            If DrawFlag Then
                  Line -(X, Y)
            End If

            If LineFlag Then
                  TempColor = ForeColor
                  TempMode = DrawMode
                  ForeColor = BackColor
                  DrawMode = 7          'Xor mode
                  Line (AnchorX, AnchorY)-(CurrentX, CurrentY)
                  Line (AnchorX, AnchorY)-(X, Y)
                  ForeColor = TempColor
                  DrawMode = TempMode
            End If

      End If
End Sub

Private Sub Form_MouseUp(Button As Integer, Shift As Integer, X As Single,
➥Y As Single)
      If Button = 1 Then       'Checking to see if button released
                               'is the left button
            If LineFlag Then
                  Line (AnchorX, AnchorY)-(X, Y)
            End If
      End If
End Sub
```

Drawing Boxes

You can draw boxes by using the Line method, as long as you specify the B parameter. It will be simple, in fact, to add this capability to your code. Wherever lines were drawn before, the same thing can be used for boxes after BoxFlag is tested and found to be True. The two places where the Line method has already been used are the MouseMove and MouseUp events, as follows:

```
Private Sub Form_MouseMove(Button As Integer, Shift As Integer, X As Single,
➥Y As Single)
     Dim TempColor As Long
     Dim TempMode As Integer

     If Button = 1 Then        'Left Button Is pressed

          If DrawFlag Then
                Line -(X, Y)
          End If

          If LineFlag Then
                TempColor = ForeColor
                TempMode = DrawMode
                ForeColor = BackColor
                DrawMode = 7         'Xor mode
                Line (AnchorX, AnchorY)-(CurrentX, CurrentY)
                Line (AnchorX, AnchorY)-(X, Y)
                ForeColor = TempColor
                DrawMode = TempMode
          End If

     End If
End Sub

Private Sub Form_MouseUp(Button As Integer, Shift As Integer, X As Single,
➥Y As Single)
     If Button = 1 Then     'Checking to see if button released
                            'is the left button
          If LineFlag Then
                Line (AnchorX, AnchorY)-(X, Y)
          End If
     End If
End Sub
```

All you need to do is repeat the line code for boxes by using the **B** parameter and checking for the
BoxFlag. Add that code like this:

```
Private Sub Form_MouseMove(Button As Integer, Shift As Integer, X As Single,
➥Y As Single)
     Dim TempColor As Long
          Dim TempMode As Integer

     If Button = 1 Then        'Left Button Is pressed

          If DrawFlag Then
                Line -(X, Y)
          End If

          If LineFlag Then
                TempColor = ForeColor
                TempMode = DrawMode
                ForeColor = BackColor
                DrawMode = 7         'Xor mode
                Line (AnchorX, AnchorY)-(CurrentX, CurrentY)
                Line (AnchorX, AnchorY)-(X, Y)
                ForeColor = TempColor
                DrawMode = TempMode
          End If
```

```
        If BoxFlag Then
                TempColor = ForeColor
                TempMode = DrawMode
                ForeColor = BackColor
                DrawMode = 7     'Xor mode
                Line (AnchorX, AnchorY)-(CurrentX, CurrentY), , B
                Line (AnchorX, AnchorY)-(X, Y), , B
                ForeColor = TempColor
                DrawMode = TempMode
        End If

     End If
End Sub

Private Sub Form_MouseUp(Button As Integer, Shift As Integer, X As Single,
➥Y As Single)
        If Button = 1 Then      'Checking to see if button released
                                'is the left button

            If LineFlag Then
                Line (AnchorX, AnchorY)-(X, Y)
            End If

            If BoxFlag Then
                Line (AnchorX, AnchorY)-(X, Y), , B
            End If

        End If
End Sub
```

That's the only change you have to make. Now your Paint program can draw freehand, lines, and boxes. There are some other Visual Basic drawing routines that you can make use of, though. How about adding circles to the application?

"Stretching" Graphics Figures on the Screen

You could use this code to "stretch" rectangles on the screen. In fact, you could make the rectangle dotted as it is stretched by setting its DrawStyle to 1, and then resetting it back to its original value when the user is finished. You could even let users select portions of the drawing in this way. They could stretch a rectangle into place, and then the program would read all the enclosed pixels using the Point() method. Finally, those pixels could be transferred to other locations by using PSet().

Drawing Circles

As you discovered in the last chapter, drawing circles with the Circle method is not very difficult. In the Paint application, you can use the anchor point as the center of the circle and draw the circle out to the mouse pointer's location when the user releases the button. To begin, check whether the CircleFlag is set to True in the MouseUp event procedure:

```
Private Sub Form_MouseUp(Button As Integer, Shift As Integer, X As Single,
➥Y As Single)
        If Button = 1 Then        'Checking to see if button released
                                   'is the left button

                If LineFlag Then
                        Line (AnchorX, AnchorY)-(X, Y)
                End If

                If BoxFlag Then
                        Line (AnchorX, AnchorY)-(X, Y), , B
                End If

                If CircleFlag Then
                        :
                End If

        End If
End Sub
```

Add the code that will draw the circle, using (AnchorX,AnchorY) as the center point and the distance from (AnchorX,AnchorY) to the current location, (X,Y), as the radius.

```
Private Sub Form_MouseUp(Button As Integer, Shift As Integer, X As Single,
➥Y As Single)
        If Button = 1 Then        'Checking to see if button released
                                   'is the left button

                If LineFlag Then
                        Line (AnchorX, AnchorY)-(X, Y)
                End If

                If BoxFlag Then
                        Line (AnchorX, AnchorY)-(X, Y), , B
                End If

                If CircleFlag Then
                        Radius = Sqr((AnchorX - X) ^ 2 + (AnchorY - Y) ^ 2)
                        :
                End If

        End If
End Sub
```

Next, draw the circle by using (AnchorX,AnchorY) as the center point and the distance from (AnchorX,AnchorY) to the current location, (X,Y), as the radius.

```
Private Sub Form_MouseUp(Button As Integer, Shift As Integer, X As Single,
➥Y As Single)
        If Button = 1 Then        'Checking to see if button released
                                   'is the left button

                If LineFlag Then
                        Line (AnchorX, AnchorY)-(X, Y)
                End If
```

```
        If BoxFlag Then
                Line (AnchorX, AnchorY)-(X, Y), , B
        End If

        If CircleFlag Then
                Radius = Sqr((AnchorX - X) ^ 2 + (AnchorY - Y) ^ 2)
                Circle (AnchorX, AnchorY), Radius
        End If

    End If
End Sub
```

The Sqr function is being used here to find square roots, and the ^ operator is used to square the quantities. The variable Radius needs to be declared. Move to the Paint.bas Code window and declare the new variable there, at the end of the variable declarations that already exist:

```
Public AnchorX As Integer
Public AnchorY As Integer
Public DrawFlag As Boolean
Public LineFlag As Boolean
Public BoxFlag As Boolean
Public CircleFlag As Boolean
Public TextFlag As Boolean
Public Radius As Single
```

The result of all this is that the Paint program will now draw circles, as in Figure 10.6.

Figure 10.6.
The Paint application with the Box and Circle command buttons operational.

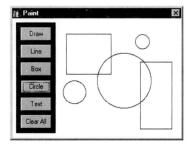

As with the line and box drawing, the application can draw the intermediate circles as the user drags the mouse. To do that, you have to modify the MouseMove event. The code to add should check whether CircleFlag is set. Also, as with the previous drawing tools, the foreground color and current drawing mode need to be saved while the circles are drawn, and then restored when the user is finished.

```
Private Sub Form_MouseMove(Button As Integer, Shift As Integer, X As Single,
➡Y As Single)
        Dim TempColor As Long
        Dim TempMode As Integer

    If Button = 1 Then        'Left Button Is pressed

            If DrawFlag Then
                    Line -(X, Y)
            End If
```

```
If LineFlag Then
        TempColor = ForeColor
        TempMode = DrawMode
        ForeColor = BackColor
        DrawMode = 7           'Xor mode
        Line (AnchorX, AnchorY)-(CurrentX, CurrentY)
        Line (AnchorX, AnchorY)-(X, Y)
        ForeColor = TempColor
        DrawMode = TempMode
End If

If BoxFlag Then
        TempColor = ForeColor
        TempMode = DrawMode
        ForeColor = BackColor
        DrawMode = 7     'Xor mode
        Line (AnchorX, AnchorY)-(CurrentX, CurrentY), , B
        Line (AnchorX, AnchorY)-(X, Y), , B
        ForeColor = TempColor
        DrawMode = TempMode
End If

If CircleFlag Then
        TempColor = ForeColor
        TempMode = DrawMode
        ForeColor = BackColor


                :


        ForeColor = TempColor
        DrawMode = TempMode
End If

    End If
End Sub
```

As before, giving the appearance of stretching a graphics figure is really a matter of erasing the old figure and drawing the new one. To do that, use the Xor Pen and draw the old circle like this:

```
Private Sub Form_MouseMove(Button As Integer, Shift As Integer, X As Single,
➥Y As Single)
    Dim TempColor As Long
    Dim TempMode As Integer

    If Button = 1 Then       'Left Button Is pressed

            If DrawFlag Then
                    Line -(X, Y)
            End If

            If LineFlag Then
                    TempColor = ForeColor
                    TempMode = DrawMode
                    ForeColor = BackColor
                    DrawMode = 7         'Xor mode
                    Line (AnchorX, AnchorY)-(CurrentX, CurrentY)
                    Line (AnchorX, AnchorY)-(X, Y)
                    ForeColor = TempColor
                    DrawMode = TempMode
            End If
```

```
            If BoxFlag Then
                    TempColor = ForeColor
                    TempMode = DrawMode
                    ForeColor = BackColor
                    DrawMode = 7     'Xor mode
                    Line (AnchorX, AnchorY)-(CurrentX, CurrentY), , B
                    Line (AnchorX, AnchorY)-(X, Y), , B
                    ForeColor = TempColor
                    DrawMode = TempMode
            End If

            If CircleFlag Then
                    TempColor = ForeColor
                    TempMode = DrawMode
            ForeColor = BackColor
                    DrawMode = 7      'Xor mode
                    Radius = Sqr((AnchorX - CurrentX) ^ 2 +
                    ➥(AnchorY - CurrentY) ^ 2)
            Circle (AnchorX, AnchorY), Radius


                      :

                    ForeColor = TempColor
                    DrawMode = TempMode
            End If

      End If
End Sub
```

Then the new circle is drawn and the mouse cursor position is stored in (CurrentX, CurrentY) for the next time. Those final lines of code and the entire MouseMove event procedure appears as follows:

```
Private Sub Form_MouseMove(Button As Integer, Shift As Integer, X As Single,
➥Y As Single)
      Dim TempColor As Long
      Dim TempMode As Integer

      If Button = 1 Then        'Left Button Is pressed

            If DrawFlag Then
                    Line -(X, Y)
            End If

            If LineFlag Then
                    TempColor = ForeColor
                    TempMode = DrawMode
                    ForeColor = BackColor
                    DrawMode = 7            'Xor mode
                    Line (AnchorX, AnchorY)-(CurrentX, CurrentY)
                    Line (AnchorX, AnchorY)-(X, Y)
                    ForeColor = TempColor
                    DrawMode = TempMode
            End If

            If BoxFlag Then
                    TempColor = ForeColor
                    TempMode = DrawMode
                    ForeColor = BackColor
```

```
                        DrawMode = 7      'Xor mode
                        Line (AnchorX, AnchorY)-(CurrentX, CurrentY), , B
                        Line (AnchorX, AnchorY)-(X, Y), , B
                        ForeColor = TempColor
                        DrawMode = TempMode
                End If

                If CircleFlag Then
                        TempColor = ForeColor
                        TempMode = DrawMode
                        ForeColor = BackColor
                        DrawMode = 7      'Xor mode
                        Radius = Sqr((AnchorX - CurrentX) ^ 2 +
                        ➥(AnchorY - CurrentY) ^ 2)
                        Circle (AnchorX, AnchorY), Radius
                        Radius = Sqr((AnchorX - X) ^ 2 + (AnchorY - Y) ^ 2)
                        Circle (AnchorX, AnchorY), Radius
                        CurrentX = X
                        CurrentY = Y
                        ForeColor = TempColor
                        DrawMode = TempMode
                End If

        End If
End Sub
```

The last of the tools is Text. The Text tool will let the user draw text directly in the graphics area.

Drawing Text

When the user clicks the Text button in the toolbox, that button gets the focus. Until another tool from the toolbox is selected, each key that the user strikes can be read and placed in code in the `cmdText_KeyPress()` event. That code skeleton looks like this:

```
Private Sub cmdText_KeyPress(KeyAscii As Integer)

End Sub
```

Because the text is printed at the current graphics position and the user sets that position with a `MouseDown` event, the application only has to complete these three steps:

1. Let the user select the Text tool.

2. Wait for the user to click somewhere in the graphics area.

3. Print whatever the user types.

A simple line of code will suffice here.

```
Private Sub cmdText_KeyPress(KeyAscii As Integer)
        Print Chr$(KeyAscii);
End Sub
```

That's all there is to it. Everything the user types is sent to the current Paint document as long as the Text button in the toolbox retains the focus. Now the Paint application toolbox is entirely functional, as you can see in Figure 10.7.

Figure 10.7.
The Paint application with all tools operational.

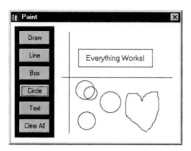

You could even add a text cursor—an insertion point—to this program with a little more work. The entire program, as it stands, appears in Listing 10.3 and Listing 10.4.

Listing 10.3. The Paint.bas of the Paint application with the Toolbox completed.

```
Option Explicit

Public AnchorX As Integer
Public AnchorY As Integer
Public DrawFlag As Boolean
Public LineFlag As Boolean
Public BoxFlag As Boolean
Public CircleFlag As Boolean
Public TextFlag As Boolean
Public Radius As Single

Public Sub FindTheFlag(Which As String)

        Which = UCase$(Which)

        DrawFlag = False
        LineFlag = False
        BoxFlag = False
        CircleFlag = False
        TextFlag = False

        Select Case Which
                Case "DRAW"
                        DrawFlag = True

                Case "LINE"
                        LineFlag = True

                Case "BOX"
                        BoxFlag = True

                Case "CIRCLE"
                        CircleFlag = True

                Case "TEXT"
                        TextFlag = True
```

continues

Listing 10.3. **continued**

```
            Case Else
                    MsgBox "We goofed here, Frodo!"

        End Select

End Sub
```

Listing 10.4. **The code for frmPaint of the Paint application.**

```
Option Explicit

Private Sub cmdBox_Click()
      FindTheFlag "BOX"
End Sub

Private Sub cmdCircle_Click()
      FindTheFlag "CIRCLE"
End Sub

Private Sub cmdClear_Click()
      Cls
End Sub

Private Sub cmdDraw_Click()
      FindTheFlag "DRAW"
End Sub

Private Sub cmdLine_Click()
      FindTheFlag "LINE"
End Sub

Private Sub cmdText_Click()
      FindTheFlag "TEXT"
End Sub

Private Sub cmdText_KeyPress(KeyAscii As Integer)
      Print Chr$(KeyAscii);
End Sub

Private Sub Form_MouseDown(Button As Integer, Shift As Integer, X As Single,
➥Y As Single)
      If Button = 1 Then   'Left button pressed
              AnchorX = X
              AnchorY = Y
              CurrentX = X
              CurrentY = Y
      End If
End Sub

Private Sub Form_MouseMove(Button As Integer, Shift As Integer, X As Single,
➥Y As Single)
      Dim TempColor As Long
      Dim TempMode As Integer

      If Button = 1 Then       'Left Button Is pressed
```

```
        If DrawFlag Then
                Line -(X, Y)
        End If

        If LineFlag Then
                TempColor = ForeColor
                TempMode = DrawMode
                ForeColor = BackColor
                DrawMode = 7          'Xor mode
                Line (AnchorX, AnchorY)-(CurrentX, CurrentY)
                Line (AnchorX, AnchorY)-(X, Y)
                ForeColor = TempColor
                DrawMode = TempMode
        End If

        If BoxFlag Then
                TempColor = ForeColor
                TempMode = DrawMode
                ForeColor = BackColor
                DrawMode = 7    'Xor mode
                Line (AnchorX, AnchorY)-(CurrentX, CurrentY), , B
                Line (AnchorX, AnchorY)-(X, Y), , B
                ForeColor = TempColor
                DrawMode = TempMode
        End If

        If CircleFlag Then
                TempColor = ForeColor
                TempMode = DrawMode
                ForeColor = BackColor
                DrawMode = 7    'Xor mode
                Radius = Sqr((AnchorX - CurrentX) ^ 2 +
                ➡(AnchorY - CurrentY) ^ 2)
                Circle (AnchorX, AnchorY), Radius
                Radius = Sqr((AnchorX - X) ^ 2 + (AnchorY - Y) ^ 2)
                Circle (AnchorX, AnchorY), Radius
                CurrentX = X
                CurrentY = Y
                ForeColor = TempColor
                DrawMode = TempMode
        End If

     End If
End Sub

Private Sub Form_MouseUp(Button As Integer, Shift As Integer, X As Single,
➡Y As Single)
     If Button = 1 Then        'Checking to see if button released
                               'is the left button

        If LineFlag Then
                Line (AnchorX, AnchorY)-(X, Y)
        End If

        If BoxFlag Then
                Line (AnchorX, AnchorY)-(X, Y), , B
        End If
```

continues

Listing 10.4. **continued**

```
            If CircleFlag Then
                    Radius = Sqr((AnchorX - X) ^ 2 + (AnchorY - Y) ^ 2)
                    Circle (AnchorX, AnchorY), Radius
            End If


        End If
End Sub
```

Now that the toolbox is finished, the next step is to add a File menu that will let the user save an image to disk, open a file, print, and select drawing colors.

Saving the Paint Image on Disk

You need to add a file menu to the Paint application, so select `frmPaint` and bring up the Menu Editor.

Design a menu using the following table. When you are through, your Paint template should look like Figure 10.8.

Caption	Name	Indentation	Other Information
&File	mnuFile	0	(None)
&Save File…	mnuFileSave	1	Shortcut: Ctrl+S
&Load File…	mnuFileLoad	1	Shortcut: Ctrl+L
-	mnuSep1	1	(None)
E&xit	mnuFileExit	1	Shortcut: Ctrl+X

Figure 10.8.
The Paint template with a File menu added.

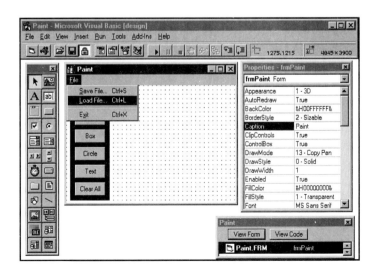

As always, the Exit item is very easy to complete. Just add the `End` statement to the code template as follows:

```
Private Sub mnuFileExit_Click()
     End
End Sub
```

Adding an Undo Item

You could even add an Undo item to the Paint application's menu by adding another form that is never shown. Whenever the user would choose a drawing tool, for example, a copy of the current picture would be transferred from `frmPaint` to the invisible form. Then if the user selected the Undo item, a copy of the picture from the invisible form would be transferred to `frmPaint`, restoring the image.

Now you should make the Save File... item active. Find the `mnuFileSave_Click()` event in the Code window:

```
Private Sub cmdFileSave_Click()

End Sub
```

When the user selects this item, the application should get the filename and then save the image. In fact, you have already developed two forms that deal with the issues of saving and loading files for you: `frmLoad` and `frmSave` from the Editor application. To save files, add the Save.frm file to the Paint application. After loading the file into your application, save it with a new name using the Save File As... item from the Visual Basic File menu. Rename the file PaintSave.frm. That way, Save.frm in the Editor application will not be overwritten.

After the user types the name of the file, the program should save the image using the name in `txtFileName`. The Paint application image can be saved using the `SavePicture` statement when the OK button is clicked.

The original code in the `frmSave` Code window appears as follows:

```
Option Explicit

Private Sub cmdCancel_Click()
     Unload cmdCancel.Parent
End Sub

Private Sub cmdOK_Click()

     On Error GoTo FileError

     Open txtFileName.Text For Output As #1        'Open file
     Print #1, frmNotePad.txtPadText.Text              'Write document
     Close #1                          'Close file

     Unload cmdOK.Parent
```

```
        Exit Sub

FileError:
        MsgBox "File Error", 48, "Editor"    'MsgBox for file error
        Resume Next

End Sub
```

In the Paint application, however, you want to use the `SavePicture` statement instead of the `Print` `#` statement. `SavePicture` saves a graphic from a form object, picture box control, or image control to a file. Its syntax works like this:

```
SavePicture picture, stringexpression
```

The `SavePicture` statement syntax uses these parts:

- *picture*—A picture or image property from which the graphics file is to be created.
- *stringexpression*—A filename of the graphics file to save.

You can use `SavePicture` in the `cmdOK_Click()` event as follows:

```
Private Sub cmdOK_Click()

        On Error GoTo FileError
            SavePicture frmPaint.Image, txtFileName.Text
        Unload cmdOK.Parent

        Exit Sub

FileError:
        MsgBox "File Error", 48, "Paint Program"    'MsgBox for file error
        Resume Next

End Sub
```

Note that the name in the error message also changed from `"Editor"` to `"Paint Program"`.

All that remains is to make the File menu's Save File… item active. You can do that by adding the following line of code to the `mnuFileSave_Click()` event:

```
Private Sub mnuFileSave_Click()
        frmSave.Show
End Sub
```

Now when a user decides to save her graphics work, she can click the Save File… item on the File menu and the Save File… dialog box will appear on the screen. The user then types a filename, which is read from the text box and then passed on to `SavePicture`. And that's it. Now you can open the graphics file that was just saved.

Reading the Image Back from the Disk

To read files from disk, you can use the frmLoad dialog box from the Editor application. Add that file, Load.frm, to the Paint application. Then save the form under a new name, PaintLoad.frm, using the Save File As... option from the Visual Basic File menu. Now double-click on the OK button in the Load Form... dialog box to bring up that button's Click procedure. The code originally written in that event appears as follows:

```
Private Sub cmdOK_Click()
      Dim TheFile As String

      On Error GoTo FileError

      If (Right(dirLook.Path, 1) = "\") Then
            TheFile = dirLook.Path + filFind.FileName

      Else
            TheFile = dirLook.Path + "\" + filFind.FileName

      End If

      Open TheFile For Input As #1
      frmNotePad.txtPadText.Text = Input(LOF(1), #1)        'Read File
      Close #1                      'Close File

      Unload cmdOK.Parent

      Exit Sub

FileError:
      MsgBox "File Error", 48, "Editor"    'MsgBox for file error
      Resume Next

End Sub
```

You might recall that the code, as written for the Editor application, spends a little time making sure that the pathname is correct; then it reads the file using the Input # statement.

In the Paint application, the code will be changed to read in a picture rather than a text file. In particular, the LoadPicture function will be used. LoadPicture loads a graphic into a form object, picture box control, or image control. Its syntax looks like this:

```
LoadPicture([stringexpression])
```

LoadPicture syntax uses one argument, *stringexpression*, which is the name of a graphics file to be loaded.

You have to assign the return value from `LoadPicture()` to the `Picture` property of an object—in this case, `frmPaint`. The code in `cmdOK_Click()` can be modified as follows:

```
Private Sub cmdOK_Click()
     Dim TheFile As String

     On Error GoTo FileError

     If (Right(dirLook.Path, 1) = "\") Then
           TheFile = dirLook.Path + filFind.FileName

     Else
           TheFile = dirLook.Path + "\" + filFind.FileName

     End If

     frmPaint.Picture = LoadPicture(TheFile)

     Unload cmdOK.Parent

     Exit Sub

FileError:
     MsgBox "File Error", 48, "Paint Program"    'MsgBox for file error
     Resume Next

End Sub
```

Again, notice that the name in the error message was changed from `"Editor"` to `"Paint Program"`.

Finally, to make this form appear on the screen when the user clicks the Load File... item on the File menu, the following line of code should be added to the `frmPaint mnuFileLoad_Click()` event:

```
Private Sub mnuFileLoad_Click()
     frmLoad.Show
End Sub
```

Now images created in the Paint application can be saved to disk and retrieved, as shown in Figure 10.9.

Figure 10.9.
*The Paint application with
the File menu completely
operational.*

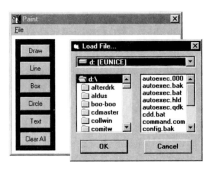

You can add more power to your application relatively easily. For example, you could add a control panel that would change the color used for drawing. That's the next topic of discussion.

A Little About the Graphics Image Format Generated by the Paint Application

The disk format created by the SavePicture statement is .bmp (bitmap). This format can be read by many other paint applications, such as Microsoft Paint that comes with Windows 95. This means that you could open a .bmp file created in Microsoft Paint in your Paint application and vice versa.

Changing the Drawing Color

In Chapter 7, you designed a Control Panel application, complete with a control panel that changed a number of main window properties, including its color. To do that, you used a number of scrollbars that could be manipulated by the user. It is easy to modify that form for use here. Then, a user of your Paint application can set the color she wants to draw with.

Load the file Panel.frm into the Paint project using the Add File... item from the Visual Basic File menu. Then change the file's name to PaintControl.frm by selecting the Save File As... option. The Control Panel should look like the one in Figure 10.10.

Figure 10.10.
The custom Control Panel, newly added to the Paint application.

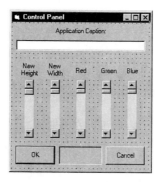

The Control Panel has a number of items that are not needed for the Paint program: scrollbars to change the main window's height and width, and a text box to change the main window's name. You can remove those controls, and then move the other controls around to fill up the box, as in Figure 10.11. In particular, notice that the label that displays the new color, lblNewColor, is enlarged. Also, the label whose caption reads Application Caption is changed to New Drawing Color.

Figure 10.11.
The Control Panel modified for the Paint application.

To recap, working down frmControlPanel from the top, the controls' properties should be set as follows:

Object	Property	Setting
Form	Caption	Control Panel
	MaxButton	False
	MinButton	False
	Name	frmControlPanel
Label	Alignment	2-Center
	Caption	New Drawing Color:
	Name	Label1
Label	BorderStyle	1-Fixed Single
	Caption	(None)
	Name	lblNewColor
Label	Alignment	2-Center
	Caption	Red
	Name	Label4
Scroll Bar	LargeChange	20
	Max	255
	Min	0
	Name	vsbNewRed
	SmallChange	10
Label	Alignment	2-Center
	Caption	Green
	Name	Label5

Object	Property	Setting
Scroll Bar	LargeChange	20
	Max	255
	Min	0
	Name	vsbNewGreen
	SmallChange	10
Label	Alignment	2-Center
	Caption	Blue
	Name	Label6
Scroll Bar	LargeChange	20
	Max	255
	Min	0
	Name	vsbNewBlue
	SmallChange	10
Command Button	Caption	OK
	Default	True
	Name	cmdOK
Command Button	Cancel	True
	Caption	Cancel
	Name	cmdCancel

On the Control Panel, there are scrollbars to change the color and a bordered label, lblNewColor, to show the new color that the user is selecting. After the drawing color is set, the user clicks OK to make it active. At that point, the new drawing color—the ForeColor property of frmPaint—should be set.

The code originally written for the cmdOK_Click() event of frmControlPanel appears as follows:

```
Private Sub cmdOK_Click()
      frmTestWindow.Caption = txtNewCaption.Text
      frmTestWindow.Height = vsbNewHeight.Value
      frmTestWindow.Width = vsbNewWidth.Value
      frmTestWindow.BackColor = RGB(vsbNewRed.Value, vsbNewGreen.Value,
      ➥vsbNewBlue.Value)
      frmControlPanel.lblNewColor.BackColor = frmTestWindow.BackColor
      frmControlPanel.Hide
End Sub
```

Modify that code to transfer the scrollbar's new color values to frmPaint.ForeColor, like this:

```
Private Sub cmdOK_Click()
    frmPaint.ForeColor = RGB(vsbNewRed.Value, vsbNewGreen.Value,
    ➡vsbNewBlue.Value)
    Unload cmdOK.Parent
End Sub
```

Also, make sure that any reference to `frmTestWindow` is removed from the Control Panel's `cmdCancel`
`Click` event, as follows:

```
Private Sub cmdCancel_Click()
    frmControlPanel.Hide
End Sub
```

The new Control Panel is all set. All that remains is to make it active when the user selects an item
from the File menu. Go back to `frmPaint` and open the Menu Editor. Move the highlight bar in the
large list box at the bottom to the last item, `E&xit`. Press the button labeled Insert. A new line appears above Exit. Add a new menu item captioned New Drawing Color…, and then add another
menu item, a separator bar. Set these two new items as follows:

Caption	Name	Indentation	Other Information
&New Drawing Color…	mnuFileColor	1	Shortcut: Ctrl+N
-	mnuSep2	1	(None)

The Menu Editor as it stands so far appears in Figure 10.12.

Figure 10.12.
*The Menu Editor dialog box,
showing the menu for
`frmPaint`.*

Close the Menu Editor and open the Code window by clicking on the menu item you just added:

```
Private Sub mnuFileColor_Click()

End Sub
```

Two things should happen here: The current drawing color (frmPaint's ForeColor property) should be loaded into lblNewColor on the Control Panel, and the Control Panel should appear on the screen. The following code takes care of that:

```
Private Sub mnuFileColor_Click()
        frmControlPanel.lblNewColor.BackColor = ForeColor
        frmControlPanel.Show
End Sub
```

Now the user can design multicolored graphics in your Paint application. Give it a try yourself. Select the New Drawing Color… item from the File menu. The Control Panel appears on the screen. Manipulate the scrollbars until you have a new drawing color you like, and then click OK. When you draw again, you will see that the drawing color has been switched to the new color you just selected. The Paint program as it stands with its save and load files dialog boxes and new color capabilities appears in Table 10.6 and Listing 10.5 through Listing 10.9.

Table 10.6. The menu design of the frmPaint form.

Caption	Name	Indentation	Other Information
&File	mnuFile	0	(None)
&Save File…	mnuFileSave	1	Shortcut:Ctrl+S
&Load File…	mnuFileLoad	1	Shortcut: Ctrl+L
-	mnuSep1	1	(None)
&New Drawing Color…	mnuFileColor	1	Shortcut: Ctrl+N
-	mnuSep2	1	(None)
E&xit	mnuFileExit	1	Shortcut: Ctrl+X

Listing 10.5. The code for paint.bas in the Paint application.

```
Option Explicit

Public AnchorX As Integer
Public AnchorY As Integer
Public DrawFlag As Boolean
Public LineFlag As Boolean
Public BoxFlag As Boolean
Public CircleFlag As Boolean
Public TextFlag As Boolean
Public Radius As Single
```

continues

Listing 10.5. continued

```
Public Sub FindTheFlag(Which As String)

        Which = UCase$(Which)

        DrawFlag = False
        LineFlag = False
        BoxFlag = False
        CircleFlag = False
        TextFlag = False

        Select Case Which
                Case "DRAW"
                        DrawFlag = True

                Case "LINE"
                        LineFlag = True

                Case "BOX"
                        BoxFlag = True

                Case "CIRCLE"
                        CircleFlag = True

                Case "TEXT"
                        TextFlag = True
                Case Else
                        MsgBox "We goofed here, Frodo!"

        End Select

End Sub
```

Listing 10.6. The code for the PaintLoad form of the Paint application.

```
Option Explicit

Private Sub cmdCancel_Click()
      Unload cmdCancel.Parent
End Sub

Private Sub cmdOK_Click()
      Dim TheFile As String

      On Error GoTo FileError

      If (Right(dirLook.Path, 1) = "\") Then
            TheFile = dirLook.Path + filFind.FileName

      Else
            TheFile = dirLook.Path + "\" + filFind.FileName

      End If

      frmPaint.Picture = LoadPicture(TheFile)
```

```
        Unload cmdOK.Parent

        Exit Sub

FileError:
        MsgBox "File Error", 48, "Paint Program"    'MsgBox for file error
        Resume Next

End Sub

Private Sub dirLook_Change()
        filFind.Path = dirLook.Path
End Sub

Private Sub drvChange_Change()
        dirLook.Path = drvChange.Drive
End Sub

Private Sub filFind_DblClick()
        cmdOK_Click
End Sub
```

Listing 10.7. **The code for the paintsave.frm form of the Paint application.**

```
Option Explicit

Private Sub cmdCancel_Click()
        Unload cmdCancel.Parent
End Sub

Private Sub cmdOK_Click()

        On Error GoTo FileError
        SavePicture frmPaint.Image, txtFileName.Text
        Unload cmdOK.Parent

        Exit Sub

FileError:
        MsgBox "File Error", 48, "Paint Program"    'MsgBox for file error
        Resume Next

End Sub
```

Listing 10.8. **The code for the frmControlPanel form of the Paint application.**

```
Option Explicit

Private Sub cmdCancel_Click()
        frmControlPanel.Hide
End Sub
```

continues

Listing 10.8. **continued**

```
Private Sub cmdOK_Click()
        frmPaint.ForeColor = RGB(vsbNewRed.Value, vsbNewGreen.Value,
        ➥vsbNewBlue.Value)
        Unload cmdOK.Parent
End Sub

Private Sub vsbNewBlue_Change()
        lblNewColor.BackColor = RGB(vsbNewRed.Value, vsbNewGreen.Value,
        ➥vsbNewBlue.Value)
End Sub

Private Sub vsbNewGreen_Change()
        lblNewColor.BackColor = RGB(vsbNewRed.Value, vsbNewGreen.Value,
        ➥vsbNewBlue.Value)
End Sub

Private Sub vsbNewRed_Change()
        lblNewColor.BackColor = RGB(vsbNewRed.Value, vsbNewGreen.Value,
        ➥vsbNewBlue.Value)
End Sub
```

Listing 10.9. **The code for the frmPaint form of the Paint application.**

```
Option Explicit

Private Sub cmdBox_Click()
        FindTheFlag "BOX"
End Sub

Private Sub cmdCircle_Click()
        FindTheFlag "CIRCLE"
End Sub

Private Sub cmdClear_Click()
        Cls
End Sub

Private Sub cmdDraw_Click()
        FindTheFlag "DRAW"
End Sub

Private Sub cmdLine_Click()
        FindTheFlag "LINE"
End Sub

Private Sub cmdText_Click()
        FindTheFlag "TEXT"
End Sub

Private Sub cmdText_KeyPress(KeyAscii As Integer)
        Print Chr$(KeyAscii);
End Sub
```

```
Private Sub Form_MouseDown(Button As Integer, Shift As Integer, X As Single,
➥Y As Single)
      If Button = 1 Then   'Left button pressed
               AnchorX = X
               AnchorY = Y
               CurrentX = X
               CurrentY = Y
      End If
End Sub

Private Sub Form_MouseMove(Button As Integer, Shift As Integer, X As Single,
➥Y As Single)
      Dim TempColor As Long
      Dim TempMode As Integer

      If Button = 1 Then        'Left Button Is pressed

            If DrawFlag Then
                  Line -(X, Y)
            End If

            If LineFlag Then
                  TempColor = ForeColor
                  TempMode = DrawMode
                  ForeColor = BackColor
                  DrawMode = 7          'Xor mode
                  Line (AnchorX, AnchorY)-(CurrentX, CurrentY)
                  Line (AnchorX, AnchorY)-(X, Y)
                  ForeColor = TempColor
                  DrawMode = TempMode
            End If

            If BoxFlag Then
                  TempColor = ForeColor
                  TempMode = DrawMode
                  ForeColor = BackColor
                  DrawMode = 7     'Xor mode
                  Line (AnchorX, AnchorY)-(CurrentX, CurrentY), , B
                  Line (AnchorX, AnchorY)-(X, Y), , B
                  ForeColor = TempColor
                  DrawMode = TempMode
            End If

            If CircleFlag Then
                  TempColor = ForeColor
                  TempMode = DrawMode
                  ForeColor = BackColor
                  DrawMode = 7     'Xor mode
                  Radius = Sqr((AnchorX - CurrentX) ^ 2 +
                  ➥(AnchorY - CurrentY) ^ 2)
                  Circle (AnchorX, AnchorY), Radius
                  Radius = Sqr((AnchorX - X) ^ 2 + (AnchorY - Y) ^ 2)
                  Circle (AnchorX, AnchorY), Radius
                  CurrentX = X
```

continues

Listing 10.9. continued

```
                    CurrentY = Y
                    ForeColor = TempColor
                    DrawMode = TempMode
            End If

        End If
End Sub

Private Sub Form_MouseUp(Button As Integer, Shift As Integer, X As Single,
➥Y As Single)
        If Button = 1 Then       'Checking to see if button released
                                 'is the left button

            If LineFlag Then
                    Line (AnchorX, AnchorY)-(X, Y)
            End If

            If BoxFlag Then
                    Line (AnchorX, AnchorY)-(X, Y), , B
            End If

            If CircleFlag Then
                    Radius = Sqr((AnchorX - X) ^ 2 + (AnchorY - Y) ^ 2)
                    Circle (AnchorX, AnchorY), Radius
            End If

        End If
End Sub

Private Sub mnuFileColor_Click()
        frmControlPanel.lblNewColor.BackColor = ForeColor
        frmControlPanel.Show
End Sub

Private Sub mnuFileExit_Click()
        End
End Sub

Private Sub mnuFileLoad_Click()
        frmLoad.Show
End Sub

Private Sub mnuFileSave_Click()
        frmSave.Show
End Sub
```

Your Paint application is becoming very polished! But it is missing one important feature—printing. Adding print capabilities to the project is not difficult. It's time to move on and do just that.

Printing the Paint Application's Graphics

As you discovered in the previous chapter, the printer can be used as an object and any of the graphics methods—PSet, Line, Circle, Print, and so on—can be used with it. There is a very simple way to print the graphics in the Paint application: by using the PrintForm method. This method prints everything in the client area of a window. However, this includes all of the controls that are on the form, too. Because you do not want the toolbox to print, you can make it temporarily invisible by setting the command buttons' Visible properties to False.

To begin, add a Print item to frmPaint's File menu. Open the Menu Editor and click on the E&xit item in the lower list box. Press the Insert button as you did before, and then add a new menu item, Print. After that item, add another separator bar. The settings for these two menu items should be as follows:

Caption	Name	Indentation	Other Information
&Print	mnuFilePrint	1	Shortcut Ctrl+P
-	mnuSep3	1	(None)

Next, click the new menu item, Print, to bring up this Sub procedure code skeleton:

```
Private Sub mnuFilePrint_Click()

End Sub
```

First, you have to hide the command buttons and rectangle that make up the toolbox:

```
Private Sub mnuFilePrint_Click()
        cmdDraw.Visible = False
        cmdLine.Visible = False
        cmdBox.Visible = False
        cmdCircle.Visible = False
        cmdText.Visible = False
        cmdClear.Visible = False
        shpRectangle.Visible = False

        :

End Sub
```

Next, the graphics area can be printed using the `PrintForm` method. Then the command buttons and rectangle should become visible again.

```
Private Sub mnuFilePrint_Click()
      cmdDraw.Visible = False
      cmdLine.Visible = False
      cmdBox.Visible = False
      cmdCircle.Visible = False
      cmdText.Visible = False
      cmdClear.Visible = False
      shpRectangle.Visible = False

      PrintForm

      cmdDraw.Visible = True
      cmdLine.Visible = True
      cmdBox.Visible = True
      cmdCircle.Visible = True
      cmdText.Visible = True
      cmdClear.Visible = True
      shpRectangle.Visible = True
End Sub
```

When the user prints using the new code you just wrote, Visual Basic automatically pops a small window on the screen (as shown in Figure 10.13), indicating that the application is printing. This window even includes a button that lets the user cancel at any time.

Figure 10.13.
The Paint application printing.

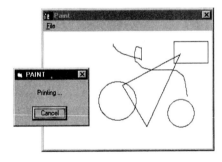

That's it for printing from the Paint application. The next—and last—capability that should be added to the project is Windows Clipboard interaction.

Using the Windows Clipboard

The Clipboard can be used to transfer data back and forth between Windows applications. The PrintScreen button on the keyboard can be pressed, for example, to take a snapshot of the screen and paste it automatically into the Clipboard. If Windows Paintbrush were open, that screen snapshot could then be pasted into the current document.

It's time to add this kind of power to your Paint application. Visual Basic supports a Clipboard object with the methods listed in Table 10.7.

Table 10.7. Clipboard object methods.

Method	Description
Clear	Clears the Clipboard.
GetData	Gets the graphics data in the Clipboard.
GetFormat	Gets the Clipboard format (text or graphics).
GetText	Gets the text in the Clipboard.
SetData	Pastes graphics data to the Clipboard.
SetText	Pastes text to the Clipboard.

There are three ways that the Clipboard object is usually used: to transfer text, graphics, or code. Because you are designing a paint application, you will be interested in graphics. The two Clipboard methods you will use are `GetData` and `SetData`.

To use the Clipboard, just add two more items to the File menu: Copy and Paste. Also, another separator bar will be needed. These items should be placed above the Print item on the File menu. Their settings are as follows:

Caption	Name	Indentation	Other Information
&Copy	mnuFileCopy	1	Shortcut: Ctrl+C
Pas&te	mnuFilePaste	1	Shortcut: Ctrl+V
-	mnuSep4	1	(None)

Notice that the shortcut keys assigned to Copy and Paste are the typical windows settings, Ctrl+C and Ctrl+V, respectively. The completed menu appears in Figure 10.14.

To get going on this, take a look at the `GetData` method. This method returns a graphic from the Clipboard object. The `GetData` method syntax works like this:

`object.GetData (format)`

The `GetData` method syntax has these parts:

- *object*—A required object expression that evaluates to an object.
- *format*—An optional constant or value that specifies the Clipboard graphics format, as described in Settings. Parentheses must enclose the constant or value. If *format* is 0 or omitted, `GetData` automatically uses the appropriate format.

Figure 10.14.
The completed frmPaint
File menu.

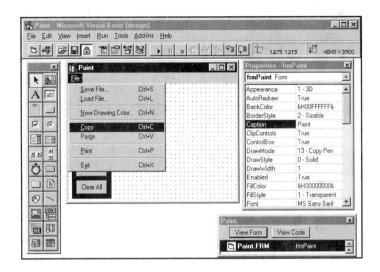

The settings for `format` are as follows:

Constant	Value	Description
vbCFBitmap	2	Bitmap (.bmp files)
vbCFMetafile	3	Metafile (.wmf files)
vbCFDIB	8	Device-independent bitmap (DIB)
vbCFPalette	9	Color palette

To get the current graphic from the Clipboard and paste it into the Paint application, the following line of code should be added to the `mnuFilePaste_Click()` event:

```
Private Sub mnuFilePaste_Click()
      Picture = Clipboard.GetData()
End Sub
```

Now look at the process of pasting a graphic into the Clipboard. To do that, you will use the `SetData` method. This method puts a picture on the Clipboard object using the specified graphic format. The `SetData` method syntax appears as follows:

`object.SetData data, format`

The `SetData` method syntax has these parts:

- *object*—A required object expression that evaluates to an object.

- *data*—A required argument. It is the graphic to be placed on the Clipboard object.

- *format*—An optional constant or value that specifies one of the Clipboard object formats recognized by Visual Basic, as described in Settings. If *format* is omitted, `SetData` automatically determines the graphic format.

In this case, `Data` refers to the `Image` property of the form, `frmPaint.Image`. The Paint application graphic can be pasted to the Clipboard by adding the following code to the `mnuFileCopy Click` event:

```
Private Sub mnuFileCopy_Click()
    Clipboard.SetData frmPaint.Image
End Sub
```

Now the user can copy to and paste from the Clipboard, enabling communication to other Windows applications. All the code for the program appears in Table 10.8 and Table 10.9, and in Listings 10.10 through 10.14 and an example of what the program looks like when running is in Figure 10.15. You've come a long way with this program. You learned how to use the mouse to draw freehand, lines, boxes, and circles. Also, you discovered how to position text, how to save and retrieve graphics from disk, how to print, and how to use the Clipboard. Congratulations!

Adding More to the Paint Application

You could add more features to the Paint program, including Cut, vertical and horizontal scrollbars, and custom images for the tools in the toolbox. The possibilities are endless!

Figure 10.15.
The completed Paint application.

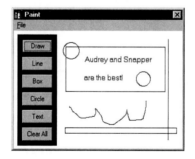

Table 10.8. The visual implementation of frmPaint.

Object	Property	Setting
Form	AutoRedraw	True
	BackColor	White
	BorderStyle	2-Sizable
	Caption	Paint
	MousePointer	2-Cross
	Name	frmPaint

continues

Table 10.8. continued

Object	Property	Setting
Command Button	Caption	Draw
	MousePointer	1-Arrow
	Name	cmdDraw
Command Button	Caption	Line
	MousePointer	1-Arrow
	Name	cmdLine
Command Button	Caption	Box
	MousePointer	1-Arrow
	Name	cmdBox
Command Button	Caption	Circle
	MousePointer	1-Arrow
	Name	cmdCircle
Command Button	Caption	Text
	MousePointer	1-Arrow
	Name	cmdText
Command Button	Caption	Clear
	MousePointer	1-Arrow
	Name	cmdClear
Shape	BackColor	Dark Blue
	BackStyle	1-Opaque
	BorderWidth	2
	BorderColor	Dark Blue
	Name	shpRectangle
Form	Appearance	1-3D
	BorderStyle	3-Fixed Dialog
	Caption	Load File…
	Name	frmLoad
Drive List Box	Name	drvChange
Directory List Box	Name	dirLook
File List Box	Name	filFind

Object	Property	Setting
Command Button	Caption	OK
	Default	True
	Name	cmdOK
Command Button	Cancel	True
	Caption	Cancel
	Name	cmdCancel
Form	Appearance	1-3D
	BorderStyle	3-Fixed Dialog
	Caption	Save File...
	Name	frmSave
Label	Alignment	2-Center
	Caption	Save File As:
	Name	lblSave
Text Box	Name	txtFileName
	Text	(None)
Command Button	Caption	OK
	Default	True
	Name	cmdOK
Command Button	Cancel	True
	Caption	Cancel
	Name	cmdCancel
Form	Caption	Control Panel
	MaxButton	False
	MinButton	False
	Name	frmControlPanel
Label	Alignment	2-Center
	Caption	New Drawing Color
	Name	Label1
Label	BorderStyle	1-Fixed Single
	Caption	(None)
	Name	lblNewColor

continues

Table 10.8. continued

Object	Property	Setting
Label	Alignment	2-Center
	Caption	Red
	Name	Label4
Scroll Bar	LargeChange	20
	Max	255
	Min	0
	Name	vsbNewRed
	SmallChange	10
Label	Alignment	2-Center
	Caption	Green
	Name	Label5
Scroll Bar	LargeChange	20
	Max	255
	Min	0
	Name	vsbNewGreen
	SmallChange	10
Label	Alignment	2-Center
	Caption	Blue
	Name	Label6
Scroll Bar	LargeChange	20
	Max	255
	Min	0
	Name	vsbNewBlue
	SmallChange	10
Command Button	CaptionDefault	OK
	Name	True
		cmdOK
Command Button	Cancel	True
	Caption	Cancel
	Name	cmdCancel

Table 10.9. The menu on `frmPaint`.

Caption	Name	Indentation	Other Information
&File	mnuFile	0	(None)
&Save File…	mnuFileSave	1	Shortcut: Ctrl+S
&Load File…	mnuFileLoad	1	Shortcut: Ctrl+L
-	mnuSep1	1	(None)
&New Drawing Color…	mnuFileColor	1	Shortcut: Ctrl+N
-	mnuSep2	1	(None)
&Copy	mnuFileCopy	1	Shortcut: Ctrl+C
Pas&te	mnuFilePaste	1	Shortcut: Ctrl+V
-	mnuSep3	1	(None)
&Print	mnuFilePrint	1	Shortcut: Ctrl+P
-	mnuSep4	1	(None)
E&xit	mnuFileExit	1	Shortcut: Ctrl+X

Listing 10.10. The code for the Paint.bas module of the Paint application.

```
Option Explicit

Public AnchorX As Integer
Public AnchorY As Integer
Public DrawFlag As Boolean
Public LineFlag As Boolean
Public BoxFlag As Boolean
Public CircleFlag As Boolean
Public TextFlag As Boolean
Public Radius As Single

Public Sub FindTheFlag(Which As String)

    Which = UCase$(Which)

    DrawFlag = False
    LineFlag = False
    BoxFlag = False
    CircleFlag = False
    TextFlag = False
```

continues

Listing 10.10. continued

```
        Select Case Which
                Case "DRAW"
                        DrawFlag = True

                Case "LINE"
                        LineFlag = True

                Case "BOX"
                        BoxFlag = True

                Case "CIRCLE"
                        CircleFlag = True

                Case "TEXT"
                        TextFlag = True

                Case Else
                        MsgBox "We goofed here, Frodo!"

        End Select

End Sub
```

Listing 10.11. The code for the **paintload** form of the Paint application.

```
Option Explicit

Private Sub cmdCancel_Click()
        Unload cmdCancel.Parent
End Sub

Private Sub cmdOK_Click()
        Dim TheFile As String

        On Error GoTo FileError

        If (Right(dirLook.Path, 1) = "\") Then
                TheFile = dirLook.Path + filFind.FileName

        Else
                TheFile = dirLook.Path + "\" + filFind.FileName

        End If

        frmPaint.Picture = LoadPicture(TheFile)

        Unload cmdOK.Parent

        Exit Sub

FileError:
```

```
        MsgBox "File Error", 48, "Paint Program"    'MsgBox for file error
        Resume Next

End Sub

Private Sub dirLook_Change()
      filFind.Path = dirLook.Path
End Sub

Private Sub drvChange_Change()
      dirLook.Path = drvChange.Drive
End Sub

Private Sub filFind_DblClick()
      cmdOK_Click
End Sub
```

Listing 10.12. The code for the **paintsave** form of the Paint application.

```
Option Explicit

Private Sub cmdCancel_Click()
      Unload cmdCancel.Parent
End Sub

Private Sub cmdOK_Click()

      On Error GoTo FileError
      SavePicture frmPaint.Image, txtFileName.Text
      Unload cmdOK.Parent

      Exit Sub

FileError:
      MsgBox "File Error", 48, "Paint Program"    'MsgBox for file error
      Resume Next

End Sub
```

Listing 10.13. The code for the **frmControlPanel** form of the Paint application.

```
Option Explicit

Private Sub cmdCancel_Click()
      frmControlPanel.Hide
End Sub
```

continues

Listing 10.13. continued

```
Private Sub cmdOK_Click()
      frmPaint.ForeColor = RGB(vsbNewRed.Value, vsbNewGreen.Value,
      ➥vsbNewBlue.Value)
      Unload cmdOK.Parent
End Sub

Private Sub vsbNewBlue_Change()
      lblNewColor.BackColor = RGB(vsbNewRed.Value, vsbNewGreen.Value,
      ➥vsbNewBlue.Value)
End Sub

Private Sub vsbNewGreen_Change()
      lblNewColor.BackColor = RGB(vsbNewRed.Value, vsbNewGreen.Value,
      ➥vsbNewBlue.Value)
End Sub

Private Sub vsbNewRed_Change()
      lblNewColor.BackColor = RGB(vsbNewRed.Value, vsbNewGreen.Value,
      ➥vsbNewBlue.Value)
End Sub
```

Listing 10.14. The code for the frmPaint form of the Paint application.

```
Option Explicit

Private Sub cmdBox_Click()
      FindTheFlag "BOX"
End Sub

Private Sub cmdCircle_Click()
      FindTheFlag "CIRCLE"
End Sub

Private Sub cmdClear_Click()
      Cls
End Sub

Private Sub cmdDraw_Click()
      FindTheFlag "DRAW"
End Sub

Private Sub cmdLine_Click()
      FindTheFlag "LINE"
End Sub

Private Sub cmdText_Click()
      FindTheFlag "TEXT"
End Sub

Private Sub cmdText_KeyPress(KeyAscii As Integer)
      Print Chr$(KeyAscii);
End Sub

Private Sub Form_MouseDown(Button As Integer, Shift As Integer, X As Single,
➥Y As Single)
      If Button = 1 Then   'Left button pressed
            AnchorX = X
```

```
                AnchorY = Y
                CurrentX = X
                CurrentY = Y
          End If
End Sub

Private Sub Form_MouseMove(Button As Integer, Shift As Integer, X As Single,
➥Y As Single)
        Dim TempColor As Long
        Dim TempMode As Integer

        If Button = 1 Then        'Left Button Is pressed

                If DrawFlag Then
                        Line -(X, Y)
                End If

                If LineFlag Then
                        TempColor = ForeColor
                        TempMode = DrawMode
                        ForeColor = BackColor
                        DrawMode = 7         'Xor mode
                        Line (AnchorX, AnchorY)-(CurrentX, CurrentY)
                        Line (AnchorX, AnchorY)-(X, Y)
                        ForeColor = TempColor
                        DrawMode = TempMode
                End If

                If BoxFlag Then
                        TempColor = ForeColor
                        TempMode = DrawMode
                        ForeColor = BackColor
                        DrawMode = 7     'Xor mode
                        Line (AnchorX, AnchorY)-(CurrentX, CurrentY), , B
                        Line (AnchorX, AnchorY)-(X, Y), , B
                        ForeColor = TempColor
                        DrawMode = TempMode
                End If

                If CircleFlag Then
                        TempColor = ForeColor
                        TempMode = DrawMode
                        ForeColor = BackColor
                        DrawMode = 7     'Xor mode
                        Radius = Sqr((AnchorX - CurrentX) ^ 2 +
                        ➥AnchorY - CurrentY) ^ 2)
                        Circle (AnchorX, AnchorY), Radius
                        Radius = Sqr((AnchorX - X) ^ 2 + (AnchorY - Y) ^ 2)
                        Circle (AnchorX, AnchorY), Radius
                        CurrentX = X
                        CurrentY = Y
                        ForeColor = TempColor
                        DrawMode = TempMode
                End If

        End If
End Sub
```

continues

Listing 10.14. **continued**

```
Private Sub Form_MouseUp(Button As Integer, Shift As Integer, X As Single,
➥Y As Single)
        If Button = 1 Then          'Checking to see if button released
                                    'is the left button

                If LineFlag Then
                        Line (AnchorX, AnchorY)-(X, Y)
                End If

                If BoxFlag Then
                        Line (AnchorX, AnchorY)-(X, Y), , B
                End If

                If CircleFlag Then
                        Radius = Sqr((AnchorX - X) ^ 2 + (AnchorY - Y) ^ 2)
                        Circle (AnchorX, AnchorY), Radius
                End If

        End If
End Sub

Private Sub mnuFileColor_Click()
        frmControlPanel.lblNewColor.BackColor = ForeColor
        frmControlPanel.Show
End Sub

Private Sub mnuFileCopy_Click()
        Clipboard.SetData frmPaint.Image
End Sub

Private Sub mnuFileExit_Click()
        End
End Sub

Private Sub mnuFileLoad_Click()
        frmLoad.Show
End Sub

Private Sub mnuFilePaste_Click()
        Picture = Clipboard.GetData()
End Sub

Private Sub mnuFilePrint_Click()
        cmdDraw.Visible = False
        cmdLine.Visible = False
        cmdBox.Visible = False
        cmdCircle.Visible = False
        cmdText.Visible = False
        cmdClear.Visible = False
        shpRectangle.Visible = False

        PrintForm

        cmdDraw.Visible = True
        cmdLine.Visible = True
        cmdBox.Visible = True
        cmdCircle.Visible = True
        cmdText.Visible = True
```

```
        cmdClear.Visible = True
        shpRectangle.Visible = True
End Sub

Private Sub mnuFileSave_Click()
        frmSave.Show
End Sub
```

Before leaving the subject of drawing graphics, there is one more thing that you should consider: the measurement scale used in an application.

Graphics Scaling

So far, you have used the Visual Basic default measurement, twips. But you aren't stuck with twips forever! In fact, if you do quite a bit of graphics programming in Visual Basic, there are times when you will want to use other unit systems. Suppose that you want to draw a grid on the screen. You will have to specify where the lines are to be placed. If you use twips, your measurements will be converted by the program to pixels. This can cause problems. If the twip spacing between the grid lines turns out to not be a whole number of pixels (39.4, for example), the lines will not always be the same distance apart on the screen. And, if the grid spacing is small, this effect will be very noticeable.

Instead, the best thing to do would be to use a pixel scale and work with pixels for the rest of the project. To do that, you would have to set the form's `ScaleMode` property. This property is available for picture boxes, forms, and the `Printer` object. The settings for `ScaleMode` are listed in Table 10.10.

Table 10.10. Settings for the `ScaleMode` property.

Setting	Description
0	Indicates that one or more of the `ScaleHeight`, `ScaleWidth`, `ScaleLeft`, and `ScaleTop` properties are set to custom values.
1	Twip. There are 1440 twips per inch, and 567 twips per centimeter. This is the default.
2	Point. There are 72 points per inch.
3	Pixel. This is the smallest unit of monitor or printer resolution.
4	Character. The scale is as follows: horizontal = 120 twips per unit; vertical = 240 twips per unit.
5	Inch.
6	Millimeter.
7	Centimeter.

Finding the Pixel Dimensions of the User's Screen

To find the size of the current screen in pixels, use the `Screen` object and check the `Screen.Width` and `Screen.Height` properties.

Besides these predefined scales—points, pixels, centimeters, and so on—using `ScaleMode = 0`, you could design your own measurement scale. For example, this capability could make drawing graphs very easy if a unit system were set up so that both the X and Y dimensions were exactly 100 units. To plot a point at (56,93) on the graph, the `PSet` method would look like this: `PSet(56,93)`. A scale can be set by simply setting the `ScaleWidth` and `ScaleHeight` properties of the form or picture box. Then, to make that form or picture box 100×100 units, both `ScaleWidth` and `ScaleHeight` should be set to `100`.

Setting a custom measurement scale has another use, also. If a custom scale is set up for an application and the user resizes a window, no changes would be needed to send graphics to the screen. For instance, if a window is 100×100 units and the user doubles the size of the window, the window is still 100×100 units.

Well, that's it for graphics, the Paint application, and the mouse. It's time to move on for some behind-the-scenes work that is very important but never seen by the user. Chapter 11 takes a look at advanced data handling.

Summary

In this chapter, you saw how to use the mouse by adding code to the mouse events `MouseDown`, `MouseUp`, and `MouseMove`. Using these events and the skills learned in the previous chapter, you developed a large-scale Paint application. The size of the program displayed the usefulness of modular code, which divides code into smaller, manageable sections. Also, the modular code is much easier to debug and maintain. This is all a part of good programming practice.

A few other techniques you discovered were stretching a graphics figure on the screen, changing the mouse cursor from an arrow to a cross, and modifying the graphics scale for an application. These graphics techniques will come in handy in many programs. Your programming skills and techniques are advancing nicely!

New Events	Description
MouseDown	This event fires when a mouse cursor is located over a form or control and a mouse button is pressed.
MouseMove	This event occurs when the mouse cursor moves over a control or form.
MouseUp	This event fires when a depressed mouse button is released.

New Properties	Description
MousePointer	This property sets the mouse cursor for the control or form.
ScaleMode	This property returns or sets a value indicating the unit of measurement for coordinates of an object when using graphics methods or when positioning controls.

New Statements	Description
SavePicture	This statement saves a graphic from a form object, picture box control, or image control to a file.

New Methods	Description
Clear	This method clears the Windows Clipboard.
Cls	This method clears the graphics from a form or picture box.
GetData	This method gets graphics data from the Windows Clipboard.
GetFormat	This method gets the Clipboard format (text or graphics).
GetText	This method gets the text from the Windows Clipboard.
PrintForm	This method sends a bit-by-bit image of a form object to the printer.
SetData	This method places graphics data into the Windows Clipboard.
SetText	This method pastes text to the Windows Clipboard.

New Functions	Description
LoadPicture	This function loads a graphic into a form object, picture box control, or image control.

11

Advanced Data-Handling, Sorting, and Storing a Spreadsheet Program

In this chapter you will see how to organize data for maximum power in your Visual Basic projects. These are techniques that all Visual Basic programmers should know. They include the following:

- Using the currency variable type
- Learning more about arrays
- Organizing data using a shell sort
- Organizing data using a quick sort
- Creating a working spreadsheet application
- Learning how binary trees can help
- Getting the most from data structures
- Using a linked list
- Understanding a circular buffer

This chapter develops some useful programs, including working examples of a shell sort, a quick sort, and a fast data-search algorithm. In addition, you will put to work in a functioning spreadsheet program the Grid control that comes with Visual Basic. In general, you will find that organizing your data for easy access can be crucial in program development for speed in both program coding and execution.

Organizing data at the beginning of an application is half the battle. It's an important topic. The way data is set up in a database program, for example, can make the difference between programming success and failure. If there are 31 uncoordinated data arrays with different indices to keep track of, there is certainly a high probability of failure. On the other hand, if the arrays were condensed into one array of data structures, there would be more chance of success. And an application written this way would be easier to maintain.

You don't have to write a database program to take advantage of these techniques. Almost all applications use and manipulate data of some type, and organizing it so that it's easily accessed is a skill no programmer should be without. For instance, a program that asks Yes/No questions of the user—as some artificial intelligence expert systems do—cries out for you to use binary trees. You would not know this if you had never heard of binary trees. You will soon find that the skills learned here will come to you naturally as you begin to expect more from your Visual Basic applications.

In this chapter you will work through many data organization methods. You will discover the most useful ways to arrange data, including arrays, data structures, linked lists, circular buffers, and binary trees. Programmers should be familiar with these common methods of arranging data and not be forced to continually reinvent the wheel.

In this chapter you will also learn two fast sorting methods in addition to a fast searching algorithm that explores sorted arrays. At the end of the chapter you will use the Visual Basic Grid control to create a working spreadsheet program. With all of these interesting topics ahead, why wait? First, a short recap about variables and then on to arrays.

A Variable Review

As you might recall from previous chapters, especially Chapter 4, "Programming in Visual Basic," the most elementary method used to organize data is to store the data in simple variables. In Visual Basic applications, these variables are declared as different types and include many you have already used: `Integer`, `Boolean`, `Long`, `Single`, `Double`, `Variant`, `Currency`, `String`.

You might not be too familiar with one of these: `Currency`. As the name implies, it is a variable that stores amounts of money. In the following example, the results are printed to the nearest cent as shown in Figure 11.1.

```
Option Explicit

Private Sub Form_Activate()
    Dim Savings As Currency
    Dim Rent As Currency
    Dim Food As Currency
    Dim Bills As Currency

    Savings = 6000#
    Rent = 775#
    Food = 124.5
    Bills = 513.72

    Savings = Savings - Rent
    Savings = Savings - Food
    Savings = Savings - Bills

    Print
    Print
    Print
    Print Tab; "Money left: $ "; Savings

End Sub
```

You might have noticed in the preceding code that there is a `#` character after two of the monetary values—`Savings` and `Rent`—and also that `Food` is valued at `124.5`. When you enter the code in the `Form_Activate()` event and type in the values `6000.00`, `775.00`, and `124.50`, Visual Basic automatically adds the `#` character as a place holder after currency values ending with .00, truncating those zeros and any other zeros after the decimal place.

Figure 11.1.
The test Savings Left
application running.

The preceding code example prints the amount of savings that remains after paying food, rent, and bills. For most purposes, you can think of the `Currency` variable as a more accurate `Long` variable with four decimal places added to it, although the last two decimal places are for internal accuracy only.

The next step up in Visual Basic data handling is to use something that you have already used: *arrays*.

Arrays

In several previous chapters you used arrays to organize data. The following is a code example that uses an array. The code prints a display of yesterday's and today's sales.

```
Option Explicit

Private Sub Form_Activate()
        Static Array(10, 2) As Currency
        Dim Sales As Integer
        Dim Day1Total As Currency
        Dim Day2Total As Currency
        Dim PrintSum As Currency

        'Today's sales
        Array(1, 1) = 10#
        Array(2, 1) = 53#
        Array(3, 1) = 7.17
        Array(4, 1) = 9.67
        Array(5, 1) = 87.99
        Array(6, 1) = 14#
        Array(7, 1) = 91.19
        Array(8, 1) = 12.73
        Array(9, 1) = 1.03
        Array(10, 1) = 5.04

        'Yesterday's sales
        Array(1, 2) = 9.67
        Array(2, 2) = 10.23
        Array(3, 2) = 8.97
        Array(4, 2) = 10#
        Array(5, 2) = 78.33
        Array(6, 2) = 17#
        Array(7, 2) = 91.36
        Array(8, 2) = 12.73
        Array(9, 2) = 16.12
        Array(10, 2) = 7.98

        Print
        Print Tab(20); "Sales (in $)"
        Print
        Print Tab(3); "Today"; Tab(33); "Yesterday"
        Print Tab(3); "-----"; Tab(33); "---------"
        Print

        For Sales = 1 To 10
            Print Tab(3); Array(Sales, 1); Tab(33); Array(Sales, 2)
        Next Sales

        Print Tab(3); "-------"; Tab(33); "-------"

        Day1Total = 0
```

```
        Day2Total = 0

        For Sales = 1 To 10
              Day1Total = Day1Total + Array(Sales, 1)
              Day2Total = Day2Total + Array(Sales, 2)
        Next Sales

        Print Tab(3); Day1Total; " = Today's Total"; Tab(33); Day2Total;
        ➥" = Yesterday's Total"
        Print
End Sub
```

The result of this code appears in Figure 11.2.

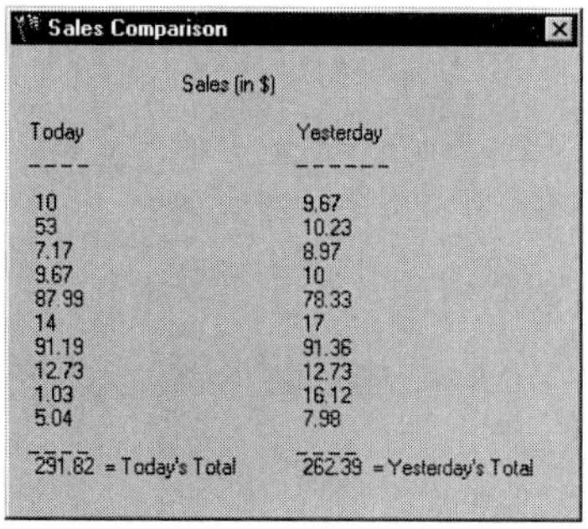

Figure 11.2.
*The test Sales application,
showing two days' total sales
using an array.*

In the preceding code, an array of ten rows and two columns is set up. Each column displays the sales figures for one day. Notice that the array is declared as static, like this:

```
Static Array(10, 2) As Currency
```

The reason this array is declared using Static instead of Dim is that in Visual Basic a fixed-size array used in a non-static procedure must be declared Static. If the entire procedure were declared Static, then the array could be declared using either Dim or Static. When an array is declared Static, it means that the values in the array will not change between calls to the procedure. In the array declaration, the array is set up using (10, 2). The number 10 represents the number of rows in the array and 2 represents the number of columns. Using this format, parallel operations can be performed on parallel sets of data, such as adding the columns of sales to produce the day's total. The code in the preceding example that does that is as follows:

```
   :

For Sales = 1 To 10
     Print Tab(3); Array(Sales, 1); Tab(33); Array(Sales, 2)
Next Sales

   :
```

As you might recall from Chapter 4, it is possible for you to create your own user-defined data structures. The following section is a brief review of how to do so.

User-Defined Data Structures

Standard data types can be grouped together to create a new type of data. For example, to define a `Type` named `Person`, use the following code:

```
Type Person
    FirstName As String * 20
    LastName As String * 20
End Type
```

Variable-length strings can be used in `Type` statements except when variables are used as records in random-access files. The data structure created by the preceding code stores a person's first and last names. A variable of this type could be set up, or even more powerfully, an array of variables of `Person` type could be created:

```
Type Person
    FirstName As String * 20
    LastName As String * 20
End Type

Public People(10) As Person
```

The people making up the array could then be referenced in the following way:

```
People(1).FirstName = "Hacker"
People(1).LastName = "Warbler"

People(2).FirstName = "Eunice"
People(2).LastName = "Dunwoodie"

People(3).FirstName = "Fairweather"
People(3).LastName = "Smith"

Print People(1).FirstName
```

This might seem like all there is to working with data structures. You know what variable types are, how to create your own variable types, and how to create arrays, or sets, of variables. What else could there be? Well, get ready for a jump. Think of this like the jump you made when you went to algebra. There are other types of data structures that allow you more flexibility in terms of how much memory you use to store your variables. The first one we are going to look at is a linked list.

Linked Lists

Linked lists are good for organizing data items in sequential chains (especially if there are a number of such chains to manage) and for using space efficiently.

Linked lists work this way: Each data item has a pointer pointing to the next data item. This pointer is an index of some sort that references the next data item. The next item in the list is found by going to the location that the current record points to. Another data item can be added to the list at any time, as long as the current pointer is updated to point to the new data item. If you were to draw a linked list it would look like Figure 11.3.

Figure 11.3.
A pictorial representation of
a linked list, using pointers.

Because the last pointer in the chain in Figure 11.3 is a null pointer with a value of zero, a program will know that the list is finished when it reaches the null pointer.

An important example of a linked list in your computer is the File Allocation Table (FAT) on disks. The FAT is a linked list of the clusters allocated to files for storage. Files are stored cluster-by-cluster, and for each cluster on the disk there is one entry in the FAT. We're going to examine how the computer uses linked lists in the FAT to maintain the location of our files.

What Is a Disk Cluster?

A *cluster* is the minimum size disk storage allocation. On 1.4MB, high-density, 3 1/2-inch diskettes, one cluster equals one sector; thus, the number of bytes per cluster and bytes per sector is the same: 512. Because one cluster equals 512 bytes, the amount of free space on 1.4MB diskettes is always reported in units of 512 bytes. On a large hard disk, one greater than 500 MB, the cluster size is 32KB. This means that every file will take up at least 32KB of disk space no matter how small it is.

For the computer to determine which cluster a file is stored in (this occurs, for example, when a Word Processing program opens a file), the cluster number is retrieved from the directory entry. Suppose that this cluster number is 2. This means that the first section of the file is stored in cluster 2 on the disk. This number is also the key to the FAT. The next cluster occupied by the file can be found by looking in cluster 2's entry in the FAT, as in Figure 11.4.

Figure 11.4.
A pictorial representation of
a pointer in the Fat
Allocation Table (FAT).

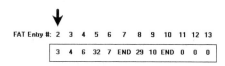

As in Figure 11.4, the number 2 cluster entry in the FAT holds 3, which is the number of the next cluster the file occupies on the disk. To find the cluster after 3, check the entry in the FAT for cluster 3, as shown in Figure 11.5.

Figure 11.5.
The FAT pointer from
cluster 2 to cluster 3 to
cluster 4.

The entry for cluster 3 holds 4, so the next section of the file can be found in cluster 4. To continue from there, check the number in the FAT entry for cluster 4, as in Figure 11.6. That number is 6.

Figure 11.6.
Checking cluster 4 for the
pointer to the file's next
cluster.

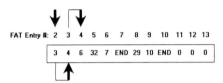

The computer continues this process until it reaches the end-of-file mark in the FAT, as shown in Figure 11.7.

Figure 11.7.
Coming to the end of the line
in the file's FAT clusters.

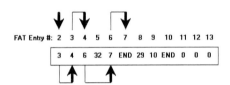

The file that has been traced through the preceding figures is stored in clusters 2, 3, 4, 6, and 7. Notice that 5 was already taken by another file, which is also weaving its own thread of clusters through the FAT at the same time. You should use linked lists such as this one when memory or disk space needs to be used efficiently—which is always—and when there is a number of sequential data chains that have to be tracked. When the file in the previous example is deleted, for instance, its entries in the FAT can be overwritten and those clusters used by another file.

Now for an example of a linked list in Visual Basic. Suppose there are two distinct career paths that have to be tracked:

- Supervisor Z Director Z Vice President Z President
- Lieutenant Z Captain Z Major Z Colonel

Note that moving to the right on either career track is a "step up the ladder," a move to a higher level.

The various levels of each career track can be connected using a linked list. To do that, start by setting up a variable of type `Person` in a module, like this:

```
Type Person

  Rank As String * 20
  SuperiorPointer As Integer

End Type
```

> **Tip:** For short exercises like these where you want to test some code without a lot of hassle you can declare the type with the `private` keyword so that it will enable you to put the type declaration in the general definitions section of a form.
>
> The `type` declaration would look like this:
>
> ```
> Private Type Person
>   Rank As String * 20
>   SuperiorPointer As Integer
> End Type
> ```

Then, in the test form's code window, fill the `Rank` fields in any order because the `SuperiorPointer` variable will keep them straight.

```
Static People(10) As Person

    People(1).Rank = "Supervisor"
    People(2).Rank = "Major"
    People(3).Rank = "Director"
    People(4).Rank = "President"
    People(5).Rank = "Captain"
    People(6).Rank = "Vice President"
    People(7).Rank = "Colonel"
    People(8).Rank = "Lieutenant"
```

For each entry in `People()`, there is also a "superior" position. For example, the superior of the entry in `People(1)`, `"Supervisor"`, is located in `People(3)`, `"Director"`. To link the entries in each of the two chains, the superior rank needs to be "pointed at" using the `SuperiorPointer` variable, like this:

```
    People(1).SuperiorPointer = 3
    People(2).SuperiorPointer = 7
    People(3).SuperiorPointer = 6
    People(4).SuperiorPointer = 0
    People(5).SuperiorPointer = 2
    People(6).SuperiorPointer = 4
    People(7).SuperiorPointer = 0
    People(8).SuperiorPointer = 5
```

Now that all the items in the two lists are linked, you can choose a number, 1 or 2, to get the program to work its way through the first or second linked list, printing the various rank names as it sorts. In the following code, 1 has been chosen as the career track and is represented by the variable `CareerTrack`.

```
Dim CareerTrack As Integer
```

```
CareerTrack = 1

Do
     Print People(CareerTrack).Rank     'Print results
     CareerTrack = People(CareerTrack).SuperiorPointer
Loop While CareerTrack <> 0
```

When this program runs it prints career track 1, as shown in Figure 11.8.

Figure 11.8.
The sample linked list
program showing career
track 1.

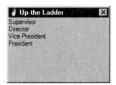

Note that the application needs to know in advance that career track 1 starts with `People(1).Rank` and that career track 2 starts with `People(8).Rank`. (Check the code, `People(1).Rank = Supervisor` and `People(8).Rank = Lieutenant`.) After that, the application could work its way up either chain of command. As it does so, it prints the current rank then gets the pointer for the next rank—the array index number found using the `SuperiorPosition` variable—at the same time.

Circular Buffers

Another data structure that programmers often use is an array with special pointers so that items in the array are inserted in such a way that the first item in the array is the first out. This is called FIFO (First In First Out). Normally, these arrays are set up as circular buffers. You can continue to put data in them as long as you do not exceed the maximum number of positions in the array. Arrays are generally used for circular buffers because they have very efficient execution speed when compared with more complex data types such as linked lists. The most familiar circular buffer in your computer is the keyboard buffer.

While one part of the operating system is putting key codes in the keyboard buffer, another part of the operating system is taking them out. The location in the buffer in which the next key code will be placed is called, appropriately enough, the *head*. The location from which the next key code is read is called the *tail*.

When characters are typed, the head advances. When they are read, the tail advances. As the keyboard buffer is written to and read from the head and tail march around. Each data location can be either head or tail. When the buffer is filled, the head comes up behind the tail—rather like a dragon patting itself on its head with its tail—and the buffer-full warning beeps.

The question that might be in your mind now is, how is this circular if you're using an array? That's a good question, and it's simple to answer. As the head and the tail are moved, you check to see if they are at the end of the array before adding them. If they are, then instead of adding one to them one is set to the beginning of the array again. This might seem strange, but it works as long as the head does not pass the tail. This is called *buffer overrun* and, in the case of the keyboard buffer, causes the computer to beep.

You can use circular buffers at different rates when part of an application is writing data and another part is reading it. First, the location of the head and tail positions must be stored. Then, after the data is in the buffer, advance the head. When data is retrieved, advance the tail. This way, the same amount of memory space can be used for both reading and writing.

Circular Lists

A close cousin of the circular buffer is the circular list, which has many of the same properties as a circular buffer. However, there are some differences.

Circular lists are less efficient in terms of processing time than circular buffers. However, they are more flexible in that the size of a circular list can be changed during runtime; a circular buffer's size is generally fixed during run-time.

Circular lists are used when processing power is not as important as the capability for the list to change size during run-time.

The primary problem with linked lists, circular buffers, and circular lists, however, is that all access to their data is sequential. To find the last entry in a linked list, for example, a program has to begin at the first entry and work its way back. That method is fine for files tracked through the FAT, where every FAT entry is needed before the entire file can be read, but it is a terrible method if an application is looking for one specific record. A better way to store the data is to make a *binary tree*.

Binary Trees

Binary trees differ from linked lists in that the data is ordered. To start, a linked list would look something like Figure 11.9.

Figure 11.9.
A drawing of a linked list.

You can add to a linked list and make a *doubly linked list*, as shown in Figure 11.10.

Figure 11.10.
An illustration of a doubly linked list.

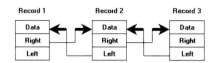

In Figure 11.10 there are two pointers in each record. One scans up the chain and the other scans down. A doubly linked list can be used when you need to be able to maneuver backward as well as forward in a list, or whenever you expect to be frequently deleting entries in the middle of the list. A doubly linked list has many uses, but it still is not a binary tree. To help the example, the values -5, 0, and 2 have been added to the data fields in Figure 11.11.

Figure 11.11.
A data field value is added to each record.

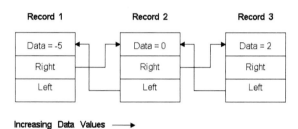

Notice that a hierarchy has been constructed based on the data values, because the records have been arranged from left to right in increasing order: -5, 0, 2. The record with the data value closest to the median data value becomes the *root* of the binary tree. (See Figure 11.12.) Notice that the previous and next pointers of the linked list now become left and right pointers. This is the convention used to name binary tree pointers.

Figure 11.12.
The binary tree's root.

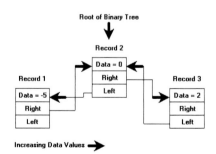

Record 2 has become the root of the binary tree because it has the data value closest to the middle of all three records. To find a record with a data value of -5, for example, the program would start at the root—record 2—which has a data value of 0. Because -5 is less than 0, the next record searched would be to the left, because data values decrease to the left. Therefore, the record to the left of record 2 is record 1, which has a value of -5. The program would then realize that it had found the target value.

In order to find the record with a data value of -5, the computer, using a binary tree, only needs to search through two records instead of three. This might seem like small potatoes, but imagine searching a list like the following one:

First Name = "Denise"
Age = 23

First Name = "Ed"
Age = 46

First Name = "Niki"
Age = 47

First Name = "Dennis"
Age = 42

First Name = "Doug"
Age = 33

First Name = "Margot"
Age = 27

First Name = "Jon"
Age = 41

First Name = "Cheryl"
Age = 28

Suppose that it is your job to coordinate this list and find a person with a specific age. To construct a binary tree, pick the person with an age closest to the median. In this case Doug, who is 33, is the closest. You can put the tree together as in Figure 11.13. There are many possible variations. Also, note that each successive node is the root of a lower binary tree.

Figure 11.13.
A binary tree.

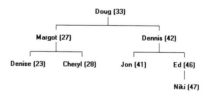

Now the search can begin with Doug and continue until the program finds the person with the required age. For example, to find the person who is 46 years old, the search would start at the top with Doug, who is 33. Because 46 is greater than 33, the search would move to the right from Doug to Dennis, who is 42, then on to Ed, who is 46. Because Ed's age equals the required age, 46, the search would be over.

Now put this example into code. Start a new Visual Basic project. Now define a new Person Type that has two pointers—one to the next-older Person, and one to the next-younger. This code goes in the general declarations section:

```
Private Type Person
    FirstName As String * 20
    Age As Integer
    NextYoungerPerson As Integer
    NextOlderPerson As Integer
End Type
```

Next, change the Name and Caption properties of the default form to frmTree and Binary Tree Example, respectively. Then save the project; save the form as BTree.frm, and the project as BTree.vbp.

Now, use the newly defined type, Person, in the Form_Activate() procedure:

```
Private Sub Form_Activate()
    Static People(10) As Person

    People(1).FirstName = "Denise"
    People(1).Age = 23
    People(1).NextYoungerPerson = 0
    People(1).NextOlderPerson = 0

    People(2).FirstName = "Ed"
    People(2).Age = 46
    People(2).NextYoungerPerson = 0
    People(2).NextOlderPerson = 3

    People(3).FirstName = "Niki"
    People(3).Age = 47
    People(3).NextYoungerPerson = 0
    People(3).NextOlderPerson = 0

    People(4).FirstName = "Dennis"
    People(4).Age = 42
    People(4).NextYoungerPerson = 7
    People(4).NextOlderPerson = 2

    People(5).FirstName = "Doug"
    People(5).Age = 33
    People(5).NextYoungerPerson = 6
    People(5).NextOlderPerson = 4

    People(6).FirstName = "Margot"
    People(6).Age = 27
    People(6).NextYoungerPerson = 1
    People(6).NextOlderPerson = 8

    People(7).FirstName = "Jon"
    People(7).Age = 41
    People(7).NextYoungerPerson = 0
    People(7).NextOlderPerson = 0
```

```
    People(8).FirstName = "Cheryl"
    People(8).Age = 28
    People(8).NextYoungerPerson = 0
    People(8).NextOlderPerson = 0

End Sub
```

Add the code that will search for the first person who is 46 years old. First, the program needs to start at the root and check to see whether that person is 46. Then it loops through the records on the tree until it finds the record that matches the search value of 46. The following declarations need to be placed after the definition of the People variable:

```
Dim BinaryTreeRoot As Integer
    Dim CurrentRecord As Integer
```

The following code needs to go after all of the people have been defined, at the end of the routine:

```
    BinaryTreeRoot = 5  'Doug is about the median age

    Print
    Print "Searching for a person 46 years old..."
    Print

    CurrentRecord = BinaryTreeRoot

    Do
        Select Case People(CurrentRecord).Age
            Case 46
                Print "That person is: "; People(CurrentRecord).FirstName
                Exit Do

            Case Is < 46
                CurrentRecord = People(CurrentRecord).NextOlderPerson

            Case Is > 46
                CurrentRecord = People(CurrentRecord).NextYoungerPerson

            Case Else
                MsgBox "Internal Error!" 'Program should never reach here!

        End Select

    Loop While CurrentRecord <> 0
```

That is how to search through a binary tree. The program just keeps going until it finds what it is looking for or runs out of branches. The result of this program is shown in Figure 11.14.

In a professional program you would want to check to see if no one was found by checking to see if the current record is 0 after the loop, but because you're just exploring how binary trees work you've not done this.

Figure 11.14.
The test Binary Tree
application running.

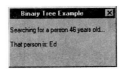

Congratulations! You've begun to order data with binary trees. This means that you have established the relative position of a record with respect to its two neighbors. However, what if all the data needs to be sorted?

Sorting data is a common task. It is the next step in this chapter's progress through the area of advanced data-handling. Sorting data should be explored in depth because it is such a common programming task. Therefore, on to working through two good sorting algorithms: shell sorts and quick sorts.

Shell Sorts

The standard shell sort is a popular programming tool. It works like this: Suppose that there is a one-dimensional array with the following values in it:

8 7 6 5 4 3 2 1

To sort this list in ascending order, divide it into two partitions, as shown in Figure 11.15.

Figure 11.15.
An array divided into two
partitions.

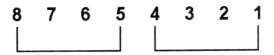

Next, compare the first element of the first partition to the first element of the second partition, as in Figure 11.16.

Figure 11.16.
A comparison of the first
element of each partition.

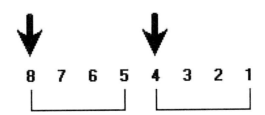

In this case, 8 is greater than 4, so the elements are switched and the next pair is compared, as shown in Figure 11.17.

Figure 11.17.
*Comparing the second
element of each partition.*

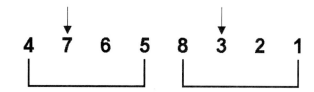

Again, because 7 is greater than 3, the two elements are swapped and the program goes on. (See Figure 11.18.)

Figure 11.18.
*The third elements are
compared then swapped.*

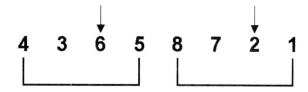

The third elements of each partition, 6 and 2, are again switched, and the last pair is examined. (See Figure 11.19.)

Figure 11.19.
*The final elements of the
partition are examined and
their positions switched.*

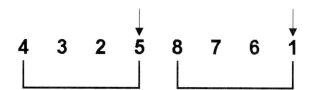

After the final pair is swapped, the list order looks like this:

4 3 2 1 8 7 6 5

Although this is somewhat better than before, the job is certainly not finished. The next step is to change to smaller partitions—three elements per partition—and repeat the process by comparing 4 with 1, and then when those swap places, 4 with 6. (See Figure 11.20.) This is not the most efficient shell sort, but it is easy to see how one works this way.

Figure 11.20.
*The list is split into smaller
partitions and the comparison begins again, this time
comparing 4 with 1, then
when those swap places, 4
with 6.*

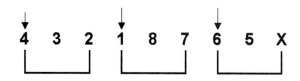

Therefore, 1 and 4 switch positions, but 4 and 6 do not. Then the next elements of each partition—3, 8, and 5—are compared. (See Figure 11.21.)

Figure 11.21.
The second elements in each partition are compared.

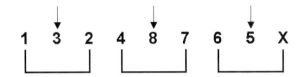

After the second elements are compared, 3 and 8 do not switch positions, but 8 and 5 do. Next, the final element in each partition is compared. (See Figure 11.22.) Note that in the very last case, 7 is compared with the x, which represents nothing.

Figure 11.22.
The last elements of each partition are compared.

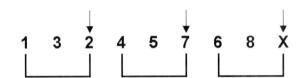

In this final comparison, nothing swaps places; therefore, the shell sort moves to the next smaller partition size, two elements per partition, and starts the process again, comparing 1 with 2, 2 with 5, and 5 with 6. (See Figure 11.23.)

Figure 11.23.
The list is grouped into smaller partitions and the comparison begins again.

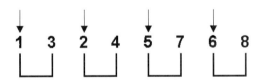

During this comparison no position changes are made. Therefore, the comparison shifts to the second element of each partition: 3, 4, 7, and 8, as shown in Figure 11.24.

Figure 11.24.
The second element of each partition is compared.

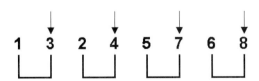

Again, no elements exchange position. At this point, the list is in this order:

1 3 2 4 5 7 6 8

This is quite a bit closer to the desired order, but it's still not quite right. Therefore, the shell sort moves down to the next partition size—one element per partition—and compares each element (see Figure 11.25).

Figure 11.25.
The list is broken down into
smaller partitions with one
element per partition, and
then each element is
compared.

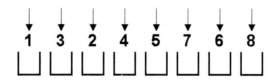

After the last comparison the 3 swaps positions with 2 and 7 switches places with 6. Finally, the order is as desired:

1 2 3 4 5 6 7 8

That is how a standard shell sort works (although the computer would be much faster than the explanation). Now put this to work in code. Begin by starting a new project and changing the `Name` and `Caption` property of the default form to `frmShellSort` and `Shell Sort Example`. Next, save the form and project as ShelSort.frm and ShelSort.vbp, respectively.

Now declare an array and fill it with values that happen to be as far from ascending order as they could possibly be.

```
Private Sub Form_Activate()
    Static Array(1 to 9) As Integer

    Array(1) = 9
    Array(2) = 8
    Array(3) = 7
    Array(4) = 6
    Array(5) = 5
    Array(6) = 4
    Array(7) = 3
    Array(8) = 2
    Array(9) = 1


End Sub
```

Why not print the values on the form for comparison later to the sorted list? The declaration belongs immediately beneath the declaration for the array:

```
Dim I As Integer
```

The rest of the code belongs under the assignment of values to the array items.

```
    Print
    Print Tab(10); " I"; Tab(24); "Array (I)"
    Print Tab(9); "---"; Tab(24); "---------"
    Print
```

```
For I = 1 To 9
    Print Tab(10); I; Tab(26); Array(I)
Next I

Print
Print Tab(10); " Sorting..."
```

Now the shell sort needs to be implemented. You do this by determining the number of items in the array and dividing it up as you saw before.

In the loop, the application should pass the variable `PartitionSize` and subtract one from it every time; thus, decreasing the partition size every time the loop starts again. Add the following to the declarations section of the procedure:

```
Dim NumPartitions As Integer
    Dim PartitionSize As Integer
    Dim NumItems As Integer
    Dim Low As Integer
```

The rest of the code needs to be inserted at the end of the procedure:

```
NumItems = UBound(Array, 1)
    PartitionSize = Int((NumItems + 1) / 2)

    Do
        NumPartitions = (NumItems + 1) / PartitionSize
        Low = 1
        For I = 1 To NumPartitions - 1

        Next I
        PartitionSize = PartitionSize - 1
    Loop While PartitionSize > 0
```

Next, the program has to loop over each element in the current partition and compare it to the corresponding element in the next position. This is the element-by-element comparison that will go from Array(Low) to Array(High) in the current partition. Low is the array index at the beginning of the partition and High is the element index at the end. Thus, the application will compare each element to the corresponding one in the next partition. Finally, if the element in the later partition is smaller than the element in the current one, the program has to switch their positions. To make these changes, add the following code to the declarations section:

```
Dim J As Integer

    Dim High As Integer
    Dim Temp As Integer
```

```
The following code needs to be inserted in the middle of the loop:
➥High = Low + PartitionSize - 1

            If High > NumItems - PartitionSize Then
```

```
        High = NumItems - PartitionSize
    End If

    For J = Low To High
        If Array(J) > Array(J + PartitionSize) Then

            Temp = Array(J)
            Array(J) = Array(J + PartitionSize)
            Array(J + PartitionSize) = Temp

        End If
    Next J

    Low = Low + PartitionSize
```

Therefore, the program loops over partition sizes, over each partition, and then finally over each element in the current partition, swapping it with its counterpart in the next partition if necessary.

The final code that needs to be added at the end of the Form_Activate() event is the code that prints the sorted list. That code and the entire program appears in Listing 11.1. Table 11.1 shows the property settings for the application. An example of the output is shown in Figure 11.26.

Figure 11.26.
*The Shell Sort sample
application running.*

Table 11.1. The Shell Sort sample application (ShelSort.vbp).

Object	Property	Setting
Form	AutoRedraw	True
	BorderStyle	3-Fixed Dialog
	Caption	Shell Sort Example
	Name	frmShellSort

Listing 11.1. The complete code for the sample application.

```
Option Explicit

Private Sub Form_Activate()
    Static Array(9) As Integer
    Dim I As Integer
    Dim J As Integer
    Dim Temp As Integer
    Dim NumPartitions As Integer
    Dim PartitionSize As Integer
    Dim NumItems As Integer
    Dim Low As Integer
    Dim High As Integer

    Array(1) = 9
    Array(2) = 8
    Array(3) = 7
    Array(4) = 6
    Array(5) = 5
    Array(6) = 4
    Array(7) = 3
    Array(8) = 2
    Array(9) = 1

    Print
    Print Tab(10); " I"; Tab(24); "Array (I)"
    Print Tab(9); "----"; Tab(24); "--------"
    Print

    For I = 1 To 9
        Print Tab(10); I; Tab(26); Array(I)
    Next I

    Print
    Print Tab(10); " Sorting..."

    NumItems = UBound(Array, 1)
    PartitionSize = Int((NumItems + 1) / 2)

    Do
        NumPartitions = (NumItems + 1) / PartitionSize
        Low = 1
        For I = 1 To NumPartitions - 1
            High = Low + PartitionSize - 1

            If High > NumItems - PartitionSize Then
                High = NumItems - PartitionSize
            End If

            For J = Low To High
                If Array(J) > Array(J + PartitionSize) Then
                    Temp = Array(J)
                    Array(J) = Array(J + PartitionSize)
                    Array(J + PartitionSize) = Temp
                End If
            Next J

            Low = Low + PartitionSize
```

```
      Next I
      PartitionSize = PartitionSize - 1
Loop While PartitionSize > 0

Print
Print Tab(10); " I"; Tab(24); "Array (I)"
Print Tab(9); "-----"; Tab(24); "-------"
Print

For I = 1 To 9
      Print Tab(10); I; Tab(26); Array(I)
Next I

End Sub
```

Run the application now and see if the shell sort works correctly.

Quick Sorts

In addition to shell sorts, another popular sorting algorithm is the quick sort. Quick sorts works like this:

1. You find a key value or test value to use to compare values. The best value in this case would be the median value of the array elements. In practice, though, a random entry is normally chosen. In the discussion to follow, you will choose a value from the center of the array.

2. Next, the program divides the array into two partitions: those values less than the test value and those greater than the test value. In the age example used in the previous section, a quick sort program would move upward in the array until it came to the first value that is greater than the test value. Then it would move down the array, beginning from the end, until it found a number less than the test value and swapped the two values. The program would continue until all the numbers in the first partition were less than the test value, and all the numbers in the second partition were greater.

3. The same steps would be applied to each partition. A new test value would be selected from each partition and each partition would be broken up into two new partitions. One of these new partitions would hold the numbers that were less than the test value, and the other partition would hold those that were greater. The program would continue in that way, splitting partitions continuously, until just two numbers were in a partition. At that point, the program would compare and switch them, if necessary.

You might have noticed that each subsequent step is a quick sort. In other words, an array is divided into two partitions less than and greater than the test value. Each partition is then broken into two partitions, a new test value is found for each partition, and so on. In this way quick sorts easily lend themselves to recursion, and this is the way they are usually coded. Because Visual Basic supports recursion, the quick sort you develop in this part of the chapter is no exception.

What Is Recursion All About?

If the term *recursion* is new to you, you should know that it refers to a routine that calls itself. If a programming task can be divided into a number of identical levels, the task can be dealt with recursively. Every time the routine calls itself it deals with a deeper level. After the final level is reached, control returns through each successive layer back to the beginning.

Now put this in code. Start a new project and change the default form's Name and Caption properties to frmQuickSort and QuickSort Example. Save the form and project as QuickSort.frm and QuickSort.vbp, respectively. Because this routine is recursive, you will need to set up a routine called SortQuick() that will be called from the main program (this routine calls itself repeatedly, or recursively). Add that subroutine to the code window by choosing Procedure from the Insert menu. Then add the array arguments that can be passed to the Sub procedure when it is called, like this:

```
Private Sub SortQuick(Array() As Integer, SortFrom As Integer,
➥SortTo As Integer)

End Sub
```

To make the quick sort happen, you just pass the array name to sort, the index where the sorting will begin—SortFrom—and the index where the sorting will end—SortTo. Working this way is useful when there is a particular partition of an array that needs to be sorted.

Start with the final case SortQuick() will have to handle: a partition of only two elements.

In this case, each element is compared to its neighbor—the only other element in this partition—and they are swapped, if necessary. That's all there is to the final case in the quick sort algorithm.

If the partition size is greater than two, however, the values need to be sorted from Array(SortFrom) to Array(SortTo) while being compared to a test value. Then each partition needs to be divided into two new partitions, and SortQuick() must be called again on every partition.

Here's how that process works. First, a test value has to be picked and the present partition is divided into two new partitions based on that test value. Next, the program starts by moving up from the bottom of the partition and stops at any values greater than the test value.

The program should also sort from the top of the partition down in the same pass, looking for the first value that's smaller than the test value. If the program finds any numbers that should be swapped between partitions, it does so, and then moves on to the next elements.

The program continues until the first index being compared is the same second index and two partitions have been created. Next, the routine calls itself (SortQuick()) again for each of the resulting partitions. (Note that these partitions can be of unequal size.) The following is the completed SortQuick routine:

```
Private Sub SortQuick(Array() As Integer, SortFrom As Integer,
➥SortTo As Integer)
      Dim Temp As Integer
      Dim I As Integer
      Dim J As Integer
      Dim AtRandom As Integer
      Dim Test As Integer

      Select Case SortFrom
            Case Is >= SortTo
                  Exit Sub

            Case Is = SortTo - 1   'Final Case
                  If Array(SortFrom) > Array(SortTo) Then
                        Temp = Array(SortFrom)
                        Array(SortFrom) = Array(SortTo)
                        Array(SortTo) = Temp
                  End If
                  Exit Sub

            Case Else   'Split the problem
                  AtRandom = (SortFrom + SortTo) \ 2
                  Test = Array(AtRandom)
                  Temp = Array(AtRandom)
                  Array(AtRandom) = Array(SortTo)
                  Array(SortTo) = Temp

                  Do
                        For I = SortFrom To SortTo - 1
                              If Array(I) > Test Then
                                    Exit For
                              End If
                        Next I

                        For J = SortTo To I + 1 Step -1
                              If Array(J) < Test Then
                                    Exit For
                              End If
                        Next J

                        If I < J Then
                              Temp = Array(I)
                              Array(I) = Array(J)
                              Array(J) = Temp
                        End If

                  Loop Until I >= J

                  Temp = Array(I)
                  Array(I) = Array(SortTo)
                  Array(SortTo) = Temp

                  SortQuick Array(), SortFrom, I - 1
                  SortQuick Array(), I + 1, SortTo

      End Select

End Sub
```

That's all there is to it. The sort continues recursively until it gets down to the final case where the partition size is 1 and the final swaps are completed.

Now add something to sort. Add the following code to the frmQuickSort Load() event. (This is same array that was sorted in the Shell Sort example.)

```
Private Sub Form_Load()
Static Array(1 to 9) As Integer
        Dim I As Integer

        Array(1) = 9
        Array(2) = 8
        Array(3) = 7
        Array(4) = 6
        Array(5) = 5
        Array(6) = 4
        Array(7) = 3
        Array(8) = 2
        Array(9) = 1

        Print
        Print Tab(10); " I"; Tab(24); "Array (I)"
        Print Tab(9); "-----"; Tab(24); "-------"
        Print

        For I = 1 To 9
                Print Tab(10); I; Tab(26); Array(I)
        Next I

        SortQuick Array(), 1, UBound(Array, 1)

        Print
        Print Tab(10); " Sorting..."

        Print
        Print Tab(10); " I"; Tab(24); "Array (I)"
        Print Tab(9); "-----"; Tab(24); "-------"
        Print

        For I = 1 To 9
                Print Tab(10); I; Tab(26); Array(I)
        Next I

End Sub
```

That's all there is to it. Before you run the application to test it out, make sure the form's AutoRedraw property is set to True, otherwise the graphics won't be redrawn when the form is covered up. See Figure 11.27 for what the output should be.

The complete code for this project appears in Listing 11.2. Table 11.2 shows the settings for the form's properties.

Figure 11.27.
The Quick Sort application running.

Table 11.2. The Quick Sort sample application (QSort.vbp).

Object	Property	Setting
Form	AutoRedraw	True
	BorderStyle	3-Fixed Dialog
	Caption	Quick Sort Example
	Name	frmQuickSort

Listing 11.2. The complete code for **frmQuickSort**.

```
Option Explicit

Private Sub Form_Load()
        Static Array(1 to 9) As Integer
        Dim I As Integer

        Array(1) = 9
        Array(2) = 8
        Array(3) = 7
        Array(4) = 6
        Array(5) = 5
        Array(6) = 4
        Array(7) = 3
        Array(8) = 2
        Array(9) = 1

        Print
        Print Tab(10); " I"; Tab(24); "Array (I)"
        Print Tab(9); "-----"; Tab(24); "-------"
        Print
```

continues

Listing 11.2. continued

```
        For I = 1 To 9
                Print Tab(10); I; Tab(26); Array(I)
        Next I

        SortQuick Array(), 1, UBound(Array, 1)

        Print
        Print Tab(10); " Sorting..."

        Print
        Print Tab(10); " I"; Tab(24); "Array (I)"
        Print Tab(9); "-----"; Tab(24); "-------"
        Print

        For I = 1 To 9
                Print Tab(10); I; Tab(26); Array(I)
        Next I

End Sub

Private Sub SortQuick(Array() As Integer, SortFrom As Integer, _
                SortTo As Integer)
        Dim Temp As Integer
        Dim I As Integer
        Dim J As Integer
        Dim AtRandom As Integer
        Dim Test As Integer

        Select Case SortFrom
                Case Is >= SortTo
                        Exit Sub

                Case Is = SortTo - 1  'Final Case
                        If Array(SortFrom) > Array(SortTo) Then
                                Temp = Array(SortFrom)
                                Array(SortFrom) = Array(SortTo)
                                Array(SortTo) = Temp
                        End If
                        Exit Sub

                Case Else    'Split the problem
                        AtRandom = (SortFrom + SortTo) \ 2
                        Test = Array(AtRandom)
                        Temp = Array(AtRandom)
                        Array(AtRandom) = Array(SortTo)
                        Array(SortTo) = Temp

                        Do
                                For I = SortFrom To SortTo - 1
                                        If Array(I) > Test Then
                                                Exit For
                                        End If
                                Next I

                                For J = SortTo To I + 1 Step -1
                                        If Array(J) < Test Then
                                                Exit For
```

```
                                End If
                        Next J

                        If I < J Then
                                Temp = Array(I)
                                Array(I) = Array(J)
                                Array(J) = Temp
                        End If

                Loop Until I >= J

                Temp = Array(I)
                Array(I) = Array(SortTo)
                Array(SortTo) = Temp

                SortQuick Array(), SortFrom, I - 1
                SortQuick Array(), I + 1, SortTo

        End Select

End Sub
```

That's it for sorting. Both the shell sort and the quick sort are pretty fast—the one you should use depends on the application. You might want to try them both and use the faster of the two.

Searching Your Data

Now that you have ordered data, searching through it becomes much easier. If the data is unordered, you would have no choice but to check one value after another until a match is found. That's exactly what happens in the following program:

```
Option Explicit

Private Sub Form_Load()
        Static Array(1 to 9) As Integer
        Dim I As Integer

        'Unordered Search

        Array(1) = 9
        Array(2) = 8
        Array(3) = 7
        Array(4) = 6
        Array(5) = 5
        Array(6) = 4
        Array(7) = 3
        Array(8) = 2
        Array(9) = 1

        Print
        Print
        Print Tab(10); "Searching the unordered list for the value 1."
        Print

        For I = LBound(Array, 1)To UBound(Array, 1)
```

```
        If Array(I) = 1 Then
                Print Tab(10); "Value of 1 is in element:   "; I
        End If
    Next I

End Sub
```

The program in Figure 11.28 just keeps scanning the list of values until it finds what it's looking for.

Figure 11.28.
An unordered search sample application running.

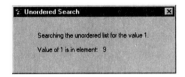

On the other hand, programs can be constructed much more intelligently when searching a sorted list. For example, if a sorted array had the following values in it:

1 2 3 4 5 6 7 8 9 10 11 12 13 14 15

and the program was searching for the entry with 10 in it, the application could begin at the center of the list, as in Figure 11.29.

Figure 11.29.
A program searches for the entry that has a value of 10 by beginning the search as close to the center of the list as possible.

Because 10 is greater than 8, the program will divide the array into two parts, using 8 as the dividing line, and check the midpoint of the array's upper section (see Figure 11.30).

Figure 11.30.
The program divides the list into two and checks the midpoint value of the upper part.

Then, because 10 is less than 12, the program will move down and cut the remaining distance in half, and finally find the correct value (see Figure 11.31).

In this way the program zeroes in on the number, cutting down the quantity of values that have to be checked. Now see how this works in a program. Start a new project and change the `Name` and `Caption` properties of the default form to `frmOrdered` and `Ordered Search Example`. Then save the form as OrdSrch.frm and the project as OrdSrch.vbp.

Figure 11.31.
*The final step divides the
upper partition into two parts
and finds the correct value.*

Next, set up the array to be searched. In this example, have the program search an array of nine elements for the entry with a value of 8.

First the program needs to cut the array into two partitions and check the value that is at the midpoint—TestIndex. Then the search should begin. The program should continue looping over the partition size. If the partition size becomes zero without finding the specified value, then that value is not in the array.

The program has to check whether it has found the target. If so, it can quit. If not, it has to go on to the next iteration of the loop, setting TestIndex to the midpoint of either the upper or lower partition, and divide that partition into two new partitions. If the target is a bigger value than the value at the current array location, the program needs to move to the partition containing higher values.

On the other hand, if the search value is smaller than the compared element the program needs to move to the lower partition, which holds the lower values.

The program should continue until it finds what it is searching for or until the partition becomes zero, which means that the searched value does not exist in the array. If the program is not successful, though, it should perform two final tests: it should check the search value against the first and last entries in the array. The reason for this is that the algorithm demands that all numbers checked be *straddled* by two other values. That is true of every element in the array except for the first and last ones. If the program did not find what it was looking for, these two values must be explicitly checked. The output of the project is shown in Figure 11.32. The completed code for the application is available in Listing 11.3. Table 11.3 shows how the form's properties should be set.

Figure 11.32.
*The Ordered Search
application running.*

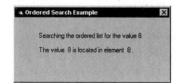

Table 11.3. The Ordered Search sample application (OrdSrch.vbp).

Object	Property	Setting
Form	AutoRedraw	True
	BorderStyle	3-Fixed Dialog
	Caption	Ordered Sort Example
	Name	frmOrdered

Listing 11.3. The complete code for OrdSrch.frm.

```vb
Option Explicit

Private Sub Form_Load()
    Static Array(9) As Integer
    Dim Partition As Integer
    Dim SearchValue As Integer
    Dim TestIndex As Integer

    'Ordered Search

    Array(1) = 1
    Array(2) = 2
    Array(3) = 3
    Array(4) = 4
    Array(5) = 5
    Array(6) = 6
    Array(7) = 7
    Array(8) = 8
    Array(9) = 9

    SearchValue = 8
    Print
    Print
    Print Tab(10); "Searching the ordered list for the value 8."
    Print

    Partition = (UBound(Array, 1) + 1) \ 2
    TestIndex = Partition

    Do
        Partition = Partition \ 2
            If Array(TestIndex) = SearchValue Then
                Print Tab(10); "The value "; SearchValue; _
                    "is located in element "; TestIndex; "."
Exit Do
            End If

            If Array(TestIndex) < SearchValue Then
                TestIndex = TestIndex + Partition
            Else
                TestIndex = TestIndex - Partition
            End If

    Loop While Partition > 0

    'Can only find straddled numbers, so add these tests:
    If Array(1) = SearchValue Then
        Print Tab(10); "The value "; SearchValue; "is located in element 1."
    End If

    If Array(UBound(Array, 1)) = SearchValue Then
        Print Tab(10); "The value "; SearchValue; _
            "is located in element "; UBound(Array, 1); "."
    End If

End Sub
```

That is how an ordered search works. This technique could come in useful in many applications that need to search through extensive lists.

Now to delve into a spreadsheet application. That's the next, and final, topic of discussion in this chapter.

A Sample Spreadsheet Application

A spreadsheet application seems quite appropriate as the final example of advanced data handling. Creating such a program is easy with the Microsoft Grid control. To get going on this application, start a new project and change the Name and Caption properties of the default form to frmSpread and Spreadsheet, respectively. Then save the form as Ssheet.frm and the project as Ssheet.vbp.

Now add the Grid control to the project by selecting the Custom Controls option from the Tools menu or by pressing Ctrl+T on the keyboard, or by using the pop-up menu. The Custom Controls dialog box opens. Scroll down the Available Controls list box until you find Microsoft Grid Control (Grid32.ocx). Select it, and then click OK. Notice that the Visual Basic Toolbox stretches to accommodate the new grid tool at the bottom.

Next, using the Grid tool that you just added to the project, draw a grid on frmSpread. Change the objects' properties to match those listed in Table 11.4.

Table 11.4. Properties for frmSpread.

Object	Property	Setting
Form	AutoRedraw	True
	BorderStyle	3-Fixed Dialog
	Caption	Spreadsheet
	Name	frmSpread
Grid	BackColor	White
	Cols	7
	Name	grdSpread
	Rows	7
	ScrollBars	0-None

When you are finished, the spreadsheet template should look something like Figure 11.33.

Figure 11.33.
The Spreadsheet template.

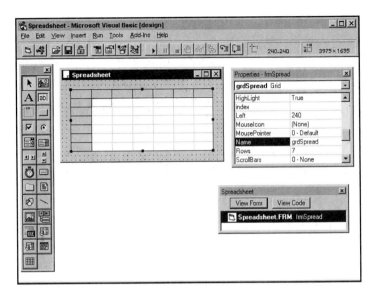

The application can now refer to the individual cells in the spreadsheet by making a particular cell the *current* cell. (Making a cell current is like moving the focus to a form or control.) To do that, you need to set only the grid's Row and Col properties. Row and Col are completely different properties from the Rows and Cols properties that are available in the Properties Window. (This is a bit confusing, isn't it!) Here's the difference between the two sets of properties:

- The Cols and Rows properties can be set at design-time (hence, they are available in the Properties Window). These properties set the total number of columns and rows available on a Grid control.

- The Col and Row properties set the active cell in a Grid control and are not available at design-time.

Suppose that you want to keep track of expenses such as these:

$400	Rent
$100	Food
$80	Car
$15	Phone
$10	Gas
?	Total

These expenses can be tracked by first labeling the cells in the spreadsheet using the Form_Load() event. All you need to do is label the rows with numbers and the columns with letters. This is the standard way spreadsheets are labeled. Then you need to enter the preceding list. That process appears as follows:

```
Private Sub Form_Load()
    Static Items(6) As String
    Dim Setup As Integer

    Items(1) = "Rent"
    Items(2) = "Food"
    Items(3) = "Car"
    Items(4) = "Phone"
    Items(5) = "Gas"
    Items(6) = "Total"

    grdSpread.Row = 1

    For Setup = 1 To 6
        grdSpread.Col = 0
        grdSpread.Row = Setup
        grdSpread.Text = Str$(Setup)
        grdSpread.Col = 2
        grdSpread.Text = Items(Setup)
    Next Setup

    grdSpread.Col = 1
    grdSpread.Row = 0

    For Setup = 1 To 6
        grdSpread.Col = Setup
        grdSpread.Text = Chr$(Asc("A") - 1 + Setup)
    Next Setup

    grdSpread.Row = 1
    grdSpread.Col = 1

End Sub
```

Run the application now to see how the code sets the grid rows and columns. The result of the code appears in Figure 11.34.

Figure 11.34.
The completed Spreadsheet template.

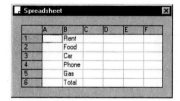

Now the program can read the numbers as they are entered in the data cells and keep a running total in the bottom box called Total. That process is performed by the grdSpread_KeyPress() event. Whenever a KeyPress() event occurs, the program should replace the typed number in the appropriate cell and update the running total at the bottom of the column (the grid control does not do this automatically). Therefore, first add the characters that the user types to the current cell in the following way:

```
grdSpread.Text = grdSpread.Text & Chr$(KeyAscii)
```

As the user types, the values appear in the current cell. The user can then change to another cell, using the mouse or by pressing the arrow keys. Next, the program should update the running total in column A. First, save the current cell's `Row` and `Col` values.

```
Private Sub grdSpread_KeyPress(KeyAscii As Integer)
    Dim OldRow As Integer
    Dim OldCol As Integer
    :

    grdSpread.Text = grdSpread.Text + Chr$(KeyAscii)
    OldRow = grdSpread.Row
    OldCol = grdSpread.Col

    :

End Sub
```

Then all the numbers in column A should be added and looped over.

All that remains is to place the sum of the values into the Total cell and restore the original current cell. The keypress routine that will enable you to edit the grid appears like this:

```
Private Sub grdSpread_KeyPress(KeyAscii As Integer)
    Dim OldRow As Integer
    Dim OldCol As Integer
    Dim RowIndex As Integer
    Dim Sum As Integer

    grdSpread.Text = grdSpread.Text & Chr$(KeyAscii)
    OldRow = grdSpread.Row
    OldCol = grdSpread.Col

    grdSpread.Col = 1 'Add numbers to first column
    grdSpread.Row = 0
    Sum = 0

    For RowIndex = 1 To 5
        grdSpread.Row = RowIndex
        Sum = Sum + Val(grdSpread.Text)
    Next RowIndex

    grdSpread.Row = 6
    grdSpread.Text = Str$(Sum)
    grdSpread.Row = OldRow
    grdSpread.Col = OldCol

End Sub
```

Now the spreadsheet works. As the user types the values in the first column, a running total appears in the Total cell, as in Figure 11.35.

Figure 11.35.
The Spreadsheet application running.

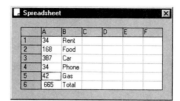

As you can imagine, this program is easily adaptable for many applications—anywhere there is a need for a spreadsheet. Note, however, that connecting cells together, as you have done by keeping a running total in the Total cell, has to be programmed into the code unless you write a program smart enough to read spreadsheet formulas as the user types them directly. Table 11.5 shows how the properties of the controls should be set. The application's code appears in Listing 11.4.

Table 11.5. The Spreadsheet application. (Ssheet.vbp)

Object	Property	Setting
Form	AutoRedraw	True
	BorderStyle	3-Fixed Dialog
	Caption	Spreadsheet
	Name	frmSpread
Grid	BackColor	White
	Cols	7
	Name	grdSpread
	Rows	7
	ScrollBars	0-None

Listing 11.4. The complete code for Ssheet.frm.

```
Option Explicit

Private Sub Form_Load()
    Static Items(1 to 6) As String
    Dim Setup As Integer

    Items(1) = "Rent"
    Items(2) = "Food"
    Items(3) = "Car"
    Items(4) = "Phone"
    Items(5) = "Gas"
    Items(6) = "Total"
```

continues

Listing 11.4. **continued**

```
        grdSpread.Row = 1

    For Setup = 1 To 6
        grdSpread.Col = 0
        grdSpread.Row = Setup
        grdSpread.Text = Str$(Setup)
        grdSpread.Col = 2
        grdSpread.Text = Items(Setup)
    Next Setup

    grdSpread.Col = 1
    grdSpread.Row = 0

    For Setup = 1 To 6
        grdSpread.Col = Setup
        grdSpread.Text = Chr$(Asc("A") - 1 + Setup)
    Next Setup

    grdSpread.Row = 1
    grdSpread.Col = 1

End Sub

Private Sub grdSpread_KeyPress(KeyAscii As Integer)
    Dim OldRow As Integer
    Dim OldCol As Integer
    Dim RowIndex As Integer
    Dim Sum As Integer

    grdSpread.Text = grdSpread.Text & Chr$(KeyAscii)
    OldRow = grdSpread.Row
    OldCol = grdSpread.Col
    grdSpread.Col = 1 'Add numbers to first column
    grdSpread.Row = 0
    Sum = 0

    For RowIndex = 1 To 5
        grdSpread.Row = RowIndex
        Sum = Sum + Val(grdSpread.Text)
    Next RowIndex

    grdSpread.Row = 6
    grdSpread.Text = Str$(Sum)
    grdSpread.Row = OldRow
    grdSpread.Col = OldCol

End Sub
```

That's it for the spreadsheet application, and advanced data-handling and sorting. In this chapter you have seen a few popular methods for handling numeric data. When you design code, it is always important to organize the data correctly. As mentioned at the beginning of the chapter, that can be half the battle of writing a successful program. The next chapter covers program debugging and error-handling.

Summary

You learned several data-handling techniques in this chapter, including how to use arrays, linked lists, doubly linked lists, binary trees, and circular buffers. You learned how to use the Grid control to quickly create a functioning spreadsheet application. In addition, you saw some useful sorting algorithms: the shell sort and the quick sort. And you even developed your own ordered search program. As you might imagine, it is much easier to search through ordered data than through un-ordered data. If a program maintains long data lists, you might keep it sorted using one of the techniques learned here and then search through it using an ordered search.

The skills picked up in this chapter can be applied to any program that maintains more than a rudimentary amount of data. Obviously, this includes database programs, but it also applies to data-entry applications, disk-optimizing programs, which maintain linked lists of a file's various parts on disk, mail-merge programs, arcade-style games, and others. Binary trees, for example, are very common when data can be distinguished on the basis of a yes-no answer. Data-handling can be tricky, but with the techniques learned here you're ready to manage many kinds of applications.

New Properties	Description
Col	The column number of the current cell in a Grid control. Available only at runtime.
Cols	The total number of columns specified for a Grid control. This property is available at design-time.
Row	The row number of the current cell in a Grid control. Available only at runtime.
Rows	The total number of rows specified for a Grid control. This property is available at design-time.

New Functions	Description
LBound	Returns the minimum value an array index can take.
UBound	Returns the maximum value an array index can take.

12

Error-Handling and Debugging

There are three kinds of errors you might encounter in Visual Basic projects:

- Syntax and compile errors
- Run-time errors
- Logical errors

Compile errors result from improperly constructed code. Examples include incorrectly entered keywords, omitted punctuation in a Visual Basic statement, mismatched `If` and `End Ifs`, and incorrectly spelled variables. This kind of error is easily dealt with if you follow some simple practices. In order to quickly catch and fix compile errors, you should require variable declarations in projects and get Visual Basic to automatically check for syntax errors.

Variable declaration is required in projects with the `Option Explicit` statement added at the beginning of every module in a project. To turn this on, select Options from the Tools menu. When the Options dialog box opens, select the Environments Tab Sheet. Select Require Variable Declarations by making sure that its box is checked. This will automatically insert an `Option Explicit` statement at the beginning of every new form or module in a project.

The effect of requiring variable declarations is to disallow implicit variable declarations. (For more information on this topic, see Chapter 4, "Programming in Visual Basic.") This means that a program containing undeclared variables cannot be run. Also, typographic errors in variable names will be pinpointed immediately (which is a very handy time-saving feature).

The Auto Syntax Check option works in much the same way. This option is also set on the Environments Tab Sheet. To turn it on, make sure the Display Syntax Errors box is checked. You should routinely work with this setting enabled. It can save a lot of time and grief. When syntax checking is enabled, Visual Basic will display an error message and highlight the offending code as soon as you enter a syntax error in the Code window. Let's look at two examples of how it works.

Type `If` in a form click event. Now suppose that you forget to put in the expression that was to be evaluated, and you go to do something else. When your cursor leaves the line, you will get an error message as in Figure 12.1. The incomplete `If` statement will be highlighted.

Figure 12.1.
*The Visual Basic syntax
error message box.*

Delete the incomplete If statement and add a MsgBox statement with no message. Try to run the project. If you have syntax checking on, you will get a message saying Argument not optional with the incomplete MsgBox statement, as shown in Figure 12.2.

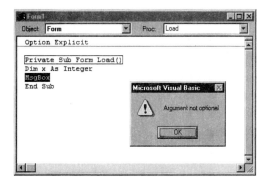

Figure 12.2.
Another Visual Basic error message box.

Setting the variable declaration and syntax checking on makes it easy to take care of syntax, compile, and spelling errors.

This chapter will show you how to handle the other two types of errors in Visual Basic: *run-time errors* and *logical errors*. Run-time errors are detected by Visual Basic and are caused when a statement attempts an operation that is impossible to carry out. An example of this would be a statement that attempted to divide by zero, or one that attempted to open a nonexistent file. In particular, the chapter will cover these topics:

- Handling run-time errors without crashing
- Using Visual Basic's Debugger
- How to use breakpoints
- The Debug window
- Trappable errors
- Error codes
- Converting error codes into English messages
- How to test your programs
- The Err object
- How to create an error
- How to write working error-handlers
- Using the Resume and Resume Next statements

There are a few demonstration programs in this chapter. You will also see how to add error-handling to a few programs written in previous chapters. When it comes to debugging, however, the programs you write—such as an investment calculator—will have a few bugs in them. You will have to find and eliminate these bugs. Mostly, what you will be learning in this chapter are new skills: error-handling and debugging. These skills are invaluable to programmers. You'll find yourself using them time and time again, especially if you develop programs longer than two dozen lines or so.

Any program that handles files should include some file error-handling because that's one of the most common types of run-time errors. Such errors include a disk becoming filled up or not being placed in a drive, a file not being found, or a nonexistent record being requested. Instead of letting Visual Basic handle errors like these (by default, Visual Basic displays error information useful only to the programmer), your programs should be capable of handling them—for example, by telling the user to put a disk in the drive, if this is necessary. With that in mind, this chapter includes a complete generic error-handling routine for file errors.

In Visual Basic, there are some excellent ways to handle errors. This means that your programs don't have to simply crash. (Rather unprofessional, don't you think?) Even more importantly, you should make sure that there are no logical errors in your programs. Users might sometimes be able to fix run-time errors, but they won't be able to do anything about logical errors. For these reasons, the skills developed in this chapter are necessary ones for the programmer to cultivate and use.

Even the best programmers make errors. Clearly, the longer the program is, the more complex the code will be. This makes it even more likely that as your projects get longer, errors will appear. Errors come in several different flavors: those that cause design-time errors, those that cause run-time errors, and those that make your programs produce incorrect or unexpected results (logical errors). Visual Basic handles the first type, design-time errors, by refusing to run programs until they're fixed and offers assistance in the form of error messages. The second two types, run-time errors and logical errors, are left up to the programmer to fix and are the primary subject of this chapter.

A run-time error is what Visual Basic refers to as a *trappable error*. Visual Basic recognizes that there is an error and allows you to trap it and take some corrective action. (Untrappable errors usually occur only at design-time.) Logical errors are different because Visual Basic usually does not recognize that there is a problem, and the code still does not operate as intended. For example, if you had a function called Counter that was supposed to increase an internal counter and return its current value every time it was called, it might look like this:

```
Function Counter()
    Dim CounterValue As Integer

    CounterValue = CounterValue + 1
    Counter = CounterValue
End Function
```

However, there is a bug here: CounterValue is not declared Static. Thus, every time this function is called, CounterValue starts at 0. The function then adds 1 to CounterValue, so 1 is returned every time. A function that simply returns 1 every time it is called does not generate a run-time error, but in light of its intended purpose, contains a bug.

You will be able to find trappable errors without difficulty, because Visual Basic generates them. Visual Basic knows exactly when they occur and allows you, the programmer, to take some action.

However, logical errors are another story. In their case, you will have to use Visual Basic's debugging capabilities to find out what went wrong and work your way through the program slowly, possibly even statement by statement. Good programmers learn these debugging skills. The best thing of all, of course, is to write programs that produce as few errors as possible. When errors do happen, they should be easy to find and fix. You should aim for this. But when bugs do creep in, you must know how to deal with them. The first topic in this chapter deals with testing the programs you write.

A Guideline for Testing Programs

When programs run, they usually operate on ranges of data. For example, a program might read the value of an integer ranging from -32,768 to 32,767 entered by the user. (Remember that if the value could not vary, there would be no point in reading it.) The limits of that value, -32,768 and 32,767, are called its *bounds*. When trying to check your programs for potential problems, it is important that you cover the entire range of such values. That does not normally mean checking every value between -32,768 and 32,767, but it does mean checking values at the bounds of the possible range for the variable, as well as some mid-range values and any other values that are likely to make problems. A great many logical errors are caused by *one-off* conditions. This means that a counter or loop is off by one. One-off errors should be suspected whenever there is a logical error with a loop or counter involved.

For example, suppose that a program reads a value that represents the number of students in a class. Perhaps after adding all the students' test scores, the user would like to divide by this value to find the class average. This is no problem for 15 or 20 students, but what if the user enters 0? Even though it is in the allowed range for unsigned integers, dividing by this value will result in an error. Or, what if the students' test scores were stored in another unsigned integer and it was found that as the number of students increased, the division did not give the desired accuracy? Checking a program's bounding values like this is vitally important. In general, there will be bounds for every crucial variable, and every combination of these values should be checked when running a program to see how they interact. This is particularly important when it comes to array indices.

Mid-range values should be checked as well. It might turn out that some combination of such values will also generate unexpected errors. The longer you test a program under usual and unusual operating circumstances, the more confidence you will have in it. As programs get more complex, the testing period normally gets longer. This is why major software companies often send out thousands of preliminary versions of their software for testing by programmers. These preliminary software versions are called *betas*. The final software package is usually called the *gamma* or *gold* version. Software companies also use error-testing programs that automatically input every possible value to test the software.

In addition, you should attempt to duplicate every run-time problem that might occur to see how a program will react. File operations are great at generating such errors. For example, what if a floppy disk is full and the user tries to write to it? What if the specified input file doesn't exist? What if the specified file to write to is read-only? What if the floppy disk has been removed? What if the user asks the application to write record -15 in a file? Of course, it is hard to generate every conceivable set of problematic circumstances, but the closer you come, the more polished and professional your application will be.

First, a brief discussion about `Resume`, `Resume Next`, and `Resume Line` and how these statements can effect error-handlers in your applications.

The *Resume* Statement

You might recall that some error-handling was built into the Editor application. The reason for this was because file-handling is such a notorious source of possible errors (as is handling input from the keyboard). Note the line at the end of the error-handler in the Editor application. You used the `Resume Next` statement (which is the same for both `frmLoad` and `frmSave`). The following code is from the `frmLoad cmdOK_Click()` event:

```
Private Sub cmdOK_Click()
    Dim TheFile As String

    On Error GoTo FileError

    If (Right(dirLook.Path, 1) = "\") Then
        TheFile = dirLook.Path + filFind.FileName

    Else
        TheFile = dirLook.Path + "\" + filFind.FileName

    End If

    Open TheFile For Input As #1
    frmNotePad.txtPadText.Text = Input(LOF(1), #1)       'Read File
    Close #1                                             'Close File
    Unload cmdOK.Parent

    Exit Sub

FileError:
    MsgBox "File Error", 48, "Editor"                    'MsgBox for file error
    Resume Next

End Sub
```

Instead of `Resume Next`, you could have used `Resume`. However, this would have different consequences. (`Resume Next` will be discussed shortly.) The simple statement `Resume` will retry the operation that caused the error after the user takes a corrective action. When Visual Basic encounters a `Resume` statement in an error-handler (such as after an `On Error GoTo` type of routine has been set up and entered), it leaves the error-handler and returns to the statement that caused the error. In other words, `Resume` allows the user to retry an operation. Suppose that you had used `Resume` in the error-handler instead. When the `Resume` statement is encountered, the program would jump back to the following line (in bold):

```
Private Sub cmdOK_Click()
    Dim TheFile As String

    On Error GoTo FileError

    If (Right(dirLook.Path, 1) = "\") Then
        TheFile = dirLook.Path + filFind.FileName

    Else
        TheFile = dirLook.Path + "\" + filFind.FileName

    End If

    Open TheFile For Input As #1
    frmNotePad.txtPadText.Text = Input(LOF(1), #1)     'Read File
    Close #1                                           'Close File
    Unload cmdOK.Parent

    Exit Sub

FileError:
    MsgBox "File Error", 48, "Editor"                  'MsgBox for file error
    Resume

End Sub
```

If the user had a problem opening the file, the application would display an error message, let the user take some corrective action, and then try opening the file again. Note, however, that this is a potential problem. If the user decides not to open the file after all, there should be some way to exit the `Sub` procedure. That could be added by using a message box that has two buttons (OK and Cancel), instead of just one (OK). The response could also be read in at the same time using the `MsgBox()` function. (You might recall that `MsgBox` has two forms. It can be used either as a statement if no reply is expected, or as a function if input is desired from the user.)

```
Private Sub cmdOK_Click()
    Dim TheFile As String
    Dim Response As Integer

    On Error GoTo FileError

    If (Right(dirLook.Path, 1) = "\") Then
        TheFile = dirLook.Path + filFind.FileName

    Else
        TheFile = dirLook.Path + "\" + filFind.FileName

    End If

    Open TheFile For Input As #1
    frmNotePad.txtPadText.Text = Input(LOF(1), #1)     'Read File
    Close #1                                           'Close File
    Unload cmdOK.Parent
```

```
        Exit Sub

FileError:
        Response = MsgBox(Msg$, 49, "Editor")
        Resume

End Sub
```

Here a message box of type parameter 48 (an exclamation point symbol) +1 (including both OK and Cancel buttons) is being passed. And the user's response is placed in the variable Response. If the user selects the OK button, this response will equal 1; if she selects the Cancel button, it will equal 2. The code can be modified to retry the problematic operation if the user selects the OK button like this:

```
Private Sub cmdOK_Click()
        Dim TheFile As String
        Dim Response As Integer

        On Error GoTo FileError

        If (Right(dirLook.Path, 1) = "\") Then
            TheFile = dirLook.Path + filFind.FileName

        Else
            TheFile = dirLook.Path + "\" + filFind.FileName

        End If

        Open TheFile For Input As #1
        frmNotePad.txtPadText.Text = Input(LOF(1), #1)      'Read File
        Close #1                                            'Close File
        Unload cmdOK.Parent

        Exit Sub

FileError:
        Response = MsgBox(Msg$, 49, "Editor")
        If Response = 1 Then
            Resume
        Else
            :
        End If
End Sub
```

In this case, if the user chooses OK, the program moves back to the same line that caused the error—most likely, the Open statement—and tries again. On the other hand, if the user chooses the Cancel button, the application should exit the Sub procedure entirely. However, it is not good to rely on the End Sub statement at the end of the procedure. If Visual Basic is in an error-handler and reaches the end of the procedure without finding a Resume statement, it will stop everything and helpfully point out that there is no Resume statement in the error-handler. (It will even do this in compiled code, placing a special No Resume window on the screen.)

In this case though, you should not use Resume if the user chooses Cancel because there are some errors that a user can't fix at this level. For example, if the error occurred because the file was too big to fit into memory, the user will have to leave this procedure (`cmdOK_Click()`), select a new file, and then select the OK button again. To leave this procedure without messages about the lack of a `Resume` statement, you need to add `Exit Sub`, like this:

```
Private Sub cmdOK_Click()
    Dim TheFile As String
    Dim Response As Integer

    On Error GoTo FileError

    If (Right(dirLook.Path, 1) = "\") Then
        TheFile = dirLook.Path + filFind.FileName

    Else
        TheFile = dirLook.Path + "\" + filFind.FileName

    End If

    Open TheFile For Input As #1
    frmNotePad.txtPadText.Text = Input(LOF(1), #1)      'Read File
    Close #1                                            'Close File
    Unload cmdOK.Parent

    Exit Sub

FileError:
    Response = MsgBox(Msg$, 49, "Editor")
    If Response = 1 Then
        Resume
    Else
        Exit Sub
    End If
End Sub
```

This avoids the potential `No Resume` message from Visual Basic and fixes the problem. In fact, there are other ways of handling `Resume` statements as well. Visual Basic supports two variations of `Resume`: the one you used in the Editor application (`Resume Next`), and `Resume Line`.

Resume Next and Resume Line

Sometimes, you do not want an application to keep retrying the operation that caused the error. One alternate method that you have already seen is to leave the procedure entirely and let the user select some other action. Two other methods are `Resume Next` and `Resume Line`. The `Resume Next` statement makes Visual Basic resume with the statement following the one that caused the error, by simply skipping the statement that produced the problem. You used `Resume Next` in the error-handler of the Editor Application. If an error did occur in that program, the application would simply continue with the next statement.

Here's another example, using `Resume Next`. One common method in Visual Basic of determining whether a file exists on disk is to create a deliberate, trappable error. You might recall that in almost all `Open` modes—`For Random`, `For Binary`, and so on—the file is automatically created if it doesn't already exist. On the other hand, if the user opened a file for input, Visual Basic would generate a trappable error if the file did not exist. It does not make sense to create the file from scratch if the application is about to read from it. You can use that error to indicate whether the file exists. Write a function called Exist(), which takes a filename as its argument and returns True if the file exists or False otherwise. The code could look something like this:

```
Private Sub Form_Load()

    If Exist("c:\autoexec.bat") Then
        Print "Boot batch file exists."
    End If

End Sub
```

To add this function at the form level, select the Procedure item from the Insert menu. The Insert Procedure dialog box opens. Change the Type option button that says Function and make sure the Scope of the procedure is Public. Then type the name of the procedure, Exist, in the text box at the top of the dialog box. Click OK. The following code skeleton appears:

```
Public Function Exist()

End Function
```

Give this function the argument FileName As String, and set up the error-handler in the following way:

```
Public Function Exist(FileName As String)

    On Error GoTo DoesNotExist
    :
    Exit Function

    DoesNotExist:
    :

End Function
```

If there is no error, a value of True should be returned. So set Exist to True. That way, the program will try to open the file.

```
Public Function Exist(FileName As String)

    On Error GoTo DoesNotExist

    Exist = True      'Set to True
    Open (FileName) For Input As #200    'unlikely to conflict
    :
    Exit Function

DoesNotExist:
    :
    Resume Next

End Function
```

In this example, the program opens the file as #200 because that file number is unlikely to conflict with other file numbers used elsewhere in the program.

Finding the Next Unused File Number

In a professional application, it is better to use the Visual Basic FreeFile function to find the next available (unused) file number rather than a fixed value such as 200.

If the file does not exist, the program should go to the location DoesNotExist, where Exist will be set to False. Then Resume Next should be added to move the program along.

```
Public Function Exist(FileName As String)

    On Error GoTo DoesNotExist

    Exist = True                         'Set to True
    Open (FileName) For Input As #200    'unlikely to conflict
    :
    Exit Function

DoesNotExist:
    Exist = False    'Set to False
    Resume Next

End Function
```

Other Possible Errors

In the preceding example, it was assumed that the error occurred because the file was not found. In an actual application, however, the file might not be able to be opened for a variety of reasons such as the disk does not respond, device user-interface error, and so on. To make sure that the file is simply "Not Found," you might add a line in the error-handler to make sure that Err = 53. This is the error generated when a file is not found, as shown later in Table 12.1.

At this point, Exist holds the correct value, True or False. All that remains is to close the file and exit the function, which can be done in the following way:

```
Public Function Exist(FileName As String)

    On Error GoTo DoesNotExist

    Exist = True    'Set to True
    Open (FileName) For Input As #200    'unlikely to conflict
    Close #200
    Exit Function
```

```
DoesNotExist:
     Exist = False    'Set to False
     Resume Next

End Function
```

Checking Whether a File Exists

Here are some other ways to check whether a file exists on disk:

1. Use the `Dir$()` function. This function simply returns an empty string, `""`, if the file does not exist.

2. Use the `FileLen()` function. `FileLen()` returns the length of a file in bytes. If the file does not exist, it returns 0. The following is a listing for an `Exist` function based on `FileLen()`:

```
Public Function Exist(F As String) As Boolean
   Dim X As Long

   On Error Resume Next

   X = FileLen(F)
   If X Then
        Exist = True
   Else
        Exist = False
   End If
End Function
```

Now `Exist()` is ready to go. Normally, it is better to move to an entirely different portion of the code to take some alternative action, and let the user know that the application is doing so. That is what the `Resume Line` statement does. With it, you can specify the line number where execution is resumed. For example, you might decide that the Editor application should always try to open and load a default file named File.txt when the application opens. To do that, you could add this code to the `Form_Load()` event:

```
Private Sub Form_Load()

    Open "c:\windows\file.txt" For Input As #1 'Open File

    frmNotePad.txtPadText.Text = Input$(LOF(1), #1) 'Read File in
    Close #1 'Close File

End Sub
```

On the other hand, if there was an error, you might want to open the Load File… dialog box on the screen. First, set up the error-handler:

```
Private Sub Form_Load()
    On Error GoTo FileError

    Open "c:\windows\file.txt" For Input As #1       'Open File
```

```
    frmNotePad.txtPadText.Text = Input$(LOF(1), #1) 'Read File in
    Close #1 'Close File
    Exit Sub

        :

FileError:

        :

End Sub
```

Then the program could resume to another part of the procedure entirely, using a `Resume Line` statement. The following code would open the Load File dialog box on the screen:

```
Private Sub Form_Load()
    On Error GoTo FileError

    Open "c:\windows\file.txt" For Input As #1        'Open File

    frmNotePad.txtPadText.Text = Input$(LOF(1), #1) 'Read File in
    Close #1 'Close File
    Exit Sub

Here: frmLoad.Show
    Exit Sub

FileError:
    Resume Here

End Sub
```

That's almost it for `Resume`, `Resume Next`, and `Resume Line`. There is one more point that needs to be considered.

Suppose that `Procedure1` calls `Procedure2` as shown in Figure 12.3.

Figure 12.3.
A drawing showing
Procedure1 calling
Prodedure2.

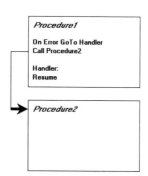

Next, assume that an error occurs while the program is in `Procedure2`, but `Procedure2` has no error-handler. Visual Basic would work its way back up the calling ladder, searching for an error-handler. In this case, an error-handler is found in `Procedure1`, as shown in Figure 12.4.

Figure 12.4.

A pictorial representation of Visual Basic searching for, and finding, an error-handler.

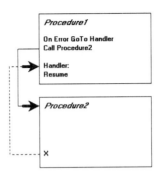

In this case, Procedure1 is handling Procedure2's error. If an error-handler is left out of Procedure2, you should be aware of this. Statements such as Resume Next in Procedure1's error-handler can cause unexpected or even disastrous results.

Visual Basic lends a hand when it comes to certain types of errors, though, and those errors are called *trappable errors*. First, take a look at how to handle them.

Handling Run-Time Errors

If a user asked the Editor application to read a file on a floppy disk that has been removed, she would get a message box like the one in Figure 12.5, informing her that there was a file error.

Figure 12.5.

The Editor application's file error message.

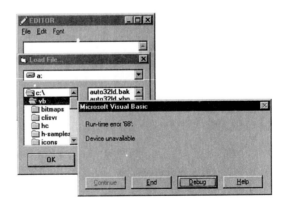

This type of error is easily intercepted. The following section is a quick recap of how it was done in the Editor application.

The *On Error GoTo* Statement

Trappable errors are caught with an On Error GoTo statement. For example, here is how it was used in the Editor application in frmLoad:

```
Private Sub cmdOK_Click()
    Dim TheFile As String

    On Error GoTo FileError

    If (Right(dirLook.Path, 1) = "\") Then
        TheFile = dirLook.Path + filFind.FileName

    Else
        TheFile = dirLook.Path + "\" + filFind.FileName

    End If

    Open TheFile For Input As #1
    frmNotePad.txtPadText.Text = Input(LOF(1), #1)      'Read File
    Close #1                                            'Close File
    Unload cmdOK.Parent

    Exit Sub

FileError:
    MsgBox "File Error", 48, "Editor"    'MsgBox for file error
    Resume Next

End Sub
```

When Visual Basic generates a trappable error after executing a statement like this in a procedure, control jumps to the specified label—in this case, FileError. That is exactly what the GoTo statement does. It transfers control to a new location in a procedure. Its syntax works like this:

GoTo *line*

The GoTo statement uses one argument, *line*, which can be any line label or line number. A line label can be any combination of characters that starts with a letter and ends with a colon. A line number can be any combination of digits that is unique to the module where it is used.

One thing you should note is that GoTo can branch *only* to lines within the procedure where it appears.

Here, the On Error GoTo statement is executed first, setting up the error-handling routine. Note also that the Sub procedure is exited before reaching that routine. That way, the error-handling code is not inadvertently executed. The procedure is set up much like a procedure that has subroutines, which are handled with the GoSub statement in Visual Basic. GoSub branches to and returns from a subroutine within a procedure. Its syntax appears as follows:

```
GoSub line
    :
line
    :
Return
```

Like the GoTo statement, the GoSub statement also uses one argument: *line* can be any line label or line number.

GoSub and Return can be used anywhere in a procedure, but GoSub and the corresponding Return must be in the same procedure.

Because the code in an error-handling routine—as well as the code in a GoSub subroutine—is in the same Sub or Function procedure, this code shares all the variables of the Sub or Function procedure. That means that the routine will have access to variables that might be of value in fixing the error.

Note also that On Error GoTo statements can be overridden with later statements of the same kind. This is useful if the application has entered a different part of the code with different potential errors and you want to use a different error-handler. However, not too much has happened here. Only the fact that an error occurred has been recognized. The next step is to discover what the error was and then to take action, if possible.

Turning Error-Handling Off

If you want to, you can even turn error-handling off. Just execute the statement On Error GoTo 0 in your program.

The *Err* Object

The Err object can be used to determine what error occurred. The Err object's properties and methods can be used and accessed with the dot operator like those of any other object. You might recall numerous examples of the *Object.Property* and *Object.Method* syntax. In this case, the Err object syntax looks like this:

```
Err[.{property ¦ method}]
```

One of the error object's most important properties (and its default) is Number, which returns or sets an error number. Many error numbers are predefined in Visual Basic. Some of the most common ones appear in Table 12.1. (For a complete list, search the Visual Basic Help file for "Trappable Errors.")

You should also know about the Err.Description property. This property contains a description of the error. For example, Err.Description for Error Number 11 is Division by zero.

The Err Object

The Err object is new to Version 4 of Visual Basic. It provides greater ease and richness of options for error trapping.

In previous versions of Visual Basic, the Err function returned the current error number. Error$(Err) returned the description of the error.

The old syntax can still be used. Because Number is the default property of the Err object, omitting a property altogether will return the error number. This means that the Error function will still return a description of the current error when it is called with Err as an argument.

However, you are probably better off using and getting to know the new Visual Basic 4 way of handling errors. This means using the Err object.

Table 12.1 shows some common trappable errors in Visual Basic. This is an abbreviated list. The entire list is available in the Visual Basic Help file and includes the following:

- DDE and form-related messages
- OLE automation messages
- Grid messages
- OLE control messages
- Common dialog control messages

Table 12.1. Some common trappable errors.

Error Number	Description
3	Return without GoSub
5	Invalid procedure call
6	Overflow
7	Out of memory
9	Subscript out of range
10	This array is fixed or temporarily locked
11	Division by zero
13	Type mismatch
14	Out of string space
18	User interrupt occurred
20	Resume without error

continues

Table 12.1. continued

Error Number	Description
28	Out of stack space
35	Sub, Function, or Property not defined
47	Too many DLL application clients
48	Error in loading DLL
49	Bad DLL calling convention
51	Internal error
52	Bad file name or number
53	File not found
54	Bad file mode
55	File already open
57	Device I/O error
58	File already exists
59	Bad record length
61	Disk full
62	Input past end of file
63	Bad record number
67	Too many files
68	Device unavailable
70	Permission denied
71	Disk not ready
74	Can't rename with different drive
75	Path/File access error
76	Path not found
90	With...End With block error
91	Object variable not set
92	For loop not initialized
93	Invalid pattern string
94	Invalid use of Null

The Err Object

The Err object has the properties and methods shown in Tables 12.2 and 12.3.

Table 12.2. The Err object's properties.

Property	Data Type	Purpose
Number	Long	Returns or sets the error number.
Source	String	Name of the current Visual Basic project.
Description	String	Contains a description of the error based on the error number. If this string doesn't exist, Description contains the string "User-Defined Error".
HelpFile	String	Project's Help file.
HelpContext	String	Help file context ID.

Table 12.3. The Err object's methods.

Method	Purpose
Clear	Clears the Err object after an error has been handled. This method is equivalent to the Err = 0 statement in previous versions of Visual Basic. Visual Basic calls the Clear method automatically whenever any kind of Resume, Exit Sub, Exit Function, Exit Property, or On Error statement has been executed.
Raise	Generates a run-time error. Optionally, it can be used to set the Err object's properties.

Why not use the Err object to update the Editor application? That way it can indicate exactly what error occurred. Open the Editor application in Visual Basic. (You might want to rename the project and its associated forms so that they are not overwritten.) Then modify the frmLoad cmdOK_Click() event as follows:

```
Private Sub cmdOK_Click()
    Dim TheFile As String

    On Error GoTo FileError

    If (Right(dirLook.Path, 1) = "\") Then
        TheFile = dirLook.Path + filFind.FileName

    Else
        TheFile = dirLook.Path + "\" + filFind.FileName

    End If
```

```
      Open TheFile For Input As #1
      frmNotePad.txtPadText.Text = Input(LOF(1), #1)      'Read File
      Close #1                                            'Close File
      Unload cmdOK.Parent

      Exit Sub

FileError:
      'MsgBox for file error
      MsgBox "File Error " & Str$(Err.Number) & " "
      ⮡& Err.Description, 48, Error.Source
      Resume Next

End Sub
```

Add the same line of code to the `frmSave cmdOK_Click()` event also:

```
Private Sub cmdOK_Click()

      On Error GoTo FileError

      Open txtFileName.Text For Output As #1      'Open file
      Print #1, frmNotePad.txtPadText.Text        'Write document
      Close #1                                    'Close file

      Unload cmdOK.Parent

      Exit Sub

FileError:
      'MsgBox for file error
      MsgBox "File Error " & Str$(Err.Number) & " "
      ⮡& Err.Description, 48, Error.Source
      Resume Next

End Sub
```

To test this out, make an .exe file for the Editor application. Next, run the .exe from the Windows 95 desktop. Type a little in the Editor's text box, and then save the file on a floppy disk. Now remove the disk from the drive. Using the Load File dialog box, try to read the file. A message box appears on the screen, displaying the message `Device appears unavailable`.

Even if the user has no knowledge of Visual Basic or computers, the explanation `Device Unavailable` is certainly an improvement over the cryptic message `File Error 68`, and it might help the user to remedy the situation by replacing the disk in the A: drive.

How To Create an Error Condition

Routines in your programs that handle errors themselves must be thoroughly debugged and tested. But how are you going to do this without being able to cause every possible error that might come up? Truthfully, you don't even want to think about causing some of them, such as a hard drive with no more space on it. Others will happen whether you want them to or not. The fact remains that in order to successfully create error-handling routines, you must first be able to create errors.

Fortunately, as you will see in a few seconds, the `Err` object makes this very easy. You are about to write a small program, the first part of an application that demonstrates general error-handling, which will cause the error of choice to be generated. The `.Raise` method will be applied to the `Err` object to do this (although you could alternatively set the `Err.Number` property directly.)

Start a new project and change the default form's `Name` and `Caption` properties to `frmErrorHandler` and `Error Demonstration`, respectively. Then save the form as ErrorHandler.frm and the project as ErrorHandler.vbp. Place a text box and two buttons on the form in roughly the same positions shown in Figure 12.6. Then change the controls' properties to reflect those in the table below. (The table works from the top of the form down.)

Figure 12.6.
The ErrorHandler form template.

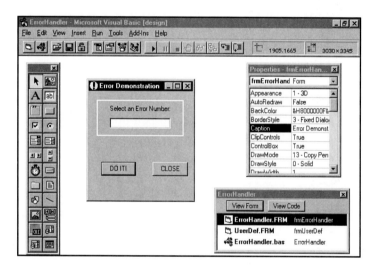

Object	Property	Setting
Form	BorderStyle	3-Fixed Dialog
	Caption	Error Demonstration
	Name	frmErrorHandler
Label	Alignment	2-Center
	Caption	Select an Error Number:
	Name	Label1
Text Box	Name	txtError
	Text	(None)
Shape	BorderColor	White
	BorderWidth	2
	Name	Shape1

continues

Object	Property	Setting
Command Button	Caption	DO IT!
	Default	True
	Name	cmdDoIt
	Cancel	True
	Caption	CLOSE
	Name	cmdClose

This program generates a specified error. That means that the user will type the error number in txtError and press the DO IT! button to see what error is generated. The main event that will handle the code is cmdDoIt_Click(). Also, cmdClose_Click() should be made active. Add the code for both events as follows:

```
Private Sub cmdClose_Click()
    Unload cmdClose.Parent
End Sub

Private Sub cmdDoIt_Click()
    On Error Resume Next
    Err.Clear
    Err.Raise Val(txtError.Text)
    MsgBox "You have generated error number " & Str$(Err.Number) &_
    ➡" ; Description: " & Err.Description & " error.", 64, "Error Demo"
End Sub
```

Now run the project. Enter a trappable error number such as 11 (which is a Divide by Zero error) in the next box. Then press the DO IT! command button. A message box will appear on the screen describing the error as in Figure 12.7. Try a few different numbers (perhaps from Table 12.1) to test the program.

Figure 12.7.
The error-handling program creating a trappable error.

With this application, you are able to create an error of your own choosing. This is an extremely useful technique. Now that you know how to create simulated errors, you are ready to move to the topic of error-handling routines.

Creating Customized Error-Handlers

When creating your own error-handler, there are some errors that can be expected to happen more often than others. You might want to make special provisions for handling them. For example, if a program were writing files, you might anticipate error 61, Disk Full. If that error occurred, the program could send up a message box saying The disk is full. Please delete some files and click OK. The user would then know to clear some disk space. (In a case like this one, you should also include a Cancel button. That way, if the user wanted to, she could cancel the file writing operation instead.) Then, after the user clicks OK, she could go back and try the operation again.

Let's look at an example of a custom error-handler in code. When a program loads files, these are some errors and messages that the Err object would be most likely to display. Table 12.4 shows some of those possible messages.

Table 12.4. Some possible file errors.

Error Number	Description
52	Bad File Name or Number
54	Bad File Mode (File opened for wrong kind of access)
55	File already open
57	Device I/O error
61	Disk full
62	Input Past End of File
64	Bad File Name
68	Device unavailable
71	Disk not ready
72	Disk Media error
76	Path Does Not Exist

You might want to write your own error-handling routine to implement trapping these particular errors. Add a new module to the ErrorHandler project. Change its Name property to ErrorHandler, and save it as ErrorHandler.bas. In the new module's Code window, insert a public function by selecting the Procedure item from the Insert menu. Call the function FileErrors. After the function's code skeleton appears in the Code window, add the code that sets up error constants, checks for the error by using a Case Select statement, and then sends up an error message using the appropriate error. The following code does just that. It might seem lengthy, but it covers all 11 errors in Table 12.4.

```
Public Function FileErrors(errVal As Long) As Integer

    Const ERR_DEVICEUNAVAILABLE = 68
    Const ERR_DISKNOTREADY = 71
    Const ERR_DEVICEIO = 57
    Const ERR_DISKFULL = 61
    Const ERR_BADFILENAME = 64
    Const ERR_BADFILENAMEORNUMBER = 52
    Const ERR_PATHDOESNOTEXIST = 76
    Const ERR_BADFILEMODE = 54
    Const ERR_FILEALREADYOPEN = 55
    Const ERR_INPUTPASTENDOFFILE = 62
    Const MB_ICONEXCLAMATION = 48

    Dim msgType As Integer, Msg As String, Response As Integer

    'Return Value     Description
    ' 0           Repeat
    ' 1           Resume
    ' 2           Unrecoverable error - Resume Next
    ' 3           Unrecognized error

    msgType = MB_ICONEXCLAMATION

    Select Case errVal
        Case ERR_DEVICEUNAVAILABLE                      ' Error #68
            Msg = "That device appears unavailable."
            msgType = MB_ICONEXCLAMATION + 5

        Case ERR_DISKNOTREADY                           ' Error #71
            Msg = "Insert a disk in the drive and close the door."
            msgType = MB_ICONEXCLAMATION + 5

        Case ERR_DEVICEIO                               ' Error #57
            Msg = "Internal disk error."
            msgType = MB_ICONEXCLAMATION + 5

        Case ERR_DISKFULL                               ' Error #61
            Msg = "Disk is full. Continue?"
            msgType = MB_ICONEXCLAMATION + 2

        Case ERR_BADFILENAME, ERR_BADFILENAMEORNUMBER   ' Errors #64 & 52
            Msg = "That file name is illegal."

        Case ERR_PATHDOESNOTEXIST                       ' Error #76
            Msg = "That path doesn't exist."

        Case ERR_BADFILEMODE                            ' Error #54
            Msg = "Can't open your file for that type of access."
            msgType = MB_ICONEXCLAMATION + 2

        Case ERR_FILEALREADYOPEN                        ' Error #55
            Msg = "This file is already open."

        Case ERR_INPUTPASTENDOFFILE                     ' Error #62
            Msg = "This file has a nonstandard end-of-file marker, "
            Msg = Msg + "or an attempt was made to read beyond "
            Msg = Msg + "the end-of-file marker."
```

```
            Case Else
                FileErrors = 3
                Exit Function

        End Select

        Response = MsgBox(Msg, msgType, "Disk Error")

        Select Case Response
            Case 4                ' Retry buttons.
                FileErrors = 0

            Case 5                ' Ignore button.
                FileErrors = 1

            Case 1, 2, 3          ' Cancel, OK,Abort buttons.
                FileErrors = 2

            Case Else
                FileErrors = 3
        End Select
    End Select

End Function
```

The 11 errors that the preceding code handles include quite a few of the more common file and disk access errors. But you could, of course, add more errors to the routine if you like. And, if you wanted to handle particular errors or conditions in a different way, with a different message or action, you could do that also.

Now add a few more controls and a bit more code to the ErrorHandler form for testing the file errors.

Add a frame, another command button, and an array of option buttons (optErr(0), optErr(1), and optErr(2)) to the form. Place them in the approximate positions indicated by Figure 12.8, moving the DO IT! and CLOSE command buttons down. Then change the control's properties to match the following table.

Object	Property	Setting
Frame	Caption	Type of Error-handling:
	Name	Frame1
Option Button	Caption	File Error Handling Routine
	Index	0
	Name	optErr
	Value	True
Option Button	Caption	General Error Routine
	Index	1
	Name	optErr

continues

Object	Property	Setting
Line	BorderColor	White
	Name	Line1
Option Button	Caption	User Defined Errors
	Index	2
	Name	optErr
Command Button	Caption	SET
	Name	cmdSet

Figure 12.8.

The ErrorHandler application with a frame and array added to the form template.

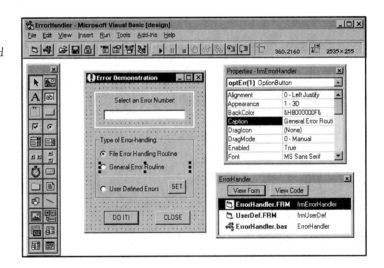

Change the cmdDoIt_Click() procedure as follows to add the code that will activate the first option button captioned File Error Handling Routine:

```
Private Sub cmdDoIt_Click()
    Dim RetVal As Integer

    On Error Resume Next
    Err.Clear
    Err.Raise Val(txtError.Text)

    If optErr(0).Value Then 'File Error Routine
        RetVal = FileErrors(Err.Number)

            ' Return Value    Means
            ' 0               Repeat
            ' 1               Resume
            ' 2               Unrecoverable error - Resume Next
            ' 3               Unrecognized error
```

```
      Select Case RetVal
            Case 0
                  cmdDoIt_Click

            Case 1
                  Resume

            Case 2
                  MsgBox "Unrecoverable Error!"
                  Resume Next

            Case 3
                  MsgBox "Unrecognized Error!"

            Case Else
                  MsgBox "Internal Error: should not reach this place."
      End Select

   ElseIf optErr(1).Value Then        'General Error Routine

      :

   ElseIf optErr(2).Value Then        'User-Defined Error Routine

      :

   End If

End Sub
```

The preceding code sets the value of a new variable, `RetVal`, and then uses a `Select Case` statement depending upon `RetVal`'s value. That's all there is to setting the code for the first option button, `optErr(0)`. Run the application now and test the new code by entering a file or disk error number from Table 12.4 in the text box. When you do, be sure that the File Error Handling Routine option is selected as it is in Figure 12.9. Then click `cmdDoIt` and see what happens.

Figure 12.9.
The ErrorHandler application with added error creation options.

You'll come back to this soon and add two more interesting error-handling routines that correspond to the other option buttons used in this demonstration program.

But first, why not add this file error module to the Editor program?

Adding an Error Handler to the Editor Application

Open the Editor application, and add the ErrorHandler.bas file to the project by selecting the Add File… item from the File menu. (You might want to rename this module using the Save File As… option on the File menu. If you do, change the path to match that of the Editor application. That way, there will be a permanent copy of the module there with that application.)

Modify the code in the `cmdOK_Click()` procedure of `frmSave` as follows:

```
Private Sub cmdOK_Click()
    On Error GoTo FileError

    Open txtFileName.Text For Output As #1  'Open file
    Print #1, frmNotePad.txtPadText.Text        'Write document
    Close #1

    Unload cmdOK.Parent
    Exit Sub

FileError:
    Dim RetVal As Integer

    RetVal = FileErrors(Err.Number)

    ' Return Value    Means
    ' 0               Repeat
    ' 1               Resume
    ' 2               Unrecoverable error - Resume Next
    ' 3               Unrecognized error

    Select Case RetVal
        Case 0
            cmdOK_Click

        Case 1
            Resume

        Case 2
            MsgBox "Unrecoverable Error!"
            Resume Next

        Case 3
            MsgBox "Unrecognized Error!"

        Case Else
            MsgBox "Internal Error: should not reach this place."
    End Select

End Sub
```

Go ahead and try it out. Try to save your work in drive A: without a disk in the drive, and you'll get a message like the one in Figure 12.10.

Figure 12.10.
The Editor application with
an improved error-handler in
`frmSave`.

Next, modify `frmLoad`. You must change the `cmdOK_Click()`, `drvChange_Change()`, and `drvLook_Change()` procedures to reflect the error-handling modifications. Here is what the code in `frmLoad` should look like now:

```
Option Explicit

Private Sub cmdCancel_Click()
    Unload cmdCancel.Parent
End Sub

Private Sub cmdOK_Click()
    Dim TheFile As String

    On Error GoTo FileError

    If (Right(dirLook.Path, 1) = "\") Then
        TheFile = dirLook.Path + filFind.FileName
    Else
        TheFile = dirLook.Path + "\" + filFind.FileName
    End If

    Open TheFile For Input As #1
    frmNotePad.txtPadText.Text = Input(LOF(1), #1) 'Read File
    Close #1     'Close File

    Unload cmdOK.Parent
    Exit Sub

FileError:
    Dim RetVal As Integer

    RetVal = FileErrors(Err.Number)

    ' Return Value    Means
    ' 0               Repeat
    ' 1               Resume
    ' 2               Unrecoverable error - Resume Next
    ' 3               Unrecognized error

    Select Case RetVal
        Case 0
            cmdOK_Click
```

```
        Case 1
            Resume

        Case 2
            MsgBox "Unrecoverable Error!"
            Resume Next

        Case 3
            MsgBox "Unrecognized Error!"

        Case Else
            MsgBox "Internal Error: should not reach this place."
    End Select

End Sub

Private Sub dirLook_Change()

    On Error GoTo FileError2:

    filFind.Path = dirLook.Path
    Exit Sub

FileError2:
    Dim RetVal As Integer

    RetVal = FileErrors(Err.Number)

    ' Return Value    Means
    ' 0               Repeat
    ' 1               Resume
    ' 2               Unrecoverable error - Resume Next
    ' 3               Unrecognized error

    Select Case RetVal
        Case 0
            cmdOK_Click

        Case 1
            Resume

        Case 2
            MsgBox "Unrecoverable Error!"
            Resume Next

        Case 3
            MsgBox "Unrecognized Error!"

        Case Else
            MsgBox "Internal Error: should not reach this place."
    End Select

End Sub

Private Sub drvChange_Change()

    On Error GoTo FileError3:
```

```
        dirLook.Path = drvChange.Drive
        Exit Sub

FileError3:
        Dim RetVal As Integer

        RetVal = FileErrors(Err.Number)

        ' Return Value      Means
        ' 0                 Repeat
        ' 1                 Resume
        ' 2                 Unrecoverable error - Resume Next
        ' 3                 Unrecognized error

        Select Case RetVal
            Case 0
                cmdOK_Click

            Case 1
                Resume

            Case 2
                MsgBox "Unrecoverable Error!"
                Resume Next

            Case 3
                MsgBox "Unrecognized Error!"

            Case Else
                MsgBox "Internal Error: should not reach this place."
        End Select

End Sub

Private Sub filFind_DblClick()
        cmdOK_Click
End Sub
```

Great! Just to see what you've done, run the program and try loading a file from the A: drive when no floppy disk is present. See Figure 12.11 to see what error-handling capabilities you have built into the Editor application.

Figure 12.11.
The new error-handling capabilities built into the file loading portion of the Editor application.

You have added truly sophisticated error-handling to the Editor program. Because you merely added the generic file error-handler from the ErrorHandler.bas file and a few lines of code, you can see how easy it is to do this kind of thing. This same module could be used over and over in other applications that need error-handling.

Finishing the Error-Handling Application

Now you return to the error-handler application. Reopen ErrorHandler.vbp. It's time to experiment with some other generalized ways to handle errors.

Add a new procedure to the ErrorHandler module by opening that Code window and selecting the Procedure item from the Insert menu. Create a public `Sub` procedure called `ShowError`. Then click OK. Now add the following code to the new `ShowError` `Sub` procedure:

```
Public Sub ShowError()
    Dim S As String
    Dim Crlf As String

    Crlf = Chr(13) + Chr(10)
    S = "The following Error occurred:" + Crlf + Crlf

    'add the error string
    S = S + Err.Description + Crlf

    'add the error number
    S = S + "Number: " + CStr(Err.Number)

    'beep and show the error
    Beep

    MsgBox S, 64, "General Error Demo"

    Resume Next

End Sub
```

Next, add a call to the `ShowError` procedure in `frmErrorHandler`'s `cmdDoIT_Click()` event, as follows:

```
Private Sub cmdDoIt_Click()
    Dim RetVal As Integer

    On Error Resume Next
    Err.Clear
    Err.Raise Val(txtError.Text)

    If optErr(0).Value Then 'File Error Routine
        RetVal = FileErrors(Err.Number)

            ' Return Value      Means
            ' 0                 Repeat
            ' 1                 Resume
            ' 2                 Unrecoverable error - Resume Next
            ' 3                 Unrecognized error
```

```
        Select Case RetVal
            Case 0
                cmdDoIt_Click

            Case 1
                Resume

            Case 2
                MsgBox "Unrecoverable Error!"
                Resume Next

            Case 3
                MsgBox "Unrecognized Error!"

            Case Else
                MsgBox "Internal Error: should not reach this place."
        End Select

    ElseIf optErr(1).Value Then          'General Error Routine

        ShowError

    ElseIf optErr(2).Value Then          'User-Defined Error Routine

        :

    End If

End Sub
```

You're ready to try it out now. Make sure that the General Error option is selected, pick a good error number, and press the DO IT! command button. Something similar to Figure 12.12 will appear.

Figure 12.12.
With the ShowError
*procedure added to the Error
module, the General Error
Routine is functional.*

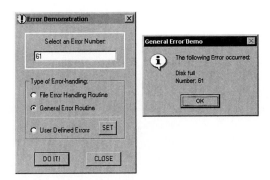

Although this general error routine doesn't do too much besides opening a nice box with a helpful message, it is useful because it is so generally applicable. You can just plug it into almost any kind of project. If there are one or two errors that you need to handle in a special way, you can test for them with an If…Then or Select Case statement, and let the rest be handled by the general error routine.

The next capability to add to this demonstration program is a method for creating and displaying *user-defined* errors.

A user-defined error is one you invent yourself. It is used when you need the ability to trap errors that aren't built into Visual Basic and the `Err` object.

The `Err.Raise` method is used to assign user-defined error numbers and descriptions. You can use any unoccupied error number you like between `0` and `65,535`, inclusive. (This is the valid range of values for the `Err.Number` property.) For example, there are no predefined error numbers `0,1,2,` or `21-27`. For that matter, you could change the description of an existing error number, but there would rarely be much point in doing so.

A Visual Basic Programming Tip

To avoid any possibility of conflicting with predefined error numbers, start your user-defined error numbers at the highest possible number: `65,535`. Then work your way down from there.

Now it's time to add the user-defined error capabilities to your demonstration program. Add a new form to your project and change its `Name` and `Caption` properties to `frmUserDef` and `User-Defined Error`, respectively. Then save the form as UserDef.frm. Place two text boxes—one for the user-defined error number and one for the user-defined string definition—on the form and add labels above each one. Also, put a command button captioned OK on the form. For placement, use Figure 12.13 as a guide. Then use the following table to set the controls' properties.

Figure 12.13.
The User-Defined Error form template.

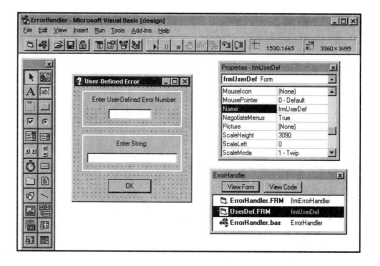

Object	Property	Setting
Form	BorderStyle	3-Fixed Dialog
	Caption	User-Defined Error
	Name	frmUserDef
Label	Alignment	2-Center
	Caption	Enter User-Defined Error Number:
	Name	Label1
Text Box	Name	txtErrNum
	Text	(None)
Shape	BorderColor	White
	BorderWidth	2
	Name	Shape1
Label	Alignment	2-Center
	Caption	Enter String:
	Name	Label2
Text Box	Name	txtErrString
	Text	(None)
Shape	BorderColor	White
	BorderWidth	2
	Name	Shape2
Command Button	Caption	OK
	Default	True
	Name	cmdOK

Now add code to the form's events as follows:

```
Option Explicit

Private Sub cmdOK_Click()
    gErrNum = Val(txtErrNum.Text)
    gErrStr = txtErrString.Text
    frmErrorHandler!txtError = txtErrNum.Text
```

```
        Unload cmdOK.Parent

End Sub

Private Sub txtErrNum_Click()
     txtErrNum.Text = ""
End Sub

Private Sub txtErrString_Click()
     txtErrString.Text = ""
End Sub
```

Next, add two public declarations and a new public Sub procedure called UserError to the ErrorHandler.bas module as follows:

```
Option Explicit

Public gErrNum As Long
Public gErrStr As String

Public Sub UserError()
     Dim s As String
     Dim CRLF As String

     On Error Resume Next

     CRLF = Chr(13) + Chr(10)

     Err.Clear
     Err.Raise gErrNum, , gErrStr
     s = "The following Error occurred:" + CRLF + CRLF

     'add the error string
     s = s + Err.Description + CRLF

     'add the error number
     s = s + "Number: " + CStr(Err.Number)

     'beep and show the error
     Beep

     MsgBox s, 64, "USER Error Demo"

     Resume Next

End Sub
```

Change frmErrorHandler by adding the following call to the cmdSet_Click() procedure:

```
Private Sub cmdSet_Click()
     frmUserDef.Show vbModal
End Sub
```

Finally, you need to modify the code in frmErrorHandler's cmdDoIt_Click() sub procedure so that it calls the new UserError routine as follows:

```
Private Sub cmdDoIt_Click()
    Dim RetVal As Integer

    On Error Resume Next
    Err.Clear
    Err.Raise Val(txtError.Text)

    If optErr(0).Value Then 'File Error Routine
        RetVal = FileErrors(Err.Number)

        ' Return Value      Means
        ' 0                 Repeat
        ' 1                 Resume
        ' 2                 Unrecoverable error - Resume Next
        ' 3                 Unrecognized error

        Select Case RetVal
            Case 0
                cmdDoIt_Click

            Case 1
                Resume

            Case 2
                MsgBox "Unrecoverable Error!"
                Resume Next

            Case 3
                MsgBox "Unrecognized Error!"

            Case Else
                MsgBox "Internal Error: should not reach this place."
        End Select

    ElseIf optErr(1).Value Then       'General Error Routine

        ShowError

    ElseIf optErr(2).Value Then       'User-Defined Error Routine

        UserError

    End If

End Sub
```

Your error demonstration program now has the capability to define and display user-defined errors. Go ahead and check it out now. An example of how the program works is shown in Figures 12.14 through 12.16. Be sure to select the User Defined Errors option button and assign your error using the SET command button. The complete code appears in Table 12.5 and Listings 12.1 through 12.3.

Figure 12.14.
Entering a user-defined error in the ErrorHandler application.

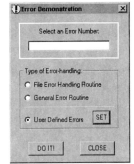

Figure 12.15.
The user-defined error set and displayed by the ErrorHandler application.

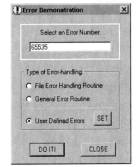

Figure 12.16.
Another example of a user-defined error.

Table 12.5. The visual definition of the Error Handler form.

Object	Property	Setting
Form	BorderStyle	3-Fixed Dialog
	Caption	Error Demonstration
	Name	frmErrorHandler
Label	Alignment	2-Center
	Caption	Select an Error Number:
	Name	Label1

Object	Property	Setting
Text Box	Name	txtError
	Text	(None)
Shape	BorderColor	White
	BorderWidth	2
	Name	Shape1
Frame	Caption	Type of Error-handling:
	Name	Frame1
Option Button	Caption	File Error Handling Routine
	Index	0
	Name	optErr
	Value	True
Option Button	Caption	General Error Routine
	Index	1
	Name	optErr
Line	BorderColor	White
	Name	Line1
Option Button	Caption	User Defined Errors
	Index	2
	Name	optErr
Command Button	Caption	SET
	Name	cmdSet
Command Button	Caption	DO IT!
	Default	True
	Name	cmdDoIt
Command Button	Cancel	True
	Caption	CLOSE
	Name	cmdClose
Form	BorderStyle	3-Fixed Dialog
	Caption	User-Defined Error
	Name	frmUserDef

continues

Table 12.5. continued

Object	Property	Setting
Label	Alignment	2-Center
	Caption	Enter User-Defined Error
	Name	Number:
		Label1
Text Box	Name	txtErrNum
	Text	(None)
Shape	BorderColor	White
	BorderWidth	2
	Name	Shape1
Label	Alignment	2-Center
	Caption	Enter String:
	Name	Label2
Text Box	Name	txtErrString
	Text	(None)
Shape	BorderColor	White
	BorderWidth	2
	Name	Shape2
Command Button	Caption	OK
	Default	True
	Name	cmdOK

Listing 12.1. The code in the module ErrorHandler.bas.

```
Option Explicit

Public gErrNum As Long
Public gErrStr As String

Public Function FileErrors(errVal As Long) As Integer

    Const ERR_DEVICEUNAVAILABLE = 68
    Const ERR_DISKNOTREADY = 71
    Const ERR_DEVICEIO = 57
    Const ERR_DISKFULL = 61
    Const ERR_BADFILENAME = 64
```

```
        Const ERR_BADFILENAMEORNUMBER = 52
        Const ERR_PATHDOESNOTEXIST = 76
        Const ERR_BADFILEMODE = 54
        Const ERR_FILEALREADYOPEN = 55
        Const ERR_INPUTPASTENDOFFILE = 62
        Const MB_ICONEXCLAMATION = 48

        Dim msgType As Integer, Msg As String, Response As Integer

        'Return Value        Description
        ' 0                  Repeat
        ' 1                  Resume
        ' 2                  Unrecoverable error - Resume Next
        ' 3                  Unrecognized error

        msgType = MB_ICONEXCLAMATION

        Select Case errVal
            Case ERR_DEVICEUNAVAILABLE                    ' Error #68
                Msg = "That device appears unavailable."
                msgType = MB_ICONEXCLAMATION + 5

            Case ERR_DISKNOTREADY                         ' Error #71
                Msg = "Insert a disk in the drive and close the door."
                msgType = MB_ICONEXCLAMATION + 5

            Case ERR_DEVICEIO                             ' Error #57
                Msg = "Internal disk error."
                msgType = MB_ICONEXCLAMATION + 5

            Case ERR_DISKFULL                             ' Error #61
                Msg = "Disk is full. Continue?"
                msgType = MB_ICONEXCLAMATION + 2

            Case ERR_BADFILENAME, ERR_BADFILENAMEORNUMBER    ' Errors #64 & 52
                Msg = "That file name is illegal."

            Case ERR_PATHDOESNOTEXIST                     ' Error #76
                Msg = "That path doesn't exist."

            Case ERR_BADFILEMODE                          ' Error #54
                Msg = "Can't open your file for that type of access."
                msgType = MB_ICONEXCLAMATION + 2

            Case ERR_FILEALREADYOPEN                      ' Error #55
                Msg = "This file is already open."

            Case ERR_INPUTPASTENDOFFILE                   ' Error #62
                Msg = "This file has a nonstandard end-of-file marker, "
                Msg = Msg + "or an attempt was made to read beyond "
                Msg = Msg + "the end-of-file marker."

            Case Else
                FileErrors = 3
                Exit Function

        End Select
```

continues

Listing 12.1. **continued**

```
        Response = MsgBox(Msg, msgType, "Disk Error")

        Select Case Response
            Case 4          ' Retry buttons.
                FileErrors = 0

            Case 5          ' Ignore button.
                FileErrors = 1

            Case 1, 2, 3    Cancel, OK,Abort buttons.
                FileErrors = 2

            Case Else
                FileErrors = 3
        End Select

End Function

Public Sub ShowError()
    Dim s As String
    Dim CRLF As String

    CRLF = Chr(13) + Chr(10)
    s = "The following Error occurred:" + CRLF + CRLF

    'add the error string
    s = s + Err.Description + CRLF

    'add the error number
    s = s + "Number: " + CStr(Err.Number)

    'beep and show the error
    Beep

    MsgBox s, 64, "General Error Demo"

    Resume Next

End Sub

Public Sub UserError()
    Dim s As String
    Dim CRLF As String

    On Error Resume Next

    CRLF = Chr(13) + Chr(10)

    Err.Clear
    Err.Raise gErrNum, , gErrStr
    s = "The following Error occurred:" + CRLF + CRLF

    'add the error string
    s = s + Err.Description + CRLF

    'add the error number
    s = s + "Number: " + CStr(Err.Number)
```

```
        'beep and show the error
        Beep

        MsgBox s, 64, "USER Error Demo"

        Resume Next

End Sub
```

Listing 12.2. **The complete code for** `frmUserDef`.

```
Option Explicit

Private Sub cmdOK_Click()
    gErrNum = Val(txtErrNum.Text)
    gErrStr = txtErrString.Text
    frmErrorHandler!txtError = txtErrNum.Text

    Unload cmdOK.Parent

End Sub

Private Sub txtErrNum_Click()
    txtErrNum.Text = ""
End Sub

Private Sub txtErrString_Click()
    txtErrString.Text = ""
End Sub
```

Listing 12.3. **The code for** `frmErrorHandler`.

```
Option Explicit

Private Sub cmdClose_Click()
    Unload cmdClose.Parent
End Sub

Private Sub cmdDoIt_Click()
    Dim RetVal As Integer

    On Error Resume Next
    Err.Clear
    Err.Raise Val(txtError.Text)

    If optErr(0).Value Then 'File Error Routine
        RetVal = FileErrors(Err.Number)

        ' Return Value        Means
        ' 0                   Repeat
        ' 1                   Resume
        ' 2                   Unrecoverable error - Resume Next
        ' 3                   Unrecognized error
```

continues

Listing 12.3. **continued**

```
        Select Case RetVal
            Case 0
                cmdDoIt_Click

            Case 1
                Resume

            Case 2
                MsgBox "Unrecoverable Error!"
                Resume Next

            Case 3
                MsgBox "Unrecognized Error!"

            Case Else
                MsgBox "Internal Error: should not reach this place."
        End Select

    ElseIf optErr(1).Value Then        'General Error Routine
        ShowError

    ElseIf optErr(2).Value Then        'User-Defined Error Routine
        UserError

    End If
End Sub

Private Sub cmdSet_Click()
    frmUserDef.Show vbModal
End Sub
```

That's it for coverage of trappable errors in Visual Basic. There's more to finding and eliminating errors than this, though. It's time to turn to debugging.

Using the Visual Basic Debugging Tools

Logical errors in a program are usually harder to find than compile or run-time errors. A logical error could be buried deep in a long chain of complex statements. Fortunately, Visual Basic provides some debugging tools that you can use to help locate and even fix errors in logic.

Using Text Boxes and Message Boxes in Debugging

Text boxes can make excellent debugging tools if used to print out intermediate results in a program. To use text boxes, simply add a few extra text boxes to an application and print out crucial values in them as the program runs. For example, you might want to see what is happening to a variable that is supposed to be counting keystrokes: Is it increased every time the user presses a key? Or, you might want to make sure that the program is reading mouse cursor coordinates correctly in a `MouseDown()` event by displaying them in text boxes as well. In general, temporary text boxes can provide a window into what's happening behind the scenes in an application. That is what debugging is all about.

The `MsgBox` function can be used for this purpose, as well. It is very easy to insert temporary message boxes that output variable values.

For the purposes of exploring debugging, create a list of 10 or so names that needs to be alphabetized:

John
Tim
Edward
Samuel
Frank
Todd
George
Ralph
Leonard
Thomas

Please note that in this example, explicit declaration of variables is not required. As you will see, the first bug found is caused by the unintended confusion between the variables `Tmp$` and `Temp$`. Had explicit declaration been required, in all likelihood this bug would never have made it into the program.

Start by setting up an array to hold all the names in the `Form_Click()` event:

```
Private Sub Form_Click()
    Static Names(10) As String

    Names(1) = "John"
    Names(2) = "Tim"
    Names(3) = "Edward"
    Names(4) = "Samuel"
    Names(5) = "Frank"
    Names(6) = "Todd"
    Names(7) = "George"
    Names(8) = "Ralph"
    Names(9) = "Leonard"
    Names(10) = "Thomas"

    :

End Sub
```

Then arrange them in alphabetical order using a loop sort:

```
Private Sub Form_Click()
    Static Names(10) As String

        Names(1) = "John"
        Names(2) = "Tim"
        Names(3) = "Edward"
        Naes(4) = "Samuel"
        Names(5) = "Frank"
        Names(6) = "Todd"
        Names(7) = "George"
        Names(8) = "Ralph"
        Names(9) = "Leonard"
        Names(10) = "Thomas"

        For I = I To 10
            For J = I To 10
                If Names(I) > Names(J) Then
                    Temp$ = Names(I)
                    Names(J) = Names(J)
                    Names(J) = Tmp$
                End If
            Next J
        Next I

        :

End Sub
```

Note here that the > logical operator is used to compare strings. This is perfectly legal in Visual Basic and enables the program to determine the string's alphabetical order. Finally, print out the result, name by name, by adding the following code:

```
Private Sub Form_Click()
    Static Names(10) As String

        Names(1) = "John"
        Names(2) = "Tim"
        Names(3) = "Edward"
        Names(4) = "Samuel"
        Names(5) = "Frank"
        Names(6) = "Todd"
        Names(7) = "George"
        Names(8) = "Ralph"
        Names(9) = "Leonard"
        Names(10) = "Thomas"

        For I = I To 10
            For J = I To 10
                If Names(I) > Names(J) Then
                    Temp$ = Names(I)
                    Names(J) = Names(J)
                    Names(J) = Tmp$
                End If
            Next J
        Next I
```

```
Names(3) = "Edward"
Names(4) = "Samuel"
Names(5) = "Frank"
Names(6) = "Todd"
Names(7) = "George"
Names(8) = "Ralph"
Names(9) = "Leonard"
Names(10) = "Thomas"

For I = I To 10
    For J = I To 10
        If Names(I) > Names(J) Then
            Temp$ = Names(I)
            Names(J) = Names(J)
            Names(J) = Tmp$
        End If
    Next J
Next I

For K = 1 To 10
    Print Names(K)
Next K

End Sub
```

Misspelling a variable's name is extremely common when implicit variable declaration is used. Visual Basic does not complain about such errors because it assumes that a new variable, Tmp$, is being implicitly declared and sets that new variable to the empty string, "".

Using the Option Explicit Command

The best way to avoid such errors is to use the Option Explicit command. This prevents you from declaring variables implicitly. Visual Basic will then flag as syntax errors variables that are not explicitly declared.

You can actually fix this problem without stopping the program. Just open Visual Basic's Run menu, where you will see three choices highlighted: Break, End, and Restart. Select Break to temporarily stop the program. Now you can change the code and then continue with program execution. In Break mode, Visual Basic usually allows programming changes up to the level of declaring new variables. In this case, just edit the code to change Tmp$ to Temp$, as shown in Figure 12.19.

Quicker Access to Debugging Commands

You can also use the last five buttons in the toolbar for debugging: Toggle Breakpoint, Instant Watch, Calls, Step In, and Step Over.

Figure 12.19.

Editing code while an
application is running.

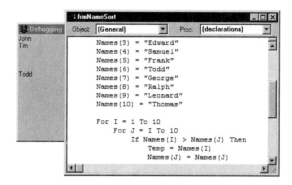

The code in the `Form_Click()` event should now look like this:

```
Private Sub Form_Click()
    Static Names(10) As String

    Names(1) = "John"
    Names(2) = "Tim"
    Names(3) = "Edward"
    Names(4) = "Samuel"
    Names(5) = "Frank"
    Names(6) = "Todd"
    Names(7) = "George"
    Names(8) = "Ralph"
    Names(9) = "Leonard"
    Names(10) = "Thomas"

    For I = I To 10
        For J = I To 10
            If Names(I) > Names(J) Then
                Temp$ = Names(I)
                Names(J) = Names(J)
                Names(J) = Temp$
            End If
        Next J
    Next I

    For K = 1 To 10
        Print Names(K)
    Next K

End Sub
```

It's time to stop fooling around with implicit variable declaration and declare the variables explicitly. Add `Option Explicit` at the top of the Code window, and then declare the variables like this:

```
Option Explicit

Private Sub Form_Click()
    Static Names(10) As String
    Dim I As Integer
```

```
    Dim J As Integer
    Dim K As Integer
    Dim Temp As String

    Names(1) = "John"
    Names(2) = "Tim"
    Names(3) = "Edward"
    Names(4) = "Samuel"
    Names(5) = "Frank"
    Names(6) = "Todd"
    Names(7) = "George"
    Names(8) = "Ralph"
    Names(9) = "Leonard"
    Names(10) = "Thomas"

    For I = I To 10
        For J = I To 10
            If Names(I) > Names(J) Then
                Temp = Names(I)
                Names(J) = Names(J)
                Names(J) = Temp
            End If
        Next J
    Next I

    For K = 1 To 10
        Print Names(K)
    Next K

End Sub
```

If the variables had been declared in this fashion right from the beginning, the misspelled variable name would never have happened. Visual Basic would have caught the error immediately.

Let the program continue by selecting the Continue item from the Run menu. After you do, click the form to see whether the change from Tmp to Temp made a difference. The name list appears as in Figure 12.20.

Figure 12.20.
The sample Name Sort application, running after the variable Tmp is changed.

Well, the change you made did have an effect, but the result is clearly not right yet. The obvious problem in the program is that the entries in the Names() array are being filled incorrectly. To check what is happening, you should watch the array elements as they are filled. You can do that by setting a *breakpoint*. A breakpoint halts program execution when it is reached. Stop the program and set a breakpoint by moving the cursor on the screen down to the line that reads If Names(I) > Names(J) Then:

```
Private Sub Form_Click()
    Static Names(10) As String
    Dim I As Integer
    Dim J As Integer
    Dim K As Integer
    Dim Temp As String

    Names(1) = "John"
    Names(2) = "Tim"
    Names(3) = "Edward"
    Names(4) = "Samuel"
    Names(5) = "Frank"
    Names(6) = "Todd"
    Names(7) = "George"
    Names(8) = "Ralph"
    Names(9) = "Leonard"
    Names(10) = "Thomas"

    For I = I To 10
        For J = I To 10
            If Names(I) > Names(J) Then
                Temp = Names(I)
                Names(J) = Names(J)
                Names(J) = Temp
            End If
        Next J
    Next I

    For K = 1 To 10
        Print Names(K)
    Next K

End Sub
```

Now press F9 or select Toggle Breakpoint from the Run menu. The selected `If...Then` statement appears in bold to indicate that a breakpoint has been set, as shown in Figure 12.21.

Figure 12.21.
A breakpoint set in the Name Sort code.

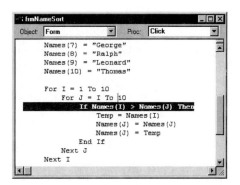

Now set a watch over the array variables `Names(I)` and `Names(J)`. Select the Add Watch... item from the Tools menu. Type `Names(I)` into the Expression list box and make sure that the Watch Type is set to Watch Expression, as in Figure 12.22. (You can automatically place the `Names(I)` array in the

Expression list box on the Add Watch dialog box if you select Names(I) with the mouse before opening the Add Watch dialog box.)

Figure 12.22.
The Add Watch dialog box.

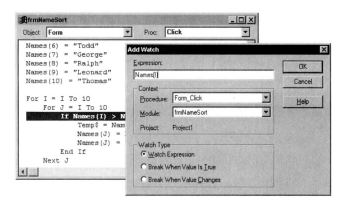

When you are finished, click OK. Repeat the process again for the array variable Names(J).

Run the program by selecting Start from the Run menu. Program execution starts and continues until it reaches the breakpoint. The breakpoint line, If Names(I) > Names(J) Then, is outlined with a border, as in Figure 12.23. Check the values of Names(I) and Names(J) in Visual Basic's Debug window.

The Two Panes of the Debug Window

The appearance of the Debug window has changed with Visual Basic 4. There are two panes. The execution point of your code appears in the lower pane. The upper pane shows the value of the expressions you have decided to watch.

The Debug window lets the programmer check the values of a program while in a *break state*. The break state happens when you select Break from the Run menu or when the program reaches a breakpoint. Check the upper pane of the Debug window for the values of the watched variables Names(I) and Names(J). As usual, two quotation marks represent an empty string. In this case, that means that there is nothing in either variable as in Figure 12.23.

The empty strings indicate that the If Names(I) > Names(J) Then statement is comparing nothing. The values in Names(I) and Names(J) are not valid. At this point, both I and J are supposed to point at the first element in the array. Both I and J should be 1. Hence, the line of code that initializes I has to be changed as follows:

```
Private Sub Form_Click()
    Static Names(10) As String
    Dim I As Integer
    Dim J As Integer
```

```
Dim K As Integer
Dim Temp As String

Names(1)  = "John"
Names(2)  = "Tim"
Names(3)  = "Edward"
Names(4)  = "Samuel"
Names(5)  = "Frank"
Names(6)  = "Todd"
Names(7)  = "George"
Names(8)  = "Ralph"
Names(9)  = "Leonard"
Names(10) = "Thomas"

For I = 1 To 10
    For J = I To 10
        If Names(I) > Names(J) Then
            Temp = Names(I)
            Names(J) = Names(J)
            Names(J) = Temp
        End If
    Next J
Next I

For K = 1 To 10
    Print Names(K)
Next K

End Sub
```

Figure 12.23.
The Debug window, showing no contents for `Names(I)` *and* `Names(J)`.

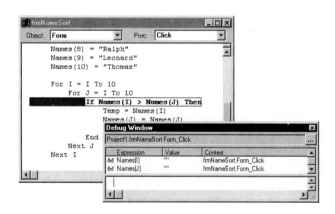

However, when you make the change and run the program the result is still wrong as shown in Figure 12.24. (Note that Toggle Breakpoint, F9, on the Run Menu toggles the breakpoint you set to Off, or you can remove all breakpoints by selecting Clear All Breakpoints from the Run menu.)

Obviously, a problem still exists. Examine the only other part of the program, the part where the actual elements are switched. Add a breakpoint at the end of the element-switching section. Select the code line `Names(J) = Temp` and put a breakpoint there as shown in Figure 12.25.

Figure 12.24.
The Name Sort result after the variable I is initialized to 1.

Figure 12.25.
A breakpoint added at the end of the element-switching section.

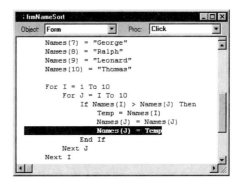

Now run the program. Execution halts at the breakpoint—the line that reads Names(J) = Temp. Examine Names(I) and Names(J) in the Debug window, as shown in Figure 12.26. One variable has a value of "John", and the other "Edward".

Figure 12.26.
The Debug window showing the values of Name(I) and Name(J).

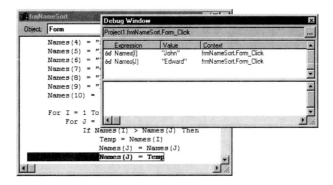

The exchange of array elements is supposed to go as follows:

1. The value that is in Names(I) should be placed in the variable Temp.

2. Then the element in Names(J) should be copied and placed in Names(I).

3. Finally, the value stored in Temp should be passed to Names(J).

At the breakpoint shown in Figure 12.25, everything has happened except the final step. The program is about to move the value stored in Temp to Names(J).

Therefore, one would expect Names(I) and Names(J) to hold the same value, but they do not. Names(I) holds "John" and Names(J) holds "Edward". Something is definitely wrong. Look back one line in the code to the following:

```
Private Sub Form_Click()
     Static Names(10) As String
     Dim I As Integer
     Dim J As Integer
     Dim K As Integer
     Dim Temp As String

     Names(1) = "John"
     Names(2) = "Tim"
     Names(3) = "Edward"
     Names(4) = "Samuel"
     Names(5) = "Frank"
     Names(6) = "Todd"
     Names(7) = "George"
     Names(8) = "Ralph"
     Names(9) = "Leonard"
     Names(10) = "Thomas"

     For I = 1 To 10
          For J = I To 10
               If Names(I) > Names(J) Then
                    Temp = Names(I)
                    Names(J) = Names(J)
                    Names(J) = Temp
               End If
          Next J
     Next I

     For K = 1 To 10
          Print Names(K)
     Next K

End Sub
```

Ah, there's the problem! This line should read Names(I) = Names(J). Make that change. The complete, bug-free code is as follows:

```
Private Sub Form_Click()
     Static Names(10) As String
     Dim I As Integer
     Dim J As Integer
     Dim K As Integer
     Dim Temp As String

     Names(1) = "John"
     Names(2) = "Tim"
     Names(3) = "Edward"
     Names(4) = "Samuel"
```

```
        Names(5) = "Frank"
        Names(6) = "Todd"
        Names(7) = "George"
        Names(8) = "Ralph"
        Names(9) = "Leonard"
        Names(10) = "Thomas"

        For I = 1 To 10
            For J = I To 10
                If Names(I) > Names(J) Then
                    Temp = Names(I)
                    Names(I) = Names(J)
                    Names(J) = Temp
                End If
            Next J
        Next I

        For K = 1 To 10
            Print Names(K)
        Next K

End Sub
```

The result of the bug-free code appears in Figure 12.27.

Figure 12.27.
*The Name Sort application
running without any bugs.*

Congratulations on a successful debugging job! As you can see, there are some powerful debugging tools available in Visual Basic, including the Debug window and breakpoints. In fact, these tools have even more capabilities. For example, a program can be executed line by line and the values of variables can be changed while a program is running. In the following section, you will see those features in action as you debug an Investment Calculator application.

Debugging an Investment Calculator

Suppose that you decide to write a small investment calculator program that would project an investment's value after a certain number of years. Presume that the investment is $1,000 at 7 percent for 12 years. Compounded annually, that investment would be worth the following:

$\$1,000.00 \times (1 + .07)^{12} = \$2,252.19$

```
    For K = 1 To 10
        Print Names(K)
    Next K

End Sub
```

Unfortunately, the window in Figure 12.17 is the result of the program when the user clicks the form with the mouse.

Figure 12.17.

The Name Sort sample
application running, but
with a bug.

Figure 12.17 looks a little incomplete, to say the least! It is time to debug. In fact, you can start debugging without even stopping the program. To do that, select the Code item from the Visual Basic View menu, or press F7. The `Form_Click()` `Sub` procedure opens, as shown in Figure 12.18.

Figure 12.18.

The Code window open
while the Name Sort
program is running.

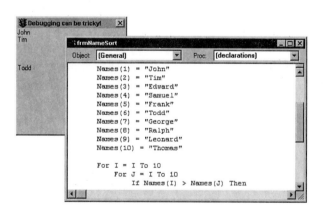

Visual Basic gives the programmer the chance to scan code for possible errors while a program is running. When you do that, you might spot one error right away by just reading the code. In particular, when the program is switching elements around in the array, it loads them temporarily into a variable named `Temp$`. But when they are loaded back into the array, the program uses a (misspelled) variable named `Tmp$`:

```
Private Sub Form_Click()
    Static Names(10) As String

    Names(1) = "John"
    Names(2) = "Tim"
```

Begin by putting the calculator template together. Start a new project and place three text boxes on the form to hold the three values: Investment ($1,000.00), InterestRate (7 percent), and Years (12). The calculation that the program should perform looks like this:

$$\text{Result} = \text{Investment} \times (1 + \text{InterestRate}/100)^{\text{Years}}$$

Add four text boxes and one command button to the form as shown in Figure 12.28. Also, add the labels that appear to the left of the text boxes. Change the controls' properties to match those listed in the following table. (The table works its way down from the top of the form.)

Figure 12.28.
The completed Investment Calculator template.

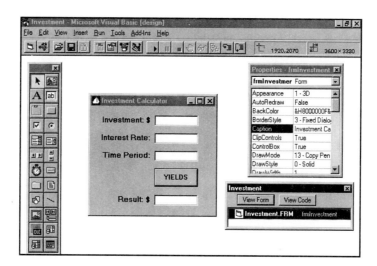

Object	Property	Setting
Form	Appearance	1-3D
	BorderStyle	3-Fixed Dialog
	Caption	Investment Calculator
	Name	frmInvestment
Label	Alignment	1-Right Justify
	Caption	Investment: $
	Font	Size: 10 pt
		Style: Bold
	Name	Label1
Text Box	Name	txtInvestment
	TabIndex	0
	Text	(None)

continues

Object	Property	Setting
Label	Alignment	1-Right Justify
	Caption	Interest Rate:
	Font	Size: 10 pt
		Style: Bold
	Name	Label2
Text Box	Name	txtInterestRate
	TabIndex	1
	Text	(None)
Label	Alignment	1-Right Justify
	Caption	Time Period:
	Font	Size: 10 pt
		Style: Bold
	Name	Label3
Text Box	Name	txtYears
	TabIndex	2
	Text	(None)
Command Button	Caption	YIELDS
	Default	True
	Font	Style: Bold
	Name	cmdYields
Label	Alignment	1-Right Justify
	Caption	Result: $
	Font	Size: 10 pt
		Style: Bold
	Name	Label4
Text Box	Locked	True
	Name	txtResult
	TabStop	False
	Text	(None)

Save the project by selecting the Save Project… item from the Visual Basic File menu. Save the form and project as Investment.frm and Investment.vbp, respectively. Then lock the controls on the form so that they are not inadvertently moved. The investment calculator template is all set.

Now, put the code behind the form. To use the calculator, the user places the investment amount in the top text box, the interest rate in the next text box, and the number of years the investment will last in the third text box. Then she clicks the YIELDS button to see the result in the bottom box. That means that all the action will take place in cmdYields_Click(). Double-click on that button to bring up the Code window and the associated event code skeleton:

```
Private Sub cmdYields_Click()

End Sub
```

Start writing code by converting the text entered in the text boxes into numeric values:

```
Private Sub cmdYields_Click()
    Investment = Val(txtInvestment.Text)
    InterestRate = Val(txtInterestRate.Text)
    Years = Val(txtYears.Text)

    :

End Sub
```

Next, add the code that performs the calculation:

```
Private Sub cmdYields_Click()
    Investment = Val(txtInvestment.Text)
    InterestRate = Val(txtInterestRate.Text)
    Years = Val(txtYears.Text)
    Result = Investments * (1 + InterstRate / 100) ^ Years

    :

End Sub
```

Finally, add the line of code that displays the result:

```
Private Sub cmdYields_Click()
    Investment = Val(txtInvestment.Text)
    InterestRate = Val(txtInterestRate.Text)
    Years = Val(txtYears.Text)
    Result = Investments * (1 + InterstRate / 100) ^ Years
    txtResult.Text = Format$(Result, "###,###,##0.00")
End Sub
```

(Please note that for the purposes of this demonstration, the Option Explicit keywords that require explicit variable declaration have not been used. If they had been, the bugs that you will find in a few minutes would have never happened!)

Give the calculator a try now. Run the program and enter values in each text box. To follow the previous example, use $1,000.00 at 7 percent for 12 years. Then press the YIELDS command button. Oops! Something is wrong. The result in the lower text box reads $0.00, as shown in Figure 12.29. Obviously, there's a problem; it's time to debug.

Figure 12.29.
The Investment Calculator with a bug.

Start by placing a breakpoint (by using F9 or Toggle Breakpoint on the Run menu) in the first line of the cmdYields_Click() procedure as in Figure 12.30.

Figure 12.30.
A breakpoint added to the first line of the `cmdYields_Click()` *procedure.*

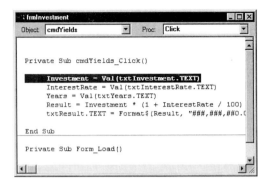

When the program reaches this point, it will automatically break. As shown in Figure 12.31, use the Add Watch... item on the Tools menu to add watches to the various variables: `Investment`, `InterestRate`, `Years`, and `Result`.

Figure 12.31.
Adding Watches to debug the Investment Calculator application.

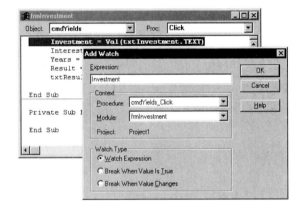

Run the application now and place the same values in the text boxes. Then click the YIELDS command button. When you do, the program reaches the breakpoint and stops. Now single step through the code one line at a time by using the F8 key or selecting the Step Into item from the Run menu. Press F8 once to execute the first line. The box around the first line—as is usual for a breakpoint— moves to the second line, indicating where the program is, as shown in Figure 12.32. Note also that the text of the first line stays bold, indicating that there is still a breakpoint there.

After executing the first line, check the value of the watched variable `Investment` in the Debug window. As shown in Figure 12.32, `Investment` holds a value of `1000`, as it should.

The next step is to set the interest rate by stepping the program forward one more line. Do that by pressing F8 again. Then check the value of the watched variable `InterestRate` in the Debug window. This value should read `7`, as it does in Figure 12.33.

Figure 12.32.
Stepping through the buggy Investment Calculator program. The watched variable Investment holds the correct value, 1000.

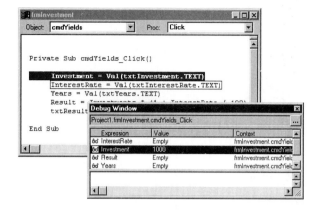

Figure 12.33.
After stepping one more line into the program, the value of the watched variable InterestRate reads 7, as it should.

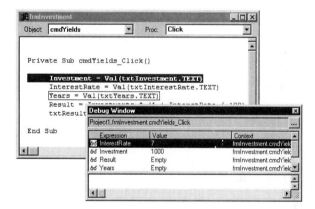

Everything seems correct so far. Check the value of the next watched variable, Years, by pressing F8 again to step the program ahead one more line. Check the Debug window. The variable Years certainly does hold the value 12, as in Figure 12.34. This is correct. Hence, it should be concluded that the line of code that fills the value for the variable Years is correct.

Figure 12.34.
The application stepped one more line. The watched variable Years does indeed hold the proper value.

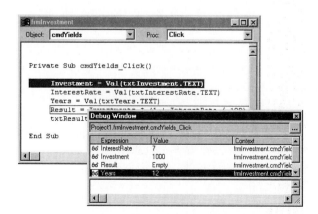

To continue the process, press F8 once again to execute the fourth line in the code. This line sets the value for the variable `Result` after performing the calculation. Check the Debug window again to see what value the watched variable `Result` holds. (This is shown in Figure 12.35.)

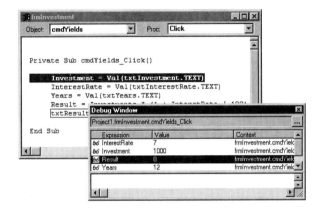

Figure 12.35.
The program stepped one more line, thus setting the value of the watched variable Result.

There is a problem there! For some reason, the value for `Result` is `0`. This is definitely wrong. Check the line of code for any kind of mistake: Is the formula that is supposed to determine the investment return wrong? Is a variable name misspelled?

```
Private Sub cmdYields_Click()
    Investment = Val(txtInvestment.Text)
    InterestRate = Val(txtInterestRate.Text)
    Years = Val(txtYears.Text)
    Result = Investments * (1 + InterstRate / 100) ^ Years
    txtResult.Text = Format$(Result, "###,###,##0.00")
End Sub
```

There are two problems in the code line, and they both deal with misspelled variable names. The first one is `Investments`; it should really be `Investment`. Because the variables in the application were implicitly declared, when Visual Basic encountered the variable name `Investments` instead of `Investment`, it assumed that this was a different variable. The other problem is the variable `InterestRate`. In the buggy line of code, this variable was misspelled `InterstRate`. In the Debug window, change those two variable names to what they should be: `Investment` and `InterestRate`.

Because you have already executed that line by stepping through it, you can't execute it again without starting from the top of the `cmdYields_Click()` procedure. Stop the program and return to the design desktop. Remove the breakpoint from the code by selecting Clear All Breakpoints from the Run menu. Then run the application again using the same values. When you do, you will see that the calculator comes up with the correct result, as in Figure 12.36.

Actually, the two bugs that you found would have never crept into the code in the first place if explicit variable declaration had been required.

Figure 12.36.
The bug-free Investment Calculator application.

As you can see, single stepping like this can be a powerful debugging tool that gives you, the programmer, a picture of what a program is doing line by line. In general, you now have a good idea of the debugging capabilities found in Visual Basic. If an error is suspected in a program's logic, breakpoints can be set to stop the code at strategic locations. This enables you to check what is happening. In addition, variable values can be determined using the Watch feature of the Debug window. To further locate the problem, you can even step through the code line by line.

Break Mode Debugging Commands: *Step Over, Step To Cursor,* and *Set Next*

In fact, there are a number of other powerful debugging commands that are now available in Visual Basic 4 when you are in break mode. They are all available on the Run menu:

- `Step Over` (Shift+F9)—Similar to `Step Into` except that when the current statement contains a call to a procedure, `Step Over` executes the called procedure as a unit and then returns to the next statement in the current module.

- `Step To Cursor` (Ctrl+F8)—Selects a statement further down the code where you want execution to stop. `Step To Cursor` helps you leap over large blocks of code that you do not want to view.

- `Set Next` (Ctrl+F9)—Sets a different line of code to execute next (must be within the current procedure). `Set Next` allows you to back up in the debugging process.

- `Show Next`—Places the cursor on the line that will execute next.

About Debugging and Mouse or Keyboard Input

There is one problem that should be mentioned before finishing with debugging and moving on to the next chapter. Because Visual Basic programs are event-driven, there are a few considerations that must be taken into account. If you place a breakpoint in a

> MouseDown or KeyPress event procedure and you release the mouse button or key while the program is in a break state, you might never get a MouseUp or KeyUp event when the code continues. In other words, keep in mind that Visual Basic programs respond to the computer environment, and if you change that environment while debugging, it might result in unexpected consequences.

That's it for coverage of debugging and error-handling. The next chapter, "Connecting to Other Window Applications: DDE," examines Dynamic Data Exchange. This is for communication between Windows applications.

Summary

This chapter started by giving some very simple guidelines that will help to avoid compile and syntax errors. Part of the chapter dealt with handling two types of errors that might occur: trappable run-time errors and logical errors. Another section of the chapter discussed the new Err object. You saw how trappable errors could be handled using the statements On Error GoTo and Resume. When these statements are used along with error-handling code, a program will not have to come to a halt if an unforeseen circumstance causes problems. Instead, the problem can be fixed by the programmer, or the program can inform the user of the problem, allowing her to fix it. This is especially important when programs are sent out for others to use. Programs that can handle errors are termed *robust*. You have seen that fixing a program's logical bugs is made easier by using the debugging tools and techniques available in Visual Basic. These tools include the Debug window, breakpoints, single-stepping, and Watch. In particular, you used the Debug window to watch variables as a program executed, after setting a breakpoint to halt the program at a strategic code line. These tools and methods are very powerful and are now a part of your Visual Basic programming techniques.

New Statements	Description
On Error GoTo *line*	Enables the error-handling routine that starts at *line*, which is any line label or line number. Thereafter, if a run-time error occurs, control branches to *line*, making the error-handler active. The specified line must be in the same procedure as the On Error statement; otherwise, a compile-time error occurs.
On Error Resume Next	Specifies that when a run-time error occurs, control goes to the statement immediately following the statement in which the error occurred; thus, execution continues. It's recommended to use this form rather than On Error GoTo when accessing objects.
On Error GoTo 0	Disables any enabled error-handler in the current procedure.

New Statements	Description
Resume [0]	If the error occurred in the same procedure as the error-handler, execution resumes with the statement that caused the error. If the error occurred in a called procedure, execution resumes at the statement that last called out of the procedure containing the error-handling routine.
Resume Next	If the error occurred in the same procedure as the error-handler, execution resumes with the statement immediately following the statement that caused the error. If the error occurred in a called procedure, execution resumes with the statement immediately following the statement that last called out of the procedure containing the error-handling routine (or On Error Resume Next statement).
Resume *line*	Execution resumes at *line*, which is a line label or line number. The argument line must be in the same procedure as the error-handler.

New Object	Description
Err	Contains information about run-time errors. Accepts the Raise and Clear methods for generating and clearing run-time errors. The properties of the Err object are set by the generator of an error—Visual Basic, an OLE object, or the programmer.

The following properties are associated with the Err object:

Property	Description
Description	A string corresponding to the return of the Error function for the specified Number, if this string exists. If the string does not exist, Description contains User-defined error.
HelpContext	The Visual Basic Help file context ID for the error corresponding to the Number property.
HelpFile	The fully qualified drive, path, and filename of the Visual Basic Help file.
Number	A value specified as argument to the Error statement. Its value corresponds to the value returned by the Err function in previous versions of Visual Basic.
Source	The name of the current Visual Basic project.

13

Connecting to Other Windows Applications: DDE

Visual Basic programs run in a multitasking operating environment along with other Windows applications. Because of this, data can be easily exchanged by copying and pasting information from one program to another. Visual Basic programs can extract data from other applications, automatically update them with new data, and even send commands or keystrokes to manipulate data by remote control. All this can be achieved using the programming link called *Dynamic Data Exchange (DDE)*. Although DDE is an older inter-application communications standard dating to the earliest versions of Windows, it remains a useful technique in many situations.

This chapter shows you how to connect Visual Basic applications to other Windows programs—both those written in Visual Basic and others, including WordPad—by transferring data and commands to and from each application. The chapter covers the following topics:

- What is Dynamic Data Exchange (DDE)?
- How DDE works
- Creating DDE links at design-time
- DDE link properties
- DDE link events
- Run-time Client links
- Handling DDE errors
- Sending commands to other applications

In this chapter you will learn how to communicate and exchange data, in addition to commands, with other Windows programs. This can be extremely useful if you want to coordinate the use of several applications into one. For example, a program could have a few sections of Excel worksheets on the same master form, as well as a few documents from Microsoft Word for Windows and some Visual Basic graphs.

DDE is a very useful technique that relies on *links* between a Visual Basic program and others. You will discover that there are a number of ways to set up such links. You could link a text box to a WinWord document, for instance, or to a few cells in an Excel spreadsheet. You will also learn how to link applications at design-time by using Visual Basic's *Paste Link* menu item. You will create a DDE mini-application that will show the user how each type of link works. Then you will set up DDE links between your application and Program Manager to add a new program folder to the Program menu item found under the Windows 95 Start button.

What is Dynamic Data Exchange (DDE)?

One benefit of the Windows 95 operating environment is that it *multitasks*. This means that it can run several different applications at one time, making it substantially different from DOS. This Windows capability raises some interesting possibilities for program interaction. What if two applications could communicate in some way, for example, by passing data and instructions back and forth? If this were possible, each application could handle the tasks that it was best at—those for which it was designed. For instance, a spreadsheet could manipulate data in cells, a word processor could format data into documents, and the power and flexibility of both would be increased by working together. All of this is possible under Windows 95 in a process called *Dynamic Data Exchange (DDE)*.

DDE is a mechanism supported by the Windows 95 operating system that enables two applications to *talk* to each other by continuously and automatically exchanging data. DDE automates the manual cutting and pasting of data between applications, providing a faster vehicle for updating information.

First, you will begin by establishing a DDE link between your program and WordPad. You will see how DDE works by setting up *conversations*.

Next, you will discover how to let users set up their own DDE links between the controls in your applications and those of other applications. Also, you will find out how to open a Windows application that is supposed to be communicating with your Visual Basic program, but is not because it isn't running.

Finally, you will learn about some advanced DDE topics, including how to send actual commands to other applications—creating a new Explorer folder, for example—and how to handle DDE errors. With all this in store, it's time to start by examining what exactly makes DDE work.

How DDE Works

Windows applications exchange data by engaging in a DDE *conversation*. This is similar to a conversation between two people. The application that initiates the conversation is called the *destination application*, or simply the *destination*. The application responding to the destination is called the *source application*, or the *source*. (This terminology might seem a bit counter-intuitive, but it will make sense in a few minutes.) An application can engage in several conversations at one time, acting as the destination in some and the source in others. There is nothing special about an application that makes it a destination or source; these are merely roles that many applications can adopt. A diagram of a DDE conversation appears in Figure 13.1.

Figure 13.1.
A pictorial representation of destination and source applications and the data flow direction.

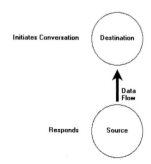

Source and Destination Applications: New DDE Terminology

In previous versions of VB, the DDE destination was called the *client* and the source was called the *server*.

In Visual Basic any text box, picture box, or label can be the destination in a conversation—whereas any form can be the source.

When a destination application begins a DDE conversation, it must specify

- The name of the source application that it wants to talk to
- The subject of the conversation, called the *topic*

If a source application receives a request for a conversation concerning a topic it recognizes, it responds and a conversation begins. Once established, a conversation cannot change applications or topics. The combination of application and topic uniquely identifies the conversation and remains constant the entire time. If either the destination or source changes application or topic, the conversation ends.

During the conversation, the destination and source can exchange information about one or more *items*. An item is a reference to information that is meaningful to both applications. Either the destination or source can change the item without affecting the state of the conversation. The communications flow is shown in Figure 13.2.

Figure 13.2.

The destination and source applications engaged in a DDE conversation, exchanging items.

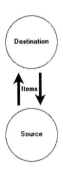

Together, the application, topic, and item serve to uniquely identify the information passed between the applications.

The Application Name

Every application that can be a DDE source has a unique *application name*. Usually, this is the executable filename without the extension. For example, Excel.exe would be called Excel. The names of a few Microsoft applications are listed in the Table 13.1.

Table 13.1. A few DDE application names.

Application	DDE Application Name
Microsoft Access	MSAccess
Microsoft Excel	Excel
Microsoft FoxPro for Windows	FoxPro
Microsoft Project	Project
Microsoft Windows Program Manager	ProgMan
Microsoft WordPad	WordPad
Microsoft Word for Windows	WinWord

How Do You Find the DDE Application Name for an Application that Is Not on the List in Table 13.1?

The answer to this question is that the information should be supplied in the application's documentation. Another place to look, though, is in the RegEdit utility. RegEdit.exe should be located in your Windows directory. To find an installed application name, start the RegEdit application and select HKEY_LOCAL_MACHINE. Then move down through the tree structure by selecting Software | Microsoft | Windows | App Paths. Another place to look in the Local Machine directory is Shared Tools | Shared Tools Location. The Registry is discussed in detail in Chapter 16.

You should also know that DDE application names, like most Visual Basic names, are not case-sensitive. Thus, Excel, excel, and EXCEL all refer to Microsoft Excel.

When a form in a Visual Basic application is the source in a conversation, its application name is the name you choose for the application when creating the .exe file. If you are running the application within Visual Basic, the application name is the name of the project without a filename extension.

The Topic

The *topic* defines the subject of a DDE conversation and is usually some information unit that is meaningful to the source application. Most applications recognize a document name as the topic for a DDE conversation. For example, Excel recognizes a filename ending with .xls or .xlc. Microsoft Word recognizes filenames ending with .doc or .dot.

Many applications that perform DDE support a topic called *System*. This topic can be used to request information from an application. You can provide a System topic in your own Visual Basic application by including a form with its `LinkTopic` property set to `System` and adding controls with names corresponding to various system items.

The Item

The *item* identifies the piece of information actually being passed during the DDE conversation. For instance, Word for Windows recognizes any bookmark in a document specified by the LinkTopic as an item in a conversation. Excel recognizes cell references, such as A1D5, as items in a conversation.

When a control in a Visual Basic application is the conversation destination, the control defines the item for the conversation by setting the `LinkItem` property for that control.

When a form in a Visual Basic application is the source in a conversation, the name of each text box, label, and picture on the form can be the item for a DDE conversation.

Dynamic Data Exchange Links

A DDE conversation is often referred to as a *link* because the two applications are linked by the data they are exchanging. There are three types of links, each distinguished by how the source updates the destination when data in the source changes:

- *Automatic link*—the source supplies data to the destination every time the data defined by the `LinkItem` property changes.
- *Manual link*—the source supplies data only when the destination requests it.
- *Notify link*—the source notifies the destination when the data changes but supplies data only when the destination requests it.

Automatic, Notify, and Manual Links: New DDE Terminology

In previous versions of Visual Basic, DDE links were called *hot*, *warm*, or *cold*, depending upon the frequency of information passed. In Visual Basic 4, a hot link is called an *automatic link*, a warm link is now referred to as a *notify link*, and a cold link is called a *manual link*.

Creating DDE Links at Design-Time

While designing a Visual Basic application, you can create data links to other applications that support DDE. These links are saved as values in the various `Link` properties of the forms and controls in your application. Thus, they are automatically re-established when the application runs. This is convenient, because you do not have to write any code to allow your application to perform DDE conversations with other applications.

This convenience, however, comes at the expense of some flexibility, because these links cannot be changed without writing code to do so. You will probably want to establish links at run-time so that you can handle errors and control certain actions, such as tracking the order in which the links are established. Nevertheless, you can learn quite a bit about DDE by creating links at design-time.

Design-Time Destination Links

Establishing DDE links at design-time is very easy in Visual Basic. For example, suppose that you had a Microsoft Word document saved as a Word document called DDE_Link.doc. You might want to establish a link between the text in that document and a text box, txtTest, in a Visual Basic program you are designing. If you were to establish such a link, it would remain part of the program when it ran. (You should note that automatic links can be established only at design-time.) This type of connection is called a *destination link*. A destination link is one in which your application—the destination—is the application requesting information, and the other is the source.

OLE Links in Microsoft Word 6.x and Above

The shortcut method described in this section for creating DDE linked items does not work with Word versions 6.x. As of the Word 6.0 release, the application no longer uses DDE links when copying information to the clipboard. Instead it uses OLE links. (In order to perform DDE with Word 6.x, you must set up the links manually.)

Also, Microsoft Word comes with several specialized tools: WordArt, Equation, and Graph. These tools have been included with Visual Basic 4 as OLE Objects. They can be added to the Visual Basic Toolbar like any other custom control and added to a form just by double-clicking on them. The MS-Word-related Visual Basic custom objects found in the Custom Controls dialog box include Microsoft Word 6.0 Document, Microsoft Word 6.0 Picture, Microsoft WordArt 2.0, Microsoft Equation 2.0, and Microsoft Graph 5.0. These exciting new tools are discussed in the next Chapter 14, "Connecting to Other Windows Applications: Object Linking and Embedding 2."

In this case, txtTest will receive what is in DDE_Link.doc; thus txtTest is the destination, and DDE_Link.doc is the source. To establish this simple link, start Visual Basic and WordPad. Create a document in WordPad called DDE_Link.doc and type a few lines. Select all the text that you just typed and copy it, using the Copy item from WordPad's Edit menu. This action transfers the text to the Clipboard and establishes WordPad as the data source.

The next step is to set up the link with txtTest. Add a text box to the default form in Visual Basic and change its Name property to txtText. Then select the Paste Link item from Visual Basic's Edit menu. This item is active only if the Clipboard data conforms to the DDE link standards. If the link is successful, the value of the txtTest Text property will change to display the current state of the data in the source application. After you select Paste Link, the link is formed and the text in DDE_Link.doc appears in txtTest, as shown in Figure 13.3. If you edit the text in DDE_Link.doc, the text in txtTest will change automatically to reflect the editing.

Figure 13.3.

A design-time destination link between a Visual Basic text box, txtTest, and a Windows 95 WordPad document, DDE_ Link.doc.

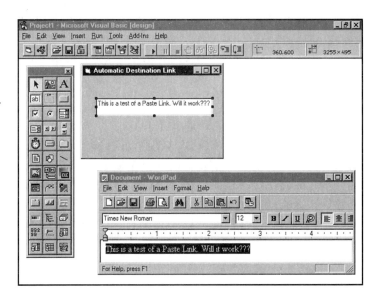

You should note that this is an automatic link. Once the link is established, the value of the control will change whenever the data in the source application changes. This will happen when your Visual Basic application is running, causing a Change event, and while you are building applications.

Design-Time Links Are Cut Briefly when an Application Opens

If you run a program with a design-time link in the Visual Basic environment, VB has to cut the link temporarily when it switches from design-time to run-time. Most, but not all, applications, such as WordPad or Excel, will attempt to re-establish the link.

This automatic link is saved with the form and is permanent. This means that whenever the form is opened at design-time or loaded at run-time, it attempts to re-establish the conversation with the source application. If the source application is running and recognizes the topic, the conversation is re-established. If the source application is not running or does not respond to the topic, Visual Basic generates an error.

Manual Links Cannot Be Added at Design-Time

A manual link cannot be set up at design-time because some code is needed to maintain a manual link. In particular, the `LinkRequest` method must be present in code to request data updates.

There are several events associated with Visual Basic destination applications. Their names and descriptions appear in Table 13.2.

Table 13.2. DDE destination control events.

Event	Description
LinkOpen	This event occurs when a control successfully initiates a DDE conversation.
LinkClose	This event occurs when a DDE conversation is ended for any reason.
LinkError	This event is recognized only as the result of a DDE-related error that occurs when no Visual Basic code is being executed. The error number is passed as an argument.
LinkNotify	If the `LinkMode` property of a control is set to `3-Notify`, the `LinkNotify` event occurs whenever the source has new information to supply to the control.

Providing Data Through Links

If you want a Visual Basic application to supply data to other applications, you should create a *source link*. A source link is a connection wherein the other application—the destination—requests data from your application—the source. As with destination links, source links can be created at design-time and made a permanent part of the Visual Basic application. To create a source link, the project containing your application must be open in the Visual Basic environment and the other application must be running, also.

Why not try this out with Microsoft Excel? (This, of course, assumes that you have Excel installed on your computer.)

Start a new Visual Basic project and make sure that Excel is running. Place a text box on the VB form and change its `Text` property to `Does this work?`. Now select the form. Set its `LinkMode` property to `1-Source`. Then select the text box and copy the control by selecting Copy from the Visual Basic Edit menu.

In Excel, select the destination for the data by clicking a cell. Then go into the application's Edit menu and select Paste Special. A Paste Special dialog box appears on the screen with two option buttons—Paste (the default) and Paste Link—and a large list box. Select Paste Link and click OK. The DDE link is established, and the text from the Visual Basic text box appears in the selected cell as shown in Figure 13.4.

Figure 13.4.
A Visual Basic text box source linked to Microsoft Excel.

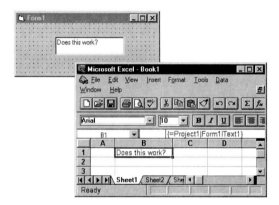

If the link is successful, the value of the control—in this case, the `Text` property of the text box—will be displayed in the destination application's cell. Once you have established an automatic link between a control in your application and a destination application, Visual Basic will automatically supply new data to the destination application every time the value of the control changes. You can change the value of the control at design-time and watch as Visual Basic supplies the new data to the other application. Try that with the Excel example, now. Change the `Text` property of the text box and watch as the DDE link automatically updates the text appearing in the linked Excel cell.

There are several events associated with Visual Basic applications that are used as source applications. They are shown in Table 13.3.

Table 13.3. DDE source form events.

Event	Description
LinkOpen	This event occurs when a destination application initiates a conversation.
LinkClose	This occurs if a destination application ends its conversation.
LinkError	As with a destination link, this event is recognized only as the result of a DDE-related error that occurs when no Visual Basic code is being executed. The error number is passed as an argument.
LinkExecute	This event occurs when a destination application sends a command string to be executed by the source application.

The DDE Link Properties

Using Copy and Paste Link to establish DDE conversations is fine for learning about DDE or for quick programming tasks, but these commands are not flexible enough for most sophisticated applications. In addition, they do not allow for conversations with other applications that support DDE but do not provide Copy and Paste Link commands.

To create and use DDE conversations from code, or to manually establish conversations without using Paste Link, you must use the Link properties associated with forms and controls: LinkTopic, LinkItem, and LinkMode.

The *LinkTopic* Property

LinkTopic specifies a control's DDE conversation. When a control is engaged in a DDE conversation with another application, the LinkTopic property contains the name of that application and the topic of the conversation. To set LinkTopic for a destination control, use a string with the following syntax:

```
application¦topic
```

The LinkTopic property has the following parts:

- *application*—this is the name of the application from which data is requested—usually the executable filename without an extension—for example, Excel (for Microsoft Excel). The pipe character, | (character code 124), separates the application from the topic. (This character is often located on the keyboard on the same key as the backslash, \, character.)
- *topic*—this is the fundamental data grouping used in the source application; for example, a worksheet in Microsoft Excel.

Thus, following the conventions of the property syntax, the source application is separated from the topic by a pipe character. A link to Excel might look like this:

```
Excel¦c:\excel\vouchers.xls
```

This property can be set for any text box, label, or picture box. If you know the application name for an application and a topic it supports, you can establish a DDE conversation with that application.

If a Visual Basic application is used as a source application, the destination application uses the value of the LinkTopic property on the source form to establish the conversation. The LinkTopic property of a form specifies the topic that the form will respond to in a DDE conversation. The names of individual controls on the form define the items that other applications can use in DDE conversations.

The *LinkItem* Property

A control's LinkItem property specifies the item for the conversation, defined by the LinkTopic property for that control. The setting of this property varies depending on the source application. For instance, if the topic of a conversation with Excel is a spreadsheet, the LinkItem could be

A1D5

This would point the information being passed to cell A1D5.

The *LinkMode* Property

If you try setting the LinkTopic and LinkItem properties, you will discover that nothing happens. This is because the conversation must be initiated by the LinkMode property. This property has three settings: 1-Automatic, 2-Manual, and 3-Notify. The LinkMode property is normally set to the default, 0-None. When it is set to Automatic, Manual, or Notify, Visual Basic immediately tries to initiate the conversation specified in the LinkTopic property. If the source application specified in the LinkTopic property is not running, Visual Basic generates an error as shown in Figure 13.5.

Figure 13.5.
The error generated by a non-existent source application.

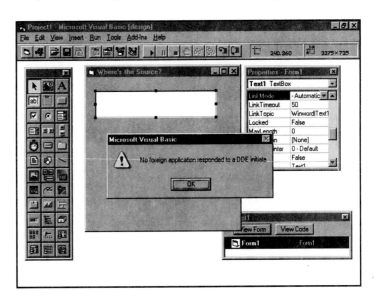

If the LinkMode property is set to 1-Automatic, whenever the data specified by the combination of the LinkTopic and LinkItem properties changes, the control receives the new data and a Change event is generated for that control. If the LinkMode property is set to 2-Manual or 3-Notify, the control is not updated automatically and the LinkRequest method must be used to obtain new information from the source.

When the value of LinkTopic changes, Visual Basic automatically ends the conversation and resets LinkMode to 0-None. It is good programming practice, though, to explicitly set LinkMode to None before changing the LinkTopic property. Once a new value is set for LinkTopic, a new conversation can be established by setting LinkMode to Automatic, Manual, or Notify again.

Preset Constants for the LinkMode Property Settings

In Visual Basic 4, there are preset constants available for the LinkMode property settings. They are as follows:

Constant	Setting	Description
vbLinkNone	0	No DDE link.
vbLinkAutomatic	1	An automatic DDE link is established.
vbLinkManual	2	A manual DDE link is established.
vbLinkNotify	3	A notify DDE link is established.

If a Visual Basic application is used as a source application, the destination application also uses the value of the LinkMode property on the source form to establish the conversation. Similar to a Visual Basic destination application, a Visual Basic source application is usually set to 0-None. If LinkMode is set to 1-Source, the controls on the form will supply data to any destination that establishes a DDE conversation with them. If LinkMode is set to None at design-time, its value cannot be changed at run-time. Otherwise, if the property is set to Source at design-time, its value can be freely changed between None and Source at run-time.

Setting Automatic, Manual, and Notify Links

When a control's LinkTopic property is set to a valid value—a combination of a running application's name and a topic that the application recognizes—and the LinkItem property is also set to a valid value for that LinkTopic, an automatic link can be established by setting the LinkMode property for that control to Automatic.

A *manual link* can be created by setting the LinkMode property to 2-Manual. When the property is set to manual, a conversation exists, but the control does not automatically receive new information every time it changes. To obtain the most recent data, the code must include the LinkRequest method.

The other possible setting for the LinkTopic property is Notify. A *notify link* is almost the same as a manual link except that the source notifies the destination when information changes. This notification occurs in the destination application as a LinkNotify event. When this occurs, the LinkRequest method should again be used to get the most recent data.

The following mini-application demonstrates the three possible link types. It uses a second application created in Visual Basic as the source. Therefore, the demonstration application acts as the destination and calls the source application when it runs. Then the user can choose the type of link she would like to establish by selecting different option buttons in the destination program window. Depending upon the link selected, the data is updated in various ways.

To get going on this, start a new Visual Basic project. This first project will be the source application that the destination program will call. Change the default form's Caption and Name properties to Source and frmMain, respectively. Then save the form as Source.frm and save the project as Source.vbp. Next, position a test box on the form as in Figure 13.6, and change the form and control properties to reflect those in Table 13.4.

Figure 13.6.
The Source application template.

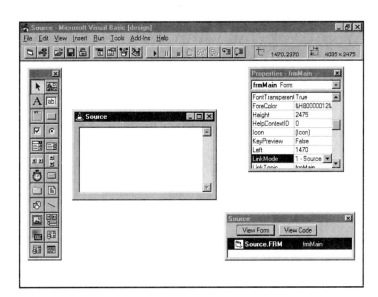

Table 13.4. The visual implementation of the main form.

Object	Property	Setting
Form	BorderStyle	3-Fixed Dialog
	Caption	Source
	LinkMode	1-Source
	LinkTopic	frmMain
	Name	frmMain
Text Box	MultiLine	True
	Name	txtBox
	ScrollBars	2-Vertical
	Text	(None)

The only code in this project checks to see if a second version of this application is running. If so, the focus is shifted to that second version and it is closed. The code to do that should go into the Form_Load() event as follows:

```
Option Explicit

Private Sub Form_Load()
    Dim SaveTitle As String

    'The following code will keep the application
    'from running twice

    If App.PrevInstance Then
        SaveTitle = App.Title
        App.Title = "... duplicate instance."
        frmMain.Caption = "... duplicate instance."
        AppActivate SaveTitle
        SendKeys "% R", True
        End
    End If

End Sub
```

That's all there is to the source. Save the project and then make an .exe file of it by selecting the Make EXE File item from the File menu. Name the executable file Source.exe. After you have done that, start another new application. This one is going to become the destination.

Change the default form's Name and Caption properties to frmDestination and Destination, respectively. Then save the form as Destination.frm and the project as Destination.vbp. Now add a text box, three option buttons, and two command buttons to the form. Place them on the form in roughly the same positions as those in Figure 13.7. Then use Table 13.5 to set the controls' properties. (The table works its way down the form from the top.)

Figure 13.7.
The Destination program template.

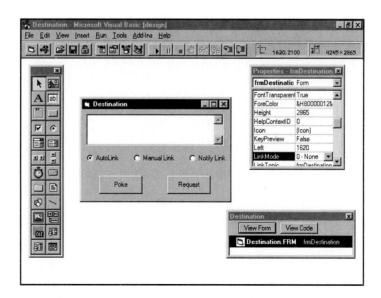

Table 13.5. The visual implementation of the destination form.

Object	Property	Setting
Form	BorderStyle	3-Fixed Dialog
	Caption	Destination
	LinkTopic	frmDestination
	Name	frmDestination
Text Box	MultiLine	True
	Name	txtDestination
	ScrollBars	2-Vertical
	Text	(None)
Option Button	Caption	Auto Link
	Name	optAutoLink
Option Button	Caption	Manual Link
	Name	optManualLink
Option Button	Caption	Notify Link
	Name	optNotifyLink
Command Button	Caption	Poke
	Name	cmdPoke
Command Button	Caption	Request
	Name	cmdRequest

The code for this application is straightforward. When an option button is selected for a particular type of link—automatic, manual, or notify—that option button's Click event is activated, triggering the code that sets up that link with the source application. Add that code to the option buttons' Click events like this:

```
Private Sub optAutoLink_Click()
    cmdPoke.Visible = True
    cmdRequest.Visible = False        'No need for button with vbLinkAuto link
    txtDestination.LinkMode = vbLinkNone        'Clear DDE Link
    txtDestination.LinkMode = vbLinkAutomatic      'Reestablish LinkMode
End Sub

Private Sub optManualLink_Click()
    cmdPoke.Visible = True
    cmdRequest.Visible = True         'Make Request button valid
    txtDestination.LinkMode = vbLinkNone        'Clear DDE Link
    txtDestination.LinkMode = vbLinkManual      'Reestablish new linkmode
End Sub
```

```
Private Sub optNotifyLink_Click()
    cmdPoke.Visible = False
    cmdRequest.Visible = True                'Make Request button valid
    cmdRequest.Enabled = False
    txtDestination.LinkMode = vbLinkNone         'Clear DDE Link
    txtDestination.LinkMode = vbLinkNotify    'Reestablish new linkmode
End Sub
```

Next, add the code that makes the notify link inform the destination application that the source application has changed. In this sample application, this notification will take the shape of a message box, telling the user that the source has changed.

```
Private Sub txtDestination_LinkNotify()
    Beep
    Beep
    Beep
    MsgBox "Attention: You Have a Message!"
    Beep
    cmdRequest.Enabled = True
End Sub
```

This destination application will automatically open the source program that you created a few minutes ago. (That way the user does not have to worry about starting the source application.) The code that does this should be placed in the Form_Load() event, like this:

```
Private Sub Form_Load()
    Dim I As Long

    'This procedure will start the VB Source application
    ➥that was created earlier

    I = Shell("c:\vb\programs\source.exe", vbNormalFocus)
    'make sure the path in the above line is correct for your computer!

    I = DoEvents()           'Causes windows to finish processing the Shell cmd

    'Clear the DDE link if exists
    txtDestination.LinkMode = vbLinkNone
    'Set up the link
    txtDestination.LinkTopic = "Source¦FrmMain"
    'Set link to source text box
    txtDestination.LinkItem = "TxtBox"
    'Establish a Manual DDE link
    txtDestination.LinkMode = vbLinkManual
    'Set option button
    optManualLink.Value = True

End Sub
```

The final sections of code should go in the command buttons' `Click` events. When the user presses cmdRequest, she is requesting a data update from the source application (this button is only active for manual and notify links). The other command button, cmdPoke, performs a very interesting task. The data flow in a DDE conversation is usually from the source application to the destination application. However, the destination application can also send data to the source. This is called *poking* data. It is performed using the `LinkPoke` method, which sends the control's value to the source application, updating the data that is referred to by the `LinkItem` property. The code for these two command buttons is as follows:

```
Private Sub cmdPoke_Click()
      'With any DDE link, this button will be visible, and when
      'selected it will poke information from Destination
      'application to the Source application

      txtDestination.LinkPoke
   End Sub

Private Sub cmdRequest_Click()
      'With a Manual DDE link, this button will be visible, and when
      'selected it will request an update of information from the Source
      'application to the Destination application

      txtDestination.LinkRequest
End Sub
```

That's all there is to it! The destination application is complete. Take it for a test spin; check out the different link options and how they affect data updating. Playing with this application is a very good way to learn about DDE because it shows you what the various kinds of links events do. An example of each of the types of links appears in Figures 13.8 through 13.11. Figure 13.8 shows an automatic link that updates automatically. Figure 13.9 shows a manual link, where the application must specifically request to be updated. Figure 13.10 shows a notify link, which is the same as a manual link except that it receives messages from the source application. Figure 13.11 shows the result of poking a message back along the DDE channel.

Figure 13.8.
The Destination and Source applications running and connected with an automatic link.

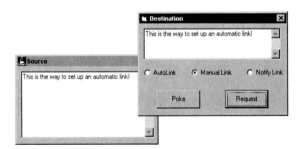

Figure 13.9.
The Destination and Source applications connected with a manual link.

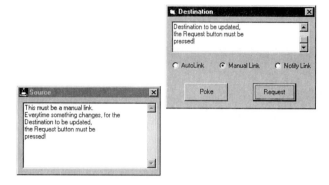

Figure 13.10.
The two applications connected with a notify link. Notice the message box informing the user that the source has changed.

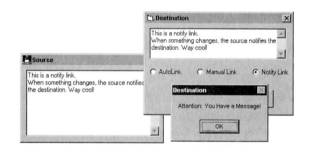

Figure 13.11.
Poking data back to the Source.

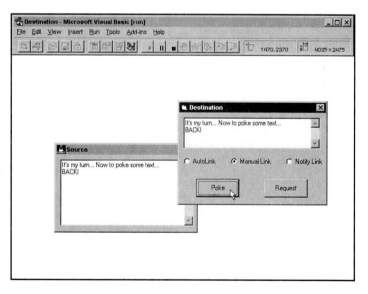

The complete visual design and code for this DDE example appears in Tables 13.6 and 13.7 and Listing 13.1 and Listing 13.2.

The control on the Source application form should be set as shown in Table 13.6.

Table 13.6. The main form for the DDE Mini-Application.

Object	Property	Setting
Form	BorderStyle	3-Fixed Dialog
	Caption	Source
	LinkMode	1-Source
	LinkTopic	frmMain
	Name	frmMain
Text Box	MultiLine	True
	Name	txtBox
	ScrollBars	2-Vertical
	Text	(None)

Listing 13.1. The code for the main form of the DDE Mini-Application.

```
Option Explicit

Private Sub Form_Load()
    Dim SaveTitle As String

    'The following code will keep the application
    'from running twice

    If App.PrevInstance Then
        SaveTitle = App.Title
        App.Title = "... duplicate instance."
        FrmMain.Caption = "... duplicate instance."
        AppActivate SaveTitle
        SendKeys "% R", True
        End
    End If

End Sub
```

Table 13.7. The visual design of the frmDestination form.

Object	Property	Setting
Form	BorderStyle	3-Fixed Dialog
	Caption	Destination
	LinkTopic	frmDestination
	Name	frmDestination

Object	Property	Setting
Text Box	MultiLine	True
	Name	txtDestination
	ScrollBars	2-Vertical
	Text	(None)
Option Button	Caption	Auto Link
	Name	optAutoLink
Option Button	Caption	Manual Link
	Name	optManualLink
Option Button	Caption	Notify Link
	Name	optNotifyLink
Command Button	Caption	Poke
	Name	cmdPoke
Command Button	Caption	Request
	Name	cmdRequest

Listing 13.2. The complete code for `frmDestination`.

```
Application.Option Explicit

Private Sub cmdPoke_Click()
    'With any DDE link, this button will be visible, and when
    'selected it will poke information from Destination
    'application to the Source application

    txtDestination.LinkPoke
    End Sub

Private Sub cmdRequest_Click()
    'With a Manual DDE link, this button will be visible, and when
    'selected it will request an update of information from the Source
    'application to the Destination application

    txtDestination.LinkRequest
End Sub

Private Sub Form_Load()
    Dim I As Long

    'This procedure will start the VB Source application
    ➡that was created earlier

    I = Shell("c:\vb\programs\source.exe", vbNormalFocus)
    'make sure the path in the above line is correct for your computer!
```

continues

Listing 13.2. **continued**

```
    I = DoEvents()              'Causes windows to finish processing the Shell cmd

    txtDestination.LinkMode = vbLinkNone        'Clear the DDE link if exists
    txtDestination.LinkTopic = "Source¦frmMain"         'Sets up link
    txtDestination.LinkItem = "TxtBox"          'Set link to source text box
    txtDestination.LinkMode = vbLinkManual      'Establish a Manual DDE link
    optManualLink.Value = True                  'Set option button

End Sub

Private Sub optAutoLink_Click()
    cmdPoke.Visible = True
    cmdRequest.Visible = False          'No need for button with vbLinkAuto link
    txtDestination.LinkMode = vbLinkNone            'Clear DDE Link
    txtDestination.LinkMode = vbLinkAutomatic       'Reestablish LinkMode
End Sub

Private Sub optManualLink_Click()
    cmdPoke.Visible = True
    cmdRequest.Visible = True                'Make Request button valid
    txtDestination.LinkMode = vbLinkNone            'Clear DDE Link
    txtDestination.LinkMode = vbLinkManual      'Reestablish new linkmode
End Sub

Private Sub optNotifyLink_Click()
    cmdPoke.Visible = False
    cmdRequest.Visible = True                'Make Request button valid
    cmdRequest.Enabled = False
    txtDestination.LinkMode = vbLinkNone            'Clear DDE Link
    txtDestination.LinkMode = vbLinkNotify      'Reestablish new linkmode
End Sub

Private Sub txtDestination_LinkNotify()
    Beep
    Beep
    Beep
    MsgBox "Attention: You Have a Message!"
    Beep
    cmdRequest.Enabled = True
End Sub
```

The *LinkTimeout* Property

Some applications take longer to respond to DDE conversations than others. If an application takes too long to respond, Visual Basic generates a trappable run-time error—error number 286. You can adjust the amount of time Visual Basic waits for a response by setting a control's LinkTimeout property. The values for the property are tenths of a second, and the default value is 50 tenths, or five seconds. This is adequate for conversations with most applications, but you can adjust it as necessary. If LinkTimeout is set to -1, Visual Basic waits for 65,535 tenths of a second, or approximately one hour and forty-nine minutes for a response from the other application before it generates an error.

Recovering From an Apparent Freeze During a DDE Conversation

If a Visual Basic application seems to freeze during a DDE conversation and you do not want to wait for a time-out error to occur, you can recover by pressing the Esc key. This interrupts any pending DDE operations in Visual Basic and generates a trappable run-time error—error number 287.

Several Methods and One Function that Work with DDE

DDE gives you, the programmer, the ability to manipulate other applications by remote control. Once the destination link is set up with another application, you can send data, request data, and send commands to the destination applications. Just as with Source.vbp in the DDE example earlier, when an application is the source in a conversation, the destination can also be notified when data has changed.

Often a conversation cannot be initiated because the source application is not running. If this is the case, Visual Basic will generate a trappable run-time error. You can trap this like any other run-time error and start the source application by using the Shell function. You might recall the Shell application you built back in Chapter 7. The Shell function would work the same way here with the following syntax:

```
Shell(pathname[, windowstyle])
```

The Shell function uses the following arguments.

- *pathname*—the name of the program to execute and any required arguments or command-line switches; might include directory or folder and drive. It can also be the name of a document that has been associated with an executable program.

- *windowstyle*—this argument can have these values:

Constant	Value	Description
vbNormalFocus	1	Window has the focus and is restored to its original size and position.
vbMinimizedFocus	2	Window is displayed as an icon with focus.
vbMaximizedFocus	3	Window is maximized with focus.
vbNormalNoFocus	4	Window is restored to its most recent size and position. The currently active window remains active.
vbMinimizedNoFocus	6	Window is displayed as an icon. The currently active window remains active.

Notice how the `Shell` function was used in the preceding DDE application to open Source.exe:

```
Private Sub Form_Load()
    Dim I As Long

    'This procedure will start the VB Source application
    ➥that was created earlier

    I = Shell("c:\vb\programs\source.exe", vbNormalFocus)
    'make sure the path in the above line is correct for your computer!

    I = DoEvents()            'Causes windows to finish processing the Shell cmd

    :

End Sub
```

The call opens the source application with focus and at its normal size—not minimized or maximized.

The `LinkPoke` method also used in the sample DDE application *pokes* data from the destination application back at the source. `LinkPoke` transfers the contents of a label, picture box, or text box control to the source application in a DDE conversation. Its syntax works like any other method—`Object.Method`—as follows:

object.LinkPoke

Typically, information in a DDE conversation flows from source to destination. However, `LinkPoke` enables a destination object to supply data to the source. Not all source applications accept information supplied this way. If the source application doesn't accept the data, an error occurs.

The next method that works with DDE linking is `LinkRequest`. This method is used to update the destination application when a manual or notify link has been established. With either of these link types, data is not automatically updated. The application must explicitly ask the source to update the control by calling LinkRequest.

Any application that supports DDE can receive commands from a Visual Basic destination application. Once the destination link is established with another application, the `LinkExecute` method can be used on the control maintaining the link. For instance, the destination could send a macro command to Excel to close an active worksheet through its own control—suppose it is a text box on the destination form named `txtLink`—like this:

```
txtLink.LinkExecute "[File.Close()]"
```

You should note that every application accepts different command strings. Usually, the documentation that comes with an application will tell you what commands it will accept.

The final method, `LinkSend`, notifies other applications that data has changed. When a form in a Visual Basic application is acting as the source in a DDE conversation, Visual Basic takes care of most of the details for you. For instance, if a destination application initiates a conversation with a text box control on the form, Visual Basic automatically updates the destination in the case of an automatic link, or in the case of a notify link, Visual Basic notifies the destination when data changes.

However, Visual Basic does not do this with a picture box. The contents of a picture box can be large and it can take many graphics methods to complete a change to a picture. Because of this, the source application might waste time and resources updating every DDE destination each time a pixel in the picture changed. Instead, any Visual Basic DDE destinations can be updated explicitly by executing the LinkSend method.

It's time to put all of these properties, events, and methods to work in an application. How about something that communicates with Program Manager and places a new program folder and executable application on the Windows 95 Start menu? (Yes, Virginia, there is a Program Manager in Windows 95; the executable still lives in the Windows directory.)

What Does Program Manager Do in Windows 95?

Program Manager still makes groups, though the new Windows 95 term for groups is *folders*. Program Manager oversees the contents of the *Program* menu located under the Start button. So, instead of using Program Manager to navigate through the Windows environment (as it was used in Windows 3.x), the user now goes to the Program menu item, where all Program Manager folders are located. When a new folder is added to Program Manager, that folder is also automatically added to the Program menu.

This project will be constructed in three parts:

1. The first part opens Program Manager and adds a new folder that the user will name. Simultaneously, this folder will be added to the Program menu item found under the Windows 95 Start button.

2. Then the application's capabilities will be extended to add an executable application to the new Program Manager folder, and consequently add that executable to the new folder on the Program menu.

3. Finally, the project will be expanded to alphabetically list all Program folders found under the Start button on the user's computer.

(You might want to test out Program Manager for yourself, to see what kind of groups you have on your computer. To run the application, go to the Windows directory and double-click Progman.exe.)

To get going with all of this, start a new Visual Basic project. Change the default form's Name and Caption properties to frmPMFolder and Let's Talk to Program Manager!, respectively. Then save the form as PM.frm and the project as PM.vbp.

Next, add two labels, a text box, two command buttons, and a rectangle on the form. Position them approximately in the same positions as those shown in Figure 13.12. Change the controls' properties to match those in the Table 13.8. (The table works from the top of the form down.)

Figure 13.12.
The first stage of the PM application template.

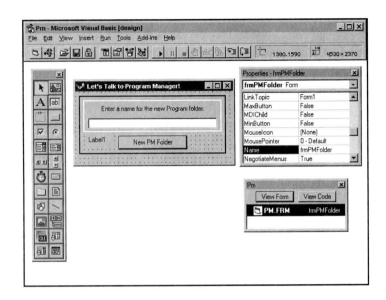

Table 13.8. The visual design of the PM application.

Object	Property	Setting
Form	BorderStyle	3-Fixed Dialog
	Caption	Let's Talk to Program Manager!
	Name	frmPMFolder
Shape	BorderColor	White2
	BorderWidth	
	Name	Shape1
Label	Alignment	2-Center
	Caption	Enter a name for the new Program folder:
	Name	lblName
Text Box	Name	txtNewPMFolder
	Text	(None)
Label	Caption	Label1
	Name	Label1
	Visible	False
Command Button	Caption	Do It!
	Default	True
	Name	cmdDoIt

Object	Property	Setting
Command Button	Cancel	True
	Caption	Close
	Name	cmdClose

Now to add the behind-the-scenes wiring. First, write the code that closes the form when the user clicks the Close button. In the Code window, add that code to the cmdClose_Click() procedure as follows:

```
Private Sub cmdClose_Click()
    Unload cmdClose.Parent
End Sub
```

The user will enter a name for a new Program Manager group in txtNewPMFolder and click the Do It! button. So, the action happens when the command button's Click event is activated—a new Program folder is created. To make the code more modular, place all the code that does this in a separate Sub procedure called CreateProgManFolder. (You'll write this procedure in just a minute.) Add the call to the procedure like this:

```
Private Sub cmdDoIt_Click()
    CreateProgManFolder Me, Trim$(txtNewPMFolder.Text), "myapp.grp"
End Sub
```

Next, write the CreateProgManFolder Sub procedure. Add that new procedure by selecting Procedure from the Insert menu. Then name the procedure CreateProgManFolder, make sure that it is public, and click OK. The procedure's code skeleton will appear in the code window:

```
Public Sub CreateProgManFolder()

End Sub
```

You may be curious about one of the labels that you added to the form. It is just a default label, Label1, with a caption the same as its name. You might have also noticed that its Visible property is set to False. Because the application that you are writing is going to become the destination application in a DDE link, some control has to be available to create the link between the application and Program Manager. That is what the label is for. At run-time the label will be invisible, but is there to create the DDE conversation. So the code has to include LinkMode, LinkTopic, and LinkTimeout settings to make the DDE link work. It also includes a function called DoEvents, which will make the Visual Basic application yield system resources to enable the Program Manager to complete its tasks. (The DoEvents function is discussed in more detail in the next section about DDE error-handling.) Some programmers use asterisks, *, or dashes, -, to separate module descriptions from code. That technique will be used in this example. So, see if you like this particular style. Add the code that creates the DDE link using the invisible label:

```
Public Sub CreateProgManFolder(f As Form, gpName As String, gpPath As String)

    '.............................................................
    ' Procedure: CreateProgManFolder
    ' Arguments: f       The Form where Label1 exists
    '            gpName      A string that contains the group name
    '            gpPath      A string that contains the group file
    '                    name  i.e. 'myapp.grp'
    '.............................................................
    Dim Count As Integer, Doze As Integer
    Screen.MousePointer = 11


    '.............................................................
    'A label control is used to generate the DDE messages
    '.............................................................
    On Error Resume Next


    '..................................
    ' Set LinkTopic to PROGRAM MANAGER
    '..................................
    f.Label1.LinkTopic = "ProgMan¦Progman"
    f.Label1.LinkMode = vbLinkManual      '2

    For Count = 1 To 10              'Loop to ensure that there is enough
                                     'time to process
        Doze = DoEvents()            'DDE Execute. This is redundant
                                     'but needed for debug windows.
    Next

    f.Label1.LinkTimeout = 100

    :

End Sub
```

Now add the code that creates the new Program folder and resets the `LinkMode` and `LinkTimeout` properties:

```
Public Sub CreateProgManFolder(f As Form, gpName As String, gpPath As String)

    '.............................................................
    ' Procedure: CreateProgManFolder
    ' Arguments: f       The Form where Label1 exists
    '            gpName      A string that contains the group name
    '            gpPath      A string that contains the group file
    '                    name  i.e. 'myapp.grp'
    '.............................................................
    Dim Count As Integer, Doze As Integer
    Screen.MousePointer = 11


    '.............................................................
    'A label control is used to generate the DDE messages
    '.............................................................
    On Error Resume Next
```

```
'--------------------------------
' Set LinkTopic to PROGRAM MANAGER
'--------------------------------
f.Label1.LinkTopic = "ProgMan¦Progman"
f.Label1.LinkMode = vbLinkManual    '2

For Count = 1 To 10      'Loop to ensure that there is enough
                         'time to process
    Doze = DoEvents()    'DDE Execute. This is redundant
                         'but needed for debug windows.
Next

f.Label1.LinkTimeout = 100

'------------------
' Create program folder
'------------------
f.Label1.LinkExecute "[CreateGroup(" + gpName + Chr$(44) + gpPath + ")]"

'---------------
' Reset properties
'---------------
f.Label1.LinkTimeout = 50
f.Label1.LinkMode = vbLinkNone      '0

Screen.MousePointer = 0
End Sub
```

That's all there is to it! The first part of this application is ready to roll. Try it out. Run the program
and make a new Program folder with a name of your choice. Figure 13.13 shows that the folder is
simultaneously added to the Programs menu item found under the Start button.

Figure 13.13.
The first part of the PM
application complete and
running.

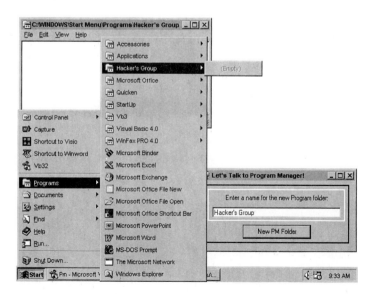

Now that the user can open a new program folder, she should also be able to add an executable item to that folder. To add that to the code, the form needs to be expanded. Stretch it down, toward the bottom of the screen. Move the Close command button down to the bottom and delete the Do It! command button. Add a new command button directly below txtNewPMFolder and change its Caption, Default, and Name properties to New PM Folder, True, and cmdNewFolder, respectively. Then go into the code to the now defunct cmdDoIt_Click() procedure. Copy the code line calling the Sub procedure CreateProgManFolder. Now completely delete that procedure. Find the Click event for the new command button, cmdNewFolder. Paste the line of code that you just copied into that event. It should look now appear as follows:

```
Private Sub cmdNewFolder_Click()
    CreateProgManFolder Me, Trim$(txtNewPMFolder.Text), "myapp.grp"
End Sub
```

Go back to the form and draw a rectangle around the entire group of controls. Change this rectangle's BorderWidth property to 2 and its BorderColor to Navy. This rectangle will separate this first section of the form from the new controls that you are about to draw.

Using Figure 13.14 as a guide, add the new controls listed in Table 13.9. (Figure 13.14 also shows the controls added in the third stage of the PM application, but you don't have to worry about these quite yet.)

Figure 13.14.
The second stage of the PM application template.

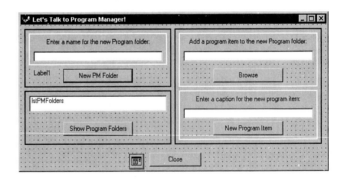

Table 13.9. The visual design of the PM application.

Object	Property	Setting
Shape	BorderColor	Navy
	BorderWidth	2
	Name	Shape3
Shape	BorderColor	White
	BorderWidth	2
	Name	Shape4

Object	Property	Setting
Label	Alignment	2-Center
	Caption	Add a program item to the new Program folder:
	Name	Label2
Text Box	Name	txtNewItem
	Text	(None)
Command Button	Caption	Browse
	Name	cmdBrowse
Shape	BorderColor	White
	BorderWidth	2
	Name	Shape5
Label	Alignment	2-Center
	Caption	Enter a caption for the new program item:
	Name	Label3
Text Box	Name	txtCaption
	Text	(None)
Command Button	Caption	New Program Item
	Name	cmdItem
Common Dialog	DefaultExt	Exe
	DialogTitle	Enter Program File Name!
	Name	CommonDialog1

Now for the code behind these new controls. When the user adds a new item to the new Program folder, she enters a filename in txtNewItem by either typing the information or by pressing the Browse button to find the correct executable file. So first, add the code that makes the Browse command button work. (Note that this code uses the common dialog control to open a file dialog box.)

```
Private Sub cmdBrowse_Click()
    CommonDialog1.FileName = ""
    CommonDialog1.Flags = 4096
    'Demonstration flags set to 4096 so that user can only enter
    'existing files

    CommonDialog1.Filter = "Programs (*.exe)   ¦ *.exe"
    CommonDialog1.ShowOpen

    If CommonDialog1.FileName <> "" Then
        txtNewItem.Text = CommonDialog1.FileName
    End If

End Sub
```

The next step for the user would be to enter a name for the new item that will go into the folder. So, she enters the name in txtCaption. Then, when the user is finished, she will click the New Program Item command button to create the new Program folder item. Again, the code's action centers around a command button's click event—in this case, cmdItem_Click(). To continue the theme of modularity in this program, the click event should call a Sub procedure that will create the new item. Why not call the procedure CreateProgManItem? Add that call as follows:

```
Private Sub cmdItem_Click()
    CreateProgManItem Me, Trim$(txtNewItem.Text), Trim$(txtCaption.Text)
End Sub
```

Here is how to write the procedure CreateProgManItem. Add this new subroutine by selecting Procedure from the Insert menu. The code template should appear as follows:

```
Public Sub CreateProgManItem()

End Sub
```

The code for this procedure is essentially the same as the code you wrote for CreateProgManFolder except that it opens a new item when the LinkExecute method is called. That line of code is in bold below. The entire code for the subroutine is as follows:

```
Public Sub CreateProgManItem(F As Form, ExePath As String, ItemCap As String)

    '-----------------------------------------------------------
    ' Procedure: CreateProgManItem
    '
    ' Arguments:    F         The form where Label1 exists
    '           ExePath       A string that contains the command line
    '                         for the item/icon.
    '                         i.e. c:\myapp\setup.exe'
    '           ItemCap       A string that contains the item's caption
    '-----------------------------------------------------------


    Screen.MousePointer = 11


    '-------------------------------------------------------------------
    ' Windows requires DDE in order to create a program group and item.
    ' Here, a Visual Basic label control is used to generate the DDE messages
    '-------------------------------------------------------------------
    On Error Resume Next
    Dim count As Integer, doze As Integer

    '--------------------------------
    ' Set LinkTopic to PROGRAM MANAGER
    '--------------------------------
    F.Label1.LinkTopic = "ProgMan¦Progman"
    F.Label1.LinkMode = vbLinkManual    '2

    For count = 1 To 10       'Loop to ensure that there is enough
                              'time to process
        doze = DoEvents()     'DDE Execute. This is redundant
                              'but needed for debug windows.
    Next
```

```
F.Label1.LinkTimeout = 100


'------------------------------------------------
' Create Program Item, one of the icons to launch
' an application from Program Manager
'------------------------------------------------
F.Label1.LinkExecute "[AddItem(" + ExePath + Chr$(44) +
➡ItemCap + Chr$(44) + ",,)]"


'----------------
' Reset properties
'----------------
F.Label1.LinkTimeout = 50
F.Label1.LinkMode = vbLinkNone        '0

Screen.MousePointer = 0

End Sub
```

That's all there is to it! The second part of the application is ready to roll. Figure 13.15 shows the program in action; try it out. First, add a new folder to the Program menu, and then add a new item to your folder.

Figure 13.15.
The second part of the PM application complete and running.

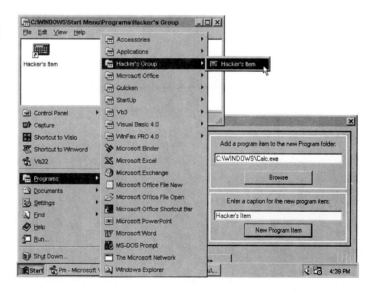

Now on to the third and final part of the application. This time, the extended functionality of the application moves in the direction of the Start button's Program menu itself. This next part lists every available Program folder in alphabetical order. This shouldn't be hard at all!

Stretch the form horizontally and move the entire group of controls—bounding rectangles and all—that makes a new item to the right of the form, as in Figure 13.14. Then add a new boundary rectangle to enclose the controls you are about to draw. Change the new rectangle's BorderWidth property to 2 and the BorderColor to Navy. Then add a list box and command button within that border. Position them as shown in Figure 13.14, and change their properties to match Table 13.10.

Table 13.10. More controls for the PM application.

Object	Property	Setting
Shape	BorderColor	Navy
	BorderWidth	2
	Name	Shape6
List Box	Name	lstPMFolders
	Sorted	True
Command Button	Caption	Show Program Folders
	Name	cmdShowPM

The only action in this section of the application happens when the user presses the Show Program Folders command button. Then the Click event associated with that button should call a subroutine that gets all the names of the Program folders and places the names into the list box, lstPMFolders. Because lstPMFolders' Sorted property is set to True, the control will automatically alphabetize the list for you. Enter the code that will call this routine, aptly named GetFolders, (and clears the list box, also) like this:

```
Private Sub cmdShowPM_Click()
    lstPMFolders.Clear
    GetFolders
End Sub
```

Here is the last bit of code for this application. Create a new Sub procedure called GetFolders. Its code skeleton should appear as follows:

```
Public Sub GetFolders()

End Sub
```

This routine is going to establish a link with Program Manager to request the Program folder data. Then it will place the information in the list box, lstPMFolders. In keeping with the idea of modularity, make the first task—creating the link with Program Manager—a separate subroutine that GetFolders calls. Name the routine GetLinkData. (You will write this DDE linking routine in a few minutes.) Add that call to the GetFolders Sub procedure, as follows:

```
Public Sub GetFolders()
    '-----------------------------------------------------
    'Load program folder names from ProgMan
    '-----------------------------------------------------
    GetLinkData "PROGMAN"

    :

End Sub
```

After the `GetFolders` routine links with Program Manager and retrieves the Program folder data from `GetLinkData`, all that is left to do is place each item into the list box. That can be accomplished like this:

```
Public Sub GetFolders()
    '-------------------------------------------------------------
    'Load program folder names from ProgMan
    '-------------------------------------------------------------
    GetLinkData "PROGMAN"

    Dim count As Integer, Temp As String, CRLF As String

    CRLF = Chr$(13) + Chr$(10)
    Temp = Label1
    count = InStr(Temp, CRLF)


    '-------------------------------------------------------------
    ' Add each name to sorter list box
    '-------------------------------------------------------------
    Do While count
        lstPMFolders.AddItem Left$(Temp, count - 1)
        Temp = Mid$(Temp, count + 2)
        count = InStr(Temp, CRLF)
    Loop

End Sub
```

Now for the final piece of code—the `GetLinkData` Sub procedure. All this does is establish the link between your Visual Basic application and Program Manager, and requests the Program folder information. This task can be completed using the properties discussed in this chapter—such as `LinkTopic`, `LinkItem`, and `LinkRequest`. Add that code like this:

```
Public Sub GetLinkData(Item As String)
    '-------------------------------------------------------------
    'Establish DDE link with ProgMan
    'Request Item
    '-------------------------------------------------------------
    Label1.LinkTopic = "ProgMan|Progman"
    Label1.LinkItem = Item$
    Label1.LinkMode = vbLinkManual      '2
      Label1.LinkRequest
    On Error Resume Next
    Label1.LinkMode = vbLinkNone        '0
    On Error GoTo 0
End Sub
```

The PM application is now complete. Why not run it and try the new capability that you just built in—press the Show Program Folders command button and watch your application fly!

The complete code for this application appears in Listing 13.3 and Figure 13.16 shows how the program looks when it is running. The controls' properties on frmPMFolder should be set as shown in Table 13.11.

Figure 13.16.
The completed PM application running, showing a list of available Program folders.

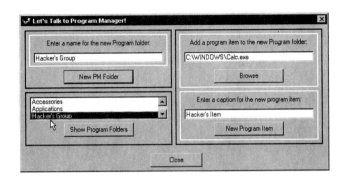

Table 13.11. The PM Application.

Object	Property	Setting
Form	BorderStyle	3-Fixed Dialog
	Caption	Let's Talk to Program Manager!
	Name	frmPMFolder
Shape	BorderColor	White
	BorderWidth	2
	Name	Shape1
Label	Alignment	2-Center
	Caption	Enter a name for the new Program folder:
	Name	lblName
Text Box	Name	txtNewPMFolder
	Text	(None)
Label	Caption	Label1
	Name	Label1
	Visible	False
Command Button	Caption	New PM Folder
	Default	True
	Name	cmdNewFolder
Command Button	Caption	Close
	Name	cmdClose
Shape	BorderColor	Navy
	BorderWidth	2
	Name	Shape2

Object	Property	Setting
Shape	BorderColor	Navy
	BorderWidth	2
	Name	Shape3
Shape	Name	Shape4
Label	Alignment	2-Center
	Caption	Add a program item to the new Program folder:
	Name	Label2
Text Box	Name	txtNewItem
	Text	(None)
Command Button	Caption	Browse
	Name	cmdBrowse
Shape	Name	Shape5
Label	Alignment	2-Center
	Caption	Enter a caption for the new program item:
	Name	Label3
Text Box	Name	txtCaption
	Text	(None)
Command Button	Caption	New PM Item
	Name	cmdItem
Common Dialog	DefaultExt	Exe
	DialogTitle	Enter Program File Name!
	Name	CommonDialog1
Shape	BorderColor	Navy
	BorderWidth	2
	Name	Shape6
List Box	Name	lstPMFolders
	Sorted	True
Command Button	Caption	Show Program Folders
	Name	cmdShowPM

Listing 13.3. **The complete code associated with `frmPMFolder`.**

```
Option Explicit

Private Sub cmdBrowse_Click()
    CommonDialog1.FileName = ""
    CommonDialog1.Flags = 4096
    'Demonstration flags set to 4096 so that
    'user can only enter existing files

    CommonDialog1.Filter = "Programs (*.exe)   ¦ *.exe"
    CommonDialog1.ShowOpen

    If CommonDialog1.FileName <> "" Then
        txtNewItem.Text = CommonDialog1.FileName
    End If

End Sub

Private Sub cmdClose_Click()
    Unload cmdClose.Parent
End Sub

Public Sub CreateProgManFolder(F As Form, gpName As String, gpPath As String)

    '-----------------------------------------------------------
    ' Procedure: CreateProgManFolder
    ' Arguments: f          The Form where Label1 exists
    '            gpName      A string that contains the group name
    '            gpPath      A string that contains the group file
    '                        name  i.e. 'myapp.grp'
    '-----------------------------------------------------------
    Dim count As Integer, doze As Integer
    Screen.MousePointer = 11

    '----------------------------------------------------------------------
    'A label control is used to generate the DDE messages
    '----------------------------------------------------------------------

      On Error Resume Next

    '--------------------------------
    ' Set LinkTopic to PROGRAM MANAGER
    '--------------------------------
    F.Label1.LinkTopic = "ProgMan¦Progman"
    F.Label1.LinkMode = vbLinkManual    '2

    For count = 1 To 10        'Loop to ensure that there is
                               'enough time to process
        doze = DoEvents()      'DDE Execute. This is redundant
                               'but needed for debug windows.
    Next

    F.Label1.LinkTimeout = 100

    '--------------------
    ' Create program folder
    '--------------------
    F.Label1.LinkExecute "[CreateGroup(" + gpName + Chr$(44) + gpPath + ")]"
```

```
      '----------------
      ' Reset properties
      '----------------
      F.Label1.LinkTimeout = 50
      F.Label1.LinkMode = vbLinkNone          '0

      Screen.MousePointer = 0
End Sub

Private Sub cmdItem_Click()
    CreateProgManItem Me, Trim$(txtNewItem.Text), Trim$(txtCaption.Text)
End Sub

Private Sub cmdNewFolder_Click()
    CreateProgManFolder Me, Trim$(txtNewPMFolder.Text), "myapp.grp"
End Sub

Public Sub CreateProgManItem(F As Form, ExePath As String, ItemCap As String)

      '--------------------------------------------------------
      ' Procedure: CreateProgManItem
      '
      ' Arguments:   F          The form where Label1 exists
      '              ExePath    A string that contains the command line
      '                         for the item/icon.
      '                         i.e. c:\myapp\setup.exe'
      '              ItemCap    A string that contains the item's caption
      '--------------------------------------------------------

      Screen.MousePointer = 11

      '------------------------------------------------------------------
      ' Windows requires DDE in order to create a program group and item.
      ' Here, a Visual Basic label control is used to generate the DDE messages
      '------------------------------------------------------------------
      On Error Resume Next
      Dim count As Integer, doze As Integer

      '-------------------------------
      ' Set LinkTopic to PROGRAM MANAGER
      '-------------------------------
      F.Label1.LinkTopic = "ProgMan¦Progman"
      F.Label1.LinkMode = vbLinkManual    '2

      For count = 1 To 10       'Loop to ensure that there is enough
                                'time to process
          doze = DoEvents()     'DDE Execute. This is redundant
                                'but needed for debug windows.
      Next

      F.Label1.LinkTimeout = 100

      '------------------------------------------------
      ' Create Program Item, one of the icons to launch
      ' an application from Program Manager
      '------------------------------------------------
      F.Label1.LinkExecute "[AddItem(" + ExePath + Chr$(44) +
    ➥ItemCap + Chr$(44) + ",,)]"
```

continues

Listing 13.3. continued

```
    '----------------
    ' Reset properties
    '----------------
    F.Label1.LinkTimeout = 50
    F.Label1.LinkMode = vbLinkNone        '0

    Screen.MousePointer = 0

End Sub


Private Sub cmdShowPM_Click()
    lstPMFolders.Clear
    GetFolders
End Sub

Public Sub GetFolders()
    '----------------------------------------------------------
    'Load program folder names from ProgMan
    '----------------------------------------------------------
    GetLinkData "PROGMAN"

    Dim count As Integer, Temp As String, CRLF As String

    CRLF = Chr$(13) + Chr$(10)
    Temp = Label1
    count = InStr(Temp, CRLF)
    '----------------------------------------------------------
    ' Add each name to sorter list box
    '----------------------------------------------------------
    Do While count
        lstPMFolders.AddItem Left$(Temp, count - 1)
        Temp = Mid$(Temp, count + 2)
        count = InStr(Temp, CRLF)
    Loop

End Sub

Public Sub GetLinkData(Item As String)
    '----------------------------------------------------------
    'Establish DDE link with ProgMan
    'Request Item
    '----------------------------------------------------------
    Label1.LinkTopic = "ProgMan¦Progman"
    Label1.LinkItem = Item$
    Label1.LinkMode = vbLinkManual       '2
    Label1.LinkRequest
    On Error Resume Next
    Label1.LinkMode = vbLinkNone         '0
    On Error GoTo 0
End Sub
```

The PM application can be used to add executable items to the StartUp submenu found under the Programs menu item. To do that, type `StartUp` in the text box that creates a new program folder; then press the New PM Folder command button. The code automatically locates the StartUp folder and opens it in Program Manager. The next step is to add an executable item to that folder, using the Add Program Item text box to the right of the PM form. Then enter a name for that new item and press the New Program Item command button. The new item appears simultaneously in the Program Manager StartUp folder and the StartUp folder located as a subfolder under the Program menu item. This technique could be used in your setup routine if you had an application that you always wanted to load when Windows 95 started up.

The following section offers a brief discussion about handling DDE errors.

Handling DDE Errors

Errors can occur sometimes when a Visual Basic application is performing DDE. The types of errors that can occur can be divided into two groups: errors that occur in statements, functions, or expressions within executing code, and errors that happen when no code is being executed.

The first type of error is no different from any other run-time error and can be handled with standard error-handling statements and functions.

The second error group might seem rather unusual. How can an error occur if there isn't any code executing? It seems rather illogical. But, you must remember that Visual Basic is always performing a variety of tasks, even when a program's code is not executing. For example, Visual Basic updates automatic links whenever data changes. This can cause many errors to occur: The data might be in the wrong format, or it may be so large that copying it causes the operating environment to run out of memory. This can be handled by generating a `LinkError` event. You could write an event procedure to handle this event like any other. Some DDE errors are listed in the Table 13.12. You can make use of these errors in the same way you did in Chapter 12, "Error-Handling and Debugging."

Table 13.12. **Some Visual Basic DDE errors.**

Error	Description
280	DDE channel not fully closed; awaiting response from foreign application.
281	No more DDE channels.
282	No foreign application responded to a DDE initiate.
283	Multiple applications responded to a DDE initiate.
284	DDE channel locked.
285	Foreign application won't perform DDE method or operation.

continues

Table 13.12. continued

Error	Description
286	Time-out while waiting for DDE response.
287	User pressed Esc key during DDE operation.
288	Destination is busy.
289	Data not provided in DDE operation.
290	Data in wrong format.
291	Foreign application quit.
292	DDE conversation closed or changed.
293	DDE method invoked with no channel open.
294	Invalid DDE Link format.
295	Message queue filled; DDE message lost.
296	PasteLink already performed on this control.
297	Can't set LinkMode; invalid Link Topic.
298	DDE requires Ddeml.dll.
320	Can't use character device names in filenames: 'item'.
321	Invalid file format.

If a Visual Basic application is engaged as a destination in a DDE conversation and an error occurs when no Visual Basic code is executing, the LinkError event occurs. Because the destination in a DDE conversation is always a control in a Visual Basic application, the LinkError event would be a control event.

On the other hand, if a Visual Basic application were acting as the source in a DDE conversation and an error occurred when no Visual Basic code was executing, the LinkError would occur as a form event.

In both cases, the errors would be handled the same—with some error-trapping code placed in the appropriate controls' LinkError event. For a destination application, this might be a text box named txtEmployee—hence the event would be txtEmployee_LinkError(). For a source application, this might be frmPayroll_LinkError(). Some possible error-handling code could appear as follows:

```
Private Sub frmPayroll_LinkError(ErrorNumber As Integer)
    Dim Msg
    Const conOutOfMemory = 11

    Select Case ErrorNumber
        Case conOutOfMemory
            Msg = "Not enough memory to perform DDE."

        Case vbDataTransferFailed
            Msg = "Destination tried unsuccessfully to poke data."
```

```
        Case vbDDESourceClosed
            'Source form LinkMode property set to None.
            Msg = "Destination trying unsuccessfully to connect."

        Case Else
            Msg = "Unexpected DDE Error: " & ErrorNumber
    End Select

    If ErrorNumber <> vbWrongFormat Then
        'Ignore WrongFormat errors because several may be generated
        'until the source and destination agree on a common format.
        MsgBox Msg, MB_IconExclamation, App.EXEName & " DDE Failure."
    End If

End Sub
```

Although a Visual Basic application appears to be completely separate from all other applications that are running, remember that they are all running on the same computer. To run simultaneously, the applications must share the computer's resources. When a Visual Basic application is waiting for an event to occur, it automatically shares the computer's resources with other running applications. A Visual Basic application also yields to other applications whenever it performs a DDE operation.

Most applications can respond at that time, but some might be unable to complete their side of the DDE conversation. This would cause a time-out error. To avoid this, you can add the DoEvents function to your error-handling code.

DoEvents passes control to the operating system, and control is not returned until the operating system has finished processing the events in its queue. You should note that some applications have more work to do to keep up their end of a DDE conversation, and one call to DoEvents will not be enough. So, if you get a bunch of run-time errors indicating that the other applications are busy or not handling DDE properly, try placing a call—or several calls—to DoEvents in your error-handling code.

Summary

In this chapter you saw that DDE can be used as a mechanism for extracting data from other applications, sending data to other applications, and even sending commands or keystrokes to other applications. Although DDE is a useful technique for this kind of simple communication between applications, in many situations you might be better off using Object Linking and Embedding (OLE).

OLE, the subject of the next chapter, is a technology that is fully supported in Windows 95. The future of DDE support is unclear. As you saw in this chapter, Word for Windows 6.x no longer supports pasting of automatic DDE links (WinWord 2 supported this). To Paste Link from Word 6.x in a Visual Basic application at design-time, you must now use the OLE object control. Where goes WinWord, so go other applications.

What exactly *is* DDE good for? As this chapter has shown, DDE provides quick, simple links to other applications for the sole purpose of exchanging data. One application that comes with Windows 95 that uses DDE is the card game Hearts. The Hearts application uses DDE links to connect up to four computer stations (if four human players are not present, the computer takes over the extra hands) to one another across a network. Another apt use for DDE is retrieving financial information such as stock quotes. There are several applications available in the software marketplace that do just this. These programs use DDE to link to and query an online service for specified stock quotes. Then, when the information has been retrieved, the applications use DDE to poke these current stock quotes to a companion accounting program. These links are fast, dependable, and efficient.

As opposed to DDE, OLE is an industry standard intended to be used by applications to provide objects in a consistent way so that other applications can communicate with them and use the tools they provide.

You will soon see the tremendous power and flexibility of the OLE technology. Using the OLE container control you can embed any object that supports OLE automation—for example, an Excel spreadsheet or a WinWord document—in your Visual Basic applications. Using OLE automation, you can also borrow the functionality, such as macro language commands and formatting tools, of another application.

It's time to move on and explore the wonderful power of OLE!

New Events	Description
LinkClose	Occurs when a DDE conversation terminates. Either application in a DDE conversation may terminate a conversation at any time.
LinkError	Occurs when there is an error during a DDE conversation. This event is recognized only as the result of a DDE-related error that occurs when no Visual Basic code is being executed. The error number is passed as an argument.
LinkExecute	Occurs when a command string is sent by a destination application in a DDE conversation. The destination application expects the source application to perform the operation described by the string.
LinkNotify	Occurs when the source has changed the data defined by the DDE link if the LinkMode property of the destination control is set to 3-Notify.
LinkOpen	Occurs when a DDE conversation is being initiated.
New Properties	Description
LinkItem	Returns or sets the data passed to a destination control in a DDE conversation with another application.
LinkMode	Returns or sets the type of link used for a DDE conversation and activates the connection. Enables a *destination control* on a Visual Basic form to initiate a conversation, as specified by the control's LinkTopic and LinkItem properties. Enables a destination application to initiate a conversation with a Visual Basic source form, as specified by the destina-

tion application's `application¦topic!item` expression.

New Properties	Description
LinkTimeout	Returns or sets the amount of time a control waits for a response to a DDE message.
LinkTopic	For a destination control, it returns or sets the source application and the topic (the fundamental data grouping used in that application). Use LinkTopic with the LinkItem property to specify the complete data link.

New Statements	Description
AppActivate	Activates an application window.
SendKeys	Sends one or more keystrokes to the active window as if typed at the keyboard.

New Methods	Description
LinkExecute	Sends a command string to the source application in a DDE conversation.
LinkPoke	Transfers the contents of a label, picture box, or text box control to the source application in a DDE conversation.
LinkRequest	Asks the source application in a DDE conversation to update the contents of a label, picture box, or text box control.
LinkSend	Transfers the contents of a picture box control to the destination application in a DDE conversation.

New Function	Description
DoEvents	Yields execution so that the operating system can process other events.

14

Connecting to Other Windows Applications: OLE 2

Object Linking and Embedding (OLE) is a technique that enables applications to work together when handling and displaying data. As the name implies, OLE either links or embeds an object in another application in order to share data. The OLE tools available with Visual Basic 4 make it easy to link or embed data from other Windows programs into your own Visual Basic applications. OLE, now in version 2, is similar to DDE in some ways—in fact, DDE was used as the base mechanism for OLE 1.0—but it is different in many others. The topics covered in this chapter include:

- What is Object Linking and Embedding (OLE)?
- A comparison of OLE 1.0 and OLE 2.0
- The Windows 95 Registry
- Methods and properties associated with OLE
- The OLE Container Control
- OLE Automation: operating objects from other applications
- The invisible OLE interface
- An introduction to custom class modules
- Creating custom properties and methods
- Building an OLE Server
- Registering an OLE Server in the Windows 95 Registry

Suppose that you would like to write an application that includes several graphs, charts, spreadsheets, some nifty, eye-catching type, and even a media clip that includes sound and video. And then, when the application was running, wouldn't it be great if the user could simply double-click any one of these objects and modify it to suit her needs—changing a chart's data, updating a spreadsheet? That is exactly what OLE can do for your applications.

It sounds difficult, doesn't it? It really isn't. This chapter presents the fundamental concepts and terms used with OLE, including some hot Visual Basic 4 updates, and then moves on to create a quick sample application with a linked object created at design time. After that, you will learn about embedded objects, along with how to build linked and embedded objects at run-time. Finally, you will discover how to create your own OLE Server using a class module, set your own custom properties and methods, and connect it all to your own controlling application. With that in mind, it's time to get going.

What is Object Linking and Embedding (OLE)?

OLE is a method that enables different applications to work together and share data. A Visual Basic *OLE Container Control* is used to contain this data from another application by either linking or embedding the data into a Visual Basic program.

OLE Client Control is Now Called OLE Container Control

In previous versions of Visual Basic, the object that contains the linked or embedded data was called an *OLE Client Control*. With Visual Basic 4 this name has been changed to *OLE Container Control*.

You might find it interesting to pull the name "Object Linking and Embedding" apart. The term *object* means nothing more than a discrete unit of data supplied by another program. An application can *expose*—make available—many types of objects. For example, a spreadsheet program could expose a worksheet, macro sheet, chart, cell, or range of cells. Each one of these would be considered a different type of object.

Every OLE object has a *class*. The application that provides the object's data and the type of data the object contains determines the object's class. An object is derived from its class. The distinction between class and object is important. Think of it in terms of the relationship of shirts and a shirt pattern. The shirt pattern is a class. It defines the shape and size of shirts. The shirts are objects. In other words, a class is a format of how the data will appear. An object is data that adheres to the class' format.

There are two ways to share data with OLE, by *linking* or by *embedding*. These are two distinct methods of sharing data. You cannot link and embed an object at the same time; it is either linked or embedded. The difference between these two is the place where the data is stored and whether other applications have access to it.

New Terminology: Controlling Applications and Object Applications

In Visual Basic 3, a program that provided access to an object was called either a Source Application or a Server. With the advent of Visual Basic 4, this name has been changed to *Object Application*.

Also, an application used to contain OLE objects was formerly called a *Destination Application* or a *Client*. With Visual Basic 4 this name has been changed to *Controlling Application*.

When an object is linked, a placeholder for the linked object is inserted in the application, not the actual data itself. For instance, when a range of spreadsheet cells is linked to a Visual Basic application the data associated with the cells is stored in another file. Only a link to the data and an image of the data are stored in the OLE container control. The user of an application with a linked object can activate the object by double-clicking on it, for example, and the application will automatically start. The data in the application can then be edited, but this editing is performed in a separate window outside the OLE container control.

The data from an object that is linked to a Visual Basic application can be accessed from any other application that contains links to that data, and that data can be changed from within any of them. The data exists in only one place, however: in the *object application*. The object application is the source program that provides the object.

Registering an Application's Object Library in the Windows 95 Registry

The object that you want to place in an OLE container control must be in your computer's system registry. When you install an application that supplies the objects you want to use in a project, that application should register its object library on your system. That way, the objects will appear in the Insert Object dialog box that appears when an OLE container control is added to a form. (This dialog box is also available through the OLE container control's pop-up menu.) The Windows 95 Registry, how to register objects, and the OLE container control's pop-up menu will be discussed shortly. (Registering your own OLE Servers will be discussed later in the chapter.)

When an OLE container control is used to create an embedded object, every bit of data associated with the object is copied into the control and held there. If the OLE container control is saved, the saved file contains the name of the application that supplied the object, the object's data, and a metafile image of the object. Because of this, embedded objects greatly increase file size.

Note: If you need to use embedded objects but don't want the overhead of a metafile or rendered image of the data, select the display as icon option. This only works, however, if you do not need to see the embedded object before you start to edit it.

Using Insertable Objects Instead of the OLE Container Control to Embed Data

Instead of using the OLE container control, you can embed data from another application by using registered OLE Servers on your computer. By selecting the insertable objects checkbox in the Custom Controls dialog box, you will see a list of the applications on your system that support OLE and what document types they support. An example of what you might see if you have Windows 95 and Office installed appears here:

- Media Clip
- Microsoft Equation 2.0
- Microsoft Excel 5.0 Chart

- Microsoft Excel 5.0 Worksheet
- Microsoft Excel Macrosheet
- Microsoft Graph 5.0
- Microsoft Word 6.0 Document
- Microsoft Word 6.0 Picture
- Microsoft WordArt 2.0
- MS PowerPoint 4.0 Presentation
- MS PowerPoint 4.0 Slide
- Package
- Paintbrush Picture
- Video Clip
- Wave Sound
- WordPad Document

To use one of these objects, add it to the Visual Basic Toolbox by selecting it in the Custom Control dialog box found under the Tools menu. You must make sure that the checkbox Insertable Objects is checked. For instance, suppose that you added a Microsoft Graph button to the Toolbox. This control would give you the functionality of the Graph application without having to write the code to create that graph. You will read about several of these tools later in Chapter 18, "Using Custom Controls," and in Chapter 20, "Multimedia."

Unlike linked objects, no other application has access to the data in an embedded object. The only way to get to an embedded object is through the controlling application. Linked objects exist only as files on disk. Therefore, they can only be accessed by an application using the OLE Server that controls the embedded object. This means that you can use an embedded OLE object when you want only your application to maintain data produced and edited by another application.

There are three ways to create an OLE object in Visual Basic.

1. Add the object to the Toolbox using the Custom Controls command on the Tools menu, and then draw the object directly on a form. This method embeds the object within the form interface in your application.

2. Use the CreateObject or GetObject functions to create the object in code. This technique creates the object in a running instance of the application that provides the object. (More about these functions in the section titled "Creating Embedded Objects at Design Time.")

3. Embed or link the object within an OLE container control. This technique enables you to change objects on the form at run-time, create linked objects, and bind the OLE container control to a Data control.

A Brief Comparison of OLE 1.0 and OLE 2.0

The original version of OLE, version 1.0, introduced the important concept of linking or embedding an object into an application. When OLE 1.0 arrived on the scene, it appeared to be a souped-up version of DDE. The technology at that point was thought of as merely a way to create applications that supported what was called "Compound Documents." With OLE 1.0, the user activated an embedded object and the object application opened in its own window. To the user it appeared that the embedded object temporarily lifted itself from its place on the controlling application.

With the arrival of OLE 2.0 in Visual Basic 3, many things changed. The embedded object remained in its container control. When a user clicked an OLE 2.0 object (suppose it was a spreadsheet), OLE would replace the controlling application's menu with that of the object's application, letting the user manipulate the embedded object as if she were running the application directly.

And now the OLE 2 tools available in Visual Basic 4 have been improved radically with the addition of Class Modules, OLE Automation, and if you have the Professional or Enterprise Editions, the ability to create OLE Servers.

Class modules enable the programmer to create any kind of OLE object. A class module is essentially the "blueprint" for objects created for an object application. And programmers can create custom properties or methods for objects made with class modules.

This new module type ties in with *OLE Automation*. OLE Automation is used by applications to expose their OLE objects to development tools, macro languages, and other applications that support OLE Automation. OLE Automation defines how code is shared between applications and how an application can be controlled from other applications. Many applications out in the marketplace today have taken advantage of OLE Automation to use code from other applications. For instance, you could create an OLE *Automation object* named MyObject, using a class module. (An Automation object is an object that is exposed to other applications.) Then, you could write code to manipulate your Automation object from another application.

What OLE Automation and OLE Servers Can (and Cannot) do in Visual Basic 4

OLE Automation is implemented independently from the rest of OLE. With Visual Basic 4, you can create object applications in the form of .exe files that supply *object libraries*. You cannot create an object application as a dynamic-link library (.dll) with Visual Basic 4.

Also, OLE Servers cannot function as insertable controls. They cannot provide objects that can be linked or embedded into the documents of other applications In other words, at this time Visual Basic 4 is not capable of creating an OLE custom control (.ocx). This is still best done using C++ and is discussed in Chapter 19.

An extension of OLE Automation and class module flexibility is the new Visual Basic capability to create OLE Servers. An application that exposes objects to other applications is called an OLE Server or an OLE Automation Server. In other words, your custom OLE Server is, itself, an object application. And you, the programmer, can decide which options you choose to implement—the objects (classes) can be used only by the application in which they are defined, or they can be exposed for use by other applications.

Therefore, at this point there are two OLE sisters, if you will, that represent the OLE technology available in Visual Basic 4. One sister is familiar; she's been with Visual Basic for quite a while. This OLE lady uses OLE container controls to link or embed data in applications. The other OLE sister, the little sister, is much more mysterious and new to Visual Basic, in fact. She works independently from her older OLE sibling, using OLE Automation, making custom OLE objects, and creating OLE Servers. (And like any child, this younger sister will grow and change with future versions of Visual Basic.) To start off, take a look at the familiar older sister. It's time to explore linking and embedding using OLE container controls.

OLE Sample Programs Supplied with Visual Basic 4

Included with Visual Basic 4 are several OLE-based applications. They are located in the Samples directory under OleAuto, OleCont, and OleServ. Run them, see how they work, and look at the code. As the saying goes, pictures—or a code listing—can be worth a thousand words.

The OLE Container Control

The OLE container control is used to hold data from other applications by linking or embedding that data into your Visual Basic applications. As discussed earlier, the primary difference between a linked and embedded object is where the object's data is stored. Data associated with a linked object is managed by the application that created it and is stored outside the OLE container control. Data associated with an embedded object is held in the OLE container control and can be saved with the Visual Basic application.

Before an Object Can Be Placed in an OLE Container Control, the Object Must Be in the Windows 95 Registry

When an application that supplies OLE objects is installed on your system, that application should register its object library with your system registry. That way, the application's objects will appear in the Insert Object dialog box. You can use RegEdit.exe to search the system registry for an object, but if you do open it, be very careful when you change the registry's contents. Make a backup of the current registry first.

To make a backup of the registry, run RegEdit.exe. Select the Export Registry File item from the Registry menu. An Export Registry File dialog box will open on the screen. In the Export Range area, select the All option button to back up the entire registry, or select the Selected Branch option button to back up a particular branch of the registry tree. Type in a filename (this backup will have a .reg file suffix). Press Save.

To restore the Registry from a backup, run RegEdit.exe and select Import Registry File from the Registry menu. Find the .reg file, and then click Open.

The Windows 95 Registry will be discussed in the section on the Windows 95 Registry later in this chapter.

The OLE container control lets you add objects from other applications to your Visual Basic programs. A container control can hold only one object at a time. There are several ways to make a linked or embedded object in the OLE container control. The method you use will depend on whether you want to create a linked or embedded object at design-time or run-time.

Creating Linked Objects at Design-Time

Start a new Visual Basic project and find the OLE container tool in Visual Basic's Toolbox. Select it and draw an OLE container control on the default form in the design window. When you do, an Insert Object dialog box will appear on the screen, as in Figure 14.1, that presents a list of objects available for linking or embedding in the application.

Figure 14.1.
The Insert Object dialog box, showing a list of objects available for OLE linking or embedding.

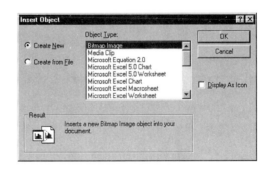

At this point you can either pick an object to insert or choose the Cancel button. Press Cancel in the dialog box. This closes the Insert Object dialog box, leaving an empty OLE container control on the form.

When a linked or embedded object is created, it contains the name of the application that supplied the object, its data (or in the case of a linked object, a reference to the data), and an image of the data. There are three properties that correspond to the name, reference, and image. They are Class, SourceDoc, and SourceItem. These properties are set automatically when you insert an object into an OLE container control at design-time. (Class, SourceDoc, and SourceItem are fully discussed in the following section of this chapter.)

An object that supports OLE can be dragged into an OLE container control at design-time. Try that right now. Click on the empty OLE container control in the open Visual Basic project. Change its SizeMode property to 1-Stretch. Now, open a folder that contains a Word document. Click on the folder and drag the document's icon onto the empty OLE container control in the open Visual Basic project. When the document icon passes into the container control area, it changes from the familiar, blue-aqua W to a small dashed rectangle under the pointer arrow. Release the left mouse button, and drop the icon onto the control. It takes a few seconds for the object to establish itself, but when it does, you're looking at your Word document as in Figure 14.2.

Figure 14.2.
A Word for Windows
document dragged onto an
OLE container control.

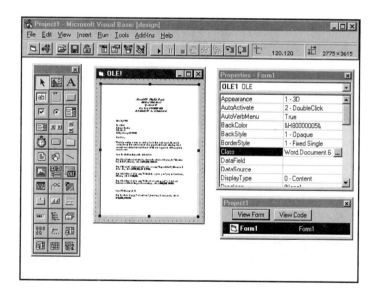

Scroll up the OLE container control's Properties list until you find the Class property. Notice that this property has automatically been set to Word.Document.6. Now scroll down to the OLETypeAllowed property. The default setting for this property is 2-Either. This is where you would set whether the Word document is 0-Linked or 1-Embedded.

Select the OLE container control on the form and delete it. Now add a new OLE container control to the form. Again, the Insert Object dialog box appears on the screen. This time you are going to create a linked object using the Insert Object dialog box. Select the Create from File radio button. Select the Link check box, as shown in Figure 14.3. Then press the Browse button. A Browse dialog box opens. Choose an object that you would like to link to this OLE container control. (The same document that was dragged onto the previous container control will be used here.) After you have selected the object—spreadsheet, word processing document, chart, graph, and so on—press the Insert button to return to the Insert Object dialog box.

Figure 14.3.
The Insert Object dialog box with a file selected to be linked to an OLE container control.

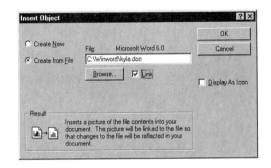

Notice that at the bottom of the dialog box the Result frame displays a description of what will happen if you press OK. You're all set. Press OK. The dialog box closes and the linked object appears on the form in the container control as in Figure 14.4.

Figure 14.4.
A Word for Windows document linked to an OLE container control.

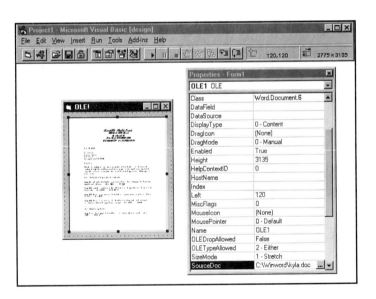

If you look at the OLE container control's Properties window you will notice that the Class property has automatically been set to Word.Document.6, and the SourceDoc property has been set to the path of the linked document.

When you use a linked object in an application, every user who runs your program must have access (a valid pathname) to the linked file and a copy of the application that created the file. If not, when your application is run an image of the original data will be displayed, but the user will not be able to modify the data. And the user will not see changes that might have been made to the linked data.

If you do use a linked object in an application, be aware that it is possible for that object's data to be changed by another application when your application is not running. If this happens, the next time your application is run the most current data will not appear automatically in the OLE container control. To display the updated data, use the Update method. The Update method will retrieve the current data from the application that supplied the object and update the graphic data display in the OLE container control. Its syntax works like any other method.

`object.Update`

Also, if the user wants to save any changes to linked data, she must use the Save command from the object application's File menu.

Next is a brief discussion of a new Visual Basic feature: the pop-up menu associated with the OLE container control. After that, it is time to embed an object (how about a video clip with sound.)

Suppose that you put an OLE container control on a form and choose not to link or embed an object when the Insert Object dialog box appears on the screen. Or suppose that after you have embedded or linked an object you decide that the data in the container is wrong; you want to use a different object. You've got an OLE container control on the form, but how do you get to that Input Object dialog box? Use the new OLE container control pop-up menu.

Click on the sample OLE container control that is holding the Word document to select it. With your mouse pointer anywhere over the control, click the right mouse button. The OLE container control's pop-up menu appears as shown in Figure 14.5.

Figure 14.5.
The pop-up menu associated with the OLE container control.

The pop-up menu contains some interesting items.

- Cut, Copy, and Paste are old friends; these items affect the control itself. They will either cut or copy the OLE container control, and then paste the original or a copy onto the form. (If you paste a copy on the form, Visual Basic will automatically ask whether you want to create an array.)

- The Delete command completely removes the control from the form, View Code will open the Code Window, displaying the OLE container control's code, and Align to Grid will snap the control to the nearest grid points.

- Insert Object will delete the existing object and then open the Insert Object dialog box, enabling you to create a new object in its place.

- The Paste Special command is used to paste an object from the Clipboard into the OLE container control. This command is enabled only if there is data pasted into the Clipboard; for instance, a range of cells from Excel.

- The next four commands toggle on the menu depending upon the state of the control's object. Delete Embedded Object or Delete Linked Object are used to delete an existing object. The control itself will remain on the form. Create Link will appear only if the SourceDoc property is set. Create Embedded Object will appear only if either the Class or SourceDoc properties are set.

- Edit actually enables you to edit the data contained in the control. Depending upon whether the data is linked or embedded, an instance of the application where the data was created will appear either in its own window or in the OLE container control.

- And, finally, the Open command will open the application where the data was created, regardless of whether the object is linked or embedded, enabling you to edit the data in the native application.

The last two items are determined by the application that created the object. For example, if a word processing application was the originator, then the menu would display Edit and Open. If a multimedia application created a .wav file, the menu would display Play and Edit.

Now on to embedding an object at design-time in the sample OLE container control. Then, after a discussion about creating linked or embedded objects at run-time, the chapter will move to an interesting program. This application will use OLE Automation and class modules to create a custom OLE object and expose custom properties and methods to other applications, and then move to creating an OLE Server.

Creating Embedded Objects at Design-Time

When you create an embedded object you can either embed existing data from a file or create a new, empty OLE container control that can be filled with data later. Usually, embedded objects that display existing data are created at design-time. That way, you can effectively create your program's user interface by moving and correctly sizing the OLE container control and other controls on the form.

Unlike the data in a linked object, the data in an embedded object is not automatically saved. Thus, if you want changes made by the user to appear the next time your application is run, you must use the `SaveToFile` method to save the data. `SaveToFile` works like this:

`object.SaveToFile filenumber`

The `SaveToFile` method syntax has the following parts:

- `object`—an object expression.
- `filenumber`—a required numeric expression specifying the file number used when saving an object. This number must correspond to an open, binary file.

This method is used to save OLE objects. If the object is linked (`OLEType = 0`) then only the link information and an image of the data is saved to the specified file. The object's data is still maintained by the application that created the object. If the object is embedded (`OLEType = 1`) then the object's data is maintained by the OLE container control and can be saved by your Visual Basic application.

To load an object saved to a data file use the `ReadFromFile` method. `ReadFromFile` works like any other method, like this:

`object.ReadFromFile filenumber`

The `ReadFromFile` method syntax has the following parts:

- `object`—An object expression.
- `filenumber`—A required numeric expression specifying the file number used when loading an object. This number must correspond to an open, binary file.

Now, move back to the OLE container control that is holding the linked Word for Windows document. It's time to embed an interesting video clip into the control. Click on the OLE container control to select it, and then set its `OLETypeAllowed` property to `1-Embedded`. Next, position the mouse pointer anywhere over the container control and click the right mouse button. Select the Insert Object command from the pop-up menu. Click the Create from File option button and then click the Browse button. Now select the file to embed. In this case, use a sample media clip file that comes with Windows 95. Move to the Windows directory, find the Media folder, and double-click it. Select the Skiing.avi file and press Insert. Finally, choose OK to create the embedded object. Your display should then look similar to the one in Figure 14.6.

Figure 14.6.
The Skiing.avi file embedded in an OLE container control.

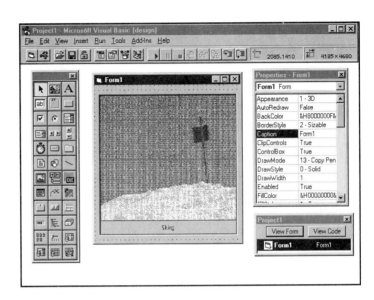

A snowy scene fills the OLE container control and a panel at the bottom of the scene contains the caption Skiing. To play the video clip (if you have a sound card and speakers, turn the speakers on—this file also includes an accompanying sound byte) by using the pop-up menu again. Activate the pop-up menu and select the Play command. The captioned panel at the bottom of the OLE container control changes to a mini control panel, containing Play and Stop buttons (the Play button toggles to Pause after the clip starts) and a slider indicating the video sequence position as in Figure 14.7.

Figure 14.7.
The Skiing.avi file playing.

You can also play the clip when this test application is running. To do so, just run the sample project and either use the pop-up button to access the Play command or double-click the OLE container control.

Creating Linked or Embedded Objects at Run-Time

Methods and properties are used in code to create linked or embedded objects at run-time. Table 14.1 contains OLE container control properties, and Table 14.2 contains OLE container control methods. To see a complete list, use Visual Basic's On-Line Help.

Table 14.1. OLE container control properties.

Property	Description
AutoActivate	Returns or sets a value that enables the user to activate an object by double-clicking the OLE container control or by moving the focus to the OLE container control.
Class	Identifies the type of object held by the OLE container control.
DataField	Specifies the field name that is used to retrieve the value of a control.
DataSource	Specifies the record set that is used to bind data to the OLE container control.
DisplayType	Specifies whether the object should be displayed with content of the object or just as the icon of the OLE Server.
Object	A run-time, read-only property indicating the active class. To use this property, the OLE container control must contain an object that is programmable.
OLEType	Returns the status of the object in an OLE container control. This property is not available at design-time; it is read-only at run-time.
OLETypeAllowed	Determines the type of object you can create: 0 = Linked, 1 = Embedded, or 2 = Either.
OLEDropAllowed	If this property is set to True, a user can drag and drop an insertable object's icon into the OLE container control at run-time. This has the same effect as copying an object onto the Clipboard and the application calling the Paste method on the OLE container control.
SizeMode	Determines how an object's icon or data image is displayed in the OLE container control. The settings are as follows:
	0 (Clip)—The object is displayed in its actual size. If the object is larger than the OLE container control its image is clipped by the control's borders.

continues

Table 14.1. continued

Property	Description
	1 (Stretch)—The object's image is sized to fill the OLE container control. The image may not maintain the original proportions of the object.
	2 (Autosize)—The OLE container control is resized to display the entire object. This is the default.
	3 (Zoom)—The object is resized to fill the OLE container control as much as possible while still maintaining the original proportions of the object.
SourceDoc	When you create a linked object, this property determines which source file to link. When you create an embedded object, this property determines the file to use as a template.
SourceItem	This property is for linked objects only. It specifies the data to link within a file.

Table 14.2. OLE container control methods.

Method	Description
CreateEmbed	Creates an embedded object.
CreateLink	Creates a linked object.
DoVerb	Opens an object for an operation, such as editing. Its syntax is as follows:
	object.DoVerb (*verb*)
	The DoVerb method syntax has these parts:
	• *object*—An object expression.
	• *verb*—An optional argument. The verb of the object to execute. If the verb is not specified, the default verb is executed. The value of this argument can be one of the standard verbs supported by all objects or an index of the ObjectVerbs property array.
InsertObjDlg	Displays the Insert Object dialog box, enabling the user to select the object that will be inserted into the OLE container control at run-time.
PasteSpecialDlg	Displays the Paste Special dialog box, enabling the user to copy the contents of the Clipboard into the OLE container control at run-time.

The OLE Container Control's New Methods: The `Action` Property is Now Passé

In previous Visual Basic versions, the OLE container control's `Action` property was used to create objects at run-time. The `Action` property is included in Visual Basic 4 for backward compatibility. It is best to use the new methods `CreateEmbed`, `CreateLink`, `DoVerb`, `InsertObjDlg`, and `PasteSpecialDlg` instead.

Along with the properties listed in Table 14.1 are a completely new set of OLE container control constants for several properties. They are explained in Table 14.3.

Table 14.3. Visual Basic constants that correspond to certain OLE container control properties.

Constant	Value	Description
PROPERTY: `AutoActivate`		
`vbOLEActivateManual`	0	OLE object isn't automatically activated.
`vbOLEActiveGetFocus`	1	Object is activated when the OLE container control gets the focus.
`vbOLEActivateDoubleclick`	2	Object is activated when the OLE container control is double-clicked.
`vbOLEActivateAuto`	3	Object is activated based on the object's default method of activation.
PROPERTY: `DisplayType`		
`vbOLEDisplayContent`	0	Object's data is displayed in the OLE container control.
`vbOLEDisplayIcon`	1	Object's icon is displayed in the OLE container control.
PROPERTY: `OLETypeAllowed`		
`vbOLEEither`	2	OLE container control can contain either a linked or an embedded object.
PROPERTY: `OLEType`		
`vbOLELinked`	0	OLE container control contains a linked object.
`vbOLEEmbedded`	1	OLE container control contains an embedded object.

continues

Table 14.3. continued

Constant	Value	Description
vbOLENone	3	OLE container control does not contain an object.
PROPERTY: SizeMode		
vbOLESizeClip	0	Object's image is clipped by the OLE container control's borders.
vbOLESizeStretch	1	Object's image is sized to fill the OLE container control.
vbOLESizeAutoSize	2	OLE container control is automatically resized to display the entire object.
vbOLESizeZoom	3	Object's image is stretched but in proportion.
PROPERTY: UpdateOptions		
vbOLEAutomatic	0	Object is updated each time the linked data changes.
vbOLEFrozen	1	Object is updated whenever the user saves the linked document from within the application in which it was created.
vbOLEManual	2	Object is updated only when Action property is set to 6 (update).

To see an entire list of OLE container control constants use either the Visual Basic Object Browser or On-Line Help.

Now it's time to use some of these properties, methods, and constants. You will write a mini demonstration program that will create either linked or embedded objects at run-time and display the object's class and source document (if there is one).

Start a new Visual Basic project. Change the default form's Name and Caption properties to frmOLETest and Run-Time OLE, respectively. Then use the Save Project item on the File menu to save the form as RunTime OLE.frm and the project as RunTime OLE.vbp. Add an OLE container control to the form. When the Insert Object dialog box appears on the screen, select Cancel. That way, the container will be empty.

Using Figure 14.8 and the following table as a guide, draw the necessary controls on the form and set their properties as shown in the table. (The OLE container control is set to a specific size because it will be used in code later; set the measurements for the control then resize your form accordingly.)

Object	Property	Setting
Form	Caption	Run-Time OLE
	Name	frmOLETest
OLE Container Control	Height	2412
	Left	120
	Name	oleTest
	SizeMode	3-Zoom
	Top	120
	Width	5652
Command Button	Caption	Insert OLE Data
	Default	True
	Name	cmdInsert
Command Button	Caption	Display Object Specs
	Enabled	False
	Name	cmdSpecs
Command Button	Caption	Close
	Name	cmdClose

Figure 14.8.
The completed frmOLETest *form.*

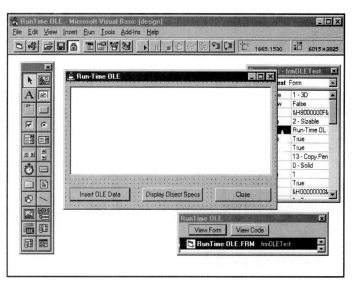

When you are satisfied with the form's design, lock the controls. That way, they won't be inadvertently moved.

This mini-application is very straightforward. When the user presses the Insert OLE Data command button, a simple Data form will appear on the screen. This form will be used to enter the data type desired (linked or embedded) and dictate the data's appearance (as an icon or graphically displayed). After the user makes her selections and presses OK, the Insert Object dialog box will open and she can use it to add the data to the OLE container control. As soon as the OLE container control is holding data, the Display Object Specs command button will be enabled. When pressed, this command button will bring up a message box that displays the data's class and its source document (if there is one). From there, the user can insert other objects and generally have a good time fooling around with the program.

First, set the code that will close the form and end the application when the user presses the Close button.

```
Private Sub cmdClose_Click()
    Unload cmdClose.Parent
End Sub

Private Sub Form_Unload(Cancel As Integer)
    End
End Sub
```

The program is first activated when the user presses the Insert OLE Data button. Double-click that button to open the Code Window and the button's code skeleton.

```
Private Sub cmdInsert_Click()

End Sub
```

This button calls a form named frmType that enables the user to select the type of data to be inserted into the OLE container control. (You will create this form in just a minute.) Add the code to call that form.

```
Private Sub cmdInsert_Click()
    frmType.Show
End Sub
```

Now, add the code that will bring up a message box when cmdSpecs is pressed. The message box will display the data's Class property and SourceDoc property, if it has one. (An embedded object that is created using an OLE compatible application, such as Excel or Word, will not have a SourceDoc property because the embedded object is based on an application, not a document.) Also, the message contained in the message box would get very long and difficult to read if it is placed in one line. You can use a hacker's trick to split up the lines. Declare Msg as a string and then create the long message by adding each subsequent line using a plus sign, (+). That code looks like this:

```
Private Sub cmdSpecs_Click()
    Dim Crlf, Msg As String
    'Crlf = carriage return plus line feed
    Crlf = Chr(10) + Chr(13)

    'a hacker trick: stacking message!
    'makes a long message easier to read
```

```
    Msg = "The Class of this object is: "
    Msg = Msg + oleTest.Class + Crlf

    'If the embedded or linked data is not from a file
    'then the SourceDoc property will be empty
    If oleTest.SourceDoc <> "" Then
        Msg = Msg + "The SourceDoc is: "
        Msg = Msg + oleTest.SourceDoc + Crlf
    End If

    MsgBox Msg, 64, "OLE Object Properties"
End Sub
```

The last thing left to do with this form is to make sure it's centered when it opens and also be certain that the OLE container control's `SizeMode` property is initially set to Zoom. Add that code like this:

```
Private Sub Form_Initialize()
    oleTest.SizeMode = vbOLESizeZoom
End Sub

Private Sub Form_Load()
    Me.Top = (Screen.Height - Me.Height) / 2
    Me.Left = (Screen.Width - Me.Width) / 2
End Sub
```

Now create the form that sets the data type and calls the Insert Object dialog box. Add a form to the project by selecting Form from the Insert menu. Change its `Name` and `Caption` properties to `frmType` and `OLE Object Type`, respectively. Using the Save File item on the File menu, save the it as OLE Type.frm.

Add the controls shown in Figure 14.9, placing them roughly as illustrated.

Figure 14.9.
The OLE Object Type form.

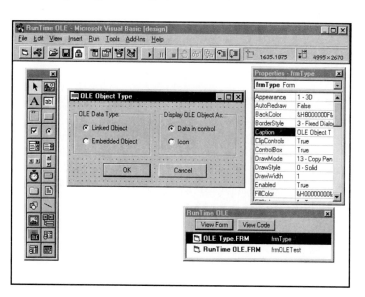

Next, set the controls' properties as follows:

Object	Property	Setting
Form	BorderStyle	3-Fixed Dialog
	Caption	OLE Object Type
	MaxButton	False
	MinButton	False
	Name	frmType
Frame	Caption	OLE Data Type:
	Name	Frame1
Option Button	Caption	Linked Object
	Index	0
	Name	optType
	Value	True
Option Button	Caption	Embedded Object
	Index	1
	Name	optType
Frame	Caption	Display OLE Object As:
	Name	Frame2
Option Button	Caption	Data in control
	Index	0
	Name	optDisplay
	Value	True
Option Button	Caption	Icon
	Index	1
	Name	optDisplay
Command Button	Caption	OK
	Default	True
	Name	cmdOK
Command Button	Cancel	True
	Caption	Cancel
	Name	cmdCancel

When you are satisfied with the form's design, lock the controls using the Lock Controls button on the Toolbar or the pop-up menu.

Referencing Objects Repeatedly Using the `With...End With` Statement

A very handy, time-saving statement has been included in Visual Basic 4: `With...End With`. The `With` statement works like this:

```
With object        [statements]End With
```

The `With` statement syntax has these parts:

* `object`—The name of an object or a user-defined type.

* `statements`—One or more statements to be executed on object.

The `With` statement enables you to perform a series of statements on a specified object without requalifying the name of the object again and again. For example, if you have a number of different properties to change on a single object, it is more convenient to place the property assignment statements within the `With` control structure, referring to the object once instead of referring to it with each property assignment.

Here's how that looks in code. First, the old way with a control requalified again and again (notice all the typing):

```
frmOLETest.oleTest.DisplayType = vbOLEDisplayContent
frmOLETest.oleTest.SizeMode = vbOLESizeZoom
frmOLETest.oleTest.Top = 120
frmOLETest.oleTest.Left = 120
frmOLETest.oleTest.Height = 2412
frmOLETest.oleTest.Width = 5652
```

Now, the same code using the `With` statement:

```
With frmOLETest.oleTest
      .DisplayType = vbOLEDisplayContent
      .SizeMode = vbOLESizeZoom
      .Top = 120
      .Left = 120
      .Height = 2412
      .Width = 5652
End With
```

To complete this form, first add the code that closes the form if the user decides to press the Cancel button. Also, center the form when it loads.

```
Private Sub cmdCancel_Click()
    Unload cmdCancel.Parent
End Sub

Private Sub Form_Load()
    Me.Top = (Screen.Height - Me.Height) / 2
    Me.Left = (Screen.Width - Me.Width) / 2
End Sub
```

With this form the user selects either an embedded or linked data object and its appearance—either as an icon or graphically displayed. All the action really happens when the user presses the OK button.

The first thing you must do is set up the `If...Then` statements that correspond to the user's choice of option buttons. That code skeleton looks like this:

```
Private Sub cmdOK_Click()

    If optType(0) Then
        :
    Else
        :
    End If

    If optDisplay(0) Then
        :
    Else
        :
    End If

    :
End Sub
```

Then add the code to select the data type that the user wants, using the `OLETypeAllowed` property:

```
If optType(0) Then
        frmOLETest.oleTest.OLETypeAllowed = 0   'linked
    Else
        frmOLETest.oleTest.OLETypeAllowed = 1   'embedded
    End If
```

Next, add the code that determines the data display (an icon or graphical representation). If the user decides she wants an icon, the OLE container control should resize itself to the icon. It would look pretty silly if the icon expanded itself to fill the container. To resize the container to icon size, use the `SizeMode` property. Use the `With...End With` statement to cut down on the typing:

```
If optDisplay(0) Then
        :
    Else                                'show icon
        With frmOLETest.oleTest
            .DisplayType = vbOLEDisplayIcon
            .SizeMode = vbOLESizeAutoSize
        End With
    End If
```

Now, suppose that the user decides she wants the data to show graphically. The code has to do two things:

1. Make sure that the `SizeMode` property is set to Zoom; this way, the data will stretch proportionately to the control.

2. Be certain that the container control is its original size. If an icon was selected for the previous linked or embedded object, the OLE container control resized itself to accommodate the icon. This smaller control could contain the data in a graphical form, but it would be awfully small.

Resizing the control is as simple as using the OLE container control's original `Top`, `Left`, `Height`, and `Width` properties.

```
If optDisplay(0) Then              'show data contents
        With frmOLETest.oleTest
            .DisplayType = vbOLEDisplayContent
            .SizeMode = vbOLESizeZoom
            .Top = 120        'making control full size to fit form
            .Left = 120
            .Height = 2412
            .Width = 5652
        End With
    Else                               'show icon
        With frmOLETest.oleTest
            .DisplayType = vbOLEDisplayIcon
            .SizeMode = vbOLESizeAutoSize
        End With
    End If
```

Write the final lines of code that close frmType, call the Input Options dialog box using the InsertObjDlg method, and enables cmdSpecs on frmOLETest. cmdSpecs is the command button used to see the statistics of the OLE object. cmdSpecs is enabled only if the Class property of the OLE container control holds something. This accounts for the possibility of the user selecting Cancel in the Input Object dialog box and thus not having actually inserted an object.

```
cmdOK.Parent.Hide
    frmOLETest.oleTest.InsertObjDlg

    If frmOLETest.oleTest.Class <> "" Then
        'Enable Display Object Specs command button
        frmOLETest.cmdSpecs.Enabled = True
    End If
```

That's it! Run the mini-application and try it out. Figure 14.10 shows an example of the mini-application having an object inserted. See what happens when you select linked or embedded objects. How does the Input Object dialog box differ?

Figure 14.10.
The Run-Time OLE
application in action,
selecting linked, graphically
displayed data.

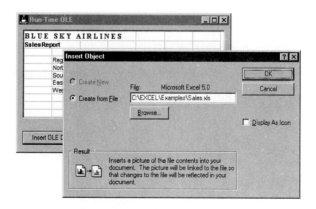

Figure 14.11 shows an Excel spreadsheet in the mini-application.

Figure 14.11.
The linked data in the OLE
container control.

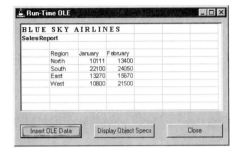

Figure 14.12 shows a Microsoft chart that was inserted as an icon.

Figure 14.12.
Embedded data displayed
with an icon.

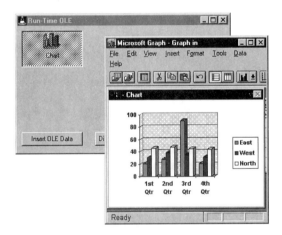

Figure 14.13 shows how you can use the pop-up menu to edit the object.

Figure 14.13.
Using the right mouse button
pop-up menu to edit the
embedded data.

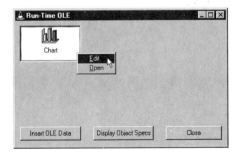

The complete code listing for this demonstration application is available in Listing 14.1.

Listing 14.1. **The code for frmOLETest.**

```
Option Explicit

Private Sub cmdClose_Click()
    Unload cmdClose.Parent
End Sub

Private Sub cmdInsert_Click()
    frmType.Show
End Sub

Private Sub cmdSpecs_Click()
    Dim Crlf, Msg As String
    'Crlf = carriage return plus line feed
    Crlf = Chr(10) & Chr(13)

    'a hacker trick: stacking message!
    'makes a long message easier to read
    Msg = "The Class of this object is: "
    Msg = Msg & oleTest.Class & Crlf

    'If the embedded or linked data is not from a file
    'then the SourceDoc property will be empty
    If oleTest.SourceDoc <> "" Then
        Msg = Msg & "The SourceDoc is: "
        Msg = Msg & oleTest.SourceDoc & Crlf
    End If

    MsgBox Msg, 64, "OLE Object Properties"
End Sub

Private Sub Form_Initialize()
    oleTest.SizeMode = vbOLESizeZoom
End Sub

Private Sub Form_Load()
    Me.Top = (Screen.Height - Me.Height) / 2
    Me.Left = (Screen.Width - Me.Width) / 2
End Sub

Private Sub Form_Unload(Cancel As Integer)
    End
End Sub
```

And, the code for frmType is shown in Listing 14.2.

Listing 14.2. **The code of the frmType—OLE Object Type form.**

```
Option Explicit

Private Sub cmdCancel_Click()
    Unload cmdCancel.Parent
End Sub

Private Sub cmdOK_Click()
```

continues

Listing 14.2. continued

```
        If optType(0) Then
            frmOLETest.oleTest.OLETypeAllowed = 0   'linked
        Else
            frmOLETest.oleTest.OLETypeAllowed = 1   'embedded
        End If

        If optDisplay(0) Then            'show data contents
            With frmOLETest.oleTest
                .DisplayType = vbOLEDisplayContent
                .SizeMode = vbOLESizeZoom
                .Top = 120       'making control full size to fit form
                .Left = 120
                .Height = 2412
                .Width = 5652
            End With
        Else                             'show icon
            With frmOLETest.oleTest
                .DisplayType = vbOLEDisplayIcon
                .SizeMode = vbOLESizeAutoSize
            End With
        End If

        cmdOK.Parent.Hide
        frmOLETest.oleTest.InsertObjDlg

        If frmOLETest.oleTest.Class <> "" Then
            'Enable Display Object Specs command button
            frmOLETest.cmdSpecs.Enabled = True
        End If
End Sub

Private Sub Form_Load()
    Me.Top = (Screen.Height - Me.Height) / 2
    Me.Left = (Screen.Width - Me.Width) / 2
End Sub
```

The following section discusses a part of Windows 95 that is directly linked to OLE Automation and custom OLE Servers: the Registry.

The Windows 95 Registry

The Windows 95 Registry is the centralized information repository that Windows 95–compliant applications use to store and retrieve initialization information.

A Warning About Altering the Registry!

It's okay for you to look through the Registry using RegEdit.exe, but be *very careful* if you alter anything. Be prudent and make a backup first. Normally, configuration changes should be made with the Windows 95 Control Panel tools or other tools that know how to properly store values in the Registry. If you make errors while you change values with RegEdit.exe, *you will not be warned.* The Registry Editor does not understand or recognize errors in syntax or other semantics.

In effect, the Registry can be used in an analogous fashion to the .ini files (called Profile Strings) used under Windows 3.*x*. Each key in the Registry is similar to a bracketed heading in an .ini file, and the entries under each heading are similar to values in the Registry. You should know, though, that Registry keys can contain subkeys, even though .ini files do not support nested headings. Registry values can also consist of binary data rather than the simple strings representing values in .ini files. Also, individual preferences for several users of the same computer can be stored in the Registry; this would take some doing with .ini files.

Note: Complete information about the Registry from the perspective of a power user is included in *Peter Norton's Complete Guide to Windows 95* (Sams 1995). This would be an invaluable reference if you plan on editing the Registry yourself.

At this point, Microsoft is discouraging the use of .ini files in favor of Registry entries, although some applications, particularly 16-bit Windows-based programs, need to continue using .ini files for now. However, you need to be aware that even Visual Basic still uses an .ini file. (This is discussed in Chapter 22, "Creating an Installation Program,")

The Registry is structured as a set of six subtrees of keys that contain databases specific to the computer and the user. Each individual key can contain data items called value entries and, as mentioned earlier, can contain subkeys. In the Registry structure, keys are analogous to directories, and the value entries are analogous to files.

Here's an overview of the six subtrees:

- **Hkey_Local_Machine**—This key contains specifications for the computer, drivers, and other system settings. This is computer-specific information about the type of hardware installed, how ports are mapped, how the software is currently configured, and other information.

- **Hkey_Classes_Root**—This key contains the same data as it did in Windows 3.1. It contains essential information about OLE and association mappings that enable Windows 95 to support drag-and-drop operations, Windows 95 shortcuts (which are, in fact, OLE links) and core aspects of the new Windows 95 user interface.

- **Hkey_Users**—This key contains information about all the users who log onto the computer. It includes both user-specific and generic user information. The information is made up of default settings for applications, event schemes, desktop configurations, and so on.

- **Hkey_Dyn_Data**—This key contains the dynamic status information for various devices and is used as part of the Plug and Play information. This information might change as new devices are added to or removed from the system.

- **Hkey_Current_Configuration**—This key points to a branch of Hkey_Local_Machine\Config that contains information about the computer's current hardware configuration.

- **Hkey_Current_User**—This key points to a branch of Hkey_Users for the user who is currently logged on.

What does all this have to do with Visual Basic programming and OLE, you ask? In the next section, "Using OLE Automation," your OLE Server application must be registered in the Registry so that its objects are available to the controlling application. The questions are, how does one do this, and where does the custom OLE Server appear in the Registry? Another question you might ask is "If an OLE Server is being debugged and tested, wouldn't that make for a big bunch of useless Registry entries that would gum up the system?"

To answer the first question, it's easy to register a custom OLE Server (you'll develop a project shortly that creates an OLE Server). To do so, create an .exe file of the project. Make sure the OLE Server application is not running in the Visual Basic development environment. This is important because the temporary Windows Registry entries created by the run-time application will conflict with the permanent entries created for the executable version of the OLE Server. Click the Start button on the Windows 95 Taskbar, and choose the Run item. In the Open text box enter the path and name of the .exe file (or use the Browse button to find it). Place the cursor in the Open text box and move all the way to the end of the path/filename. Add the /REGSERVER command line parameter to the end of the line, as shown in the following code (suppose that the following line is your file's path and name):

```
c:\vb\programs\MyServer.exe /REGSERVER
```

This should only go in the setup program of an OLE Server. Do it once for your users! You certainly don't want to use it every time you run an executable. When an OLE Server is running in the Visual Basic environment, Visual Basic temporarily registers the server in the system Registry.

Question number two: Where is the registration for the OLE Server placed when it is registered? It goes into the Hkey_Classes_Root subtree. The CLSID (Class ID) key of the Root entry matches the CLSID of the OLE Server. Also, an entry for the OLE Server goes into Typelib, which is also found under Hkey_Classes_Root subtree.

And, finally, yes, the Registry would get filled with a bunch of useless registrations if you are not careful about unregistering outdated .exe files. You unregister an .exe file by using the Run item found under the Start button. Using the Browse button to move through the directory structure, find the .exe file that you want to unregister. When you've found it, select it, and then press OK. This returns you to the Run dialog box. Place the cursor in the Open text box, listing the outdated

.exe file and move it to the end of the path/filename. Add the /UNREGSERVER command line parameter to the end of the line like this (suppose that the following line is your file's path and name):

```
c:\vb\programs\MyServer.exe /UNREGSERVER
```

This switch removes the registration of the .exe file.

As mentioned earlier, Visual Basic creates a temporary Registry entry for an OLE Server when the OLE Server is running in the Visual Basic environment. The minute that server project is ended, that temporary registration is cut off.

It's time to move on to a look at OLE Automation and creating your own OLE Server.

OLE Automation

OLE Automation is used by applications to provide objects to other programs, development tools, and languages. For example, a spreadsheet application can provide a chart, cell, or range of cells as different types of objects. A word processing program could provide sentences, bookmarks, or paragraphs as objects. And you, the programmer, could use the power of a spreadsheet object to store data in a spreadsheet format and execute macros on each cell, or use a word processing object to create and present a table from data in your application. That's what OLE Automation is all about: it is a standard that defines how code is shared between applications and how an application can be controlled from other applications. A diagram of this appears in Figure 14.14.

Figure 14.14.
A pictorial representation of the use of OLE Automation to communicate between applications.

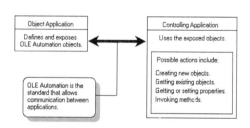

How about a quick demo-application to show you the incredible power of OLE Automation? (In order to create this application, you must have Microsoft Excel installed on your computer.) Start a new project and change the Caption and Name properties of the default form to OLE Automation and frmAutomation, respectively. Now save the form as OLE Automation.frm and the project as OLE Automation.vbp. Add three text boxes, two labels, and two command buttons to the form. Using Figure 14.15 and the following table, roughly position the controls and set their properties.

Figure 14.15.
*FrmAutomation designed
and ready to go.*

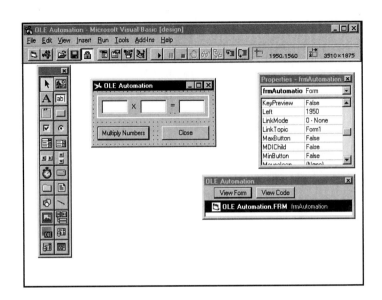

Object	Property	Setting
Form	BorderStyle	3-Fixed Dialog
	Caption	OLE Automation
	Name	frmAutomation
Text Box	Name	txtMultiplier1
	Text	(None)
Label	Caption	x
	Font	Size: 12
	Name	Label1
Text Box	Name	txtMultiplier2
	Text	(None)
Label	Caption	=
	Font	Size: 12
	Name	Label2
Text Box	Locked	True
	Name	txtResult
	Text	(None)
Command Button	Caption	Multiply Numbers
	Default	True
	Name	cmdMultiply

Command Button	Caption	Close
	Name	cmdClose

Now attach Excel's object library to the project by selecting References from the Tools menu. When you do, the References dialog box appears on the screen, as shown in Figure 14.16.

Figure 14.16.
The References dialog box.

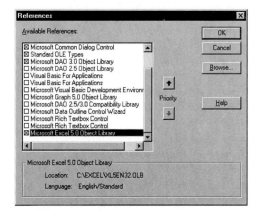

Scroll down the list until you find the Microsoft Excel 5.0 Object Library. (If you don't see it and you have Excel installed on your machine, then use the Browse button to find Excel5.olb.) Select the Excel object library by checking the box, and then press OK.

Now open up the Object Browser (either press F2 or select it from the View menu). Press the arrow to the right of the Libraries/Projects list box and scroll down until you find the Excel listing and select it. When you do, all of Excel's exposed classes, modules, properties, and methods appear in the Object Browser. If you wanted to, you could select a method or property and choose Paste from the Edit menu to automatically add the syntax to your code.

First off, make the Close button operational, as in the following code:

```
Private Sub cmdClose_Click()
    Unload cmdClose.Parent
End Sub

Private Sub Form_Unload(Cancel As Integer)
    End
End Sub
```

The `CreateObject` function is used to create an OLE Automation object. Its syntax works like this:

```
CreateObject(class)
```

The `class` argument uses the syntax *appname.objecttype* (that is, `Excel.Sheet`) and has these parts:

- *appname*—The name of the application providing the object.
- *objecttype*—The type or class of object to create.

Another function used in OLE Automation is `GetObject`. The `GetObject` function retrieves an OLE Automation object from a file. Its syntax works this way:

```
GetObject([pathname][, class])
```

The `GetObject` function syntax uses the following named arguments:

- *pathname*—The full path and name of the file containing the object to retrieve. If *pathname* is omitted, *class* is required.
- *class*—A string representing the class of the object.

As with the `CreateObject` function, the class argument uses the syntax *appname.objecttype* and has these parts:

- *appname*—The name of the application providing the object.
- *objecttype*—The type or class of object to create.

Note: When you use the `GetObject` function and do not include the class of the object to be activated, then the default object of the specified file is activated.

In this case, use `CreateObject` to open Excel because you won't be working with an existing file. All the action in this application occurs when the user presses the Multiply Numbers button. Add the `CreateObject` function to the command button's `Click` event.

```
Private Sub cmdMultiply_Click()
    Dim XL As Object

    'Open Excel
    Set XL = CreateObject("Excel.Sheet")

    :
End Sub
```

This opens Excel invisibly. Make it visible and equate two specific cells, A1 and A2, to the text boxes `txtMultiplier1` and `txtMultiplier2`.

```
Private Sub cmdMultiply_Click()
    Dim XL As Object

    'Open Excel
    Set XL = CreateObject("Excel.Sheet")

    'Make Excel visible
    XL.Application.Visible = True

    'Equate the first two text boxes to specific cells
    XL.Cells(1, 1).Value = txtMultiplier1.Text
    XL.Cells(2, 1).Value = txtMultiplier2.Text

    :
End Sub
```

Finally, multiply the two numbers in Cell A3 and place the result in txtResult. Then, close Excel and release the object variable by setting it equal to Nothing. Those final lines of code, plus the complete code listing, is shown in Listing 14.3.

Listing 14.3. The OLE automation application (OLE Automation.vbp).

```
Option Explicit

Private Sub cmdClose_Click()
    Unload cmdClose.Parent
End Sub

Private Sub cmdMultiply_Click()
    Dim XL As Object

    'Open Excel
    Set XL = CreateObject("Excel.Sheet")

    'Make Excel visible
    XL.Application.Visible = True

    'Equate the first two text boxes to specific cells
    XL.Cells(1, 1).Value = txtMultiplier1.Text
    XL.Cells(2, 1).Value = txtMultiplier2.Text

    'Multply the numbers and display the result
    XL.Cells(3, 1).Formula = "=R1C1 * R2C1"
    txtResult.Text = XL.Cells(3, 1)

    'Close Excel
    XL.Application.Quit

    'Release the object variable
    Set XL = Nothing
End Sub

Private Sub Form_Unload(Cancel As Integer)
    End
End Sub
```

That's it! Run the application and enter a number in the first two text boxes; then click the Multiply Numbers button and watch Excel do the work, as shown in Figure 14.17!

No OLE 2 Network Support, Yet

OLE 2 does not offer the capability to share objects across a network. This functionality is planned for future versions of OLE.

This was just a simple demonstration of multiplying two numbers. Imagine what you could do with the full power of Excel available to your applications!

Figure 14.17.
The OLE Automation demo program running.

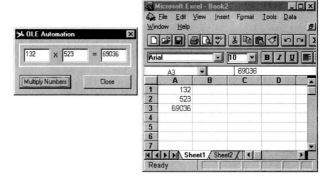

You should know that the `GetObject` function does not open files in all applications. For instance, to load a file in Microsoft Word 6.0, you would have to use the `CreateObject` function to start Word, and then open the file using the WordBasic method `FileOpen`. That code might look something like this:

```
Dim WinWord As Object
Set WinWord = CreateObject ("Word.Basic")        'Starts a copy of Word
WinWord.FileOpen Name:= "C:\MyFile.doc"          'Opens the file MyFile.doc
```

Note: Word's support of OLE Automation has been very different from the implementation of OLE automation in other applications. It appears that the Word developers don't want to adopt OLE automation, but are being required to. Expect that Word's OLE Automation will improve in future versions.

The `Set` statement used in the preceding code and in the OLE Automation demo-application assigns an object reference to a variable or property. Its syntax works like this:

```
Set objectvar = {[New] objectexpression ¦ Nothing}
```

The `Set` statement syntax has these parts:

- *objectvar*—The name of the variable or property; it follows standard variable naming conventions.

- `New`—A keyword used to create a new instance of a Visual Basic object or an externally creatable OLE Automation object. The `New` keyword cannot be used to create new instances of any intrinsic data type and cannot be used to create dependent OLE Automation objects.

- *objectexpression*—An expression consisting of the name of an object, another declared variable of the same object type, or a function or method that returns an object of the same object type.

- `Nothing`—Discontinues association of *objectvar* with any specific object. Assigning *objectvar* to `Nothing` releases all the system and memory resources associated with the previously referenced object when no other variable refers to it.

Class modules can be used to define classes, or "blueprints," of objects. You can also create your own properties and methods that can be used with objects at run-time. One of the primary ideas of Object-Oriented Programming (OOP) is that all of the data and procedures related to a particular object are kept together with the object itself. It's more modular that way. This is why an object's properties and methods are defined in the same class module that defines the object's class.

Class modules are almost the same as forms. The exception is that class modules are not visible at run-time, whereas forms can be. Each class module defines one class; you can have more than one class module in a project. The `Sub` and `Function` procedures in a class module are the class's methods. The module-level variables and Property procedures in a class module are the properties of the class. You can also set the properties of the class module itself to further define the behavior of the class:

- The `Creatable` property determines whether applications outside your project can declare new instances of your class.
- The `Public` property determines whether other applications can write code to invoke the properties and methods of your class.
- The `Name` property determines the name of the class.

Just like a form at design-time, each class module is a separate class. To create an object from a new class at run-time, use the `New` keyword with the following syntax:

```
Dim variable As New class
```

For instance, to create an object called `Cookie` from a class module called `CookieCutter`, you would use the following statement:

```
Dim Cookie As New CookieCutter
```

The easiest way to define the properties of an object that you create using a class module is by using public variables, like this:

```
Public Ingredients As String
Public NumEggs As Integer
```

Then, you could put the following code in the `Form_Click` event to create an instance of a class and set its property values:

```
Dim SandTart As New Class1
SandTart.Ingredients = "Flour, sugar, butter"
SandTart.NumEggs = 3
```

The Property Procedures

The `Property` keyword is used in the following contexts: the `Property Get` statement, the `Property Let` statement, and the `Property Set` statement. These `Property` statements are used to manipulate and set properties for an object. They are somewhat involved, but very important.

Property Set

`Property Set` is normally used in tandem with `Property Get`. `Property Set` declares the name, arguments, and code that form the body of a `Property` procedure. `Property Set` attaches the reference to an object. Its syntax is as follows:

```
[Public ¦ Private][Static] Property Set name [(arglist)]
    [statements]
    [Exit Property]
    [statements]
End Property
```

The `Property Set` statement syntax has the following parts:

- `Public`—This indicates that the `Property Set` procedure is accessible to all other procedures in all modules. If used in a private module (one that contains an `Option Private` statement), the procedure is not available outside the project.

- `Private`—This indicates that the `Property Set` procedure is accessible only to other procedures in the module where it is declared.

- `Static`—This indicates that the `Property Set` procedure's local variables are preserved between calls. The `Static` attribute doesn't affect variables that are declared outside the `Property Set` procedure, even if they are used in the procedure.

- *name*—This is the name of the `Property Set` procedure; it follows standard variable naming conventions, except that the name can be the same as a `Property Get` or `Property Let` procedure in the same module.

- *arglist*—A list of variables representing arguments that are passed to the `Property Set` procedure when it is called. Multiple arguments are separated by commas. The last argument is the object reference used on the right-hand side of an object reference assignment.

- *statements*—Any group of statements to be executed within the body of the `Property Set` procedure.

The *arglist* argument has the following syntax and parts:

```
[ByVal ¦ ByRef] varname[( )][As type]
```

- `ByVal`—Indicates that the argument is passed by value.

- `ByRef`—Indicates that the argument is passed by reference.

- *varname*—The name of the variable representing the argument; follows standard variable naming conventions.

- *type*—A data type of the argument passed to the Property Set procedure; can be Byte, Boolean, Integer, Long, Currency, Single, Double, Date, String (variable length only), Object, Variant, a user-defined type, or an object type.

You should know that every Property Set statement must define at least one argument for the procedure it defines. That argument (or the last argument, if there is more than one) contains the actual object reference for the property when the procedure defined by the Property Set statement is invoked. If a procedure is not explicitly specified Public or Private, it is public by default.

Viewing Property Set, Property Get, and Property Let in Code. (Sometimes it's Not Easy!)

If you use Full Module View when writing code—in other words, all routines are shown in the Code Window at once—then you should have no problem viewing the paired statements Property Set and Property Get, or Property Get and Property Let. These statements will appear alphabetically below one another.

However, if you like to view the code one procedure at a time and use these paired statements, both might not be visible at the same time. (Yes, this is odd!) To toggle between the paired statements, click the procedure name in the Code Window's Procedure list box where the two statements are located.

Property Get

The Property Get statement declares the name, arguments, and code that form the body of a Property procedure. Property Get retrieves the value of a property. Its syntax is as follows:

```
[Public ¦ Private][Static] Property Get name [(arglist)][As type]
    [statements]
    [name = expression]
    [Exit Property]
    [statements]
    [name = expression]
End Property
```

The Property Get statement syntax has these parts:

- Public—This indicates that the Property Get procedure is accessible to all other procedures in all modules. If used in a private module (one that contains an Option Private statement), the procedure is not available outside the project.

- Private—This indicates that the Property Get procedure is accessible only to other procedures in the module where it is declared.

- *Static*—This indicates that the `Property Get` procedure's local variables are preserved between calls. The `Static` attribute doesn't affect variables that are declared outside the `Property Get` procedure, even if they are used in the procedure.

- *arglist*—A list of variables representing arguments that are passed to the `Property Get` procedure when it is called. Multiple arguments are separated by commas. The name and data type of each argument in a `Property Get` procedure must be the same as the corresponding arguments in a `Property Let` procedure (if one exists).

- *type*—A data type of the value returned by the `Property Get` procedure; can be `Byte`, `Boolean`, `Integer`, `Long`, `Currency`, `Single`, `Double`, `Date`, `String` (except fixed-length), `Object`, `Variant`, or user-defined type. Arrays of any type cannot be returned, but a `Variant` containing an array can. The return type of a `Property Get` procedure must be the same data type as the last (or sometimes the only) argument in a corresponding `Property Let` procedure (if one exists) that defines the value assigned to the property on the right-hand side of an expression.

- *statements*—Any group of statements to be executed within the body of the `Property Get` procedure.

- *expression*—A value of the property returned by the procedure defined by the `Property Get` statement.

The *arglist* argument has the following syntax and parts:

```
[ByVal | ByRef] varname[( )][As type]
```

- `ByVal`—This argument indicates that the argument is passed by value.

- `ByRef`—This indicates that the argument is passed by reference.

- *varname*—The name of the variable representing the argument; follows standard variable naming conventions.

- *type*—A data type of the argument passed to the `Property Get` procedure; can be `Byte`, `Boolean`, `Integer`, `Long`, `Currency`, `Single`, `Double`, `Date`, `String` (variable-length only), `Object`, `Variant`, a user-defined type, or an object type.

Like `Property Set`, `Property Get` is set to a default of `Public`, if `Public` or `Private` are not explicitly specified. Also, like a `Sub` and `Property Let` procedure, a `Property Get` statement is a separate procedure that can take arguments, perform a series of statements, and change the values of its arguments. However, unlike a `Sub` or `Property Let`, you can use `Property Get` on the right-hand side of an expression in the same way you use a function or a property name when you want to return the value of a property.

Property Let

Finally, the `Property Let` statement declares the name, arguments, and code that form the body of a `Property Let` procedure. `Property Let` assigns a value to a property. Its syntax is the same as `Property Set`.

```
[Public ¦ Private][Static] Property Let name [(arglist)]
    [statements]
    [Exit Property]
    [statements]
End Property
```

The `Property Let` statement syntax uses these parts:

- `Public`—This indicates that the `Property Let` procedure is accessible to all other procedures in all modules. If used in a private module (one that contains an `Option Private` statement), the procedure is not available outside the project.

- `Private`—This indicates that the `Property Let` procedure is accessible only to other procedures in the module where it is declared.

- `Static`—This indicates that the `Property Let` procedure's local variables are preserved between calls. The `Static` attribute doesn't affect variables that are declared outside the `Property Let` procedure, even if they are used in the procedure.

- *name*—This is the name of the `Property Let` procedure; it follows standard variable naming conventions, except that the name can be the same as a `Property Get` or `Property Set` procedure in the same module.

- *arglist*—A list of variables representing arguments that are passed to the `Property Let` procedure when it is called. Multiple arguments are separated by commas. The name and data type of each argument (except the last one) must be the same as the corresponding arguments in a `Property Get` procedure. The last argument is the value assigned to the property on the right-hand side of an expression. The data type of the last (or sometimes only) argument must be the same as the return type of the corresponding `Property Get` procedure.

- *statements*—Any group of statements to be executed within the body of the `Property Let` procedure.

The *arglist* argument has the following syntax and parts:

```
[ByVal ¦ ByRef] varname[( )][As type]
```

- `ByVal`—Indicates that the argument is passed by value.
- `ByRef`—Indicates that the argument is passed by reference.

- *varname*—The name of the variable representing the argument; follows standard variable naming conventions.
- *type*—A data type of the argument passed to the `Property Let` procedure; can be `Byte`, `Boolean`, `Integer`, `Long`, `Currency`, `Single`, `Double`, `Date`, `String` (variable-length only), `Object`, `Variant`, a user-defined type, or an object type.

Wow! With all that information out on the table, it's time to create a custom object with properties and methods.

Defining Classes and Creating Objects

Here's a simple Visual Basic example to get you going. Start Visual Basic and change the `Name` and `Caption` properties of the default form to `frmHouse` and `Creating Objects`, respectively. Save the form as Objects.frm and the project as Objects.vbp.

Now add two labels and two command buttons to the form. Set their properties as follows, an example of what the form should look like appears in Figure 14.18:

Object	Property	Setting
Form	Caption	Creating Objects
	Name	frmHouse
Label	BackColor	White
	BorderStyle	1-Fixed Single
	Caption	(None)
	Name	lblKitchen
Label	BackColor	White
	BorderStyle	1-Fixed Single
	Caption	(None)
	Name	lblLivingRoom
Command Button	Caption	Create Kitchen
	Name	cmdKitchen
Command Button	Caption	Create Living Room
	Name	cmdLivingRoom

Now add a class module to the project by selecting Class Module from the Insert menu. Change the class module's `Name` property to `Room` and save it as Room.cls.

This application will use the class module `Room` to define the `Room` class, from which you will create two objects, `Kitchen` and `LivingRoom`.

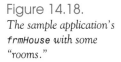

Figure 14.18.
The sample application's
frmHouse *with some*
"rooms."

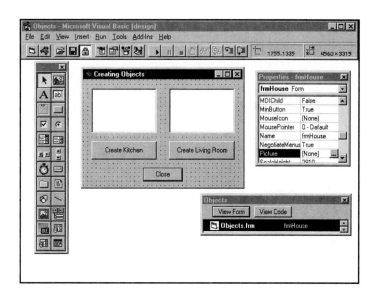

When the user presses the Create Kitchen button, an instance of the Room class is created and the value of a custom property, CurrentRoom, is set as Kitchen. A message box will go up on the screen, displaying the capacity of Kitchen, and then lblKitchen will change color and display the name of the Room. Add that code, along with the code for cmdClose, in frmHouse's Code Window like this:

```
Private Sub cmdKitchen_Click()
    Dim Kitchen As New Room
    Kitchen.Capacity = 10            'sets property value
    Set House.CurrentRoom = Kitchen     'calls Property Set
    MsgBox "The kitchen's capacity is " & House.CurrentRoom.Capacity
    House.CurrentRoom.TurnOnLights 1   'calls method
End Sub

Private Sub cmdClose_Click()
    Unload cmdClose.Parent
End Sub

Private Sub Form_Unload(Cancel As Integer)
    End
End Sub
```

Now add the following declarations to the frmHouse module:

```
Dim objectX As Room
Public House As New frmHouse
```

The second command button, cmdLivingRoom, does essentially the same thing as cmdKitchen, except that it creates a second instance of the class Room, the LivingRoom.

```
Private Sub cmdLivingRoom_Click()
    Dim LivingRoom As New Room
    LivingRoom.Capacity = 15              'sets property value
    Set House.CurrentRoom = LivingRoom    'calls Property Set
```

```
        MsgBox "The living room's capacity is " & House.CurrentRoom.Capacity
        House.CurrentRoom.TurnOnLights 2          'calls method
End Sub
```

Next, add the procedures—Property Get and Property Let—that assign the instance of the Room class—Kitchen or LivingRoom—to the CurrentRoom property of House. With the frmHouse Code Window open add Property Get by selecting Procedure from the Insert menu. Select the Public and Property option buttons, and type CurrentRoom into the Name text box. Press OK. Property Get is added to the Code Window (at the same time Property Let is also automatically added). Now add the following code to these procedures:

```
Public Property Get CurrentRoom()
    Set CurrentRoom = objectX      'accepts passed in argument
End Property

Public Property Set CurrentRoom(x As Room)
    Set objectX = x                'sets a reference to an object
End Property
```

The final code needs to go into the class module, Room. First, add a declaration that creates the Capacity property for Room objects.

```
'Creates Capacity property for Room objects
Public Capacity As Integer
```

Now, add the method TurnOnLights that sets the color of the rooms and caption properties of the label controls.

```
Public Sub TurnOnLights(x As Integer)
    Select Case x
        Case 1
            With frmHouse.lblKitchen
                .BackColor = vbBlue
                .ForeColor = vbWhite
                .Caption = "Kitchen!"
            End With

        Case 2
            With frmHouse.lblLivingRoom
                .BackColor = vbYellow
                .ForeColor = vbBlack
                .Caption = "Living Room!"
            End With
    End Select
End Sub
```

There! You've used a class module to create a Room class, and then used the Room class to create two objects, Kitchen and LivingRoom. Each of these objects have a Capacity property and call the custom method TurnOnLights. Run the application and try it out! You'll see something similar to Figure 14.19.

Figure 14.19.
The Create Objects
application running.

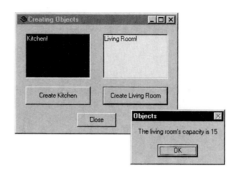

Listings 14.4 and 14.5 show the complete code for this demo-application.

Listing 14.4. The Room class module of Create Objects (Objects.vbp).

```
Option Explicit

'Creates Capacity property for Room objects
Public Capacity As Integer

Public Sub TurnOnLights(x As Integer)
    Select Case x
        Case 1
            With frmHouse.lblKitchen
                .BackColor = vbBlue
                .ForeColor = vbWhite
                .Caption = "Kitchen!"
            End With

        Case 2
            With frmHouse.lblLivingRoom
                .BackColor = vbYellow
                .ForeColor = vbBlack
                .Caption = "Living Room!"
            End With
    End Select
End Sub
```

Listing 14.5. Code for **frmHouse** of Create Object.

```
Option Explicit

Dim objectX As Room
Public House As New frmHouse

Private Sub cmdClose_Click()
    Unload cmdClose.Parent
End Sub
```

continues

Listing 14.5. **continued**

```
Private Sub cmdKitchen_Click()
    Dim Kitchen As New Room
    Kitchen.Capacity = 10              'sets property value
    Set House.CurrentRoom = Kitchen    'calls Property Set
    MsgBox "The kitchen's capacity is " & House.CurrentRoom.Capacity
    House.CurrentRoom.TurnOnLights 1   'calls method
End Sub

Private Sub cmdLivingRoom_Click()
    Dim LivingRoom As New Room
    LivingRoom.Capacity = 15               'sets property value
    Set House.CurrentRoom = LivingRoom     'calls Property Set
    MsgBox "The living room's capacity is " & House.CurrentRoom.Capacity
    House.CurrentRoom.TurnOnLights 2       'calls method
End Sub

Public Property Get CurrentRoom()
    Set CurrentRoom = objectX      'accepts passed in argument
End Property

Public Property Set CurrentRoom(x As Room)
    Set objectX = x               'sets a reference to an object
End Property

Private Sub Form_Unload(Cancel As Integer)
    End
End Sub
```

Now that you have used a class module to create objects, a property, and method, it's time for you to create your own OLE Server.

Passing Parameters

When you pass parameters to and from object applications and client applications you must use the intrinsic Visual Basic variable types; for example, integer, long, byte, string, and object. This might seem obvious, but how do you pass a form as a parameter? It must be passed as an object.

Creating a Custom OLE Server

By creating and using class modules in your Visual Basic code, you gain the advantages of code re-usability and modularity. Therefore, if you turned that application into an OLE Server you would raise this advantage to the next level. Other programmers can create objects using the classes that your custom OLE Servers expose.

All this harks back to OLE Automation. The objects that an OLE Server exposes to other applications are called OLE Automation objects. And an application can expose any number of objects that its programmer desires. OLE Automation defines two types of members that the programmer can expose for an object: methods and properties. Therefore, your application becomes an OLE Server when you expose its objects and their properties and methods. The combination of methods and properties an application exposes is called an *interface*. Each class module in a project defines a single object and a single interface, and setting a class module's `Public` property to `True` exposes the object for external use.

> OLE Automation is implemented independently from the rest of OLE. In other words, it is not connected to the usage of Visual Basic OLE container controls. Providing objects that can be linked or embedded (for instance, using the OLE container control) into other applications' documents is a function that is not included in OLE Servers created with Visual Basic 4.

An OLE Server exposes objects for use by other applications. Programs or programming tools that access those objects are called *controlling applications*, or *OLE Automation controllers*. The controlling application decides which objects to use and when to use them.

The Center Form Application, Part 1

To create an example OLE Server, start a new Visual Basic project. Remove the default form from the project. This OLE Server is not going to have a visible user-interface; it is going to expose a method that centers the controlling application. Save the project as Center Form—Server.vbp.

Now add a standard module to the project and save it as Center Form—Server.bas. This module will contain the `Sub Main` procedure. (You must have a module containing a `Sub Main` procedure for this to work.) Open the module's Code Window and enter the following code:

```
Option Explicit

Public Sub Main()

End Sub
```

You can leave the module's `Name` property as `Module1`. That's it for the standard module. Now add a Class Module, using the Insert menu. Change its `Name` property to CenterForm, its `Public` property to `True`, and its `Instancing` property to 2-Creatable MultiUse.

The Instancing property controls when and how an object can be created by a controlling application. This property's settings are as follows:

- 0-Creatable. This means that other applications cannot use the New operator nor the Dim statement's New keyword to create objects from the class.

- 1-Creatable SingleUse. This setting means that other applications can create objects from the class, but any given instance of the OLE Server can provide only one object of this class.

- 2-Creatable MultiUse. This means that other applications can create objects from the class and the OLE Server can provide any number of objects, regardless of how many applications request them.

Next, in the class module's Code Window create the Sub procedure that will become the CenterForm method (notice that the form is passed as an object).

```
Option Explicit

Public Sub CenterForm(Frm As Object)
    Frm.Move (Screen.Width - Frm.Width) / 2, (Screen.Height - Frm.Height) / 2
End Sub
```

That's it for the code for the OLE Server. The next thing you need to do is set the project options for your OLE Server. Select the Options item from the Visual Basic Tools menu. The Options dialog box opens on the screen. Select the Project tab. Now, make sure that your Project tab sheet is set to the following:

1. Because the application does not need to show a start-up form, the Start-up Form list box at the top left of the tab sheet should read Sub Main. Many OLE Servers operate, as this one does, behind the scenes. Other OLE Servers show a main window only if the user starts them by double-clicking the application icon. If OLE starts a server in response to a request from another application, the server does not show any interface.

2. Type Center in the Project Name text box. The project name you enter here identifies your OLE Server in the System Registry.

3. Make sure the Start Mode is set to OLE Server. This is very important! Usually, OLE automatically closes a server that has objects which are not being requested by other applications. This means that if the Start Mode were set to Standalone instead of OLE Server, every time you ran your OLE Server in the Visual Basic development environment, OLE would close it. Therefore, when the Start Mode is set to OLE Server, Visual Basic keeps your application running even though there aren't any applications requesting objects from it. This gives you time to switch to your controlling application.

4. Finally, type Center Form in the Application Description text box. This is the text that users of your OLE Server will see in the References and Object Browser dialog boxes.

When you are finished, the Project tab sheet should look like the one in Figure 14.20.

Figure 14.20.
The completed Project tab sheet in the Options dialog box.

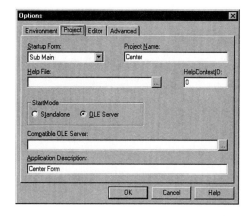

Now that you have set the project options, open the Object Browser (which is found under the View menu). Use the arrow to the right of the Libraries/Project list box to view the entire list. There's your server complete with its modules and methods. This is shown in Figure 14.21.

Figure 14.21.
The Object Browser showing the new OLE Server CenterForm.

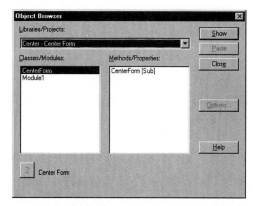

Running Multiple Instances of Visual Basic

It is now possible to run multiple instances of Visual Basic. This is especially useful when you are designing OLE Server applications. There is no need to continually create .exe files of the OLE Server in order to test it. First, start one instance of Visual Basic and run the server application, then minimize it. Then, start a second instance of Visual Basic and run the controlling application. That's all there is to it!

Run the OLE Server application. Just as it should, nothing (except the Debug and Project Windows) appears on the screen. With the OLE Server application running, minimize this instance of Visual Basic. Now, double-click the Visual Basic 4 icon to open another instance of Visual Basic. This is where you are going to create the controlling application.

This time you are going to need the default form. So add a command button to the form and change the objects' properties as shown in the following table:

Object	Property	Setting
Form	BorderStyle	3-Fixed Dialog
	Caption	Center Form
	Name	frmCenter
Command Button	Caption	Center Form
	Default	True
	Name	cmdCenter

Save the form and project as Center Form - Controller.frm and Center Form - Controller.vbp, respectively. Now add the code that calls the center form method to the `cmdCenter Click` event.

```
Option Explicit

Private Sub cmdCenter_Click()
    Dim x As Center.CenterForm
    Set x = CreateObject("Center.CenterForm")
    x.CenterForm frmCenter
End Sub
```

That's all there is to it. All you need to do now, before you run the controlling application, is to add the reference to the OLE Server that is running minimized. Choose References from the Tools menu. Scroll down the references list. Center Form, the application description of the OLE Server (that you typed in the Application Description text box on the Project tab sheet of the Object dialog box) is there on the Available References list. Select it and put an X in its check box, and then click OK as in Figure 14.22.

Figure 14.22.
The References dialog box, with the selected Center Form reference.

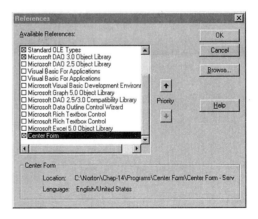

If you open the Object Browser now, you will discover that Center Form is available in the Project/ Libraries list box. When selected, the module CenterForm and its CenterForm method are displayed.

Run the test application and press the center form button, as was done in Figure 14.23. Did the form get centered? If so, you just put your OLE Server to use!

Figure 14.23.
The OLE Server running minimized with the controlling application using its CenterForm method.

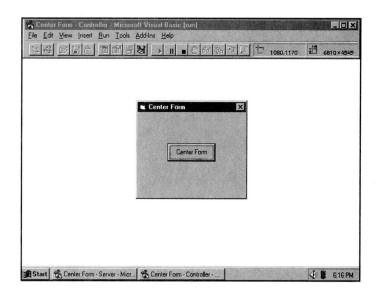

Preserving References to Custom OLE Servers

Just because you set the reference once to your OLE Server in the controlling application, do not expect this reference to be there every time. Visual Basic only creates a temporary entry in the Registry. When the server application is shut down (or changed) that temporary registration is destroyed. If you change the OLE Server or the controlling application at all, the reference to the server in the controlling application will be missing.

To restore the reference, open the References dialog box. In the Available References list box, the reference to the OLE Server will be marked as missing (it will literally say MISSING:x; where x is the server's application description). Uncheck the missing reference, and then click OK. Now, open the References dialog box again. The new reference should be available on the list without the MISSING message. Select it, and then press OK.

How about making this OLE Server do something more, perhaps create a method that is used to add two numbers together and then set a custom Additive property?

Public Constants in Class Modules

In Visual Basic 4, `Public` constants cannot be exposed in class modules. However, constants can be distributed for the OLE Server using a standard module or text file that other programmers can include in their Visual Basic projects.

The Center Form Application, Part 2

To see how to extend a class, start out by adding the new property to the server application that will be set with the result of the user's number added to 42. Open the class module's Code window and insert a new property by selecting Procedure from the Insert menu. Be sure to pick the Public and Property options, and then type `Additive` into the Name box. Click OK. Add the following code to the new property's code skeleton:

```
Public Property Let Additive(i As Integer)
     sum = i
End Property
```

Next, create the method that will add 42 with the user's number. Add a new public function by selecting Procedure from the Insert menu. Make sure that the Public and Function option buttons are selected, and then type the name `ShowSum`. Add the following code to the new function:

```
Public Function ShowSum() As Integer
     ShowSum = sum + 42
End Function
```

Declare the variable sum in the General Declarations section of the class module.

```
Option Explicit

Private sum As Integer
```

That's all the code you need for the new property and method. Save the OLE Server, and then run it and minimize this instance of Visual Basic. If you don't have another instance of Visual Basic running with the controlling application opened, start another instance of Visual Basic and open Center Form - Controller.vbp. (If you do have the controlling application opened in a minimized instance of Visual Basic, it's time to maximize it.)

Add a new command button to `frmCenter`. Change its `Caption` property to `Add 42 to Number` and its `Name` property to `cmdAddNum`, the frmCenter form should now look like Figure 14.24.

Figure 14.24.
*The controlling application
with the new command
button, cmdAddNum.*

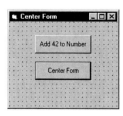

When the user presses this command button the application will ask the user for a number to add to 42. Then it will call the new method that adds the numbers, sets the `Additive` property, and displays the property's value in a message box. Add that code like this:

```
Option Explicit

Public x As Object

Private Sub cmdAddNum_Click()
    Dim j As Integer
    Dim MyValue, Message, Title, Default, Msg As String

    Message = "Enter a numerical value for additive property"   'Set prompt
    Title = "Additive Property Demo"                            'Set title
    Default = "10"                                              'Set default
    MyValue = InputBox(Message, Title, Default)
x.Additive = Val(MyValue)                                    'SET PROPERTY
    j = x.ShowSum                                               'CALL METHOD
    MsgBox "You property value is" + Str$(j), 48, "Addtive Property + 42"
End Sub

Private Sub Form_Load()
    Set x = CreateObject("Center.CenterForm")      'Creating object
End Sub

Private Sub Form_Unload(Cancel As Integer)
    Set x = Nothing      'Releasing object
End Sub
```

And that's it! Because you have changed both the server and controlling application you will have to reset the reference to the server. Open the References dialog box by selecting that item on the Tools menu. Uncheck the missing reference to Center Form and press OK. Now, open the References dialog box again. Select the restored Center Form reference, and then press OK. Run your controlling application as in Figures 14.25 and 14.26.

Figure 14.25.
The input box requesting a number to add to 42.

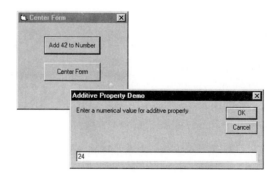

Figure 14.26.
The resulting sum is set as the server's `Additive` *property and displayed in a message box.*

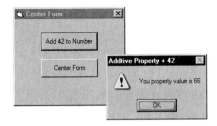

Listing 14.6. **The Ole server class module of Center Form (Part 2 - Server.vbp.).**

```
Option Explicit

Private sum As Integer

Public Sub CenterForm(Frm As Object)
    Frm.Move (Screen.Width - Frm.Width) / 2, (Screen.Height - Frm.Height) / 2
End Sub

Public Function ShowSum() As Integer
    ShowSum = sum + 42
End Function

Public Property Let Additive(i As Integer)
    sum = i
End Property
Listing 14.X. Module1 of Center Form
Option Explicit

Public Sub Main()
    'You have to have this blank module if you don't
    'have a start-up form for the application
End Sub
```

Listing 14.7 shows the code in the controlling application.

Listing 14.7. **The frmCenter form of the Center Form Controller (Center Form, Part 2 - Controller.vbp).**

```
Option Explicit

Public x As Object

Private Sub cmdAddNum_Click()
    Dim j As Integer
    Dim MyValue, Message, Title, Default, Msg As String

    Message = "Enter a numerical value for additive property"    'Set prompt
    Title = "Additive Property Demo"    'Set title
    Default = "10"                      'Set default
    MyValue = InputBox(Message, Title, Default)
```

```
        x.Additive = Val(MyValue)         'SET PROPERTY
        j = x.ShowSum                     'CALL METHOD
        MsgBox "You property value is" + Str$(j), 48, "Addtive Property + 42"
End Sub

Private Sub cmdCenter_Click()
        Dim x As Center.CenterForm
        Set x = CreateObject("Center.CenterForm")
        x.CenterForm frmCenter
End Sub

Private Sub Form_Load()
        Set x = CreateObject("Center.CenterForm")
End Sub

Private Sub Form_Unload(Cancel As Integer)
        Set x = Nothing      'release object
End Sub
```

Now add a few more features to the OLE Server: opening a blank OLE dialog box up on the screen and then adding a method that nudges the controlling application's `frmCenter` to the left.

The Center Form Application, Part 3

To make the final addition to this application, close down the instance of Visual Basic that is running the controlling application. That way there will be only one instance of Visual Basic open—the one running the OLE Server application.

Maximize the server instance of Visual Basic and press the End button to return to the design desktop. Use the Insert menu to add a form to the server. Set the new form's `Caption` property to `Blank form for Demo!`, the `BorderStyle` property to `3-Fixed Dialog`, and the `Name` property to `frmDialog`. Save the form as Dialog Form, Part 3 - Server.frm. Close the blank form and move to the class module's Code Window. This is where you will enter the code that will show the blank form. Add a new method, `ShowForm`, to the code like this:

```
Public Sub ShowForm()
        frmDialog.Show
End Sub
```

That's all you need for the server. Run the server application and minimize this instance of Visual Basic.

Start another instance of Visual Basic and open the controlling application. When the user presses the Show OLE Form command button, the controlling application will use the `ShowForm` method to bring up the blank form you just added to the OLE Server. Add this third command button and position it as shown in Figure 14.27.

Figure 14.27.
The third command button,
cmdShow, added to the
controlling application's
frmCenter form.

Change the command button's `Caption` property to Show OLE Form and its `Name` property to cmdShow. Now add the code to the `cmdShow Click` event that uses the new `ShowForm` method.

```
Private Sub cmdShow_Click()
    x.ShowForm
End Sub
```

That's all there is to it! Make sure the reference to your server application isn't missing (it probably will be because you changed both the server and controlling applications). Once you've re-established the reference, run the controlling application and pull up that blank OLE form, as in Figure 14.28.

Figure 14.28.
After Show OLE Form is
pressed, the controlling
application uses the custom
method ShowForm to open a
blank OLE form.

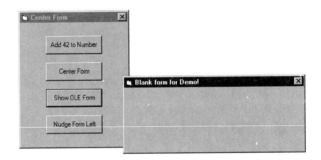

Close down the instance of Visual Basic that is running the controlling application. Maximize and return to the server's Visual Basic design desktop. It's time to add the final feature to this OLE Server/controlling application demonstration.

In the class module's Code Window, add the custom method that will nudge the controlling application's form to the left, like this:

```
Public Sub MoveLeft(Target As Object, i As Integer)
    Target.Left = Target.Left - i
End Sub
```

That's all the server needs. Run it and minimize that instance of Visual Basic.

Start a second instance of Visual Basic again and open the controlling application. Add a final command button to the form and change its `Caption` and `Name` properties to `Nudge Form Left` and `cmdNudge`, respectively.

Now add the code that uses the new MoveLeft method (remember that the unit of measurement used here is twips).

```
Private Sub cmdNudge_Click()
    x.MoveLeft Me, 100
End Sub
```

The controlling application is finished. Re-establish the reference to the OLE Server, and then run the application and try out all the command buttons.

This is shown in Table 14.4, Listing 14.8, and Listing 14.9.

Table 14.4. The blank form in Center Form, Part 3 (Center Form, Part 3 - Server.vbp).

Object	Property	Description
Form	BorderStyle	3-Fixed Dialog
	Caption	Blank form for Demo!
	Name	frmDialog

Listing 14.8. The code for Module1 (the standard module).

```
Option Explicit

Public Sub Main()
    'You have to have this blank module if you don't
    'have a start-up form for the application
End Sub
```

Listing 14.9. The code for the class module, CenterForm.

```
Option Explicit

Private sum As Integer

Public Sub CenterForm(Frm As Object)
    Frm.Move (Screen.Width - Frm.Width) / 2, (Screen.Height - Frm.Height) / 2
End Sub

Public Function ShowSum() As Integer
    ShowSum = sum + 42
End Function

Public Property Let Additive(i As Integer)
    sum = i
End Property

Public Sub ShowForm()
    frmDialog.Show
End Sub
```

continues

Listing 14.9. continued

```
Public Sub MoveLeft(Target As Object, i As Integer)
    Target.Left = Target.Left - i
End Sub
```

Table 14.5. The frmCenter Forms of the Center Form - Controller Application, Part 3 (Center Form, Part 3 - Controller).

Object	Property	Setting
Form	BorderStyle	3-Fixed Dialog
	Caption	Center Form
	Name	frmCenter
Command Button	Caption	Add 42 to Number
	Name	cmdAddNum
Command Button	Caption	Center Form
	Default	True
	Name	cmdCenter
Command Button	Caption	Show OLE Form
	Name	cmdShow
Command Button	Caption	Nudge Form Left
	Name	cmdNudge

Listing 14.10. The complete code for frmCenter.

```
Option Explicit

Public x As Object

Private Sub cmdAddNum_Click()
    Dim j As Integer
    Dim MyValue, Message, Title, Default, Msg As String

    Message = "Enter a numerical value for additive property"   'Set prompt
    Title = "Additive Property Demo"                            'Set title
    Default = "10"                                              'Set default
    MyValue = InputBox(Message, Title, Default)
    x.Additive = Val(MyValue)                                   'SET PROPERTY
    j = x.ShowSum                                               'CALL METHOD
    MsgBox "You property value is" + Str$(j), 48, "Addtive Property + 42"
End Sub

Private Sub cmdCenter_Click()
    Dim x As Center.CenterForm
```

```
    Set x = CreateObject("Center.CenterForm")
    x.CenterForm frmCenter
End Sub

Private Sub cmdNudge_Click()
    x.MoveLeft Me, 100
End Sub

Private Sub cmdShow_Click()
    x.ShowForm
End Sub

Private Sub Form_Load()
    Set x = CreateObject("Center.CenterForm")
End Sub

Private Sub Form_Unload(Cancel As Integer)
    Set x = Nothing      'release object
End Sub
```

That's it for this chapter. OLE 2.0 in all its incarnations—from OLE container controls to OLE Automation and custom OLE Servers—certainly has plenty to offer! Chapter 15, "Advanced Control and Form Handling" focuses on special features of Visual Basic 4, which can improve the look of your applications and make them easier to handle.

Summary

In this chapter you discovered the many faces of OLE 2.0. After experimenting with linking and embedding objects in OLE container controls at design-time, you went on to learn the many properties and methods associated with OLE. Then, using a quick demo application, you linked and embedded data in an OLE container control at run-time. From there, the chapter's material touched on OLE Automation, the Windows 95 Registry and how to register a custom OLE Server in the Registry. Finally, you used a class module to create your own OLE Server application and ran a second instance of Visual Basic to design and run a controlling application that called the server's methods and properties.

OLE container controls can be used to instantly add the power and flexibility of word processing, spreadsheet, and chart applications (to name a few) to your programs. There's no need for you to create and code a spreadsheet; all you have to do is link or embed one into an OLE container control.

OLE Automation adds another dimension to programming by making the exposed objects of other applications available in your applications. Along with this goes the new Visual Basic 4 capability to create OLE Servers. It's now possible to create OLE Server application modules that can be immediately plugged into a controlling application. No bugs, no debugging mess, just instant functionality plugged into your controlling applications.

New Objects	Description
OLE Container Control	This control lets you add insertable objects to your forms in Visual Basic applications.

New Properties	Description
Action	The Action property is included only for compatibility with earlier Visual Basic versions. In previous versions of Visual Basic, this property set a value that determined an action; it was not available at design time and was write-only at run-time.
Class	An OLE object is derived from its class. The application that provides the object's data and the type of data the object contains determines the object's class. For example, the class of an Excel 5.0 spreadsheet would be Excel.Sheet.5.
DataField	Returns or sets a value that binds a control to a field in the current record.
DataSource	Binds the current control to a database by setting a value that specifies the Data control. Not available at run-time.
DisplayType	Returns or sets a value indicating whether an object displays its contents or an icon. 0-Content is the default. When the OLE container control contains an object, the object's data is displayed in the control. 1-Icon displays an icon in the OLE container control when the control contains an object.
Object	This property returns the object in an OLE container control. It is not available at design-time; it is read-only at run-time. This property can be used to specify a desired object in an OLE Automation task.
OLETypeAllowed	This property returns or sets the type of object the OLE container control can contain.
OLEDropAllowed	This property returns or sets a value that determines whether an OLE container control can be a drop target for OLE drag-and-drop operations.
SizeMode	This property returns or sets a value specifying how the OLE container control is sized or how its image is displayed when it contains an object.

New Properties	Description
SourceDoc	This property returns or sets the filename to use when you create an object. For backward compatibility with the Action property, use the SourceDoc property to specify the file to be linked.
SourceItem	This property returns or sets the data within the file to be linked when you create a linked object. The OLETypeAllowed property must be set to 0-Linked or 2-Either when using this property. Use the SourceDoc property to specify the file to link.
Verb	The Verb property is included for compatibility with the Action property in earlier Visual Basic versions. For current functionality, use the DoVerb method. This property was used in previous version of Visual Basic to return or set a value specifying an operation to perform when an object was activated using the Action property.

New Keywords	Description
New	The New keyword is used in conjunction with the following statements: Dim, Private, Public, Set, and Static.
Nothing	The Nothing keyword in Visual Basic is used to disassociate an object variable from any actual object. For example, when you use the Set statement to assign Nothing to an object variable, the code would look like this: `Set MyObject = Nothing`

New Statements	Description
Property Get	Declares the name, arguments, and code that form the body of a Property procedure, which gets the value of a property.
Property Let	Declares the name, arguments, and code that form the body of a Property Let procedure, which assigns a value to a property.
Property Set	Declares the name, arguments, and code that form the body of a Property procedure, which sets a reference to an object.
Set	Assigns an object reference to a variable or property.
With...End With	The With statement enables you to perform a series of statements on a specified object without requalifying the name of the object. Here's an example:

New Statements	Description

```
With frmBigForm.lblMyLabel
    .BackColor = vbBlue
    .ForeColor = vbWhite
    .Height = 234
    .Width = 832
    .Caption = "This is my
        wonderful label!"
End With
```

New Methods	Description
CreateEmbed	Creates an embedded object.
CreateLink	Creates a linked object.
DoVerb	Opens an OLE object for an operation, such as editing.
InsertObjDlg	Displays the Insert Object dialog box, which enables the user to select the object type to be inserted into an OLE container control at run-time.
PasteSpecialDlg	Displays the Paste Special dialog box. This enables the user to copy the contents of the Clipboard into an OLE container control at run-time.
ReadFromFile	Loads an object from a data file created using the SaveToFile method.
SaveToFile	Saves an object to a data file.
SaveToOLE1File	Saves an object in the OLE file format.
Update	Retrieves the current data from the application that supplied the object and displays that data as a graphic in the OLE container control.

New Functions	Description
CreateObject	Creates an OLE Automation object.
GetObject	Retrieves an OLE Automation object from a file.

15

Advanced Control and Form Handling

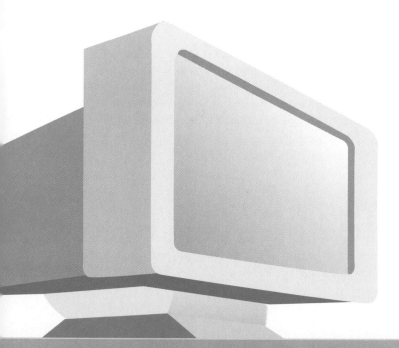

In this chapter, I'll show you some exciting advanced and professional methods of handling controls and forms in Visual Basic. In particular, these are the topics to be covered:

- Passing controls to procedures
- Dragging and dropping Visual Basic controls
- Ensuring automatic and correct resizing of controls
- Changing the tab order of controls, revisited
- Passing variables between forms
- Setting up arrays of forms
- Generating forms from code modules
- About class modules and custom properties
- The forms collection property
- The Multiple Document Interface (MDI) application form
- Using the Me keyword to identify forms
- External resource files

In Chapter 11, you saw a good deal about advanced data handling. There is another aspect of Visual Basic that follows from advanced data handling, and that is advanced control and form handling. In this chapter, I'll take you through advanced techniques for handling controls and forms, much as I did in Chapter 11 for data handling. The techniques you'll look at fall into two broad categories: those to improve communications between the different parts of a Visual Basic application (for example, between procedures and controls) and those that apply to groups of similar items, such as collections of controls and arrays of forms.

As an introduction to these topics, I'll show you what goes into designing and creating a simple desktop organizer: one that lets the user drag a couple of controls—each corresponding to an application program—around on a form. This Desktop Organizer acts a little like the Windows Start menu. Unlike the Start menu, however, the Desktop organizer enables the user to organize executable files in Windows by dragging them around a window and placing them in one of two boxes, labeled Business and Home. The Desktop organizer demonstrates a good bit about advanced techniques in working with controls, techniques we can then extend to forms.

A Desktop Organizer Example

Here, the names like Solitaire and Calculator refer to Windows applications, as they might in the Windows Start menu. The goal here is to allow the user to click one such name and drag it into the other box (for example, from Business to Home or the other way around).

When the user releases the mouse button, the application name stays put.

In this way, users can organize their applications. When the user double-clicks an application name, the Desktop organizer program should start the application up (I'll use the Shell( ) function to do that). Let's see how to make this work.

To enable dragging and dropping of the filenames in the organizer window, I'll use the DragMode property that most controls have, along with the form's DragDrop event. That is, I'll store the names of the applications such as Calculator and Solitaire in labels and make it possible for the user to drag these labels around the window by setting their DragMode property correctly. In addition, when the user stops dragging them across the window and drops them, I'll have the program react to the Form DragDrop event that Visual Basic will generate. I'm going to use labels instead of text boxes to hold the application names because the user can modify text in text boxes, and would rightly expect that any modification made should be reflected in the program; that is, changing Calculator to Control Panel should result in the Control Panel being launched rather than the Calculator.

To start, I'll draw the two boxes in which the application labels are organized. I label them Business and Home. It will prove much easier to draw the boxes rather than to use frames, because frames are controls, each of which has its own DragDrop event. In that case, I would have to coordinate three events: Label1_DragDrop, Label2_DragDrop, and Form_DragDrop. I simply draw the two boxes.

Then the only event I'll have to worry about when the user drags an application name around is Form_DragDrop( ). I'll draw the two boxes in the Form_Load( ) event, using graphics methods like those discussed in Chapter 9. After setting the form's AutoRedraw property to True, I can print the labels Business and Home with the following code, tying them to the size of the window. (If this same code is added to the Form_Resize event, the user can resize the window as well, without altering the relative positions of the labels.)

```
Private Sub Form_Load ( )
    CurrentY = ScaleWidth / 20
    CurrentX = ScaleWidth / 9
    Print "Business";
    CurrentX = 5 * ScaleWidth / 9
    Print "Home"
        :
```

Matching Controls' Sizes to Their Form's Size

If I were using actual Visual Basic controls here, I could have them resized in the Form_Resize event by updating their Width and Height properties. I could also rely on the Elastic OLE Custom Control (OCX), a third-party Visual Basic custom control produced by VideoSoft.

Now, because Business and Home are the names of the two boxes themselves, I need to make them stand out from the application names, which will be inside the boxes. To do that, I'll increase the font size of these names from 8.25 points to 12 points using the form's FontSize property. Next, I draw the boxes themselves using the Line method with the B option. I use relative coordinates to tailor the boxes to the size of the form, like so:

```
Private Sub Form_Load ( )
    CurrentY = ScaleWidth / 20
    CurrentX = ScaleWidth / 9
    Print "Business";
    CurrentX = 5 * ScaleWidth / 9
    Print "Home"
    Line (ScaleWidth / 9, 2 * ScaleHeight / 9)-
        (4 * ScaleWidth / 9, 8 * ScaleHeight / 9), , B
    Line (5 * ScaleWidth / 9, 2 * ScaleHeight / 9)-
        (8 * ScaleWidth / 9, 8 * ScaleHeight / 9), , B
End Sub
```

In addition, I can give the form the caption Desktop Organizer. At this point, when the program runs, the user sees something like Figure 15.1.

Figure 15.1.
Beginning the Desktop Organizer.

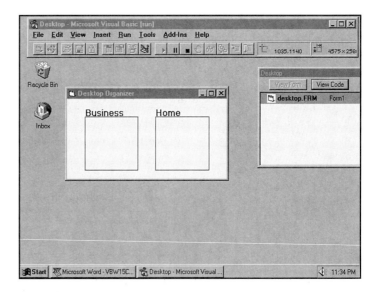

I still need to add the labels holding the application names, to make it possible to drag them around the window, and to start the corresponding application when the user double-clicks one of them. To do that, I create four new labels, giving each the name LLL to create a control array. In addition, I give each of them a caption corresponding to the names of Windows applications. As shown, I use Solitaire, Calculator, Minesweeper, and Paintbrush in this example. Now when the user runs the program, the Desktop Organizer looks like the one shown in Figure 15.2.

Figure 15.2.

The Desktop Organizer with
program labels attached.

Next, I'll take up the dragging process. The properties, events, and methods of dragging appear in Table 15.1. One property of most controls is the DragMode property; this property indicates how controls will respond when the user attempts to drag them around with the mouse. If you set a control's DragMode property to Automatic (such as DragMode = 1), the user can drag the control around at any time. This sounds like what I want except for one thing: When a control's DragMode is Automatic, the control does not respond to any mouse events, except attempts to drag it. In the present case, as in most programs, I want to use the controls for other things besides dragging them around; specifically, I want the user to be able to double-click the labels and start the corresponding application. So an automatic drag mode isn't the way to go. Table 15.1 shows, among other things, the other choices I have for DragMode.

Table 15.1. Control dragging methods, properties, and events.

Drag method	Controls dragging if control's DragMode is set to Manual (0); Control.Drag 0 cancels the drag operation; Control.Drag 1 starts it (moves the mouse cursor to the control and attaches the control to it); and Control.Drag 2 ends dragging. (Drag is only needed when a control's DragMode is manual, but you can use it if DragMode is Automatic (1) also.)
DragDrop event	Occurs when a control is dropped on an object.
DragIcon property	Indicates the icon you want used as the user drags a control around.
DragMode property	Set to Manual (0—the default) or Automatic (1) to control dragging of controls. If a control's DragMode is automatic, the user can drag it at any time (and the control does not respond to normal mouse input like clicks). If you use manual drag mode, the dragging is under your control with the Drag method.
DragOver event	Occurs when a control is dragged over an object (such as a form or control).

As it turns out, I want to use manual dragging—such as, DragMode is set to Manual (0—the default). When a user presses a mouse button while the mouse cursor is on top of a control whose DragMode is set to Manual, a MouseDown( ) event is generated. I can take advantage of that fact to enable dragging at that time, using the Drag method (whose job is exactly that—to enable dragging). The sequence of events goes like this. The user moves the mouse cursor on top of a label and presses a mouse button. At that point, a *LLL_MouseDown( )* event is generated, where *LLL* is the name of the control array containing the labels. In that event procedure, I have the program execute this statement: LLL(Index).Drag 1, which starts dragging (associates the label with the mouse cursor). Here, Index is the index value of the selected label in the control array; it is passed in LLL_MouseDown( ). In code, that looks like this:

```
Private Sub Form_Load ( )
    CurrentY = ScaleWidth / 20
    CurrentX = ScaleWidth / 9
    Print "Business";
    CurrentX = 5 * ScaleWidth / 9
    Print "Home"
    Line (ScaleWidth / 9, 2 * ScaleHeight / 9)-
        (4 * ScaleWidth / 9, 8 * ScaleHeight / 9), , B
    Line (5 * ScaleWidth / 9, 2 * ScaleHeight / 9)-
        (8 * ScaleWidth / 9, 8 * ScaleHeight / 9), , B
End Sub

Private Sub LLL_MouseDown (Index As Integer, Button As Integer, Shift As
Integer, X As Single, Y As Single)
  LLL(Index).Drag 1
        :
End Sub
```

Now the user is able to drag the label around. When this happens, a shady outline is displayed connected to the mouse cursor; it follows the mouse cursor around. The default outline shape is simply a fuzzy box the size of the control itself. Instead of this, I can specify a DragIcon (one of the drag properties associated with most controls). For example, here I might use one of the icons in Visual Basic's icon library. In particular, I'll use one of the drag-drop icons (DRAG2PG, for instance). The result within the running Organizer program is shown in Figure 15.3.

In Figure 15.3, I'm dragging the Calculator label—but note that the control itself (that is, the label with the displayed name Calculator) stayed behind. I can fix that by making the label invisible when I start dragging its outline. I do this in the MouseDown event:

```
Private Sub Form_Load ( )
    CurrentY = ScaleWidth / 20
    CurrentX = ScaleWidth / 9
    Print "Business";
    CurrentX = 5 * ScaleWidth / 9
    Print "Home"
    Line (ScaleWidth / 9, 2 * ScaleHeight / 9)-
        (4 * ScaleWidth / 9, 8 * ScaleHeight / 9), , B
    Line (5 * ScaleWidth / 9, 2 * ScaleHeight / 9)-
        (8 * ScaleWidth / 9, 8 * ScaleHeight / 9), , B
End Sub
```

```
Private Sub LLL_MouseDown (Index As Integer, Button As Integer, Shift As Integer, X As
Single, Y As Single)
  LLL(Index).Drag 1
  LLL(Index).Visible = 0
End Sub
```

Figure 15.3.
Dragging with the Desktop Organizer.

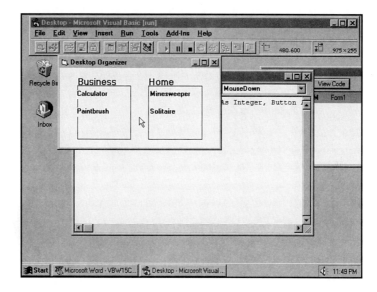

The next step is to respond when the user releases the mouse button, dropping the label in its new position. When that happens, a DragDrop( ) event is generated. The information that Visual Basic passes to the DragDrop event procedure must contain three items: the x coordinate of the mouse cursor when the control was dropped, the y coordinate of the cursor, and some indication of what control was actually dropped. Remember, this is a Form_DragDrop event, and forms can hold many controls. You have to specify which was actually dropped.

To indicate what control was dropped, Visual Basic passes a type of argument that we haven't seen before; it actually passes the control itself as an argument. That is, this is the way the DragDrop event procedure looks:

```
Sub Form_Load ( )
    CurrentY = ScaleWidth / 20
    CurrentX = ScaleWidth / 9
    Print "Business";
    CurrentX = 5 * ScaleWidth / 9
    Print "Home"
    Line (ScaleWidth / 9, 2 * ScaleHeight / 9)-
        (4 * ScaleWidth / 9, 8 * ScaleHeight / 9), , B
    Line (5 * ScaleWidth / 9, 2 * ScaleHeight / 9)-
        (8 * ScaleWidth / 9, 8 * ScaleHeight / 9), , B
End Sub
```

```
Sub LLL_MouseDown (Index As Integer, Button As Integer, Shift As Integer, X As Single, Y
As Single)
  LLL(Index).Visible = 0
  LLL(Index).Drag 1
End Sub

Sub Form_DragDrop (Source As Control, X As Single, Y As Single)
        :
End Sub
```

Note the first argument, Source, which is passed As Control (that is, as a Visual Basic control.) Inside the Sub procedure Form_DragDrop( ), you can use Source entirely as if it were a Visual Basic control like any other. For example, if the dropped control were a text box, you could examine its text property—Source.Text—and so on.

This brings up an interesting point. How exactly do you know what type of control was dropped? You know you can pass controls to procedures and functions; this is one of the most important of our advanced control-handling techniques. To make it work, though, you have to know something about which control was passed. Names such as Text1 or Label1 are not available at run-time in Visual Basic. However, you can determine the type of control with the Typeof keyword. For example, if I wanted to make sure that the dropped control was a label, I could do this:

```
Sub Form_DragDrop (Source As Control, X As Single, Y As Single)
    If TypeOf Source Is Label Then
        :
    End If
End Sub
Note the syntax here:
If TypeOf Source Is Label Then
        :
        'Perform actions  :
End If
```

Here, I use the TypeOf, Label, and Is keywords (note that you use Is, not =, with TypeOf) to check the type of the control named Source. Besides Label, the other keywords you can check passed controls against are CheckBox, ComboBox, CommandButton, DirListBox, DriveListBox, FileListBox, Frame, HScrollBar, Label, ListBox, Menu, OptionButton, PictureBox, TextBox, Timer, or VScrollBar.

When the program encounters a DragDrop event, the user has dropped the label he or she was dragging. Thus, I must now do two things here: Make the original label visible again, and terminate dragging (disconnect the label outline from the mouse cursor) with the Drag method, like this:

```
Sub Form_DragDrop (Source As Control, X As Single, Y As Single)
    If TypeOf Source Is Label Then
        Source.Drag 2
        Source.Visible = -1     'True
        :
        :
    End If
End Sub
```

You might be surprised to learn that Visual Basic does not move the label that was dragged to the new location when it was dropped. The reason is that this gives you, the programmer, more control over what actually happens in your programs. For instance, you might not want to reposition the control where it was dropped, because it might have been dropped in some illegal region of your application. (You probably don't want command buttons on top of your picture boxes, for example.) Instead, you are responsible for moving the control to its new location if you really want it there, and rejecting the move if you don't. You accomplish the actual relocation with the Move method, which Visual Basic uses to move objects around.

To use Move correctly, I need to have saved the original location of the mouse cursor in the control that was dragged at the time of the MouseDown event so that I can restore the control with respect to the cursor's new position. You see, I only get the mouse cursor's position in the DragDrop event, so I have to figure out the control's new position from that. But the cursor could have been anywhere inside the control to drag it—upper-left corner, center, and so on—which means that it's hard to know how to position the control with respect to the cursor. For this example, however, I'll just make the assumption that the mouse cursor was roughly in the middle of the label when dragging started and position the label accordingly like this:

```
Sub Form_DragDrop (Source As Control, X As Single, Y As Single)
    If TypeOf Source Is Label Then
        Source.Drag 2
        Source.Visible = -1      'True
        Source.Move (X - Source.Width / 2), (Y - Source.Height / 2)
    End If
End Sub
```

That's almost it for this application. All that remains is making the four labels' DblClick( ) procedure active so that the user can start the applications by double-clicking the label. Because I have left the labels' DragMode as Manual, the labels can still recognize mouse events like double-clicks. I simply add the code necessary to the procedure LLL_DblClick( ).

However, there is a problem: What application do I start? As in the Windows Start menu, it isn't necessarily the case that the names in the labels correspond to the actual names of the applications' executable files. When you add an application to the Start menu, Windows must know both the name you want for its shortcut—say, Calculator—and the actual name of its executable file (path and filename): c:\windows\calc.exe (although having to know the actual filename of an application is something that Windows 95 shields you from). Besides the name in the label, you need the path and filename information.

As mentioned, not even the names of controls such as Text1 or Picture1 are preserved at run-time. However, the need to associate text information with a control like this is frequent, especially when you pass controls. You might want to know which particular control was passed. Using TypeOf won't help you if you've several controls of the same type. So Visual Basic provides the Tag property, which is a property of all controls. The Tag property enables you to associate a text string with a control. A common use of the Tag property is to store the control's name so that you can see which control you are working with at run-time. Here, I'll store the path and filenames of each application in the matching label's Tag property. To do that, I simply place the correct text string in each label's Tag property, as shown in Table 15.2. You might need to correct the path if Windows is not stored in the Windows directory of your C drive.

Table 15.2. Settings for Desktop Organizer's **Tag** Properties.

Label Name	Label Caption	Tag Property
LLL(1)	Calculator	c:\windows\calc.exe
LLL(2)	Paintbrush	c:\windows\pbrush.exe
LLL(3)	Minesweeper	c:\windows\winmine.exe
LLL(4)	Solitaire	c:\windows\sol.exe

That's it. All I have to do now is add one line to the `LLL_DblClick( )` `Sub` procedure like this, completing the program, which appears in Listing 15.1:

```
Sub LLL_DblClick (Index As Integer)
    Resultval% = Shell(LLL(Index).Tag, 1)
End Sub
```

Listing 15.1. Desktop.Mak.

```
Form Form1 -----------------------------
    AutoRedraw      =    -1  'True
    Caption         =    "Desktop Organizer"

Label LLL
        Caption        =    "Calculator"
        Tag            =    "c:\windows\calc.exe"
        Index          =    1

Label LLL
        Caption        =    "PaintBrush"
        Tag            =    "c:\windows\pbrush.exe"
        Index          =    2

Label LLL
        Caption        =    "Minesweeper"
        Tag            =    "c:\windows\winmine.exe"
        Index          =    3

Label LLL
        Caption        =    "Solitaire"
        Tag            =    "c:\windows\sol.exe"
        Index          =    4

Sub Form_Load ( )
    CurrentY = ScaleWidth / 20
    CurrentX = ScaleWidth / 9
    Print "Business";
    CurrentX = 5 * ScaleWidth / 9
    Print "Home"
    Line (ScaleWidth / 9, 2 * ScaleHeight / 9)-
        (4 * ScaleWidth / 9, 8 * ScaleHeight / 9), , B
    Line (5 * ScaleWidth / 9, 2 * ScaleHeight / 9)-
        (8 * ScaleWidth / 9, 8 * ScaleHeight / 9), , B
End Sub
```

```
Sub LLL_MouseDown (Index As Integer, Button As Integer, Shift As Integer, X As Single, Y
As Single)
    LLL(Index).Visible = 0
    LLL(Index).Drag 1
End Sub

Sub Form_DragDrop (Source As Control, X As Single, Y As Single)
    If TypeOf Source Is Label Then
        Source.Drag 2
        Source.Visible = -1
        Source.Move (X - Source.Width / 2), (Y - Source.Height / 2)
    End If
End Sub

Sub LLL_DblClick (Index As Integer)
    Resultval% = Shell(LLL(Index).Tag, 1)
End Sub
```

The second argument to `Shell( )` indicates how I want the application to start. I pass a 1 so that it starts in an open window. Now the Desktop Organizer is ready to launch applications.

Reaching a Passed Control's Parent Window

If you have been passed a control—named, say, `Source`—in a `Sub` procedure or in a function and need to work with some of the properties of the form it's on (you might change the form's `BackColor` property), you can address that form with the `Parent` keyword like this: `Parent.Source.BackColor = NewColor&`.

Passing Controls to Procedures

Of course, you can pass controls to procedures and functions yourself. It is advisable to set up procedures or functions that can accept controls as arguments in two cases: when you have a number of controls and you want to perform the same (but multiple) actions on each one, such as initializing them, or when you don't know which control you will be expected to work on. An example of the second case might be a procedure to print strings in picture boxes. That code looks like this:

```
Form1 General Declarations ----------------------------------

    Dim StringToPrint As String        'Form-wide variable

Form1 ----------------------------------

    Sub Form_Load ( )
    PString$ = "Now is the time for all good men..."

    StringToPrint = PString$
    PrintLine$ = ""
```

```
NextWord$ = GetWord$( )
Do While NextWord$ <> ""
    Temp$ = PrintLine$ + NextWord$
    If Picture1.TextWidth(Temp$) > Picture1.ScaleWidth Then
    Picture1.Print PrintLine$    'Print before too long
    PrintLine$ = NextWord$
    Else
    PrintLine$ = Temp$
    End If
    NextWord$ = GetWord$( )
    Loop
Picture1.Print PrintLine$    'Print remainder.
End Sub

Function GetWord$ ( )
    If InStr(StringToPrint, " ") = 0 Then
        GetWord$ = StringToPrint
    StringToPrint = ""
    Else
GetWord$ = Left$(StringToPrint, InStr(StringToPrint, " "))
    StringToPrint = Right$(StringToPrint, Len(StringToPrint) -
InStr(StringToPrint, " "))
    End If
End Function
```

Here, the code prints a text string in a picture box whose name is `Picture1`. This code would be much more useful if you could write a general `Sub` procedure called `PrintString( )` that would print text in any picture box. To let it print in any picture box, you can pass the picture box as an argument like this:

```
Sub PrintString(PBox As Control, PString As String)

End Sub
```

Inside `PrintString( )`, you can refer to the picture box simply as `PBox`. For the actual body of the procedure, simply borrow code from the preceding, like this (everything after the first line of the `Form_Load( )` procedure), just changing all references to `Picture1` to `PBox`:

```
Sub PrintString(PBox As Control, PString As String)

    StringToPrint = PString    PrintLine$ = ""
    NextWord$ = GetWord$( )
    Do While NextWord$ <> ""
        Temp$ = PrintLine$ + NextWord$
        If PBox.TextWidth(Temp$) > PBox.ScaleWidth Then
        PBox.Print PrintLine$    'Print before it gets too long
        Else
        PrintLine$ = Temp$
        End If
        NextWord$ = GetWord$( )
        Loop

        PBox.Print PrintLine$        'Print remainder
    End Sub
```

And that's it. Now you have set up `PrintString( )`, a general word-wrapping routine for printing in picture boxes. You can call it with a single line in the `Form_Load( )` procedure like this. (This line replaces the original line in the `Form_Load( )` event that did the same thing.)

```
Sub Form_Load ( )
    Call PrintString(Picture1, "Now is the time for all good men...")
End Sub
```

Passing Forms as Arguments to Procedures

You can actually pass forms to `Sub` procedures and functions. This is very useful if you have a number of forms that you want to apply the same set of operations to or to coordinate in some way. Because you can pass a form to a `Sub` or function in one line, that `Sub` or function might contain many lines of code. That is, the more windows you have to handle in the same way, the more economical it becomes to package the form-handling code in a single procedure. For example, suppose you had a program that maintained four windows, named Form1 through Form4. With the click of one button, you should be able to arrange all these windows in a cascade, as well as to make them all the same size.

Start by making sure that all windows appeared in the screen. Form1 is the startup form here; if you wanted another form to be the startup form, you can use the Set Startup Form… in Visual Basic's Run menu:

```
Sub Form_Load ( )
    Form2.Show
    Form3.Show
    Form4.Show
End Sub
```

Now you might have a button labeled Cascade which, when clicked, will arrange the four windows in a cascade. Next, design a `Sub` procedure named, say, `Cascade( )` that will arrange the windows. You can pass forms using the `As Form` declaration in `Cascade( )` definition. You can use that `Sub` procedure like this when the Cascade button (whose name is `Command1`) is clicked:

```
Sub Form_Load ( )
    Form2.Show
    Form3.Show
    Form4.Show
End Sub

Sub Command1_Click ( )
    Cascade Form1
    Cascade Form2
    Cascade Form3
    Cascade Form4
End Sub
        :
```

Note that I'm passing the four forms, Form1 to Form4, to Cascade( ). I can start Cascade( ) like this (here I'm associating it with the startup form, Form1, but I could put it in a module as well):

```
Sub Cascade (TheForm As Form)

End Sub
```

The form is passed as TheForm; now I'm able to refer to it in Cascade( )'s code as TheForm.

Next, work on positioning the form. Because I want to cascade the forms, I have to retain the upper-left position of each form between calls, so I make those coordinates Static:

```
Sub Cascade (TheForm As Form)
    Static TopX, TopY As Integer
        :
End Sub
```

Now I can position TheForm like this:

```
Sub Cascade (TheForm As Form)
    Static TopX, TopY As Integer
    TheForm.Move TopX, TopY
        :
End Sub
```

Then I update the top-left coordinates for the next form. To do that, I need the height and width of the screen, which I can find with the Screen object. The width of the screen is held in Screen.Width, and the height in Screen.Height. I use them like this:

```
Sub Cascade (TheForm As Form)
    Static TopX, TopY As Integer
    TheForm.Move TopX, TopY
    TopX = TopX + Screen.Width / 10
    TopY = TopY + Screen.Height / 10
        :
End Sub
```

Finally, I change the form's size so that each will be uniform, like this:

```
Sub Cascade (TheForm As Form)
    Static TopX, TopY As Integer
    TheForm.Move TopX, TopY
    TopX = TopX + Screen.Width / 10
    TopY = TopY + Screen.Height / 10
    TheForm.Width = Screen.Width / 4
    TheForm.Height = Screen.Height / 4
End Sub
```

When the user clicks the button labeled Cascade, the four windows arrange themselves neatly, because I'm passing these forms, one after the other, to Cascade( ), which moves and resizes them. Note that Form1 will appear on top because it receives the focus when the Cascade( ) Sub procedure finishes; you might give another window the focus with the SetFocus method.

Consider another example. Suppose you wanted a Sub procedure in a module that would change the Title of a form to Hello. You might call this Sub procedure CallHello( ) and start like this:

```
Sub CallHello ( )
    :
```

I have to indicate what type of argument is passed to CallHello. It happens to be a form, which looks like this:

```
Sub CallHello (TheForm As Form)
    :
```

Now I'm free to refer to the form that was passed to the procedure as TheForm. If I want to change TheForm's Caption property to Hello, I could do it like this:

```
Sub CallHello (TheForm As Form)
    TheForm.Caption = "Hello."
End
```

At this point, I have to pass a form to CallHello( ). I might do that in a Form_Click( ) event like this:

```
Sub Form_Click( )

End
```

Here, I want to pass the current form to CallHello( ) —but how do we do that? I can't use a line like CallHello Form1, where Form1 is the name of the form, because many copies of Form1 may be running and Visual Basic won't know which one I mean. Instead, I use a special keyword that applies to any form, which is Me. The keyword Me always refers to the currently active form. So to change the current form's caption to Hello, when the click event occurs, I can do this:

```
Sub Form_Click( )
    CallHello Me
End
```

That is all there is to it. Now you can pass forms and refer to the current form as well.

Creating an Array of Forms

It might surprise you to learn that you can even set up an array of forms in Visual Basic. Let's say that you want to create such an array in Form1's Form_Click( ) event:

```
Sub Form_Click( )

End
```

First, set up an array of forms called TheForms( ) (using Static so that they will stay around after you leave this event procedure), like this:

```
Sub Form_Click( )
    Static TheForms(5) As Form
    :
End
```

With forms, having declared the array does not mean the forms actually exist. You have to set aside memory and actually create the forms with the Set and New keywords, which allocates space for the elements in this array.

Now that you are about to create a form, the question is: "What type of form shall it be?" You can't just give it type `Form` because there are so many types, sizes, and colors of forms that Visual Basic wouldn't know what you mean. Instead, you specify a type of form that already exists, such as `Form1`. You do that like this:

```
Sub Form_Click( )
    Static TheForms(5) As Form
    Set TheForms(1) = New Form1
:
End
```

Now `TheForms(1)` exists, and it is a perfect copy of `Form1`. To display it (although it will overlap the current `Form1` on the screen) you can do this:

```
Sub Form_Click( )
    Static TheForms(5) As Form
    Set TheForms(1) = New Form1
        TheForms(1).Show
End
```

Using `Set` along with `New`, you can create a new instance of any form from within a code module, letting your program user clone forms at run-time.

Working with Multiple Controls

That's it for advanced form handling for the moment. Let's go back to controls; there is more to advanced control handling to come, having to do mainly with working with more than one control. For example, you can determine what the active control (the one with the focus) is at any time. This turns out to be most useful.

Determining Which Control Is Active

You have seen the `Screen` object before. The width and height of the screen are stored in the `Screen.Width` and `Screen.Height` properties. However, there is another useful property of the `Screen` object: `Screen.ActiveControl`. This property holds the currently active control. Using it, you can refer to the properties of that control in the normal way. For example, if the active control were a text box, you could refer to its `Text` property like this:

```
Screen.ActiveControl.Text.
```

Using `Screen.ActiveControl` is useful if you have a number of similar controls and have to make use of them outside their event procedures. For example, let's say that we had a number of text boxes in a window. Suppose you also have an Edit menu with two items in it: Copy (Copy selected text to the clipboard) and Paste (Paste text from the clipboard).

Now, when the user marks text in one of the text boxes and selects, say Copy from the Edit menu, he or she wants to copy the selected text to the clipboard. However, the program is not within an event procedure connected with either text box when the user selects the Copy item in the File menu. Thus, the program has to determine which text box the user wants to select text from. That is done by checking which text box is currently active—which one has the focus. The program can do that by checking Screen.ActiveControl. A line like this will do the trick:

```
Clipboard.SetText Screen.ActiveControl.SelText
```

Determining Which Form is Active

Besides Screen.ActiveControl, you can also determine which form is the currently active one—that is, which form has the focus—by checking Screen.ActiveForm. Screen.ActiveForm holds the Me value for the current form. In addition, you can check how many forms the current application has by checking the Forms collection like this: Forms.Count. You can use the Forms collection to perform some action on every form within an application. The number of controls in a given form, say Form1, is stored in Form1.Count.

Changing the Tab Order

Another topic that you saw only briefly before concerns the tab order of the controls in a window. For example, let's say that we had three command buttons in a window.

Because these controls were added in the order Command1, Command2, and Command3, they are arranged in a certain tab order. We've left Command1 as the default button (which you can change by setting another button's Default property to True), so when the program starts, Command1 will have the focus (and be surrounded by a thick black border). As is normal in Windows, the user can move to the next control in the tab order by pressing the Tab key; in this case, that's Command2. Pressing the Tab key again will move the focus to Command3.

Visual Basic keeps track of the order with the TabIndex property. You can change the tab order at run-time by placing new values in the TabIndex properties. For example, when the user clicks Command1, you might execute this code:

```
Sub Command1_Click( )
    Command2.TabIndex = 2
    Command3.TabIndex = 1
End Sub
```

Handling Controls That Overlap

Besides tab order, controls that overlap have a `Zorder`. Setting a control's `Zorder` to 0 places it on top of the other controls it overlaps.

It is also worth noticing that if you want to remove one of the buttons (or any control) from the tab order—which means that it cannot receive the focus—you can set its `TabStop` property to `False`. Another way of doing this is to set its `Enabled` property to `False`, which grays out the button's caption and makes sure that the button can't receive the focus.

Working with Multiple Forms

Returning to forms now, there are a number of ways in which you can work with more than one form within an application. You've seen already how you can generate additional instances of a form from within code, using the `Set` and `New` keywords with a variable of type `Form`. There are other ways to generate additional forms within an application. You can also have these forms communicate data to each other, a topic we'll look at first.

Passing Data Between Forms

Suppose you have an item of data—perhaps some text input by the user—that you would like to send from the form on which it was entered to another form. How might you go about this? One way might be to create a global variable—that is, a single variable to which both forms have access (along with, of course, every other form and module in the project). This isn't the ideal solution, though, especially if you want to keep the original variable contents unchanged in the first form while you make changes in the second. Besides, global variables are usually frowned upon as poor programming practice.

Instead, you can create a more localized kind of variable; one that can still be accessed from outside its parent form, but that can't destroy anyone else's data if the variable itself is modified. You do this using the `Public` keyword within the `Declarations` section of a `Form` module, as in

```
Public ParameterVariable as Integer
```

The variable `ParameterVariable` behaves very much like a function parameter in this case. As far as accessing it goes, it behaves exactly like a property. Supposing the variable was declared within `Form2` and you wanted to change its contents from `Form1`, you would do it like this:

```
Form2.ParameterVariable = 35
```

If you had a variable with the same name in `Form1`, executing the preceding statement would do nothing to its contents. Declaring and using variables in this way lets you pass data among forms without resorting to global variables.

More on the Forms Collection

In an earlier sidebar on determining the active form, I casually mentioned the Forms collection as something you can use to make a single change to every form within a project. I should explain this more fully.

The Forms collection is an object possessed by every Visual Basic project. It consists of all the loaded forms within the project. The Forms collection has a single property, called `Count`, which contains the number of forms currently loaded.

The Forms collection acts like an array of forms; thus, `Forms(0)` refers to the first loaded form. You could use this index with a `For...Next` loop to make some change to every form in the collection, as in

```
Private Sub Command1_Click ()
    Dim I       ' Declare variable.
    For I = 0 To Forms.Count - 1
        Forms(I).Caption = "I'm Form #" & I
    Next I
End Sub
```

Another way to use the Forms collection would be to set the active windows on an application's Window menu. Working through a loop like that just shown, you could copy the caption from each active window and use this caption to replace the relevant caption on the Window menu. A line to do that might look like the following:

```
mnuWindowItem1.Caption = Forms(I).Caption
```

You would need to have set aside enough items at design time; you should also make them not visible until filled with a form caption.

Another Way to Get Multiple Forms: The MDI Interface

Working with `Set` and `New` within a code module, you can have an application generate many instances of a single form. Each such instance behaves like a clone of the original, with its own menu (if any), controls, and procedures just like the form out of which it was cloned. Although this may be adequate for some purposes, it isn't for others.

Think of your word processor. You can probably open more than one document with it at a time. Each document appears in its own window—in effect, within its own form in Visual Basic parlance.

Yet each of these windows differs from the main program window. (In my word processor, only the main window contains a menu and command buttons.) Clearly, the program doesn't clone document windows off the main window. Although it might maintain a definition of a separate document window, and clone new windows off that, this still wouldn't work right; my document windows are entirely contained within my word processor's program window, and can't be removed from it. Can this be done in Visual Basic?

In fact, it can, if you rely on the Multiple Document Interface (MDI). MDI refers to a special form that you can include in a project; you add an MDI form using the MDI Form command in the Visual Basic Insert menu. Figure 15.4 shows what the MDI form looks like.

Figure 15.4.
The MDI form in a new project.

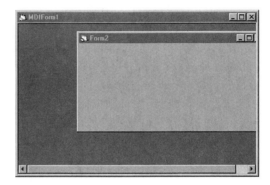

The MDI form (there can be only one such form per project) acts like a container for other forms, just as a form acts as a container for controls. A form is made to be contained by the MDI form by setting its `MDIChild` property to `True`.

You'll note from Figure 15.4 that the single form contained with the MDI Form shown, called `Form2`, has been dragged over so that its right edge is past the right edge of the MDI form itself. `Form2` is clipped; it doesn't hang off the edge. This demonstrates that `Form2` is contained within the MDI form.

You could use the MDI form as an application's program window, letting each form contained within it act as a document window. As for document windows, you might generate them in code using an existing template form. (This template form need not be shown.) For example, the code to enable a New Window command might look like this:

```
Private Sub mnuFileNewWindow_Click(DocWindow as Form)
Set DocWindow as New Form1
DocWindow.Show
End Sub
```

So much for working with multiple forms. The last topics in this chapter deal, in a sense, with both multiple forms and multiple controls, as they're advanced techniques that apply to programs as a whole.

Advanced Program Techniques

The last set of advanced techniques I'm going to show you have global implications. They include creating your own object classes (with methods and properties you define), relying on external resource files, and using conditional compilation to create different versions of an application.

Class Modules and Custom Properties

A single Visual Basic control or form represents, of course, an instance of a class. When you add a form to a project, for example, what you're doing is creating a new object based on the definition for the class form. The same holds true for creating controls.

A class, among other things, contains definitions for properties and methods. Properties are defined as public variables of various data types (frequently `Integer` and `String`). Methods are defined using `Sub` procedures.

If you like, you can actually create your own object classes. You do so using the Class Module command from the Visual Basic Insert menu. Within a class module, you define `Public` variables and procedures that define the class's properties and methods. To use this class within a program, you must create instances of it. You can do this using object variables declared to have the same type as your class, and by using `Set` and `New` to create an instance. If your class were called `MyObject`, such code might look like this:

```
Dim NewObject as MyObject
Set NewObject as New MyObject
```

Using External Resource Files

Suppose you suddenly found out your nifty new Visual Basic application is wanted overseas. The only problem is, it's wanted in French. You don't know the language. Although you could have a consultant go through your program and try to translate it, the process could prove tedious if the consultant isn't a programmer. What's more, you might not want to let him look at your source code anyway. What to do?

Had you been clever, you could have designed your program in such a way that no changes need to be made to the source code in order to have the program translated into another language. You do that by maintaining all the program's strings in a separate file called a resource file. You load text items, such as menu and command button captions, into the appropriate places by referring to the resource file.

A resource file can hold strings, pictures, and raw binary data. You access these items with the `LoadResString()`, `LoadResPicture()`, and `LoadResData()` functions.

You can have only one resource file in a project. If you attempt to add additional resource files, you'll get an error message.

To create a resource file, you should create a file (*.RC) containing all the strings within your application. You'll need to rely on the Windows Software Development Kit (SDK) to determine the form this file should take. You have to associate a number (ID) with each resource. You use this resource ID number to reference individual resources within your Visual Basic code.

You must then use a resource compiler to convert the resource source file into an actual resource file (*.RES). A resource compiler is included with Visual C++. (I'll talk about the C programming language and its relationship to Visual Basic starting with Chapter 17.)

By the way, you can't use resource ID 1; that's reserved for the application icon. You'll get an error message if your code attempts to load resource ID 1.

Once created, you must add the resource file to a project before you can use `LoadResString()` to get data from it. You use the Add File command in the Visual Basic File menu. In the Add File dialog box that appears, select Resource Files (*.RES) in the List Files of Type box. Next, select the particular resource file you want to add to the project, then click OK. You can read more about using resource files in the documentation for the Windows SDK.

Multiple Program Versions: Using Conditional Compilation

As a last advanced technique topic, in a chapter where I've talked a lot about multiple this and multiple that, it only seems fitting that we look at multiple versions of one program from a single set of source code files. Why might you want to do so? Well, for one thing, you might want to provide a version of your application for all those folks who have yet to make the leap to Windows 95. (Some suggest this will be a large crew for some time.) To do this, you need to create both 16- and 32-bit versions of your application.

Although you could change the relevant statements by hand, a better way is to set your program up so that the actual code used to construct an executable application is contingent on what version you want to produce. You do this using conditional compilation statements. A conditional compilation block looks like this:

```
#If expression Then
    statements
[#ElseIf expression-n Then
    [elseifstatements]]
[#Else
    [elsestatements]]
#End If
```

Note that a conditional compilation block looks much like an If…Then…Else block, except for the presence of the number sign. Only statements whose test expression evaluates to True are compiled; the rest are ignored. The test condition usually relies on what conditional compilation constant has been defined using #Const. Consider the following:

```
#Const Win32
#If Win16 Then
     ' statements exclusive to 16-bit
#ElseIf Win32 Then
     ' statements exclusive to 32-bit
#Else
     ' statements for somebody else
#End If
```

In this case, only the statements in the block introduced by #ElseIf Win32 are compiled and put into the executable program. As you'll see in Chapter 17, you do need this kind of capability to prepare multiple program versions for different flavors of Windows, because certain very useful functions have different locations in their 16- and 32-bit versions.

That's it for this coverage of advanced control and form handling. In the next chapter, I'll look at using Visual Basic to work with databases.

Summary

Here you've become familiar with some advanced methods of working with forms and controls. I demonstrated how to pass both forms and controls to procedures and how to work with them in those procedures. You have also seen how to set up an array of forms (much like our earlier control arrays), how to use the Me keyword to refer to the current form, and how to find a passed control's parent form (with the Parent keyword). I also showed you how to enable dragging and dropping of Visual Basic controls on a form and to put together a desktop organizer program that took advantage of these techniques. You learned how to determine a control's type at run-time, how to determine which control is active in a form—and how to determine which form is active on the screen (*active* means has the focus). I showed you how to change the tab order of controls on a form and by seeing how to use the TabStop property to make sure that certain controls never get the focus. We looked at passing variables between forms, and at working with multiple forms using the MDI interface. I finished up with a brief look at external resource files and at conditional compilation.

New Events	Description
DragDrop	Occurs when a control is dropped on an object.
DragOver	Occurs when a control is dragged over an object (form or control).

New Properties	Description
ActiveControl	This property holds a form's currently active control (the one with the focus). You can refer to its properties like this: `Form1.ActiveControl.Text`.
ActiveForm	Holds the currently active form on the screen or in an MDIForm. You can refer to its properties like this: `Screen.ActiveForm.Caption`.
DragIcon	Indicates the icon you want used as the user drags a control around.
DragMode	Set to manual (0—the default) or automatic (1) to control dragging of controls. If a control's `DragMode` is automatic, the user can drag it at any time (and the control does not respond to normal mouse input like clicks). If you use manual drag mode, the dragging is under your control with the `Drag` method.
TabStop	If `True`, means this control can receive the focus; if `False`, it cannot (`True` or `False` only).
Zorder	Determines the position of a control on or under overlapping controls. Setting a control's `Zorder` to `0` places it on top of the other controls it overlaps.

New Methods	Description
Drag	Controls dragging if control's `DragMode` is set to Manual (0); `Control.Drag 0` cancels the drag operation, `Control.Drag 1` starts it (moves the mouse cursor to the control and attaches the control to it) and `Control.Drag 2` ends dragging. (`Drag` is only needed when a control's `DragMode` is manual, but you can use it if `DragMode` is Automatic (1) also).

16

Linking to Databases

In this chapter you'll learn how to access external databases from within a Visual Basic program. Topics covered include

- Microsoft Access and the Jet database engine
- Using the data control to access databases
- The new Visual Basic 4 Data-Bound controls
- Visual Basic and SQL (Structured Query Language)
- The ODBC (Open DataBase Connectivity) engine
- DynaSets and Snapshots
- Third-party data-aware products

In Chapters 13 and 14, I showed you how to connect to other Windows applications. In this chapter, I want to consider an important variant of such connectivity: accessing external database documents. Databases are very important tools within many organizations. Getting needed data out of them effectively is both important and sometimes tricky to accomplish. Fortunately for programmers, Visual Basic includes a number of features that make database access relatively simple to program. The features include its close relationship with the Microsoft Access database program, a data control that can be used to access database information and display it within other controls, and the capability to work with ODBC and SQL drivers to access and manage data in relational databases.

The data-access capabilities contained within the Professional Edition of Visual Basic are designed to work with both remote and client/server databases. A set of DLL files constitutes the "engine" with which Visual Basic programs can access remote database files. The Professional Edition also has the capability to connect to a client/server database, phrasing queries to the remote server. Although you can't construct a database server of your own using the Professional Edition, the Visual Basic Enterprise Edition contains a set of remote database objects that give you much greater access to the client/server model. In this chapter, I'll concentrate on the database-access capabilities offered by the Professional Edition. We'll start by looking at what makes Visual Basic and Microsoft Access so close.

About Visual Basic and Microsoft Access

Microsoft Access is a database program; you use it to create collections of organized data items. These items, of course, are called *records*. Each record has the same form and consists of one or more pieces, each of which stores a particular kind of data. These record pieces are referred to as *fields*.

It's likely none of this is new to you. What might be new is the information that Visual Basic and Microsoft Access have a deep affinity for each other. As Microsoft is the developer of both, this isn't necessarily surprising. What the two programs share is the code to access database files. In a nutshell, this means that, with just a little help, a Visual Basic application can easily link up with a database written in Microsoft Access. (Such files are usually identified by the extension .mdb.) Visual Basic is designed to use one of Access' pieces directly. This piece is called the Jet database engine. It really is all of the database code for Access. The rest of Access is really the visual interface. The fact that Visual Basic integrates directly into the Jet database engine means that Visual Basic integrates very well into Access environments. Taken together, the different routines and capabilities shared by Access and Visual Basic constitute the Microsoft Jet database engine.

The Jet Database Engine

Visual Basic links up with databases by using the Microsoft Jet database engine. The Jet engine is a database-management system that retrieves data from and stores data in both user and system databases. You can think of it as a component with which other data access systems are built. These include, of course, Microsoft Access and Visual Basic.

The Jet database engine does not always follow the client/server database model. Instead, it is a database engine local to the computer on which it's running. It is contained in a set of DLL files that are linked into your Visual Basic programs when they're run. The Jet engine contains all of the code necessary to access, interpret, and present data from a remote database file. The Jet database engine also has the capability to access data from ODBC data sources.

You, as a Visual Basic programmer, can access the capabilities of the Jet database engine in a number of ways. One way is to use the engine's *Data Access Object model* (DAO). The DAO offers an organized hierarchy of data-access object classes, starting with the DBEngine class at the top and working down to individual fields at the bottom.

The latest, 32-bit version of the Jet engine, Version 3.0 (the one included with the Professional Edition), has added a number of new classes to this model, including the Workspace class (an instance of a *workspace* constitutes a single session with a particular database, in which a user is identified by name and password, among other things).

Tip: Visual Basic and Access are extremely similar when it comes to designing code and applications. Their code is now almost wholly transportable, they each have workspaces, and the form design is very similar. Depending upon your application you may want to prototype it in Access. A prototype in Access might be easier to work with since all of the data management tools are right there.

When you've completed your application you could move it to Visual Basic for added speed, or simply purchase the Access Developer's Kit and convert your Access application into something that you can ship out.

The Jet database engine provides other new features including cascading updates and deletes, programmatic access to referential integrity, and improved query speed. If you own Microsoft Access 2.0, you can also work with security settings in a Jet database. The Jet engine also supports database replication and direct manipulation of replicated databases from within your Visual Basic programs.

You should note that the Jet database engine also comes in another flavor, Version 2.5. This is the 16-bit version of the engine. Versions 2.5 and 3.0 are functionally compatible, meaning you can create 16- and 32-bit versions of your Visual Basic database-access programs using the same programming code.

Using the Data Control

Although you must use the Jet database engine's DAO model to access many of its capabilities, probably the simplest way to harness the power of the Jet engine within a Visual Basic program is by using the *data control*. The data control enables you to establish links to database files created by Microsoft Access and a number of other database programs. You display information from records in the database through *bound controls*—text boxes, labels, and picture boxes, for example—that are bound to the database control and set to display specified database fields. The control itself enables you to page around in the database to examine individual records. Figure 16.1 shows a working data control bound to two text labels.

Figure 16.1.
A data control with two bound labels.

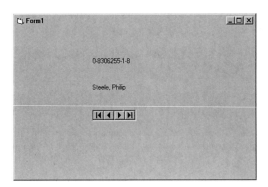

You need to take only a few steps to use the database control to create a link to an outside database. They are as follows:

1. Draw a data control on the appropriate form.

2. Set the DatabaseName and RecordSource properties of the data control to the database you want to view.

3. Draw controls on the form in which to display database information. Bind each control to the data control by putting the data control's name into the control's `DataSource` property.

4. For each such control, set the `DataField` property to display the desired field within the database.

All of these steps bear looking into a little more closely, so we'll do so now.

Linking to an Outside Database

After you've drawn a data control on your form, the first thing to do is link it to an outside database document. All you really need to do is fill in a database name to the `DatabaseName` property of the data control. If you're not linking to a Microsoft Access database, you must specify with the `Connect` property of the data control the type of database to use. When you click in the Properties window to select the `Connect` property, it will drop down to show a list of available database types. These include the various versions of dBASE, Excel, FoxPro, Lotus, and Paradox, along with plain text.

Another property to set is `RecordSource`. This property selects a table containing selected field names from the database. If you connect to a database at design-time, a list of available tables appears in the drop-down list for this property.

If desired, you can have your program set any of these properties at run-time. You need to use the `Refresh` method on the data control to actually open the specified database after these properties have been set.

Creating and Binding Control Objects

Before you can view or modify records from a database, you must create areas in which the record's fields can be shown. You do this using (usually text) controls from the Visual Basic toolbox. The controls you use depend on the kind of data you want to display. To display text data and enable the user to edit it, for example, you'd use text boxes.

Three Bound Controls: DBList, DBCombo, and DBGrid

New to Version 4 of Visual Basic are three bound data controls: DBList, DBCombo, and DBGrid. DBList is a list box like we saw back in Chapter 7; DBCombo is a data-bound combo box, a topic also covered in Chapter 7. The difference is that DBList and DBCombo are automatically filled with data from the appropriate `RecordSet` object; you don't use the `AddItem` method to get data into them. The two can also be used to pass one selected item on to a second data control for further processing.

Table 16.1 shows properties that apply to these new bound data controls.

Table 16.1. Bound data controls properties.

Property	Meaning
DataSource	Name of data control to be updated when a selection is made.
DataField	Name of database field to be updated in RecordSet specified by DataSource.
RowSource	Name of the data control to be used as a source for the list portion of the control.
ListField	Name of field in the RecordSet specified by RowSource to be used to fill the list. This is usually a non-coded description.
BoundColumn	Name of database field in RecordSet specified by RowSource to be passed back to the DataField once a selection is made.
BoundText	Text value of BoundColumn field. After a selection is made, this value is returned to the DataSource to update the DataField field.
Text	Text value of the currently selected list item.
MatchEntry	How to search the list.
SelectedItem	Bookmark of the selected item in the RecordSet specified by the RowSource property.
VisibleCount	The number of items fully or partially visible in the list.
VisibleItems	Array of bookmarks, one for each visible item in the list.

The DBGrid control, on the other hand, enables you to present data in tabular form, as a series of rows and columns. It looks like the ordinary Grid control, but you can set the DBGrid control's DataSource property to a data control so that the control is automatically filled and its column headers set automatically from a data control's RecordSet object.

After you create controls for the various fields you want to display from each database record, you must bind each control to the data control. You do this by entering the name of the data control (the default name for the first data control is Data1) into the DataSource property for each control.

The last thing to do is to set which field to display in the control. You set this with the control's DataField property. If you set this property at design-time and have already set which database and database table to use, the available fields appear in the drop-down list next to the property name.

Note that, as with the name of the database and the name of the database table, you can supply field names to display at run-time.

Manipulating Database Records

At run-time, the user clicks one of the four buttons on the data control to move among records in the database. The leftmost button moves to the first record, the second moves back one record, the third moves forward one record, and the rightmost moves to the last record. Note that you could set the caption on the control to show the name of the database being browsed.

These buttons are functional "right out of the box"; you don't have to write any code to enable the user to move among records.

You can do more than just look at records, however. If you use text boxes to display text fields from a database, you can enable the user to save any modifications made in these boxes back to the original database. You can also enable the user to add and delete records. Visual Basic provides three methods that work on the data control's RecordSet property to provide this functionality. These methods are shown in the following table.

Method	Effect
AddNew	Adds a new record to the database record set. The contents of all bound controls are immediately cleared to show this new record is blank.
Update	Saves any changes back out to the database record set. Although you could invoke this method to save changes, note that all changes are saved immediately and automatically if the user clicks a button on the data control to move to another record.
Delete	Removes the current record from the database record set.

Working with Other Database Engines

In addition to working with Access, FoxPro, and other database applications' files, Visual Basic can be adapted to work with other database engines. This includes working in client/server mode, in which your Visual Basic application passes queries on to a remote database and database engine. The two most important ways of doing so are through the SQL and ODBC standards. What's more, you can design a single application that can access multiple database engines.

About Structured Query Language

Structured Query Language (SQL) is a language used in querying, updating, and managing relational databases. You can use this language to retrieve, sort, and filter specific data to be extracted from a given database. You can think of SQL as a way of asking questions of a remote database. The answer you get is a set of records that match the criteria you specify in your SQL "question."

Visual Basic's SQL capability is implemented through the ODBC architecture, which you'll learn about a little more in a bit. What's important to know about ODBC as it relates to SQL is that there are different levels of compliance possible; each level up is a superset of the previous level. Visual Basic's SQL capability includes all of the minimum SQL grammar, along with most of the statements in the core and extended ODBC grammars, subject to some exceptions and limitations as outlined in Table 16.2.

Table 16.2. Visual Basic SQL limitations.

Visual Basic SQL Limitation	Description
Batched SQL statements	Such statements can't include CREATE VIEW.
CURDATE scalar function	The SQL Server driver doesn't support the SQL_DATE data type; thus, the CURDATE scalar function must return a value of type SQL_VARCHAR instead of type SQL_DATE.
CURTIME scalar function	The SQL Server driver doesn't support the SQL_TIME data type; thus, the CURTIME scalar function must return a value of type SQL_VARCHAR instead of type SQL_TIME.
SIGN scalar function	If the argument of the function is a real number, the SIGN function returns a value of type SQL_FLOAT.
Unsupported SQL Statement	Description
CREATE INDEX	There is no support for the ASC and DESC clauses. Attempts to use them will cause a syntax error.
DELETE	The clause WHERE CURRENT OF cursor-name isn't supported.
DROP INDEX	Table-name.index-name must be used instead of index-name.
IEF	No clauses supported.
MAX, MIN	No support for the DISTINCT keyword.
SELECT	The FOR UPDATE OF clause isn't supported.
UPDATE	The clause WHERE CURRENT OF cursor-name isn't supported.

Now that we're past these limitations, let's look at working with SQL. SQL queries are constructed from a set of keywords. These keywords include

```
SELECT fieldlist

FROM tablenames IN databasename

WHERE searchconditions

GROUP BY fieldlist
```

```
HAVING searchconditions

ORDER BY fieldlist
```

You can use SQL SELECT statements in Visual Basic where you might use a table name, query name, or field name. For example, you can use an SQL statement in place of a table name when setting the RecordSet property. You could, of course enable an SQL-savvy user to perform such an action directly by typing such a query into a text box. Your application would then retrieve the query from the text box and pass it to the appropriate property or method.

An SQL *query* consists of a simple text string; you can use the concatenation operator along with string variables to build such a string within your code. A simple SQL query might look like the following:

```
"SELECT * FROM Clients ORDER BY [Last Name];"
```

This SQL query creates a collection of records—a record set, in other words. In this query, the database table Clients is being consulted for all records; these records are to be ordered by the Last Name field. A little later, when we talk about creating record sets, we'll see how to pass such a query along to the database.

About Open Database Connectivity

Open Database Connectivity (ODBC) is a protocol that enables your Visual Basic applications to connect to a variety of external database servers or files. ODBC drivers used by the Microsoft Jet database engine enable access to Microsoft SQL Server and several other external databases.

Your Visual Basic applications can connect to any database with an ODBC driver installed on your or your user's system. You can connect to ODBC database tables in a variety of ways. This includes using the data control to open either an attached ODBC table or the ODBC database directly.

Before any of your applications can access an ODBC database, the ODBC drivers must be installed and a *Data Source Name* (DSN) created using the Control Panel. Reference to an ODBC database requires you to use the DSN. It contains the linkage information used by the ODBC drivers and the Microsoft Jet database engine to establish a connection to the database. When you are ready to open an ODBC database, use the DSN in the Connect property of the data control. For more information on both SQL and ODBC, consult the Visual Basic Data Access guide.

About Dynasets and Snapshots

The result of any query on a database, whether it's phrased in SQL or in another language, will be a collection of records that match the query; for example, all employees with the last name "Brown" who've been at the company five years or more. The Visual Basic Jet database engine maintains the records returned in answer to a query in an object called a *record set*.

Record sets come in different flavors. A *Snapshot* is a static set of records; Snapshots cannot be updated. In a *Dynaset*, on the other hand, the Jet engine doesn't really bring in the required records; rather, it maintains pointers to them. You can think of these pointers as being similar to bookmarks in the original database. Because Dynasets use pointers, you can have your application update any and all records within the Dynaset. You can't update records within a Snapshot.

Table-, Dynaset- and Snapshot-Type `RecordSet` Objects

The version of the Jet database engine from Visual Basic's previous editions supported the Table, Dynaset, and Snapshot data-access objects. In Visual Basic 4 and Version 3.0 of the Jet engine, these objects are subsumed in the `RecordSet` object. There is continued support for these objects in Version 3.0 of the engine, but they are NOT the same as the table-type, dynaset-type, and snapshot-type `RecordSet` objects from Version 3.0 of the engine.

To create either of these record sets, you must use a variable of type `RecordSet` in a statement with the `OpenRecordSet` method. For example, consider creating a Dynaset using the simple SQL query you saw earlier in the chapter. First, the appropriate object variables must be declared:

```
Dim TheDB as Database, Rset as RecordSet, SQLStatement as String
```

The variable `TheDB` refers to a database object; it'll be used to open the actual database. The variable `Rset` is a `RecordSet` object; it will point to the created Dynaset. `SQLStatement` is a string in which the query is to be stored.

The following code initializes the database variable, moves the SQL query into the string variable `SQLStatement`, and then constructs a Dynaset on the query:

```
Set TheDB = DBEngine.Workspaces(0).OpenDatabase("MyData.MDB")
SQLStatement = "SELECT * FROM Clients ORDER BY [Last Name];"
Set Rset = TheDB.OpenRecordSet(SQLStatement)
```

To create a Snapshot, on the other hand, you must include the keyword `dbOpenSnapshot`, as follows:

```
Set TheDB = DBEngine.Workspaces(0).OpenDatabase("MyData.MDB")
SQLStatement = "SELECT * FROM Clients ORDER BY [Last Name];"
Set Rset = TheDB.OpenRecordSet(SQLStatement, dbOpenSnapshot)
```

To use your newly created record set in a program, you can assign it to the `RecordSet` property of a data control, as follows:

```
Data1.RecordSource = Rset
```

The previous record set is removed from the data control and replaced by the results of your query. Contents of the query must be shown in one or more bound controls, of course. The `Field` property of these controls must be set to the field you want to display for each record in the record set.

There are a number of methods and properties you can use on a `RecordSet` object to manipulate the data it contains. Table 16.3 lists just a few of them.

Table 16.3. Record set methods and properties.

Record set Method/Property	Purpose
BOF property	Set to True if the current record is the first in the record set.
EOF property	Set to True if the current position in the record set is after the last record.
Filter property	Used to exclude specified records from the record set. Set to a string specifying which records to exclude. A second record set must be created after the Filter property is set, using the OpenRecordSet method on the first to create the second, filtered record set.
FindFirst method	Finds first record in a record set to match a specified search criterion. Sets the current position to that record, if any is found. The search criterion is specified as a string variable containing the specifications for the search.
FindLast method	Finds last record in a record set to match a specified search criterion. Sets the current position to that record, if any is found. The search criterion is specified as a string variable containing the specifications for the search.
FindNext method	Finds the next record in a record set to match a specified search criterion. Sets the current position to that record, if any is found. The search criterion is specified as a string variable containing the specifications for the search.
FindPrevious method	Finds first preceding record in a record set to match a specified search criterion. Sets the current position to that record, if any is found. The search criterion is specified as a string variable containing the specifications for the search.
MoveFirst method	Moves current record position to first record in the record set.
MoveLast method	Moves current record position to last record in the record set.
MoveNext method	Moves current record position to the next record in the record set.
MovePrevious method	Moves current record position to preceding record in the record set.
RecordCount property	Number of records in the record set.
Sort property	Sets how to organize the records in a record set. Sort should be set to a string specifying the sort criteria, usually the name of a field by which to sort.

The following bit of code opens a database, creates a record set on it using an SQL query, finds a record matching a specific criterion, moves to the record following that record, and sets the data control Data1 to show the resulting record set:

```
Dim TheDB as Database, Rset as RecordSet, SQLStatement as String, FindRec as String
Set TheDB = DBEngine.Workspaces(0).OpenDatabase("MyData.MDB")
SQLStatement = "SELECT * FROM Clients ORDER BY [Last Name];"
Set Rset = TheDB.OpenRecordSet(SQLStatement)
FindRec = "Last Name = Davis"
Rset.FindFirst FindRec
Rset.MoveNext
Data1.RecordSource = Rset
```

Note: When you want to get rid of a record set (or even an open database), you can use the Close method to release it.

A Working Database Program

Let's try to put to work the things we've seen in this chapter. You'll recall that back in Chapter 7 we started to develop a simple database program that did not rely on the data control or any other data-aware controls from Visual Basic 4. We further modified that database program in Chapter 8. Let's modify that program yet again so that it does use the data control.

First, create a copy of that project and each of its associated form and code module files, except for frmSave and frmLoad. These two should be removed from the new project. (Use the Remove File command in the Visual Basic File menu.) Give the new project the name Databas32. The startup form, frmDatabase, should be made slightly larger. Double-click the data control tool to add a data control. Position it as shown in Figure 16.2.

Figure 16.2.
Modifying the startup form for the new database program.

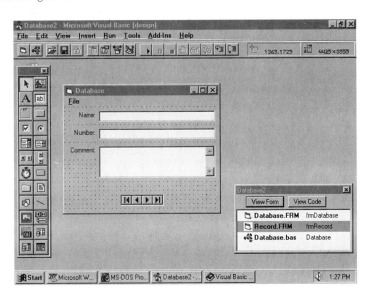

The three text boxes on this form—txtNameField, txtNumberField, and txtCommentField—need to be bound to Data1. To do that, set the DataSource property for each of these controls to Data1.

Now we have to specify which database to open. Although we could set the DatabaseName property of the control Data1 at design-time, it would really be better to give the user a choice of databases to open. We can do that by presenting a common dialog box when the user chooses Load File... from the File menu, and then using the choice made to set Data1's DatabaseName property. To add a common dialog control to frmDatabase, just double-click the control's icon on the toolbox.

Now we must enable this common dialog box. We have to set the dialog box's Filter property so that only database files are shown. We can then present the dialog box and have the user's choice become the basis of Data1's DatabaseName property. The relevant code, which we add to the mnuFileLoad_Click() procedure, looks like this:

```
CommonDialog1.Filter = "Access Database (*.MDB) ¦ *.MDB"
    CommonDialog1.ShowOpen
    Data1.DatabaseName = CommonDialog1.filename
    Data1.Refresh
```

Remember that you must use the Refresh method on the data control to have it accept the new DatabaseName setting.

Now we must identify a source of records for Data1 to use. The different record tables available in the selected database can be found in the TableDefs collection. We can use the Name property of the first item in the TableDefs collection as a record source. The code to do that takes just two lines:

```
Data1.RecordSource = Data1.Database.TableDefs(0).Name
    Data1.Refresh
```

Now we need to have the three bound text boxes set to display the first three fields in the selected database. This we do by setting the DataField property for each text box, using the Fields collection within the TableDefs collection. (Note that if there aren't three fields in the first table of the selected database, the user will get an error message. Fortunately, the example database included with Visual Basic does work. That database file is called Biblio.mdb.) So the code to set the fields to display in the three bound text boxes looks like this:

```
txtNameField.DataField = Data1.Database.TableDefs(0).Fields(0).Name
txtNumberField.DataField = Data1.Database.TableDefs(0).Fields(1).Name
txtCommentField.DataField = Data1.Database.TableDefs(0).Fields(2).Name
```

It would be nice to have the three labels for these fields display the actual field names. We can do that with the following code:

```
Label1 = Data1.Database.TableDefs(0).Fields(0).Name
Label2 = Data1.Database.TableDefs(0).Fields(1).Name
Label3 = Data1.Database.TableDefs(0).Fields(2).Name
```

That's all it takes to enable the mnuFileLoad_Click() procedure. Now, it would be nice to give the user the capability to search records in the database file. To do that, we have to modify the frmRecord form and the existing mnuFileFind_Click() procedure.

What we'll do is give the user a choice of which field to search. We'll do this using the existing list box on the form, lstName. Make the form slightly larger, add a text box into which the user can type the search text, and then include labels for both boxes. Figure 16.3 shows the results of these changes.

Figure 16.3.
A modified form for searching the current database.

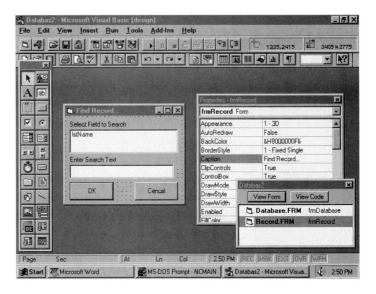

Now we have to modify the code for the OK button, cmdOk_Click(). We must build a search criterion out of the field name chosen by the user, and the search text entered. We then use this criterion string with the FindNext method. After that, we hide the form frmRecord and redisplay frmDatabase. The code looks like this:

```
Dim Criterion As String
    Criterion = "" & lstName.List(lstName.ListIndex) & "= " & "'" & Text1.TEXT & "'" &
""
    frmDatabase.Data1.Database.RecordSets(0).FindNext Criterion
    frmRecord.Hide
    frmDatabase.Show
```

What's being built into the string variable Criterion is a search string, such as "Author = 'Davis, Harold'". The string is then used to search the first record set in the Record sets collection for the current database file.

The File Find capability isn't quite ready. We have to make sure that the correct field choices appear in the lstName list box, using the AddItem method. Exactly where you do this is the tricky part; you can't do it when the program first starts because the wrong field names will appear. You have to wait until a database file is loaded. The logical place to add the required code would seem to be with the mnuFileLoad_Click() procedure. It looks like this:

```
frmRecord.lstName.AddItem Label1
frmRecord.lstName.AddItem Label2
frmRecord.lstName.AddItem Label3
```

These three lines add the text from the three field labels to the lstName list box.

Now the program user can find a given record within the database file.

There are some other modifications to make to bring this program up to speed. The code to add a new item to the database is now entirely wrong. You need to replace all instances of the current code in the procedure `mnuFileAdd_Click()` with the following single line:

```
Data1.AddNew
```

The existing code for the procedure `mnuFileSave_Click()` can be enabled replaced with

```
Data1.Update
```

That's really all it takes to completely convert the database program to work with the data control and with its underlying Jet database engine capabilities.

Data-Aware Products from Third-Party Developers

You aren't limited to using the data control (and others) within Visual Basic when you want to work with outside data. Third-party data-aware products include the BVSP control from Borland, the CDB database engine for Windows, and the QuadPro SQL/Win SQL driver. As always, you can find out more about these (and other) data-aware controls by looking into the appropriate areas on CompuServe or America Online.

Summary

In this chapter, we took a brief look at connecting to outside databases from within Visual Basic programs. After I introduced you to the Microsoft Jet database engine and described its relationship to Microsoft Access and Visual Basic, you saw how to use the data control to connect to an outside database. From there, we moved to a brief discussion of connecting to outside database drivers, such as SQL and the ODBC driver. After talking about Dynasets and Snapshots, we mentioned the existence of some third-party add-ons you can use to expand your data-aware capabilities. The following list shows some new properties and methods you've learned in this chapter.

New Properties	Description
DatabaseName	A property of the data control, used to set what database document to access.
DataField	Property of a bound control; sets which field in the current record will be shown by that control.

DataSource	Property used to bind a data-aware control to a data control; after this, the control can display information from a database linked to that control.
RecordCount	Number of records in the current record set.
RecordSource	Property of the data control, used to establish which record set to view. Can be an SQL query.

New Methods	Description
Close	Close open database or record set.
OpenDatabase	Method applicable to the current workspace; opens the specified database file. Use with SET and an object variable of type Database to create a reference to the database
OpenRecordSet	Method applicable to an open database, creates a record set according to specified criteria; this might include an SQL query. Use with SET and an object variable of type RecordSet to create a reference to the record set.

17

Linking to C and to Windows Directly

In this chapter, you will see how to connect your programs directly to C-language programs and to the Windows library functions. This includes creating and using OLE custom controls (OCXs). In particular, we will cover these topics:

- Creating C library functions
- Declaring external functions in Visual Basic
- A screen-capture program
- Writing a dynamic link library
- Calling C code directly from Visual Basic
- Passing parameters to C functions
- Introducing OLE Controls: What they are and how they're made
- Using callbacks and third-party callback utilities

To begin, we'll create a new program that extends Visual Basic by making use of the Windows library functions. As you will see, these library functions are available to all Windows programs, which means that they are available to your Visual Basic programs as well. All you have to do is inform Visual Basic about the characteristics of the Windows library function(s) you will be using, and then you are free to call them.

We will make use of these functions to extend Visual Basic considerably. For example, we will write a screen-capture program here to do two things that are normally impossible in Visual Basic: draw on the screen outside the Visual Basic window and copy graphics from areas outside this window. By developing these methods of interfacing to the Windows library functions, your programs can be extended immeasurably. In other words, if it can be done in Windows, your program will be able to do it.

In addition, you will see how to connect your Visual Basic code to code you have written in C. Many people who program in C would like to use Visual Basic because developing programs with it is so easy, but they have great amounts of C code they would have to rewrite. Using the skills I teach here, they will be able to interface Visual Basic directly to their C code.

We have gone far with Visual Basic—about as far as the language itself permits, in fact. At this point, you have seen almost all of the keywords in action. The actual language is not designed to get extraordinarily complex, but there is a great deal more to come. We can go beyond the language itself, extending it through its own external interface system.

We will look at two ways of using that interface system in this chapter: connecting to Windows system calls (that is, the system calls that Visual Basic itself uses to create programs), and connecting to your own C routines. You won't need any additional software to connect to Windows system calls; however, you will need some additional software to connect your code to C. Visual Basic can link to external code as long as it is in .dll—or dynamic link library—format.

The dynamic link library format is a special Windows file format that you will learn more about later in this chapter; it can become quite complex. Dynamic link libraries are specially set up so that Windows programs can call the routines inside them. They are called dynamic link libraries because these links between Windows program and library routines are made at run-time, not at the time when the program's .exe file is made, as is the case with DOS programs. It turns out that there are many routines (several thousand) in dynamic link libraries that come with Windows already, and you can use them to extend Visual Basic. After we do that here, you will see how to create your own dynamic link libraries, containing your own code (written in C) so that you can link your own external routines into Visual Basic.

No extra software is required to work with Windows system calls. Although you don't have to have the documentation for those calls, it helps to have the OLE Control Development Kit (CDK), because it includes the file Win32api.txt, which defines all of the Windows system calls as Visual Basic needs them defined. As it turns out, the CDK also contains documentation for all Windows system calls.

To create dynamic link libraries, as we will do in this chapter, you will definitely need something extra: a programming package that is capable of creating them. For clarity, in this chapter we will use one of Microsoft's own C packages—Microsoft Visual C++ for Windows. In order to follow along, you will also need a knowledge of C and, preferably, experience in Windows programming. Working with OLE custom controls (OCXs) doesn't absolutely require that you use Visual C++, but doing so makes this work easier because it gives you access to a range of tools offered by Microsoft.

Linking Visual Basic Programs with Windows 95

Visual Basic gives you a surprising amount of utility for a relatively simple language, primarily because its I/O capabilities (that is, forms and controls) are so well developed and easy to use. However, there are some things that general Windows programs do that Visual Basic can't do because of built-in limitations. For example, there is no provision in Visual Basic to write to areas of the screen outside of a Visual Basic program's window, as it is possible to do in a general Windows program. However, it turns out that you can call the same Windows routines that Visual Basic calls, and through this mechanism you can do (almost) anything that a general Windows program can do.

A Screen-Capture Program

Let's look at an example of this, preferably an example that goes beyond the bounds of conventional Visual Basic programming and that does something interesting at the same time. For instance, we can develop a screen-capture program that enables us to capture a selected portion of the Windows screen. That is, we can use the mouse cursor to move to a location on the screen (inside our program's window) and to press the left mouse button. At that point, we should be able to stretch a rectangle around the region of the screen we want to capture. When we release the mouse button, that section of the screen should then appear inside our form.

This requires us to do a couple of things that are normally impossible in Visual Basic: stretch (draw) a rectangle anywhere on the screen, including wholly or partly outside our program's window; and copy an image—a bitmap—from any location on the screen into our form. We might not be able to do this in standard Visual Basic, but by taking the initiative, we can extend it ourselves.

About Available Windows Documentation

If you want to link to Windows system calls like this yourself, you should get a complete set of documentation that lists them all. The Windows interface is referred to as the Windows Application Programming Interface—the Windows API—and documentation covering it is available from many sources, including the Windows SDK.

Declaring External Code

Before looking at a screen-capture program, let's start our introduction to the Windows API with something more modest. Suppose we want to make the computer emit a beep whenever a mouse button goes down with the pointer inside our Visual Basic program window. Using purely Visual Basic code, we could do it like this:

```
Private Sub Form_MouseDown (Button As Integer, Shift As Integer, X As Single, Y As
Single)

    Beep

End Sub
```

This will certainly get the computer to beep when a mouse button is pressed if the mouse cursor is inside our program's window. However, this is a very boring beep: its duration and tone are fixed, and they depend strictly on the type of computer we're running. Apart from sounds like chimes and bells—a whole different type of animal—we've all heard fancy beeps emitted by different programs. Surely these beeps don't come from the Visual Basic Beep command. So how are they obtained?

Windows actually provides thousands of functions for us to take advantage of programs like those written with Visual Basic. Taken together, these functions constitute the *Windows Application Program Interface* (API). The Windows API is one way through which an application can work directly with the Windows operating system. Among the many functions contained in the API is one called Beep(), which plays a beep of a specified tone and duration.

If we represent the tone by the X coordinate of the mouse pointer and the duration by the Y coordinate, we could modify the previous MouseDown event as follows:

```
Private Sub Form_MouseDown (Button As Integer, Shift As Integer, X As Single, Y As
Single)

    Beep(X,Y)

End Sub
```

As it stands, however, we cannot run our program and get the results we want because Visual Basic has never heard of our version of the Beep() function. If you try to run the program, you just get the regular old beep. We have to indicate that Beep() is a function in the Windows API. To do this, we must write a function declaration that tells Visual Basic where to find the Beep() function. All such function definitions must appear in code modules.

Any function in the Windows API is contained in one of the Windows *dynamic link libraries* (DLLs). Again, a DLL is a library of routines loaded and linked into applications at run-time. In a Visual Basic declaration for an API function, we must indicate in which DLL the function resides. There are three primary dynamic link libraries for use with Windows 95: User32, GDI32 (Graphics Device Interface), and Kernel32. It turns out that Beep() is in the Kernel32 DLL. You can determine which library holds what routines by consulting the Windows documentation.

Thus, we declare the Beep() DLL function to Visual Basic with a statement like

```
Declare Function Beep Lib "kernel32"
```

This function definition is incomplete, however, because we haven't provided any arguments to the function. It turns out that this function expects arguments, passed as long integers, for the tone and duration of the sound. Further, it, along with most API calls, expects these arguments to be passed by value. In general, the Windows routines we are interfacing to expect us to pass everything by value except for arrays and structures (we say that Windows uses the *Pascal calling convention*). The Visual Basic convention is to pass by reference, which means that we will usually have to place the ByVal keyword before arguments when declaring them so that Visual Basic passes them by value, like this:

```
Declare Function Beep Lib "kernel32" (ByVal dwFreq As Long, ByVal dwDuration As Long)
```

Finally, we have to indicate the return value of the function we are declaring. Because it is a function, it will have a return value; if it were a Sub procedure, it would have none. Beep() returns a long integer value; its meaning is of no importance. The complete declaration looks like the following:

```
Declare Function Beep Lib "kernel32" (ByVal dwFreq As Long, ByVal dwDuration As Long) as
➡Long
```

There's one last thing. Although we've provided a new definition for Beep(), Visual Basic is still going to use the old Beep command in its place. In order to get around this, we must provide an alias to the `Beep` command. This is done using, you guessed it, the `Alias` keyword. Many API functions have aliases that let you get around the existence of keywords. Unfortunately, `Beep()` does not. You can, however, specify which number function `Beep()` is within the kernel32 DLL; this is called using its *ordinal number*. The working function definition becomes

```
Declare Function Beep Lib "kernel32" Alias "Beep#nnn" (ByVal dwFreq As Long, ByVal
➥dwDuration As Long) as Long
```

Now we can run the program. When we do, we get a beep when the mouse button goes down. The tone depends on how close to the window's top the pointer is when the mouse button is pressed; the duration depends on the pointer's horizontal position.

Using Predefined Declarations: WIN32API.TXT

Declarations like the preceding one for `Beep()` can get a little tedious to write, especially when they are long like the one for `BitBlt()`, which we will use later:

```
Declare Function BitBlt Lib "GDI" (ByVal hDestDC As Integer, _
                            ByVal X As Integer, ByVal Y As Integer, _
                            ByVal nWidth As Integer, _
                            ByVal nHeight As Integer,_
                            ByVal hSrcDC As Integer, _
                            ByVal XSrc As Integer, _
                            ByVal YSrc As Integer,
                            ByVal dwROP As Long) As Integer
```

Fortunately, the Windows system calls are already declared for us in a file that comes with the Visual Basic Control Development Kit (the CDK) in a file named Win32api.txt. You can take the declaration of any Windows routine you want out of that file and place it into a module. A very handy thing to use in this regard is the API viewer application. Using this application, you can search for any API call by name and then copy its declaration. Figure 17.1 shows the API viewer set to show WIN32API.TXT.

Note: The API Loader will prompt you to create a database of the text file to improve its loading speed. However, you shouldn't do this unless you don't need your computer for a couple of hours (or was it days). This is an extremely lengthy process... for no apparent reason.

Copying a function definition with the API Viewer is easy: find the function name in the scrolling list at the top, click to select it, and then click the Add button. Then click Copy. You can then switch to Visual Basic and paste the definition into a code module.

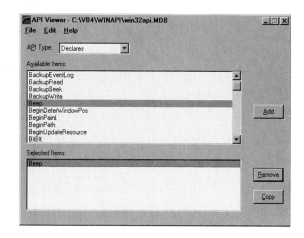

Figure 17.1.
The Windows API viewer application, showing the contents of WIN32API.TXT.

If you don't have the WIN32API file, you will have to create your own declarations from the Windows programming documentation.

About Callback Functions

Some functions in the Windows API require the pointer to address in memory of a function as a parameter; these are *callback* functions because the API function is, in a sense, calling back a function in the program calling it in turn. Providing proper function addresses can be tricky. Fortunately, there are third-party add-ins that simplify this process. Desaware offers a package called SpyWorks that includes, among many other things, a custom control called Cbk.ocx that provides a pool of addresses, any one of which can be used as a callback function, and thus provided as a parameter to an API function requiring it.

Starting the Screen-Capture Program

To implement our screen-capture program, give the program the name Screen Capture. The program waits until the mouse goes down somewhere in its window. The form for this window has the following properties:

Object	Property	Setting
Form	Caption	Screen Capture
	BorderStyle	0
	Left	0
	Top	0
	ScaleMode	3

Now when the mouse button goes down, we will store the location at which it does so as an anchor point, as we did in our Paint program. We can set up a structure to hold this and other points in the module like this (some Windows routines expect us to pass a point structure like this, as you will see in a minute):

```
'Module -------------------------------

Type ApiPoint
     X As Integer
     Y As Integer
End Type
```

Next, we set up a form-level variable of that type in the (declarations) part of Form1's (general) object like this:

```
'Form1 Form-level Declarations ---------------------------------

Dim Anchor As ApiPoint
```

Now we can store the *anchor point* (that is, one corner of the screen section that we want to capture) when the mouse button goes down like this in the MouseDown event:

```
Private Sub Form_MouseDown (Button As Integer, Shift As Integer, X As Single, Y As
Single)

     Anchor.X = X
     Anchor.Y = Y
          :

End Sub
```

Note, however, that these coordinates are with respect to the upper-left corner of Form1's client area. To work with the whole screen, we will have to use screen coordinates, which are required by the Windows functions we will be calling. In addition, most Windows screen manipulation uses pixel measurements, not twips; that's the reason we changed Form1's ScaleMode property to 3 (that is, pixels). X and Y will be reported to us in pixels, not twips, which is what we will need to pass to Windows.

Now that we are using pixels, there is an easy way to change from client-area coordinates (called *client coordinates*) to screen coordinates. We can use the Windows ClientToScreen Sub procedure like this, where we pass the Anchor point structure (which is what ClientToScreen requires—a point structure) like this:

```
Sub Form_MouseDown (Button As Integer, Shift As Integer, X As Single, Y As Single)

     Anchor.X = X
     Anchor.Y = Y
     ClientToScreen hWnd, Anchor
          :

End Sub
```

> ### Winapi.txt has all the Structures Windows Requires
>
> The structures required by Windows calls—such as the preceding Point structure—are defined in Win32api.txt.

This converts the point stored in the Anchor structure to screen coordinates. Note that we also have to declare ClientToScreen in our code module, like this:

```
'Module -------------------------------

Type ApiPoint
     X As Integer
     Y As Integer
End Type

Declare Sub ClientToScreen Lib "User" (ByVal hWnd As Integer,
     lpPoint As ApiPoint)
```

You might also note that Windows routines expect us to pass structures to them by reference, not by value, so we omit the ByVal keyword when we declare the point structure here.

Next, we want to stretch a rectangle around the screen when the user moves the mouse cursor. This procedure breaks down as follows:

First, we will have to draw a box from the anchor point to the mouse cursor's current location, which we will store in a point structure named Current. Current is just another instance of the type ApiPoint.

After we draw the box, we should store the current location in another structure, which we can call OldCurrent. In other words, the box we just drew extends from Anchor to OldCurrent.

When the mouse cursor moves, there will be a new Current position, so we want to redraw the box from Anchor to OldCurrent, erasing it.

Finally, we want to redraw the box from Anchor to the new Current, giving the impression of stretching it.

To start, we can store the Anchor point in the OldCurrent structure when the mouse goes down, so when we erase the box from Anchor to OldCurrent, we will have values to work with:

```
Sub Form_MouseDown (Button As Integer, Shift As Integer, X As Single, Y As Single)

    Anchor.X = X
    Anchor.Y = Y
    ClientToScreen hWnd, Anchor
OldCurrent.X = Anchor.X
    OldCurrent.Y = Anchor.Y
         :

End Sub
```

We can define `OldCurrent`—and `Current` as well—the current location of the mouse cursor—as form-level variables like this:

```
'Form1 Form-level Declarations ----------------------------------

Dim Anchor As ApiPoint
Dim Current As ApiPoint
Dim OldCurrent As ApiPoint
```

We also need to indicate the start of the capture process, after the mouse button goes down. We indicate that by setting a flag named `CapFlag` like this:

```
Sub Form_MouseDown (Button As Integer, Shift As Integer, X As Single, Y As Single)

    Anchor.X = X
    Anchor.Y = Y
    ClientToScreen hWnd, Anchor
    OldCurrent.X = Anchor.X
    OldCurrent.Y = Anchor.Y
    CapFlag = -1          'True

End Sub
```

That flag is also a form-level variable that we can store like this:

```
'Form1 Form-level Declarations ----------------------------------

Dim Anchor As ApiPoint
Dim Current As ApiPoint
Dim OldCurrent As ApiPoint
Dim CapFlag As Integer
```

Note that we should also initialize `CapFlag` to `0` when the form is first loaded like this:

```
Sub Form_Load ()

CapFlag = 0

End Sub
```

At this point, we have started the capture process. But we still need to stretch a rectangle around the screen. This is something that happens as the mouse moves; thus, let's work on the `MouseMove` event first. To do that, we will have to see how to draw anywhere on the screen in Windows.

Accessing the Screen Directly in Windows

To stretch a rectangle around the screen, we will use the `MouseMove` event as follows:

```
Sub Form_MouseMove (Button As Integer, Shift As Integer, X As Single, Y As Single)

End Sub
```

Note that we should only draw our rectangle if we are capturing (that is, if the mouse button went down), which we can check with `CapFlag`:

```
Sub Form_MouseMove (Button As Integer, Shift As Integer, X As Single, Y As Single)

     If CapFlag Then
          :
     End If

End Sub
```

We begin by storing the current location of the mouse cursor in the `Current` point structure and by converting it to screen coordinates with `ClientToScreen`:

```
Sub Form_MouseMove (Button As Integer, Shift As Integer, X As Single, Y As Single)

     If CapFlag Then
          Current.X = X
          Current.Y = Y
          ClientToScreen hWnd, Current
               :
     End If

End Sub
```

Next, we have to draw the rectangle. To do any drawing with the Windows system calls, we have to have a *device context handle*, which tells the program where to draw. We can't use the device context handle of our program's main window, because we would only be able to draw inside it. That is why we are restricted to drawing inside it in Visual Basic. Instead, we can actually get a device context handle to the entire screen using the `CreateDC()` function, which is declared as follows:

```
Declare Function CreateDC Lib "GDI" (ByVal lpDriverName As String,
ByVal lpDeviceName As Any, ByVal lpOutPut As Any,
ByVal lpInitData As Any) As Integer
```

The first argument, `lpDriverName`, of type `String`, is supposed to carry the DOS filename of the device driver for the new device for which we are trying to create a device context. Actually, it is a long pointer to a string (in the C programming language, a pointer holds the address of the object pointed to, not the object itself). It turns out that when we use `ByVal` with a string argument, Visual Basic automatically passes the string using conventions appropriate for a C-style string, so we are set—all we have to do is put the name of a device driver into a string and pass that.

Usually, you use `CreateDC()` to create device contexts for devices not originally designed into Windows, provided the manufacturer supplies a Windows device driver file. However, Windows already has a few default device drivers here, and one of them is "Display." That is, if we pass "Display" as `lpDriverName`, we will get a device context handle to the entire screen. That is exactly what we want, because we want to work with the entire screen. After we have a device context to the screen, which we will call `hDCScreen`, we can draw anywhere on it.

The remaining arguments are these: `lpDeviceName` is normally a pointer to a string that holds the name of the device (for example, "AllPro LaserWriter"); `lpOutPut` is normally a pointer to a string that specifies the output device (for example, a DOS filename or a physical device); and `lpInitData` is a long pointer to a device initialization data structure. Because we are using a default device name (that is, "Display"), we will pass NULL pointers (that is, `0&`, because long pointers are two words long), as indicated by the Windows documentation for these three arguments. When we need to pass a pointer to a Windows function, it will often accept a NULL pointer instead, usually meaning that we want to use a default value or that the argument doesn't apply. All this means that we want to use `CreateDC()` like this:

```
hDCScreen = CreateDC("Display", NULL, NULL, NULL)
```

We will have to be a little careful when passing NULL pointers; to see why, let's take a look at each of the arguments in turn. You might notice that the first argument, `lpDriverName`, is of type `String`. The Windows routines expect strings to be passed in ASCIIZ format—that is, as ASCII strings with a terminating 0 byte (the last byte is simply `0`, not `Chr$(0)`). As mentioned, the `ByVal` argument, used with `As String`, indicates to Visual Basic that it should pass the string as an ASCIIZ (that is, C-style) string.

About .dll Files Written For Visual Basic

If you come across a .dll file specially written for Visual Basic (not C) that accepts strings, you don't have to pass them using the `ByVal` keyword at all. Just declare them `As String`, and Visual Basic will pass them as Visual Basic strings.

You might notice that the remaining arguments are passed `As Any`. This is a special declaration that removes type restrictions on those arguments and will enable us to pass NULL pointers. Originally, these arguments were all declared `As String` (which is the way you will find them in Winapi.txt):

```
Declare Function CreateDC Lib "GDI" (ByVal lpDriverName As String, _
             ByVal lpDeviceName As String, ByVal lpOutPut As String, _
             ByVal lpInitData As String) As Integer
```

However, if we want to pass a pointer as a NULL pointer, we have to declare the corresponding argument `As Any` in Visual Basic (if we left it `As String` and passed a `0` value, Visual Basic, expecting a string, would generate an error):

```
Declare Function CreateDC Lib "GDI" (ByVal lpDriverName As String, _
             ByVal lpDeviceName As Any, ByVal lpOutPut As Any,
             ByVal lpInitData As Any) As Integer
```

That is the way to handle NULL pointers. In addition, we have to pass the actual argument—`0&`—with `ByVal` when we use it so that the `0&` argument is passed directly. Now that we have removed the type restrictions, we can use `CreateDC()` like this:

```
Sub Form_MouseMove (Button As Integer, Shift As Integer, X As Single, Y As Single)

    Dim hDCScreen As Integer

    If CapFlag Then
        Current.X = X
        Current.Y = Y
```

```
ClientToScreen hWnd, Current
hDCScreen = CreateDC("DISPLAY", ByVal 0&, ByVal 0&, ByVal 0&)
    :
```

The only other data item to be careful of when passing to Windows calls are arrays. In Visual Basic, you can pass an entire array to a `Sub` procedure or function by including a set of empty parentheses after the array name, but you can't do that when calling a Windows procedure. In C, you pass a pointer to an array, not the whole thing, and Visual Basic enables you to do this by passing the first element of the array by reference (do not use `ByVal`) like this:

```
WinResult% = WinFunc(my_array(1))
```

In other words, the Windows routine will get what it needs (a pointer to the array) if you pass the first element of the array by reference instead of by value. (Passing *by reference* actually means passing by pointer—that is, by address.) You can pass properties by value (declare the argument with `ByVal`), but note that you cannot pass forms or controls.

We have already covered strings, handles, and NULL pointers, so you are in good shape. A summary of declarations appears in Table 17.1. Note that if you have the file Winapi.txt, you won't need to worry about declarations, because they are all supplied for you. This file is included with Visual Basic 4.

Table 17.1. Windows API declaration conventions.

To Pass	Use This Declaration
Arrays	Pass first array element
Controls	Cannot be passed to the Win API
Forms	Cannot be passed to the Win API
Handles	`ByVal Integer`
Numbers	`ByVal NumberType` (`ByVal Integer/Long/Single/Double`, and so on)
NULL Pointers	`As Any` (and pass `ByVal &0` in the call)
Properties	`ByVal PropertyName`
Strings	`ByVal String`
Win Structs	`As StructName` (defined in Winapi.txt: that is, as `ApiPoint`)

At this point, then, we also should add `CreateDC()` to our module:

```
'Module --------------------------------

Type ApiPoint
    X As Integer
    Y As Integer
End Type
```

```
Declare Sub ClientToScreen Lib "User" (ByVal hWnd As Integer, lpPoint As ApiPoint)
Declare Function CreateDC Lib "GDI" (ByVal lpDriverName As String,
ByVal lpDeviceName As Any, ByVal lpOutPut As Any,
ByVal lpInitData As Any) As Integer
```

Now we add our handle to the screen, hDCScreen. Windows functions that draw or manipulate graphics images demand that you pass a device context handle to them every time you use them (because you can have many such device contexts open in Windows). In fact, we will use hDCScreen right away. Here, in the MouseMove event, we are supposed to be enabling the user to stretch a rectangle across the screen, enclosing the area that we are supposed to capture.

If you think about it, drawing such a rectangle means first erasing the previous rectangle (from the Anchor point to the OldCurrent point) and then drawing a new one (from the Anchor point to the new Current point). To make sure that we can erase our previous lines simply by drawing over them, we can make the drawing mode Not Pen (as we've seen previously, Not Pen makes the pen draw the inverse of what's on the screen). There is one pen per device context. As you might suspect, all Visual Basic objects that have pens are really Windows device contexts, and we can change the one in our screen device context to Not Pen with SetROP2(), whose name means "set binary raster operation." If we pass a value of 6 (this and other values can be found in the Windows documentation) to SetROP2(), we will indicate that we want to use the Not Pen for this device context:

```
Sub Form_MouseMove (Button As Integer, Shift As Integer, X As Single, Y As Single)

    Dim hDCScreen As Integer

    If CapFlag Then
    Current.X = X
    Current.Y = Y
    ClientToScreen hWnd, Current
    hDCScreen = CreateDC("DISPLAY", ByVal 0&, ByVal 0&, ByVal 0&)
    Dummy% = SetROP2(hDCScreen, 6)
        :
    End If
End Sub
```

Then we add SetROP2(()) to our module:

```
'Module --------------------------------

Type ApiPoint
    X As Integer
    Y As Integer
End Type

Declare Sub ClientToScreen Lib "User" (ByVal hWnd As Integer, lpPoint As ApiPoint)
Declare Function CreateDC Lib "GDI" (ByVal lpDriverName As String,
ByVal lpDeviceName As Any, ByVal lpOutPut As Any,
ByVal lpInitData As Any) As Integer
Declare Function SetROP2 Lib "GDI" (ByVal hDC As Integer,
ByVal nDrawMode As Integer) As Integer
```

SetROP2() returns the current value of the device context's pen, and it is usually a good idea to save that value before changing to a new pen so that you can change back afterward (that is, some other part of the program might not expect a Not Pen here). Here, however, we are going to destroy this device context before leaving this event procedure, so we just place the old pen value in a dummy variable and continue. Next, we should erase the old box that goes from (Anchor.X, Anchor.Y) to (OldCurrent.X, OldCurrent.Y). To do that, we can move to the anchor point with the Windows function MoveTo(), which works just like setting the CurrentX and CurrentY properties of an object (in fact, when you set those properties, that's exactly what Visual Basic is doing). Because all of our points are already stored in screen coordinates, we can move to the Anchor point like this:

```
Sub Form_MouseMove (Button As Integer, Shift As Integer, X As Single, Y As Single)

    Dim hDCScreen As Integer

    If CapFlag Then
    Current.X = X
    Current.Y = Y
    ClientToScreen hWnd, Current
    hDCScreen = CreateDC("DISPLAY", ByVal 0&, ByVal 0&, ByVal 0&)
    Dummy% = SetROP2(hDCScreen, 6)
    Dummy2& = MoveTo(hDCScreen, Anchor.X, Anchor.Y)
        :
    End If

End Sub
```

And we add MoveTo() to the module:

```
'Module --------------------------------

Type ApiPoint
    X As Integer
    Y As Integer
End Type

:
        :
Declare Function MoveTo Lib "GDI" (ByVal hDC As Integer,
ByVal X As Integer, ByVal Y As Integer) As Long
```

MoveTo() returns a long value—two 16-bit words—whose upper word holds the old y-coordinate and whose lower word holds the previous x-coordinate. Again, we will place that value in a dummy variable and continue. The next step is to erase the box, and we do that simply by drawing it with Not Pen, using the Windows LineTo() function like this:

```
Sub Form_MouseMove (Button As Integer, Shift As Integer, X As Single, Y As Single)

    Dim hDCScreen As Integer

    If CapFlag Then
    Current.X = X
    Current.Y = Y
    ClientToScreen hWnd, Current
    hDCScreen = CreateDC("DISPLAY", ByVal 0&, ByVal 0&, ByVal 0&)
    Dummy% = SetROP2(hDCScreen, 6)
    Dummy2& = MoveTo(hDCScreen, Anchor.X, Anchor.Y)
    Dummy% = LineTo(hDCScreen, OldCurrent.X, Anchor.Y)
    Dummy% = LineTo(hDCScreen, OldCurrent.X, OldCurrent.Y)
    Dummy% = LineTo(hDCScreen, Anchor.X, OldCurrent.Y)
```

```
        Dummy% = LineTo(hDCScreen, Ancho
                  :
        End If

End Sub
```

And we add `LineTo()` to our module:

```
'Module --------------------------------

Type ApiPoint
    X As Integer
    Y As Integer
End Type

    :
            :
Declare Function LineTo Lib "GDI" (ByVal hDC As Integer,
ByVal X As Integer, ByVal Y As Integer) As Integer
```

Now that the old box from `Anchor` to `OldCurrent` has been erased, we update the `OldCurrent` point (so that the next time the mouse moves, we will erase the box we are about to draw) like this:

```
Sub Form_MouseMove (Button As Integer, Shift As Integer, X As Single, Y As Single)

    Dim hDCScreen As Integer

    If CapFlag Then
    Current.X = X
    Current.Y = Y
    ClientToScreen hWnd, Current
    hDCScreen = CreateDC("DISPLAY", ByVal 0&, ByVal 0&, ByVal 0&)
    Dummy% = SetROP2(hDCScreen, 6)
    Dummy2& = MoveTo(hDCScreen, Anchor.X, Anchor.Y)
    Dummy% = LineTo(hDCScreen, OldCurrent.X, Anchor.Y)
    Dummy% = LineTo(hDCScreen, OldCurrent.X, OldCurrent.Y)
    Dummy% = LineTo(hDCScreen, Anchor.X, OldCurrent.Y)
    Dummy% = LineTo(hDCScreen, Anchor.X, Anchor.Y)
    OldCurrent.X = Current.X
    OldCurrent.Y = Current.Y
              :
    End If

End Sub
```

And now we can draw the new box from `Anchor` to `Current` this way:

```
Sub Form_MouseMove (Button As Integer, Shift As Integer, X As Single, Y As Single)

    Dim hDCScreen As Integer

    If CapFlag Then
    :
    :
    OldCurrent.X = Current.X
    OldCurrent.Y = Current.Y
    Dummy2& = MoveTo(hDCScreen, Anchor.X, Anchor.Y)
    Dummy% = LineTo(hDCScreen, Current.X, Anchor.Y)
    Dummy% = LineTo(hDCScreen, Current.X, Current.Y)
    Dummy% = LineTo(hDCScreen, Anchor.X, Current.Y)
```

```
        Dummy% = LineTo(hDCScreen, Anchor.X, Anchor.Y)
        :
        End If

End Sub
```

The final step is to destroy our screen device context, now that we don't need it any longer. We can do that with `DeleteDC()`:

```
Sub Form_MouseMove (Button As Integer, Shift As Integer, X As Single, Y As Single)

        Dim hDCScreen As Integer

        If CapFlag Then
        Current.X = X
        Current.Y = Y
        ClientToScreen hWnd, Current
        hDCScreen = CreateDC("DISPLAY", ByVal 0&, ByVal 0&, ByVal 0&)
        Dummy% = SetROP2(hDCScreen, 6)
        Dummy2& = MoveTo(hDCScreen, Anchor.X, Anchor.Y)
        Dummy% = LineTo(hDCScreen, OldCurrent.X, Anchor.Y)
        Dummy% = LineTo(hDCScreen, OldCurrent.X, OldCurrent.Y)
        Dummy% = LineTo(hDCScreen, Anchor.X, OldCurrent.Y)
        Dummy% = LineTo(hDCScreen, Anchor.X, Anchor.Y)
        OldCurrent.X = Current.X
        OldCurrent.Y = Current.Y
        Dummy2& = MoveTo(hDCScreen, Anchor.X, Anchor.Y)
        Dummy% = LineTo(hDCScreen, Current.X, Anchor.Y)
        Dummy% = LineTo(hDCScreen, Current.X, Current.Y)
        Dummy% = LineTo(hDCScreen, Anchor.X, Current.Y)
        Dummy% = LineTo(hDCScreen, Anchor.X, Anchor.Y)
        Dummy% = DeleteDC(hDCScreen)
        End If

End Sub
```

It is Important to Deallocate Windows Handles

If your Windows programs crash, one reason may be that you are not deallocating handles. If you do not delete the device context with `DeleteDC()` at the end of `MouseMove()` and keep allocating new device context handles when you enter the `MouseMove` event, Windows will soon run out of handle space in memory, and everything will come to a halt.

And, of course, we add `DeleteDC()` to our module as well:

```
'Module --------------------------------

Type ApiPoint
        X As Integer
        Y As Integer
End Type

:
        :
Declare Function DeleteDC Lib "GDI" (ByVal hDC As Integer) As Integer
```

At this point, we can already draw rectangles on the screen just by running our program, pressing the mouse button at some screen location, and dragging the resulting rectangle.

Now we are prepared to start work on the MouseUp event. When the user releases the mouse button, she wants us to capture the screen image that appears in the rectangle bounded by Anchor and Current. To do that, we will use the BitBlt() function, which lets us copy bitmaps.

The first thing in the MouseUp event is to check whether we are capturing screen data—that is, if CapFlag is True—and we check that like this:

```
Sub Form_MouseUp (Button As Integer, Shift As Integer, X As Single, Y As Single)

    If CapFlag Then
        :
    End If

End Sub
```

If so, then we are expected to capture the image, ending the capture process. We can set CapFlag to False:

```
Sub Form_MouseUp (Button As Integer, Shift As Integer, X As Single, Y As Single)

    If CapFlag Then
    CapFlag = 0
    :
    End If

End Sub
```

Next, we update the current point and get a device context handle to the screen again:

```
Sub Form_MouseUp (Button As Integer, Shift As Integer, X As Single, Y As Single)

    Dim hDCScreen As Integer

    If CapFlag Then

    CapFlag = 0
    Current.X = X
    Current.Y = Y
    ClientToScreen hWnd, Current
    hDCScreen = CreateDC("DISPLAY", ByVal 0&, ByVal 0&, ByVal 0&)
        :
    End If

End Sub
```

Now we have to erase the last rectangle left on the screen as a result of the last MouseMove event, and we do that like this:

```
Sub Form_MouseUp (Button As Integer, Shift As Integer, X As Single, Y As Single)

    Dim hDCScreen As Integer

    If CapFlag Then
```

```
        CapFlag = 0
        Current.X = X
        Current.Y = Y
        ClientToScreen hWnd, Current
        hDCScreen = CreateDC("DISPLAY", ByVal 0&, ByVal 0&, ByVal 0&)
        Dummy% = SetROP2(hDCScreen, 6)
        Dummy2& = MoveTo(hDCScreen, Anchor.X, Anchor.Y)
        Dummy% = LineTo(hDCScreen, OldCurrent.X, Anchor.Y)
        Dummy% = LineTo(hDCScreen, OldCurrent.X, OldCurrent.Y)
        Dummy% = LineTo(hDCScreen, Anchor.X, OldCurrent.Y)
        Dummy% = LineTo(hDCScreen, Anchor.X, Anchor.Y)
            :
        End If

End Sub
```

Now we are ready to copy the screen image to our form using the BitBlt() procedure. To use BitBlt(), we have to know the width of the bitmap we want to copy, which is the width Abs(Anchor.X - Current.X), and the height, which is Abs(Anchor.Y - Current.Y). In addition, we have to know the bitmap's upper-left coordinate in screen coordinates, and that looks like this:

```
Sub Form_MouseUp (Button As Integer, Shift As Integer, X As Single, Y As Single)

    Dim hDCScreen As Integer

    If CapFlag Then

    CapFlag = 0
    Current.X = X
    Current.Y = Y
    ClientToScreen hWnd, Current
    hDCScreen = CreateDC("DISPLAY", ByVal 0&, ByVal 0&, ByVal 0&)
    Dummy% = SetROP2(hDCScreen, 6)
    Dummy2& = MoveTo(hDCScreen, Anchor.X, Anchor.Y)
    Dummy% = LineTo(hDCScreen, OldCurrent.X, Anchor.Y)
    Dummy% = LineTo(hDCScreen, OldCurrent.X, OldCurrent.Y)
    Dummy% = LineTo(hDCScreen, Anchor.X, OldCurrent.Y)
        Dummy% = LineTo(hDCScreen, Anchor.X, Anchor.Y)
      MapWidth% = Abs(Anchor.X - Current.X)
      MapHeight% = Abs(Anchor.Y - Current.Y)
    If Anchor.X < Current.X Then
        UpperLeftX% = Anchor.X
    Else
        UpperLeftX% = Current.X
    End If
    If Anchor.Y < Current.Y Then
        UpperLeftY% = Anchor.Y
    Else
        UpperLeftY% = Current.Y
     End If
     :
    End If

End Sub
```

The last thing to do is to use BitBlt(), which takes arguments like this:

```
Declare Function BitBlt Lib "GDI" (ByVal hDestDC As Integer, ByVal X As Integer, _
        ByVal Y As Integer, ByVal nWidth As Integer, ByVal nHeight As Integer, _
```

```
    ByVal hSrcDC As Integer, ByVal XSrc As Integer, ByVal YSrc As Integer, _
    ByVal dwROP As Long) As Integer
```

In order, these arguments refer to the destination device context handle for the copied bitmap (which will simply be the hDC property of our form so that the bitmap will appear there), the new (x, y) location of the bitmap in the destination (which we can make (0, 0), that is, the upper left of our form), the width and height of the bitmap, the source device context handle (that is, hDCScreen), the location of the bitmap in the source device context, and a final argument that indicates what we want done with the bitmap (we will pass a value of &HCC0020, which indicates that we want the bitmap copied from the source to the destination—this value is also stored as the constant SRCCOPY in Win32api.txt). Finally, we delete our screen device context and we are done:

```
Sub Form_MouseUp (Button As Integer, Shift As Integer, X As Single, Y As Single)

    Dim hDCScreen As Integer

    If CapFlag Then
    CapFlag = 0
    Current.X = X
    Current.Y = Y
    ClientToScreen hWnd, Current
    hDCScreen = CreateDC("DISPLAY", ByVal 0&, ByVal 0&, ByVal 0&)
    Dummy% = SetROP2(hDCScreen, 6)
    Dummy2& = MoveTo(hDCScreen, Anchor.X, Anchor.Y)
    Dummy% = LineTo(hDCScreen, OldCurrent.X, Anchor.Y)
    Dummy% = LineTo(hDCScreen, OldCurrent.X, OldCurrent.Y)
    Dummy% = LineTo(hDCScreen, Anchor.X, OldCurrent.Y)
    Dummy% = LineTo(hDCScreen, Anchor.X, Anchor.Y)
    MapWidth% = Abs(Anchor.X - Current.X)
    MapHeight% = Abs(Anchor.Y - Current.Y)
    If Anchor.X < Current.X Then
        UpperLeftX% = Anchor.X
    Else
        UpperLeftX% = Current.X
    End If
    If Anchor.Y < Current.Y Then
        UpperLeftY% = Anchor.Y
    Else
        UpperLeftY% = Current.Y
    End If
    Dummy% = BitBlt(hDC, 0, 0, MapWidth%, MapHeight%, hDCScreen,
    UpperLeftX%, UpperLeftY%, &HCC0020)
    Dummy% = DeleteDC(hDCScreen)
    End If

End Sub
```

The final listing appears in Listing 17.1. We can see the operation of our screen capture program in Figure 17.2. In Figure 17.2 we've captured the project window of the Capture project. It is a success. We can capture any rectangular region of the screen with it.

Figure 17.2.
Our screen-capture program at work.

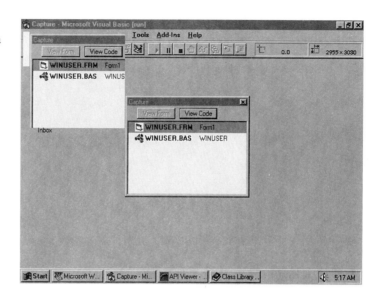

Listing 17.1. The screen-capture program.

```
Form Form1 ----------------------------------
Caption          =          "Screen Capture"

Capture.Bas ----------------------------------

Type ApiPoint
     X As Integer
     Y As Integer
End Type

Declare Sub ClientToScreen Lib "User" (ByVal hWnd As Integer, lpPoint As ApiPoint)
Declare Function CreateDC Lib "GDI" (ByVal lpDriverName As String, _
        ByVal lpDeviceName As Any, ByVal lpOutPut As Any, _
        ByVal lpInitData As Any) As Integer
Declare Function SetROP2 Lib "GDI" (ByVal hDC As Integer, _
        ByVal nDrawMode As Integer) As Integer
Declare Function MoveTo Lib "GDI" (ByVal hDC As Integer, _
        ByVal X As Integer, ByVal Y As Integer) As Long
Declare Function LineTo Lib "GDI" (ByVal hDC As Integer _,
        ByVal X As Integer, ByVal Y As Integer) As Integer
Declare Function DeleteDC Lib "GDI" (ByVal hDC As Integer) As Integer
Declare Function BitBlt Lib "GDI" (ByVal hDestDC As Integer, _
        ByVal X As Integer,
 ByVal Y As Integer, ByVal nWidth As Integer, _
        ByVal nHeight As Integer, ByVal hSrcDC As Integer, _
        ByVal XSrc As Integer,
 ByVal YSrc As Integer, ByVal dwROP As Long) _
        As Integer
```

continues

Listing 17.1. **continued**

```
'Form1 Form-level Declarations ----------------------------------
'Set Form ScaleMode to Pixel

Dim Anchor As ApiPoint
Dim Current As ApiPoint
Dim OldCurrent As ApiPoint
Dim CapFlag As Integer

'Form1 --------------------------------

Sub Form_Load ()

    CapFlag = 0

End Sub

Sub Form_MouseDown (Button As Integer, Shift As Integer, X As Single, Y As Single)

    Anchor.X = X
    Anchor.Y = Y
    ClientToScreen hWnd, Anchor
    OldCurrent.X = Anchor.X
    OldCurrent.Y = Anchor.Y
    CapFlag = -1          'True

End Sub

Sub Form_MouseMove (Button As Integer, Shift As Integer, X As Single, Y As Single)

    Dim hDCScreen As Integer

    If CapFlag Then
    Current.X = X
    Current.Y = Y
    hDCScreen = CreateDC("DISPLAY", ByVal 0&, ByVal 0&, ByVal 0&)
    ClientToScreen hWnd, Current
    Dummy% = SetROP2(hDCScreen, 6)
    Dummy2& = MoveTo(hDCScreen, Anchor.X, Anchor.Y)
    Dummy% = LineTo(hDCScreen, OldCurrent.X, Anchor.Y)
    Dummy% = LineTo(hDCScreen, OldCurrent.X, OldCurrent.Y)
    Dummy% = LineTo(hDCScreen, Anchor.X, OldCurrent.Y)
    Dummy% = LineTo(hDCScreen, Anchor.X, Anchor.Y)
    OldCurrent.X = Current.X
    OldCurrent.Y = Current.Y
    Dummy2& = MoveTo(hDCScreen, Anchor.X, Anchor.Y)
    Dummy% = LineTo(hDCScreen, Current.X, Anchor.Y)
    Dummy% = LineTo(hDCScreen, Current.X, Current.Y)
    Dummy% = LineTo(hDCScreen, Anchor.X, Current.Y)
    Dummy% = LineTo(hDCScreen, Anchor.X, Anchor.Y)
    Dummy% = DeleteDC(hDCScreen)
    End If

End Sub

Sub Form_MouseUp (Button As Integer, Shift As Integer, X As Single, Y As Single)
```

```
Dim hDCScreen As Integer

If CapFlag Then
CapFlag = 0
Current.X = X
Current.Y = Y
ClientToScreen hWnd, Current
hDCScreen = CreateDC("DISPLAY", ByVal 0&, ByVal 0&, ByVal 0&)
Dummy% = SetROP2(hDCScreen, 6)
Dummy2& = MoveTo(hDCScreen, Anchor.X, Anchor.Y)
Dummy% = LineTo(hDCScreen, OldCurrent.X, Anchor.Y)
Dummy% = LineTo(hDCScreen, OldCurrent.X, OldCurrent.Y)
Dummy% = LineTo(hDCScreen, Anchor.X, OldCurrent.Y)
Dummy% = LineTo(hDCScreen, Anchor.X, Anchor.Y)
MapWidth% = Abs(Anchor.X - Current.X)
MapHeight% = Abs(Anchor.Y - Current.Y)
If Anchor.X < Current.X Then
    UpperLeftX% = Anchor.X
    Else
    UpperLeftX% = Current.X
End If
If Anchor.Y < Current.Y Then
    UpperLeftY% = Anchor.Y
Else
    UpperLeftY% = Current.Y
End If
Dummy% = BitBlt(hDC, 0, 0, MapWidth%, MapHeight%,
    hDCScreen, UpperLeftX%, UpperLeftY%, &HCC0020)
Dummy% = DeleteDC(hDCScreen)
End If

End Sub
```

That's it for our exploration of connecting Visual Basic to the Windows system calls. Next, we will see how to connect Visual Basic to routines written in C.

Connecting Visual Basic to C

We can, of course, create our own dynamic link libraries. This is especially useful because it enables us to link C code that we already have into Visual Basic. In this section, you will see how to do this by constructing a sample C function named CInterface() (because you can use it as a C interface template, replacing its code with your own). To do that, we will use Microsoft's Visual C++ for Windows and keep the C programming to a minimum. Accordingly, the function CInterface() will only do something minimal. Let's have it accept a long integer argument and return the same long integer after incrementing it by one. After the C interface is all set up, of course, you can use your own C code for the body of this function.

In order to create a dynamic link library file, the C source file only needs to have three parts: a LibMain() function (note that in C, unlike Visual Basic, all procedures are functions) that performs whatever initialization we need, the externally callable functions that make up the library itself (here, only the function `CInterface()`), and a Windows exit procedure whose name must be `WEP()`. In fact, there is a default `WEP()` function in the Windows library already, and we will specify that we want to use that later. That leaves us with only two functions to write: `WinMain()` and `CInterface()`. We can put them in a file named Cuser.C and work on that file in Visual C++.

To start creating Cuser.C (and therefore our .dll file, Cuser.dll), we must include the C header file Windows.H, which we can do with the C preprocessor statement like this:

```
#include <Windows.H>
```

Next, we define the `LibMain()` function so that it accepts these arguments:

```
#include <Windows.H>

int FAR PASCAL LibMain(HANDLE hModule, WORD wDataSeg,
        WORD cbHeapSize, LPSTR lpszCmdLine)
{

}
```

In `LibMain()`, you can perform initialization for the rest of the functions in your dynamic link library (that is, treat it something like a `Form_Load` event), because it is called when the library is first loaded. To indicate that the initialization went successfully, you return a value of `TRUE` (which has the value `1` in Visual C++, not `-1` as in Visual Basic). Because we don't have to perform any initialization here, we will just return a value of `TRUE`:

```
#include <Windows.H>

int FAR PASCAL LibMain(HANDLE hModule, WORD wDataSeg,
        WORD cbHeapSize, LPSTR lpszCmdLine)
{
    return TRUE;
}
```

Next, we have to set up our function `CInterface()`. This function is supposed to take a long argument, which we can call `arg1`, and pass a long argument back, so we set it up like this:

```
#include <Windows.H>

int FAR PASCAL LibMain(HANDLE hModule, WORD wDataSeg,
        WORD cbHeapSize, LPSTR lpszCmdLine)
{
    return TRUE;
}

long FAR PASCAL CInterface(long arg1)
{

}
```

Our goal is simply to return `arg1 + 1`, so we can do that like this:

```
#include <Windows.H>

int FAR PASCAL LibMain(HANDLE hModule, WORD wDataSeg,
        WORD cbHeapSize, LPSTR lpszCmdLine)
{
```

```
        return TRUE;
}

long FAR PASCAL CInterface(long arg1)
{
        return (arg1+1);
}
```

And we are done with Cuser.C, which appears in Listing 17.2; that is all the C code we need for a dynamic link library. Note that real library functions are supposed to be bulletproof, so in a real library function, we'd have to check whether or not adding 1 to arg1 would cause an overflow and, if so, indicate that in some fashion.

Listing 17.2. Cuser.C.

```
#include <Windows.H>

int FAR PASCAL LibMain(HANDLE hModule, WORD wDataSeg,
        WORD cbHeapSize, LPSTR lpszCmdLine)
{
        return TRUE;
}

long FAR PASCAL CInterface(long arg1)
{
        return (arg1+1);
}
```

Visual C++ will also need a .def file in order to create a working dynamic link library (.dll) file. In that file, Cuser.def, we indicate with the following lines that we want to create a dynamic link library that can be used in Windows and that will operate in protected mode:

```
LIBRARY    CUSER

EXETYPE    WINDOWS

PROTMODE
   :
```

Next, we give Windows the capability to move our code and data around in memory as it requires and to allocate a small amount of memory for free usage by our code in a C-style heap:

```
LIBRARY    CUSER

EXETYPE    WINDOWS

PROTMODE

CODE       PRELOAD MOVEABLE DISCARDABLE
DATA       PRELOAD SINGLE
SEGMENTS   'WEP_TEXT' FIXED PRELOAD

HEAPSIZE   1024
   :
```

How to Get More Memory in Windows

Extra memory from the heap can be allocated for your program if you use the `LocalAlloc()`/ `GlobalAlloc()` set of Windows functions; it is inadvisable to use the traditional C `malloc()`/ `free()` functions in Windows.

Finally, we indicate that we want to use the default `WEP()` function and that we want to export (that is, make available to the rest of the Windows system) our function `CInterface()` like this:

```
LIBRARY    CUSER

EXETYPE    WINDOWS

PROTMODE

CODE       PRELOAD MOVEABLE DISCARDABLE
DATA       PRELOAD SINGLE
SEGMENTS 'WEP_TEXT' FIXED PRELOAD

HEAPSIZE 1024

EXPORTS
     WEP         @1 RESIDENTNAME
     CInterface  @2
```

And that's it for the .def file, which appears in Listing 17.3.

Listing 17.3. Cuser.def.

```
LIBRARY    CUSER

EXETYPE    WINDOWS

PROTMODE

CODE       PRELOAD MOVEABLE DISCARDABLE
DATA       PRELOAD SINGLE
SEGMENTS 'WEP_TEXT' FIXED PRELOAD

HEAPSIZE 1024

EXPORTS
     WEP         @1 RESIDENTNAME
     CInterface  @2
```

About Libraries that Include More than One Function

If your library includes more than just one function, list them under the `CInterface` line as `@3`, `@4`, and so on.

Visual C++ keeps track of which files to use in creating Cuser.dll by using a .mak file for the Cuser project, just as we would in Visual Basic. However, the C++ Cuser.mak file is more complex than the one for Visual Basic. This file indicates which Visual C++ files are used to create Cuser.dll, what linker and library options are required, and so on. And that's all there is to it; this is a very small project as .dll libraries go. To create the .mak file itself, you must use Visual C++ to create a new project and include the appropriate files (Cuser.C, Cuser.def) within it. Refer to the Visual C++ documentation for more information on creating .mak files.

Now that we have the three files Cuser.C, Cuser.def, and Cuser.mak, we can create Cuser.dll with Visual C++. To do that, simply load the Cuser project using the MSVC Project menu's Open… item to open Cuser.mak.

To make Cuser.dll, select the Project… item in the MSVC Options menu, indicating that you want to create a .dll file by clicking the correct buttons in the resulting window.

Finally, select the Build item in MSVC's Project menu, which creates Cuser.dll. Now we have created our own .dll file, ready to be used. To use it, place it in a directory that Windows will search for dynamic link libraries—c:\windows or c:\windows\system, for example.

The Visual Basic Part of the Code

Now start Visual Basic so that you can use our Cuser.dll library. Call the new Visual Basic project Vbcuser.mak for Visual Basic C user, giving Form1 the caption C Interface and setting its AutoRedraw property to True. Next, add a command button (Command1) and a text box (Text1).

We can use the command button to call CInterface(), and we can display the value we get back in the text box to make sure that it's incremented each time. Before doing anything else, we can declare the Cuser.dll function CInterface() in the module, Vbcuser.bas:

```
'Module -------------------------------

Declare Function CInterface Lib "Cuser.Dll" (ByVal x&) As Long
```

Next, we can declare a form-level variable called TheVal, initialize it to 1 in Form_Load, display it in the text box, and instruct the user to click the button to increment the displayed value:

```
Dim TheVal As Long

Sub Form_Load ()
    Print "Click the button to interface to C"
    Print "and increment the displayed value."
    TheVal = 1
    Text1.Text = Str$(TheVal)
End Sub
```

Now, when the user clicks the button Command1, we can call `CInterface()` to increment `TheVal` and display its new value like this:

```
Dim TheVal As Long

Sub Form_Load ()
     Print "Click the button to interface to C"
     Print "and increment the displayed value."
     TheVal = 1
     Text1.Text = Str$(TheVal)
End Sub

Sub Command1_Click ()
     TheVal = CInterface(TheVal)
     Text1.Text = Str$(TheVal)
End Sub
```

That's all there is to it. When the user runs the program, it displays a value of 1. When she clicks the button, we pass that 1 to `CInterface( )`, where it's incremented and passed back. Then we display the resulting 2 and so on; each time the user clicks the button, we call our .dll routine so that the displayed value is incremented. Of couse, you wouldn't ever really call a .dll that performs so simple a task however; I am illustrating the concept of making DLL calls. The final listing of vbcuser appears in Listing 17.4.

Listing 17.4. Vbw17cd4.txt.

```
Form Form1 --------------------------------
     Caption      =       "C Interface"

CommandButton Command1
     Caption      =       "Click Me"

TextBox Text1
     TabIndex     =       0

'Module ------------------------------

Declare Function CInterface Lib "Cuser.Dll" (ByVal x&) As Long

'Form1 Declarations ------------------------------

Dim TheVal As Long

'Form1 ------------------------------

Sub Form_Load ()
     Print "Click the button to interface to C"
     Print "and increment the displayed value."
     TheVal = 1
     Text1.Text = Str$(TheVal)
End Sub

Sub Command1_Click ()
     TheVal = CInterface(TheVal)
     Text1.Text = Str$(TheVal)
End Sub
```

That's all there is to creating our own .dll files, which let us link C code directly into Visual Basic. There is another way of communicating with the Windows API, however, that uses the extended capabilities of C++. This method makes use of the Microsoft Foundation Classes (MFC).

About the Microsoft Foundation Classes

Most active Windows programming work these days uses the object-oriented flavor of C, C++, and relies heavily on object classes. Fortunately for us, Microsoft has done a lot of work in this area and has created an extensive set of object classes for use in Windows programming. The company refers to this set of classes as the Microsoft Foundation Classes (MFC).

The MFC provides an application framework that provides all the code needed to support a Windows application using C++. (In fact, a judicious programmer can make the same MFC source code work for the Macintosh as well.) The app framework takes care of all the overhead you'd otherwise have to manage within a Windows application, which can be considerable.

Central to understanding the use of the MFC are the concepts of *classing* and *encapsulation*. Each MFC class represents a sort of definition for a particular kind of object—a window or a menu, for instance. Each class contains member functions that represent actions that can be performed on that object. These functions are thus conceptually similar to Visual Basic object methods. The classes themselves are arranged hierarchically; each class can be thought of as an instance of yet another class (except the first, or *foundation*, class), inheriting from that class certain general characteristics while adding new ones particular to its specific function.

Much of the MFC actually is intended to work with the Windows API. We say that the MFC *encapsulates* API functions; this means that the functions are presented and handled in object-oriented form. In practical terms, this means that much of the API grunge work, such as docking and undocking toolbars, is handled for you automatically.

Why is the MFC of importance to you as a Visual Basic programmer? For one thing, using it can simplify certain aspects of creating DLLs, as much of the overhead work is handled by the MFC class structure. The MFC also turns out to be quite handy when you want to create your own OLE custom controls, a subject we'll consider in depth in Chapter 19. The MFC is included as part of the OLE CDK, and includes a ControlWizard that uses the MFC to help you create custom controls easily.

You have come far in this chapter; you have seen how to use the vast wealth of Windows functions in the dynamic link libraries that come with Windows and how to create your own dynamic link libraries as well, including using MFC. In the next chapter, you will see how to extend Visual Basic even more when we start adding the custom controls that Microsoft supplies in the Visual Basic Professional Edition.

Summary

You have learned two major new skills: how to connect your programs both to the Windows library functions and to C code that you write yourself. In particular, we developed a screen-capture program that used the Windows library calls to do a number of things not usually allowed in Visual Basic, including drawing outside our window and copying graphics from the screen outside our window. By doing this, we created an interesting program, and you saw how to set up the interface to Windows library calls simply by declaring them to Visual Basic—in addition, you saw how to get a handle to the whole screen in Windows by referencing the Display object.

The Windows library functions are stored in dynamic link libraries. After you saw how to connect to such libraries, your next step was to write dynamic link libraries yourself so that you could connect your Visual Basic programs to some C code that you had written. You also saw how to pass parameters back and forth between C and Visual Basic. Together, these techniques augment Visual Basic tremendously—now you can call any Windows function you want (which means that if you can do it in Windows, you can do it in Visual Basic), and you can also interface to C, which is the language in which Windows programs are often written. A review of the new functions we explored appears below.

New Windows	Functions
BitBlt GDI library	Copies bitmaps between device contexts. The arguments are these: the destination device context handle for the copied bitmap, the new (x, y) location of the bitmap in the destination, the width and height of the bitmap, the source device context handle, the location of the bitmap in the source device context, and an argument that indicates what we want done with the bitmap (for example, a value of &HCC0020 indicates that we want the bitmap copied from the source to the destination—this value is also stored as the constant SRCCOPY in Winapi.txt). Use it like this: ```BitBlt(ByVal hDestDC As Integer, ByVal X As Integer, ByVal Y As Integer, _` ` ByVal nWidth As Integer, ByVal nHeight As Integer, _` ` ByVal hSrcDC As Integer, ByVal XSrc As Integer, _` ` ByVal YSrc As Integer, _` ` ByVal dwROP As Long) As Integer```
ClientToScreen	User library. Converts coordinates pointed to by lpPoint from client area to screen. Use it like this: ```ClientToScreen (ByVal hWnd As Integer, _` ` lpPoint As ApiPoint)```

CreateDC	GDI library. Creates a device context. Use it like this: ```CreateDC (ByVal lpDriverName As String,_ ByVal lpDeviceName As Any, ByVal lpOutPut As Any,_ ByVal lpInitData As Any) As Integer```
DeleteDC	GDI library. Deletes the device context whose handle you pass. Use it like this: ```DeleteDC (ByVal hDC As Integer) As Integer```
LineTo	GDI library. Draws a line from the current graphics position to (x, y). Use it like this: ```LineTo (ByVal hDC As Integer, ByVal X As Integer, ByVal Y As Integer) As Integer```
MoveTo	GDI library. Sets the location of the current graphics position. Use it like this: ```MoveTo (ByVal hDC As Integer, ByVal X As Integer, ByVal Y As Integer) As Long```

New Windows Functions

SetROP2	GDI library. Sets binary raster drawing operation for a device context. Use it like this: ```SetROP2 (ByVal hDC As Integer, ByVal nDrawMode As Integer) As Integer```

18

Using Custom Controls

If you want to do something with Visual Basic that was not originally designed into the programming environment—for example, generate reports based on database information or add a video clip—you can probably find a third-party custom control that will add the functionality you need. There are hundreds of third-party controls on the market, and adding them to your Visual Basic projects is easy. This chapter will show you how to install custom controls and discuss the third-party controls that ship with Visual Basic's Professional and Enterprise Editions. The topics covered in this chapter include

- A custom control overview
- Updating the Notepad to show key status
- 3-D buttons
- The common dialog control revisited
- The Sheridan Tabbed Dialog control (Tabctl32.ocx)
- Using older .vbx custom controls with Visual Basic 4 and Windows 95

Microsoft provides a series of professional-level controls in the Visual Basic Professional and Enterprise Editions. Customized controls can augment the controls already available in Visual Basic, dramatically extending project development and flexibility. The Professional and Enterprise Editions also include the OLE Custom Development Kit (OLE CDK) for creating your own custom controls. Creating custom controls will be discussed in depth in the next chapter.

This chapter discusses and demonstrates some of the custom controls that come with Visual Basic 4, including the key status control, 3-D buttons, and the pre-written dialog boxes (called common dialog boxes) that will let you pop font, file open, file save, and color selection dialog boxes on the screen from a single control. (The file open aspect of this control was discussed in Chapter 8.) These new controls will be put to use upgrading one of the programs from Chapter 9; the Editor application will be updated, making use of the key status control to show what state the keyboard is in.

About Custom Controls

The focus of this chapter is on the Professional and Enterprise Editions' custom controls. You'll find that using them is as simple as using other controls in Visual Basic. (In fact, you used several of these controls already, such as the animated button control in Chapter 9 and the common dialog control in Chapter 8.) To use a custom control that is in your Visual Basic toolbox, just select the custom control you want to use, draw it on the form, and then add the appropriate Visual Basic code for it. Some controls, such as the key status control, don't even require code to be useful.

16- and 32-Bit OLE Custom Controls

Previously, Visual Basic custom controls came in files with the extension .vbx. For Visual Basic 4, Microsoft has migrated to a new control standard—.ocx. These OLE custom controls generally come in two flavors: a 16-bit version and a 32-bit version. There are .ocx versions of all the custom .vbx controls found in Visual Basic 3.0. In addition to taking advantage of Microsoft's OLE architecture, .ocx controls are more powerful because they can be used in any application capable of containing an OLE object.

Visual Basic 4's Professional and Enterprise Editions come with 22 custom controls, ranging from fancy 3-D command buttons to a control for loading and playing multimedia files. Some of the .ocx files containing these controls actually contain a group of related controls. For example, The Sheridan 3D Controls (Threed16.ocx or Threed32.ocx) contains a group of 3-D button controls, including a command button, panel, and check box.

Table 18.1 lists many of the custom controls included in the Professional and Enterprise Editions of Visual Basic.

Table 18.1. Professional/Enterprise Edition custom controls by file (32-bit versions).

Custom Control	File	Description
Crystal Report Control	Crystl32.ocx	This control is actually two items rolled up in one. First, Crystal Reports is a powerful Windows report writer that you can use to design reports for your application's users. Second, the Crystal Custom Control is a set of tools that lets you build the connection between your application and the print engine. For more information, see VB's online help under "Crystal Custom Control for Visual Basic."
Desaware Animated Button Control	Anibtn32.ocx	This control is a button that can have multiple faces loaded in as frames. (See the sample application in Chapter 9.)

continues

Table 18.1. continued

Custom Control	File	Description
Microhelp Gauge	Gauge32.ocx	The gauge control creates user-defined gauges with a choice of linear (filled) or needle styles.
Microhelp Key State Control	Keysta32.ocx	Key status control—shows state of Caps Lock, Num lock, and so on.
Microsoft Comm Control	Mscomm32.ocx	The communications control provides serial communications for your application by allowing the transmission and reception of data through a serial port.
Microsoft Common Dialog Control	Comdlg32.ocx	Common dialog box control. (See Chapter 8.)
Microsoft Data Bound List Control	Dblist32.ocx	This .ocx contains two controls: DBList and DBCombo. The DBList and DBCombo controls are different from the standard ListBox and ComboBox controls in that they are automatically filled from a recordset instead of through the use of the `AddItem` method.
Microsoft Grid Control	Grid32.ocx	The grid control displays a series of rows and columns; the intersection of a row and column is a cell. The contents of each cell can be read and set in code.
Microsoft MAPI Controls	Msmapi32.ocx	The Messaging Application Program Interface (MAPI) controls enable you to create a mail-enabled Visual Basic MAPI application. There are

Custom Control	File	Description
		two MAPI custom controls contained in this .ocx: MAPI Session and MAPI Messages. The MAPI Session control establishes a MAPI session, and the MAPI Messages control then enables the user to perform a variety of messaging system functions.
Microsoft Masked Edit Control	Msmask32.ocx	The masked edit control provides restricted data input as well as formatted data output.
Microsoft Multimedia Control	Mci32.ocx	The multimedia MCI control manages the recording and playback of multimedia files on Media Control Interface (MCI) devices. (This control is discussed in Chapter 20.)
Microsoft Outline Control	Msoutl32.ocx	The outline control is a special type of list box that displays items in a hierarchical list. This is useful for showing directories and files in a file system.
Microsoft Picture Clip Control	Picclip32.ocx	The picture clip control allows the programmer to select an area of a source bitmap and then display the image of that area in a form or picture box.
Microsoft Rich Text Box Control	Richtx32.ocx	The RichTextBox control allows the user to enter and edit text while also providing more advanced formatting features than the conventional TextBox control.

continues

Table 18.1. continued

Custom Control	File	Description
Microsoft Windows Common Controls	Comctl32.ocx	Windows 95 controls, including a progress bar, toolbar, and tabstrip. This group of controls is discussed in Chapter 3.
Microsoft RemoteData Control	Msrdc32.ocx	This control provides access to data stored in a remote ODBC data source. The RemoteData control enables you to move from row to row in a result set and to display and manipulate data from the rows in data-bound controls.
Outrider Spin Button Control	Spin32.ocx	The spin button control is a spinner control you can use with another control to increment and decrement numbers. It can also be used to scroll back and forth through a range of values or a list of items.
Pinnacle - BPS Graph Control	Graph32.ocx	The graph control lets you design graphs interactively on your forms. At run-time, new data can be sent to the graphs; the user can also draw graphs, print them, copy them onto the Clipboard, or change graph styles and shapes.
Sheridan 3D Controls	Threed32.vbx	This .ocx contains a group of 3-D controls, including a check box, panel, option button, and pushbutton.

Custom Control	File	Description
Sheridan Tabbed Dialog Control	Tabctl32.ocx	This custom control sets up tabbed pages that can be styled to look exactly like those found in Windows 95.

For more information on any of the custom controls, look in Visual Basic's online help.

Remember that the custom controls that ship with Visual Basic are only the tip of the iceberg. There are hundreds of third-party controls available in the marketplace designed for specific programming needs. To find out about available custom controls, check out the vendors' support forums available on CompuServe. Also, magazines devoted to Visual Basic and Windows 95 programming are a good source for information.

Installing Custom Controls

Although some of the Professional and Enterprise Editions' custom controls are preloaded for you when you begin a new project, not all of them are. Consequently, before you can use a custom control you must make sure that it has been loaded into your Visual Basic project. Add custom controls using the Custom Control dialog box, which is accessed using the Tools menu. Figure 18.1 shows the Custom Controls dialog box.

Figure 18.1.
Adding custom controls to the current project using the Custom Controls dialog box.

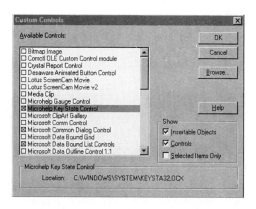

For controls that are already included in a project, the check box next to the control's name is filled in with an X. To add a control not currently available, simply find its name and check the box. If you have installed a control onto your system but do not see it on the Available Controls list, use the Browse button to locate the file. You should know that a custom control that is added to a project will appear only in that project. If you want a certain custom control automatically added to every new project, you will need to modify the Autoload.vbp file found in your Visual Basic directory.

How to Set Up Automatic Loading of .ocx Files

You can change what OLE Control files are automatically loaded when Visual Basic starts a new project by changing the Auto32ld.vbp file (for 32-bit projects) or Autoload.vbp (for 16-bit projects) in your Visual Basic directory.

To add or remove an .ocx from the autoload procedure, start Visual Basic and select Open from the File menu. Move to the directory where Visual Basic resides on your system and then select either Auto32ld.vbp (for 32-bit projects) or Autoload.vbp (for 16-bit projects). After you have selected either of these files, click OK in the Open dialog box. The Auto32ld application opens. Now add or delete custom controls to this application as you would in any of your projects. Using the Custom Controls dialog box accessed through Tools | Custom Controls…, select the controls to delete or add. When you are finished, click OK. Save the project, and then exit it by starting a new project. The controls that you added or deleted from the autoload procedure are now automatically added to (or have been removed from) the default toolbox.

Distributing Applications with Custom Controls

When you add a custom control to a project, you don't actually add the control's code. You are simply establishing access to the control from within your Visual Basic project. Although this saves disk space, because only one copy of the control is needed on your computer no matter how many programs it's used in, it means that you must take special steps when you distribute any application that uses this custom control.

Why do you have to distribute the control? Well, the target machine might not have the control loaded onto its system. Generally, a target machine will have only the appropriate file if the Visual Basic 4 Professional or Enterprise Editions are installed, or if another installed application uses the control. So, when you distribute a custom-control based on a Visual Basic 4 application, you must include the appropriate .ocx file(s) with the installation. These files have to be installed in the target computers, usually in the Windows\System directory or in a directory created for your application. This is discussed in detail along with setup programs in Chapter 22.

Custom Control Examples

Although this chapter cannot demonstrate every custom control that is listed in Table 18.1—that would be rather lengthy—several custom controls are discussed. You will find that the general principles involved in these examples apply to the use of most custom controls. (Also, several of the controls listed in Table 18.1 are discussed elsewhere in the book.)

Updating the Notepad Application Using Key Status Controls

The first custom control example involves Microhelp's Key State Control (Keysta32.ocx). You might recall that you developed an updated Editor application in Chapter 9. Using this project and the custom control, you will add a few easy-to-read key state indicators to the right side of the Editor form.

Start Visual Basic and open the Editor3 project. Next, add the Microhelp Key State Control, using the Custom Controls... dialog box found under Tools | Custom Controls. When you add the control to the Editor application, the project's toolbox stretches to accommodate the new tool, as shown in Figure 18.2.

Figure 18.2.
The Microhelp Key State
Control added to the toolbox.

To add the key state controls to the Editor form, stretch the form to the right, making it wider. Double-click the Key Status tool in the toolbox to add the control to the form. A default-sized Key State control appears in the middle of the form. Move that first Key State control to the right of the text box. Add two more Key State controls in the same way, positioning them in a column below the first one. When you are finished, your form should look something like the one shown in Figure 18.3.

Figure 18.3.
The three Key State controls
added to the Editor form.

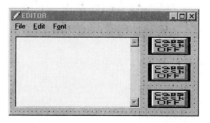

By default, each key state control shows the Caps Lock state; if you were to run this program, each key state control would change automatically as the Caps Lock state toggled, alternately showing Caps Lock ON and Caps Lock OFF. However, three controls doing the same thing is a little repetitive; these controls can be set to watch other key states as well.

As you might expect, each custom control comes with its own set of properties and methods. Most custom controls support a standard set of properties and methods. Some standard properties include Caption, DragIcon, DragMode, Enabled, FontName, Height, hWnd (window handle), Index (for control arrays), Left, MousePointer, Name, TabIndex, TabStop, Tag, Top, Visible, and Width. Some standard methods include Click, DragOver, GotFocus, KeyDown, KeyPress, KeyUp, LostFocus, MouseDown, MouseUp, MouseMove, and Move. Not all custom controls support every one of these properties and methods, but most will. To see all the properties for a new control that are available at design-time, you can check the Properties window; the properties for the Key State control are shown in Figure 18.4. (To see all the methods for a custom control, look in the Code window.)

Figure 18.4.
The Key State control's properties.

Change the middle Key State control from 0-Caps Lock to 1-Num Lock, using its Style property, as shown in Figure 18.5.

Figure 18.5.
Setting the Key State control's Style property.

Now, set the bottom Key State control's Style property to 3-Scroll Lock. Finally, set the AutoSize property for all three Key State controls to True.

That's all there is to it! There is no code involved in operating these three controls. Run the Editor3 application and try out the Key State controls by pressing the Caps Lock, Num Lock, and Scroll Lock buttons on your keyboard. (See Figure 18.6.)

Figure 18.6.
The Editor application and its three Key State controls in action.

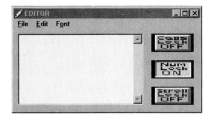

Buttons with a 3-D Appearance

There is an entire series of Sheridan Software 3-D controls in Visual Basic's Professional and Enterprise Editions, and they are all packed into the file Threed32.ocx. The 3-D controls appear in the toolbox as shown in Figure 18.7. They include a 3-D check box, 3-D command button, 3-D frame, 3-D option button, 3-D panel, and 3-D group pushbutton.

Figure 18.7.
The Sheridan 3D controls.

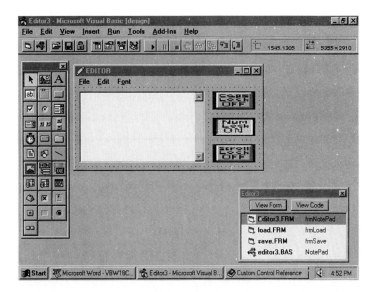

By using these controls, you can create some good 3-D effects. For example, the 3-D panel can give the appearance of a panel that is slightly or greatly raised (or lowered) from the surface of your window. Using this panel, you can set text or graphics off nicely. In addition, these controls support a 3-D font.

There are other types of buttons in Visual Basic's Professional and Enterprise Editions as well. Some have been used in previous chapters. For example, in Chapter 9, the Moon Phase application used the Desaware Animated Button Control (Anibtn32.ocx) to display a series of pictures that created an animation using a timer.

About Prewritten Dialog Boxes

Visual Basic 4 provides you with five prewritten dialog boxes in the Comdlg32.ocx—Common Dialog Box—custom control. (The open file version of this dialog box was used in Chapter 8.) These dialog boxes are shown in Table 18.2.

Table 18.2. The Common Dialog control `Action` property values.

Dialog Box	Action Property Values
None	0
File Open Dialog	1
File Save Dialog	2
Color Selection Dialog	3
Font Selection Dialog	4
Print Dialog	5
Show Winhelp.exe	6

(The Common Dialog `Action` property returns or sets the type of dialog box to be displayed and is available only at run-time.)

The Common Dialog `Action` Properties

With Visual Basic 4, the `Action` properties can be accessed with greater ease using the following methods: `ShowOpen`, `ShowSave`, `ShowFont`, `ShowColor`, `ShowPrinter`, and `ShowHelp`. These updated methods are discussed in Chapter 8.

Common Dialog Boxes and Flags

By setting the `Action` property using the values from Table 18.2 like this:

```
object.Action = [value]
```

you can tell the Common Dialog control which dialog box to display.

Each kind of dialog box—such as File Open, Color Selection, and Print—uses different flags to set the options used in that dialog box. These flags can be easily found using either of two tools: VB's online Help (look under the "Flags" topic and then select the type of dialog box you are interested in) or the Object Browser found under the View menu (select MSComDlg in the Libraries/Projects list box).

For example, here are a few flags that a Font dialog can use:

Flag	VB Constant	Integer Value	Hex Value
Makes the dialog box list the available printer and screen fonts.	cdlCFBoth	3	&H3&
Specifies that the dialog box enables strikethrough, underline, and color effects.	cdlCFEffects	256	&H100&
Specifies that the dialog box allows only the selection of scalable fonts.	cdlCFScalableOnly	131072	&H20000&
Specifies that the dialog box allows only the selection of TrueType fonts.	cdlCFTTOnly	262144	&H40000&

If you wanted to set several of the font flags' constants in code, you would use the Or connector like this:

```
CommonDialog1.Flags = cdlCFBoth Or cdlCFEffects Or cdlCFTTOnly
CommonDialog1.Action = 4      'sets the control as a Font dialog
```

Or you could add up all the integer values and set the same three flags like this:

```
CommonDialog1.Flags = 262403
CommonDialog1.Action = 4      'sets the control as a Font dialog
```

To set the flags at run-time, use the Common Dialog control's Custom property. Select the tab for the type of dialog box that you would like to use, and then type in the flag's combined integer value into the Flags text box.

Using Common Dialogs to Display Windows Help

Note in particular that if you set a Common Dialog control's Action property to 6, it displays Windows help— Winhelp.exe. This is a useful asset to many Windows programs, especially if you have a Windows help (.hlp) file ready for your program (this will be discussed in Chapter 21).

The Common Dialog Demo application featured in Chapter 8 uses many of these techniques—the Action property, flags, and constants.

The Sheridan Tabbed Dialog Control (Tabctl32.ocx)

The Sheridan Tabbed Dialog control is a very useful addition to Visual Basic 4 for use with Windows 95. This control provides a way to let the user select from among related options within the context of a single form or dialog box. Windows 95 makes extensive use of the tab metaphor in its user interface. An example of this is shown in Figure 18.8.

Figure 18.8.
A tab control used in Windows 95.

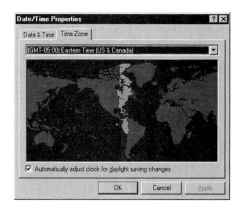

In the Windows 95 Control Panel and elsewhere, the tab control is used to group related options. This is especially useful when there are many related control options to set. Presenting them all at once on a single form can be overwhelming to the user. Instead, the options can be sorted into broad groups and displayed on a single tab page. You can display either an image or a caption or both on a tab, as well as set its appearance. The tab tool itself, once drawn on a form, acts as a container for other controls. It is really very easy to use this control. Why not check it out?

Start a new Visual Basic project and add the Sheridan Tabbed Dialog control (Tabctl32.ocx) to your toolbox using the Custom Controls... item found on the Tools menu. When the control has been added to the toolbox, double-click it to create a default-sized tabbed dialog control. You can then resize the control so it looks like the one in Figure 18.9.

Notice that the control default is set to three tabs—Tab 0, Tab 1, and Tab 2. Even at design-time, the tabs are already operational. Click one of the tabs that does not have focus to give it focus, and bring it to the front of the tab group.

Figure 18.9.
A Sheridan Tabbed Dialog control dropped on a form.

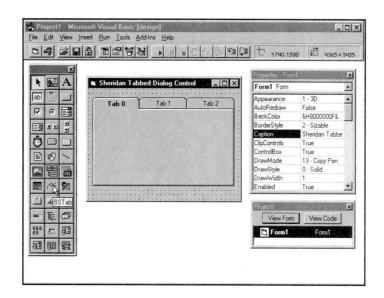

There are several properties that quickly give this tab control a customized, professional appearance. The following summarizes some of these properties:

Property	Description
ForeColor	Sets the tabs' font color.
Picture	Adds an image to the tab that is selected.
Style	Sets the way the tabs look. There are two settings for this property: `0-MS Office Tabbed Dialog` and `1-Windows 95 Property Page`.
TabHeight	Sets the tabs' height.
TabMaxWidth	Sets the tabs' maximum width.
TabOrientation	Determines where the tabs appear on the dialog box. There are four settings for this property: `0-Tabs on Top`, `1-Tabs on Bottom`, `2-Tabs on Left`, and `3-Tabs on Right`.
Tabs	Sets the number of tabs shown in the dialog box.
TabsPerRow	Sets the number of tabs allowed per row.

Click the `Style` property and check out the two possible settings. Change the number of tabs from the default of 3 and change the number of tabs available per row. Play with the other properties and see what you can come up with.

The tabbed dialog control lets you quickly and easily match the tabbed dialogs found in both Windows 95 and Microsoft Office interfaces. This gives your programs a look and response that is consistent with other professional Windows 95 applications.

About Backward Compatibility: Using .vbx Controls with Visual Basic 4

As a final thought regarding custom controls in Visual Basic, the continued viability of .vbx controls should be considered. This isn't really about using existing Microsoft controls such as the common dialog control; all of these have been updated to the new OLE Control standard. Instead, this refers to existing third-party controls written under the old .vbx format.

Many developers have a great deal of work (and money!) invested in their .vbx controls, and were upset when Microsoft changed the rules of the game by switching to the OLE Control standard. Not that this was done without warning: Microsoft has been advocating OLE and telling the world of their intentions for OLE custom controls for years. Still, many developers have continued to worry about the viability of their products in the new OLE custom-control Windows 95 world.

The good news is that programmers invested in .vbx technology do not need to panic—yet. Existing .vbx-based custom controls can be used with Windows 95 and with Visual Basic 4, with one provision: The programmer will have to use the 16-bit version of Visual Basic 4 and produce 16-bit applications. (.vbxs were created before 32-bit PC operating systems were a reality, and can't work within a 32-bit application context.) For the developer, Microsoft has included control wizards in the OLE CDK to assist with migrating existing .vbx controls to the new OLE Control format. While using .vbxs with Windows 95 is possible for now, Microsoft is making no promises for future versions of its operating systems. Developers had best move to the OLE control standard as soon as they can.

As you can see, custom controls can be very useful; there is a rich set of resources here, ready for use by the Visual Basic programmer. In fact, custom controls are not only useful, they can even be designed by the programmer—you! That is exactly what the next chapter is all about.

Summary

This chapter took a look at the many third-party custom controls that ship with the Professional and Enterprise Editions of Visual Basic 4. In particular, the chapter focused on the Key State control, 3-D controls, the common dialog control, and the tabbed dialog control.

These controls are only a few of the myriad custom controls available in the Visual Basic marketplace. Instead of having to work around a specific project development problem because Visual Basic does not include a particular functionality, a third-party control can most likely be found and used to surmount the problem. Whether you want to add the look of Windows 95 to your applications, generate Database reports, link lists, create an on-line help system, or add fax capabilities to your projects—with third-party custom controls, you can do it!

New Properties	Description
Action	CMDialog property that determines what kind of dialog box appears. See Table 18.2 for the available choices.
DialogTitle	Holds the title to be used in a common dialog box control.
FileName	Holds the filename in file-oriented common dialog controls.
Flags	Set of flags used to communicate with CMDialog controls. See Chapter 8 for a complete list.
Font3D	Holds the 3-D font setting for 3-D button controls.
Frame	Holds the current frame of an Animated Button control; animation occurs when you flip through these frames.
Style	Sets the desired key for a Key State control.

19

Creating Custom Controls

In this chapter, I'll expand the discussion of custom controls from the previous chapter to show you how to create custom controls of your own. Topics covered include

- Designing a new control for Visual Basic
- What it takes to support a control in Visual Basic
- Designing a control's toolbox bitmap
- Using a new control
- VBXs versus OLE Controls (OCXs)
- About the OLE CDK

Here I'm actually going to create and implement a custom control for Visual Basic, just like the key status control or a 3-D command button from the preceding chapter. Along the way, you'll see how the process of writing and supporting such a new control works in code. With the programming done, anyone will be able to add the new control to the Visual Basic toolbox; Visual Basic programmers will be able to double-click the tool and draw its control on a form. The newly drawn control will have its own events and properties, each fully supported by Visual Basic. Properties will appear in the Properties window to be set at design-time or in code.

You can see the inherent power behind this way of programming—you can design a custom control to accomplish almost any important task, such as encrypting files, searching entire hard disks for data, supporting pop-up help—the sky's the limit. The real beauty is that after you've created a working control, you can then incorporate it into any Visual Basic project where its services might be required, saving you a lot of programming time on subsequent projects because you won't find yourself reinventing the wheel. And your custom control's usability needn't be limited to your own projects. There is a thriving market for such add-on controls for Visual Basic; you might find yourself with a marketable, as well as useful, tool on your hands.

Note: Note that this chapter's examples are written almost entirely in C, which is the standard development language in Windows when you want to go past what's possible in Visual Basic. Refer to Chapter 17, "Linking to C and to Windows Directly," for more information on working with C in a Visual Basic context.

For purposes of introducing you to the inner workings of a custom control, I'm going to take you through the long way of creating such a control. Later in this chapter, I'll introduce you to a part of the Visual Basic Professional Edition that makes custom control creation considerably easier.

Creating a Custom Control

Now it's time to see how to create custom Visual Basic controls, just like the ones used in the previous chapter. The result will be a new custom control file—an .ocx file—that a user can add to programs simply by using Visual Basic's Custom Control... command in the Tools menu. When the user adds the .ocx file, the new control will be added as a tool in the toolbox.

Before beginning, though, you'll need some additional software. This chapter relies on the Visual Basic *Object Linking and Embedding Custom Development Kit* (OLE CDK), which is included in the Visual Basic Professional Edition. You will also need a package that can create dynamic link libraries, such as Microsoft Visual C++ (used in Chapter 17). It will also be handy to have the Windows 95 Software Development Kit (SDK). With all that in mind, I'll now show you how to start designing a custom control.

A Simple Control Example

Let's create a control to draw a simple geometrical figure—for example, a box. It would seem logical to call it a box control. The control will draw a box, either colored blue or left blank, within the bounds of the tool on a form. The box will be slightly smaller than the control, allowing for room for the user to click inside and outside of it. The box control will also register when a user clicks on it, determining whether the click came inside the box or outside of it (but still on the control). Not terribly useful, perhaps, but it will illustrate the process of creating a control without introducing too many programming complications.

To begin, I'll define a custom property for this control—let's say `BoxColor`—that specifies whether the box in the center of the control will be colored or left blank (that is, white). That is, if `Box1.BoxColor` is set to `True` (at design-time or at run-time), the box in the center of the control will be colored blue. The finished box tool will also determine whether the user clicked the control, and if she did, whether she clicked inside the box. This leads to two new custom events, `ClickInside` (the box) and `ClickOutside` (of the box but still inside the control), that might be used this way in a Visual Basic program:

```
Sub Box1_ClickOutside ( )
    'Visual Basic code
End Sub

Sub Box1_ClickInside ( )
    'Visual Basic code
End Sub
```

For example, the program could beep once if the user clicks outside of the box (but still in the control) and twice if she clicks inside the box. The code to make this work looks like this:

```
Sub Box1_ClickOutside ( )
     Beep
End Sub

Sub Box1_ClickInside ( )
     Beep
     Beep
End Sub
```

For the preceding Visual Basic code to work, I have to make a file called Box.ocx, the custom control file that lets the user create box controls. Obviously, I can't just pop out to the Windows desktop and create a new file named Box.ocx. In fact, to make Box.ocx, six files are required, which must then be compiled using Visual C++. The relevant files are as follows:

- Init.C—Initializes and registers the control with Visual Basic
- Box.C—The control's event and message handler
- Box.H—Header file: holds prototypes and variable declarations
- Box.Rc—Holds bitmap information for the control's toolbox bitmaps
- Box.Def—Specifies creation of a Windows DLL library
- Makefile—Used by Visual C++ to produce Box.ocx

The logical place to start is with Init.C, which holds the initialization code for the Box custom control.

Initializing and Registering a Control

The first step in setting up a custom control is to register its properties and events with Visual Basic using VBRegisterModel( ); this is what happens in the program Init.C. The required information is passed in a series of structures: properties in a PROPINFO structure, events in an EVENTINFO structure, and the two combined in a MODEL structure that is passed to VBRegisterModel( ). (By the way, the word *model* here refers to the class of control being registered.) We'll look at each of the structures in turn in the next few sections of this chapter.

Registering a Property

Information about the Box control's BoxColor property is contained in a PROPINFO structure, which looks like this:

```
typedef struct tagPROPINFO
{
     PSTR    npszName;      /* Property name                    */
     FLONG   fl;            /* PF_ flags                        */
     BYTE    offsetData;    /* Offset into structure            */
     BYTE    infoData;      /* 0 or _INFO value for bitfield    */
     LONG    dataDefault;   /* 0 or _INFO value for bitfield    */
     PSTR    npszEnumList;  /* NULL or a near ptr to a string   */
```

```
/* containing values for prop. listbox */
    BYTE    enumMax;      /* Maximum legal value for enum.    */
}
PROPINFO;
```

The second field, f1, holds the flags that tell Visual Basic how this property acts; the available flags appear in Table 19.1. This table shows that it's possible to create properties that are only accessible at run-time, or that cannot be changed at run-time, and so on. You might also note from looking at the table that Visual Basic will communicate with the tool itself in a series of messages (each of which has the prefix VBM_). This means the tool will be processing both normal Windows messages (WM_ messages) and Visual Basic messages (VBM_ messages). Windows itself communicates by sending messages to an application. Visual Basic also uses its own set of messages to communicate with the OCX. I'll have more to say about Visual Basic messages later in this chapter.

Table 19.1. **Visual Basic property flags.**

Property Flag	Means
DT_HSZ	Property is a string.
DT_SHORT	Property is a short.
DT_LONG	Property is a long.
DT_BOOL	Property is a Boolean.
DT_COLOR	Property is a color value.
DT_ENUM	Property is an enumeration.
DT_REAL	Property is a real value.
DT_XPOS	Property is x coordinate in twips.
DT_XSIZE	Property is x size in twips.
DT_YPOS	Property is y coordinate in twips.
DT_YSIZE	Property is y size in twips.
DT_PICTURE	Property is a picture.
PF_fPropArray	Property is an array (must use DATASTRUCT to get or set property values).
PF_fSetData	Set property by setting data in programmer-supplied data structure.
PF_fSetMsg	VBM_SETPROPERTY when attempting to set property.
PF_fNoShow	Do not show property in the Properties window.
PF_fNoRuntimeW	Property is read-only at run-time.
PF_fGetData	Get property value from programmer-supplied data.
PF_fGetMsg	VBM_GETPROPERTY message is sent when property value is requested.
PF_fSetCheck	VBM_SETPROPERTY message is sent before property is set.

continues

Table 19.1. **continued**

Property Flag	Means
PF_fSaveData	Save property setting along with form when file is saved to disk.
PF_fSaveMsg	VBM_SAVEPROPERTY/VBM_LOADPROPERTY sent when property value is saved or loaded to/from file.
PF_fGetHszMsg	VBM_GETPROPERTYHSZ sent when property value is displayed in the Properties window.
PF_fUpdateOnEdit	Property is updated as characters are typed in the Settings box of the Properties window.
PF_fEditable	Enable programmer to edit text in Settings box.
PF_fPreHwnd	Load property before control's window structure is created.
PF_fDefVal	Avoid saving and loading property to and from disk when it is equal to dataDefault in the PROPINFO structure.
PF_fNoInitDef	Do not load property from dataDefault in PROPINFO when loading control.

In the case of the Box control, I'll make the BoxColor property a short value. To keep track of all of the Box control's properties (such as BoxColor), I'll set up a BOX structure, something like this:

```
typedef struct tagBOX
{
    RECT    rectDrawRegion;
    SHORT   BoxColor;
} BOX;
```

Here, I store both the box's dimensions and the current value of BoxColor inside the BOX's structure. I place the BOX structure's definition in the file Box.H, the header file that holds C function proto-types and variable definitions. The RECT type in the preceding definition is actually the Windows rectangle type, in which I can store the dimensions of the box. The definition for this structure is as follows:

```
typedef struct tagRECT
    {
    int    left;
    int    top;
    int    right;
    int    bottom;
    } RECT;
```

I'll also ask Visual Basic to store the settings of the control's properties in a BOX structure. Then, when a property is changed, Visual Basic will return a pointer to its internal BOX structure, from which I can read the appropriate values. That is, Visual Basic enables me to configure the data structure that it will use to store a control's properties in a manner I find most convenient. I do that by setting up the structure named BOX. I can then specify that Visual Basic should update the Box control's properties in its internal structure, or that the control itself will handle this. The choice depends on the setting of the property's PF flags, as indicated in Table 19.1. This example uses the PF_fGetData flag, which indicates to Visual Basic that the control will be responsible for updating its internal BOX structure (as opposed to using PF_fSetData, which causes Visual Basic to handle that update itself). The control will also use PF_fSetMsg, which means that the control will get a VBM_SETPROPERTY message when a property changes. By reading the new value of the property as passed to the control, the control's code will be capable of determining whether to update Visual Basic's internal BOX structure.

To let Visual Basic set up such a structure internally, I'll have to let Visual Basic know how big a BOX structure is. After I do, Visual Basic will set aside that many bytes in its own memory. Next, I have to let Visual Basic know what data items are in the structure and at what locations. To indicate that, I will pass the offset of the various properties in the structure to Visual Basic.

In this way, Visual Basic sets up its own BOX structure the way I want it. When it has to update the data in it, it will pass back a pointer to that structure, along with the new value of the property that has changed.

The next step, then, is to pass the offset of BoxColor in a BOX structure to Visual Basic; I do that with a PROPINFO structure (I must pass one PROPINFO (property information) structure for each of the Box control's properties), the generic form of which looks like this:

```
typedef struct tagPROPINFO
{
    PSTR    npszName;       /* Property name                          */
    FLONG   fl;             /* PF_ flags                              */
    BYTE    offsetData;     /* Offset into structure                  */
    BYTE    infoData;       /* 0 or _INFO value for bitfield          */
    LONG    dataDefault;    /* 0 or _INFO value for bitfield          */
    PSTR    npszEnumList;   /* NULL or a near ptr to a string         */
                            /* containing values for prop. listbox    */
    BYTE    enumMax;        /* Maximum legal value for enum.          */
}
PROPINFO;
```

In the case of the BoxColor property, I fill the fields of this structure as follows (notice that I'm passing the offset of BoxColor inside the BOX structure here):

```
#include <windows.h>
#include "vbapi.h"
#include "box.h"

PROPINFO Property_BoxColor =
{
    "BoxColor",
    DT_SHORT | PF_fGetData | PF_fSetMsg | PF_fSaveData,
    (USHORT)&(((BOX *)0)->BoxColor), 0, /* get offset */
    0,
    NULL, 0
};
```

Note also that I've included Windows.H here in Init.C; this is a header file with Windows system data definitions. I've also included Box.H, where the BOX structure is declared, and Vbapi.H. This last file, Vbapi.H, holds the prototypes for the functions that I will need to interface with Visual Basic (these functions are prefixed with VB; for example, VBRegisterModel( )) you'll see such functions throughout this chapter.

Now I can add additional properties. Visual Basic provides a number of pointers to default PROPINFO structures for some standard properties, as shown in Table 19.2. I can use some of them to easily include a number of standard Visual Basic properties—such as Name, Index, BackColor, Left, Top, Width, Height, Visible, Parent, DragMode, DragIcon, and Tag. In this way, Visual Basic has already done a lot of work for me—I can use the default PROPINFO structures for each of these properties.

To create this list of properties (in preparation for passing them to Visual Basic in VBRegisterModel()), I have to set up a NULL-terminated array of pointers to PROPINFO structures (one pointer per property). I'll call this array of pointers Box_Properties[ ]. I will include a pointer to the PROPINFO property I declared for BoxColor (I called that PROPINFO structure Property_BoxColor) as well as the predefined pointers to the other properties I want in the control. The predefined pointers are of type PROPINFO, so the array of pointers to PROPINFO structures, which I'm calling Box_Properties[ ], looks like this:

```
#include <windows.h>
#include "vbapi.h"
#include "box.h"

PROPINFO Property_BoxColor =
{
    "BoxColor",
    DT_SHORT ¦ PF_fGetData ¦ PF_fSetMsg ¦ PF_fSaveData,
    (USHORT)&(((BOX *)0)->BoxColor), 0, /* get offset */
    0,
    NULL, 0
};

PPROPINFO Box_Properties[] =        <—
{                                    :
    PPROPINFO_STD_NAME,              :
    PPROPINFO_STD_INDEX,             :
    PPROPINFO_STD_BACKCOLOR,         :
    PPROPINFO_STD_LEFT,              :
    PPROPINFO_STD_TOP,               :
    PPROPINFO_STD_WIDTH,             :
    PPROPINFO_STD_HEIGHT,            :
    PPROPINFO_STD_VISIBLE,           :
    PPROPINFO_STD_PARENT,            :
    PPROPINFO_STD_DRAGMODE,          :
    PPROPINFO_STD_DRAGICON,          :
    PPROPINFO_STD_TAG,               :
    &Property_BoxColor,              :
    PPROPINFO_STD_HWND,              :
    NULL                             :
};
```

Table 19.2. Predefined properties in the Visual Basic CDK.

Property	Constant defined in Vbapi.h
Name	PPROPINFO_STD_NAME
Index	PPROPINFO_STD_INDEX
BackColor	PPROPINFO_STD_BACKCOLOR
ForeColor	PPROPINFO_STD_FORECOLOR
Left	PPROPINFO_STD_LEFT
Top	PPROPINFO_STD_TOP
Width	PPROPINFO_STD_WIDTH
Height	PPROPINFO_STD_HEIGHT
Enabled	PPROPINFO_STD_ENABLED
Visible	PPROPINFO_STD_VISIBLE
MousePointer	PPROPINFO_STD_MOUSEPOINTER
Caption	PPROPINFO_STD_CAPTION
FontName	PPROPINFO_STD_FONTNAME
FontBold	PPROPINFO_STD_FONTBOLD
FontItalic	PPROPINFO_STD_FONTITALIC
FontStrike	PPROPINFO_STD_FONTSTRIKE
FontUnder	PPROPINFO_STD_FONTUNDER
FontSize	PPROPINFO_STD_FONTSIZE
TabIndex	PPROPINFO_STD_TABINDEX
Parent	PPROPINFO_STD_PARENT
DragMode	PPROPINFO_STD_DRAGMODE
DragIcon	PPROPINFO_STD_DRAGICON
BorderStyleOff	PPROPINFO_STD_BORDERSTYLEOFF
TabStop	PPROPINFO_STD_TABSTOP
Tag	PPROPINFO_STD_TAG
Text	PPROPINFO_STD_TEXT
BorderStyleOn	PPROPINFO_STD_BORDERSTYLEON

Now I'm set as far as properties go. The next step is to register the control's events, including ClickInside and ClickOutside.

Registering an Event

To register events, I have to put together an array of EVENTINFO structures, each of which is defined like this in Vbapi.H:

```
typedef struct tagEVENTINFO
{
    PSTR        npszName;      /* Event procedure name              */
    USHORT      cParms;        /* Number of parameters to pass to it */
    USHORT      cwParms;       /* Number of words in parameters     */
    PWORD       npParmTypes;   /* List of parameters by type        */
    PSTR        npszParmProf;  /* Event parameter profile string    */
    FLONG       fl;            /* EF_ flags                         */
}
EVENTINFO;
```

The ClickOutside event doesn't need any parameters passed to it. I indicate that by placing 0s or NULLs in its EVENTINFO structure:

```
EVENTINFO Event_ClickOutside =
{
    "ClickOutside",
    0,
    0,
    NULL,
    NULL
};
```

On the other hand, I'll add parameters in the ClickInside event, passing the x and y coordinates of the mouse cursor like this (in Visual Basic):

```
Sub Box1_ClickInside (X As Single, Y As Single)
    Beep
    Beep
End Sub
```

To enable this feature, I have to indicate the type of arguments I want passed to the event procedure, their numbers, and their names, all in the EVENTINFO structure. Visual Basic has defined these constants in Vbapi.H, which enables me to specify the data types of the arguments I will pass:

ET_I2	16-bit signed integer scalar or array variable
ET_I4	32-bit signed integer scalar or array variable
ET_R4	32-bit real scalar or array variable
ET_R8	64-bit real scalar or array variable
ET_CY	64-bit currency scalar or array variable
ET_SD	String scalar or array variable
ET_FS	Fixed-length string variable

Thus, in the ClickInside() event, I will pass two arguments for a total of four words. Each will be a 32-bit single, and the argument list will be "X As Single, Y As Single" like this:

```
WORD Paramtypes_ClickInside[] = {ET_R4, ET_R4};

EVENTINFO Event_ClickInside =
{
    "ClickInside",             /* Name of event                 */
    2,                         /* Pass 2 parameters             */
    4,                         /* Total number of words to pass */
    Paramtypes_ClickInside,    /* Parameter specification       */
    "X As Single,Y As Single"  /* Argument names                */
};
```

As you might expect, there are a number of predefined events (just as there were predefined properties); these appear in Table 19.3. If you use them, Visual Basic automatically adds support for them to your control. For the Box control, I'll add DragDrop and DragOver.

Table 19.3. Predefined **EventInfo** pointers.

Event	Predefined EventInfo Pointer
Click	PEVENTINFO_STD_CLICK
DblClick	PEVENTINFO_STD_DBLCLICK
DragDrop	PEVENTINFO_STD_DRAGDROP
DragOver	PEVENTINFO_STD_DRAGOVER
GotFocus	PEVENTINFO_STD_GOTFOCUS
KeyDown	PEVENTINFO_STD_KEYDOWN
KeyPress	PEVENTINFO_STD_KEYPRESS
KeyUp	PEVENTINFO_STD_KEYUP
LostFocus	PEVENTINFO_STD_LOSTFOCUS
MouseDown	PEVENTINFO_STD_MOUSEDOWN
MouseMove	PEVENTINFO_STD_MOUSEMOVE
MouseUp	PEVENTINFO_STD_MOUSEUP

As with properties, I have to set up an array of pointers (here to EVENTINFO structures) so that I can assemble all events in one place. And, as before, I will use some default pointers (type PEVENTINFO) to include the standard events I have decided on (DragDrop and DragOver). That means that the array of pointers to EVENTINFO structures, which I can call Box_Events[ ] (the counterpart of Box_Properties[ ]), will look like this in Init.C:

```
#include <windows.h>
#include "vbapi.h"
#include "box.h"

PROPINFO Property_BoxColor =
{
:
```

```
    :
};

PPROPINFO Box_Properties[] =
{
    PPROPINFO_STD_NAME,
        :
        :
    NULL
};

WORD Paramtypes_ClickInside[] = {ET_R4, ET_R4};

EVENTINFO Event_ClickOutside =
{
    "ClickOutside",
    0,
    0,
    NULL,
    NULL
};

EVENTINFO Event_ClickInside =
{
    "ClickInside",
    2,
    4,
    Paramtypes_ClickInside,
    "X As Single,Y As Single"
};

PEVENTINFO Box_Events[] =
{
    &Event_ClickInside,
    &Event_ClickOutside,
    PEVENTINFO_STD_DRAGDROP,
    PEVENTINFO_STD_DRAGOVER,
    NULL
};
```

Now I have all of my control properties in one array, `Box_Properties[ ]`, and all of my control events in another, `Box_Events[ ]`. The final step is to place pointers to those arrays in a larger MODEL structure and pass it to `VBRegisterModel( )`. The MODEL structure looks like this:

```
typedef struct tagMODEL
{
    USHORT      usVersion;          /* VB version used by control         */
    FLONG       fl;                 /* Bitfield structure                 */
    PCTLPROC    pctlproc;           /* the control proc.                  */
    FSHORT      fsClassStyle;       /* window class style                 */
    FLONG       flWndStyle;         /* default window style               */
    USHORT      cbCtlExtra;         /* # bytes alloc'd for HCTL structure */
    USHORT      idBmpPalette;       /* BIT MAP id for tool palette        */
    PSTR        npszDefName;        /* default control name prefix        */
    PSTR        npszClassName;      /* Visual Basic class name            */
    PSTR        npszParentClassName; /* Parent window class if subclassed  */
    NPPROPLIST  npproplist;         /* Property list                      */
    NPEVENTLIST npeventlist;        /* Event list                         */
    BYTE        nDefProp;           /* index of default property          */
    BYTE        nDefEvent;          /* index of default event             */
```

```
        BYTE        nDefValue;              /* index of default control value   */
}
MODEL;
```

Here we will store the current Visual Basic version, a pointer to the routine that we will use to handle events for our control. The routine itself will be named `BoxCtlProc( )` and will be in Box.C. I'll use the default Windows style of the control (that is, each control is itself a window, as you might expect) and the size of the data structure to store data about the control, the name of the control, the name of the control class being set, and pointers to the `PROPINFO` and `EVENTINFO` arrays I have already set up. I'll name this model structure `modelBox`, because it determines the model (that is, class) of the box control:

```
MODEL modelBox =
{
    VB_VERSION,                 /* VB version */
    0,                          /* No additional params */
    (PCTLPROC)BoxCtlProc,       /* Control's event proc */
    CS_VREDRAW | CS_HREDRAW,    /* Window class style */
    WS_BORDER,                  /* Window style */
    sizeof(BOX),                /* Size of BOX */
    IDBMP_BOX,                  /* Resource number of tool box bit map */
    "Box",                      /* Control name prefix (—> Box1, Box2...) */
    "BoxClass",                 /* Name of our control class */
    NULL,                       /* No parent class */
    Box_Properties,             /* Point to properties we want */
    Box_Events,                 /* Point to events we want */
    IPROP_BOX_COLOR,            /* index of default property     */
    IEVENT_BOX_CLICKINSIDE,     /* index of default event        */
    IPROP_BOX_COLOR             /* index of default control value */
};
```

Omitting the Border in Your Custom Control

If you don't want to include a border around your control, you can omit the `WS_BORDER` flag in the preceding code, setting that value to `0L` instead.

Note that when I pass the size of the control's data structure—`sizeof(BOX)`—Visual Basic sets aside that many bytes, in effect duplicating that structure. As mentioned, I also tell Visual Basic the byte offset of each property in that data structure (that is, I pass it in the `PROPINFO` structures), so it knows where to store them. Later, I will be able to get a pointer to that internal Visual Basic structure, and that is where I can read or write the data that Visual Basic will associate with the control. One of the preceding values, `IDBMP_BOX`, is a resource number that you haven't seen yet but that I will define soon. This resource number corresponds to the bitmap I want to use for the Box control tool in Visual Basic's toolbox. I will add `IDBMP_BOX` later (after designing the corresponding bitmap).

This `MODEL` structure is the structure that will be passed to `VBRegisterModel( )`. Let's examine that process now. Because Box.ocx is set up as a dynamic link library, the first thing that will occur when the .ocx file is loaded is a call to a function named `LibMain( )`, where I can perform initialization. `LibMain( )` must be put in Init.C.

In fact, I'll set up LibMain( ) now. A number of parameters will be passed that I won't actually use, but I'll go ahead and copy over all unused parameters to avoid unused parameter warning messages from the compiler. Following that, I'll execute UnlockData(0), which simply makes sure that the corresponding data segment will not be locked in place when not used. In addition, I will need the instance handle, hMod. When the control is registered, this handle is passed in LibMain( ). I save it in the variable hmodDLL like this:

```
MODEL modelBox =
{
    VB_VERSION,
    0,
    (PCTLPROC)BoxCtlProc,
    CS_VREDRAW | CS_HREDRAW,
    WS_BORDER,
    sizeof(BOX),
    IDBMP_BOX,
    "Box",
    "BoxClass",
    NULL,
    Box_Properties,
    Box_Events,
    IPROP_BOX_COLOR,
    IEVENT_BOX_CLICKINSIDE,
    IPROP_BOX_COLOR
};

HANDLE hmodDLL;            /* Instance handle */

int FAR PASCAL LibMain
(
    HANDLE hModule,
    WORD   wDataSeg,
    WORD   cbHeapSize,
    LPSTR  lpszCmdLine
)
{
    wDataSeg    = wDataSeg;
    cbHeapSize  = cbHeapSize;
    lpszCmdLine = lpszCmdLine;

    hmodDLL = hModule;

    return 1;
}
```

I use the instance handle hmodDLL when I register the control using VBRegisterModel(). After LibMain() returns, I will get a call to the function VBINITCC( ). It is here that I will call VBRegisterModel( ). I pass it hmodDLL, the instance handle (I can have multiple instances of the program running, so I need an instance handle), and a pointer to modelBox. The MODEL structure for the Box control thus looks like this:

```
MODEL modelBox =
{
    VB_VERSION,
    :
```

```
        IPROP_BOX_COLOR
};

HANDLE hmodDLL;          /* Instance handle  */

int FAR PASCAL LibMain
{
 :
}

BOOL FAR PASCAL _export VBINITCC
(
    USHORT usVersion,
    BOOL   fRuntime
)
{
    fRuntime  = fRuntime;
    usVersion = usVersion;

    return VBRegisterModel(hmodDLL, &modelBox);
}
```

This registers the control. That is all for Init.C. Now Visual Basic is aware of the control, including all of its properties and events. To make those events and properties active, Visual Basic will send messages (letting me know what's going on with the control) to the function BoxCtlProc( ), which was registered previously. I will handle those messages in that function, taking the correct action as needed (for example, turning the control's box blue if BoxColor becomes True or causing a ClickInside event if the user clicks inside the box).

The entire listing for Init.C is in Listing 19.1. You might have noticed that one of the items placed in the MODEL structure is IDBMP_BOX; this identifies the bitmap file to associate with the tool. Visual Basic uses that bitmap in the toolbox; so let's see how to create it next.

Listing 19.1. OCX initialization (Init.C).

```
#include <windows.h>
#include "vbapi.h"
#include "box.h"

PROPINFO Property_BoxColor =
{
    "BoxColor",
    DT_SHORT ¦ PF_fGetData ¦ PF_fSetMsg ¦ PF_fSaveData,
    (USHORT)&(((BOX *)0)->BoxColor), 0, /* get offset to BoxColor */
    0,
    NULL, 0
};

PPROPINFO Box_Properties[] =
{
    PPROPINFO_STD_NAME,
    PPROPINFO_STD_INDEX,
    PPROPINFO_STD_BACKCOLOR,
    PPROPINFO_STD_LEFT,
```

continues

Listing 19.1. continued

```
        PPROPINFO_STD_TOP,
        PPROPINFO_STD_WIDTH,
        PPROPINFO_STD_HEIGHT,
        PPROPINFO_STD_VISIBLE,
        PPROPINFO_STD_PARENT,
        PPROPINFO_STD_DRAGMODE,
        PPROPINFO_STD_DRAGICON,
        PPROPINFO_STD_TAG,
        &Property_BoxColor,
        PPROPINFO_STD_HWND,
        NULL
};

WORD Paramtypes_ClickInside[] = {ET_R4, ET_R4};

EVENTINFO Event_ClickOutside =
{
        "ClickOutside",
        0,
        0,
        NULL,
        NULL
};

EVENTINFO Event_ClickInside =
{
        "ClickInside",
        2,
        4,
        Paramtypes_ClickInside,
        "X As Single,Y As Single"
};

PEVENTINFO Box_Events[] =
{
        &Event_ClickInside,
        &Event_ClickOutside,
        PEVENTINFO_STD_DRAGDROP,
        PEVENTINFO_STD_DRAGOVER,
        NULL
};

MODEL modelBox =
{
        VB_VERSION,
        0,
        (PCTLPROC)BoxCtlProc,
        CS_VREDRAW | CS_HREDRAW,
        WS_BORDER,
        sizeof(BOX),
        IDBMP_BOX,
        "Box",
        "BoxClass",
        NULL,
        Box_Properties,
        Box_Events,
        IPROP_BOX_COLOR,
```

```
        IEVENT_BOX_CLICKINSIDE,
        IPROP_BOX_COLOR
};

HANDLE hmodDLL;                  /* Instance handle  */

int FAR PASCAL LibMain
(
    HANDLE  hModule,
    WORD    wDataSeg,
    WORD    cbHeapSize,
    LPSTR   lpszCmdLine
)
{
    wDataSeg    = wDataSeg;
    cbHeapSize  = cbHeapSize;
    lpszCmdLine = lpszCmdLine;

    hmodDLL = hModule;

    return 1;
}

BOOL FAR PASCAL _export VBINITCC
(
    USHORT usVersion,
    BOOL   fRuntime
)
{
    fRuntime  = fRuntime;
    usVersion = usVersion;

    return VBRegisterModel(hmodDLL, &modelBox);
}
```

Designing a Control's Toolbox Bitmap

Now we can actually design a bitmap for the toolbox. Fortunately, the CDK comes with several sample bitmaps that can be modified. For example, in the directory c:\vb\cdk\pix, I find Pixcd.Bmp. This I copy and rename to Boxcu.Bmp. Next, I load the image file into the SDKPaint program or the Image Editor in the Windows SDK and change the figure in it to a simple box for the Box control. When I am done editing these bitmaps with SDKPaint or the Image Editor, I simply save it to disk. That's it; I have created the icon I need.

After creating the bitmap file, I can assign the corresponding bitmap an arbitrary resource number like this in Box.H:

```
#define IDBMP_BOX        5000            /* boxcu.bmp */


typedef struct tagBOX
{
    RECT     rectDrawRegion;
```

```
    SHORT   BoxColor;
} BOX;
```

Then I have to associate this resource ID with the bitmap file itself, which I do in Box.Rc like this:

```
IDBMP_BOX          BIT MAP  DISCARDABLE "boxcu.bmp"
```

In fact, that is all I will need in Box.Rc (one of our six files for Box.ocx), because the bitmaps are the only resources I will use here.

The Box Control Procedure

The second C procedure we will need, now that our Box control is installed, is Box.C, which handles the operation of Box controls. This is where the function BoxCtlProc( ) is, and where Visual Basic will pass messages intended for the control. I start Box.C by including the files I will need:

```
#include <windows.h>
#include "vbapi.h"
#include "box.h"
        :
        :
```

Next come the prototypes of the functions I will use in this code in addition to BoxCtlProc( ). I won't put these prototypes in Box.H because these functions are designed to help BoxCtlProc( ) and are entirely internal to Box.C. These functions are PaintBox(), which will paint box controls; InBox(), which will let me determine whether a mouse event occurred inside or outside of the box in the middle of the control (that is, that's the difference between ClickInside( ) and ClickOutside( )); FireClickInside( ), which lets me fire, or cause, a Visual Basic event—in this case, ClickInside( ); and FireClickOutside( ).

```
#include <windows.h>
#include "vbapi.h"
#include "box.h"

VOID NEAR PaintBox(PBOX pbox, HWND hwnd, HDC hdc);
BOOL NEAR InBox(PBOX pbox, SHORT x, SHORT y);
VOID NEAR FireClickInside(HCTL hctl, SHORT x, SHORT y);
VOID NEAR FireClickOutside(HCTL hctl);
        :
        :
```

Previously, I set up a BOX structure to store the properties of the Box control like this:

```
typedef struct tagBOX
{
    RECT    rectDrawRegion;
    SHORT   BoxColor;
} BOX;
```

As you've seen, Visual Basic will set up the same structure internally. When necessary, it will pass a pointer to that structure (that is, for me to set values in or to read the values that I have set previously), which means that it will be useful to define a type of pointer to BOX called PBOX in Box.H.

```
#define IDBMP_BOX          5000              /* boxcu.bmp */


typedef struct tagBOX
{
    RECT     rectDrawRegion;
    SHORT    BoxColor;
} BOX;

typedef BOX FAR * PBOX;
```

Note that this is the type of argument I can pass to PaintBox( ) and InBox( )—passing them the BOX pointer I got from Visual Basic. Next in Box.C comes BoxCtlProc( ) itself; this is where I process messages sent to the control. These messages are of two kinds: WM_ messages that come from Windows (such as WM_PAINT) and VBM_ messages that come from Visual Basic itself (such as VBM_DRAGDROP, which means that the control was just dropped).

I'll start BoxCtlProc( ) now. There are five parameters passed to that function: hctl, the control handle that Visual Basic gives to the control; hwnd, the Windows handle to the control; msg, the message intended for the control (for example, WM_PAINT, WM_SIZE, or messages from Visual Basic such as VBM_SETPROPERTY); wp, a message parameter (that is, either the customary wparam parameter from Windows for WM_ messages or additional information from Visual Basic for VBM_ messages); and lp (that is, the customary lparam or additional Visual Basic information for VBM_ messages).

```
#include <windows.h>
#include "vbapi.h"
#include "box.h"

VOID NEAR PaintBox(PBOX pbox, HWND hwnd, HDC hdc);
BOOL NEAR InBox(PBOX pbox, SHORT x, SHORT y);
VOID NEAR FireClickInside(HCTL hctl, SHORT x, SHORT y);
VOID NEAR FireClickOutside(HCTL hctl);

LONG FAR PASCAL _export BoxCtlProc(HCTL hctl, HWND hwnd, USHORT msg,
    USHORT wp, LONG lp)
    :
```

In general, you pass hctl to Visual Basic API functions and hwnd to Windows API functions, although they both refer to the same control. In fact, hctl returns the pointer to Visual Basic's internal BOX structure that we need. To get that pointer, I simply dereference hctl with the VBDerefControl( ) function. That is, I get the pointer to Visual Basic's currently active BOX structure like this:

```
#include <windows.h>
    :
    :
LONG FAR PASCAL _export BoxCtlProc(HCTL hctl, HWND hwnd, USHORT msg,
    USHORT wp, LONG lp)
{
    PBOX pbox;
    LPRECT prect;

    /* Note: Must again dereferece hctl whenever we invalidate */
    /* pbox—including after calls to VB API */
    pbox = (PBOX)VBDerefControl(hctl);
    :
```

Note that you should use VBDerefControl( ) again after every time you do something that might cause Visual Basic to change the BOX structure in some way—including calls to the Visual Basic API. This API provides you with the means of connecting to Visual Basic through such functions as VBXPixelsToTwips( ) or VBFireEvent( ), both of which you'll see soon.

Now that I have a pointer (pbox) to the Box control's data, I can start interpreting the message sent with a switch statement:

```
#include <windows.h>
#include "vbapi.h"
#include "box.h"
    :
    :
    pbox = (PBOX)VBDerefControl(hctl);

    switch (msg){
    :
    :
```

For example, when the control is first created, I get a WM_CREATE message, as would any normal Windows program. I can perform initialization when I get that message; for example, I might set the BoxColor property to FALSE to start:

```
#include <windows.h>
#include "vbapi.h"
#include "box.h"
    :
    :
    pbox = (PBOX)VBDerefControl(hctl);

    switch (msg){
    case WM_CREATE:                 /* Perform initialization here */
       pbox->BoxColor = FALSE;
       break;
```

This is the way that I will interface to the BoxColor property:

```
pbox->BoxColor
```

because it enables me to set or reset Visual Basic's own internal setting of that property.

Next, I'll handle the case in which the control was (re)sized—the WM_SIZE case. In that case, I want to fill in or update the RECT structure in which I store the size of the box inside the control, which I have called rectDrawRegion in the BOX structure (from Box.H).

```
#define IDBMP_BOX        5000            /* boxcu.bmp */

typedef struct tagBOX
{
    RECT      rectDrawRegion;
    SHORT     BoxColor;
} BOX;

typedef BOX FAR * PBOX;
```

I can do that by getting a pointer to `rectDrawRegion` in Visual Basic's `BOX` structure. This rectangle defines the box inside the control. When I get a resize event, I will have to adjust its coordinates accordingly (because I will have to redraw the box in `WM_PAINT` events, which will read its size from this same `RECT` structure). Because the control is simply a window, I can find its (new) size with the Windows function `GetClientRect()`. After that, all that remains is to recalculate the size of the box in the control (making it occupy the middle region of the control) and store it in Visual Basic's `BOX` data structure like this:

```
#include <windows.h>
#include "vbapi.h"
#include "box.h"
    :
    :
    switch (msg){
    case WM_CREATE:              /* Perform initialization here */
       pbox->BoxColor = FALSE;
       break;

    case WM_SIZE:               /* Our control was (re)sized */
       prect = &pbox->rectDrawRegion;

       GetClientRect(hwnd, prect);        /* Draw box in the control */
       prect->left = prect->right / 4;
       prect->right = 3 * prect->right / 4;
       prect->top = prect->bottom / 4;
       prect->bottom = 3 * prect->bottom / 4;
       break;
          :
```

That also means that when I paint, I will be able to use the coordinates in the `BOX` structure. In fact, I'll add the `WM_PAINT` case now. I set up a separate `Paint` function called `PaintBox()`, because it's usually convenient to call such a function from several places in the program. We will pass the pointer to the box structure—`pbox`—to `PaintBox()`, along with a handle to the device context, `hdc`, in which it's supposed to paint.

That means that I can set up the `WM_PAINT` case easily. If the `wp` parameter is nonzero, it means that I am being asked to print on the printer, and `wp` holds the correct device context handle. Otherwise, I can simply use `BeginPaint()` and `EndPaint()` (as I would normally) to get a device context handle, like this:

```
#include <windows.h>
#include "vbapi.h"
#include "box.h"
    :
    :
    pbox = (PBOX)VBDerefControl(hctl);

    switch (msg){
case WM_CREATE:               /* Perform initialization here */
        pbox->BoxColor = FALSE;
        break;

case WM_SIZE:                /* Our control was (re)sized */
        prect = &pbox->rectDrawRegion;
```

```
        GetClientRect(hwnd, prect);          /* Draw box in the control */
        prect->left = prect->right / 4;
        prect->right = 3 * prect->right / 4;
        prect->top = prect->bottom / 4;
        prect->bottom = 3 * prect->bottom / 4;
        break;

    case WM_PAINT:                 /* Repaint our control */
        if (wp)
        PaintBox(pbox, hwnd, (HDC)wp);      /* Printer */
        else{
        PAINTSTRUCT ps;

            BeginPaint(hwnd, &ps);
            PaintBox(pbox, hwnd, ps.hdc);
            EndPaint(hwnd, &ps);
        }
        break;
        :
```

Now I have to set up PaintBox(), which does the real work. Even so, all I really have to do in PaintBox() is to find the coordinates of the box that I set in WM_SIZE and draw a rectangle. That looks like this, when I find the coordinates of the rectangle in the BOX structure pointed to by pbox and draw it:

```
VOID NEAR PaintBox (PBOX pbox, HWND hwnd, HDC hdc)
{
    LPRECT  prect = &pbox->rectDrawRegion;

    Rectangle(hdc, prect->left, prect->top, prect->right, prect->bottom);
}
```

You might recall, however, that the box is supposed to be colored blue (that is, RGB(0, 0, 255)) if the BoxColor property is set. That property will be stored in the box structure's BoxColor field like this:

```
typedef struct tagBOX
{
    RECT      rectDrawRegion;
    SHORT     BoxColor;
} BOX;

typedef BOX FAR * PBOX;
```

So, I can check it like this in PaintBox() (using the standard Windows functions CreateSolidBrush() and SelectObject() as needed to color the box blue):

```
VOID NEAR PaintBox (PBOX pbox, HWND hwnd, HDC hdc)
{
    HBRUSH  hbr;
    HBRUSH  hbrOld = NULL;
    LPRECT  prect = &pbox->rectDrawRegion;

    f(pbox->BoxColor){
        hbr = CreateSolidBrush(RGB(0, 0, 255)); /* Blue brush */
        hbrOld = SelectObject(hdc, hbr);
    }
    Rectangle(hdc, prect->left, prect->top, prect->right, prect->bottom);
```

```
        if(pbox->BoxColor){
            SelectObject(hdc, hbrOld);          /* Restore old brush */
        }
}
```

That takes care of the WM_PAINT case. Next, let's handle the case when the mouse button goes down in the control. In that case, I will get a WM_MOUSEDOWN message; now I have to determine whether the mouse went down inside the box in the control (that is, I will have to fire a ClickInside event) or not (ClickOutside). I can use the InBox( ) function for that if I pass it the location of the mouse cursor and a pointer to the BOX structure and have it return a BOOL value (TRUE if the event occurred inside the box):

```
BOOL NEAR InBox(PBOX pbox, SHORT x, SHORT y)
{

}
```

All I need to do is get a pointer to rectDrawRegion—as before—and then check whether the mouse coordinates, x and y, indicate that the mouse cursor was inside it or not:

```
BOOL NEAR InBox(PBOX pbox, SHORT x, SHORT y)
{
    LPRECT  prect = &pbox->rectDrawRegion;

    return ((prect->left < x) & (prect->right > x) & \
        (prect->top < y) & (prect->bottom > y));
}
```

Now I can determine whether the mouse clicked inside or outside of the box in the control simply by using InBox( ). In the WM_LBUTTONDOWN case, then, I can find the x and y coordinates of the mouse click from the lp parameter—x = LOWORD(lp), and y = HIWORD(lp). If the click was indeed in the box (as determined by InBox( )), I want to fire the ClickInside event with FireClickInside(), which I will write in a moment. If the click was not inside the box, I want to use FireClickOutside(), which I will also write in a moment. In code, then, the WM_LBUTTONDOWN event looks like this:

```
#include <windows.h>
#include "vbapi.h"
#include "box.h"
    :
    :
    case WM_PAINT:                  /* Repaint our control */
        if (wp)
          PaintBox(pbox, hwnd, (HDC)wp);    /* Printer */
        else{
          PAINTSTRUCT ps;

          BeginPaint(hwnd, &ps);
          PaintBox(pbox, hwnd, ps.hdc);
          EndPaint(hwnd, &ps);
        }
        break;

    case WM_LBUTTONDOWN:            /* Button down in our control */
        if (InBox(pbox, LOWORD(lp), HIWORD(lp))){
          FireClickInside(hctl, LOWORD(lp), HIWORD(lp));
```

```
      }
      else
        FireClickOutside(hctl);
      break;
    :
```

Now let's take a look at `FireClickOutside( )`, followed by `FireClickInside( )`. If the user clicks the control, she generates a `ClickInside` or `ClickOutside` event (we decide which one). I can fire—generate—events with `VBFireEvent( )`, but how do I tell Visual Basic which event I'm firing? You might recall that I set up the array of pointers to event structures like this (in Init.C):

```
PEVENTINFO Box_Events[] =
{
    &Event_ClickInside,
    &Event_ClickOutside,
    PEVENTINFO_STD_DRAGDROP,
    PEVENTINFO_STD_DRAGOVER,
    NULL
};
H
```

Visual Basic will take them in order—which means that `ClickInside` is considered event 0 for the Box control, `ClickOutside` event 1, `DRAGDROP` event 2, and `DRAGOVER` event 3. In fact, I can define these constants in Box.H for easy reference.

```
#define IDBMP_BOX         5000

typedef struct tagBOX
{
    RECT    rectDrawRegion;
    SHORT   BoxColor;
} BOX;

typedef BOX FAR * PBOX;

#define IEVENT_BOX_CLICKINSIDE    0
#define IEVENT_BOX_CLICKOUTSIDE   1
#define IEVENT_BOX_DRAGDROP       2
#define IEVENT_BOX_DRAGOVER       3
```

Similarly, I assembled the array of properties like this (in Init.C):

```
PPROPINFO Box_Properties[] =
{
    PPROPINFO_STD_NAME,
    PPROPINFO_STD_INDEX,
    PPROPINFO_STD_BACKCOLOR,
    PPROPINFO_STD_LEFT,
    PPROPINFO_STD_TOP,
    PPROPINFO_STD_WIDTH,
    PPROPINFO_STD_HEIGHT,
    PPROPINFO_STD_VISIBLE,
    PPROPINFO_STD_PARENT,
    PPROPINFO_STD_DRAGMODE,
    PPROPINFO_STD_DRAGICON,
    PPROPINFO_STD_TAG,
    &Property_BoxColor,
    PPROPINFO_STD_HWND,
```

```
        NULL
};
```

So I can add them to Box.H as well.

```
#define IDBMP_BOX          5000

typedef struct tagBOX
{
    RECT     rectDrawRegion;
    SHORT    BoxColor;
} BOX;

typedef BOX FAR * PBOX;

#define IPROP_BOX_NAME                 0
#define IPROP_BOX_INDEX                1       :
#define IPROP_BOX_BACKCOLOR            2       :
#define IPROP_BOX_LEFT                 3       :
#define IPROP_BOX_TOP                  4       :
#define IPROP_BOX_WIDTH                5       :
#define IPROP_BOX_HEIGHT               6       :
#define IPROP_BOX_VISIBLE              7       :
#define IPROP_BOX_PARENT               8       :
#define IPROP_BOX_DRAGMODE             9       :
#define IPROP_BOX_DRAGICON            10       :
#define IPROP_BOX_TAG                 11       :
#define IPROP_BOX_COLOR               12       :
#define IPROP_BOX_HWND                13


#define IEVENT_BOX_CLICKINSIDE         0
#define IEVENT_BOX_CLICKOUTSIDE        1
#define IEVENT_BOX_DRAGDROP            2
#define IEVENT_BOX_DRAGOVER            3
```

That completes Box.H, which you can find in Listing 19.2.

Listing 19.2. Box.H.

```
#define IDBMP_BOX          5000

LONG FAR PASCAL _export BoxCtlProc(HCTL, HWND, USHORT, USHORT, LONG);

typedef struct tagBOX
{
    RECT     rectDrawRegion;
    SHORT    BoxColor;
} BOX;

typedef BOX FAR * PBOX;

#ifndef RC_INVOKED

#define IPROP_BOX_NAME                 0
#define IPROP_BOX_INDEX                1
#define IPROP_BOX_BACKCOLOR            2
#define IPROP_BOX_LEFT                 3
#define IPROP_BOX_TOP                  4
```

continues

Listing 19.2. continued

```
#define IPROP_BOX_WIDTH          5
#define IPROP_BOX_HEIGHT         6
#define IPROP_BOX_VISIBLE        7
#define IPROP_BOX_PARENT         8
#define IPROP_BOX_DRAGMODE       9
#define IPROP_BOX_DRAGICON       10
#define IPROP_BOX_TAG            11
#define IPROP_BOX_COLOR          12
#define IPROP_BOX_HWND           13

#define IEVENT_BOX_CLICKINSIDE   0
#define IEVENT_BOX_CLICKOUTSIDE  1
#define IEVENT_BOX_DRAGDROP      2
#define IEVENT_BOX_DRAGOVER      3

#endif
```

For a ClickOutside( ) event, then, I only have to fire event number IEVENT_BOX_CLICKOUTSIDE. As I set things up, ClickOutside( ) has no arguments passed to it, so I only need to use VBFireEvent( ) like this in FireClickOutSide( ) (which is called from the WM_LBUTTONDOWN case):

```
VOID NEAR FireClickOutside(HCTL hctl)
{
     VBFireEvent(hctl, IEVENT_BOX_CLICKOUTSIDE, NULL);
}
```

The first argument I pass to VBFireEvent( ) is hctl, the control's handle; the next is the number of the event (IEVENT_BOX_CLICKOUTSIDE); and the last is a pointer to the additional parameters I want to pass to the event procedure. Here, there are no additional parameters, so I'm done with FireClickOutside( ).

However, I also have to set up FireClickInside( ) in case the user clicks inside the box. For that I will need the actual mouse coordinates, because I plan to pass them to the ClickInside( ) event.

```
Sub Box1_ClickInside (X As Single, Y As Single)
     Beep
   Beep
End Sub
```

I can get the mouse coordinates from lp (that is, x = LOWORD(lp), and y = HIWORD(lp)) in the WM_LBUTTONDOWN case like this:

```
case WM_LBUTTONDOWN:           /* Button down in our control */
   if (InBox(pbox, LOWORD(lp), HIWORD(lp))){
      FireClickInside(hctl, LOWORD(lp), HIWORD(lp));
   }
   else
      FireClickOutside(hctl);
break;
```

Now I need to design FireClickInside( ) to handle and pass these parameters correctly.

```
VOID NEAR FireClickInside(HCTL hctl, SHORT x, SHORT y)
{
}
```

To pass these parameters to Visual Basic so that they will be passed to `Box1_ClickInside( )`, I have to set up a structure and pass a pointer to it when I use `VBFireEvent( )`. That structure holds the arguments to pass to the event procedure, but in reverse order. You don't have to set up an argument list if no parameters are passed to the event procedure, but `ClickInside( )` does take parameters, so I will have to set up an argument list here.

Note that the box control supports the `Index` property, which means that I can have arrays of box controls and that an index can be passed. I didn't have to take that into account before because I didn't pass a parameter structure then. That is, if your event procedure takes no parameters, you don't have to pass a parameter structure—even if you support control arrays. In that case, Visual Basic will take care of passing an index itself. But now that I am passing a parameter structure to `VBFireEvent`, it turns out that I do have to include space for a (possible) `Index` property. Because `Index` will always be passed first, it comes last here (and I give it the expected `LPVOID` type):

```
typedef struct tagCLICKINSIDEPARMS
{
    float   far *Y;
    float   far *X;
    LPVOID  Index;
} CLICKINSIDEPARMS;

VOID NEAR FireClickInside(HCTL hctl, SHORT x, SHORT y)
{

}
```

That's all there is to setting up the parameter structure. Now I just have to fill that parameter structure with the mouse cursor location and pass it to `VBFireEvent( )`. However, it is very important to note that I have to convert from the pixel coordinates that I extracted from `lp` like this:

```
case WM_LBUTTONDOWN:          /* Button down in our control */
    if (InBox(pbox, LOWORD(lp), HIWORD(lp))){
        FireClickInside(hctl, LOWORD(lp), HIWORD(lp));
    }
    else
        FireClickOutside(hctl);
    break;
```

to twips for Visual Basic. I do that with a common Visual Basic API call, `VBXPixelsToTwips( )`, like this in `FireClickInside( )`:

```
typedef struct tagCLICKINSIDEPARMS
{
    float   far *Y;
    float   far *X;
    LPVOID  Index;
} CLICKINSIDEPARMS;

VOID NEAR FireClickInside(HCTL hctl, SHORT x, SHORT y)
```

```
{
    CLICKINSIDEPARMS EventParams;
    float     VisBasX, VisBasY;

    VisBasX = (float)VBXPixelsToTwips(x);
    VisBasY = (float)VBYPixelsToTwips(y);
    EventParams.X = &VisBasX;
    EventParams.Y = &VisBasY;

    VBFireEvent(hctl, IEVENT_BOX_CLICKINSIDE, &EventParams);
}
```

That's it for `FireClickInside()`. Now I've made the two events active—`ClickInside` and `ClickOutside`. All that remains is to take care of the property, `BoxColor`, when someone changes it. To do that, I will handle the `VBM_SETPROPERTY` message, which indicates that someone has changed a property of the control. The number of the property changed is passed in `wp`, and the new value in `lp`. Here, I can handle the case in which the `BoxColor` property—to which I have given the number `IPROP_BOX_COLOR` in Box.H—changes by checking the value in `wp`. If it's equal to `IPROP_BOX_COLOR`, I should load the new setting from `lp` into the `BOX` structure. I can do that like this in Box.C:

```
#include <windows.h>
#include "vbapi.h"
#include "box.h"

VOID NEAR PaintBox(PBOX pbox, HWND hwnd, HDC hdc);
BOOL NEAR InBox(PBOX pbox, SHORT x, SHORT y);
VOID NEAR FireClickInside(HCTL hctl, SHORT x, SHORT y);
VOID NEAR FireClickOutside(HCTL hctl);

LONG FAR PASCAL _export BoxCtlProc(HCTL hctl, HWND hwnd, USHORT msg,
    USHORT wp, LONG lp)
{
    switch (msg){
    :
    :
    case WM_LBUTTONDOWN:         /* Button down in our control */
            :
            :
        break;

    case VBM_SETPROPERTY:               /* BoxColor was set */
        switch (wp){
        case IPROP_BOX_COLOR:
            pbox->BoxColor = (SHORT)lp;
            InvalidateRect(hwnd, NULL, TRUE);
            return 0;
        }
        break;
    }
    return VBDefControlProc(hctl, hwnd, msg, wp, lp);
}
```

Notice that I repaint the control when the `BoxColor` property changes (actually, I use `InvalidateRect()` so that a `WM_PAINT` message will be sent). This enables me to add or remove the blue coloring as needed. Note also that at the end of the code I used `VBDefControlProc()`, which has the same use as

`DefWindowProc( )` does in most Windows programs—that is, you pass the messages you don't want to handle on to it. That's it for Box.C, which handles the messages for our control; the full code appears in Listing 19.3. Now we are almost ready to go.

Listing 19.3. Box.C.

```c
#include <windows.h>
#include "vbapi.h"
#include "box.h"

VOID NEAR PaintBox(PBOX pbox, HWND hwnd, HDC hdc);
BOOL NEAR InBox(PBOX pbox, SHORT x, SHORT y);
VOID NEAR FireClickInside(HCTL hctl, SHORT x, SHORT y);
VOID NEAR FireClickOutside(HCTL hctl);

LONG FAR PASCAL _export BoxCtlProc(HCTL hctl, HWND hwnd, USHORT msg,
        USHORT wp, LONG lp)
{
    PBOX pbox;
    LPRECT prect;

    /* Note: Must again dereferece hctl whenever we invalidate */
    /* pbox—including after calls to VB API */
    pbox = (PBOX)VBDerefControl(hctl);

    switch (msg){
    case WM_CREATE:             /* Perform initialization here */
    pbox->BoxColor = FALSE;
    break;

    case WM_SIZE:               /* Our control was (re)sized */
    prect = &pbox->rectDrawRegion;

    GetClientRect(hwnd, prect);     /* Draw box in the control */
    prect->left = prect->right / 4;
    prect->right = 3 * prect->right / 4;
    prect->top = prect->bottom / 4;
    prect->bottom = 3 * prect->bottom / 4;
    break;

    case WM_PAINT:              /* Repaint our control */
    if (wp)
        PaintBox(pbox, hwnd, (HDC)wp);   /* Printer */
    else{
        PAINTSTRUCT ps;

        BeginPaint(hwnd, &ps);
        PaintBox(pbox, hwnd, ps.hdc);
        EndPaint(hwnd, &ps);
    }
    break;

    case WM_LBUTTONDOWN:        /* Button down in our control */
    if (InBox(pbox, LOWORD(lp), HIWORD(lp))){
        HDC hdc = GetDC(hwnd);
            /* Do work if desired */
```

continues

Listing 19.3. **continued**

```
                ReleaseDC(hwnd, hdc);
            FireClickInside(hctl, LOWORD(lp), HIWORD(lp));
        }
        else
            FireClickOutside(hctl);
        break;

        case VBM_SETPROPERTY:               /* BoxColor was set */
        switch (wp){
        case IPROP_BOX_COLOR:
            pbox->BoxColor = (SHORT)lp;
            InvalidateRect(hwnd, NULL, TRUE);
            return 0;
        }
        break;
        }
        return VBDefControlProc(hctl, hwnd, msg, wp, lp);
}

VOID NEAR PaintBox (PBOX pbox, HWND hwnd, HDC hdc)
{
    HBRUSH  hbr;
    HBRUSH  hbrOld = NULL;
    LPRECT  prect = &pbox->rectDrawRegion;

    if(pbox->BoxColor){
        hbr = CreateSolidBrush(RGB(0, 0, 255)); /* Blue brush */
        hbrOld = SelectObject(hdc, hbr);
    }
    Rectangle(hdc, prect->left, prect->top, prect->right, prect->bottom);
    if(pbox->BoxColor){
        SelectObject(hdc, hbrOld);          /* Restore old brush */
    }
}

BOOL NEAR InBox(PBOX pbox, SHORT x, SHORT y)
{
    LPRECT  prect = &pbox->rectDrawRegion;

    return ((prect->left < x) & (prect->right > x) & \
    (prect->top < y) & (prect->bottom > y));
}

VOID NEAR FireClickOutside(HCTL hctl)
{
    VBFireEvent(hctl, IEVENT_BOX_CLICKOUTSIDE, NULL);
}

typedef struct tagCLICKINSIDEPARMS
{
    float   far *Y;
    float   far *X;
    LPVOID  Index;
} CLICKINSIDEPARMS;

VOID NEAR FireClickInside(HCTL hctl, SHORT x, SHORT y)
{
```

```
    CLICKINSIDEPARMS EventParams;
    float     VisBasX, VisBasY;

    VisBasX = (float)VBXPixelsToTwips(x);
    VisBasY = (float)VBYPixelsToTwips(y);
    EventParams.X = &VisBasX;
    EventParams.Y = &VisBasY;

    VBFireEvent(hctl, IEVENT_BOX_CLICKINSIDE, &EventParams);
}
```

In fact, the code is done, but I still need to complete Box.Def, which indicates to the linker that I want to create a Windows dynamic link library. The required .def file appears in Listing 19.4 (Box.def).

Listing 19.4. Box.def.

```
LIBRARY          BOX
EXETYPE          WINDOWS
DESCRIPTION      'Visual Basic Box Custom Control'

CODE             MOVEABLE
DATA             MOVEABLE SINGLE

HEAPSIZE         2048

EXPORTS
    WEP     @1      RESIDENTNAME

SEGMENTS
    WEP_TEXT FIXED
```

The final file I need is the makefile used by the compiler. That file, simply called Makefile, is more or less standard for creating .ocx files. The Makefile specifies all that the various linkers, compilers, and libraries need to know to create Box.ocx. (See Listing 19.5.) Compiled with the Makefile, then, Box.ocx is at last ready for us to use.

Listing 19.5. The compiler makefile.

```
.SUFFIXES:  .c .def .VBX .h .lnk .map .obj .rc .res .sym

Default: box.vbx

.c.obj:
    echo >con Compiling $(<F)
    cl /c /W4 /G2cs /Zp /BATCH /Osge /GD -AS $<

box.obj: box.c box.h

init.obj: init.c box.h

box.VBX: init.obj box.obj box.lnk box.res box.def
    echo >con Linking box.VBX...
```

continues

Listing 19.5. continued

```
    link /co @box.lnk
    echo >con RCing box.VBX...
    rc -30 box.res box.VBX
    echo >con mapsyming box.VBX...
    mapsym box
    echo >con Done Linking box.VBX

box.lnk: makefile
    echo >con Making <<box.lnk
    box.obj + init.obj
    box.VBX /co /align:16 /batch /far /li /map /nod /noe /nopackc/w
    box.map
    vbapi.lib libw.lib sdllcew.lib
    box.def
<<KEEP

box.res: box.rc box.h \
    boxcd.bmp \
    boxcu.bmp \
    boxmu.bmp \
    boxeu.bmp
    echo >con Resource compiling box.RC
    rc -R $(RCINCS) box.rc
```

Using a New Custom Control

All that remains is to put Box.ocx to work. That, of course, you do in Visual Basic. Start a new project and call it Box.Mak. Now add Box.Vbx with the Visual Basic Tool menu's Custom Control… menu item. You'll see that the new control appears in the toolbox. You can create a new Box control as you would any other control—just double-click the box tool and move the Box control that appears into place on the form. Next, you can open the code window, where you will find these events, among others:

```
Sub Box1_ClickOutside ( )
End Sub
Sub Box1_ClickInside (X As Single, Y As Single)

End Sub
```

As was the original plan, put this code in the event procedures:

```
Sub Box1_ClickOutside ( )
    Beep
End Sub
Sub Box1_ClickInside (X As Single, Y As Single)
    Beep
    Beep
End Sub
```

Now, find the BoxColor property in the Properties window; when you do, you'll find that it has a setting of 0. To set the BoxColor property to True, set it to -1. At that point, the box inside the control turns blue. Finally, run the program. When you click inside the control but outside of the central box, you get a beep. When you click inside the box, you get two beeps. Box.ocx is a success—I have actually designed and implemented my own Visual Basic control, extending the language.

OLE Controls (OCXs) versus VBXs

Prior to the advent of OLE custom controls, VBX controls were the only game in town. The way to create a VBX control was very similar to that for creating an OCX control, as you might be able to tell if you have some familiarity with the former process. However, the similarities really end there.

The most important thing to keep in mind about VBXs is that they're limited to use with Visual Basic. This means that no other potential container application can work with a VBX. OCXs, on the other hand, can be used in any application that supports the OLE 2.0 architecture. For example, you might add an OCX control to a Microsoft Excel spreadsheet, enabling it with code written in Excel's version of Visual Basic for Applications. That's something you can't do with a VBX.

Another difference is that VBXs are strictly limited to use in 16-bit environments, as Windows 3.1 was. OCXs can be developed for use in either 16- or 32-bit environments. In fact, the same source code can be used to develop either control version. Don't despair over the 16-bit limitation of VBXs, though; the Visual Basic Professional Edition provides tools you can use to easily translate VBX source code into OCX form, and that also enable you to choose for what platform (16- or 32-bit) to produce OCXs. The OLE Control Development Kit is a very useful thing to have around, as you'll see next.

The OLE CDK

The OLE Control Development Kit (CDK), a part of the Visual Basic Professional Edition (it's also part of other development applications, such as Visual C++), makes it much easier to develop and implement custom controls for use within Visual Basic and elsewhere. The CDK also offers tools to help migrate existing VBX controls to the OCX standard. The OLE CDK makes use of the Microsoft Foundation Classes (MFC), which encapsulate the functions we've talked about previously in this chapter, among other things.

An important part of the OLE CDK is the ControlWizard. It takes you step by step through the process of creating an OCX, handling all of the code overhead (such as function prototypes and constant definitions) for you. You can also use the Wizard to change a VBX file into OCX form.

The steps involved in creating an OCX with the ControlWizard are as follows:

1. Create the basic control using the Wizard. This process creates all of the necessary control files as described earlier in the chapter.

2. Modify the control bitmap.

3. Modify the About dialog box.

4. Define standard properties and events.

5. Add custom properties and events.

6. Build the control.

7. Register and test the control.

The kinds of issues and procedures you need to make the control functional are the same as I showed you in the long discussion of the Box control in this chapter. The OLE CDK simply eliminates the drudge work.

Summary

Here you have seen how to design and implement a new control in Visual Basic. I showed you what it takes to support such a control and how you can indicate to Visual Basic what properties a control has, as well as what type of events it can support. I showed you how to register a control with Visual Basic, how to design its appearance by painting it on the screen, and how to handle events connected with it. You have also seen how to create bitmaps that Visual Basic will use in the toolbox as the control's icon and how to get them installed. I showed you how to link together all the control files into an .ocx file, creating a working custom control, which we then put to work. The following reviews the C functions that you learned about in this chapter.

New C Functions	Description
VBDefControlProc	Visual Basic's default control (hctl) (hwnd, msg, wp, lp) handling procedure. The parameters are the same as what are passed to a Visual Basic control procedure and should be passed along unchanged.
VBDerefControl(hctl)	Should be used whenever you do something that causes Visual Basic to change your control's data.
VBFireEvent	Fires a Visual Basic event. The hctl (hctl, IEVENT_NUMBER) parameter is the control's handle, &EventParams; IEVENT_NUMBER is the event number as registered with VBRegisterModel( ), and &EventParams is a pointer to an event parameter structure (so Visual Basic knows what values to pass to a Visual Basic event procedure).
VBXPixelsToTwips(px)	Converts the point px (a Windows point structure) from screen pixels to Visual Basic's twips.
VBRegisterModel	Used to register a control with Visual Basic (hmodDLL, &modelStruc). The hmodDLL parameter is passed to LibMain(), and modelStruc is a Visual Basic Model structure defining this control.

20 Multimedia

Multimedia applications are programs that make sounds, display graphics, and run animated videos. Today's computer users have come to expect multimedia elements in professional applications that they use—although, of course, the user's ability to take advantage of multimedia software depends on the hardware facilities of the target system. With the release of Windows 95, the baseline of users' expectations regarding the inclusion of multimedia in applications has increased greatly.

Some applications are almost entirely multimedia by their very nature. This category of program might include your favorite CD-ROM game. More commonly, however, you will find that "normal" applications are embellished with multimedia touches. For example, navigation might be made easier with graphical hot spots, or users might be rewarded for performing an action—such as backing up the program data—by hearing an inspirational chord play.

This chapter will cover the Visual Basic 4 controls that enable you to play sound files (both WAV and MIDI) and video files (AVI files). (Another control that ships with Visual Basic that is very useful for creating animated effects is the Anibutton OLE control. Creating a simple animation with this control was explained in Chapter 9, "Graphics." In fact, many of the graphics techniques that were covered in Chapter 9 come in handy when you start to design sophisticated multimedia effects.)

Using Visual Basic 4 and Windows 95, there are many different ways to access multimedia functionality—always provided, of course, that your target systems are equipped to handle multimedia (for example, have a sound card, CD-ROM, and the correct drivers).

Although multimedia facilities in Visual Basic 4 are greatly enhanced over previous versions of Visual Basic, to create professional-quality multimedia applications you would probably want to use some third-party tools in addition to those available in Visual Basic. The last section of this chapter provides an overview of what tools are available and what they do.

Some General Considerations

When you create a multimedia application, there are some general considerations you should bear in mind.

Multimedia files—graphics, sound, and video—tend to be very large. Although you can compress and on-the-fly decompress some of these files in an actual application, you'll still need a great deal of disk space to create an extensive multimedia application. As a rule of thumb, to create a CD-ROM consisting of 400 to 600 MB of data, you'd need 4 GB of hard-drive space for the source files.

Typically, one minute of video for a double-speed CD-ROM drive requires 20 to 30 MB of data. A minute of high-quality sound comes in at around 5 MB, and a full-screen, 256KB image is about 300 KB. It's much smarter to plan your space requirements in advance than to find out midway through a project that it doesn't fit onto your proposed delivery media.

What is MIDI, Anyway?

.mid files are created using the *Musical Instrument Digital Interface* (MIDI), a standardized protocol that enables computers and synthesizers to communicate. These files can be very compact compared to .avi and .wav files, and offer great sound quality. Each .mid file is divided into separate tracks, usually one "instrument" per track. (The word *instrument* is in quotes because these are sounds created by a synthesizer—that is, the synthesizer can be programmed to play a note with the same nasal quality of an oboe, but it's not really an oboe playing on the track. Likewise, .mid files cannot record singing.)

Using professional music-writing software—such as Coda Software's Finale—these files are created in one of three ways. The first is by "capturing" the sounds played all at once by a synthesizer then breaking them down into different tracks. Another method is to play and record each track individually on the synthesizer. Finally, the third technique involves actually dictating the notes, one at a time, on the computer screen—the cyberspace-era version of writing music by hand.

Don't assume that just because an application looks pretty—for example, contains multimedia elements—it will take any less careful planning and coordination to get it right. If anything, the reverse is true. By adding multimedia elements to an application, you are greatly adding to the complexity of getting the application to come out right.

It's a good idea to have a target platform in mind for your multimedia application before you start work on it—for example, a Pentium with 16 MB of RAM and a 4X CD-ROM. (Of course, this system might be too fast for multimedia written for an older, 386-based system. Special effects might rush past in the blink of an eye, too fast for the user to even see them.) If you have a target platform in mind, you can test it to see that the speed with which multimedia effects occur are what you had in mind. Obviously, if your application will be used on a wide variety of platforms—as is the case, for example, with a shrink-wrapped CD-ROM, you should test it on the entire range of possible systems on which it will be used. It is a good idea to indicate in this situation the lowest possible acceptable configuration.

One important point about multimedia that is sometimes overlooked is that you cannot use graphics, sounds, and videos in your application without a license to do so. It is potentially a very expensive mistake to suppose that you can reuse a multimedia file just because you have possession of that file. To get around this problem, you can purchase libraries of multimedia files that are licensed for unlimited re-distribution. Otherwise, you should be certain that you have a license—sometimes termed *clearance*—to distribute as part of your application any multimedia file that you did not create.

Multimedia Tools

Now we'll take a brief look at some of the multimedia tools that ship with Visual Basic 4.

The Media Player Application

Media Player is a stand-alone, OLE-enabled application that you can easily embed in Visual Basic 4 projects to enable your users to play multimedia files. You can add the Media Player application to your toolbox in three different modes. The process of adding the application is described below; the different modes are listed in Table 20.1.

Table 20.1. Different Media Player modes.

Mode	Command Switch	Effect
Media Clip	Mplayer.Exe (with no additional command-line switch)	Full Media Player application is enabled.
MIDI Sequence	Mplayer.Exe /mid	Gives you a MIDI sequence, plays sounds, extracts sound clips from full sound files; non-sound multimedia functions disabled.
Video Clip	Mplayer.Exe /avi	Video clip player; non-video functions disabled.

To install any or all of these three insertable objects, use the Custom Controls dialog box found in the Tools menu. (Adding insertable objects and custom controls is described in Chapter 18.) You should bear in mind that you can choose to install Media Player in only one mode—for example, MIDI Sequence—or you can install all three, in which case they will appear in your toolbox as three different objects with different icons representing them.

After the Media Player insertable object has been properly loaded in your toolbox, you can draw one on a Visual Basic form. To access the Media Player menus at design-time, use the right mouse button to display the pop-up menu and select Edit. This enables you to load a multimedia file into the application. Your users will play the multimedia file at run-time simply by double-clicking on the Media Player object.

Using the Media Player interface, you can quickly and easily

- Play audio, video, or animation files
- Copy a multimedia clip into a document
- Link multimedia files to a document using OLE

- Display time or tracks on a scale with a moving thumb to indicate where you are in the file
- Set auto-rewind or auto-repeat to loop multimedia files—that is, continually play a sound file
- Set volume options
- Set MIDI output properties and new instruments using external MIDI ports

It's important to understand that Media Player works very differently depending on whether you load a multimedia file—for example, a sound—at design-time or at run-time. If a file is loaded at design-time, when the user double-clicks the Media Player object at run-time, that file is the *only* file the user can play. On the other hand, if no file is loaded at design-time, double-clicking on the Media Player object at run-time causes the Media Player application to load. This application looks pretty much like a CD player. The user can select a multimedia file to open from the Media Player's menu, which is then inserted in the OLE object. Pressing the Play button plays the selected multimedia file. All of this is a lot less complicated in practice than it might sound, so try it out, play with it, and have fun with multimedia!

For an example of Media Player in use, see the section later in this chapter titled "Playing a Sound File."

Multimedia MCI Control

The Multimedia MCI control—Mci32.ocx—manages the playback and recording of multimedia files on devices that comply with the Media Control Interface (MCI) standard. In appearance, this control looks like the buttons on an old-fashioned tape deck. Pushing individual buttons sends commands to MCI devices such as sound cards, CD-ROM drives and videotape players that cause multimedia files to play. The buttons on the MCI control are Previous, Play, Pause, Back, Stop, Record, and Eject.

In order to write an application that lets a user select a button on the Multimedia MCI control, the MCI device—for example, the CD-ROM drive—must be open. In addition, the buttons that you want your users to access must, of course, be set to Visible and Enabled.

There are a number of ways to program with this control. You can use it to let users control multimedia playback; or, on the other hand, you can set it to Invisible and manipulate the control in code at run-time. In other words, an application can use the Multimedia MCI control to play multimedia devices with or without user intervention.

You should also know that you can manipulate many MCI devices from one form. Generally, one Multimedia MCI control is used per device. The type of device can be set using the DeviceType property. The syntax of a DeviceType setting command is

```
MMControl.DeviceType = DeviceString
```

`DeviceString` is a string that can contain one of the following values: `AVIVideo`, `CDAudio`, `DAT`, `DigitalVideo`, `MMMovie`, `Other`, `Overlay`, `Scanner`, `Sequencer`, `VCR`, `Videodisc`, or `WaveAudio`. If you are creating an application in which the user will play a multimedia file (this situation is termed a *simple* multimedia device) then you *must* set the `DeviceType` value to one of these settings. If you are opening a multimedia file directly by specifying the filename (termed a *compound* use of the multimedia device) you don't have to specify a `DeviceType` provided that the multimedia file type is registered with Windows 95 so that the MCI control knows what kind of device to open. (If the Multimedia MCI control cannot correctly identify the device from the filename extension—perhaps it has not been entered in the Registry—then you should use a `DeviceType` setting.)

If you are programming the Multimedia MCI control at run-time (as opposed to letting the users of your application press the control's buttons), use the `Command` property. The syntax for this command is

```
MMControl.Command = CmdString
```

The possible values for `CmdString` are listed in Table 20.1. You should know that a command entered in this fashion is executed immediately (for example, as soon as the line of code that sets it is encountered). If an error is encountered—for example, the `DeviceType` might not be set—the error-code value is stored in the `MMControl.Error` property. Many of the possible `Command` actions listed in Table 20.2 require the value of other `MMControl` properties. If so, these are listed in Table 20.2 along with the default value of the property. In some cases, if a property has no value, it will not be used. This is indicated in the table.

Table 20.2. Multimedia MCI control **Command** property values.

Command	What It Does	Properties Used
Open	Opens a device.	Notify: default is False.
		Wait: default is True.
		Shareable: ignore if no value.
		DeviceType: ignore if no value.
		FileName: ignore if no value.
Close	Closes a device.	Notify: default is False.
		Wait: default is True.
Play	Plays a device.	Notify: default is True.
		Wait: default is False.
		From: ignore if no value.
		To: ignore if no value.

Command	What It Does	Properties Used
Pause	Pauses playing or recording. If Command = Pause is executed when the device is already paused, tries to resume playing or recording.	Notify: default is False. Wait: default is True.
Stop	Stops playing.	Notify: default is False. Wait: default is True.
Back	Steps backward—for example, to the next track.	Notify: default is False. Wait: default is True. Frame: ignore if no value.
Step	Steps forward.	Notify: default is False. Wait: default is True. Frame: ignore if no value.
Prev	Goes to the beginning of the current track using the Seek command. If executed within three seconds of the Prev command, goes to the beginning of the previous track or to the beginning of the first track if at the first track.	Notify: default is False. Wait: default is True.
Next	Goes to the beginning of the next track. If at the last track goes to the beginning of the last track.	Notify: default is False. Wait: default is True.
Seek	If not playing when executed, seeks a position. If playing, continues playing.	Notify: default is False. Wait: default is True. To: ignore if no value.

continues

Table 20.2. continued

Command	What It Does	Properties Used
Record	Records.	Notify: default is True.
		Wait: default is False.
		From: ignore if no value.
		To: ignore if no value.
		RecordMode: default is 0Insert.
Eject	Ejects media.	Notify: default is False.
		Wait: default is True.
Sound	Plays a sound.	Notify: default is False.
		Wait: default is False.
		Filename: ignore if no value.
Save	Saves an open multimedia file.	Notify: default is False.
		Wait: default is False.
		Filename: ignore if no value.

Most of the other Multimedia MCI control properties mentioned on this table are pretty straightforward. You should know that the Notify property if set to True generates a Done event that occurs when the MCI event is complete. If the Wait property is set to True, execution control does not return to the application calling the Multimedia MCI control until the MCI command is complete.

For full details—and a listing of all of the control's properties, events, methods, and error codes—you should browse the control's Help file. In addition, a demonstration application ships with the Professional and Enterprise Editions of Visual Basic 4 and can be found under the VB\Samples\MCI directory.

You'll see the Multimedia MCI control in action in a few moments in the section titled "Playing Video Files."

Playing a Sound File

One way to play sound files in your applications is to use the Media Player insertable object.

Start a new project and using the Custom Controls dialog box found under the Tools menu, make sure the MIDI Sequence (Mplayer.exe /mid) has been added to your toolbox. Save the form and project as Midi.frm and Midi.vbp, respectively. Next, change the form's properties to the following:

Object	Property	Setting
Form	BorderStyle	3-Fixed Dialog
	Caption	Play a Sound!
	Name	frmMidi

Double-click on the MIDI Sequence button in the toolbox to add the object to your form. When you do, an interface panel with the usual buttons (such as Play, Stop, and Fast Forward) and several menus appears on the screen. Press the Close button on this panel to close it; then run the project. The result, playing canyon.mid, is shown in Figure 20.1. That's all there is to it—no code is necessary!

Figure 20.1.
The MIDI application running.

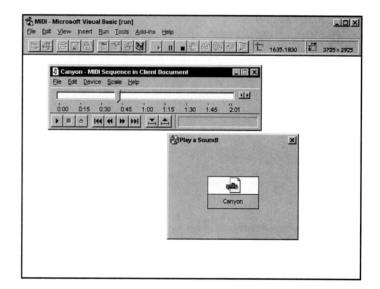

To use the sound player, just double-click on the object. The interface panel that appeared when you first added the object to the form appears on the screen again. Select the Open item from the File menu. An Open dialog box pops up on the screen. Choose a sound file to play from those loaded on your system, then press the Open button. The name of the file you selected appears below the object's icon in the form window and several buttons on the interface panel—Play, Pause, Stop, and so on—become active. Press the Play button to play your file.

Media Player's OLE Behavior

Media Player operates as an OLE server. In the context of playing multimedia files, OLE behavior may appear somewhat quirky.

Just so you know: if the user opens a sound file, plays it, and so on, and then closes the OLE server application (for example, the interface panel), a dialog box will appear on the screen asking whether the user wants to update the client document. If the user presses No, the panel disappears and the user can double-click on the object to select another file to open as before. If the user presses Yes, however, the sound file that was opened is loaded into the object for ever and ever. From then on, that is the only sound file the object will play until the Visual Basic application is closed and restarted.

You could have used Media Player to open a video file instead of a sound file. In just the same way, the Multimedia MCI control demonstration applet will open a video file in the next section. It, too, can be used to open any multimedia file, not just videos.

Playing Video Files

To get going on this quick Multimedia MCI control demo, start a new Visual Basic project. Using the Custom Controls dialog box found under the Tools menu, make sure that the Microsoft Common Dialog Control (Comdlg32.ocx) and the Microsoft Multimedia Control (Mci32.ocx) are added to your toolbox. Save the form and project as Mci.frm and Mci.vbp, respectively.

Double-click on the MCI button in the toolbox to add the control to the default form. Also, drop a common dialog control and a command button on the form. Place the controls on the form as shown in Figure 20.2, and set the properties of the objects as shown in Table 20.3.

Table 20.3. The visual design of the Video application.

Object	Property	Setting
Form	Border	3-Fixed Dialog
	Caption	Play a Video!
	Name	frmVideo
CommonDialog	DefaultExt	.avi
	DialogTitle	Open AVI File
	Filter	Video Files (*.avi) | *.avi | All Files(*.*) | *.*

Object	Property	Setting
	InitDir	C:\Windows
	Name	CommonDialog1
MCI Control	Name	MMControl1
	Visible	False
Command Button	Caption	Play
	Default	True
	Name	cmdPlay

Figure 20.2.
The MCI application at design-time.

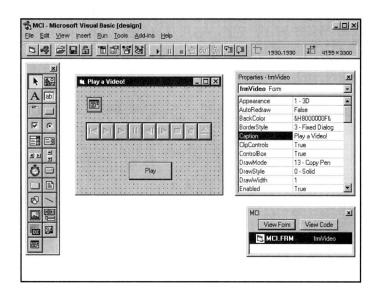

Because this application is set up to open a .avi file, you do not have to specify the `DeviceType` property of the Multimedia MCI control. The control senses automatically that `AVIVideo` is the device type to open. If you weren't specifying a file with an extension that was registered to a particular type of device player, you would have to make sure to specify the `DeviceType` property of the control before opening it.

When this application runs, the only thing the user sees is the command button with its Play caption. So, the user presses Play and the Open AVI File dialog box appears on the screen. The user selects an .avi file, then presses Open. When she presses Open, two things happen: the command button's caption changes to Stop and the .avi file plays in a window that opens on the screen. If the user wants to stop the file, all she has to do is press the Stop button.

As you probably have figured out by now, the hot spot in this application is that command button. Open the Code window and move to the command button's `Click` event. The first few lines of code should activate the common dialog controls and set the MCI player's `Wait` property to `False` so that the video can be interrupted while it is playing. Add that code like this:

```
Private Sub cmdPlay_Click()

    :
    CommonDialog1.ShowOpen
    MMControl1.Wait = False
    :

End Sub
```

Next, the code should transfer the file name that the user selects in the Open dialog box to the MCI control, change the command button's `caption property` to Stop, and play the file. That code appears as follows:

```
Private Sub cmdPlay_Click()

    :
    CommonDialog1.ShowOpen
    MMControl1.Wait = False

    If CommonDialog1.filename <> "" Then
        MMControl1.filename = CommonDialog1.filename
        cmdPlay.Caption = "Stop"
        MMControl1.Command = "OPEN"
        MMControl1.Command = "PLAY"
    End If

End Sub
```

Finally, if the user presses the Stop button, the MCI player should stop playing and close, and the command button's `Caption` property should be set back to Play. That code should go at the top of the `cmdPlay_Click()` event:

```
Private Sub cmdPlay_Click()

    If cmdPlay.Caption = "Stop" Then
        cmdPlay.Caption = "Play"
        MMControl1.Command = "STOP"
        MMControl1.Command = "CLOSE"
        Exit Sub
    End If

    CommonDialog1.ShowOpen
    MMControl1.Wait = False

    If CommonDialog1.filename <> "" Then
        MMControl1.filename = CommonDialog1.filename
        cmdPlay.Caption = "Stop"
        MMControl1.Command = "OPEN"
        MMControl1.Command = "PLAY"
    End If
End Sub
```

And that's it! Run the MCI application now and test it out. Press the Play button, find a video file to play, and enjoy the show! It should look something like Figure 20.3.

Figure 20.3.
The MCI application in action.

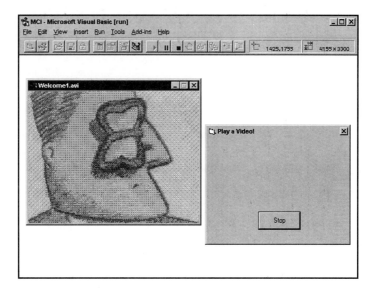

Third-Party Multimedia Tools

As you've seen in this chapter, you can put together some pretty decent multimedia applications in Visual Basic 4. But there are some specialized aspects of multimedia application development that require task-specific software. For example, in order to lay out a multimedia CD-ROM, you will need CD-ROM mastering software such as Corel Corporation's CD-Creator.

You may also want to extend the multimedia capabilities of Visual Basic. Many third-party vendors produce Visual Basic add-ons that make it easier to produce sophisticated effects. This is particularly true of sophisticated, high-resolution visual effects such as dissolves, rotations, and morphs.

Table 20.4 lists some of the leading multimedia add-ons to Visual Basic and gives you an idea of what they do.

Table 20.4. **Popular multimedia add-on products.**

Vendor	Product	Description
Arctic Software	MIDI CoolTools	A collection of Visual Basic custom controls that enable you to develop MIDI applications.
AudioFile	TalkWorks	Enables you to record, play back, and embed audio messages into Windows applications.

continues

Table 20.4, continued

Vendor	Product	Description
AutoDesk	Animation for Windows Developer Kit	Lets you add FLI and FLC animations to an application; includes a Visual Basic support layer.
Crisp Technology	JPEG Image Compressor	Custom control that supports JPEG compression and decompression.
Data Techniques	ImageMan	A library that enables you to add scanner and image-processing support to your Visual Basic applications.
First Byte	ProVoice	A library that enables you to convert text to speech from within a Visual Basic application.
Genus Microprogramming	GX Effects for Windows	A toolkit for adding multimedia effects to Windows applications.
ImageFX	FXTools/Visual Basic Professional	A suite of custom controls that add special effects such as dissolves, wipes, and so on to images, text, shapes, and video.
Iterated Systems	ColorBox for Windows	A software-development kit that enables you to integrate fractal still-image compression into your applications.
Lenel Systems International	MediaDeveloper	A development tool—with links to Visual Basic using custom controls—that enables you to create Windows applications with multimedia effects.
Looking Glass	RavenWrite	Available as a library or a custom Software control, RavenWrite is a hypermedia text engine that enables you to easily integrate graphic hot links into your applications.
Media Architect	MediaKnife/ ImageKnife	Custom controls—at press time available only in the VBX format—that enable you to create numerous visual special effects, including wipes, pushes, curtains, spirals, and sparkles.
Motion Works	MediaShop for Windows	A complete set of tools—including custom controls—for creating interactive multimedia applications.

Vendor	Product	Description
Rainbow Imaging	Picture++	An imaging library that enables you to display almost any kind of graphics file.
TegoSoft	Advanced Multimedia Control	Program helps you write applications that record sounds using a Windows-compatible sound card.
TerraTech	Dazzle/VB	A collection of custom controls for dealing with image files.
V-Graph	Multimedia Widgets	Visual Basic custom controls intended to give developers easy access to multimedia functions.

Summary

In this chapter you have had an overview of using multimedia to enhance your Visual Basic applications. Windows 95 is a rich multimedia environment, and you should certainly take the time to learn to add the flourishes and user-appeal that multimedia brings to your applications. Besides the bells and whistles, these elements make your projects more professional, polished, and appealing to the software marketplace.

21

Creating a Windows 95 Help File

There's more to a well-behaved Windows 95 program than just the code that performs its functions. You might have noticed that most Windows programs have their own help system designed to let the user who declines to read manuals know something about how each part of the program functions. The user selects an item in the application's Help menu, and a help window opens. Most applications use the built-in Windows help system, which does all the work. This engine requires only a .Hlp file, which defines the help for the application. Creating this file is the real trick to providing online help. To show you how that is done, you will develop a demonstration file named Editor.Hlp to use with the Editor application that's been put together in previous chapters. Topics covered in the process of developing this file include

- What to include in (and omit from) a good Help file
- The steps involved in creating help
- Designing hypertext links
- Enabling contents pages and keyword searches
- Using the Help compiler
- Using context-sensitive help
- Using third-party Help creation tools

You'll find that the things you must do to create and enable a help file—including providing hypertext links and keyword searches—are not very difficult. Activating the help within a Visual Basic application is also not difficult; you just use the common dialog control and the properties and methods reserved for WinHelp. Probably the greatest challenge in making a help system is the advanced planning you need to do to make sure your help is really useful for your program users.

Note: Creating online help requires two things: a word processor capable of handling Rich Text Format (RTF) and the Microsoft Windows Help Compiler. The former is something you have to provide on your own; Microsoft Word for Windows is an excellent choice, and the one used in this chapter. The help compiler is included as part of the Visual Basic Professional Edition.

Keys to Good Online Help

If you pause to think about your experiences with the help systems in different Windows applications you've used, you can probably think of several things that made each system either a good or bad source of information about its associated application. In general, a good help system should be

- **Thorough:** The system should cover every visible aspect of the application's user interface. This includes all menus and menu commands, each form, and each control on each form.

- **Flexible:** The system should provide more than one way for a user to find help on a topic. For example, a user should be able to find help for a particular control both by searching in the help's table of contents and by selecting the item in question and pressing the F1 key to obtain context-sensitive help.

- **Uncluttered:** The system should not provide help for intuitively obvious or trivial topics.

- **Concise:** Help for each individual item, ideally, shouldn't extend over more than one screen within the Help window.

- **Cross-referenced:** The system should let the user view related topics easily, usually by clicking highlighted words called hypertext links that take the user directly to help associated with the highlighted word or phrase.

It is a good idea to go through your application piece by piece (form by form, menu by menu, control by control) to determine how many help items you need. You can then determine which items should cross-reference each other. (Additional cross-references will likely suggest themselves to you as you write the help itself.) After you make some notes about what each help item should say, you're ready to begin creating the help system itself.

Steps to Creating Help

No matter the contents, the steps involved in creating a help file for any Visual Basic application are the same. They are

1. Create a word processor document that describes the help. This file includes a contents page, keywords that the user can use to find help items directly, definitions for hypertext links, and the help items themselves.

2. Convert the word processor document into RTF (Rich Text) format.

3. Prepare a Help project file that identifies the RTF file to use in creating the help.

4. Submit the help project file to the Windows Help Compiler.

5. Enable links to the finished help file within your application by providing the help file's name and other data to the common dialog control.

Creating the Text
for the Editor Help File

In order to create Editor.Hlp for the Windows help system you must first start by creating Editor.Rtf, a *rich text* file. Rich text includes all kinds of embedded items, such as footnotes and hidden text. It is the first step in creating a help file. After you create Editor.Rtf—which will specify how you want your help topics set up and in what text you want them—you will use the Help Compiler (Hc.Exe, which comes with the Visual Basic Professional Edition) along with a Help Project file (Editor.Hpj, coming up next) to create Editor.Hlp.

To create Editor.Rtf, you need a word processor capable of creating rich text files. In this example, I will use Microsoft Word for Windows Version 6.0 (other word processors can create rich text format files, so you aren't limited to using Word). If you have that package, start it in Windows now.

The first screen that the user will see might present an overview, or contents screen, something like Figure 21.1.

Figure 21.1.
A simple contents screen for editor help.

The user then can select help topics. For this example, include a section on different menu commands here. When the user clicks this item, a new screen might open, showing the available options for help on Editor commands, something like Figure 21.2.

Figure 21.2.
Commands for which help is available.

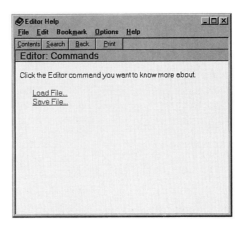

When the user clicks one of these options, such as Load File..., the appropriate help screen opens (with demonstration text only), as shown in Figure 21.3.

Figure 21.3.
Help for a selected topic.

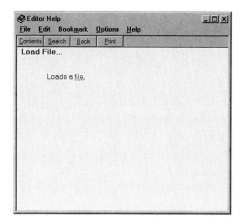

The process of moving from one screen to another in a help file (as from Figure 21.2 to 21.3) is called *jumping*. There are two kinds of jumps: jumps to another help screen and jumps to pop-up windows. You make a jump to another screen by selecting an underlined topic in Windows help; you display a pop-up window by selecting a topic with a dotted underline. Both types of underlined items appear green on a color monitor.

A *pop-up window* is a window that appears next to or below the item to which it is connected. Within a help system, pop-ups are generally used to define terminology. For example, because the word "file" in Figure 21.3 has a dotted underline under it, the user can click it for more information about the term "file," opening a pop-up window like that shown in Figure 21.4.

Figure 21.4.
A pop-up window for a selected item.

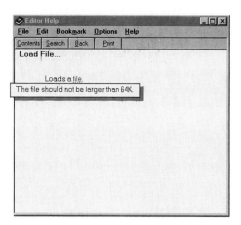

Enabling all these features is not difficult. They depend only on the way in which the Editor.Rtf file is set up.

To create the help file you just saw, first type the first screenful of information into Word now, as shown in Figure 21.1.

Next, you have to tell the help system what to do. You do this by adding *tags* to certain items, specifying what action to take when the user clicks that item. In this case, you want to jump to a new screen when the user clicks the word Commands. To indicate that, you highlight the word Commands and select the Word Format menu's Font… item. A dialog box labeled Font opens. You then select the Double Underline option in the Underline drop-down list box (this will become a single solid underline in the final help file). Click OK to close the Font dialog box.

Next, place the cursor immediately after the word Commands, open the Font dialog box again, and check the Hidden Text box in it. There must be no spaces between the word Commands and the hidden text that follows. Now you can add the jump tag, which will indicate what topic you want to jump to. Here, type `EDITOR_COMMANDS` (note that no spaces are used in a jump tag like this). That's what's involved in a jump tag: hidden text identifying the name of the help page that the help system should display when the user clicks the underlined item next to the tag.

Next, you have to create the EDITOR_COMMANDS screen (with the Load File… and Save File… jump tags). You do that by starting a new page. To insert a page break, select the Break item in Word's Insert menu. In the dialog box that opens, click the item marked Page Break and then click OK.

Now that you have started a new page you must indicate that this is the target of the jump tag you just created, using hidden text on the previous page (that is, you have to associate the page with the term EDITOR_COMMANDS). You do so using a footnote.

Thus, to associate this page of information with the jump to EDITOR_COMMANDS, place the cursor at the very beginning of the new page and select the Footnote… item in the Word Insert menu. A new dialog box labeled Footnote appears. Click the option button marked Custom Mark and type a number sign (#) in the text box next to it; then select OK to close the box.

At this point, Word cuts the window you're working on in half, displaying a new section at the bottom labeled Footnotes and placing the cursor after the mark you have selected (#, which also appears in the text you have been working on). Now type `EDITOR_COMMANDS` and return to the text window (the window above the Footnotes window) by clicking it.

By using a footnote with a # sign and by giving that footnote the text `EDITOR_COMMANDS`, you have connected the jump on the previous page to the current page. When the user clicks the word Commands, the page you have just connected to it will appear. Thus, you use a footnote using the # symbol and the appropriate page name, like EDITOR_COMMANDS, to identify jump destination pages.

There are other footnote symbols you can use here as well. For example, if you insert a footnote with the footnote mark $ and give it the text `Editor:Commands`, you give the current page a title. This title will appear in the list box when the user accesses the Search feature of Windows Help. If you add another footnote with the mark K and give it the text *Commands*, you define a keyword with which the user can search for a topic. Therefore, the $ symbol marks a title and the K symbol marks a keyword.

Finally, add the text `Editor:Commands`, the title, right after the footnotes you've inserted.

There are two jumps to be made on this new page itself, Load File... and Save File.... After double-underlining each, give these two items the tags `LOAD_FILE` and `SAVE_FILE` (as hidden text) and type the rest of the text into the window, as shown previously in Figure 21.2.

Now you need to create help screens for each of these items, Load File... and Save File.... You do that by inserting a hard page break with the Break item in the Insert menu and by typing the text of the Load File... demonstration help screen. Then connect this screen to the jump `LOAD_FILE` by inserting a footnote at the very beginning of this page with the footnote mark # as before.

Do the same for the Save File... help screen (use the text Save File... and the explanation "Saves a file."). Tie the Save File... help screen to the tag `SAVE_FILE` with another # footnote.

You're almost done with Editor.Rtf. The final step is to add a pop-up help window to the word "file" in the Load File... help screen.

Doing this is as easy as inserting the jumps you have already added. The only difference here is that instead of giving the word "file" a double underline, you give it a single underline (select the Underline option in the Format menu's Font item). Next, connect "file" to the text that will appear as you have done before, using a jump tag—which I'll call `FILE_POPUP`—and connecting that to a new page of text (insert a hard page break), which starts with a # footnote. You then give this footnote the text `FILE_POPUP`. Finally, type the text `The file should not be larger than 64K` into the `FILE_POPUP` page.

That's it; the file Editor.Rtf is done. Save this file now in .Rtf format by selecting the Save As... item in Word's File menu and by selecting Rich Text Format (the Rtf option in the Save File As Type box). (See Listing 21.1. The footnotes are included here.)

Listing 21.1. Editor Help Contents.

```
CommandsEDITOR_COMMANDS
—page break—


#$KEditor: Commands

Click the Editor command you want to know more about.
Load File...LOAD_FILE
Save File...SAVE_FILE
—page break—


# Load File...
```

continues

Listing 21.1. continued

```
     Loads a fileFILE_POPUP.
—page break—
```

```
# Save File...

     Saves a file.
—page break—
```

```
# The file should not be larger than 64K.
—page break—
```

All that remains is to convert Editor.Rtf into Editor.Hlp, which the Windows Help system will read. You do this with the assistance of a help project file, Editor.Hpj; you'll look into that next.

Creating Context-Sensitive Help

It is possible also to create context-sensitive help by using the `HelpContextID` properties of forms and controls. You can give a different number to each item for which you want to enable context-sensitive help. Doing this allows you to provide help information on a control-by-control level, which the user accesses by pressing F1 with the relevant item selected.

To enable your compiled Help file (.Hlp file) to correctly respond to context sensitive queries—as noted earlier these are set in Visual Basic using the `HelpContextID` property—you must specify the relationship between the context number and the topic it points to in the help project file (.Hpj) used to compile the finished .Hlp file. Help project files are discussed further in the section *Creating the Project File Editor.Hpj* below. This information goes in the [Map] section of the .Hpj file. For more information on how to incorporate context-sensitive help in your help files, see Chapter 6, "Creating Help Files," which can be found in the "Help Compiler Guide" documentation that comes with the Professional and Enterprise Editions of Visual Basic.

For example, to enable context-sensitive help for the Editor's Load File... command, display the Visual Basic Menu Editor, select Load File... in the scrolling area at the bottom, and then enter a context ID number for the Load File...command; you must choose a unique number (you might, for instance, make it 1001). Click OK to exit the Menu Editor. Then, outside of Visual Basic, you must set up the relationship between your newly entered context ID number for the Load File... command and the Help page containing the information you want shown when the user presses F1. Use a line like the following with the EDITOR.HPJ [MAP] section:

```
1001 = FILE_LOAD
```

Creating the Project File Editor.Hpj

The next step in creating the editor help file is to create Editor.Hpj. This file is the one to be passed to the help compiler, HC.Exe. The compiler will create Editor.Hlp. You start Editor.Hpj by indicating that you want to save a record of errors that occur during compilation in the file Editor.Err. You then specify that the title of the help system should be Editor Help, and that you do not want to compress this file (an option that can produce more compact help files). You also specify that you want to see all warnings, like this:

```
[OPTIONS]
errorlog = editor.err
title = Editor Help
compress = false
warning = 3
      :
      :
```

Next, indicate that the rich text format file that holds the help text is called Editor.Rtf.

```
[OPTIONS]
errorlog = editor.err
title = Editor Help
compress = false
warning = 3

[FILES]
editor.rtf
      :
      :
```

Finally, you can specify the location, the title (Editor Help), and the size of the help window on the screen, like this:

```
[OPTIONS]
errorlog = editor.err
title = Editor Help
compress = false
warning = 3

[FILES]
editor.rtf

[WINDOWS]
main = "Editor Help", (0,0,1023,1023 ),,, (192,192,192 )
```

That completes Editor.Hpj; it was that quick. Now that you have Editor.Rtf and Editor.Hpj, you're ready to produce the actual help file, Editor.Hlp.

Creating the Help File Editor.Hlp

I use the help compiler for Windows 95, which is called Hc.Exe. Using the Run... command in the start menu, start that program and pass it the name of the project file Editor.Hpj, like this:

```
C:\VB2\HC>HC EDITOR.HPJ
```

That's all there is to it; the help compiler creates Editor.Hlp from the two files editor.HPJ and editor.RTF. All that remains is to connect the help to the Editor itself.

Connecting Editor.Hlp to the Editor Program

Reaching the Editor.Hlp file from the Editor program is not hard. First, add a Help menu to the Editor with menu items called Contents... and Search for Help on..., as shown in Figure 21.5.

Figure 21.5.
Adding help to the menu of the Editor program.

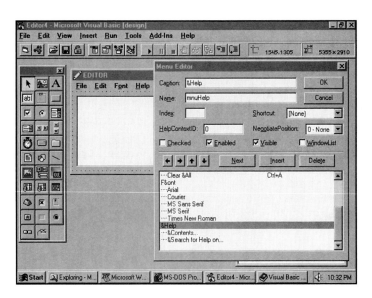

Next, choose the Contents menu item to bring up the Sub procedure `mnuHelpContents_Click()`.

```
Private Sub mnuHelpContents_Click()
    .
    .
    .
End Sub
```

When the user makes this selection you want to call up the help system. You can do this using the `ShowHelp` method of the common dialog control. First, of course, you must add a common dialog control to the Editor's form. You do this by double-clicking the Tool icon on the toolbox.

With this done, you need to enable the code that accesses the help system. There are two important properties you must set here: HelpFile, which specifies which help file to connect to (Editor.Hlp in this case), and HelpCommand, which specifies which kind of help window to open into. With these properties set you can invoke ShowHelp to bring up the help system with the correct file loaded. The necessary code looks like the following:

```
Private Sub mnuHelpContents_Click()
        CommonDialog1.HelpFile = "Editor.HLP"
        CommonDialog1.HelpCommand = cdlHelpContents
        CommonDialog1.ShowHelp
End Sub
```

This will bring the help file up on the screen. Notice that the constant cdlHelpContents is assigned to the HelpCommand property. This is one of several constants, already defined in Visual Basic, for setting what kind of help to access. The constants and their uses are shown in Table 21.1.

Table 21.1. Constants used for setting the Help common dialog properties.

Constant	Use
cdlHelpCommand	Executes a Help macro.
cdlHelpContents	Displays the Help contents topic.
cdlHelpContext	Displays Help for a particular context. When using this setting, you must also specify a context using the HelpContext property.
cdlHelpContextPopup	Displays in a pop-up window a particular Help topic identified by a context number.
cdlHelpForceFile	Ensures that the help engine displays the correct Help file. If the correct Help file is currently displayed, no action occurs. If the incorrect Help file is displayed, the engine opens the correct file.
cdlHelpHelpOnHelp	Displays Help for using the Help application itself.
cdlHelpIndex	Displays the index of the specified Help file. An application should use this value only for a Help file with a single index.
cdlHelpKey	Displays Help for a particular keyword. When using this setting, you must also specify a keyword using the HelpKey property.
cdlHelpPartialKey	Displays the topic found in the keyword list that matches the keyword passed in the dwData parameter if there is one exact match. If more than one match exists, the Search dialog box with the topics found listed in the Go To list box is displayed. If no match exists, the Search dialog box is displayed. To bring up the Search dialog box without passing a keyword, use a long pointer to an empty string.

continues

Table 21.1. continued

Constant	Use
cdlHelpQuit	Notifies the Help application that the specified Help file is no longer in use.
cdlHelpSetContents	Determines which contents topic is displayed when a user presses the F1 key.
cdlHelpSetIndex	Sets the context specified by the HelpContext property as the current index for the Help file specified by the HelpFile property.

Using the cdlHelpPartialKey constant, you can activate the Search for Help on... item as well. The code to do so looks like this:

```
Private Sub mnuHelpSearch_Click()
        CommonDialog1.HelpFile = "Editor.HLP"
        CommonDialog1.HelpCommand = cdlHelpPartialKey
        CommonDialog1.ShowHelp
End Sub
```

Let's see this at work; run the Editor now and select the Contents item in the Help menu; this brings up the help window, as first shown in Figure 21.1. The user can click the Commands item (shown underlined) to switch to another window, just as in normal Windows help. In addition, the user can select items with a dotted underline (the word "file"), bringing up a pop-up help window. The pop-up disappears when clicked. That's all there is to enabling a help system.

New Features in Windows Help

WinHelp version 4.0 includes various features that are improvements over previous versions of the Windows Help system. Using the current version of HC.EXE (the one that ships with the Professional and Enterprise Editions of Visual Basic 4) to compile your Help files enables you to include these features—making your Help files Windows 95-like in look and feel.

Enhanced features of WinHelp 4.0 (and the Windows 95 Help system) include

- Improved copy facilities
- Improved printing facilities
- New background color override
- New combined index option
- New context menu
- New context-sensitive Help access
- New Help Topics dialog box

- New key and button functions
- New Options menu
- Training cards available as a feature

Here is a look at these changes one by one.

You'll find that the Copy dialog box has been removed from WinHelp 4.0. Instead, users select the text they want to copy and then choose Copy from the menu. In addition, Help file text can be directly selected and dragged to any program that is set up as an OLE2.0 drop target.

Users can now print multiple topics by selecting a *book* in the Contents tab, and then clicking Print. Also, pop-up topics can be printed using a right-mouse button click.

If the user has changed the desktop color scheme so that the Help file appears as something other than black text on a white background, then any author-defined window background colors are ignored.

In WinHelp version 4.0, the user has the option of viewing either individual Help indexes or a combined index.

By clicking the right mouse button while viewing a Help file, the user will now activate a context menu. Commands on this menu are

- Annotate
- Copy
- Print Topic
- Font
- Keep Help On Top
- Use System Colors

In addition to accessing context-sensitive Help file capabilities using the F1 key, there are now two additional ways to activate context-sensitive Help. The user can click the ? [Question Mark] button on the application's title bar and then click an object or control. Or, the user can click the right mouse button on an object or control and select What's This? from the right mouse context menu.

The Esc key now closes open Help file windows. If there is only one Help file window open, Esc closes the Help system.

An Options Menu, which enables the user to configure the appearance and behavior of the Help file, has been added to the main Help window menu bar.

Training Cards is a new feature that allows bidirectional communication between a WinHelp file and another application. WinHelp can send a message to the application, and then the application can send a message back to the program telling it what topic to display next. You can use the

Training Cards feature to *talk* users through complex tasks. This can work much the way Wizards do. (A good example of the use of Training Cards built into Windows 95 can be found in the troubleshooting topic of the Windows 95 Help file. If you select Network Troubleshooting, Training Cards walks you through the process of getting your network connections straightened out.)

As you can see, this powerful feature set (mostly built into HC.EXE and WinHelp version 4.0, requiring no additional work on your part) can enable you to quickly put together modern Windows 95 compliant Help systems.

Third-Party Help File Tools

If all those tags and hidden text items and footnotes you need to make a Help RTF file seem tedious to manage (especially for a large project with a lot of help items), don't worry. Your desire for easier help file generation has been anticipated by a number of third-party vendors, who have prepared programs that make it a breeze to generate Windows help files. Some of these programs are even shareware available online (for example, use CompuServe's Windows File Finder and search on the keywords `help` and `authoring`).

Programs such as Doc-To_Help, ForeHelp, WhizNotes, Help Yourself, the HyperText Development Kit (HDK), HelpGen, RoboHelp, and Visual Help can take much of the guesswork out of help file authoring. Many of these programs include nifty graphical interfaces with drag and drop features that make establishing hypertext links much easier than embedding hidden text tags.

The Doc-To-Help program, for example, includes both print and online help template files. You can use this tool to help manage both online help and your product's printed manual. ForeHelp, on the other hand, is much easier to use and can be learned quickly. It isn't for use with very large help systems, however. Finally, the Hypertext Development Kit (HDK) has both object-oriented and database features. For instance, HDK warns you if you attempt to delete a linked topic from your current help. It also monitors context ID numbers and warns you of conflicts.

Again, you can find out much more about Windows Help authoring products in the relevant product areas on online services such as CompuServe and America Online.

Summary

In this chapter you have seen how to design and implement online Help in Visual Basic. After discussing some pointers regarding what a good help system should have and should avoid, you were introduced to the steps involved in creating online help. Through the medium of creating a very simple help system for the Editor application, you learned how to create the RTF file that is the basis of any help system, how to set up a project file that refers to the RTF file and sets other help system parameters, and how to compile the project and RTF files into a working Windows help file.

You then learned how to display this help file within the Windows Help engine using the common dialog control and its ShowHelp method. Finally, you briefly learned some third-party Windows Help authoring tools that can make it easier to create fully functional online help systems for your projects.

New Method	Description
ShowOpen	A method applying to the common dialog control. Using this method invokes the WINHELP.EXE help engine. The correct control properties must be set before invoking ShowOpen, such as those to set which help file to use and which help window to open.

New Properties	Description
HelpFile	Property of the common dialog control used to establish which help file to open when ShowHelp is invoked.
HelpCommand	Property of the common dialog control used to set which kind of help—contents, keyword search, and so on—to display when ShowOpen is invoked. Used with a number of predefined constants for the various help types available.

22

Creating an Installation Program

Overview

By now you should see that Visual Basic 4 offers a great many tools and capabilities to simplify as well as expand your application programming capabilities. Still, you aren't quite finished examining these capabilities yet. In this chapter, you will learn how to add that last important part of a distributable application package: a setup program.

This chapter covers the following topics:

- The nature of a setup program, and why to include one when you distribute a program
- Using SetupWizard to create application packages that you can distribute
- Elements of an installation setup
- Customizing your setup program

Suppose you've created an application in Visual Basic that you'd like to share or even sell. How do you go about distributing it? You might think you need only prepare an EXE file of your application and put it on a diskette, but things aren't that simple. You see, depending on the custom tools you use to create an application, a Visual Basic application can actually require more than a dozen separate files to be able to run on a target computer system. Most important, you cannot count on the target system having all these files in the correct location. This is especially true if your target doesn't own a copy of Visual Basic itself (which you have no way of knowing in advance).

If you were able to determine how to get all the necessary files onto a disk (perhaps you had to compress them to save room), you'd still give your client the rather difficult job of copying all these files to the correct locations on the hard disk—some files going into an application directory, others into the Windows System directory, and so on. Your user would also have to uncompress any compressed files. All this would have to be done by hand, step-by-step, relying no doubt on your written instructions. I'll wager that you know from personal experience that complicated program installation like what was just described is something users do not appreciate.

Microsoft knows it as well, and has for years. If you've installed any of its products (including, of course, Visual Basic), then you've run into its solution to the problem. All Microsoft Windows 95 (and most earlier) applications feature a single executable file, usually called Setup.exe, that you run to install the application and all its files—DLLs, custom controls, help files, and so on. Setup copies (and possibly decompresses) all the required files for you, putting each into the right place.

Microsoft has shared its knowledge of making Setup files in a nifty application named SetupWizard, a part of the Setup Kit that comes with the Visual Basic Professional Edition. The Setup Wizard just about automates the process of creating distribution disks for your Visual Basic applications. But that's not the only thing the Setup Kit offers. It also includes the source code for a customizable setup program, Setup1.vbp, which you can modify so that your setup program performs exactly as you wish it to. These tools easily enable you to create setup routines for Windows 95 applications with professional polish and features. In this chapter, I'll show you something about both the SetupWizard and how to use Setup1.vbp.

Creating a Distributable Application

If you have an interesting application you want to distribute to friends, coworkers, or even clients, you can use SetupWizard, which is included with the Visual Basic package, to make distribution disks for your program. Doing so involves these steps:

1. Find and click the SetupWizard icon.

2. Enter the path name (disk, directory, and filename) of the project file for which you want to create a distribution disk.

   Remember that the project file has an extension .VBP. Click Next to continue.

3. Select any special features supported by your application. Click Next.

4. Choose the disk drive to use and the type of disks to support. Click Next.

5. Add or remove files from the list shown as needed. Click Next to build distribution disks.

6. Follow screen prompts to create the distribution disks.

You will learn more about each step in turn.

When you first run SetupWizard, you're presented with a screen like the one shown in Figure 22.1. The first thing you're asked to do is specify what project to build the distribution disks out of.

Figure 22.1.
Selecting a project file in SetupWizard.

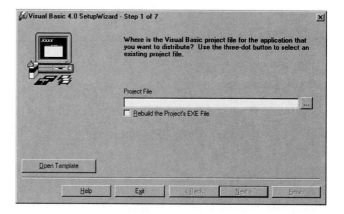

Note that you can click the ellipsis to the right of the text edit box to browse on your hard disk and find the project file you want. With this done, click the Next button.

If an up-to-date .exe file for your application isn't yet available, the SetupWizard launches Visual Basic and prepares one for you. (This always happens if you click the Rebuild the Project's EXE File checkbox on the first SetupWizard screen.) When the .exe file is ready, SetupWizard moves to step two.

In step two, you're asked if you wish to install any data access engines, as shown in Figure 22.2.

Figure 22.2.
*Selecting data access engines
to install in SetupWizard.*

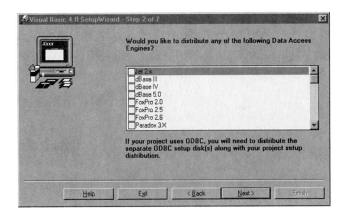

Click to select the drivers to install, if any, and then click the Next button.

In the third step of the setup process, you must determine where to save the distribution files. You can put them onto floppy disks or onto a local or network hard drive. The SetupWizard screen associated with this step is shown in Figure 22.3.

Figure 22.3.
*Selecting where to put the
distribution files.*

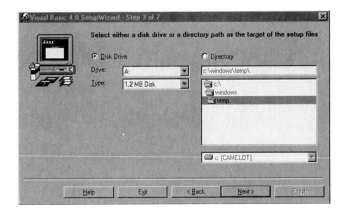

Click the option button for the destination you want. Note that you use a hard drive if you want to prepare files to distribute over a network or if you want to eventually distribute your application on CD-ROM. (Personally, I find one CD-ROM much easier to manage than thirty floppy disks.) When you're finished selecting, click the Next button.

In the fourth step of the SetupWizard process, the Wizard looks for any OLE servers that your application needs. It presents this information to you on a screen similar to that shown in Figure 22.4.

You can double-click a server's name to remove it from the list. When you're finished, click the Next button.

Figure 22.4.
SetupWizard determines which OLE servers your application needs.

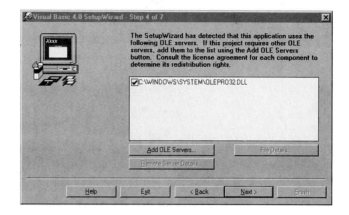

In step five of this process, the SetupWizard looks for file dependencies that your application requires in order to run on any Windows-equipped PC. It presents this information to you on a screen similar to that shown in Figure 22.5.

Figure 22.5.
SetupWizard determines what other files your application depends on to run properly.

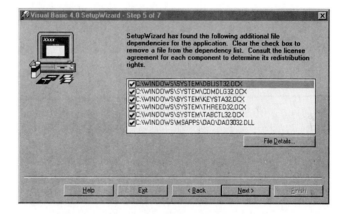

Note that you need to see whether you have the right to distribute each of these files before you proceed. You can uncheck a file to remove it from the list; however, this will undoubtedly render your application useless. When you're finished with this screen, click Next.

In the penultimate SetupWizard step, the program asks how your application is to be distributed. It does this using a screen like that shown in Figure 22.6.

If your Visual Basic program is going to be installed in a directory of its own as a standard application file, you need only click Next, taking you to the final step.

In the final SetupWizard step, you're shown all the files that your application requires, as shown in Figure 22.7.

Figure 22.6.
SetupWizard wants to know
some specifics about the
application.

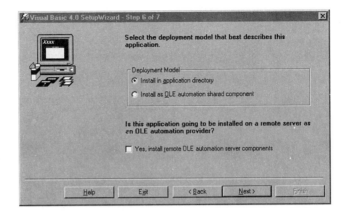

Figure 22.7.
SetupWizard shows the files
needed to build your
application setup disks.

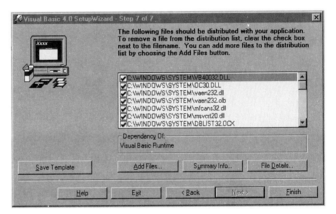

Again, you need to be certain you have the right to distribute all these files before proceeding. You can double-click an item to remove it from the list, but again, this will probably cripple your application and render it useless. Removing a file might be OK for removing certain Visual Basic DLLs (for example, VB40032.dll) when your program is going to colleagues that have Visual Basic or Visual Basic programs installed already. When you're satisfied with your file list, click the Finish button.

The SetupWizard now proceeds to build the distribution version of your application and create the appropriate setup file. If you're saving the application onto floppy disks, the SetupWizard prompts you for each disk in turn after first telling you how many are needed.

Note: If at any point you need to suspend the SetupWizard, but would like to return and pick up where you left off, click the Save Template button. This lets you save your existing setup work. You can then click Open Template on the first SetupWizard screen to open your file and proceed with your work.

That's really all there is to creating a distributable application. If you're like me, though, this may not be enough. What, for example, has SetupWizard created? Is there any way to bend this creation more firmly to one's will? In fact there is, although doing so successfully depends on knowing more about what the SetupWizard has done. It turns out that the files produced are common to any Microsoft Windows installation program, even ones that bypass the SetupWizard and rely instead on other Setup toolkit files.

Parts of an Installation Setup

In addition to your application's .exe file and any .dlls and .ocxs it needs, the SetupWizard adds several other files to the first of your distribution diskettes. The files are described in Table 22.1.

Table 22.1. Essential setup files on the first distribution diskette.

Setup File	Purpose
SETUP.EXE	A "bootstrap" program that begins the installation process; this is the program your application user should choose. After Setup installs the data needed by the installation process, this program passes control to the custom installation program, usually called Setup132.exe.
SETUP132.EXE	The custom installation program. This program does the actual work of copying files to the correct location on the user's hard disk. Note that you can customize this program; it is itself a Visual Basic program, saved as Setup1.vbp in the \SETUPKIT\SETUP1 directory of your main Visual Basic directory.
SETUP.LST	A text file that shows all the files that must be installed on the user's computer. This information is used by Setup132.exe. You can edit this information to create a more customized installation process.
SETUPKIT.DLL	A library of functions used by Setup and Setup1. This is one of the first files copied to the user's hard disk during the bootstrap part of the installation process.

Ver.dll No Longer Needed with Windows 95

Previous versions of Visual Basic installation required the dynamic link library Ver.dll, which contained functions to expand compressed files. With Windows 95, this .dll is no longer needed.

Using the preceding files, you can actually create distribution disks without even opening the SetupWizard. Of course, you need to know all the files your application requires. With all these files listed, you then determine what files to put on what disks (if more than one is needed), and modify the file Setup.lst accordingly. No changes are necessarily needed to Setup.exe and Setup132.exe.

The file Setup.lst is probably the most important part of creating an install; this file lets the rest of the Setup files know what files must be installed and where they should go. The SetupWizard creates this file for you, but you can build your own Setup.lst file if you know what you're doing.

About Setup.lst

The file Setup.lst, a text file, contains three different sections, which are described in Table 22.2.

Table 22.2. The three sections of the Setup.lst text file.

Setup.lst Section	Purpose
[BOOTSTRAP]	Lists all files that must be loaded before the application and its dependency files can be copied.
[FILES]	Files required by the application. Each file appears on a line by itself, with information identifying the file and its destination.
[SETUP]	Custom installation information, including the name of the application (appears on the Setup "splash screen," that flashy background that takes over the monitor whenever the user runs a setup program), the default application directory to use, the name of the custom setup program file (for example, Setup132.exe), info about the presence of Btrieve and ODBC drivers, and the filename for your application's executable file.

By editing Setup.lst, you can achieve a level of custom control over the installation process. In particular, modifying the [SETUP] section of this file lets you determine important things like the default destination directory (this is your suggestion for where the application should go; the user generally gets the chance to override this choice) and the application name to display during installation on the so-called splash screen. If you like, you can run the SetupWizard to create the Setup.lst file for you, and then modify the results using a text editor.

Working with Setup.lst

Information in the [FILES] section of Setup.lst takes on a special form. Each file must appear on a line by itself, in the following format:

```
Filex=y,[SPLIT],file,install,path,register,date,size,[version]
```

The parts of this line are explained in Table 22.3.

Table 22.3. Syntax of Entries in the [FILES] section of Setup.lst.

File component	Purpose
File	A keyword that appears as-is at the beginning of each line specifying a file to copy.
x	A sequence number. Values start with one; each line in the file section must be numbered in order without skipping values.
y	The disk number on which the file appears. If all files are on a single disk, then the number is always 1.
SPLIT	An optional keyword that specifies that this file has been split across disks because it's too big to fit on a single disk. Each part of a split file except the last must be tagged with this keyword.
file	The name of the file that's being copied.
install	The installation name of the file that's being copied. This differs from the name on the source diskettes if, for example, the file has been compressed. (Such files usually have the last letter in their extension replaced by an underscore.)
path	Where to install the file. Although you can specify an actual path, it's better to use one of the path macros shown in Table 22.4.
register	How to include the file in the user's system registry.
date	The last modification date of the file.
size	Size in bytes of the file.
version	Optional internal version number of the file.

The path part of a file specification line might be among the most important part of creating a good installation program. Creating the file specification line requires that you know the various macros available for specifying a copy destination, as shown in Table 22.4.

Table 22.4. Macros for specifying a destination path for installing files.

Macro	Meaning
$(WinSysPath)	The user's Windows System subdirectory.
$(WinPath)	The user's Windows directory.
$(AppPath)	The application directory specified by the user; uses the DefaultDir value in the SETUP section if the user does not specify otherwise.
$(AppPath)\SAMPLES	A samples subdirectory under the application directory.
c:\path	A literal path. Microsoft recommends against this because it forces a destination on your user.

Information in the [SETUP] portion of Setup.lst also takes a special form. The [SETUP] section defines how the setup program will look, some defaults, and some special options. The different items available are shown in Table 22.5.

Table 22.5. Meaning of items in the [SETUP] section of Setup.lst.

Item	Description
Title	Name of the application as it should appear on the Setup splash screen.
DefaultDir	Name of the default application directory. The user can override this.
Setup	Name of the custom setup program, usually Setup132.exe.
Btrieve	Set to a nonzero value if any Btrieve drivers are included in the distribution.
ODBC	Set to a nonzero value if any ODBC drivers are included in the distribution.
AppEXE	Name of the application file, such as Editor.exe.

How does all this work together? Listing 22.1 shows what a typical Setup.lst file looks like as prepared by the SetupWizard.

Listing 22.1. The Setup.lst file from the SetupWizard for the Editor application.

```
[BootStrap]
File1=1,,setup132.ex_,setup132.exe,$(WinPath),$(EXESelfRegister),,6/15/1995,
➥155648,4.0.0.2209
File2=1,,stkit432.dl_,stkit432.dll,$(WinSysPath),,$(Shared),6/15/1995,25088,
➥4.0.22.9
File3=1,,VB40032.DL_,VB40032.DLL,$(WinSysPath),,$(Shared),6/15/1995,707856,
➥4.0.22.9
File4=1,,OC30.DL_,OC30.DLL,$(WinSysPath),$(DLLSelfRegister),$(Shared),
```

```
➥3/22/1995,638464,3.10.0.0
File5=1,,vaen232.dl_,vaen232.dll,$(WinSysPath),,$(Shared),6/15/1995,10240,
➥2.0.0.5208
File6=1,,vaen232.ol_,vaen232.olb,$(WinSysPath),,$(Shared),3/22/1995,34816,
➥2.0.0.4921
File7=1,,mfcans32.dl_,mfcans32.dll,$(WinSysPath),,$(Shared),6/9/1995,133904,
➥3.2.1.0
File8=1,,msvcrt20.dl_,msvcrt20.dll,$(WinSysPath),,$(Shared),6/9/1995,253952,
➥2.11.0.0

[Files]
File1=1,,DBLIST32.OC_,DBLIST32.OCX,$(WinSysPath),$(DLLSelfRegister),$(Shared),
➥6/15/1995,140288,4.0.22.8
File2=1,,COMDLG32.OC_,COMDLG32.OCX,$(WinSysPath),$(DLLSelfRegister),$(Shared),
➥6/15/1995,84480,4.0.22.8
File3=1,,KEYSTA32.OC_,KEYSTA32.OCX,$(WinSysPath),,$(Shared),6/15/1995,115200,
➥1.0.17.0
File4=1,,THREED32.OC_,THREED32.OCX,$(WinSysPath),$(DLLSelfRegister),$(Shared),
➥6/15/1995,193536,1.0.34.0
File5=1,,TABCTL32.OC_,TABCTL32.OCX,$(WinSysPath),,$(Shared),6/15/1995,123392,
➥1.0.11.0
File6=1,,DAO3032.DL_,DAO3032.DLL,$(WinSysPath),$(DLLSelfRegister),$(Shared),
➥6/15/1995,443152,2.99.0.1806
File7=1,,MSJT3032.DL_,MSJT3032.DLL,$(WinSysPath),,$(Shared),6/15/1995,962832,
➥2.99.0.1806
File8=1,,MSJTER32.DL_,MSJTER32.DLL,$(WinSysPath),,$(Shared),6/15/1995,23824,
➥2.99.0.1806
File9=1,,MSJINT32.DL_,MSJINT32.DLL,$(WinSysPath),,$(Shared),6/15/1995,34576,
➥2.99.0.1806
File10=1,,VBAJET32.DL_,VBAJET32.DLL,$(WinSysPath),,$(Shared),6/15/1995,52584,
➥2.0.0.5208
File11=1,,VBDB32.DL_,VBDB32.DLL,$(WinSysPath),,$(Shared),6/15/1995,62016,
➥4.0.22.9
File12=1,,MSRD2X32.DL_,MSRD2X32.DLL,$(WinSysPath),,$(Shared),6/15/1995,249616,
➥2.99.0.1806
File13=1,,MSWNG300.DL_,MSWNG300.DLL,$(WinSysPath),,$(Shared),6/15/1995,292624,
➥2.99.0.1806
File14=1,,DAO2532.TL_,DAO2532.TLB,$(WinSysPath),,$(Shared),6/15/1995,48212
File15=1,,OLEPRO32.DL_,OLEPRO32.DLL,$(CommonFiles)\OleSvr,$(DllSelfRegister),
➥$(Shared),6/15/1995,74240,4.0.0.5135
File16=1,,Editor.ex_,Editor.exe,$(AppPath),$(EXESelfRegister),,8/2/1995,22528,
➥1.0.0.0

[Setup]
Title=Editor
DefaultDir=$(ProgramFiles)\Editor4
Setup=setup132.exe
AppExe=Editor.exe
```

Just to customize a little, you could change the line

```
Title=Editor
```

to something like

```
Title=Visual Basic Demonstration Editor
```

You don't have to include the word "Setup" as part of the title; Setup132.exe does this for you. Modifying this line lets you change the splash screen to say something more to your liking.

About Setup1.vbp

For the ultimate in customization, you can go directly into the Setup1.vbp file and make modifications. Any modification you make to this project file and its components will be reflected in all subsequent setup files, even those produced by the SetupWizard, unless you choose to make a copy.

In order to work with Setup1.vbp you must know a good bit about working with the Windows 95 API, a subject I first broached back in Chapter 17. A great many of the procedures in Setup1.vbp rely on Windows API functions.

As an example, you might consider changing the color of the splash screen created by Setup1.exe. The relevant code, shown next, is found in the `DrawBackGround` procedure within the form frmSetup1.

```
'Paint blue screen
'
For intY = 0 To intFormHeight Step intBANDHEIGHT
    Line (-1, intY - 1)-(intFormWidth, intY + intBANDHEIGHT), RGB(0, 0, sngBlueCur),
    ➡BF
    sngBlueCur = sngBlueCur + sngBlueStep
Next intY
```

This procedure draws the blue gradient fill shown on most current splash screens. If you change the RGB value in the following line:

```
Line (-1, intY - 1)-(intFormWidth, intY + intBANDHEIGHT), RGB(sngBlueCur, 0, 0), BF
```

you're in effect telling the procedure to draw in red, not blue. (The values given to the RGB function, integers from 0 to 255, specify the red, green, and blue components, respectively, of the color in which to draw.)

That's all there is to creating a SETUP program and distribution diskettes, even down to customizing your Setup1.exe file so it doesn't look like everyone else's. With this information, plus a help system and a working application developed with the principles shown in this book, you should be well on your way to success as a Visual Basic 4 programmer for Microsoft Windows 95. Good luck!

Summary

In this chapter you learned the importance of a good installation program. You learned how Visual Basic's SetupWizard (a part of the Professional Edition's Setup Kit) takes you step-by-step through the process of creating a distributable application package. You looked at the component files that go into an installation, along with the function of each. I took you inside the most important of these files and in the process showed you how to customize an installation and even create one without relying on the SetupWizard. Finally, you peeked inside Setup1.vbp to see something about modifying and customizing your installation even further.

A

Visual Basic Naming Requirements and Conventions

In the interest of standardization and readability, Microsoft has created naming conventions for Visual Basic. The primary objectives in creating these conventions were as follows:

- To be precise, complete, readable, memorable, and unambiguous
- To be consistent with other language conventions
- To allow for longer, more descriptive object names

The names of declared constants, variables, and procedures *must* follow the following four guidelines:

- These names must begin with a letter.
- The names cannot contain embedded periods or type-declaration characters.
- The names of constants, variables, and procedures cannot be longer than 200 characters. The names of classes, forms, modules, and controls cannot exceed 40 characters.
- The declared item names cannot use *restricted keywords*. Restricted keywords are words that Visual Basic uses as part of its language. This includes such predefined statements as If and Loop, functions such as Len and Abs, and operators such as Or and Mod.

Although it is not recommended, you can give forms and controls the same name as a restricted keyword—for instance, you could name a control Loop. The problem is that your code could not refer to the control in the usual way, because Visual Basic would assume the keyword Loop was meant. Consequently, this code would cause an error:

```
Loop.Enabled = True
```

To refer to a form or control that uses the same name as a restricted keyword, the name must be surrounded with square brackets. Thus, the following code would not cause an error:

```
[Loop].Enabled = True
```

Square brackets can only be used this way when referring to forms and controls that are named with restricted keywords. Square brackets cannot be used to declare a variable or define a procedure with the same name as a restricted keyword. Typing square brackets can get tedious, and naming forms and controls using reserved words can be confusing; thus, it is not recommended. Microsoft has included this square-bracket technique to assist programmers if, in a future Visual Basic version, a new keyword conflicts with an existing form or control name. Thus you, the programmer, could easily update your code to work with the new version.

Object-Naming Conventions

As you know, when an object—a form or control—is first created, Visual Basic sets its Name property to a default value. For example, all text boxes have their Name property initially set to Text*n*, where *n* is 1, 2, 3, and so on. The first text box drawn is automatically named Text1, the second Text2, and the third Text3.

As the creator of your program, you may want to keep the default name, although this can get confusing if several controls of the same type are added to a form. It just makes sense to change the Name properties to something more descriptive.

In addition to complying with the naming requirements stated in the previous section, Microsoft has proposed the object-naming conventions listed in Table A.1. These conventions were created with coding consistency and standardization in mind.

Table A.1. Visual Basic object-naming conventions.

Object	Prefix	Example
Check box	chk	chkFontSuperscript
Combo box	cbo	cboLanguage
Command button	cmd	cmdOK
Data	dat	datLibrary
Data-bound combo box	dbc	dbcGerman
Data-bound grid	dbg	dbgRetailPrices
Data-bound list box	dbl	dblBusinessRules
Directory list box	dir	dirChange
Drive list box	drv	drvLocate
File list box	fil	filFind
Form	frm	frmSave
Frame*	fra	fraSelectColor
Grid	grd	grdWeeklyExpenses
Horizontal scrollbar	hsb	hsbSpeed
Image	img	imgBalloon
Label*	lbl	lblDescription
Line*	lin	linHorizontal
List box	lst	lstBusinessRules
Menu	mnu	mnuEditPaste
OLE container	ole	oleChart1
Option button	opt	optYes
Picture box	pic	picStar

continues

Table A.1. continued

Object	Prefix	Example
Shape* (includes circles, squares, ovals, rectangles, rounded rectangles, and rounded squares)	shp	shpRectangle
Text box	txt	txtClientName
Timer*	tmr	tmrAlarm
Vertical scrollbar	vsb	vsbNewHeight

The objects listed with an asterisk (*) are not usually referenced in code; hence their default names don't necessarily have to be changed.

Menu-Naming Conventions

There are five guidelines that Microsoft has created when it comes to naming menu items. They are as follows:

- Item names should be unique within a menu, but can be repeated in different menus to represent similar or different actions.
- Item names can be single, compound, or multiple words.
- Use a unique mnemonic access character for each menu item name when assigning access keys and shortcut keys. This feature is for users who like to choose commands with the keyboard. An *access key* is identified with an underscore; for example, Print. No two menu titles should use the same access character. *Shortcut keys* appear to the right of the corresponding menu item and use Ctrl+*letter* or Ctrl+*function key*. For instance, Print can be run immediately when Ctrl+P is pressed. The access character for both access and shortcut keys should be the first letter of the menu title, unless another letter offers a stronger memory association. (A typical Windows convention for the Exit item usually found on the bottom of the File menu is: Access Key—Exit; Shortcut Key—Ctrl+X.)
- An ellipsis (...) should follow menu items that require more information before they can be completed. For example, Save As is always followed by an ellipsis because more information is needed to save the file. This information is normally gathered with a Save As dialog box.
- Keep the item names short. This is for easy identification for the programmer and for localization. Foreign-language versions tend to increase word length by 30 percent. Hence, long menu names could create space problems for menu items.

Table A.2 lists the menu-naming conventions created by Microsoft. These conventions should be used to set the `Name` property in the Menu Editor. By being consistent when naming menu items, these names will be placed together in Visual Basic editor routine lists, making the logic and structure of an application easier to understand.

Table A.2. Visual Basic menu-naming conventions.

Menu Element	Syntax	Example
Menu Title	mnu*MenuTitle*	mnuEdit
Menu Item	mnu*MenuTitleItem*	mnuEditPaste
Menu Array Items	mnu*MenuTitleArray*	mnuEditUndoArray
Submenu Items	mnu*MenuTitleSubmenuTitleItem*	mnuFormatFontSize

New Controls Not Listed Here

For new controls not listed in Table A.1, try to come up with a unique, three-character prefix. (But it is more important to be clear than to stick to three characters.)

Naming Routines and Variables

Variable and function names should use the following structure:

prefixBodyQualifiersSuffix

The *prefix* describes the use and scope of the variable, for instance, `cMoneyFrench` (where `c` is the prefix to indicate the currency type) and `sClientNameFirst` (where `s` is the prefix indicating the string type). These prefixes are as listed in Tables A.3, A.4, and A.5.

Table A.3. Prefixes for variable names.

Variable	Prefix	Type Character
Boolean	b	%
Byte	bt	
Currency	c	@
Date	dt	
Double	d	#
Integer	n	%

continues

Table A.3. continued

Variable	Prefix	Type Character
Long	l	&
Object	o	
Single	f	!
String	s	$
Variant	vnt	

Table A.4. Prefixes for function names.

Function	Prefix	Type
Array	a	
Database	db	
Date+Time	dt	
Dynaset	dy	
Float/Single	f	!
Handle	h	%
Index	I	%
Unsigned	u	&
Unsigned Long	ul	#
Word	w	%

Table A.5. Prefixes for variable and function scope.

Scope	Prefix
Local to module or form	m
Public (available to entire application)	p
Static variable	st
Variable passed by value (local to a routine)	v
Variable passed by reference (local to a routine)	r

The *body*, as it is defined in the format above, consists of the variable and routine names. These names should use mixed-case letters and should be as long as needed to describe their purpose. Function names should also begin with a verb, such as `InitCompanyNameArray` or `GetLinkData`. For terms that are long and frequently used, abbreviations should be used to keep the names to reasonable lengths. For instance, use `Init` for `Initialization`, `Num` for `Number`, `Tbl` for `Table`, and so on. If you do use an abbreviation, be consistent throughout your entire application. Randomly switching between `Num` and `Number` within one project can become confusing to someone trying to read your code.

Qualifiers are used to label-related variables and routines. Many times related routines and variables are used to handle a common object. It can be very helpful to use standard qualifiers to label these derivatives. At first, putting a qualifier after the body of the name may seem a bit awkward—for instance, `sGetClientNameFirst` instead of `sGetClientFirstName`, or `sGetClientNameLast` instead of `sGetClientLastName`—but this practice helps to order these names together in Visual Basic editor routine lists, making the logic and structure of an application easier to understand. Table A.6 is a short list of common qualifiers.

Table A.6. A few common Visual Basic qualifiers.

Qualifier	Description
First	The first element of a set.
Last	The last element of a set.
Next	The next element in a set.
Prev	The previous element in a set.
Cur	The current element in a set.
Max	The maximum value in a set.
Min	The minimum value in a set.

Finally, the *suffix*, in the format above, is the optional Visual Basic type character, such as $, #, and !. Refer back to the list of these characters in Table A.3. They are not used if explicit variable declaration is used.

Naming Conventions

The body of constant names should be place in uppercase, with underscores (_) separating the words. For example, `psNEW_LINE`, which refers to a newline character string that is public, or `mnCLIENT_LIST_MAX`, which refers to a local maximum client list limit that is an integer.

Adding Comments to Your Applications

To make life easier for both you and anyone reading your code, you should put a brief comment at the beginning of each procedure or function, describing what it does. Any parameters passed to the routine should be described if they are not obvious, or when specific ranges are assumed by the routine. Values returned by functions and public variables that are changed by the routine, especially through reference parameters, should be described at the beginning of the routine.

Remember: *The best documentation is self-documentation.* This means that an application's code should be so clearly and logically written that no extra comments are needed.

Index

M